Judaism: Practice and Belief
63 BCE – 66 CE

E. P. SANDERS

JUDAISM
Practice and Belief
63 BCE – 66 CE

SCM PRESS
London

TRINITY PRESS INTERNATIONAL
Philadelphia

First published 1992
Second impression with corrections 1994

SCM Press Ltd
26–30 Tottenham Road
London N1 4BZ

Trinity Press International
P.O. Box 851
Valley Forge, Pa. 19482

British Library Cataloguing-in-Publication Data
ISBN 0334 02470 6 pbk
ISBN 0334 02469 2

Library of Congress Cataloguing-in-Publication Data
ISBN 1 56338 015 3 pbk
1 56338 016 1

Sanders, E. P.
  Judaism: practice and belief, 63 BCE–66 CE/E. P. Sanders
    p. cn.
  Includes bibliographical references and index.
  ISBN 1–56338–016–1,–ISBN 1–56338–015–3 (pbk.)
    1. Judaism–History–Post-exilic period, 585 B.C.–210 A.D.
  2. Judaism–Customs and practices. 3. Jews–Social life and
  customs–70 70 A.D.   I. Title.
  BM176S257 1992   91–42481
  269′.09′014–DC20   CIP

Plans by John Flower

Typeset at The Spartan Press Ltd, Lymington, Hants
and printed in Great Britain by
Mackays of Chatham, Kent

For David Daube and W. D. Davies

Historians rarely descend to those details
from which alone
the real estate of a community can be collected.
Macaulay, 'Machiavelli'

Contents

    Practice and Belief   367
18 The Pharisees I: History   380
19 The Pharisees II: Theology and Practice   413
20 Other Pietists   452
21 Who Ran What?   458
22 Epilogue   491

    Notes   495
    Bibliography   544
    Indexes   555

Preface

This is the book I always wanted to write, or at least close to it. It deals with Judaism as a functioning religion in the early Roman period (usually called for convenience 'the first century'). Though there are substantial chapters on theology and the famous parties (Sadducees, Pharisees and Essenes), the accent is on the common people and their observances. These two emphases, I think, strike the right balance in a work on the history of a religion.

In 1966 I decided to study what I then thought of as 'practical piety'. I was fascinated by E. R. Goodenough's depiction of Judaism: rabbinic Judaism was a small island in a sea of another form of Judaism, which shared the general characteristics of Hellenistic mysticism. I thought that a study of pious practices, such as prayer, purifications and offerings to the temple, might help clarify the relationship between Palestinian and Diaspora Judaism. This is not the place to recount why I changed projects and wrote *Paul and Palestinian Judaism* instead of 'Diaspora and Palestinian Religious Practice'. I mention this only to explain that I have finally returned to a topic that I wanted to study 25 years ago, though then I would have pursued it somewhat differently. I have by no means lost confidence in the common-denominator theology that I described in *P&PJ*; on the contrary, I am more convinced than ever that a broad agreement on basic theological points characterized Judaism in the Graeco-Roman period. Now I wish to place theology into its proper historical context, religious practice.

The first draft of this book was short; I had aimed at writing an introduction to Jewish religious practice in no more than 200 pages. I soon realized, however, that my views on several crucial issues were so different from those that prevail that the reader would not know how to evaluate them if I did not discuss the sources in detail. I then determined to apply the same principle to the entire book, except for the introductory chapters on the history of the period. I have studied afresh almost every point covered in the present work, seldom relying on received scholarly opinion, and I have attempted to let the reader see how I have understood the primary sources. The consequence is that ancient sources are quoted and discussed much more fully than is usually the case in books covering such a substantial period.

One of my major aims has been to analyse divergent evidence, rather than simply citing various passages in the notes, with no indication of where the problems are.

I also decided to discuss competing interpretations of a few topics. The book kept growing. I published some of the most detailed and controversial studies separately; they are chapters II–IV of *Jewish Law from Jesus to the Mishnah: Five Studies* (1990; the topics are 'oral law'; Pharisaic purity laws; food and purity practices in the Diaspora; gifts to the temple from Diaspora Jews). Chapters II and III of that work take up two of the views of Jacob Neusner that are most relevant to the understanding of Pharisaism.

In the present book, I describe the views of other scholars and enter into debate with them only occasionally. There are many points at which more discussion of secondary literature, especially recent research, would be beneficial. Providing this benefit, however, would have doubled or tripled the size of the book and delayed it for years. With apologies to my colleagues, I have decided to publish the work as it stands. I hope some day to be able to study numerous of the sub-topics in even greater detail and add some that I have left out.

The most substantial discussions of secondary literature come in chapters 10 (priests outside the temple; scribes, teachers and magistrates), 18 (the history and influence of the Pharisees) and 21 ('Who ran what?'). In these cases, I have had to argue at length against the prevailing views, which are enshrined in volume II of Schürer's *History of the Jewish People* (now revised and updated by Geza Vermes, Fergus Millar and others) and in Jeremias' *Jerusalem in the Time of Jesus*. On these interrelated topics, the enormous weight of 150 or 200 years of academic opinion has so suppressed the most natural interpretation of some of the evidence that I have tried to show in detail what is wrong with the prevailing view.

The present work, however, is not primarily polemical. To a very large degree, it is simply different from other works in the field. It deals with numerous aspects of religious practice that other introductions to first-century Judaism do not treat, and (to repeat) it discusses the primary evidence in much greater detail.

I have benefitted from the support of several sponsors, students, friends, colleagues and assistants. Actual composition began in the summer of 1985, when I was teaching a graduate seminar at McMaster University in conjunction with my long-time colleague, Albert Baumgarten, from whom I have learned a great deal. I am grateful to McMaster University for support during that and subsequent summers. Most of the work was written while I was at Oxford, where I was stimulated by conversations with Geza Vermes, Martin Goodman, Robin Lane Fox, Fergus Millar, Angus Bowie, John

Matthews, Samuel Barnish and others. The stimulation was for the most part general rather than specific. In terms of human contact, Oxford was and remains easily the best place in the world to study this sort of topic, and I feel privileged to have had the opportunity to work there during the period 1984–1990. The Queen's College, where I was Fellow, provided a most agreeable setting, and I am grateful to the Provost and Fellows for numerous benefits, especially conversation in an atmosphere at once relaxed and challenging.

My work on this book and the previous volume of essays has been supported by the University of Oxford and Duke University, which granted leaves, the Guggenheim Foundation and the British Academy. I am extremely grateful to these institutions and their officers.

Martin Goodman and James McLaren read and commented on chapter 21, as a result of which I made several revisions (though not quite every one that they suggested). Hyam Maccoby has corresponded with me in great detail about some of the topics covered in *Jewish Law from Jesus to the Mishnah*. This has allowed me to correct a few points in the present volume. I am most appreciative of the time and energy that he has spent, and I am deeply indebted to him. I discussed most of these chapters with Margaret Davies, who also read the penultimate draft in 1990. As a result, a lot of the book is clearer than it otherwise would have been. John Bowden read the same typescript and made recommendations for revision, every one of which I have tried to follow. Rebecca Gray read two drafts, five years apart, and made several very helpful suggestions. She also assisted substantially in the final editorial revision. The reader is the beneficiary, and my own gratitude is profound. The undergraduates in 'Religion 52.3, Introduction to the New Testament' (Duke University, 1991) divided up the proof and read it. They caught several errors and infelicities; I appreciate their work very much.

Linda Foster and other members of the staff of SCM Press have been both diligent and helpful. Deborah Gray began work on the Bibliography, which was completed by Lynne Degitz and Frank Crouch, who also did the most difficult part of the work on the indexes of names and passages. My thanks to all three for their care and accuracy. Duke University generously provided funds. This assistance has saved at least six months of my life, which I am now old enough to value very highly.

Professors W. D. Davies and David Daube have done me the great honour of allowing me to dedicate the book to them. Their academic achievements, coupled with their warm and compassionate humanity, put them at the head of the list of those who have studied Judaism and Christianity in the Graeco-Roman world. This book is a very inadequate tribute, but it is the best that I can do, and I offer it to them.

List of Illustrations

Chronological Table

581 BCE	Third deportation to captivity in Babylon
550–530	Cyrus of Persia
538	Beginning of the return to Jerusalem
520–15	Rebuilding of the temple
520	Joshua, son of Jehozadak, Zadokite high priest (according to Chronicles)
458	Ezra (the date is disputed, but this is probably the one intended by the Chronicler)
333–332	Conquest of Palestine by Alexander the Great
323	Death of Alexander
c. 300–198	Palestine under Ptolemies of Egypt
c. 200	Simon II high priest
198	Palestine under Seleucids of Syria
187	Death of Antiochus III (the Great)
175–164	Antiochus IV (Epiphanes)
167–142	Hasmonean revolt
167	Profanation of the temple
166	Death of Mattathias the Hasmonean
166–160	Judas Maccabeus
164	Rededication of the temple
160–143	Jonathan
142–63	Hasmonean dominance
142–134	Simon
134–104	John Hyrcanus
104–103	Aristobulus
103–76	Alexander Jannaeus
76–67	Salome Alexandra
76–67	Hyrcanus II high priest
67–63	Aristobulus II king and high priest
63	Conquest of Judaea by Pompey
63 to 37	Somewhat confused: Roman overlordship; competition between Hyrcanus II and Aristobulus II, then between

	Hyrcanus II and Antigonus, Aristobulus' son; Parthian invasion; rise of the family of Antipater, sons Phasael and Herod
63–40	Hyrcanus II high priest and ethnarch
40–37	Antigonus high priest
37–4	Herod the Great King (appointed 40)
37–36	Hananel high priest
36	Aristobulus III high priest
36–30	Hananel again high priest
31 BCE–14 CE	Augustus (formerly Octavian) emperor
4 BCE–6 CE	Archelaus ethnarch, ruler of Judaea
4 BCE–39 CE	Antipas tetrarch, ruler of Galilee and Peraea
6–41 CE	Judaea governed directly by Roman prefects
14–37	Tiberius emperor
37–41	Gaius (Caligula) emperor
41–54	Claudius emperor
41–44	Agrippa I king, ruling over most of Herod's former kingdom
44–66	Judaea, Samaria and part of Galilee ruled directly by Roman procurators
48–66	Agrippa II given piecemeal parts of his father's kingdom
54–68	Nero emperor
66–73	The first Jewish revolt
70	The fall of Jerusalem
73 or 74	The fall of Matsada

Abbreviations

Antiq.	Josephus, *Jewish Antiquities*. Bibliography 1.
AOT	*The Apocryphal Old Testament*, ed. Sparks. Bibliography 1.
Apion	Josephus, *Against Apion*. Bibliography 1.
Arist.	*Letter of Aristeas* (in *POT*).
ASOR	American School of Oriental Research.
BA	*Biblical Archaeologist*, Baltimore.
BAR	*Biblical Archaeological Review*, Washington.
BASOR	*Bulletin of the American Schools of Oriental Research*, Baltimore.
BCE	Before the common era.
BCH	*Bulletin de Correspondance Hellénique*, Athens and Paris.
BDB	Brown, Driver and Briggs, Hebrew lexicon (Bibliography 2).
Bibl. Antiq.	Pseudo-Philo, *Biblical Antiquities* (in *OTP* II).
c.	*circa*, 'about', used to indicate an approximate date.
CD	*Covenant of Damascus* (=*Zadokite Documents*, Bibliography 1).
CE	Common era.
cf.	*Confer* (Latin = 'compare').
CHJ	*Cambridge history of Judaism*. Bibliography 2.
CRINT	Compendia Rerum Iudaicarum ad Novum Testamentum, Assen and Philadelphia.
DJD	*Discoveries in the Judaean Desert*. Bibliography 1.
DSSE³	Vermes, *Dead Sea Scrolls in English*. Bibliography 1.
Enc. Jud.	*Encyclopaedia Judaica*. Bibliography 2.
ET	English translation.
f.	'following': used after a page, verse, or paragraph number to mean 'also the next'.
Heb.	Hebrew.
HJP	Schürer, *History of the Jewish People*. Bibliography 3.
HTR	*Harvard Theological Review*, Cambridge, Massachusetts.
HUCA	*Hebrew Union College Annual*, Cincinnati.

ibid.	'The same' (Latin): used in an endnote to mean 'the same work as the one just cited'.
IDB	*Interpreter's Dictionary of the Bible*. Bibliography 2.
IEJ	*Israel Exploration Journal*, Jerusalem.
J&J	Sanders, *Jesus and Judaism*. Bibliography 3.
JB	Jerusalem Bible (an ET of the Bible).
JBL	*Journal of Biblical Literature*, Atlanta.
JESHO	*Journal of the Economic and Social History of the Orient*, Leiden.
JJS	*Journal of Jewish Studies*, Oxford.
JLJM	Sanders, Jewish Law From Jesus to the Mishnah. Bibliography 3.
Jos. and Asen.	*Joseph and Aseneth* (in *OTP* II).
JPJC	Schürer, *The Jewish People in the Time of Jesus Christ*. Bibliography 3.
JQR	*Jewish Quarterly Review*, Philadelphia.
JSJ	*Journal for the Study of Judaism*, Leiden.
JTS	*Journal of Theological Studies*, Oxford.
Jub.	*Jubilees* (in *OTP* I).
LCL	Loeb Classical Library, London and Cambridge, Massachusetts.
Life	Josephus, *The Life*. Bibliography 1.
LXX	The Septuagint (Greek translation of Hebrew Bible).
NEB	New English Bible (an ET of the Bible).
NRSV	New Revised Standard Version (an ET of the Bible).
NTS	*New Testament Studies*, Cambridge.
OTP	*Old Testament Pseudepigrapha*, ed. Charlesworth. Bibliography 1.
P&PJ	Sanders, *Paul and Palestinian Judaism*. Bibliography 3.
POT	*The Pseudepigrapha of the Old Testament in English*, ed. Charles. Bibliography 1.
Ps. Sol.	*Psalms of Solomon* (in *POT* and *OTP* II).
1QH	Hodayot: the *Thanksgiving Hymns* from Qumran (in *DSSE³*).
1QM	Milhamah: the *War Rule* from Qumran. Bibliography 1, *The Scroll of the War* . . . ed. Yadin.
1QS	Serekh: the *Community Rule* from Qumran (in *DSSE³*).
1QSa	Serekh appendix A: the *Messianic Rule* from Qumran (in *DSSE³*).
1QSb	Serekh appendix B: *Blessings* attached to IQS (in *DSSE³*).
4QMMT	Scroll of *Some of the Precepts of the Torah* from Qumran. Not yet published; see p. 528 n. 36.

4QPBless	The *Blessings of Jacob* from Qumran (in *DSSE³*).
4Q174	The *Midrash on the Last Days* from Qumran (in *DSSE³*).
4Q503	The *Daily Prayers* from Qumran (in *DSSE³*).
11QTemple	The *Temple Scroll* from Qumran. Bibliography 1, *The Temple Scroll*, ed. Yadin.
RB	*Revue Biblique*, Paris.
RSV	Revised Standard Version (an ET of the Bible).
Spec. Laws	Philo, *The Special Laws*. Bibliography 1.
Sib. Or.	*Sibylline Oracles* (in *OTP* I).
T.	*Tosefta* (before rabbinic tractate; Bibliography 1); *Testament* (before a person's name; in *OPT* II).
War.	Josephus, *The Jewish War*. Bibliography 1.

PART I
Context

I

Preview

Judaism in the period of our study was dynamic and diverse. Our first task is to understand the context in which various individuals and groups came to different views about how best to be Jewish. In Palestine, the topic spans everything from private behaviour to the Jewish state, and in the Diaspora it includes private and group behaviour. We shall not cover every possible point with equal thoroughness, and on many topics, especially socio-political questions, we shall concentrate on Palestine.

In their quest to be properly Jewish and to live as God willed, first-century Jews sometimes co-operated and compromised with one another, sometimes competed peacefully, and sometimes shed blood. Being Jewish meant living in a certain way; 'Judaism' was more a way of life than a doctrinal system. Consequently agreements and disagreements often concerned practice, which is the principal topic of our study. Underlying practice, however, were beliefs, and we shall also give an account of these.

The period requires definition. We shall consider in general the time enclosed by great revolts: the Hasmonean (or Maccabean) revolt against the Seleucids and the first Jewish revolt against Rome (c. 167 BCE to 73 or 74 CE).[1] We shall give closer attention to the Roman period (63 BCE to 74 CE) than to the Hasmonean (167–63 BCE), and we shall not discuss the first revolt (66–74 CE). Thus the study concentrates on the period that begins with the conquest of Jerusalem by the Roman general Pompey (63 BCE) and ends with the outbreak of revolt against Rome (66 CE). Even within this span, we shall pay more attention to the situation in Judaea and Galilee after the death of Herod the Great (4 BCE) than to events of the previous years. I shall use 'first-century Judaism' as a convenient term to describe the period under investigation. The phrase is intended to refer generally to the early Roman period (63 BCE–66 CE). The principal dates of the entire period are these:

167 to 142 BCE	Hasmonean revolt
142 to 63 BCE	Hasmonean dominance
63 BCE	Roman conquest under Pompey
37 to 4 BCE	Reign of Herod the Great
66 to 74 CE	First revolt against Rome

The political and military history of this period is not our major concern, and I shall try to avoid a historical summary that catalogues events – preferring, rather, to be always in pursuit of a question. Despite this preference, a certain amount of cataloguing is necessary. The reader will encounter a barrage of names, dates and events. These will be presented in tabular form from time to time, and comprehensive tables are given on pp. xvff. Some will wish to read a proper history of the period, of which several are available. Some of these are listed, with short comments, in the Bibliography.

The Jews of Palestine in our period faced the questions common to societies: foreign and domestic relations. In terms of foreign affairs, the question was how to relate to the great empires of the Mediterranean: when to fight, when to yield; when to be content with partial independence, when to seek more. In terms of internal affairs, the primary issue was who would control the national institutions: the temple, the sacrifices, the tithes and other offerings, and the administration of the law.

These two questions, throughout the period, were interrelated. Inevitably the people who controlled foreign policy also controlled – or at least had the power to control – domestic policy. This was a constant source of tension. There was no simple distinction between 'church' and 'state' or 'religion' and 'politics'. God, in the eyes of Jews, cared about all aspects of life; no part of it was outside 'religion'. Thus, in any case in which there was a choice – whether between would-be rulers, competing architectural plans for the temple, or various prohibitions on the sabbath – Jews would attempt to discern and follow *God's* will. Not infrequently they disagreed. Although often there was a good deal of tolerance, every disagreement was potentially serious, since to some it might reveal that certain others rejected the will of God. In our period, some people cared intensely about government and relations with foreign empires, and they regarded some of the alternatives as being absolutely against the will of God. Some cared relatively little about Israel's stance towards the Hellenistic monarchies or Rome but were deeply concerned about the priesthood and the calendar, which determined holy days. Rulers or leaders might be supported on one score and opposed on another. Their very success in war and diplomacy might make them suspect with regard to piety. Since God had views on everything, issues from quite diverse areas of life might become matters of religious principle. This point helps explain some of the contentiousness among Jews during the period of this study.

The history that we consider is both tense and intense, and it would be important and interesting even were its outcome less momentous than it was. As things turned out, however, first-century Jewish Palestine was the cradle of two of the West's three major religions: rabbinic Judaism and Christianity.

Sources

The principal source for the history of the period, and for its social, political and religious issues, is the work of the Jewish author, Josephus. For the Hasmonean period, I and II Maccabees are also important. Josephus, however, so determines what we know and think of the period, and the evaluation of what he wrote is so crucial to any reconstruction of it, that it will be worthwhile to give a thumbnail sketch of his career.

Joseph ben Mattathias, who subsequently became known as Flavius Josephus, was a member of the Jewish priestly aristocracy who lived from about 37 to 100 CE.[2] In an idealized sketch of his youth he says that his learning was respected by his seniors by the time he was fourteen. He later studied the various parties within Judaism and decided to follow the views of the Pharisees. When war broke out between the Jews and Rome in 66, he was assigned military responsibility for part of Galilee. After Rome's conquest of Jotapata, where he was in command, he and others formed a suicide pact. Through trickery or coincidence he and one other were the last to draw the fatal lot, and he convinced his colleague to join him in surrendering. As a captive, he found an opportunity to praise the Roman general, Vespasian, predicting that he would be emperor. When in fact Vespasian came to power in 69, he freed Josephus. Josephus was present at the siege of Jerusalem, where he served as interpreter. Among other services, he tried to convince the Jerusalemites to surrender, but he was not successful.

He moved to Rome under the patronage of Vespasian and his son Titus, members of the Flavian family, and took the name Flavius. He turned his hand to history, being aided by Greek assistants, and with access to Roman records. His first work, the *Jewish War* (hereafter *War*), was published in both Greek and Aramaic. It has two principal themes: (1) The Jewish revolt was caused partly by Roman misgovernment (on the part of a few administrators) and partly by a very small group of irresponsible Jewish brigands; most Jews wished to be loyal participants in the Empire. (2) Rome is invincible and it is futile to rebel. The Flavians had the work circulated in the Near East, probably hoping that it would discourage other nationalist uprisings.

Subsequently Josephus wrote a long explanation of and apology for Judaism, called the *Jewish Antiquities* (hereafter *Antiq.*); an apologetic and defensive account of his own life (*Life*); and a defence of Judaism against numerous criticisms, including an attack by Apion (*Against Apion*). He planned, but did not live to write, a longer explanation of Judaism, to be called *On Customs and Causes*. It seems that a preliminary outline of this work appears in the last fourth of *Apion*.

Josephus had his weaknesses and biases, but his general merit as a historian is considerable. Since in the early parts of *Antiq.* Josephus employed sources to which we have access – the Bible and I Maccabees – scholars can attain a view of how he used sources and of characteristic changes. Further, some of the account in *War* is rewritten in *Antiq.*, and some in *Life*; the dual accounts allow critical questions to be posed and often answered. Even had Josephus been a worse historian than he was, we would be bound to follow his account of events, since often there is no other. Fortunately, wherever he can be tested, he can be seen to have been a pretty fair historian.

A pretty fair historian in the Hellenistic period did not live up to the ideal of disinterested inquiry and objective reporting to which modern historians aspire (but do not fully attain). History was written with a purpose – or two or three. Josephus' purposes are often clear. We just noted two of the main themes of *War*. The message of *Antiq.* is less pro-Roman, even more clearly pro-Jewish: Judaism is an ancient and noble culture and religion, of no pernicious effect on civilization as a whole, but rather an elevating and benevolent force. Josephus again emphasizes that Jews are not overly inclined to revolution. *Apion* is an even more forceful and cogent argument in favour of Judaism. Josephus' *Life* is sometimes shamefully self-serving, though also very useful critically, because of its overlaps with *War*.

Josephus especially controlled what his characters said, as did other historians of the time. Speeches were the historian's opportunity to show command of rhetoric (highly prized in Graeco-Roman society) and to inculcate noble thoughts. The good historian, consciously or unconsciously following the advice of Thucydides, composed speeches that were appropriate to those who made them and to the occasion.[3] Josephus' greatest masterpiece is the speech that he attributes to Eleazar, a rebel leader, just before the mass suicide of the defenders of Matsada in 74. The speech can hardly have been reported to Josephus, and so he was free to have Eleazar say precisely what he wanted. He very probably used this and other speeches to say things that he could not say in his own voice. Throughout his work Josephus attacked the more ardent revolutionaries and their leaders. His intention was to argue that Jews as a whole were trustworthy members of the empire, not rebellious subjects to be watched with suspicion. Thus he characterized the rebels as no better than common criminals. Yet Eleazar's speech is full of nobility. It is eloquent in favour of Jewish freedom and the unconquerable will to escape Roman domination. Josephus, we thus learn, could in his heart admire the rebels, even the most radical. It is safe to assume that he gave to their leader an eloquent statement of their intention and goal, as they themselves saw them. That is, the speech allows the author to drop his artificial denigration of 'brigands' and to let them speak for themselves. The objective historian would write about the last hours of the doomed rebels, 'I do not know'. Josephus freely invented, but what he invented is probably truer to their spirit than any few lines of authentic shorthand could be. We may even guess that Eleazar's speech tells us something about the wider group of Jews who fought for independence – of which Josephus had been one.

It is helpful to compare Josephus' generalizations with his accounts of individual events. We shall see below, for example, that he says that the Pharisees were so popular that they always got their way. Yet it is extremely hard to find any specific incidents in which this is true. Generalizations are easier to write and more likely to reflect an author's bias than his report of individual events. Even the latter, of course, are not free from twists that the author may wish to give them, but they are more resistant to editorial shaping than are generalizations.

These two cases (Eleazar's speech and the influence of the Pharisees) are only examples. They illustrate that, though the modern historian must follow Josephus, his work can be analysed critically.[4] This is also true of the other bodies of primary literature with which we shall deal. I shall try throughout to allow the reader to see the course of critical analysis: why Josephus' word – or that of some other source – is accepted at one point but rejected at another. It is my hope to do more than to present another summary of conclusions, but rather to tackle questions, and to let the reader follow the investigation.

In addition to Josephus, the works of Philo are important, especially his treatises called *The Special Laws*. I shall use these selectively, but I shall not offer a general evaluation of them. The same is true of many of the books now included in the 'Apocrypha' and 'Pseudepigrapha'.[5] In these collections, we find 'apocalypses' or 'revelations', which do raise questions that require brief consideration. These books offer descriptions of the other world, the afterlife, God's action in the future, and other 'hidden' topics.[6] The four main apocalypses (or works with appreciable apocalyptic sections) are either too early or too late to be primary evidence for our period: *I Enoch* and *Jubilees* are too early, *IV Ezra* and *II Baruch* are too late. *Jubilees*, though it has apocalyptic sections, is full of details about practice, and we shall note some of these, especially when there are parallels in later sources (as there often are).

The subject matter of the apocalypses, however, was current in our period. I shall offer an outline of various hopes for the future (ch. 14). Other topics, such as angels and other heavenly beings, the number of heavens, and the details of the final judgment (or judgments), will appear very briefly or not at all. There are two reasons for this.

One is that I do not regard apocalyptic*ism* as an ideology that competed with other ideologies, or as a movement that included only people who were not in other movements. Jews did not have to choose between apocalypticism and worship in the temple, or between apocalypticism and the Pharisaic interpretation of sabbath law. Our ideas about Judaism are often shaped by the way people of previous centuries (both ancient and modern) preserved, organized and published Jewish literature. We have rabbinic literature, and so we speak of 'rabbinic Judaism'; apocalyptic literature, and so we speak of 'apocalyptic Judaism'. Although rabbinic literature reveals that the rabbis were aware of esoteric knowledge, it does not contain descriptions of heavenly tours. Does it, then, come from a different group? Not necessarily. People who debated details of sabbath law in the morning could have contemplated the mysteries of the heavenly chariot in the evening. The briefest glance at ancient documents will show that authors (and editors) had more than one interest. *Jubilees* contains both legal and esoteric material, and *I Enoch* includes calendrical details as well as visions of the last judgment. Paul expected a dramatic cosmic event, the return of the Lord, and he had visions and heard voices, but he was also a very practical man who could organize the details of travel plans and give concrete instructions about worship services.[7] To take an example from more recent centuries: Isaac Newton took a keen interest in apocalypses. An ancient apocalyptist may also have been a legal expert, a priest, or anything else.

The combination of topics and literary genres (in *Jubilees*, Paul's letters and elsewhere) proves beyond doubt that a type of literature does not constitute a distinct kind of Judaism. But we should not think that every author put all of his or her thoughts into one book. A person who had views on both the divine throne and sabbath law might have written them up separately. Paul wrote occasional letters, and thus discussed widely diverse topics in the same place. Some people were tidier. Isaac Newton did not publish his studies of apocalypses in the *Principia*. This fits in perfectly with everything we know about humanity: one interest does not necessarily exclude others; sometimes people categorize their interests and deal with one at a time, and sometimes not. Rabbinic literature shows a high level of categorization, which has numerous effects, one being the exclusion of apocalyptic visions.

The present study is organized according to aspects of practice. This reveals more than just my present interest. I think that the description of first-century Judaism according to the categories of surviving literature (apocalyptic, rabbinic, philosophical, mystical and the like) is an error. It makes a lot of sense to study one body of literature at a time, but it is unreasonable to think that a convenient way of arranging our own time reflects the social organization of living and breathing people in the first century. A collection of literary remains represents one of the special interests of an individual or a group; but we should not suppose that each collection corresponds to an isolated group of people who had no other ideas and who would have denounced other literary collections as belonging to a different 'Judaism', or would have found them incomprehensible.[8] This is no more true of ancient people (for example, Paul and the author of *Jubilees*) than of modern (such as Isaac Newton and every reader whose shelves contain books on different topics, arranged by subject). Thus in dealing with religious practice, I think that I am also dealing with 'apocalyptists', who, in my view, did not form separate conventicles and spend all their time contemplating the heavenly secrets.

This brings us to the second reason for not giving apocalyptic themes a separate place in this book. Once one assumes, as I do, that *anyone* may have conceived of the other world as having seven heavens, each with its own characteristic, one must immediately confess ignorance about what role visionary conceptions played in ordinary religious life. Jews did have ideas about the future (often vague ones) and sometimes we can tell that concrete actions were predicated on the basis of hopes about what God would do. We shall examine some instances. Apart from this, it is impossible to know what the practical effect was of thinking graphically and pictorially about things that lie beyond sense perception. The Essenes were greatly concerned with purity, and they also thought that angels in some way or other dwelt in their midst. Was there a causal connection? This is a topic that I shall discuss in its place; here I shall say that angels were only a part of Essene thinking about their own community and that many factors in addition to belief in angels bore on the Essenes' purity rules.

I doubt that very many Jews spent much *time* contemplating the other world. As they went about the daily business of feeding and clothing themselves, worrying about the mortgage, saying the daily prayers, and saving up for a banquet at the next festival, no doubt their concerns were sometimes lightened by the thought of angels watching over them, or by the hope of a better age. But our principal concern is precisely to consider their daily, weekly, seasonal and annual practices, as well as the beliefs that bore directly on them. If I could tie metaphysical speculation to practice, I would do it, but at the present time I am inclined to doubt that a causal connection can be demonstrated often enough to enlighten us about the motives of Jewish religious practice.[9]

Rabbinic literature poses special problems, which require a few words here and several more in other sections of the book. The rabbinic compilations (Mishnah, Tosefta, Midrashim and Talmuds) are later than our period, being no earlier than the first part of the third century CE. They certainly contain older material. Scholars of all schools accept attributions to a named Pharisee or rabbi as being fairly reliable: a rule attributed to Shammai probably reflects his view. Material attributed to a pre-70 Pharisee or to one of the earliest post-70 rabbis[10] constitutes a body of evidence that most scholars accept as representing Pharisaism. But how much of the rest is early tradition? Here there are sharp disagreements. In this study, I shall sometimes cite second-century rabbinic passages in order to illustrate points; but when I wish to derive hard information about actual practice I shall take a minimalist view of rabbinic evidence, making use only of material that can be confidently assigned to the early period. I shall especially follow this limitation in discussing the Pharisees. I know that there are many instances in which a discussion first attested in the mid-second century is substantially earlier. It sometimes happens, for example, that a debate attributed to second-century rabbis is illuminated by, or illumines, a passage in the Dead Sea Scrolls. In such cases we may assume that earlier rabbis or Pharisees also discussed the topic, even though the surviving attributions are later. For this and other reasons, I am persuaded that many early traditions in rabbinic literature are overlooked when one focuses only on passages that are attributed to pre-70 Pharisees or to early rabbis. Despite this, in the present work I take a very cautious approach to rabbinic literature, and for the most part I use only passages that are attributed to a pre-70 Pharisee or to the Houses of Hillel and Shammai.[11] Exceptions to this rule will be justified case by case.[12]

The date of rabbinic traditions, however, is not the most serious problem. The bigger issues concern *genre* and *authority*. Scholars frequently suppose that an argument in rabbinic literature is a *law* and that Pharisaic or rabbinic law determined common *practice*. The two principal books that cover more-or-less the same ground as the current volume, Schürer's *History of the Jewish People in the Age of Jesus Christ*, vol. II, and Jeremias' *Jerusalem in the Time of Jesus*, are, to different degrees, based on the assumption that rabbinic views disclose first-century practice. Indeed, most historians of Judaism assume that what people actually did corresponded to what the rabbis thought they should do, and that one discovers behaviour by determining what rabbinic opinion was. Scholarly differences about first-century practice usually spring from disagreements about what the Pharisees or rabbis thought.

The present work breaks fundamentally with that view. Rabbinic arguments are frequently only arguments, not laws, and in any case Pharisaic or rabbinic views did not *govern* first-century Jewish practice. The degree of Pharisaic influence varied from time to time and issue to issue. A lot of examples will appear in the course of this work, becoming most prominent in 'Who Ran What?' (ch. 21). I shall follow an eclectic method, attempting to discover actual practice by studying diverse, sometimes contradictory opinions in the various sources. As I indicated above, I shall try to make the line of reasoning clear, so that the conclusions can be assessed. It will not be possible to do this on every single point, but the reader will see enough instances to be able to assess the method. Those who are accustomed to deriving information about actual behaviour from rabbinic opinions may wish to begin with p. 458, 'The rabbis had laid it down'.

Besides the fact that the rabbis did not dictate practice, rabbinic legal discussions are sometimes idealistic, referring to the way things should be done, not describing how they were done. This too requires that the material be used with caution.[13] Idealism marks *all* the sources, not just rabbinic literature. Josephus' discussions of the law of Moses, for example, are not necessarily descriptions of what his contemporaries did. His narrative of events, however, gives us some control. The Mishnah contains very little narrative, but what there is makes the idealization of the more theoretical discussions stand out by contrast (see p. 420 below, on *Sanhedrin* 7.2). Further, only the Mishnah discusses an entire ideal world in the present tense, a world in which God's will is revealed through prophets, and the Urim and Thummim on the high priest's vestments still give oracular advice (*Shevuʿot* 2.2; cf. *Sanhedrin* 11.5f.).[14] Other parts of the Mishnah, however, do seem to reflect current practice, and I shall attempt to derive some of the details of sacrifice from the tractates *Tamid* and *Yoma*.

While there are a lot of differences between the present work and other introductions to first-century Judaism, the views that the Pharisees did not control Palestine,[15] and that the Mishnah does not necessarily describe general practice, may be the most important. A second distinguishing feature of this work is the effort to describe *common* Judaism, that of the ordinary priests and the ordinary people. This means that the special views of the famous parties (Pharisees, Sadducees and Essenes) are relegated to their proper place. Many scholars write on the assumption that Judaism was *divided* into parties; but the parties were quite small, and (as we shall see) none of them was able to coerce the general populace into adopting its platform. We shall try to uncover what was *common* in two senses: agreed on among the parties, agreed on by the populace as a whole.

As I shall explain more fully below, the discussion of common Judaism in Part II will include information about the Greek-speaking Diaspora. The principal focus, however, is on Palestine.

The description of common Judaism occupies over half the book. Judaism as a religion, like most other religions, is based on repeated cycles: daily, weekly, seasonal and annual observances. A description of such a religion is by definition static: repeated religious practices do not change often, and such changes as there are usually take a long time. One can, to be sure, detect changes between the Persian period and the Roman, but we shall be able to find fewer changes from the early to the late decades of the Roman period. Further, the descriptions of practice that ancient sources offer the reader are also static – this *is* the way we observe Passover – and we do not have enough such descriptions to permit much of a history of change and development. When we turn to groups (Part III), it will be possible to offer a little more analysis of chronological developments.

Although we cannot often give an evolutionary history of religious belief and observance, we are dealing with a concrete historical period, one that influenced Jewish behaviour in countless ways. For example, pilgrimage in the Roman period was not precisely the same as in the Persian period. Not only were its physical and social circumstances different, it also had *political* implications. The pilgrimage festivals, as times of national remembrance, were prime occasions for social, political and economic protest. To understand this, we must have some idea of the actual circumstances of our period. Put another way, to understand *Judaism* we must know what the Jewish *people* were doing and what others were doing that affected them. The Jews' 'religious' behaviour was closely related to the political and social environment.

Thus we need to know the history, but I do not intend to spend hundreds of pages describing it. As a compromise, we shall begin by looking at the situation that produced competing parties and groups. Focusing on some historical disputes will allow us to sketch a few salient points of political and military history, and, more importantly, to lay out some of the major issues within first-century Judaism. The parties were formed because of real issues. Once we see what they were, we can better describe common Judaism, returning to groups and sub-groups in the last part of the study.

2

The Issues that Generated Parties

The Judaism that Josephus knew as a young man – that is, Judaism in the 50s and 60s of the common era – had three main parties. He several times mentions them and twice writes fairly substantial summaries, calling them either 'parties' within the Jewish 'philosophy' or separate 'philosophies' (*War* 2.119–66; *Antiq.* 18.11–25; cf. 13.171f.; 13.297).[1] We may briefly define them as follows (partly in reliance on Josephus' summaries, but partly borrowing from our later discussion):

Sadducees: aristocrats, including aristocratic priests, who followed the biblical law but not the relatively new Pharisaic 'traditions' and who denied the resurrection. Politically, most of them saw co-operation with Rome as Israel's best policy.

Pharisees: both priests and laity, apparently mostly the latter. Few Pharisees were socially and financially prominent. They were acute interpreters of the law and were fairly rigorous in keeping it. They also had special traditions, some of which heightened, some of which relaxed the law. They believed in the resurrection. Their stance towards Herod, the Herodians and Rome is difficult to ascertain and was probably not uniform. For the most part they were willing to accept the status quo, with what degree of restlessness we do not know.

Essenes: a party of priests and laity that had more than one branch. All Essenes kept separate from other Jews to some degree. They had their own views about many matters, especially the temple and purity; and they attributed their views, in whole or in part, to Moses (or to God). One branch of the party was monastic and lived in an isolated and remote area (the Dead Sea Sect). The Sectarians thought that their leaders – priests of the house of Zadok – should rule Israel.

In his summaries, Josephus refers also to the rise of a 'fourth philosophy', which was largely Pharisaic in opinion, but whose members would accept no master but God (*Antiq.* 18.23; *War* 2.118).

There were only a few Sadducees, more than 4,000 Essenes, and (at the time of Herod) 6,000 Pharisees (*Antiq.* 13.298; 18.20; 17.42). We cannot assume that these numbers are precise, but we should accept what they imply: that relatively few Jews belonged to one of the parties and that the Pharisaic party was the largest of the three, followed by the Essenes.

In some respects party positions can be said to have originated during the biblical period, and especially during the exile,[2] but the groups as we know them from Josephus, the New Testament, the Dead Sea Scrolls and rabbinic literature – the principal bodies of primary evidence – were shaped by the events of the Hasmonean uprising against the Seleucid kingdom and the period of Hasmonean rule (briefly described below). During the course of the successful revolt, three things happened:

1. Israel re-established first religious and then political autonomy.
2. One option for Israelite life – merger into the common Hellenistic culture – was decisively rejected. Jewish life would be lived according to the law of Moses, which in some ways separates Jew from Gentile.
3. The old leadership of Israel – the Zadokite priesthood – was replaced by the Hasmonean family.

Complete autonomy, coupled with the removal of the previous leadership, led naturally to disagreements about how Jewish life should be constituted and lived, or exacerbated some of the disagreements that already existed. We shall trace enough of the history to see how the issues arose and what they were.

The Persian Period

586	Destruction of Jerusalem by Nebuchadnezzar of Babylon
581	Third deportation to captivity in Babylon
550–530	Cyrus of Persia
538	Beginning of the return to Jerusalem
520–515	Rebuilding of the temple
520	Joshua, son of Jehozadak, Zadokite high priest (according to Chronicles)
458	Ezra (the date is disputed, but this is probably the one intended by the Chronicler)
333–332	Conquest of Palestine by Alexander the Great

Some time after Cyrus of Persia allowed the Jewish leaders to return from Mesopotamia to Palestine,[3] they established what Josephus would later call a 'theocracy': local government was primarily in the hands of the high priest, who spoke for God. There was a governor, and the Jewish state could not oppose or disobey Persia, but Persia's hand did not lie heavy on Jerusalem, and the period seems to have been peaceful and relatively untroubled. The high priest was, or was considered to be, a descendant of Zadok.

The Zadokite family traced its claim to the high priesthood back to the Zadok who supported Solomon as heir to David's throne and who anointed him king (I Kings 1.28–45). After Babylonia's conquest of Judaea, during the Babylonian captivity, the prophet Ezekiel saw the Zadokite priests (of whom he was one) as having been loyal to God and thus as being worthy to retain their position when the temple was rebuilt: the temple area and the right to sacrifice would belong to

the sons of Zadok, who kept the charge of my sanctuary when the people of Israel went astray from me. [They] shall come near to me to minister to me; and they shall attend on me to offer me the fat and the blood, says the Lord God . . . (Ezek. 44.15; see also 40.44–46; 43.19; 48.11)

The high priest at the time of the rebuilding of the temple, Joshua the son of Jehozadak (Haggai 1.1), was a Zadokite (so the genealogy at the end of I Chronicles 5). Ezra, one of the leading re-founders of Israelite life, is presented as a descendant of Zadok (Ezra 7.1–6). This part of Ezra may be the work of the author of Chronicles, and the two books of Chronicles have as one of their main themes the dominance of the house of Zadok. (See, for example, the priest Azariah at the time of king Hezekiah, 715–687 BCE, II Chron. 31.9–10). One may now doubt that the high priests were actually all drawn from the family of Zadok; but later, reading Chronicles, Jews thought that this had been the case.

The Hellenistic Period and the Hasmonean Revolt

333–332	Conquest by Alexander the Great
323	Death of Alexander
c. 300–198	Palestine under Ptolemies of Egypt
c. 200	Simon II high priest
198	Palestine under Seleucids of Syria
187	Death of Antiochus III (the Great)
175–164	Antiochus IV (Epiphanes)
167	Profanation of the temple
166	Death of Mattathias
166–160	Judas Maccabeus
162–150	Demetrius I king of Syria
164	Rededication of the temple

The long and peaceful Persian period came to an end when Alexander the Great conquered Palestine in 333–332 BCE. Internally, however, there seems to have been little change, and the Zadokites still reigned supreme in Jerusalem. When, after his death, Alexander's empire was broken up by disputes and battles among his leading generals, Palestine came under the control of the Ptolemies in Egypt, but again there was little change. The Ptolemies did not interfere with domestic affairs, contenting themselves with receiving tribute, as had the Persians before them.

The descendants of Alexander's general Seleucus held Syria. During the period 202–198 BCE the greatest of them, Antiochus III, managed to wrest control of Palestine from Egypt. He was supported by, among others, the Jewish high priest Simon II, a Zadokite. It is probably this Simon who is eulogized by the sage Ben Sira, and his activities are worth citing:

> It was the High Priest Simon son of Onias
>   who repaired the Temple during his lifetime
>   and in his day fortified the sanctuary.
> He laid the foundations of the double height,
>   the high buttresses of the Temple precincts.
> In his day the water cistern was excavated,
>   a reservoir as huge as the sea.
> Anxious to save the people from ruin,
>   he fortified the city against siege (Ben Sira 50.1–4; JB)

Simon, like other high priests, served God and the people with splendour. When he emerged from the Holy of Holies on the Day of Atonement he was

> like the morning star among the clouds,
>   like the moon at the full,
> like the sun shining on the Temple of the Most High,
>   like the rainbow gleaming against brilliant clouds . . .
> like a vessel of beaten gold
>   encrusted with every kind of precious stone . . .
> when he went up to the holy altar,
>   and filled the sanctuary precincts with his grandeur . . . (Ben Sira
>   50.6–11)

Thus the Zadokite high priest was in charge in Jerusalem, and he enjoyed considerable autonomy, being able to fortify the city. In his role as high priest, of course, he presented the people's sacrifices to God and bestowed God's blessings on the people (Ben Sira 50.18–21).

There is one other way in which Ben Sira shows the broad powers of the priesthood. In his long section praising the great men of Israel's history he attributes to Aaron, the first priest, the right to teach Israel the law (45.17). We shall see that also in a later period the priesthood exercised the chief teaching, legislative and judicial powers.

Seleucid overlordship was to prove fateful for Israel. Shortly before 175 BCE there was a split in the Jewish aristocracy, between the Zadokite high priest and his brother, the latter favouring Hellenization: the adoption of Greek education, athletics and dress. He found an ally in Antiochus IV, who came to the throne of Syria in 175.

The events and the people who took part are difficult to sort out, since the sources partly disagree, and some of them seem to be confused. Fortunately, we do not need to settle precisely who did what when, and we may instead offer a general description.[4] The question of Hellenization became acute, being fiercely championed by some and bitterly opposed by others. The initiative came from Jews: some went to the king, Antiochus IV, and asked for permission 'to observe the ordinances of the Gentiles', which he granted (I Macc. 1.11–13). They built a Greek-style gymnasium, where, among other things, young men exercised nude. This brought into social prominence a crucial difference between Jew and Greek. Jewish males were circumcised, and circumcision was the primary external sign of the covenant between God and Abraham and his descendants (Gen. 17). The Greeks, believing in a whole mind in a whole body, regarded circumcision as a barbaric mutilation. Young men who wanted to fit into the Hellenistic culture 'removed the marks of circumcision' by undergoing an operation. In the minds of many they thereby 'abandoned the holy covenant' (I Macc. 1.14f.).

The conflict between the Hellenizers and those who wanted clearly distinctive Jewish identity led to conflict and bloodshed. Finally Antiochus IV forbade certain Jewish practices and even required the Jews 'to build altars and sacred precincts and shrines for idols, to sacrifice swine and unclean animals, and to leave their sons uncircumcised' (I Macc. 1.47). In the year 167 the altar of the temple in Jerusalem was defiled by pagan sacrifice (1.54). The standard of revolt was raised by one Mattathias, who was a priest, but not a Zadokite nor even an aristocrat. He and his family, including five sons, moved from Jerusalem to Modein, presumably to escape pagan practices, but foreign religion followed him there. He killed a Jew who was about to offer a pagan sacrifice, rallied others who were 'zealous for the law', and began guerilla warfare (I Macc. 2).

This family, which dominated Jewish affairs for the next hundred years, is called 'Hasmonean' after an ancestor, Hashmon, but often 'Maccabean' because of a nickname, 'the hammerer', given to Judas, the third son of Mattathias.

The original band was soon joined by 'a company of Hasideans, mighty warriors of Israel, every one who offered himself willingly for the law' (I Macc. 2.42). The word 'Hasidean' reflects the Hebrew *ḥasîdîm*, 'pious', and we have here reference to a group of people who wished to resist Hellenization and who were willing to fight and die. Though little is directly known about them, the Hasideans seem to be important for the history of the Jewish parties.[5] The influx of the pious allowed the revolutionaries wider activity, but they seem to have directed it principally against internal enemies: they 'struck down sinners in their anger and lawless men in their wrath; the survivors fled to the Gentiles for safety' (I Macc. 2.44).

Mattathias himself died shortly after starting the insurrection (in 166), and principal fame attaches to his sons. Under the leadership of Judas Maccabeus the Jews carried out military operations against the Syrians themselves. Judas' efforts met with surprising success. He regained Jerusalem (except for a citadel, the Acra, which was invested), and he purged and rededicated the temple (in 164).

Full independence, however, had not been achieved, nor was internal strife over. Antiochus IV died and his heir was a minor. One Lysias took effective control of the kingdom, raised an army, and besieged Jerusalem. Hearing of trouble at home, he offered terms; peace was temporarily established. The laws of Antiochus IV were repealed, and religious freedom was allowed, but the Jews were still under Syrian control.

Lysias did not long enjoy power. Demetrius, a member of the Seleucid family, escaped from Rome, where he was being held hostage, had Lysias and his ward, the young Antiochus V, executed, and established himself as king. Demetrius appointed as high priest Alcimus, a member of the high priestly family, but a Hellenizer. He started towards Jerusalem to assert his claims, accompanied by Bacchides, a Syrian general. At this point the Hasideans re-enter the story as a separate group:

> Then a group of scribes appeared in a body before Alcimus and Bacchides to ask for just terms. The Hasideans were the first among the sons of Israel to seek peace from them, for they said, 'A priest of the line of Aaron has come with the army, and he will not harm us'. (I Macc. 7.12–14)

The Hasideans were wrong: sixty of them were seized and killed (7.16).

It appears that we have here, not an event that led to divisions and parties, but an exemplary story that shows why they arose. The Hasmonean uprising swept together people of many shades of opinion. They need have had in common no more than a desire to abolish the hated laws of Antiochus IV. When that was done, and when a high priest of the right family was appointed, the goal of some had been achieved. It should be noted that those who held out the hand of greeting to Alcimus were apparently content even though he was known to have Hellenizing sympathies and even though he was appointed by the king of Syria. The situation that we must imagine is this: some would have held out for more, for example, a non-Hellenizing high priest, one who would destroy the gymnasium; some would want more yet, perhaps a high priest appointed by a Jewish ruler, even a puppet Jewish ruler; some would seek fully autonomy, with little regard to who was ruler and who was priest, as long as both were Jewish; some would rather have foreign domination than that of the Hasmoneans, or any other non-Davidic line; some would put up with any government and any priesthood if only peace could be restored; some would suffer anything rather than have the 'wrong' priest or ruler. Each successive step of Hasmonean success satisfied the goals of some and charged the fears of others. This is the general environment that produced the 'parties' that Josephus later summarized so neatly.

As is always the case, party labels covered a range of opinion. Not all members of modern political parties or religious denominations agree precisely with all others, and this exemplifies a general rule. Further, as we noted, most people were not members of 'parties' or 'denominations' at all. Today there is an assumption in the democratic countries that virtually all voters have primary party allegiances, though some will switch or cross lines. The electoral systems of modern states force us into thinking of nations as *consisting* of parties. In antiquity this was not so. The Greek attempt at democracy, which was short-lived, was quite different from modern democracy and was not based on competing parties. Rome, at the time of the Hasmonean revolt, was a 'Republic'; that is, it did not have a king. It was governed instead by an oligarchy, officially embodied in the Senate. The notion that a population should distribute itself among a few parties, with competing platforms, had not arisen, nor did it arise during the period that we study.

We understand the Jewish world better if we compare it to religious denominationalism, yet again there are important differences. In Europe, the United States and Canada we have large religious groupings (e.g. Protestant Christians and Catholic Christians), with many sub-divisions on the Protestant side (at least in some countries), members of other faiths, and non-believers. People who are practising members of a religion are also members of some *organization*, usually with a constitution of some sort, a bureaucracy, membership lists and the like. Those who are on no such list are not members of a religion at all. (This at least is usually the case.) We shall see in first-century Judaism fairly small but significant groups, which had special practices and beliefs, and thus a sort of separate 'constitution', and the majority, who accepted widespread and common religious practices, especially as taught and administered by the priesthood, with no denominational tag and no membership in a group other than the people of Israel. Their only constitution was the Bible as commonly interpreted. All who were Jewish were members of 'Judaism'; very few belonged to a sub-group.

Were we to survey Palestinian religion in general we would also find pagans, concentrated in a few cities. We would not find atheists. Formal atheism – the denial of the existence of a higher power – was virtually unknown in antiquity. Certainly some people lived as if there were no God, but true atheism was either non-existent or negligible.

We envisage, then, a situation in which there were many shades of opinion about 'religion' and 'politics', and in which the two were intertwined. We have also seen the formation of identifiable groups: the Hellenizers, the anti-Hellenizers and the Hasideans. During the time of military conflict, most Palestinian Jews had to chose one side or the other; they were not otherwise, however, members of 'parties'.

As the Jews watched and participated in the success of the Hasmonean revolt, and considered how things should be arranged, these seem to have been the principal questions:

1. *Hellenization*. The vengeance wreaked by the Hasmoneans and the Hasideans on those who accepted pagan practice very successfully discouraged it. Extreme Hellenization – sacrifice to foreign gods, ignoring the Jewish dietary laws and disguising the marks of circumcision – was not a continuing issue. Nor was their own 'freedom of religion': all Jews agreed that they should have their own beliefs and observances, and this was granted by everybody else until Hadrian proscribed circumcision (*c.* 130 CE). In the future there would still be questions about the introduction of Hellenistic institutions, such as games, and in general about relations between Jews and Gentiles. Could they socialize, could Jews eat Gentile food, could they intermarry? But the issues that sparked the revolt were settled by it: Jews would not engage in pagan religion, and they would not accept the most blatant and publicly obvious forms of Hellenization.

2. *The law*. The rejection of Hellenization essentially meant that Jews in Palestine would live according to the law of Moses. How strictly they would follow it, and how it would be interpreted in detail, were issues that led to much continuing controversy. But the fundamental result was clear. Later, the Hasmoneans undertook to bring all Palestine, including many Gentiles in Galilee and elsewhere, under the Mosaic law. Alexander Jannaeus (103–76) was especially successful at conquering the independent Hellenistic cities in Palestine, thus making Jewish law supreme even there. Pompey, however, restored the independence of the Hellenistic cities, and during the Roman period Jews did not force Gentiles to accept the Jewish law. There were

substantial Gentile populations in several cities, such as Caesarea (on the Mediterranean coast) and Scythopolis (Hebrew, Beth-Shean; just west of the Jordan).[6]

3. *The high priesthood.* We shall examine the continuing history and status of the office in ch. 15. Here it suffices to say that it was seen as being of crucial importance, and to many – perhaps most – was more important than the issue of military control. Many doubtless cared about the high priest's views: would he be a 'strict constructionist' of biblical law or not? Would he be open to the Hellenistic world or not? These issues mattered, but so did his lineage. We saw in the story of the Hasidean scribes (I Macc. 7.12–16) that some saw lineage as more important than policy. From 520 to 175 BCE the high priest had been (or was thought to be) a descendant of Zadok. That is a very long time, and many remained fiercely loyal to the descendants of Zadok and resented other high priests.

4. *Military control.* During the post-exilic era, under the high priesthood of the Zadokites, Judaism had gone through a long period as a rather peaceful theocracy. Throughout this time Palestine had been in some empire or other – Persia's, Alexander's, the Ptolemies', the Seleucids' – but never militarily autonomous. The local ruler had been the high priest, whose authority radiated out from the temple. He could determine what went on there and in general could control Jerusalem. He had influence and power throughout Judaea. The limited success of Judas Maccabeus in 164, therefore, in part restored the situation that had lasted since the late 500s BCE: the high priest ran the temple and Jerusalem, a remote king took care of bigger issues. Now, of course, there was a local strong man: first Judas and then two of his brothers in succession. But it was reasonable for many to wish to stop the revolt and to make peace with Syria when the temple was rededicated. The Persian and Hellenistic periods had not been all bad, and some would have been glad to return to the situation before the Hellenistic controversy and the revolt.

The Early Hasmonean Period

166–160	Judas Maccabeus	175–164	Antiochus IV (Epiphanes)
160–143	Jonathan	162–150	Demetrius I of Syria
		150–145	Alexander Balas
142–134	Simon	145–139	Demetrius II

The Hasmoneans were not content with restoring the old order. Judas showed his own ambition when he wrote to Rome and requested an alliance, a request that was granted (I Macc. 8.1). Rome even wrote to Demetrius I, threatening war if he further interfered with the Jews (I Macc. 8.31–32).

Despite this, there was further conflict between Jews and the Seleucid empire, and Judas fell in battle in the year 160. He was succeeded by his brother Jonathan, who successfully exploited internal divisions in Syria and extended his powers. Jonathan was appointed high priest by Alexander Balas, one of the contenders for the Syrian throne, in 152 (I Macc. 10.18–20). Alexander's competitor, Demetrius I, promptly offered Jonathan exemption from taxes (10.26–33). Jonathan obtained still other favours from Demetrius II, but was treacherously slain in 143. His brother Simon sought and obtained complete independence, being named 'High Priest and Friend of Kings' by Demetrius II, who also granted exemption from taxes (I Macc. 10.30–31) and the right to maintain fortresses. This was complete autonomy (142 BCE). The people 'began to engross their documents and contracts, "In the year one of Simon, great high priest, military commissioner, and leader of the Jews"' (I Macc. 13.36–42). He finally occupied the fortress Acra, the last stronghold of the Hellenizers and their Syrian supporters.

This settled for eighty years the issues that we discussed above, at least in general terms. The fall of the Acra terminated any lingering hopes that the Hellenizers still had. Jewish distinctiveness would be maintained, circumcision would be kept, and the Mosaic law would be enforced. Simon and his successors acted very much like other Hellenistic kings, and various aspects of Hellenistic culture continued to percolate through Palestine, but there would be no further effort to break down the barriers between Judaism and the rest of the Graeco-Roman world.

The issues of the high priesthood and military power were also settled. In gratitude to Simon the people of Jerusalem erected bronze tablets on Mount Zion, recounting his successes and recording that

> the Jews and their priests decided that Simon should be their leader and high priest for ever, until a trustworthy prophet should arise, and that he should be governor over them and that he should take charge of the sanctuary and appoint men over its tasks and over the country and the weapons and the stronghold, and that he should take charge of the sanctuary, and that he should be obeyed by all, and that all contracts in the country should be written in his name, and that he should be clothed in purple and wear gold. (I Macc. 14.41–43)

'High priest for ever' means that he and his descendants would be high priests. The office had been up for sale since 175, but now a decision was taken to revoke the rights of the family of Zadok. There was an escape clause in making Simon and his successors high priests: a 'trustworthy prophet' might establish otherwise.

It is noteworthy that the proclamation ties together 'leader and high priest', and only then specifies the right to control arms. That the high priest should be the leader of the nation was the natural assumption. In his office as high priest, Simon could also behave like a king, wearing purple and gold.[7] He accepted these honours in the year 140.

Simon enjoyed his success for a few years before being killed by his son-in-law (134), which shows that internecine strife was by no means over. We shall soon learn that the Hasmonean settlement was not approved by everyone.

The Period of Full Autonomy

142–134	Simon
134–104	John Hyrcanus
104–103	Aristobulus
103–76	Alexander Jannaeus
76–67	Salome Alexandra

Simon's successor was his third son, John Hyrcanus (Hyrcanus I), who had a long and successful rule, from 134 to 104. He was succeeded by his son Aristobulus (104–103), and then by another son, Alexander Jannaeus (103–76). One of these rulers first took the title 'king', but there is some uncertainty which it was.[8] It matters little. In any case Simon and his descendants were in effect kings as well as high priests.

Josephus first mentions the three parties – the Pharisees, the Sadducees and the Essenes (not the 'fourth philosophy') – when he describes the reign of Jonathan, but he offers specific stories about them only later: during the reign of John Hyrcanus (Sadducees and Pharisees) and Aristobulus (Essenes).[9] This is the principal circumstance that leads to the conclusion that it was in part the success of Jonathan and Simon that resulted in the formation of named groups. We have seen in general why this was the case, and now we shall try to be more precise.

The high priesthood was a major issue. The question of the high priest's lineage was fundamental in the case of the Essenes and possibly in the case of the Sadducees. It was an important early issue for the Pharisees. We shall take the clearest case first: the support for separate religious establishments that were ruled by Zadokites.

During the turmoil of the 170s and 160s, one of the Zadokite priests fled to Egypt and established a temple in Leontopolis.[10] There was a large Jewish population in Egypt, and the priest obviously had local support. There is some dispute as to which priest it was, a dispute that is made more difficult by the fact that Josephus' account is partially confused.[11] Many scholars think that Josephus misnumbered the priests who were named Onias, and that

Josephus' Onias III was in fact the second of the name. They hold that it was his son, Onias III (called by Josephus Onias IV), who built the temple in Egypt.[12] Others accept Josephus' numbering, and some hold that it was Josephus' Onias III who, after losing control in Jerusalem, fled to Egypt.[13] Whatever the truth of these complicated issues may be, in any case it is certain that an Onias, a Zadokite priest, fled Jerusalem and founded a rival temple in Egypt.[14]

This was not the first new temple to be built in order to provide a Zadokite with a high priesthood. In approximately 332 BCE Manasses, brother of the high priest Jaddus, arranged to have a temple built in Samaria, over which he could be high priest (*Antiq.* 11.322–4; for the background, 11.306–312). Possibly there was still another Zadokite temple. Approximately 180 BCE one Hyrcanus, the youngest son of a Zadokite high priest, fearing that his brothers would take his life, crossed the Jordan and established himself as a minor ruler at a place now known as Araq el-Emir, northeast of the Sea of Galilee. According to Josephus, he built a fortress there (*Antiq.* 12.222–34). The site has been frequently investigated, and some archaeologists think that the 'fortress' was actually a temple.[15] Even east of the Jordan he may have carried on the family profession.

In pursuit of their vocation, other members of the family – supported by some lay people, possibly some of the Hasideans – founded the Dead Sea Sect, which was a branch of the Essene party. The members of the Sect undertook to obey the law of Moses 'in accordance with all that has been revealed of it to the sons of Zadok, the Keepers of the Covenant and Seekers of His will, and to the multitude of the men of their Covenant' (1QS 5.8f.). 'Their Covenant' means 'the covenant of the sons of Zadok'. Other texts look forward to the coming of two messiahs, one a priest-messiah, the other a lay messiah, the priest being the more important of the two. In particular the messiah of Israel should defer to the priest-messiah with regard to teaching the law and judging according to it (e.g. 1QSa 2.12–21).[16]

The chief organizer of the Sect as we know it from the Dead Sea Scrolls is called 'the Teacher of Righteousness', though the roots of the Essene party may be pre-Hasmonean,[17] and it may have existed in some sense before the arrival of the Teacher. Very little is actually known of him, though there are speculative suggestions about his identity. In view of the importance of the Zadokite priests in the Sect, it is very likely that the Teacher was himself a member of that family. He was persecuted, possibly killed, by 'the wicked priest' (1QpHab. 11), who must have been one of the Hasmoneans. In view of other evidence, there are two major possibilities: he was either Jonathan or Simon, probably Jonathan.[18]

The question of Essene origins is one of unusual interest, and we shall return to it in ch. 16. The details of the origins of each of the parties, however, are peripheral to our purposes. Here the main point is that loyalty to the Zadokites resulted in one new temple, possibly two, and at least one sect.

It is possible that the Sadducees also intended to claim the authority of the Zadokite priesthood. The origin of the name 'Sadducees' cannot be determined with precision, and there are two principal possibilities, neither one entirely satisfactory from the point of view of spelling and pronunciation. One is that the party name derives from the word *tsedeq*, 'righteousness', *tsaddiq*, 'righteous'. The second possibility is derivation from the proper name Zadok. Of the two, the second is to be preferred, partly because of pronunciation. It is difficult to derive the second syllable of Sadducee from *tsedeq* or *tsaddiq*, but slightly less difficult from Zadok: in Hebrew the long *o* and long *u* are indicated by the same letter.[19]

If this etymology is right, the origin of the Sadducees as a group would be understood as follows: some priests who could trace their descent from Zadok agreed with the popular consensus that named the Hasmonean Simon 'high priest for ever' – or they went along with it. The Zadokites lost the high priesthood, but those who stayed in Jerusalem (fleeing neither to Egypt nor to the Judaean Desert) retained a good deal of wealth and power. These Zadokites joined other aristocratic priests, and they were supported by laymen who were willing or happy to accept the compromise between the Hasmoneans and this branch of the Zadokites. That is, the remaining Zadokites lent their name and prestige to the Hasmonean settlement, and in return were allowed to retain their possessions and some aspects of their former position. Those who accepted this arrangement were called 'Sadducees'. On this hypothesis, the Zadokites did not stand out as a group still seeking the high priesthood, but merged indistinguishably into the Sadducean party. Too great prominence on the part of the Zadokites would have been fatal under the Hasmoneans.

It is to be noted that the Zadokite family was a large one, and there was already a history of serious factions within it. Thus the possibility that in the 150s or 140s the family split into at least three groups (Egyptian, Essene and Sadducean) poses no intrinsic difficulty. The substantial problem with the derivation of 'Sadducee' from 'Zadok' is that we must suppose that after the accession of Simon to the high priesthood the Zadokites were prominent enough to lend their name to the aristocratic party, but not prominent enough to attract the hostile regard of successive Hasmoneans. A second difficulty is the evidence, admittedly slight, that the early Hasmonean rulers were sympathetic to the Pharisees. There are, however, no better answers to the question of the origin of the Sadducees. The proposal accepted here is etymologically superior to others (though not perfect), and it also explains the subsequent connection between the Sadducees and the eminent.

Finally, we may note that people who were probably Zadokites reappear twice in Jerusalem. After Herod the Great gained control of Jerusalem in 37 BCE he appointed Hananel, probably a member of the Zadokite family, as high priest. Hananel is said to have been a Babylonian, which presumably means that he belonged to a wing of the Zadokite family that had remained in Babylon. The last high priest to serve, Pinhas of Habta, who was chosen by the Zealots in 67 or 68 CE, was also probably a Zadokite.[20]

The Pharisaic party did not originate because of the dispute about the high priesthood, although, as we shall see below, some Pharisees had views about it. The Pharisees are usually traced to the Hasideans of I Maccabees, as are the lay or non-priestly Essenes. Not enough is known of the Hasideans to allow us to treat this as more than a hypothesis. There is one objection to it: scholars with a few fragments of information tend to suppose that they are interrelated, but this need not be the case. We do not know enough about pietist groups in the early Hasmonean period to say that the Pharisees definitely came from the one group for which we have a name.

Among the Pharisees there were both priests and non-priests, but we do not know what percentage of each. There is some evidence that early Pharisaic material focused more on the temple than did later.[21] Our information about the Pharisees increases after the reign of Herod the Great (died 4 BCE), and in the later period the party was predominantly lay. Whether lay or priestly, however, the members were scholars, careful students of the law (as were the Essenes and the priests). It is possibly important for the origins of the party that in I Macc. 7.12 the Hasideans are called 'scribes' – experts on the law.[22] Similarly, as we shall see in detail below, the Pharisees were zealous for the law and kept it strictly. These are also characteristics of the Hasideans, who early in the Maccabean revolt refused to fight on the sabbath, with the result that many were killed (I Macc. 2.29–38 specifies one thousand). We must emphasize, however, that not only the Hasideans and (later) the Pharisees were zealous for the law: so were the Essenes, and so were most Judaeans, though they may not have interpreted it as strictly as did the groups of the specially pious. Nevertheless the Hasideans and the Pharisees are singled out by their devotion to the law, and most scholars prefer a genetic explanation: the Pharisees rose from the ranks of a more general Hasidic ('pietist') movement.

Josephus' first summary of the three parties is in *Antiq.* 13.171f., at the time of Jonathan (died 143). The summary is general and could have been put anywhere, but it is nevertheless likely that the Pharisees took on social identity between 164 (the rededication of the temple) and 134 (the beginning of the reign of John Hyrcanus, the first of Mattathias' grandsons to come to power). The first concrete story about them belongs to the period of John Hyrcanus. He asked the Pharisees whether they found anything wrong in his conduct. The party 'testified to his being altogether virtuous', but one member, Eleazar, advised him to surrender the high priesthood 'and be content with governing the people'. Motivated by a Sadducee, Hyrcanus asked the Pharisees to fix Eleazar's punishment. Being mild of judgment, they proposed flogging and imprisonment in chains. Hyrcanus had wanted the death penalty; angered, he broke with the party and sided with the Sadducees (*Antiq.* 13.288–98).[23]

There is a similar story in the Talmud, according to which a Pharisee rebuked not John Hyrcanus, but his successor once removed, Alexander Jannaeus (103–76), who then executed 'all the sages of Israel' (*Kiddushin* 66a). Alexander Jannaeus, the Talmud and Josephus agree, executed numerous people. Some scholars follow the Talmud and thus put the Pharisees' first public appearance in the time of Alexander Jannaeus, but it seems better to accept Josephus, who probably had an earlier source, and place this incident early in the reign of John Hyrcanus (134–104). If this is correct, then the origin of the Pharisees as a distinct group, which is taken for granted in Josephus' story, must be dated before 134, and thus at approximately the same time as the rise of the Essenes. The Sadducees also figure in Josephus' story, and so it is likely that all three parties gained full identity at about the same time. The point of Josephus' story is to explain why Hyrcanus followed the Sadducees rather than the Pharisees.

There seems to have been little opposition to the Hasmoneans' assuming political and military control. The story about the Hasideans who accepted Alcimus as high priest (above, p. 18) shows that some were prepared to lay down their arms before political and military autonomy was achieved, and some of these were doubtless drawn into groups that emphasized obedience to the law above military autonomy, but only the Dead Sea Sect felt obliged to leave Jerusalem. The Pharisees, while critical of the Hasmoneans for assuming the high priesthood, were content to live in Jerusalem under their authority.

This complicated history can be simplified by a genealogical diagram that is based on the various possibilities and probabilities that we have discussed:

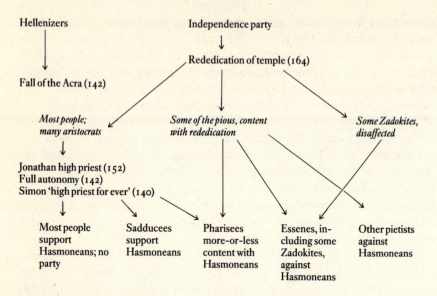

Hellenizers

Independence party

↓

Rededication of temple (164)

↓

Fall of the Acra (142)

Most people;
many aristocrats

Some of the pious, content
with rededication

Some Zadokites,
disaffected

↓

Jonathan high priest (152)
Full autonomy (142)
Simon 'high priest for ever' (140)

↓

| Most people support Hasmoneans; no party | Sadducees support Hasmoneans | Pharisees more-or-less content with Hasmoneans | Essenes, including some Zadokites, against Hasmoneans | Other pietists against Hasmoneans |

According to the diagram, the Sadducees spring from the ranks of the supporters of the Hasmoneans, being distinguished from the mass only by their social status and some of their theological views. Some members of the former high priestly family, the Zadokites, became Sadducees.

The Pharisees probably included both Hasmonean supporters and some of the Hasideans who were disenchanted with their military success and 'usurpation' of the high priesthood. On average they stood lower than the Sadducees on the socio-economic scale (two hundred years later we learn of one prominent Pharisaic family).

The Essenes were a combination of Zadokite radicals who would not compromise with the Hasmoneans and some pietists who had divergent views from other pietists, such as the Pharisees, on numerous topics. Some Essenes would not compromise at all and lived in the Judaean desert, while others lived in towns and cities, while still maintaining a higher than normal degree of separation, purity and legal rigour.

At the time of Pompey (63 BCE) we shall find unnamed pietists who regarded the Hasmoneans as wicked, but who were neither Pharisees nor Essenes.

The Hasmoneans themselves were not necessarily members of one of the named parties. We learn that Queen Salome Alexandra (76–67) was committed to the Pharisees and John Hyrcanus to the Sadducees (134–104), but otherwise there is no direct evidence of where the rulers stood via à vis the parties. Indirect evidence will show that Jannaeus and the Pharisees were enemies, and it is probable that the Pharisees allied with Hyrcanus II after

Salome Alexandra's death (on Hyrcanus II, see the next chapter; on the Pharisees, see further ch. 18).

Finally, there are 'most people', both priests and laity. They generally supported the Hasmonean family, and they considered themselves loyal to God, the Bible and Israel; but they were not members of a party.

3

Historical Outline of the Roman Period

We shall cover the remaining history with extreme economy, offering just enough information to allow the reader to identify people and events when we return to them under topical headings, where several aspects of this period will be discussed in some detail.

From the Hasmoneans to Herod

76–67 BCE	Salome Alexandra queen
76–67	Hyrcanus II high priest
67–63	Aristobulus II king and high priest
63	Conquest of Judaea by Pompey
63–40	Hyrcanus II high priest and ethnarch
40–37	Antigonus king and high priest
37–4	Herod the Great king
37–35	Hananel high priest
35	Aristobulus III high priest
35–30	Hananel again high priest

Alexander Jannaeus and Salome Alexandra had two sons, Hyrcanus II and Aristobulus II. When Alexander Jannaeus died his wife assumed the office and title of Queen, and the older son, Hyrcanus II, became high priest. When Salome died, however, Aristobulus II, the more vigorous of the two brothers, raised an army, defeated Hyrcanus II, and took both the high priesthood and the throne. Internal squabbles continued, but they were temporarily settled by Pompey, who took Jerusalem on behalf of Rome (63 BCE).

Pompey reduced the Jewish territory, assigning some of it to direct Roman rule under the legate of Syria, but he reinstated Hyrcanus II as high priest and allowed him also the title 'ethnarch', 'ruler of the people'. There now enters upon the scene the man whose family would be the dominant political force until the outbreak of the revolt 129 years later: Antipater, an Idumaean.

Idumaea was a subject region that lay just south of Judaea. It had been added to the Jewish state by John Hyrcanus (in 125), and forced conversions had followed. Antipater's father, Antipas, had been appointed administrator of Idumaea by Alexander Jannaeus (*Antiq.* 14.10). Antipater may have had the same office. He entered Judaean affairs by siding with Hyrcanus II against Aristobulus II, and after Pompey reinstated Hyrcanus II, Antipater emerged with more power. The questions of just what authority he had formally, and what were his titles from time to time, are vexed, but we do not need to settle them (see Marcus' note to *Antiq.* 14.127). Antipater now became a force in Judaea, having the military under his control.

Civil war broke out between the leading Roman generals, Pompey and Julius Caesar. Antipater shrewdly backed Caesar, using some Jewish troops, and when Caesar emerged victorious he was generous to both Hyrcanus and Antipater. Hyrcanus was confirmed in his office, and some of the land taken from the Jewish state by Pompey was restored, but Antipater was also advanced. He became virtual ruler, and he appointed two sons, Phasael and Herod, as governors. The older, Phasael, was over Judaea; the young Herod was over Galilee.

The Hasmoneans, however, were not a negligible force. They retained much of the loyalty of the populace. They were, for one thing, Jewish, while the ancestry of Antipater and his sons was doubted: the family may have been Idumaean in origin, forcibly converted.[1] Further, the Hasmonean family had once freed Israel from foreign oppression and for many years had reigned over a kingdom as large as David's, thus restoring Jewish pride.[2] Had they made a concerted and well-planned effort, they might well have resumed real power – still under Rome, to be sure, but not under Antipater and his sons. Instead, there was more strife between the two brothers. Hyrcanus II, formally in power, was apparently not forceful, but his presence kept Aristobulus from attaining power. It is very likely that both Antipater and Rome liked the situation as it was, since Hyrcanus II was not the man to try to re-establish full independence. After the assassination of Julius Caesar in 44 BCE, civil war again broke out in Rome. In the confused period that followed, Phasael and Herod more than once backed the winning side. They were counted on successively by Cassius and by Antony. Herod, further-more, astutely became engaged to a Hasmonean princess, Mariamme, which gave him a degree of standing with the many Jews still loyal to the family. Though doubtless motivated in part by political expediency, the union was, at least on Herod's part, a love match.

One further event secured for Herod the support of Rome. Parthia, a fierce military kingdom to the east of Palestine, which would remain one of Rome's principal enemies for years to come, overran the Near East, including Palestine. There the Parthians had an alliance with Antigonus, the son of Aristobulus II, who now made his own bid for power. In an attempt to make a negotiated peace, Phasael met with the Parthians. They treacherously chained and imprisoned him. He subsequently was murdered or committed suicide. The Parthians placed Antigonus on the throne. The latter had the ears (or an ear) of his uncle, Hyrcanus II, cut off, a mutilation that made him ineligible to resume the high priesthood.[3] Herod, however, escaped the Parthians and went to Rome in hope of support. Seeking a strong man to withstand the Parthian menace, later in 40 BCE the Senate named Herod 'king of the Jews', thus deposing the Hasmoneans, at least in theory. Aided by Rome, especially by troops from his friend, Antony, Herod conquered Galilee. By the Spring of 37, he was ready to besiege Jerusalem, though he paused to marry Mariamme.

The siege was eventually successful. Antigonus was taken captive and later beheaded, at Herod's request and on the orders of Antony. 'It was the first time that the Romans had executed such a sentence on a king.'[4] Herod now was king in fact as well as in name.

Herod combined extraordinary vigour with personal bravery, tactical skill, ruthlessness, and administrative gifts; and he was up to the task of being king of the Jews. The Romans left him to it, having at last found a reliable client king who could hold down the most unruly part of the empire, which they had conquered but not occupied or administered.

By the year 25 BCE Herod had won for himself a sizable kingdom, covering Palestine and some of the area east of it. In these years he had one bit of luck. In the final stage of Roman civil war, none of Herod's troops were engaged on the side of Antony and Cleopatra against Octavian. When Octavian defeated them, and thus became supreme over the entire Roman Empire (31 BCE), he confirmed Herod's large domain and the title 'king'.

In the midst of securing his realm and aiding successive Roman generals, Herod feared for his own security. The surviving Hasmoneans were the most obvious threat, since he knew that marriage into the family was not enough to secure him the loyalty of Jewish Palestine. Early in his reign he appointed Aristobulus III, Mariamme's brother, as high priest, but, when he saw how popular the young Hasmonean was, he had him drowned (35 BCE). He suspected his beloved Mariamme of being implicated in a plot against him, and he had her killed. There are two slightly different versions of the deed, which took place in either 35–34 BCE or 29 BCE. He had Hyrcanus II executed just after Octavian's defeat of Antony, probably to make sure there was no alternative to his own rule.

The execution of Mariamme, though it may have shaken his mental balance, did not lead to a diminution of his physical vigour or of his military and administrative skill. They remained high for years to come, during which he kept his diverse and difficult domain pacified, while launching one of the greatest building programmes ever undertaken by a minor king. He had work started to rebuild the temple in Jerusalem on a scale never known before, he built numerous large edifices throughout Palestine, he constructed for himself several impregnable fortresses (in case of rebellion), and he even donated temples and other buildings to cities outside Palestine. He thus enjoyed great autonomy, and he could dispose of most of the revenue of his kingdom.

As he aged, his fears for his own security became more pronounced. In the end his suspicions even extended to his sons. First to go were his two surviving sons by Mariamme, who had Hasmonean blood in their veins. He had them arrested for plotting against him – which may have been true. They were tried on Augustus' order, for Augustus would always support such an able 'friend of Rome' as Herod was. A court of Romans and of Herod's relatives found the young men guilty, and they were executed in 7 BCE. Herod directly ordered a third son to be executed just five months before his own death in 4 BCE.

The Herodians; Judaea a Province of Rome

4 BCE–6 CE	Archelaus ethnarch, ruler of Judaea
4 BCE–39 CE	Antipas tetrarch, ruler of Galilee and Peraea
6–41 CE	Judaea governed directly by Roman prefects
41–44	Agrippa I king, ruling over Herod's former kingdom
44–66	Judaea, Samaria and part of Galilee ruled directly by Roman procurators
48–66	Agrippa II given piecemeal parts of his father's kingdom
66–74	the Jewish revolt
70	the fall of Jerusalem

Herod left two wills, and Augustus finally decided to break the kingdom into three parts, which he parcelled out among three surviving sons. Archelaus received the largest share – Judaea (including Jerusalem), Samaria and Idumaea – as well as the title ethnarch. Antipas received Galilee and Peraea (east of the Jordan), and Philip several territories north and east of the Sea of Galilee. Both were given the title tetrarch, 'ruler of a fourth'.

Archelaus' career as ethnarch was not a success. Delegations of both Jews and Samaritans accused him of brutality and maladministration, and Augustus banished him to Gaul (France) in 6 CE. His territory was then directly administered by Rome, by an official called a 'prefect'. In Rome's second period of direct rule the administrator was termed 'procurator'; the latter word is sometimes incorrectly used for the prefects; thus Pilate, a prefect, has generally been called a procurator. The difficulties with terminology are not just modern. Authors who wrote in Greek did not always use the same Greek word for the each of the various Latin titles of Roman administrators. Luke used the same word for Pilate and for his superior, Quirinius, the legate of Syria (Luke 2.2; 3.1), but Josephus did much the same thing (e.g. *Antiq.* 15.345; 18.55).

The prefects resided in Caesarea, on the coast, which reduced the offence to Jewish sensibilities, according to which the world was structured in concentric circles of increasing holiness. The Holy of Holies in the temple was the very centre; Jerusalem was holier than Caesarea. The farther the Romans stayed away from the temple the better, and for the most part the Romans agreed. We shall return to other aspects of Jewish life under the Romans below.

Antipas fared much better than Archelaus. He lasted for forty-three years, until his second wife, Herodias, persuaded him to seek the title king; the result of the request was that he was deposed and exiled.

His territory was given to one of Herod's grandsons, Agrippa I, whose father was one of the sons whom Herod had executed. Agrippa was eventually entrusted with Judaea as well, but he died after a short reign.

His son, Agrippa II, was too young to be given authority, and so Rome again sent officials to govern Judaea directly. The Judaea that they governed was larger than it had been previously and included some of Galilee. Agrippa II was given increased responsibility as he matured, but most of Palestine was still under direct Roman rule when the revolt started in 66. Agrippa sided with Rome and retained some of his land after the Roman victory. The last notable Herodian, he died in approximately 100.

4

The Context of Conflict

Revolts and riots were part and parcel of life in Palestine during the Roman period, and to a considerable degree also during the Hasmonean period. It seems that every time an opportunity appeared there was an uprising of some sort. This at least is the standard view. One could, however, emphasize the other side: there were periods of strong and stable government that were marked by peace and tranquillity. During Antipas' forty-three years as tetrarch of Galilee, there seem to have been no revolts and only one notable war, which consisted of only one engagement. Despite Herod's fears, during his own reign the only wars were those in which he engaged for reasons of state – enlargement of domain or support of allies. Judaea was on the whole calm from the time Archelaus was deposed to the death of Agrippa I (from 6 to 44 CE), and for a lot of the time thereafter.

'History' has generally been understood as the story of violence and change. Social history has flourished from time to time in the nineteenth and twentieth centuries, but for the most part history has been the story of war and changes of government. That is the kind of history that Josephus wrote. But this style of narrative can be deceiving. For the relatively peaceful years 1945–1990, one could write a history full of riots and wars, even if one focused only on the stable western democracies. Such a history would obscure the degree to which domestic transquillity has prevailed. Judged by the standard of the twentieth century, first-century Palestine was not especially violent, though Josephus' history gives the impression of continual upheaval.

Besides writing a history that basically moves from war to war or riot to riot, Josephus had a more particular theory to advance: that as the great revolt of 66 drew nearer, the incidence of violence increased, spurred on by Roman mis-government and Jewish 'brigandage'. Modern scholars often accept this, and write as if there was a steady escalation of Jewish fervour for independence until finally war broke out. In fact, the revolt seems to have taken everyone by surprise, and the evidence is against the view that Jewish Palestine was steadily working itself up for war.

Yet, all this granted, one must nevertheless say that the possibility of insurrection was always present. Palestine was more like post-World War II eastern Europe than western: puppets ruled on behalf of an overwhelmingly strong foreign nation, and the imperial power could intervene at any time to impose its will. The people, left to themselves, would have preferred to be governed differently. The situation was worse yet: they would not have agreed on how to be governed. When not held down by Herod or Rome, Jews often fought among themselves. Thus we may and should doubt that the total quantity of violence was remarkable and that there was a steady escalation of revolutionary zeal, but we should accept the view that insurrection was never very far from the surface.

We cannot now say precisely what every rebel or rioter wanted. Presumably they all wanted 'freedom' – that is, they wished for society to be run according to their views rather than those of someone else. The precise changes that rebels desired varied from group to group, from person to person and from time to time.

As in ch. 1, we may distinguish internal affairs from external. Some Jews were willing to forego independence in one area if they could have it in another. Some were willing to leave to Rome, or to Herod, or to one of his successors, certain aspects of government, such as military control and foreign policy, if they would not interfere in others – especially the temple. 'Freedom' meant different things to different people.

Further, people who hoped for change disagreed very substantially with regard to what they should do. Not everyone who wanted 'freedom' is correctly called a 'rebel' or 'freedom fighter'. Some were pacifists. Of these some were willing to work within the system. Others thought that God himself would step in and take a direct hand and that they did not need to resort to arms.[1] Pacifism and going unarmed, however, did not necessarily keep safe those who were dissatisfied with the current state of affairs. Some who followed non-military paths were nevertheless cut down by the sword or executed.

In order to see the persistence of internal strife, armed uprising, and peaceful protest, as well as the periods of relative tranquillity, we shall briefly survey the major instances of conflict in the period 63 BCE–74 CE.

1. Prolonged strife between Hyrcanus II and Aristobulus II led to Roman intervention in Palestine. Both brothers sought support from the Roman general Pompey, who was then in Syria. In the end he decided on conquest, which culminated in a massacre after a lengthy siege of the temple mount (*War* 1.124–51).

2. According to the version in the *Antiquities* (14.29–60), when the delegates of Hyrcanus II and Aristobulus II were petitioning Pompey, before he decided what steps to take, 'the nation' argued a third case:

> the nation was against them both and asked not to be ruled by a king, saying that it was the custom of their country to obey the priests of the God who was venerated by them, but that these two, who were descended from the priests, were seeking to change their form of government in order that they might become a nation of slaves. (*Antiq.* 14.41)

Here the discontent was with the degree to which the Hasmoneans had become ordinary Hellenistic kings, ruling with absolute power. It appears that the Jews who made this protest would have been more comfortable with the situation of the Persian and Ptolemaic periods: a distant monarch, no close supervision of daily life, and local government by the high priest and his council. It may be this view that made many willing to admit Pompey to Jerusalem (*War* 1.142–43). They could well have reflected that the Romans would be content to collect taxes and enforce certain laws, but that they would be willing for local laws to prevail in other areas of life (as Rome often was). There was the hope that, under Roman rule, there would be greater internal freedom with regard to the observance of the Jewish law. The state would again become a theocracy, governed by the high priest and his council.

The period during which Herod was establishing his control was filled with insurgencies of various kinds. Three cases will show the range of protest and revolt.

3. Most of the civil war during the period had as its cause the conflict between Hyrcanus II and Aristobulus II, and later between Hyrcanus and Aristobulus' son Antigonus. When the Parthians invaded Syria (40 BCE), many Jews used this as an occasion to flock to Antigonus and to besiege Hyrcanus II and Phasael. Herod's troops won the day, but sixty men who were posted as guards over the captives were assaulted and burned to death. This led Herod to a massacre (*War* 1.250–2).

4. There were numerous minor uprisings. An example is that of Helix, who was defeated by Phasael (*War* 1.236f.).

5. During the year 39–38 Herod routed or destroyed many rebels in Galilee. But some, called by Josephus 'brigands', took refuge in caves that opened on to steep cliffs. Soldiers who were let down on ropes hurled firebrands into the caves, killing many. Some were taken captive. We get an idea of their temper by quoting one incident:

> Not one of them voluntarily surrendered, and of those taken by force many preferred death to captivity. It was then that one old man, the father of

seven children, being asked by them and their mother permission to leave
under Herod's pledge, killed them in the following manner. Ordering
them to come forward one-by-one, he stood at the entrance and slew
each son as he advanced. Herod, watching this spectacle from a conspicuous spot, was profoundly affected and, extending his hand to the old
man, implored him to spare his children; but he, unmoved by any word of
Herod, and even upbraiding him as a low-born upstart, followed up the
slaughter of his sons by that of his wife, and, having flung their corpses
down the precipice, finally threw himself over after them. (*War*
1.311–13)

It is evident that such people were not 'brigands'. They were unwilling to
live under Herod.

6. Herod finally pacified the kingdom, and we hear little of revolts, since
no opportunities presented themselves. One event from his last year
(5 BCE), however, may be mentioned. Herod had erected over the great
gate of the temple 'as a votive offering and at great cost, a great golden
eagle'. Two men, Judas and Matthaias, the 'most learned of the Jews and
unrivalled interpreters of the ancestral laws', who taught the youth of the
city and were beloved by many, knowing that Herod's end was near,
decided that the time had come to pull down the eagle. They inspired young
men to do this. Herod, however, was not near enough death to be
ineffective, and he had many of the protesters, including the teachers,
arrested, tried and burned alive. He also deposed the high priest, on the
grounds that he was partially responsible (*War* 1.651–5; *Antiq.* 17.149–67).

7. In 4 BCE, when Herod died, there were revolts. A group of pilgrims,
who had come to Jerusalem for the feast of Pentecost, rebelled. There
followed an uprising by the Idumaeans in Herod's mixed army of
Idumaeans and Jews, and then a revolt in Galilee led by Judas, son of
Ezekias. A Simon revolted in Peraea, east of the Jordan. Herod's heir in
Judaea, Archelaus, aided by Varus, the Roman legate in Syria, finally
restored order (*War* 2.39–79; *Antiq.* 17.271–98; 17.369f.).

8. When Augustus was considering the distribution of Herod's estate
and kingdom, a deputation of Jews pleaded that he not give power to any of
Herod's descendants. They wished what Josephus terms 'autonomy', which
turns out to mean that they asked the Romans 'to unite their country to
Syria and to entrust the administration to governors from among themselves' (*War* 2.80,91). This appeal agrees with that of 'the nation' to
Pompey (no. 2 above): the rule of a distant empire was appealing to many,
since they did not care about military success and national grandeur, but
rather – we presume – about being allowed to live according to the law.

9. Augustus, we saw above, appointed Herod's son Archelaus 'ethnarch' and made him ruler of Judaea, Samaria and Idumaea. After nine or ten years (6 CE), charges laid by deputations from Judaea and Samaria led Augustus to depose and exile him. The Emperor then sent Coponius, the first Roman prefect, to govern Judaea directly. This required a census for tax purposes, which in turn resulted in a revolt, led by Judas of Galilee (*War* 2.117f.; *Antiq.* 18.1–10).

10. When Pilate became prefect (26 CE), he ordered some of his troops to bring standards with the bust of Caesar on them into Jerusalem. A large number of Jews followed him to Caesarea and sat outside his residence for five days and nights. He summoned them to the tribunal and then had his troops surround them. When the soldiers drew their swords the Jews fell to the ground, 'extended their necks, and exclaimed that they were ready rather to die than to transgress the law'. Pilate, impressed, ordered that the standards be removed (*War* 2.169–74; *Antiq.* 18.55–9).

11. About 30 CE John the Baptist appeared in Galilee preaching the practice of 'righteousness' towards one another and 'piety' towards God, and his sermons excited the crowds. Antipas feared insurrection and had him executed (*Antiq.* 18.117–19).

12. When the emperor Gaius (Caligula) decided to have his statue erected in the temple (*c.* 41 CE), 'tens of thousands' of Jews met Petronius, the Syrian legate, at Ptolemais, asking that he slay them first. The scene was repeated at Tiberias. Petronius hesitated at the time, and the threat was later cancelled by Caligula's assassination (*Antiq.* 18.261–72; 18.305–9).

13. Under Fadus (44–46) a would-be prophet, Theudas, led a crowd to the Jordan, which he said would part on his command. The Romans sent troops, who killed many of his followers and captured others. They brought his head to Jerusalem (*Antiq.* 20.97–9; cf. Acts 5.36).

14. During the procuratorship of Felix (52–59 CE) prophets arose who led 'the multitude' into the desert, promising 'that God would there give them tokens of deliverance'. Felix sent troops 'and put a large number to the sword' (*War* 2.259f.).

15. In the same period another would-be prophet, 'the Egyptian', led many (Josephus, 30,000; Acts 4,000) in an attack on Jerusalem. The Romans killed and captured a large number, though the Egyptian escaped (*War* 2.261–3; cf. Acts 21.38).

16. When the war with Rome broke out in 66, a general assembly of the people, gathered in the temple, appointed as their leaders Ananus, the former high priest (deposed in 62) and another aristocrat, who is called Joseph son of Gorion in *War* 2.563 and Gorion son of Joseph in *War* 4.159. The other leaders were also aristocrats: the Pharisee Simeon son of Gamaliel and the

former high priest Jesus son of Gamalas (*War* 2.563; 4.158–61; *Life* 191–3, where the eminence of Simeon's family is emphasized). After Galilee fell, Zealots took refuge in Jerusalem, and eventually there was a bloody civil war that resulted in the deaths of the priestly leaders (Jesus son of Gamalas and Ananus) and thousands of their supporters (for the whole story, see *War* 4.121–365; for the deaths of the aristocratic leaders and the general slaughter of prominent families and their supporters, see esp. 4.312–16, 318, 323, 327–9, 335–44, 365).

Observations

The impression that the populace was moving ever closer to revolt is created by the events numbered 13, 14 and 15 above. Two prophets, Theudas and the Egyptian, led groups of followers to expect signs of deliverance (13 and 15), and there were others who did the same (14), all in the years 44–59 CE. The two major events of the period, however, were the protests against Pilate's standards, which probably involved mostly Jerusalemites (no. 10), and against Caligula's plan to have a statue erected in the temple (no. 12). This threat roused hostility and the fear of war even in the Diaspora (Philo, *Embassy* 213–17). These events took place in about 26 and 41 CE. They created the view that Rome might seriously interfere with the sanctity of Jerusalem and, worse, the temple. When Caligula was assassinated, everyone must have heaved a great sigh of relief; the threat of profanation had passed, and with it the threat of war. It is doubtful that the relatively minor actions of dispersing the crowds who followed would-be prophets led the general populace to think that things were getting worse and worse and that war was getting nearer and nearer.

The events that actually led to revolt were not connected with prophets and crowds of followers, were unforeseen, and took everyone by surprise. A group of Gentiles in Caesarea sacrificed birds in front of the synagogue. When the Jerusalemites heard of it, they were indignant, but they 'still restrained their feelings'. The procurator, Florus, however, at about that time took money from the temple treasury. This roused the populace greatly. He was then insulted in public. There was a massacre, followed by scourgings and crucifixions, and the fatal events were underway (*War.* 2.289–308; described more fully below, pp. 485f.). Two acts of what the Jews regarded as sacrilege, one by the procurator himself, led to the revolt. There would probably have been a revolt earlier, had Pilate persisted in displaying military standards in Jerusalem, or if Petronius had acted less cautiously. During the Roman period, tension rose and fell; it did not steadily mount. The day before Florus took the money from the temple, there was almost certainly less expectation of war than there had been fifteen years earlier, when Caligula threatened it with an 'abomination' (Dan. 9.27) almost as bad as Antiochus IV's pagan sacrifice.

We shall now attempt some summary characterizations of Jewish religio-political sentiment.

A. With regard to foreign rule: many bitterly resented it. The Hasmonean revolt was widely supported, and so was the revolt against Rome. Further, there would be another bloody attempt to gain independence from Rome in the 130s. The general desire for 'freedom' cannot be doubted.

On the other hand, foreign rule was not judged bad by everyone all the time. Some preferred foreign rule to that of a despot closer at hand and held that internal Jewish freedom – 'autonomy' – was enhanced by the rule of a distant empire (examples 2 and 8). The disagreement about what constituted worthwhile 'freedom' is evident in the tragic story of Hyrcanus II and Aristobulus II. Hyrcanus was weaker and more willing to obey stronger men – Antipater, Phasael, Herod and the Romans. He nevertheless had fair support from within Israel. Those who sided with Aristobulus (and later his son, Antigonus) were probably thereby backing a man who would fight for independence. The champions of Hyrcanus were indirectly supporting foreign domination. We recall that early in the days of the Hasmonean revolt some pious Jews were ready to stop the fight when the temple had been purged. The arguments of later generations who preferred Rome to either Hyrcanus or Aristobulus (case 2), or Rome to Archelaus (case 8), were not novel.

Josephus argues strongly that the majority of the Jews were prepared to be obedient to Rome. This is of course his own bias, but he may nevertheless be correct. Even as war grew near the chief priests were able to obtain signs of submission to Florus, the procurator, from a large number (*War* 2.320–29). It is probable that many would have been willing to remain obedient had the Romans always respected Jewish sensibilities and institutions. This is supported by the passive nature of the protests against the erection of Caligula's statue in the temple and Pilate's introduction of Roman standards into Jerusalem (examples 10 and 12). Those who protested wanted it to be clear that they did not threaten war, but were prepared to die passively rather than have the holiness of the city and the sanctuary defiled.

We should note that the Jews were not entirely unsophisticated about the nature and effectiveness of non-violent resistance. At the time of Caligula's threat to the temple they neglected their fields, even though it was time for either sowing (*Antiq.* 18.272) or harvesting (Philo, *Embassy* 249). This of course demonstrated their willingness to suffer, but it also meant that it would be impossible for Rome to collect tribute. Further, widespread hunger would lead to rioting. Petronius, the legate, realized that enforcing the order was bad policy (*Antiq.* 18.272–5).

B. There were factions in Israel that bitterly opposed one another. This is clear throughout, from the time of Antiochus IV on. When the revolt against Rome broke out internal factionalism could surface with full fury, culminating in the Zealot destruction of leading members of the Jewish aristocracy (example 16).

C. The factionalism was part of widespread unrest that erupted almost every time there was a hiatus between rulers: examples 4, 5, 7 and 9. The insurrectionists would not necessarily have agreed with one another about positive alternatives to the present situation (see B), but a lot of people were dissatisfied a lot of the time.

D. Many were susceptible to the appeal of charismatic leaders who offered the hope of divine intervention (examples 11, 13, 14 and 15).

E. Many, literally thousands, were ready to die rather than live under a regime that they did not like or tolerate offences against the institutions of Israel. Threats to the temple and to worship (6, 10 and 12) seem to have stirred more people than did military dominance (1, 3, 4 and 5), but the latter roused large numbers.

In his great apology for Judaism, *Against Apion*, Josephus emphasized Jewish willingness to die rather than to suffer godless regimes or actions:

> [We face] death on behalf of our laws with a courage which no other nation can equal. (*Apion* 2.234)

> And from these laws of ours nothing has had power to deflect us, neither fear of our masters, nor envy of the institutions esteemed by other nations. (*Apion* 2.271).

This is of course idealized: not all Jews preferred to die rather than betray the law, as the biography of Josephus shows quite well. Yet story after story reveals that his generalization is true.

Several times Josephus attributes the willingness to die rather than transgress to belief in 'a renewed existence' after death (*Apion* 2.218), and this is probably correct. We shall see that most believed in some form of afterlife. Josephus assigns this view to the leading teachers, Judas and Matthias, who persuaded some men to cut down the golden eagle over the temple (*War* 1.650), and also to the Jews who faced Petronius: 'though they regarded the risk involved in war with the Romans as great, yet [they] adjudged the risk of transgressing the Law to be far greater' (*Antiq.* 18.270), since it might cost them more than their physical existence. Zeal for God's law and his worship was one of the principal motives of the actions of many

Jews, and belief in an afterlife encouraged people to follow the law even if it meant death.

From this description of restless pursuit of the right form of government (the right policy on both internal and external issues), we turn to the relatively static world of religious practice – the daily, weekly, seasonal, annual and septennial observances required by Jewish law and kept by most Jews. This will lead us to common theology. Only then shall we return to the groups whose emergence we described in ch. 2; in the course of this examination we shall consider in more detail some aspects of the history of the period.

In proceeding in this way, we are in one sense turning from 'politics' to 'religion', but in another sense not. One of the standard problems of describing Judaism is the way in which religion and politics intertwine. The simplest way of presenting their interrelationship is to narrate historical events, as we have been doing. In chapters 2–4, summarizing the history of events, we have also been dealing with 'religion' and 'theology'. We have seen, for example, that those who wanted military affairs handled by a foreign empire sought not only 'autonomy' but also a 'theocracy' – rule by God. Some of the rebels at the time of the great revolt took as their slogan, 'no master but God'. The 'political' question was religious: which system of government was best in God's sight? which best facilitated the observance of the divine law? Yet on the other hand Jews could distinguish military control from what we would now call 'religion'. People who did not mind Roman dominance very much wanted to keep busts of Caesar out of Jerusalem.

The worship of God occupied its own sphere, or rather spheres (temple, home and synagogue), which were partially insulated from the events of the outside world, such as changes of government. The Jews, in fact, protested when outside events affected worship too strongly. In the next part, then, we shall drop the interplay between government and theology (returning to it in Part III), and deal with 'religion' in a narrow sense, beginning with the simplest and most fundamental aspect of any ancient religion: animal sacrifice. We do not turn to a different 'group'. Ancient Jews combined socio-political activity and the observance of timeless rites (as do all other people, both past and present).[2] When Aristobulus II and his followers, who had plenty of political ambition, were shut up in the temple complex by the supporters of Hyrcanus II, they paid 1,000 drachmas a head for sacrificial animals (though they were double-crossed and did not get them) (*Antiq.* 14.25–28).

Thus, though we now take leave of stories of government and military action, we are not shifting to the description of another Judaism, but to the description of what the very same Jews did when they worshipped God.

PART II
Common Judaism

5

Common Judaism and the Temple

Common, normal and normative

Within Palestine, 'normal' or 'common' Judaism was what the priests and the people agreed on. We shall see that in general Jews of the Greek-speaking Diaspora shared in this normal Judaism, although their participation in temple worship, which was an important ingredient, was restricted. In this part of our study, I shall continue to concentrate on Palestine, though I shall also illustrate the degree to which Jews of the western Diaspora shared religious practices and theological beliefs with their Palestinian contemporaries.[1] That there was a world-wide feeling of solidarity among Jews is easily proved. Scattered throughout the pages that follow we shall see payment of the temple tax by Diaspora Jews, pilgrimage to the temple from abroad, world-wide alarm at the threat of Gaius to have his statue erected in the temple, the ways in which Gentiles singled out Jews as different, the benefits that Diaspora Jews reaped when Julius Caesar was grateful to Palestinian Jews for support, and many other points.[2]

'Normal' Judaism was, to a limited degree, also 'normative': it established a standard by which loyalty to Israel and to the God of Israel was measured. Outside Palestine there could be little coercion to accept the norm, except for moral suasion, and even within Palestine there were definite limits to what could be enforced. Outside Judaea the official guardians of the religion, the priests, had little actual power after the Roman conquest. Thus whatever we find to have been 'normal' was based on internal assent and was 'normative' only to the degree that it was backed up by common opinion – which has a good deal of coercive power, but which allows individuals who strongly dissent to break away.

Jews in general believed that their sacred books were truly Holy Scripture. God gave them the law through Moses, and they were to obey it. The prophets and the other books ('writings') were also meant for guidance and instruction. Throughout the empire Jews gathered in houses of prayer on the sabbath to learn God's way. They worshipped him with prayers and offerings; and they observed holy days, which functioned either to renew their covenant with him, to celebrate great moments of the nation's past, to mark the seasons of the agricultural year and give thanks for them, or to atone for sin.

Morton Smith has encapsulated these points in a memorable sentence:

> Down to the fall of the Temple, the normative Judaism of Palestine is that compromise of which the three principal elements are the Pentateuch, the Temple, and the *'amme ha'arez*, the ordinary Jews who were not members of any sect.[3]

I would add only that most Diaspora Jews were included in this common Judaism. They were loyal to the law and also to the temple, though they could seldom attend its services. They also shared some post-biblical practices, such as attending synagogue.

There were numerous differences within 'normal Judaism', and we shall eventually consider some of them. The present emphasis, however, is on what was common.

Physically there were three foci of religion: the temple, the synagogue (or house of prayer) and the home. We shall take these in turn before asking whether or not there was a common Jewish theology. I shall now try to describe the practice and belief of the ordinary priests and the common people – not the chief priests or 'the powerful', and not the Pharisees, Sadducees or Essenes. It is much easier to write about the named groups, and so the Judaism of our period is often treated as if it were composed of members of Josephus' three parties. We shall see that it is not impossible to discuss the ordinary people, though we can seldom give names of individuals. Josephus, an aristocrat who became a Hellenistic historian, followed both traditions in usually narrating events in terms of named leading characters and 'the masses'. He seldom named even 'the powerful'. Individuals from 'the people' very occasionally have names, but no descriptions: thus Jonathan and Ananias, Pharisees 'from the lower ranks' of the populace (*hoi dēmotikoi*), were on a committee sent to investigate Josephus during the revolt (*Life* 197), but we learn nothing about them. We do learn that during the revolt common people were sometimes given places of responsibility, but this highlights the normal situation: they were generally disregarded, except when they formed large groups. Nevertheless, since the common people were actors in many of the events that Josephus describes, we can sometimes get past his indifference to them (an indifference common to many ancient historians), and we can also take some steps towards determining what the 'normal situation' was. Before the description of Jewish practice, however, it will be useful to consider wherein ancient Judaism differed from other cultures.

Sacrifice, ethics, and the distinctiveness of Judaism

To the reader who is not thoroughly acquainted with ancient religion, Judaism's emphasis on animal sacrifice may seem alien and even repugnant. In antiquity, however, it was otherwise. In Rome, Greece, Egypt, Mesopotamia and most other parts of the ancient world, religion *was* sacrifice. Below we shall discuss such topics as the sacrificial slaughter of animals; the distribution of their parts among the priest, the altar and the worshipper; support of the temple by offerings of money, animals and agricultural produce; rites of purification; and the observance of special holy days that involved additional sacrifices, dancing and music. Every element has numerous parallels in the ancient world. When Greeks or Romans commented on Judaism, they found none of this strange. The Jewish sabbath and food laws drew comment, but not sacrifices and purifications.

Thanks to fairly recent publications, Greek religious practices are easy to study at a general level. The reader of *Greek Religion* by Walter Burkert, or *The Cuisine of Sacrifice among the Greeks*, a volume of essays edited by Marcel Detienne and Jean-Pierre Vernant, will learn a lot about animal sacrifice, holy areas and purifications.[4] Jewish sacrificial practice differed from that of the Greeks in two principal ways. In the first place, in Judaism during the Roman period the view prevailed that there should be only one temple and one place of sacrifice; the last temple to be established outside Jerusalem was the Zadokite temple in Egypt (above, p. 23). The Greeks and Romans had almost countless temples, and sacrifice could be offered even where there was no temple.

Secondly, Jewish sacrificial worship was more expensive. There was a large hereditary priesthood that was supported by non-priests. In Greece and Rome priesthood was not a profession or a caste.[5] In Rome, and not infrequently in the Greek-speaking world, it was an honour to be a priest, an honour reserved for the elite; like other honorary positions it was sometimes expensive for the office holder.[6] Rulers whom we now think of as generals, conquerors, kings and emperors were also priests. Julius Caesar was a high priest (Pontifex Maximus, e.g. *Antiq.* 14.190). Alexander the Great, in his triumphant conquest of much of the known world, sacrificed regularly.[7] In Greece and Rome, it is difficult to understand just what a priest was because the 'distinction between civic magistracy and priesthood' is elusive. Those who wanted to get on in the world sought priestly appointments (e.g. Pliny the Younger).[8] In Judaism, on the other hand, priestly office was hereditary, priests were forbidden to support themselves by working the land, and the care and feeding of the priesthood were substantial costs borne by the rest of society, especially farmers. Another element that made Jewish sacrificial worship expensive was the use of holocausts, 'whole-burnt offerings', of which there were at least two each day in the Jerusalem temple. Such sacrifices were unknown in Greece.[9] In Judaism, although a majority of the sacrifices provided food for the priest and/or the worshipper, some animals were entirely consigned to the altar. In Greece all sacrificed animals were eaten, and the gods usually got only some of the bones. In this second case, the expense of religion and the importance of a priestly caste, we can find parallels to Judaism in Babylonia, Egypt and other countries.

With regard to sacrifice, priesthood and temples, Judaism was unique because it had a single temple to the one God and a centralized cult. In comparison to Greece and Rome, the size and influence of Judaism's hereditary priesthood also stand out.

Judaism was distinctive in another way. It attempted to bring the entirety of life under the heading, 'Divine Law'. As a religion, it was not strange because it included sacrifices, but because it included ethical, family and civil law as well. Jews sometimes spoke of their 'philosophy', a term that is justified by the scope of a law that includes an entire way of life.[10] Judaism was not just a 'cult'. Our word 'religion', it should be explained, though derived from the Latin *religio*, does not have a precise ancient counterpart. Despite this, it is a very useful word. In using it, we now mean 'anything having to do with God or the gods, including every topic that appears in laws or admonitions that are attributed to the deity'. In Judaism, this is more-or-less everything. Jews thought that Moses received the law from God, and they also considered the prophets and authors of other sacred Jewish writings 'inspired'.[11] Although in a very general sense Greeks might say that their laws were of divine origin (Plato, *Laws* I), they did not treat individual points as being divinely revealed, as the rest of Plato's *Laws* makes clear. Even in discussing the correct calendar of festivals and sacrifices, the Athenian says only that he and his companions would be helped by 'oracles from Delphi' (*Laws* VIII § 828): it was up to humans to determine what they should be. Similarly, Athenians did not think that the ancient reformer of the law, Solon, passed on divine commandments, and many aspects of human behaviour were governed by secular law. In the Graeco-Roman world ethics were discussed by philosophers but were not, as a rule, thought to have divine sanction, while Jews thought that the rules governing treatment of 'the neighbour' and 'the stranger' were given by God to Moses. They corresponded to God's own nature: 'You shall be holy; for I the Lord your God am holy . . . You shall love your neighbour . . . You shall love [the stranger]' (Lev. 19.2–34).

This is not to say that in Greece and Rome there were two watertight compartments, 'religion' and 'state'. On the contrary, the two were closely intertwined. All or virtually all civic activities involved sacrifice. A 'civil' court convicted Socrates of the capital offence 'atheism'. Failure to participate in civic religion and (during the Roman empire) refusal to pay appropriate homage to the Genius of Rome and the Emperor were crimes. Jews needed special exemption from pagan civic religious rites, and later Christians often ran foul of the state because they would not join in common religious acts. Today, even in the United States, where it is against the constitution to have an established religion, the Pledge of Allegiance (since the days of Eisenhower) includes the phrase 'under God'; the President says 'so help me God' in taking the oath of office, and in court witnesses take the same oath (though in recent years other oath-forms have been allowed). If one will multiply such practices by several thousand, the importance of religion in the civic life of the Roman empire will be clear.

Yet despite the omnipresence of religion in pagan culture, ancient Judaism stands out as distinctive, since all of life was not only 'under God' in general, it was regulated by divine law. Josephus put the matter precisely:

> [Moses] did not make religion [literally 'piety'] a department of virtue, but the various virtues – I mean, justice, temperance, fortitude, and mutual harmony . . . – departments of religion. Religion governs all our actions and occupations and speech; none of these things did our lawgiver leave unexamined or indeterminate . . . He left nothing, however insignificant, to the discretion and caprice of the individual. (*Apion* 2.170–3)

The Jews of our period were not entirely unable to distinguish what we now call the secular from the sacred. To take a few examples from the historical survey in Part I: The people who wanted one of the Hasmoneans to surrender the high priesthood, and to content himself with being king, made a *de facto* distinction. Similarly some wanted Palestine to be ruled by a foreign empire, so that locally they could have a 'theocracy', rule by God (as represented by the priests). Others opposed having any master other than God: there should be no 'secular' sphere. They all, however, included more things under sacred law than did the Greeks and Romans. It is particularly important that ethical behaviour was determined by divine law.

The consequence is that we begin the discussion of Jewish religious practice with the temple, but we do not end it there.

The temple

According to scripture, God had ordained the temple and its sacrifices and

had appointed its hereditary priesthood. The overwhelming impression
from ancient literature is that most first-century Jews, who believed in the
Bible, respected the temple and the priesthood and willingly made the
required gifts and offerings. There is, to be sure, a scholarly tradition
according to which this was not so. Thus Marcel Simon, in his splendid
book *Verus Israel*, wrote that 'The genuinely pious in Israel had . . . tended
to turn away from the sanctuary . . . The living center of Judaism was the
Synagogue' and that in the Diaspora 'the temple never had stood for
anything of positive value'.[12] Ancient authors (except for a very few,
discussed below) give just the opposite impression. This holds good in the
Greek-speaking Diaspora as well as in Palestine. The author of *The Letter of
Aristeas*, an Alexandrian Jew who visited Jerusalem in the second or first
century BCE,[13] wrote in glowing and devout terms about the temple service.
Philo, who made at least one pilgrimage to Jerusalem in the first half of the
first century CE, emphasized not only his own devotion but that of the
Palestinians. He contrasted the taxes paid by compulsion in the rest of the
Graeco-Roman world with those that supported the Jerusalem temple,
which were paid 'gladly and cheerfully', and which were so abundant that
even the poorest priests were 'exceedingly well-to-do' (*Spec. Laws* 1.141–4,
133). He predicted that the temple and the offerings that supported it
would endure forever (*Spec. Laws* 1.76), and he described the sacrifical
system in loving detail, emphasizing its spiritual and ethical value (*Spec.
Laws* 1.66–345).

Ancient authors indicate that most of the Jewish people supported all
aspects of temple worship. Philo wrote that throughout the empire Jews
'collect[ed] money for sacred purposes' and sent it to Jerusalem (*Embassy*
156). He called this the offerings of the 'first fruits' (so also *Spec. Laws*
1.77f.: first fruits taken by envoys from every city). According to Josephus
the Jews in Mesopotamia made 'dedicatory offerings' to the temple in
addition to payment of the temple tax of one-half shekel (two drachmas)
(*Antiq.* 18.312). The general payment of the temple tax by Jews throughout
the empire is certain. It is taken for granted in Matt. 17.24 as well as in
Josephus. The best testimony to the fact that Jews generally paid it is that
after each of the two revolts Rome ordered that it continue to be paid, but
for other purposes (*War* 7.218; Dio Cassius 66.7).[14] (For the biblical
requirement of one-half or one-third shekel, see Ex. 30.13; Neh. 10.32).

Josephus describes the high regard in which the priesthood was held
even in the Diaspora: 'wherever there is a Jewish colony, there too a strict
account is kept by the priests of their marriages'. The purpose was to assure
the purity of the priestly line, as required by biblical law (*Apion* 1.32). Philo
indicates that priests retained their status as leaders in the Diaspora

(*Hypothetica* 7.12f.), and archaeology confirms that in at least some places outside of Palestine priests were specifically designated as such.[15]

Common piety towards the temple is described in Luke 1–2. Zechariah, the father of John the Baptist, is a pious priest; Mary and Joseph devoutly bring the required offering after childbirth; Anna and Simeon frequent the temple for the purpose of worship. Luke may have invented all this freely, or he may have had a source. In either case he captured the air of devotion around the temple.

The description that has just been given is generally true: most Jews regarded the service of the temple, including the requirements to make offerings and sacrifices, as sacred, and they respected the hereditary priesthood. It is possible, however, in relying on Josephus, Aristeas, Philo and Luke, to paint too uniform and positive a picture. Josephus was himself a priest, and the two pilgrims from Alexandria may have seen the temple service through rose-coloured lenses. Philo, despite his insistence that everyone duly presented the expected offerings, and that the priesthood was therefore exceedingly prosperous, lets it slip that he has exaggerated. He speaks of 'the neglectfulness of some' which 'has brought about the impoverishment of the consecrated class' (*Spec. Laws* 1.154). Later in this study we shall see that some priests were extremely rich while some lived close to the edge of poverty. It is impossible at this remove to say how many were impoverished or nearly so, or just how many Israelites brought their tithes and offerings in full, though in due course we shall see good evidence of widespread support of most of the temple's requirements.

There are a few hints of potentially far-reaching criticism of the temple as such. Philo, writing of the Palestinian Essenes, said that they did not offer animal sacrifices, but rather 'sanctif[ied] their minds' (*Every Good Man* 75). Philo himself was pro-temple, as we saw above, and so were the Essenes. One wing of the party, the Qumran Sect, had withdrawn from the temple, but they looked forward to taking charge of it, building it to their own design and conducting its service correctly. Philo took their refusal to participate in the cult to stem from a moral objection. It is very likely that he knew of such objections, since elsewhere he wrote about Jews who proposed to take the laws only allegorically or spiritually, disregarding the letter (*Migration of Abraham* 89–93). It may be that these extreme allegorists and others wanted only the spiritualized meaning of the temple service and not the bloody reality. Philo could understand and report on that position sympathetically, though he himself thought that the laws should be observed literally as well as spiritually. He erred in ascribing this view to the Essenes, but nevertheless his reference to it probably shows that some people actually held it.[16]

The only direct evidence of Jewish opposition to the temple as such comes from Alexandria at the end of the first century, after the temple's destruction. The author of the fourth *Sibylline Oracle* seems to have opposed all temples, including the Jewish one. He regarded as 'happy' the coming days, in which, he thought, all temples would be rejected. He saw them as 'useless foundations of dumb stones . . . defiled with blood of animate creatures' (*Sib. Or.* 4.24–30).

The rest of ancient Jewish literature is favourable to the temple in theory, though criticisms of the current priesthood are fairly frequent. In a later chapter, we shall find fierce denunciations (in the *Covenant of Damascus* and the *Psalms of Solomon*), but these are based on opposition to the contemporary priesthood, and the denunciations themselves prove that the authors held the temple and its sacrifices in respect. They attacked those who, in their view, were unworthy to hold their offices and to conduct the sacrificial worship of God.

The best proof of the favourable evaluation of the temple service will appear in ch. 14, when we discuss hopes for the future. We shall see that the hope for a new, purified or glorified temple was widespread. Thus, while we may grant that there were some radicals who opposed the temple service as such, it is more important to emphasize that most Jews – who believed the Bible, in which commandments about the temple figure very large – accepted the sacrificial system as a principal aspect of the true worship of God. We now turn to a description of the temple and its service.

Appearance (illustrations on pp. 306–14)

In considering the temple service and its meaning to most Jews, it will help to have some idea of the appearance of the buildings and courts. Even before Herod's massive building programme, the temple area was impressive and strongly built. Like many temples in the ancient world, it doubled as a fortress of last resort. Pompey could attack it successfully because he used sabbaths to bring his catapults and battering rams up to the wall. He attacked, as would others, from the vulnerable side, the north, where, in addition to the wall that encompassed the temple complex, there was only a shallow ravine (*War* 1.145; *Antiq.* 14.57). The temple was protected on the east and south by steep valleys, and by a considerable valley on the west. Pompey filled the northern ravine with rubble and brought his engines to bear on the wall, which held out for some time.

General description

In the Hasmonean, Herodian and Roman periods the temple was a large, walled area, which in the Hasmonean period was almost square, *c.* 250 metres or yards × *c.* 300 metres or yards. Herod's temple was much longer, more than 400 metres or yards long. Inside the wall were one or more large courts that could hold great crowds. An interior wall enclosed the area where the business of the temple – sacrifice – was carried out. In the open air there was a large altar, a basin, a shambles (where the animals were butchered), and cooking facilities. These were directly in front of the roofed sanctuary, which was not much used. It was divided into two chambers. The outer one contained another altar and a candelabrum, the inner was empty. Only the high priest entered this inner sanctum, and he on only one day a year, the Day of Atonement. The sanctuary was shaped, ancient writers noted, like a lion, wide in front and narrow behind. The façade was *c.* 50 metres across, but then the building narrowed to 30 metres. Its roof was approximately 50 metres above the floor.[17]

There is inconsistency in both ancient and modern literature in naming the various parts of the temple complex and especially the central sanctuary. I shall use *temple complex* and *temple area* to refer to the largest enclosure, including the outside walls, the porticoes (colonnaded halls), the various courts, and the sanctuary. When it is clear from the context, I may use 'temple' to refer to the entire temple area. By *sanctuary* I mean the central building, roofed, divided into two chambers. I shall call the *first chamber* just that: the first chamber of the sanctuary. The term *Holy of Holies* refers to the second chamber, into which the high priest went once each year.

Detailed description

The precise size of the temple area in the Hasmonean period is not known. The eastern wall extended south to a point 32 metres short of Herod's eastern wall.[18] Precisely how far it reached to the north is not certain. Various builders had expanded the temple complex between the time of the initial rebuilding (completed 515 BCE) and Pompey's invasion (63 BCE). This is a description that Josephus attributes to Hecataeus of Abdera, but that was probably written by a Jewish pseudepigrapher in the first half of the second century BCE (that is, in the pre-Hasmonean or early Hasmonean period):[19]

> Nearly in the centre of the city [Jerusalem] stands a stone wall, enclosing an area about five *plethra* long and a hundred cubits broad, approached by a pair of gates. Within this enclosure is a square altar, built of heaped up stones, unhewn and unwrought; each side is twenty cubits long and the height ten cubits. Beside it stands a great edifice, containing an altar and a lampstand, both made of gold, and weighing two talents; upon these is a

light which is never extinguished by night or day. There is not a single statue or votive offering, no trace of a plant, in the form of a sacred grove or the like. Here priests pass their nights and days performing certain rites of purification, and abstaining altogether from wine while in the temple.

A *plethron* is approximately 100 feet or 30 metres (more precisely, 98 feet/ 29.87 metres). A cubit is approximately 18 inches, though the length was not completely standardized and longer cubits are known; one may conveniently think of it as either a half-yard or half-metre. Thus Pseudo-Hecataeus describes the walled area as being roughly 500 feet (150 metres) long, from north to south, and 150 feet (45 metres) across, from east to west. Subsequent builders enlarged the wall, and the Hasmoneans carried out various building projects. Just who built what cannot be determined. In his invaluable book, Th. A. Busink estimated that, before Herod's building began, the eastern and western walls were between 225 and 275 metres long and the northern and southern walls were about 300 metres (*c.* 250 yards × 325 yards).[20] This is reasonable. The distance between the eastern and western walls is what the geography requires if one is to build close to the valleys on either side. That the Hasmonean temple had an appreciable length north-south is indicated by the seam 32 metres from the southern end of the eastern wall of Herod's temple. The evidence from Josephus' account of Pompey's siege permits some firm conclusions. The supporters of Hyrcanus II opened the city to Pompey, but the supporters of Aritobulus II cut the bridge between the Upper City and the western temple wall and withstood an appreciable siege inside the temple area, during which the sacrifices were maintained (*War* 1.142f., 148). This implies that the temple complex was capacious, and further that the western wall stood near the edge of the Tyropoeon Valley; otherwise a bridge could not have connected the wall of the temple complex to the Upper City on the other side of the valley. It is also certain that the pre-Herodian eastern wall stood at the edge of the Kidron Valley. According to Josephus, shortly before the outbreak of war in 66 CE, the Jerusalemites asked Agrippa II to rebuild the eastern portico or *stoa*, a colonnaded hall that served as the top part of the temple wall. This hall, he wrote, had been built by King Solomon (*Antiq.* 20.220f.). The portico had not actually been built by Solomon, but it was pre-Herodian and had been incorporated in Herod's eastern wall: thus Herod did not expand the temple to the east.[21]

This means that before Herod the temple already had an outer court. In the days of Ezra, the area to the east (or front) of the sanctuary had been open (Ezra 10.9). Between Ezra and Herod this space, as well as small areas to the north and west of the temple, and a considerable area to the south, had been enclosed. Some of this construction had been done at the time of Antiochus III of Syria, who reigned from 223 to 187 BCE (*Antiq.* 12.141). Antiochus had forbidden non-Jews

> to enter the enclosure of the temple which is forbidden to the Jews, except to those of them who are accustomed to enter after purifying themselves in accordance with the law of the country. (*Antiq.* 12.145)

This seems to mean that there was an outer court, probably a small one, which Gentiles and impure Israelites could enter.[22]

At some point Jewish women were also admitted to the outer court. We hear of no objection to Herod's construction of a Court of the Women, and a place for women in the temple probably preceded him. According to Ex. 38.8 women could 'minister' at the 'door of the tent of meeting', that is, at the temple gate.[23] Ezra included them, as well as children old enough to understand, when he read the law (Neh. 8.2f.). It may be that women were automatically given a place in the temple area when the space outside the sanctuary was made into an outer court. They could still bring their offerings to the gate that gave admission to the area where the priests worked, and they could hear the blessings and the songs of the Levites. Probably they could also see the sacrifices, either because the top of the interior wall was low enough or because the outer court had a balcony (as it probably did in Herod's temple.)

Herod rebuilt the temple on a vast scale. Work commenced in either the eighteenth year of his reign (20/19 BCE: *Antiq.* 15.380) or the fifteenth (23/22 BCE: *War* 1.401). It was not entirely finished until just before the outbreak of the revolt, approximately 63 CE (*Antiq.* 20.219), though the major parts were completed much earlier. The sanctuary itself took a year and a half, while the outer wall, the porticoes and the courts required eight years (*Antiq.* 15.420f.).

The overall temple complex, excluding the Antonia fortress at the northwest corner, now became an irregular quadrangle measuring, very roughly, 450 metres from south to north and 300 from east to west. R. Grafman has demonstrated that the 'foot' used by Herod's builders was .31 metres, almost precisely 1 English foot.[24] The following table gives the measurements of the outer walls in metres as determined by modern archaeology and in Herodian feet as proposed by Grafman (and therefore also in English feet):

South wall (main entrance)	281 metres	900 feet
West wall	488	1,550
North wall	315	1,000

| East wall | 466 | 1,500 |
| TOTAL CIRCUMFERENCE | 1,550 | 4,900 (9/10ths mile) |

The area enclosed by the wall is 144,000 sq. metres, 169,000 sq. yards, 35 acres. Meir Ben-Dov estimates that twelve soccer fields, including the stands, would fit into the space.[25]

The outer retaining wall was characterized by Josephus as 'the greatest ever heard of' (Antiq. 15.396). Certainly it dwarfed similar walls around Greek temple complexes. The Acropolis in Athens is 240 metres long and 120 metres wide in the middle, but it tapers sharply towards each end. The wall around the temple area in Olympia was no more than 210 metres × 170.[26] In the Mediterranean world, one has to go to Egypt to find walled sacred areas larger than Herod's temple.[27] The wall that encompases the temple of Amun at Karnak takes in 30 hectares, 300,000 square metres, approximately 75 acres.[28] The Egyptian wall is not the equal of Herod's, but the enclosed space is over twice as large. Next to it are further temples in separate walls. The sanctuary at Karnak is many times larger than the Jerusalem sanctuary (see below).[29] Egypt, of course, had much greater human and financial resources than did Herod's Palestine. Further, the vast temples at Karnak and Luxor were built over several generations. Herod's temple was an extraordinary achievement. It becomes all the more remarkable when one notes that it was only one of several large construction projects.

The workmen removed previous constructions and built on bedrock. The new wall ran appreciably farther both north and south than had its predecessor, and the enclosed area was approximately doubled. The hill slopes down, falling away more sharply the farther south one goes, and the area that was to be inside the wall was filled with rubble and levelled. At its deepest point the fill was almost 40 metres deep.[30] To resist the pressure exerted by the fill, the retaining wall was built c. 5 metres thick. Josephus claimed that the largest stones in the wall were 40 cubits long (c. 20 metres/yards; War 5.189). According to Ben-Dov, the largest stone found thus far, 'unequalled in size anywhere in the ancient world' (an exaggeration), is 12 metres long × 3 high × 4 thick and weighs almost 400 tons.[31] The largest stones, of course, are found in the lower courses and on the corners. A majority of the stones, while still very large, weigh in the region of 2 to 5 tons.[32]

The stones, or at least those that would be visible, were dressed, and a smooth border was chiseled around the edges. The fit of stone to stone was virtually perfect. The result was a wall of great beauty and enormous strength, built, as were large Egyptian and Greek walls, without the use of mortar (which, as Ben-Dov points out, would have required the burning of a great deal of wood). Some of the wall still stands today and supports the present Muslim area of worship.

For much of the rest of our description, we shall not be aided by archaeology and must rely on literature. The sources do not agree, and some of the differences are substantial. There are two descriptions in Josephus: a brief one in *Antiq* 15.410–20 and a very detailed one in *War* 5.184–227. There are some disagreements between these two accounts, most notably what he writes about entering the Women's Court. The Mishnaic tractate *Middot*, 'measurements', offers a detailed description that differs from Josephus very substantially. Scholars have been debating what to make of this situation for a long time. I am, as the saying goes, 'morally certain' that the best description of Herod's temple is that of *War* 5.[33] Given the length of time the problem has been debated (Busink traces academic disagreement back to 1630), the chances of my persuading anyone who has studied the issue, and who has come to a different view, are very slight.[34]

I shall, however, briefly indicate four significant points in favour of *War* 5, the first three derived largely from Busink: (1) Where *Middot* differs from Josephus, it is usually in agreement with a biblical description of a non-Herodian temple: Solomon's or Ezekiel's (visionary) temple. The rabbis probably studied the Bible more closely than they measured the remains on the temple mount. (2) In *Middot* the temple area is not surrounded by porticoes. As we shall see, these were a large part of Herod's construction, and Josephus cannot have made them up. Remains of their columns have also been found. Busink proposes that the porticoes are missing from the temple of *Middot* because they were a main feature of pagan architecture, and the post-70 rabbi who was responsible for the tractate did not want the Jerusalem temple to be quite as close to heathen temples as it was.[35] (3) Busink, a historian of architecture, has shown that the temple of *War* 5 works architecturally. The porticoes of the height Josephus describes would have been supported by the columns he describes. It is not very difficult for a non-architect or builder to make up, out of his own head, a portico of a given length and breadth, and to say that there were a certain number of columns of a certain size. But someone who imagined such a portico would probably describe one that would not stand up, or alternatively that would have more columns than necessary. Josephus' portico is architecturally sound. More-over, parts of a column discovered by archaeologists agree with Josephus' description. This inclines one to think that he also described the rest of the temple correctly. (4) It has long been noted that, as the Roman army gets closer in Josephus' narrative of the war, his descriptions of geography improve.[36] That is, the Romans did not guess about the circumference of a

city or a fortress (which the temple mount was), or about the height and
breadth of the walls and towers they were about to assault. They studied what
they were up against. Josephus had access to Roman notebooks, and his
assistants could read them. He used these notes when writing the *War*, but
probably not when writing the *Antiquities* twenty years later. In the later work
he seems to have relied on his memory, which was not bad for a fifty-three
year old man, but which was not as good as his original sources.[37] Research in
his day was difficult. Only the theory of assistants and Roman experts, I think,
will explain the degree to which some of Josephus' description in *War* 5 is
supported by archaeology and by the study of architecture, although in other
cases he evidently went astray. He lived in Jerusalem and had served in the
temple. He had memories of details. That does not, however, explain how he
knew heights and breadths. I could not accurately describe the size of my own
house if I did not measure it, and certainly not a public building. I think that
Josephus' memory was improved by expert assistance.[38]

I do not suppose that nothing in Mishnah *Middot* correctly describes
Herod's temple. On the contrary, my understanding of Josephus' description
of the Court of the Women virtually requires me to accept the Mishnah's
statement that the women had a gallery. Busink cites other points in favour of
some of the Mishnah's details, especially those that make architectural sense.
In this description I shall rely principally on *War* 5 and usually (though not
always) on Busink's analysis of it.

The outer wall had several gates, and the inner wall, which enclosed the
temple proper, had ten (*War* 5.198). Each gate had two doors. In one of his
late, less accurate works, Josephus relates that it required two hundred men
to close the gates every day (*Apion* 2.119). Thackeray proposed that he may
have meant ten gangs of twenty men each to close the ten gates. Josephus
describes extremely heavy doors: 'sixty cubits high and twenty broad, all
gilded and almost entirely covered with plates of wrought gold'. In the *War*
they were much smaller: 30 × 15 cubits (*War* 5.202). In *Against Apion*
Josephus exaggerated: gates 60 cubits high would be higher than the wall. He
was refuting a story that an ass' head was worshipped in the temple, and that
someone had once stolen it (*Apion* 2.114). The comment on the size of the
doors shows the impossibility of anyone stealing anything from within the
temple. Taking the smaller figures of *War* 5.202, we may estimate the size of
the doors. A door 30 × 15 cubits is 13.2 metres high and 6.6 wide (about 45
feet high × 22 feet wide): approximately 87 square metres or 1000 square
feet (the same square footage as the floor of a small house today), of heavy
wood, gilded, with overlays of precious metal. One supposes that the hinges
and supporting rollers were well designed and executed. In any case, it took a
lot of men to guard and close the gates.

Much of the enormous area enclosed by the outer wall was the Court of the Gentiles, into which anyone could go except 'women during their impurity' (*Apion* 2.102–5). Worshippers or the curious entered from the south (which became, in effect, the front of the temple area), up a monumental stairway, through a triple gate, and then up a tunnel that ran under the Royal Portico, debouching on the large plaza, the Court of the Gentiles. To the west of the triple gate was a double gate, through which people left the temple area (*Middot* 2.2). The Court of the Gentiles was separated from the area reserved for Jews by a chest-high balustrade (three cubits high: 1.5 metres; 4.5 ft., *War* 5.193) with gates, on which were warning notices, some in Greek and some in Latin, forbidding Gentiles further access. One of the Greek notices has been found:

> No foreigner is to enter within the forecourt and the balustrade around the sanctuary. Whoever is caught will have himself to blame for his subsequent death.[39]

It appears that, when Judaea was directly governed by Rome, the priests were allowed to enforce this warning, though they could not otherwise sentence people to death (*War* 6.126). Peretz Segal has convincingly proposed that the priests had the authority to carry out a legal lynching: they could drag the intruder out of the holy area and split his skull with clubs.[40]

Though the temple area was entered from the south, the temple proper, where the altar and the sanctuary were, faced east and was entered from that direction. Thus Jewish worshippers walked from the southern end of the temple area towards the centre, turned left, and then proceeded from east to west. They passed the balustrade and its warning notices, went up a flight of fourteen steps, crossed a terrace ten cubits deep, went up another five steps and came to the inner wall with its ten gates. Inside this inner wall lay, first, the Court of the Women, 'open for worship to all Jewish women alike, whether natives of the country or visitors from abroad' (*War* 5.199). This was itself enclosed, and access for women was from either the north or the south: they could not use the central eastern gate. The women's court was, according to the Mishnah, provided with a gallery, so that they could see over the heads of men into the Court of the Priests (*Middot* 2.5). This is intrinsically likely, since otherwise they would have been placed in a walled box, unable to see.[41] Jewish males continued from east to west, walking past the women's gallery, which lay either side of a corridor. They ascended fifteen more steps, shallower than the previous ones, and came to the wall that separated the Women's Court from the next courts to the west. The wall was pierced by a gate. Thus there were two eastern gates, with a corridor between them. The Women's Court was divided into two sections, one to the north and one to the south of the corridor. Referring to Busink's plans, pp. 310, 312 below: Men and women went up the steps to the gate marked 19. Women detoured to right or left, entering the Women's Court by the gates numbered 20. I propose that there was a corridor from gate 19 to the next gate, 24. Men went straight through, up the steps, and through the gate at 24.[42]

This brought the men into the Court of the Israelites – that is, the court of Jewish males who were not priests or Levites. There they could listen to the singing of the Levites (minor clergy) and watch the priests at work. Between them and the Court of the Priests was only a 'low stone parapet, fair and graceful, about a cubit high' (*c.* ½ metre or yard; *War* 5.226).

In the Court of the Priests, which not even Levites could enter, were the altar, the shambles (where animals were butchered) and the laver (where the priests washed their hands and feet, Ex. 30.17–21; *Tamid* 1.4). It was here that the sacrifices were offered. Finally came the sanctuary, with twelve steps leading up to it. The front chamber of the sanctuary contained a lampstand, a table for the showbread and an altar for burning incense. The second chamber, the Holy of Holies, separated by a curtain, was empty.

Like other sanctuaries, the one in Jerusalem was not much used. The action took place in front, in the open air. In Greek sanctuaries there were usually two or three chambers, and sometimes there was difficulty of access to the second chamber. The interior was basically the residence of the statue of the deity, and usually only priests, suppliants and people seeking refuge entered. In the Parthenon, for example, which is about 31 metres across, the space between the inner columns, where the statue of Athena was, was only 9.82 metres. It was not the place for public worship. In the Jerusalem temple,

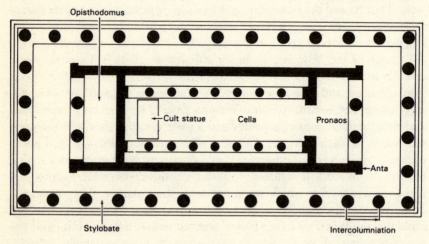

1 Normal Greek Temple Plan

the area ordinarily reserved for the cult image was the Holy of Holies, which contained 'nothing whatever'; it was 'unapproachable, inviolable, invisible to all' (*War* 5.219). Only the High Priest could enter, and he once a year, on the Day of Atonement. The rest of the sanctuary was accessible only to priests, though they performed there only a few rites. The temple service will be described below.

The façade of the front chamber of the sanctuary was 100 cubits across and 100 cubits high (44 metres or 150 feet), but behind the façade the building narrowed to 60 cubits; the ceiling was 90 or 100 cubits high.[43] Admission to this room was through two doors, covered in gold, above which were 'golden vines from which depended grape-clusters as tall as a man' (*War* 5.210). In front of the doors hung a 'Babylonian tapestry, with embroidery of blue and fine linen, of scarlet also and purple'. On it 'was portrayed a panorama of the heavens, the signs of the Zodiac excepted' (*War* 5.212f.).[44]

The interior height was divided into a lower area of 60 cubits and an upper area of 40 cubits. Along the sides of the lower area were three stories containing rooms. They occupied 20 cubits on each side, leaving the interior of the front chamber 20 cubits wide. It was 40 cubits long. There was then a curtain or veil, behind which was the Holy of Holies, which was 20 cubits square.

In the *War* Josephus claimed that some of the stones in the sanctuary were 45 cubits long, 5 cubits high and 6 cubits thick (*War* 5.224), figures that he later modified to 25 cubits $\times$ 8 $\times$ 12 (*Antiq.* 15.392). If we take the lesser length from *Antiq.* 15 and the lesser height and thickness from *War* 5, we would have measurements of *c.* 12.5 metres/yards $\times$ 2.5 $\times$ 3. This would make the stones of the sanctuary approximately the size of the largest stones that have thus far been found in the wall. Josephus may exaggerate, but his smaller figures are not impossible.

There were other rooms in the temple complex: treasury rooms were located along the inside of the inner wall, apparently built into porticoes around the Israelites' court,[45] and there were further rooms built over the inner wall. The Mishnah offers a list of functions that various rooms served. There was a dormitory where the priests who were to prepare the morning sacrifice slept; a privy; underground there was an immersion pool in case of a nocturnal emission (which resulted in impurity);[46] in another room there was a fire so that those who immersed could warm themselves. There were also rooms for the inspection of wood for the altar fire (worms rendered it invalid; it was inspected by blemished priests, who could enter the holy area but who could not sacrifice); for storing wine and oil; for salting the hides; and for rinsing the inwards of the sacrificed animals. Within the temple complex were also meeting rooms. In one, the 'Chamber of Hewn Stone', priests were inspected for fitness. According to Josephus there was also a *bouleutērion*, the room where the council, *boulē*, met.[47]

Besides the sanctuary and rooms built alongside and over walls, the only other structures in the temple complex were colonnaded halls, porticoes. We just noted porticoes along some of the interior walls. We now return to the walls and porticoes surrounding the entire temple complex. The main entrance to the temple area, as we saw above, was a monumental stairway that led to two sets of gates through the southern wall. Worshippers entered by the eastern set of gates and exited by the western. The gates were below the level of the temple courtyards, and they led to tunnels that sloped upwards and came out inside the court of the Gentiles. On the way in, people passed under the grandest of the colonnaded halls, the 'Royal Portico'. A portico (Greek, *stoa*) consists of a roof supported by columns, usually serving as a porch in front of a building, so that it has a wall on one side and is open on the other.[48] On three sides of the interior of the temple area, the porticoes were 30 cubits deep, and their roofs were supported by two rows of columns, each 25 cubits high (*c.* 15 metres/yards deep, 12.5 metres/yards high; *War* 5.190). Detailed calculations, comparison with the dimensions of other stoa, and archaeological finds indicate that Josephus gives a fairly accurate description.[49]

The Royal Portico, on the southern wall, where pilgrims approached the temple, was much grander. It had three aisles supported by four rows of columns,

> and the thickness of each column was such that it would take three men with outstretched arms touching one another to envelop it; its height was twenty-seven feet [read: cubits; see n. 54] . . . (*Antiq.* 15.413)

A reconstruction of part of a large Greek portico, depicted opposite, will give some idea of Herod's Royal Portico.

Josephus states both that the Royal Portico ran from the eastern to the western ravine and that it was a stade long. The total length of the southern wall, as we saw above, was 900 feet (*c.* 280 metres); a stade is only about 600 feet (*c.* 185 metres). Apparently the Portico did not run the full length of the wall, and Josephus' opening statement probably means 'from the eastern *towards* the western wall', rather than 'as far as the western wall'. The two outside aisles were 30 feet wide and 50 feet high (in this section, instead of 'cubit' Josephus uses the Greek or Herodian 'foot', which approximately equals the English foot). The central aisle, however, was 45 feet wide and 100 feet high. The columns were polished white marble, their capitals were carved in the Corinthian style, and the wooden ceilings of the porticoes were ornamented. With its central aisle soaring above the retaining wall, the Royal Portico was 'a structure more noteworthy than any under the sun'. 'These

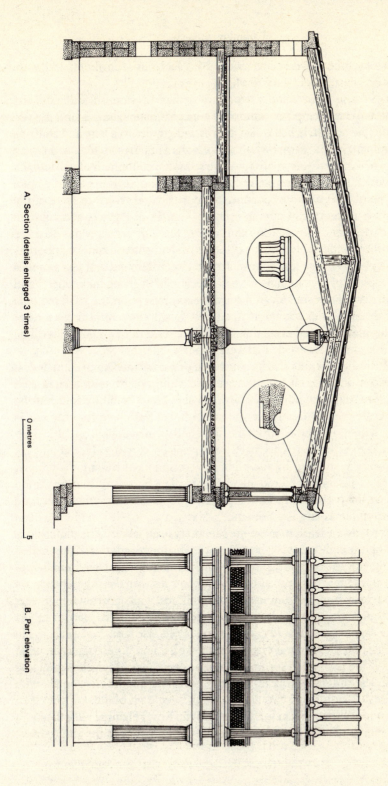

A. Section (details enlarged 3 times)

0 metres

5

B. Part elevation

structures seemed incredible to those who had not seen them, and were beheld with amazement by those who set eyes on them'.[50]

It may be useful to compare the largest hall of western antiquity, the hypostyle hall in the temple of Amun in Karnak.[51] (A comparative table is given on p. 67.) The hypostyle hall is 102 metres wide, 53 metres long and contains 134 columns. There are two rows of six columns 21 metres high. A further 122 columns, making fourteen more rows (12 rows of 9 columns, 2 of 7 columns), are 13 metres high. The capitals of the central columns represent the open papyrus plant, and the tops, opening to approximately twice the size of the column, are 15 metres in circumference. The Royal Portico, according to Josephus' description, was 186 metres long and 33 metres wide (all three aisles; perhaps wider including the columns). It had 162 columns[52] approximately 12.47 metres high and 5.55 metres in circumference.[53] If one assumes that the capitals of the columns were not reckoned in giving their height, and that on the capitals rested an architrave (beam) to support the roof, the total height of the side aisles was about 16 metres.[54] Over the central aisle a further set of columns supported a roof that was altogether about 32 metres high. The central aisles in the hypostyle hall were about 25 metres high.

The Royal Portico may also be compared to a small mediaeval cathedral. It was open on one side, it had no transept, it did not have an arched roof supported by vaulting, nor were the walls supported by buttresses, but the size and scale are not dissimilar. The cathedral at Salisbury, for example, is 137 metres long, 26 metres across the nave, and 25 metres high on the inside.

In Jerusalem, the sanctuary itself could not be very big. Herod and his advisers were restrained by the biblical description of Solomon's temple; according to Josephus, Herod justified his plan by saying that he would improve on the present inferior temple, built in adverse circumstances, and make the temple as large as Solomon's (*Antiq.* 15.386). It would have been impolitic, to say the least, to make the sanctuary itself larger. The dimensions of Solomon's temple complex, however, were no longer adequate: they suited neither the increased population of Jerusalem, nor the large number of pilgrims, nor Herod's wealth and ambition, nor his own considerable knowledge of architecture and building, nor the abilities of his architects, engineers and craftsmen. Something altogether grander was required. Herod embellished the sanctuary with gold and tapestry, but its size remained modest. He satisfied the other requirements by building the great wall, enlarging the paved platform inside the wall to accommodate the thousands of pilgrims, building the porticoes, and improving traffic flow and shopping facilities outside the temple area. That is why I have compared the hypostyle hall in the temple of Amun not with Herod's sanctuary, but with the Royal Portico. Here he could show what he could do. The Egyptian hypostyle hall is, to be sure, only one hall of a vast sanctuary that is approximately 350 metres long and 110 metres across, inside which a large European cathedral would fit quite comfortably. When one considers the advantages that the Egyptian temple had in time, manpower and money – the hypostyle hall was built by Seti I and Ramesses II – what is remarkable is that the Royal Portico stands up to the comparison so well. Aesthetically, Herod's temple is much to be preferred to the jumbled mass of the great temple at Karnak, where first one Pharaoh and then another added something on. Herod's porticoes were modelled on the elegant stoas of Greece, and the temple area displayed an admirable harmony and simplicity of design that was as efficient as it was impressive.

By the standards of classical Greece the Royal Portico might be judged excessive. Stoas of three aisles are almost unknown in the Greek-speaking world, and stoas 185 metres long are equally rare. Further, the upper half of the middle aisle of the Royal Portico was only for appearance. There was no upper floor, probably (as Busink suggests) to prevent anyone from looking over the inner wall and into the holy area.[55] On the other hand, in the Hellenistic and Roman periods there was a tendency to build temples that exceeded those of classical Greece in size. The first enormous temple was the temple of Artemis in Ephesus (fourth century BCE), which was one of the wonders of the world. Still larger temples were built at Akragas and Selinus in Sicily, Didyma in Asia Minor, and Athens (by Hadrian). If we compare Herod's construction, including the Royal Portico, with temples such as these, it will not be considered excessive.

The table below compares Herod's Royal Portico with the Portico of Attalos in Athens (two aisles and two floors; see the drawing above), the hypostyle hall in the temple at Karnak, the Parthenon (the temple of Athene in Athens), the temple of Zeus at Akragas (one of the largest temples built in the Greek-speaking world), Salisbury Cathedral, York Minster, and Temple Emanuel in New York.[56] Only the first of these is structurally the same as the Royal Portico, and the others are put in for two reasons: to give an idea of the scale of Herod's building compared to other great buildings in the Mediterranean, and to give some idea of the absolute size.

Measures are in metres.

Building	Length	Width	Number of columns	Column or interior height	Total Height
Royal portico, 3 aisles	186	33	162	12.5	32
Attalos, 2 aisles	116.5	12.5		5 lower/4 upper	12
Hypostyle, Karnak	102 [width]	53 [length]	134	21/13	25
Parthenon	70	31		10.5	
Akragas	110	53		18	
Salisbury	137	26		24.7	
York	148	36.5			
Emanuel	45.7	23.5		31.4	

It is generally accepted that the money-changers and dove-sellers whom the gospels make so famous (Mark 11.15–19 and parr.) conducted their business in the Royal Portico. It is reasonable to think that Herod knew from the outset that this trade had to take place somewhere if the temple was to function efficiently. He was interested in efficiency and traffic control, as the great care that his builders took with the streets and shops to the south and west of the temple wall demonstrates. It doubtless goes too far, however, to say that he built the Portico for the dove-sellers. He built it as the appropriate front for the temple area and to accord with his view of himself and his kingdom – and possibly even for the glory of God. Glorification of self and God not infrequently go hand-in-hand when it comes to religious architecture.

Thus far we have not discussed the overall height of the temple complex. This is a difficult topic, since the ground slopes, and since after they laid the lower courses of the walls the workmen put dirt and rubble around them. Excavations during the last twenty years, however, have revealed a lot about the southern and southwestern parts of the temple wall, which is where the ground is lowest, and where some of the main streets and shops were. Ben-Dov calculates that in the south the walls rose more than 30 metres above the paved streets, 'about the height of a ten-storey building'. 'In some places the foundations of these retaining walls reached down as far as 20 metres below the street'.[57]

Of the 30+ metres above the street, the first 19 constituted the retaining wall, which rose to the level of the paved platform inside. The depth of the fill was thus as much as 20 metres from bedrock to the street, 19 metres to the platform. Above that, as we have seen, were the porticoes, which, on the west, north and east, rose 25 cubits above the paved platform (c. 12.5 metres).[58] The central aisle of the Royal Portico was at least twice that high.

The result was that from the outside, especially from the south and east, the temple was massively imposing. On the east the wall rose some 31 metres (34 yards), and it began at the edge of a deep valley. From the south, the ground sloped more gradually, but was nevertheless substantially lower than the street at the foot of the wall. On the west there was a ravine, and on the other side of the ravine a residential area sloped up away from the temple, exceeding it in height. Nevertheless, the occupants of the Upper City looked across a ravine to the temple wall, and even to them it would have been imposing. From the distance, one saw principally the Royal Portico and the sanctuary above the walls, the one glistening white, the other gold.

The architects employed one device to make the appearance of the walls less looming. Each course was 'set about 3 centimeters further in than the one below it'.[59] The total inset from ground level to top was about 60 centimetres. This very small recess (1¼ inches, totalling 25 inches from bottom to top) would not make the temple mount 'look like the sides of a pyramid with its top lopped off', but it would keep the walls from looking as if they were falling out, on top of a person who stood near the base looking up. For a similar reason all of the outside columns of the Parthenon slant in; this keeps the temple of Athena from looking as if it is flying apart.

Inside, the temple area had a more humane aspect. The porticoes rose 12.5 metres (41 feet) from the Court of the Gentiles, but the height was softened by the open area under their roofs. We should also recall that the other courts were not only 'inner' but also 'upper': they rose above the Court of the Gentiles. The inner wall of the temple was 40 cubits (c. 20 metres/yards) high if looked at from the Court of the Gentiles, but one went up two flights of steps before going through the gate, and from the interior the wall was only 25 cubits high (12.5 metres/yards) (*War* 5.196). The Court of the Israelites was higher yet, though the sanctuary loomed above it – and well above the walls. We do not know just how high the Court of the Priests was. It was above the Court of the Women, the floor of which was above the middle of the eastern portico. (The portico was 25 cubits high; entering the Court of the Women one climbed 15 cubits.) The floor of the sanctuary may have been three-quarters of the way up the outer portico.

Finally a word about the streets and shops. Early explorers had noted two arches coming out from the side of the western wall (Robinson's and Wilson's arches). For a hundred years it was assumed that these supported bridges over the Tyropoeon Valley and connected the temple platform to the Upper City. New excavations have shown that the arches supported short bridges that spanned not the valley, but a street adjacent to the temple wall.[60] Flights of steps then led down to the street level. Robinson's arch allowed people to climb from the street along the western wall directly to the Royal Portico, without going through the main southern gates. This street (19 metres below the temple platform, c. 31 metres below the top of the western portico) had shops on both sides, backing up to the wall on one side, and cut into the arch, which is 15.2 metres broad, on the other. At the southwestern corner of the temple wall, 'West Wall Street' met another street running along the southern wall, on which there were also shops. The volume of the tourist trade probably made these very desirable locations.

Dominated by Herod's great edifice, adorned by palaces and other splendid houses, graced with abundant market space both near the temple and in the Upper City, Jerusalem doubtless was, as the Elder Pliny called it, 'by far the most illustrious city of the East'.[61]

The holiness of the temple

We have seen that the temple area consisted of areas of increasing sanctity and that admission was progressively restricted. The distinctions from area to area depended on notions of fitness and purity. Here, again, the Jewish temple was by no means unique. Limited access and purifications were common to ancient holy areas. Partly because Jews had such a high theology – the God of Israel was the only God, and he had created the heavens and earth – the rules that protected the Jerusalem temple were very exacting. Purity was so strictly observed that the inner area of the temple complex had been built by priests, 1,000 of whom Herod had ordered to be trained as masons and carpenters (*Antiq.* 15.390). This reveals that purity laws had developed. According to Ezra 3.10, when the second temple was built 'the builders laid the foundation', the priests blew trumpets and the Levites clanged cymbals. In Herod's day, laymen could not enter the court of the priests or the sanctuary itself even for the purpose of construction. Apparently we are not to think, however, that the high priest built the Holy of Holies by himself.

It is difficult for the modern westerner to imagine the feeling of sanctity that the temple inspired. It was an austere place, dedicated to the worship of the creator of the world, the God of Israel. He was regarded as mighty and holy, which includes the idea of separation from what is common. Moses, when called by God, was told to take off his shoes and to come no nearer. The call came from a bush that burned but was not consumed (Ex. 3.1–6). This was no informal, chatty visit from a god who readily took human guise, as did the gods of Greek mythology. The ideas of holiness and separation, which allowed only what was most pure to come near, informed the entire arrangement of the temple and its rites. Philo pointed out the significance of the absence of a sacred grove of trees, common to temples in the Graeco-Roman world: 'the temple which is truly holy does not seek to provide pleasure and hours of easy enjoyment but the austerity of religion (*austēran hagisteian*)' (*Spec. Laws* 1.74; cf. also Pseudo-Hecataeus, above, pp. 55f.).

The temple was holy not only because the holy God was worshipped there, but also because he *was* there. The notion of God's special presence in the temple – more precisely, in the Holy of Holies – was, we saw above, denied by some, but it was accepted by most. According to Josephus, in the good old days (the time of John Hyrcanus and before) the sardonyx on the right shoulder of the high priest's robe shone 'whenever God assisted at the sacred ceremonies' (*Antiq.* 3.215–18).[62] As Jesus put it, 'he who swears by the temple, swears by it and by him who dwells in it' (Matt. 23.21). Josephus reports that there were numerous portents of the coming destruction of the temple, one of which was that at the Feast of Weeks the priests, when they entered, heard first 'a commotion and a din', then 'a voice as of a host, "We are departing hence"' (*War* 6.300; cf. 2.539; 5.19; 5.412; *Antiq.* 20.166). Jews did not think that God was there and nowhere else, nor that the temple in any way confined him. Since he was creator and lord of the universe, he could be approached in prayer at any place. Nevertheless, he was in some special sense present in the temple. As the author of II Maccabees expressed it, 'He who has his dwelling in heaven watches over that place [the temple] itself and brings it aid'. He claimed that Heliodorus, a Seleucid official, testified that 'there certainly is about the place some power of God' (II Mac. 3.28f.). Josephus could also express God's special connection with the temple in this way; he attributes to Titus the statement that 'any deity that once watched over this place' had already ceased to do so before the Roman destruction (*War* 6.127).

God had decreed that great sanctity must govern the approach to his special dwelling. Whatever was impure must not come near him. He had ordained the progressive steps of sanctity appropriate to his worship – purity of the land, purity of Jerusalem, then the carefully controlled stages of purity within the temple. The awe and fear of him, which accompanied love and devotion, meant that the decree was kept.

As we shall see more fully below, the temple was heavily guarded, and apparently the guards even patrolled the Court of the Israelites (Philo, *Spec. Laws* 1.156). It was an offence against God for anyone other than a priest to step over the low parapet into the Court of the Priests. If even a Levite came 'near the vessels of the sanctuary or to the altar', he and the priest responsible would die (Num. 18.3). There was probably not much risk that an ordinary Jew would enter the Priests' Court, since they knew what was in the Bible and what were the laws that governed the temple. They respected its sanctity.

The purity laws, which were strictly observed and (when possible) enforced, were not primarily moral laws: impurity might be acquired when one transgressed a law, but most forms of impurity essentially had to do not with transgression but with changes of status. Purity laws affected daily life relatively little; their principal function was to regulate access to the temple, which is our present concern.[63] Josephus put it this way: '*In view of the sacrifices* the Law has prescribed purifications for various occasions: after a funeral, after child-birth, after conjugal union, and many others' (*Apion* 2.198), notably including menstruation. The purity laws are found principally in Lev. 12 (childbirth), Lev. 13–14 ('leprosy'), Lev. 15 (emissions from the body), and Num. 19 (death). (For present purposes we leave aside the laws on impure food.)

Death is the most terrifying 'change of status'; consequently corpse impurity was to be kept away from the temple and the priesthood. Priests were forbidden to contract corpse impurity except for the sake of the closest blood relations. The high priest was forbidden to contract it even when his father or mother died (Lev. 21.1–11). Corpse impurity was otherwise not wrong; on the contrary, care for the dead was considered a religious obligation. It brought one into contact with fundamental change, however, and a person in this state could not enter the temple. The impurity was acquired when one touched a corpse or was in the room with one. In first-century Palestine it was generally accepted that corpse impurity could also be contracted by 'overshadowing' the corpse or by being 'overshadowed' by the corpse. For example, walking over a grave resulted in corpse impurity by overshadowing. Tombs were whitewashed to prevent accidental contact (assumed in Matt. 23.27). Purification required seven days.

A woman was impure after childbirth, and she could not enter the temple or touch holy things. Childbirth impurity lasted either forty days (after the birth of a son) or eighty days (after the birth of a daughter). Menstruants were impure for a week, and anyone who touched a menstruant, her bed or chair was impure for a day. Contact with semen also resulted in impurity for one day. Unnatural 'discharge' of blood from a woman or semen from a man resulted in a more substantial impurity.

There were further minor impurities, such as touching the carcass of an animal, which I shall not list here. We shall see a fuller list and greater detail in ch. 12. Now we need note only that purification was achieved by bathing, washing the clothes and the passage of time, though corpse-impurity also required a special mixture of ashes and water.

All forms of impurity, most of which are connected with the main changes in life and the life-force itself, had to be kept away from what was sacred and unchanging.

Added Note: Gentiles, Purity and the Temple

The sanctity of the temple meant that Gentiles could enter only the outer court, the Court of the Gentiles, but not go further into the temple. This had not always been the case. According to Num. 15.14–16, Gentiles could bring sacrifices in the same way as Israelites. By the late third or early second century BCE, however, it was agreed that Gentiles, along with impure Israelites, could not enter the temple enclosure. Josephus quotes a proclamation by Antiochus III to that effect (*Antiq.* 12.145f.). Herod agreed: he could have hired Gentile masons to work on the temple, as (it appears) he did when building one of his palaces at Jericho, but he had priests trained as masons so that they could build the inner courts (*Antiq.* 15.390). In Herod's temple, there was a balustrade beyond which Gentiles were forbidden to pass (above, p. 61). What were the grounds of their exclusion?

Since, in general, admission to the temple was restricted by purity laws, the simplest explanation is that Gentiles were regarded as impure. There are, however, problems with this view. We shall consider the following points: (1) evidence that Jews did not think that purity laws applied to Gentiles; (2) against this, evidence that Jews at least sometimes regarded Gentiles as impure; (3) considerations that show that, in our period, there was no *general* view that Gentiles were impure.

1. Jews in general, as far back as we can see, thought that the Mosaic law was for Israelites, except when it says that it covers 'sojourners' (resident aliens, e.g. Deut. 5.14f.). Although biblical laws made most Jews impure most of the time, these laws did not apply to Gentiles.[1] To take an example from rabbinic literature: a Jewish male who stepped on the menstrual blood of a Gentile woman (outside a bathhouse, for example) was not rendered impure (at least in the view of some rabbis). Leviticus 15, according to which menstruants are impure, does not apply to Gentiles.[2] Many rabbinic scholars have been of the view that before the revolt Jews did not consider Gentiles impure. Eventually the rabbis would decide on a category, 'Gentile impurity', but these scholars maintain that there was no such category until the 'eighteen decrees', which were passed shortly before the destruction of the temple.[3]

2. In favour of the view that Gentiles were excluded from the temple because of impurity, one may cite several passages. They throw light on three legal questions, beginning with the basic one: (*a*) Was it impurity that kept Gentiles on their side of the balustrade? (*b*) If so, how serious was Gentile impurity on the standard scale of impurities? (*c*) Was Gentile impurity communicable to Jews? If they caught it, how could they get rid of it?

With regard to (*a*) and (*b*): Josephus wrote that if a senior Essene touched a lower ranking member of the sect, he bathed, 'as after contact with an alien' (*War* 2.150).[4] Although it is possible that this means that only Essenes thought that aliens conveyed impurity, it is more likely that we should apply the idea more generally: foreigners could render Jews impure. Since bathing sufficed to remove the impurity, it was light. The Essenes treated their own community as in some ways equivalent to the temple (chs 16–17), and we do not learn from this passage that any Jew who touched a Gentile would immediately bathe.

The second piece of evidence, which bears on the same two issues, is a debate between the Houses of Hillel and Shammai:

The School of Shammai say: If a man became a proselyte on the day before

Passover he may immerse himself and consume his Passover-offering in the evening. And the School of Hillel say: He that separates himself from his uncircumcision is as one that separates himself from a grave. (*Pesahim* 8.1)

The requirement of immersion means that the convert was treated as impure. The impurity was, according to the Shammaites, very light, equivalent to Jewish semen impurity. It was removed by immersion and sunset. A person could convert, immerse and eat the Passover lamb after night fell. According to the Hillelites, Gentile impurity was equivalent to corpse impurity; therefore purification required a week. Thus a person who converted and immersed on the day before Passover could not share the Passover lamb. To eat Passover, one must be rid of corpse impurity, and for that reason the Bible appoints a second Passover a month later, which those who were corpse-impure at first Passover could observe (Num. 9.9–11). The Hillelites ruled, in effect, that Gentile impurity put a convert into that category.

With regard to (*c*), whether or not Gentile impurity was communicable, Josephus' passage about the Essenes seems to imply that it was. A second passage, which is difficult and therefore interesting, seems to point in the same direction. In about 43 BCE, when Herod was merely governor of Galilee (under Hyrcanus II), he and his troops were active. They put down a minor uprising in Samaria, and then turned towards Jerusalem in order to pursue the man whom Herod suspected of having poisoned his father. It was the period before Passover. 'Hyrcanus sent orders forbidding him to intrude aliens (*allophyloi*) upon the country-folk during their period of purification' (the week before Passover, when the worshippers were being cleansed of corpse impurity) (*War* 1.229). This sounds as if, at about the time of Hillel's birth, the House of Hillel's view had already prevailed: foreigners were impure as if they were Jews who had corpse impurity, and, moreover, Gentile impurity was infectious. What is curious is the use of 'aliens' for Herod's army. His troops were probably partly Jewish and partly Idumaean. The status of Idumaeans in this period is an issue too difficult to raise here; Josephus' source may have thought of them as non-Jewish, while they may have thought of themselves as good Jews.

There is, of course, another possibility. The word 'aliens' may not convey what Hyrcanus thought. He may have presumed that Herod's Jewish soldiers had corpse impurity (he could hardly have thought anything else), and have forbidden them on that ground.

While this evidence by no means shows that there was a single law or halakhah, decreed by rabbis or Pharisees, that Gentiles were impure, they were *treated* as impure, at least when it came to the temple. The Pharisees, in fact, had nothing to do with Gentile exclusion from the temple. This is an instance that shows that some people who were not Pharisees created new laws. Exclusion of the Gentiles from the temple prevailed as early as Antiochus III.[5] Therefore the Zadokite priesthood, before the days of the Hasmoneans, had thought that Gentiles were impure, as did Herod's advisers later (presumably the priesthood, not the Pharisees).[6]

We have seen that Gentiles were *treated* as impure. Hoenig proposes that the Gentiles were not, in Jewish law, impure, but that Jews avoided various kinds of contact with them because of idolatry (n. 3 above). I am sure that idolatry was the basic problem. Further, it seems to me that Hoenig's distinction is worthwhile in two major spheres: the relations between Jews and Gentiles *in general* and the analysis of rabbinic law. Nevertheless, on the particular issue at hand, I am content to say that an exclusion that *functioned like* a purity law *was* a purity law.

3. Now we should note the degree to which Gentiles were *not* regarded as impure. Christian scholars often say that Jews would not associate with Gentiles, but that is evidently not so. In many places they lived and worked among them. I have discussed this at greater length elsewhere, and here I shall stay within the bounds of the evidence before us.[7] To deal only with the temple: there was an enormous court into which Gentiles could enter, and presumably they could buy in the shops immediately outside the temple wall. If there were a general view that Gentiles communicated impurity, they would have been kept farther away from the sanctuary than the outer court. If they could buy in the shops outside the temple, walk up the steps, and stand in the Court of the Gentiles and gawk at the porticoes, they might touch a Jew on his or her way past the balustrade. A communicable impurity would have resulted in their being kept away from the temple mount and possibly barred from Jerusalem.

We see this clearly when we compare the treatment of Gentiles with that of impure Jews. According to Josephus, Jewish 'lepers' (people with an abnormal skin condition) were expelled from the city; and Jewish menstruants, who passed on a low grade of impurity to other people (Lev. 15.19–23), were excluded from the entire temple complex.[8] Whatever it was about Gentiles that had to be kept away from the holier areas, it threatened the temple's sanctity, and the purity of worshippers, less than did Jewish menstrual blood.[9]

Hyrcanus II's decision on Herod's soldiers (assuming that he forbade them admission to the city because they were Gentiles) did not set a precedent. During Passover of the years 6–41 and 44–66 CE, Roman troops stood guard and patrolled the roofs of the temple porticoes. The high priest did not cancel Passover. Thousands of Jews flocked in to celebrate, unhindered by the presence of Gentiles who, had they been subject to it, would certainly have had corpse impurity, and who had severe cases of Gentile impurity. Possibly the soldiers moved only between the roofs of the porticoes and the Antonia fortress, never rubbing shoulders with the crowd.

To conclude: When dealing with impure Jews, we can say which impurities were communicable, because Leviticus is explicit. Further, we know how long Jewish impurities lasted and what one had to do to get rid of them. When we turn to Gentiles, we discover only one thing for sure: they were not allowed past the balustrade in the temple area. Idolatry probably was the basis of Jewish objections to Gentiles entering the temple, but in our period it seems to have been treated as creating an impurity. The evidence, however, is mixed. Gentiles had freer access to the temple than did some impure Jews, such as menstruants. This fact points towards a lack of legal clarity. What we have, really, is a single rule, Gentiles may not go beyond the barrier, without proper legal analysis and clarification. A rabbinic-style law would have determined the *severity* and *contagiousness* of the impurity, and would have related them to the various forms of Jewish impurity. The fact that the Hillelites and Shammaites did not agree is telling: things were not clearly worked out. The story about Herod's army points towards 'Hillelite' victory decades before the dispute, which means that the question was not really settled.

   The law, however, seems to have had no other effect. It is certainly possible that some Jews thought that they acquired a minor impurity if they touched a Gentile, but these same Jews thought that they acquired a minor impurity if they touched most other Jews and rather a lot of objects. Because impurity was so common, Jews in general were not afraid of it, and they did not behave in strange ways in order to avoid it. All impurities were taken care of by periodic immersions (or, in the Diaspora, other ablutions).[10]

6

The Ordinary Priests and the Levites: At Work in the Temple

As we have seen, two orders of clergy (as they would now be called) served in the temple: priests and Levites. Both positions were hereditary. According to the Bible, one of the original twelve tribes was the tribe of Levi. Moses and Aaron, his brother, were of this tribe (Ex. 2). Aaron was the first priest. His male descendants were priests, while other males of the tribe of Levi, called simply 'the Levites', were the lesser clergy (Ex. 28.1, 41; 29.9; Lev. 1.5; Num. 1.47–54; 8; 18; I Chron. 24).

The law requires that priests and Levites be wholly or partially supported by their work for the Lord. The descendants of Aaron were to have 'no inheritance' in the land. God promised the priests, 'I am your portion and your inheritance among the people of Israel' (Num. 18.20); he gave them the sacrifices and offerings to eat (Num. 18.8–13). Similarly the Levites' portion was the tithe, not land (18.21). Early in the second-temple period, Nehemiah found that the tithes were not being paid, with the result 'that the Levites and the singers, who did the work, had fled each to his field' (Neh. 13.10). This was soon corrected.

We shall see below that in our period the tithes and other contributions were made and that the priests and Levites were, on the whole, well supported. We know that some priests owned land, since Josephus refers to his own property (*Life* 422), but probably they did not work it.[1] During the long period when Jewish Palestine was a 'theocracy', governed by the high priest, which lasted from the fifth century BCE to Herod's accession as king, the biblical laws governing support of the temple and its staff had been enforced and had become habitual.[2] Herod did not relax them, but rather supported the temple in every way. His successors, both his own descendants and the Roman prefects and procurators, also looked upon the temple and the priesthood as essential to the life of the nation, and they expected the high priest to bear considerable responsibility.

In the first century, there were probably about 20,000 priests and Levites. Although I Chron. 23.3 refers to 38,000 Levites over the age of thirty (purporting to describe the time of David), it appears that in the second temple period there were relatively few. Ezra 2.36–42 and Neh. 7.39–45 list 4,289 priests and only 74 Levites, though the latter number does not include 148 singers and 138 gatekeepers (musicians and gatekeepers are sometimes considered to be Levites, as in I Chron. 23.3–5, but sometimes are listed separately). Josephus attributes to Hecataeus of Abdera the statement that 1,500 priests received tithes and administered public affairs (*Apion* 1.188). This is presumably Pseudo-Hecataeus I (first half of the second century BCE), whom we met above. His figures are either in error, or he referred only to the priests resident in Jerusalem, since there must have been more than 1,500 priests in his day.

The best estimate for our period, 20,000, is given by Josephus in *Apion* 2.108. There were, however, numerous sub-divisions, and both the work and the revenue were parcelled out. From the Bible, Josephus and the Mishnah we know that there were 24 'courses', or 'duty rosters' of priests and Levites (I Chron. 24.4; *Antiq.* 7.365; *Sukkah* 5.6), and that each course served one week. The courses were themselves divided into 'fathers' houses', which served only one day at a time.[3] It is possible that there was also a change of shifts after the morning sacrifice, some priests leaving and some coming on duty.[4] Further, while on duty the priests alternated periods of rest with periods of sacrifice. On most days only a few priests were needed to sacrifice at any one time. Had there not been a regular rotation of service, relatively few priests would have sacrificed. Sacrificing was both a privilege, since it served God, and a benefit, since it provided the priest with meat.

We shall consider the question of the number of priests and Levites more carefully. Joachim Jeremias regarded the *Letter of Aristeas* as providing better evidence than Josephus that the total number was about 20,000. We recall that its author was an Alexandrian Jew who lived in the second or first century BCE, who visited Jerusalem and described the temple service. There were more than 700 priests in attendance, in addition to 'assistants bringing forward the animals for sacrifice' (*Arist.* 95). Jeremias estimated the number of assistants at 50, and thus proposed 750 as the number of priests and Levites in each weekly course. By multiplying 750 by 24 (the number of courses), he arrived at 18,000 as the total number of priests and Levites. One can then add in musicians and gatekeepers as Levites (or, alternatively, add them to the roster of temple employees), and arrive at Josephus' figure, 20,000. The evidence from Aristeas is in fact most dubious: when we quote the passage below, the reader will see that he wrote that 700 priests were on duty at the same time, not that the weekly course consisted of 700.[5] Seven hundred at a time, however, is impossible, except at one of the festivals. One may think that this number is about right for a weekly course: 50 each shift, two shifts a day for seven days; but this argument is not aided by Aristeas' statement.

In saying that 700 at a time is impossible, I mean this: 350 priests (assuming half were resting) could not stand inside the court of the priests and sacrifice at the same time. This many or more could have sacrificed if they used the other courts, and this is what they did at Passover, a not unlikely time for the Alexandrian pilgrim to have visited. In this case, however, we still would not know how many priests there were. At Passover, all the priests were on duty, not just one course, but we do not know what kind of shifts they worked. The truth is that we cannot do better than to take Josephus' word for it. Jeremias' effort to get 'scientific' figures by revising his source is not an improvement.[6]

When on duty, some priests were accepting sacrifices, some were resting, some were inspecting sacrificial victims, others were labouring in other ways. Although we cannot be certain of numbers, there was room to butcher only a few animals simultaneously; birds were easier, since the priests could accept them by standing along the parapet, which was more than 150 metres long, without having to use the shambles. Conceivably no more than 20 or 25 priests were standing and sacrificing at any given moment on the average 'low' day, though many more than that *could* have been employed if, as seems probable, most sacrifices were birds. It is impossible to make any estimate of the number of private sacrifices on a normal day, when there were few tourists or pilgrims, and only the residents of Jerusalem and its environs needed to be served.

At the pilgrimage festivals, business accelerated; all the priests and Levites were available and worked in turn. At Passover, as we just noted, a larger portion of the temple area was used for slaughter, since the Priests' Court would not accommodate the worshippers and their lambs (*Zevahim* 5.8; see pp. 136f. below).

The work of the priesthood proper, put in terms of tasks known today, was a combination of liturgical worship and expert butchery, mostly the latter. The priests heard confessions and accepted sacrifices and offerings in the name of God. They slaughtered animals and birds and flayed (skinned) the animals and cut them up for distribution. They sprinkled or poured blood on and around the altar. They put the principal fatty pieces of the sacrificial animals on the altar: blood and fat belonged to the Lord (e.g. Lev. 3.17). In many cases priests ate most of the meat, though in the case of some sacrifices the person who brought the animal retained the bulk of the meat as food, and in others the entire animal was consumed by the flames of the altar.

As part of the temple service the priests also recited portions of scripture, prayed and burned incense. The burning of incense is prescribed by the Bible (Ex. 30.1–8; Lev. 16.13), but prayer and the recitation of scriptural passages were more recent introductions. Prayer is first mentioned, as far as I have noted, in Isa. 56.7;[7] Ben Sira (*c.* 200 BCE) refers to both prayer and singing, as well as trumpets (50.16–18). Philo attributed prayer and thanksgiving to the high priest (*Spec. Laws* 1.97; *Moses* 2.133), and he regarded the sacrifices in general as being an occasion for prayer (*Spec. Laws* 1.195). Josephus wrote that at the sacrifices 'prayers for the welfare of the community must take precedence of those for ourselves' (*Apion* 2.196). I think it probable that Josephus here referred to prayers offered by the priests, but it is possible that he meant that worshippers in general should pray for the community. It is probable that at the conclusion of the daily service, before the last incense was burned, there were prayer and scriptural passages (see the discussion of *Tamid* in ch. 7). Some aspects of this closing rite are confirmed by the book of Judith (*c.* 170–150 BCE), which mentions that the heroine prayed when 'the evening's incense was being offered in the house of God in Jerusalem' (Judith 9.1). This may reflect the priestly practice of closing prayers. We shall see below that some Jews said the *Shema* (Deut. 6.4–9) when evening approached. This too was probably in imitation of the temple service, in which, according to the Mishnah, the priests recited that and other passages after the last sacrifice. The Mishnah seems to be generally correct about the daily temple service (see ch. 7 n. 1), and below I shall summarize parts of its description.

All the work of the priests was done skilfully, devoutly and silently. These lines from *Aristeas* give the setting and something of the technique of sacrifice:

The ministration of the priests is in every way unsurpassed both for its physical endurance and for its orderly and silent service. For they all work spontaneously, though it entails much painful exertion, and each one has a special task allotted to him. The service is carried on without interruption – some provide the wood, others the oil, others the fine wheat flour, others the spices; others again bring the pieces of flesh for the burnt offering, exhibiting a wonderful degree of strength. For they take up with both hands the limbs of a calf, each of them weighing more than two talents [80 kgs/175 lbs], and throw them with each hand in a wonderful way on to the high place [of the altar] and never miss placing them on the proper spot. In the same way the pieces of the sheep and also of the goats are wonderful both for their weight and their fatness. For those, whose business it is, always select [the beasts] which are without blemish and specially fat . . . There is a special place set apart for [the priests] to rest in, where those who are relieved from duty sit. When this takes place, those who have already rested and are ready . . . rise up [spontaneously] since there is no one to give orders with regard to the arrangement of the sacrifices. The most complete silence reigns so that one might imagine that there was not a single person present, though there are actually seven hundred men engaged in the work, besides the vast number of those who are occupied in bringing up the sacrifices. Everything is carried out with reverence and in a way worthy of the great God. (*Arist.* 92–5)[8]

It is clear from this description that the priests were fit. When on duty, they were also well fed. Since only priests were allowed in the sacrificial area, they had to do all the menial tasks. While they did not themselves bring the altar wood into the temple area, they had to carry it to the room where it was sorted and inspected and then to the altar. An open fire large enough to consume the parts of animals requires a lot of wood. The priests dressed appropriately: in linen, not in wool, since the work was heavy. Ezekiel opposed sweat (44.18), but one doubts that the priests could avoid it. The sleeves of their tunics were tightly laced around their arms, and they wore breeches for greater modesty. While at work, they moved 'with unhampered rapidity', making the sacrifices, sprinkling blood, butchering the animals, burning the appropriate parts, and separating the remaining parts for their own use or that of those who brought the sacrifices (e.g. Philo, *Spec. Laws* 1.82–83).

The Levites, we have seen, assisted the priests. They sometimes helped worshippers get their animals to the Court of the Priests, and perhaps it was Levites who brought women's sacrifices from the Women's Court to the priests. Levites also carried in firewood, manned the gates and provided music. Their hymn book was the Book of Psalms, and they had to hold scrolls while they sang. We know this because, *c.* 65 CE, they petitioned to be allowed to sing from memory rather than hold the heavy scrolls. Agrippa II, whom Rome then allowed to regulate temple affairs, convened a court (a *synedrion*), which granted their request and also allowed them to wear linen. Josephus resented these changes: 'such transgression was bound to make us liable to punishment' (*Antiq.* 20.216–18).

The job of gatekeeper was important. The gates, of course, had to be closed in the evening and opened in the morning, and numerous men were required for this task. A great responsibility lay on the Levites who stood at the main entrances to the temple area, primarily the more easterly of the two sets of gates in the southern wall. We can only guess about rules for entry, but we can probably make some good guesses. The Levites at the outer gates, unlike their modern counterparts, did not have to worry about the clothing of worshippers and tourists: sandals without socks were acceptable, as were bare arms; no one wore shorts, and women did not go about in halter tops. The guards probably did, however, stop people from carrying anything in (cf. *Apion* 2.106).[9] Worshippers, of course, could bring in their offerings and a bag to carry home their portion of a shared sacrifice (if they offered one), but the temple was not a place for picnics; only holy food was admitted (*Apion* 2.108f.), and people with suspicious parcels would probably have been turned back.[10] The guards at the outer gates would not have allowed weapons (though, as the war approached, the Sicarii entered with concealed daggers and committed assassinations, *Antiq.* 20.165; cf. *War* 2.254–7).[11]

Nearby were armed guards, either Levites or additional temple servants, partly to protect the temple's great wealth, partly to prevent disturbances. Since large numbers of people gathered in the temple, the outer court was an ideal place for rousing the rabble. The author of the *Letter of Aristeas* related that in his day the temple was protected by a neighbouring citadel, which had catapults on its towers and was heavily manned (*Arist.* 100–104). In Herod's time, the situation was basically the same: the king's troops manned the Antonia fortress, which commanded the temple area. In the Roman period, the fortress was also garrisoned, in case of serious trouble, but Roman troops would not have entered the temple precincts for minor disturbances. To maintain security and discourage disturbances when large crowds came to the temple for the festivals, soldiers were posted on the roofs of the porticoes (*War* 2.224). Generally, however, the Romans left the policing of the temple and Jerusalem to the high priest, who had armed guards. Since these could not be stationed in the Antonia fortress, they were probably on duty near the gates of the temple. Philo, in describing the responsibilities of the Levites, emphasized the importance of guard duties and also indicated that there were guards at the gate through the inner wall, to check on Jewishness and purity:

> Some of these [temple attendants] are stationed at the doors as gatekeepers at the very entrances, some within in front of the sanctuary to prevent any unlawful person from setting foot thereon, either intentionally or unintentionally. Some patrol around it turn by turn in relays by appointment night and day, keeping watch and guard at both seasons. Others sweep the porticoes and the open court, convey away the refuse and ensure cleanliness. (*Spec. Laws* 1.156)

All these jobs, including the most lowly, were, in Philo's view, performed by Levites, since he continued, 'All these have the tithes appointed as their wages'. The Levites, like the priests, served in a weekly rotation of twenty-four courses.

Some priests were administrators. In the Mishnah and Tosefta there are passages that list temple officials and even name them.[12] These passages allow scholars to write such things as that Petahiah was the priest who accepted women's bird offerings and slaughtered them, or that the high priest gave the sign to Ben Arza to begin the music; that is, they allow the modern writer to add novelistic elements to the account. But the priests and Levites served in weekly courses and many of the priests' duties were allocated each day by casting lots. There probably were, however, senior administrators who, like the head treasurer, had more-or-less full-time jobs. Possibly rabbinic lists name these administrators at some given point in time (otherwise, the purpose of the lists is a mystery). If so, the statement that Petahiah was over the bird offerings does not mean that he sacrificed all the birds, but that he oversaw the procurement, sale and inspection of them. Ben Arza, in charge of the 'platform' where the musicians stood, might have been responsible for seeing that there were enough musicians each day, and that not too many were off sick. It is intrinsically likely that at any given time there were half-a-dozen or a dozen administrators, mostly priests, with two or more Levites (e.g. over the guards and over the music).

Among the full-time administrative positions, the office of chief temple treasurer was especially important.[13] The temple had vast wealth: cash, precious furnishings, and estates. This did not make it distinctive: temples ordinarily had money, both their own and private money deposited there for security. Temples were sacred in a world that believed in gods, and a temple was ordinarily a good place to put one's treasure.[14] Despite this, not everyone respected every god or God, and the temple in Jerusalem was plundered more than once.

We shall look at two stories to see whether or not we can discover the scale of the temple's wealth. Crassus (an ambitious and avaricious Roman general), intending to attack the Parthians (c. 54 BCE), raided the temple in Jerusalem on his way. Just a few years before, Pompey had entered the temple building, but he had not robbed it (*Antiq.* 14.72). Crassus, however, wanted money. He took the cash reserve, 2,000 talents, presumably in gold or silver coins.[15] A talent was a weight, about 40 kg or 88 lbs. Thus Crassus lifted about 80,000 kgs or 176,000 lbs in coin – according to the story. A lower estimate of the weight of a talent, 34.272 kgs or 75.6 lbs, would yield coins weighing 68,544 kgs, 151,200 lbs. The Guardian of Funds (variant: of Treasuries), a priest named Eleazar, hoping to keep Crassus from taking the tapestry and other valuables, such as golden vessels, weighing 8,000 talents altogether, produced a hidden bar of beaten gold worth 'many tens of thousands' of drachmas (*c.* 10,000 drachmas to the talent).[16] Though he had promised to be content, Crassus nevertheless carried off the rest of the gold from the sanctuary (*Antiq.* 14.105–109). That is, he took 10,000 talents in cash and valuables, plus the gold bar. Mary Smallwood points out that 'the figures . . . seem to belong to the realm of legend'.[17]

I am sure that Smallwood is correct. Probably Crassus did not strip the entire temple of valuables (we do not learn that fresh funds had to be found to pay for new vessels and tapestry, for example), and probably he took less than 2,000 talents in coin. The story of the golden bar, however, rings true. Though the account of Crassus' raid on the temple funds does not tell us precisely how much was there and how much he took, it and other stories of looting show that the temple had great wealth.

The second story shows that one source of income alone, the temple tax, provided a great deal of money. Cicero states that Roman administrators confiscated some of the tax: 100 Roman pounds of gold at Apamea, 20 pounds at Laodicea, 100 pounds at Adramyttium.[18] A Roman pound was approximately three-quarters of an English pound, thus about a third of a kilogram. These sums presumably were the temple tax from the regions surrounding those cities, and they by no means represent the temple's income for the year. If we were to use today's values, and calcuate an ounce of gold as worth about $400.00 US, we would arrive at the total value of $1,056,000 (220 Roman pounds of gold = 165 English pounds × 16 ounces per pound × $400). In the good old days, when gold was $35.00 an ounce, the value would have been $92,400. The confiscations were at least sizable. The real value of gold depends, of course, on such things as inflation, the price of land and the cost of food. We perhaps get a better idea of the worth of the money if we note that, after Herod's death, members of his family inherited the following annual revenues: Salome, sixty talents; Archelaus, six hundred; Antipas, two hundred; Philip, one hundred.[19] Archelaus (who became *ethnarch* and ruler of Judaea and Samaria) received about 60,000 Roman pounds, a lot more than the three confiscations produced, but much less than the amount that Crassus was said to have stolen.

We may think both that Josephus' source exaggerated Crassus' theft and that he took a great deal of wealth. On any reckoning, managing the temple's funds was a large responsibility. That there was one chief treasurer is confirmed by *War* 6.390, which relates that the man who held the office, Phineas, bought his freedom before Titus completed the conquest of Jerusalem by handing over the priests' garments, purple and scarlet cloth, cinnamon, cassia and other spices, 'other treasures' and 'numerous sacred ornaments'. By then, most of the temple wealth, as well as the property of individuals that had been lodged there for safekeeping, had already been taken by the rebels or destroyed (*War* 5.562f.; 6.157, 264, 282). Yet there was still enough to buy Phineas' freedom.

The Jerusalem temple, like any other, had 'votive offerings' (*anathēmata*). These were vessels or plaques, made of silver, gold or bronze, usually with inscriptions expressing friendship.[20] Pseudo-Hecataeus remarked on the absence of votive offerings (*Apion* 1.199). Nevertheless, even in his day there had been some, though probably they did not litter the grounds, as they did around some temples. If plaques, they would have been attached to the inner walls. Ptolemy III Euergetes, third century BCE, had given some (*Apion* 2.48); other aliens also made their contributions (*War* 2.413); Augustus himself donated vessels for wine (5.526). Spoils of war, dedicated by both the Hasmoneans and Herod, also adorned the temple walls (*Antiq.* 15.402).

The temple had to trade with local merchants and craftsmen for some items. It consumed large quantities of incense (which was burned first thing in the morning and last thing in the evening: Ex. 30.7f.; *Spec. Laws* 1.171), and it also required a good deal of cloth. Its vessels and basins (for cooking, carrying blood to the altar, and so on) needed periodic attention. The Mishnah depicts the temple as a tough trading partner: in the case of price variation between conclusion of contract and completion of sale, 'the temple always has the upper hand' (*Sheqalim* 4.9). Small tradesmen may have been made to realize that they supplied the needs of a powerful corporation, but this particular mishnah comes at the end of a chapter that contains numerous second-century disputes about how the temple managed its goods, and it is not necessarily a description of how pre-70 trade was conducted. Rather than assume gross abuse, we should think that the usual kind of symbiotic relationship existed. The temple needed tradesmen and craftsmen, and it must have paid fair prices and wages, at least on average. One may think of the relationship between governments and military suppliers in the modern world. The government complains that there are cost-overruns and sometimes assesses penalties; the suppliers complain that their profits are not adequate; they continue to do business.

Building projects also required use of local markets and workmen. According to Josephus, when the temple was finally completed, just before the outbreak of the war that would destroy it, 18,000 men were put out of work, and Agrippa II was requested to start another project to employ them. He declined to rebuild the eastern portico, but agreed to pave the city with white stone (*Antiq.* 20.219–23). Even before Herod's vast project, there had been periods of rebuilding, and the upkeep of the fabric alone required a certain number of workmen.

To complete this partial resumé of the temple's business affairs, we may note that it played some role in supplying worshippers with sacrificial victims. Scholars sometimes say that the temple or the priesthood had a monopoly on the sale of the required birds and animals. Actually, very little is known about it. We do know the general circumstances: the sacrifice had to be unblemished (Lev. 22.17–25; *Spec. Laws* 1.166).[21] Worshippers usually did not bring their own animal or bird, which might become damaged *en route*, and so be unacceptable. Most of the victims, therefore, were supplied locally. Philo, probably describing his own experience as a pilgrim, wrote that 'the most highly approved of the priests' inspected the animals. The priests wished to ensure the validity of the sacrifice and the innocence of the person who brought it: a blemished sacrifice was invalid and, worse, the person who offered it had transgressed the law. The temple inspectors examined the animals 'from the head to the extremities of the feet', including the parts 'which are concealed under the belly and thighs, for fear that some small blemish has passed unobserved' (Philo, *Spec. Laws* 1.166f.).

For the inspection that Philo describes there are four possibilities: (1) The temple could have authorized reliable sellers of sacrificial victims to sell only animals and birds that priests had previously inspected. In this case, the seller would have to give the buyer some kind of chit, indicating that the victim was unblemished. (2) The victims could have been sold in the temple area itself. If so, they would probably have been inspected in advance, but no chit would have been necessary. (3) The gatekeepers could have directed worshippers who brought birds, lambs or kids into the temple to an inspection area manned by priests in the Court of the Gentiles. (4) Possibly worshippers took their victims straight to the priest who would sacrifice them, who inspected them on the spot.

I think that we can rule out (4), inspection at the point of sacrifice. This would have slowed proceedings down greatly, and it would not have guaranteed that 'the most highly approved' priests carried out the inspection. Philo's statement implies a cadre of inspectors. There is no direct evidence in favour of (3), a station inside the Court of the Gentiles for inspecting the sacrifices (not unlike a security check at a modern airport: 'Put your case on the table and open it, please'). This would be, however, the best way of guaranteeing the absence of blemishes, and I think that it deserves consideration as the means of approving quadrupeds. We recall that, describing an earlier period, Aristeas said that 'those whose business it is' chose spotless victims (*Arist.* 93). At this point, he seems to be describing what the pilgrim could see in the temple, which places the inspection there in his day, though it gives no details.

Scholars usually hesitate only between (1) and (2): sellers authorized by the temple who traded in its precincts or nearby. The gospels depict Jesus as driving out 'those who sold and those who bought in the temple', as well as overturning 'the tables of the money-changers and the seats of those who sold pigeons' (Mark 11.15 and parallels in Matthew and Luke). John goes further:

In the temple [Jesus] found those who were selling herd-animals and flock-animals and pigeons, and the money-changers at their business. And making a whip of cords, he drove them all, with the flock and the herd, out of the temple; and he poured out the coins of the money-changers and overturned their tables. And he told those who sold the pigeons, 'Take these things away; you shall not make my Father's house a house of trade'. (John 2.14–16)[22]

There are some evident exaggerations. Mark suggests that there was ordinary trade in the temple: 'those who sold and those who bought'. John, dramatically, depicts a herd (of cattle) and a flock (of sheep and goats) standing in the temple courtyard. Jeremias, citing mostly late talmudic passages, as well as one irrelevant passage from Josephus, stated that he was

forced to conclude that in the Court of the Gentiles, in spite of the sanctity of the Temple area, there could have been a flourishing trade in animals for sacrifice, perhaps supported by the powerful high-priestly family of Annas.[23]

This is most unlikely. Common buying and selling were conducted in the shops around the outside of the temple wall (above, p. 69), a fact that reduces the possibility that they took place in the temple precincts. Stocking the temple courtyard with quadrupeds would have greatly increased the noise and commotion in an area whose sanctity and austerity were prized. Philo regarded the 'broad spaces and openness and absence of [visual] restriction on every side' as among the temple's virtues, and its quietness was also noted by pilgrims. A herd and a flock would have damaged the view and raised the background noise considerably. Worse, they would have fouled the area with urine and excrement. Philo explained that one of the reasons for the absence of the usual sacred tree or grove was that trees require fertilizer, and 'the excrements of men and irrational animals cannot be brought [into the temple] without profanity' (*Spec. Laws* 1.74f.). Having been to the temple, could he have offered this explanation if in fact fresh manure was being steadily produced? Since ruminants browse almost all day, a lot of fodder would have to be brought up, as well as straw to put under them. We would have to imagine, then, that each day drovers drove a lot of animals up the steps to Robertson's Arch, over it, and into the Royal Portico. They would also have had to bring an enormous quantity of hay and straw, and then each afternoon they would have had to clean out the litter and drive the animals back down. Herod may have known in advance that his great portico would be used for birds and money-changers, but did he build it in order to have it turned into cattle stalls? When we add these practical problems to the fact that everyone would have seen the pasturing of herds and flocks in the temple as a profanation, we may dismiss the Royal Portico or the Court of the Gentiles as the market for quadrupeds. They did not ascend the steps to the Holy Mountain.

The improbability of John's account will be further seen if we focus on his statement that Jesus drove out cattle as well as sheep and goats. The Bible never requires an ordinary individual to sacrifice a bovine. An individual could sacrifice an ox or a calf as a burnt offering or as a shared sacrifice (discussed below), but few could have afforded to do so. A bull was the sin offering of the high priest (Lev. 4.3), and a bull was also required for inadvertent transgression by the 'whole congregation of Israel' (4.13f.). Even a ruler sacrificed only a goat (4.23). On the Day of Atonement a bull was sacrificed, and at the Feast of Booths a large number were slaughtered and burnt (p. 140 below), but these were community offerings. For none of these purposes would it have been useful to make cattle available for purchase by the general public. If pastured in the Royal Portico, they would have consumed an enormous quantity of fodder, they would have fouled a great deal of straw, and they would have served no purpose. As they trudged up and down the steps each day, waiting for a wealthy person to offer one as a burnt offering, they would have been in danger of breaking a leg or otherwise being blemished, which would have rendered them invalid.

Birds are different. They were used in large numbers. They can be kept in baskets or bowls, so they do not foul the floor. Here I see no reason to reject the general view that sacrificial doves and pigeons were sold in the Royal Portico, and that money-changers were also there. (Pilgrims brought a vast diversity of coinage, and many wished to pay the temple tax on the spot; therefore money-changers were necessary.) On these two points, that is, I accept the account in the synoptic gospels.

We still do not know who sold the sacrificial victims and how worshippers obtained quadrupeds. I think it most unlikely that the temple or individual priests actually owned the birds, sheep and goats and sold them to pilgrims. It would have been against the law for priests to raise the animals, and systematic disobedience of the kind that some scholars imagine would not have been permitted. It is equally unlikely that priests served as middlemen, buying the potential victims from those who raised them and selling them to the public. Engaging in direct trade of animals would have led to specific accusations – about which the literature is silent. Probably the temple licensed dealers and inspected what they sold. Conceivably the temple charged for the licenses and for the space in the Royal Portico used by bird-sellers and money-changers, but there is no evidence either way. Pilgrims probably bought quadrupeds from dealers outside the walls of the city. While we cannot entirely rule out the possibility that the animals bore, in effect, certificates of blemishlessness, it is more likely that their suitability was confirmed when the pilgrim got his animal to the temple.

There is one interesting rabbinic passage that indicates that the sale of birds was subject to the law of supply and demand (and therefore was not monopolistic).

> Once in Jerusalem a pair of doves cost a golden *denar* [= 25 silver *denars*]. Rabban Simeon b. Gamaliel said: By this Temple! I will not suffer the night to pass by before they cost but a [silver] *denar*. He went into the court and taught: If a woman suffered five miscarriages that were not in doubt or five issues that were not in doubt, she need bring but one offering, and she may then eat of the animal-offerings; and she is not bound to offer the other offerings. And the same day the price of a pair of doves stood at a quarter-*denar* each. (*Keritot* 1.7)

The impurity under discussion is female 'discharge' – blood that was not menstruation, of which the most frequent cause was miscarriage. The impurity required a sin offering (usually two birds). The anonymous mishnah (presupposed by the above discussion) states that for five cases that *were* in doubt, a woman need bring only one pair of birds, while for five cases that *were not* in doubt, she could bring one offering and then eat a share of sacrificial food, but she still owed the other four pair of birds, to be paid for later. Simeon b. Gamaliel wished to eliminate this future obligation. The result, we are told, is that the cost of birds fell to 1/100th of the previous value.

The details are at least exaggerated. Not many women, in any one year, had five 'discharges' or miscarriages; eliminating four future offerings, thus cutting such women's total expenditure by 4/5th, could not have had such an effect on the overall price. Bird-sacrifices were required for many other purposes, and a fall of 80% in a minor category would not have been a catastrophe for dealers in pigeons. But apart from the details, the story is not unreasonable. People needed advice about what to sacrifice. They consulted experts, usually priests, but possibly non-priestly Pharisees. If their advisers told them that they need bring fewer sacrifices, they could do so with a clear conscience. The cost of sacrifices fluctuated with the market.

In any system there can be and consequently will be corruption. Below we shall consider charges that some members of the priesthood were dishonest (ch. 10; cf. 15 on the aristocrats). Some scholars, however, regard the temple *system* as being necessarily corrupt: religion should not involve business or trade; in the view of some modern critics, it should not involve the support of a central clergy. 'The whole of this traffic – money-changing, selling of doves, and market for sheep and oxen – was in itself, and from its attendant circumstances, a terrible desecration.'[24] 'When Jesus overturned the money-changers and ejected the sellers of doves from the Temple he did a service to Judaism.'[25] Jesus attacked the 'activities in which the exploitation of God's people by their priestly rulers was most visible'.[26] Whereas the 'earlier layers of the Torah' had been concerned with 'the general welfare of the people', in second-temple Judaism the taxes were 'centralized for the benefit of the Jerusalem priesthood'.[27] Thus the system itself was evil. In response to this, I shall offer a few observations that bear on the question of whether or not the system itself was 'exploitative' in the sense of forcing people to spend a lot of money on sacrifices.[28]

There is every indication that the priesthood wished to encourage people to use the temple. This goal was best served by holding down the direct costs of doing so. Leviticus led the way: a sin offering should be a quadruped; but if money were short, two birds; if even birds were too expensive, flour would do (Lev. 5.7, 11). Of the sacrifices required by biblical law, the sin offering was by far the commonest. Only in the case of dishonesty does the Bible require a guilt offering, whereas people had to bring sin offerings for several different purposes. (In ch. 7 we shall see that the term 'sin offering' is somewhat misleading.) The worshippers themselves ate the only other required sacrifices, such as the Passover lamb. Thus Leviticus, which governed sacrifice in the second-temple period, was concerned to hold down the expense.

This was very much in line with the practice of most temples. That Asclepius required only a cock was a point of pride among his devotees. Worship was thereby encouraged, which everyone involved in the cult thought was a good thing. I offer a modern analogy: every Sunday in the United States and Canada millions of Christians, both children and adults, attend Sunday School, a practice that virtually requires them to have educational literature. This literature is, in turn, produced by a publishing house owned by the denomination and is available only from that source. (Television has permitted the growth of churches led and controlled by one individual clergyman, which often sell devotional literature, among other things. I leave them aside.) The sale of religious items, even though the denomination in question has a monopoly, is not generally thought to be dishonest or exploitative. Denominations want their publishing houses to supply educational literature at a low cost, so as to encourage use of it. There must be some dishonest people engaged in all this trade, even in the major denominations, though I have never heard of any. Individual corruption would not in any case prove that Christian clergy are venal and that the whole system is rotten. Nor does the relative prosperity of the people at the top of these enterprises prove that the centralized bureacracy exploits the poor.

Modern scholars, both Jews and Christians, are inclined to see the temple system as corrupt, or as detrimental to the people's welfare, I think, because both represent movements that replaced it. We all like moral reform, and it is nice to see our spiritual ancestors as moral reformers. The first-century predecessors of modern Jews and Christians (Pharisees, rabbis, Jesus and his followers) must have thought that there was something wrong with common Judaism, the Judaism of the temple. Dishonesty, greed and corruption are universal human failings, and it is simple to say that these were *the* failings of official Judaism. Since people had to spend money to sacrifice, modern scholars target trade in sacrificial animals as the area where either dishonesty or abuse of the populace flourished. Against the suspicion that changing money and selling animals somehow enriched the priests, or was actually conducted dishonestly, I set the evidence that the populace was quick to protest any form of profanation of the temple (ch. 4). Had a chief priest owned goats, pastured them in the temple, and then, in his role as magistrate, required a lot of people to sacrifice a ram as a guilt offering, I think that we would have heard about it. Hostile modern scholars think that such things happened, but first-century Jews seem not to have thought so.

Against the much more general charges that the system was corrupt because it further impoverished the poor by requiring them to sacrifice, I set the general tendency of priesthoods to encourage use of a temple by keeping the cost of sacrifices low; the evidence of concern for the poor in Leviticus; the undoubted fact that most sacrifices were birds, not quadrupeds; and the modern analogy, which shows that religious organizations can and often do sell goods and services to a captive market without being thought of as corrupt. I doubt that the Jerusalem temple sold goods (animals and birds) to the public, but it may have licensed bird-sellers and money-changers.

In addition to these considerations, we must remember that the populace as a whole supported the temple and prized its sanctity.[29] The priesthood was devoted to the divine service. Both facts would have served to check the sort of illegal and defiling activities that are now often attributed to the chief priests (owning the flocks and herds, having a monopoly on the sale of sacrificial victims, and pasturing them in the temple). The people's pride and pleasure in the temple and its services indicate that they did not feel that 'the system' abused them.

Seeing some priests as administrators and the temple as a commercial enterprise is essential for understanding ancient Judaism, and similar descriptions are necessary in describing ancient society as a whole. If the modern critics of ancient Judaism wished to engage in a serious critique of the system, they should study it in context. Since Judaism was basically an eastern religion, its temple and priesthood could be compared to those of

Mesopotamia; the comparison will make Judaism look very, very good. Once one grants that people are going to spend money on religion one way or another, one should conclude that the temple system in first-century Judaism was pretty fair, honest and unexploitative.

To conclude our discussion of priestly jobs and responsibilities, we should return to the chief occupation of the priesthood: sacrifice and the work attendant on it. When serving in the temple, they piled the altar with firewood, cleaned off the ashes, and periodically washed the blood down the drains (*Arist.* 90). Their chief occupation, however, was to kill and butcher animals as the sacrifices ordained by God. They were devoted to his worship, which was the end that the animals and birds served. According to Josephus, during Pompey's bombardment and invasion of the temple area, the priests

> carried on their religious service uncurtailed, though enveloped in a hail of missiles. Just as if the city had been wrapt in profound peace, the daily sacrifices, the expiations and all the ceremonies of worship were scrupulously performed to the honour of God. At the very hour when the temple was taken, when they were being massacred about the altar, they never desisted from the religious rites of the day. (*War* 1. 148).

They did not grab the day's profits and run.

We shall later examine some aspects of how the priests lived and what they did most of the time, when they were not on duty. For the present, however, we shall continue to explain their most important occupation and its significance in the life of Israel.

Added Note: The Priestly Vestments

The dress of the priests, like everything else if one tries to describe it in detail, presents difficulties. According to Philo, when at work the priests wore only short linen tunics (a diminutive of *chitōn*, the word that corresponds to the Latin *tunica*) and breeches, the fabric not being specified, though linen may be implied. He emphasizes that 'in this undress, with nothing more than the short tunics, they are attired so as to move with unhampered rapidity' (*Spec. Laws* 1.83). Aristeas says that they wore tunics of fine linen that covered them to the ankles (*Arist.* 87).[1] Can we determine what they actually wore?[2] Considering the topic will help us envisage the priests at work, and it will also be helpful when we ask what ordinary people wore.

The basic biblical passage specifies four items of clothing: a tunic, a sash, head-gear, and breeches (Ex. 28.40–2). There is a similar, though more complicated list in Ex. 39.27–9. The word that I translate 'tunic' is 'coat' in the RSV; my 'sash' is usually translated 'girdle'; my 'head-gear' is often translated either 'turban' or 'cap'; occasionally someone will use 'loincloth' for 'breeches'. The subsequent description will show why I translate as I do: tunic, sash, head-gear, breeches.

Did the priests wear all four garments while sacrificing? The reports of the two pilgrims from Alexandria, Philo and Aristeas, seem to imply that they did not. Josephus' description, however, indicates that they did. Three aspects of his discussion incline me to the view that he describes what he himself actually wore and that he is not giving a literary treatment of passages in the Bible. (1) Josephus describes the clothes in the order in which the priest dressed, not the order of either Ex. 28 or 39 (breeches, tunic, sash, head-gear, rather than tunic, sash, head-gear, and breeches [Ex. 28]; tunic, head-gear, breeches, sash [Ex. 39]). (2) In the passage as a whole, he is not dependent on the LXX,[3] since the terms for the head-gear and breeches are different. He has the Hebrew in mind (see the names of the four garments, *Antiq.* 3.153, 156, 157), yet in describing the fabric he occasionally differs from the Hebrew. These minor differences show that he is not simply passing on what is in the Bible (as he sometimes does). (3) His description is so detailed that it must rest on the examination of the vestments close up: either the garments of the Jewish priests, or those of other priests.[4]

This is Josephus' description of the vestments of ordinary priests (*Antiq.* 3.152–8). Quotations are from Thackeray's translation in the LCL. First the priest puts on 'drawers covering the loins, stitched of fine spun [or twisted] linen, into which the legs are inserted as into breeches; this garment is cut short above the waist and terminates at the thighs, around which it is drawn tight'. That is, the garment is seamless, like a loincloth, but it comes down on to the thighs and serves as breeches. Josephus continues: over this the priest puts a tunic, made of fine linen of double texture, which goes down to the ankles. It has long sleeves, closely laced to the arms. It is secured to the body by a sash, wrapped twice round, going from the breast up to the armpits.[5] When the priest is not at work, the sash is tied at his chest and hangs to the ankles. When he sacrifices, however, 'he throws it back over his left shoulder'. Finally, he wears 'a cap without a peak, not covering the whole head but extending slightly beyond the middle of it'. It resembles

a coronet, consisting of a band of woven linen thickly compressed; for it is wound round and round and stitched repeatedly. This is then enveloped by a muslin veil descending from above to the forehead, thus concealing the stitches of the head-band . . . and presenting to the skull a completely even surface.

That is, he wears a simple cloth cap over a linen turban; we must call this

'head-gear'. The description of the head-gear corresponds to the complicated part of Ex. 39.27–9, which calls it 'a turban of fine linen, a head-dress of
fine linen'. The priest wore it while sacrificing: 'this head-gear is adjusted
with care so as not to slip off while the priest is busy with his sacred ministry'.

This is a convincing description. Such details as that the breeches were
drawn tight around the thighs and that the cloth cap hid the stitches on the
turban are best explained as the memories of a man who wore the clothes.
Similarly Josephus reveals practical knowledge of the care that was taken to
keep the clothing from interfering with work: the ends of the sash were
thrown over the left shoulder, the sleeves of the tunic were laced against the
arms, the bodice of the tunic was bound tightly to the chest, and the head-
gear was carefully fitted so that it would not fall off when the priest heaved a
joint of meat up on to the altar. These details show that the entire outfit was
worn, and they give us an idea of how the priests looked when at work.

No one mentions footwear at all: the priests worked barefoot. (Compare
Ex. 3.5: holy ground requires bare feet.)

Aristeas, I think, could not see the breeches and so did not mention them.
In his short description, he did not bother with the sash and cap. Philo
presents another problem. His statement that the priests wore only a short
tunic and visible breeches is eminently reasonable, and he is quite definite
about it; nevertheless, he seems to be wrong. This passage almost, not quite,
shakes my general view that, at the time he wrote the *Special Laws*, he had
made a pilgrimage. Possibly he had forgotten precisely what he had seen and
unconsciously 'dressed' the priests in costumes that he thought were
reasonable; perhaps his view of priestly garments was shaped by having seen
pagan priests in short tunics.

The fabric of the priestly garments also deserves consideration. It was of
fine linen, usually called *shesh* in Hebrew, *byssos* in Greek (e.g. Ex. 39.29;
Antiq. 3.152). There is, however, a complication. In the first list, Ex. 28, only
the fabric of the breeches is given: they are breeches of *bad*, which is plain
linen [BDB, white linen]. In Ex. 39, however, they are called 'breeches of
bad, of *shesh mishzar*'; that is, 'of plain linen, of twined fine linen'. Perhaps we
should translate *bad* as a simple generic, 'linen', and read, 'breeches of linen,
[specifically] of fine, twined linen'. Josephus is quite clear: the breeches were
of 'fine twined [or twisted] linen' (*ek bussou klōstēs*). That is, before being put
on the loom the linen thread was twined so as to be thick.

With regard to the other garments: According to both Ex. 39 and Josephus,
the tunic was of 'fine linen' (*shesh, byssos*), and Josephus adds that it was
doubled, probably by twining the thread. He also explains that the tunic was
made in two pieces, one coming down the front and one the back, joined over
the shoulders by strings. Both parts of the head-gear, according to Ex. 39,

were of 'fine linen'. According to Josephus, the turban was of 'woven linen' (he does not specify *byssos*), while the smooth covering of the head-gear was *sindōn*, 'fine cloth, usually linen' (translated 'muslin' by Thackeray). The sash, according to Ex. 39, was of 'fine twined linen' (*shesh mishzar*); according to Josephus, it had an open texture: presumably a kind of basket weave.

The sash requires further description, since it was decorated. According to Ex. 39.29, it was made of 'fine twined linen and of blue and purple and scarlet stuff, embroidered with needlework'. Josephus gives a fuller description: the sash is

> of a breadth of about four fingers and has an open texture giving it the appearance of a serpent's skin. Therein are interwoven flowers of divers hues, of crimson [Thackeray notes, 'or scarlet'] and purple, blue and fine linen, but the warp is purely of fine linen. (*Antiq.* 3.154)

This description is extremely precise. A decorative sash four fingers in breadth would be about right for a man's tunic.[6] What is most striking, however, is Josephus' knowledge of just how the sash was made. On the loom, the warp threads were *byssos*, fine linen. The weft threads provided decoration.[7] Some were of *byssos* (making the overall web *byssos*), but other weft threads provided both colour and design, 'flowers of divers hues', basically red, blue and purple.

The precise description of colours is very difficult – in fact, impossible. The biblical red is usually translated 'scarlet', while Josephus' term is usually translated 'crimson'. We cannot know precisely what reddish colour was used; there were basically two red dyes in ancient Palestine, but the shade could be altered by the use of different setting agents (mordants). Josephus, in fact, used the word 'crimson' (*phoinix* and related terms) in the *Antiquities* and 'scarlet' (*kokkos*) in the *War*.[8] The blue colour in the sashes was probably indigo. Purple is the famous 'Tyrian purple', a colour produced by a dye derived from a shellfish found off the Phoenician coast. It was widely imitated, however, and Yadin has published photographs and analysis of a first-rate imitation from the period of the second revolt (*c.* 135 CE), which was made by combining indigo and one of the red dyes (kermes).[9] On the basis of this, and taking note of the fact that even Josephus does not claim the use of authentic Tyrian purple, we may guess that in the priests' sashes the purple was produced by combining the red and blue dyes. These brightly coloured flowers stood out against the pale background of fine linen.[10]

Though nobody uses the word, the coloured threads were wool. This can be known partly from the nature of the fabrics. Linen does not readily accept dye, while the dyeing of wool was highly developed.[11] A study of the terms, however, provides further proof that the decoration was wool. Ex. 39.29

mentions 'scarlet stuff' or fabric (*tola'at shani*), and the same term is used in describing the curtain and veil of the temple (Ex. 26.31 and elsewhere). The fabric that was burned with the red heifer was the same 'scarlet stuff' (Num. 19.6); according to Josephus, it was crimson *wool* (*Antiq.* 4.80). Thus the priests' sashes combined linen and wool. This mixture is prohibited in Deut. 22.11. Both Josephus (*Antiq.* 4.208) and the Mishnah (*Kilaim* 9.1) note that only priests could wear the two together. They do not say just where, since none of the passages about the priests' garments mentions the word *wool*. We have, however, found it: wool decorated the priests' sashes.

Ezekiel, a priest who had his own views about the temple and everything connected with it, wrote that 'they shall have nothing of wool on them, while they minister at the gates of the inner court, and within' (Ezek. 44.17). Possibly he opposed using wool to decorate the sashes, but perhaps not. His concern was that 'they shall not gird themselves with anything that causes sweat' (v. 18); he may have permitted wool decoration on the sash.

With regard to the fabric, I again think that we should follow Josephus. His knowledge of how the sash was woven seems to be first-hand, and presumably he also knew what the head-gear was made of.

The priests' garments were distinctive. People ordinarily dressed in wool; thus far, only one linen garment, a child's shirt, has been discovered in Palestine, though linen wrappers, kerchiefs etc. are well-attested.[12] Ordinary people sometimes wore linen (see *War* 4.473), but wool, which in Palestine was much cheaper, predominated. Men did not usually wear breeches. The ordinary tunic of the Greek-speaking world, though made of two sheets, sewn together at the shoulders (as were the priests' tunics), did not come down to the ankle. Ordinary tunics were belted at the waist, not strapped tightly to the chest with a long sash. Most men did not wear head-gear, and certainly not of the elaborate kind described by Josephus. Finally, Jews did not mix wool and linen in the same garment, a biblical prohibition that archaeological discoveries show was observed, though the mixture was extremely common elsewhere, since in this way plain linen could be decorated with coloured wool.[13]

Let us finally ask about the colour of the linen. In an earlier publication, I erroneously wrote that in Jerusalem only the priests wore white until the Levites were given permission to do so *c.* 65 (*Antiq.* 20.216–218), and that, since the Essenes wore white (*War* 2.123), they imitated the priesthood.[14] I erred in conflating the Levites' request to wear *linen*, not white, with the Essenes' white garb. That is, I thought that the priestly tunic of *byssos* was regarded as 'white', and so I put the two passages together. Further study allows me to correct this error, but I wish to explain the point, since colour is evidently significant.

Linen, if untreated, is off-white, bone-white, or slightly yellowish; in Yadin's colour charts, the wool samples that are closest to the colour of some of the unbleached linen appear to have been dyed with yellow. Some of the linen, however, could pass as 'white'. The question is whether or not ancient Jews thought of it as white. In describing the curtain in Solomon's temple, Josephus says that it was made of 'the most gleaming (*lamprotatos*) and softest *byssos*' (*Antiq.* 8.72). This sounds very much like white, but another passage about the veil of the temple (this time, Herod's temple), proposes that the colours are symbols of the cosmos: the scarlet, blue and purple symbolize fire, air, and sea, while the *byssos* symbolizes the earth (*War* 5.213). Here it appears that Josephus equates the colour of linen with the earth, which would make it light brown, or brownish yellow, but this may not be the point of the symbolism. The parallel passage in *Antiq.* 3.183 says that *byssos* symbolizes the earth 'because from it springs up the flax'; that is, in this case it is not the colour that is symbolic. We are still not certain whether or not Josephus and others thought of untreated linen as white.

The evidence that I consider the best proof that linen was not thought of as being white consists of the few passages in which 'white' is specified; since some garments are called 'white', and the priests' are not, it seems likely that 'white' was exceptional and worthy of remark. According to Josephus (not the Bible), when David learned that Bathsheba's child had died, he changed from a black garment to a white one (*Antiq.* 7.156). Similarly Archelaus, after mourning his father, changed into white and went to the temple (*War* 2.1). After the destruction of Jerusalem, one Simon, hoping to escape by 'creating a scare', dressed in a short white tunic and put over it a purple mantle and appeared at the site of the temple (*War* 7.29). I am not sure whom he was imitating, but apparently it was not a priest. These references to white do not yet prove the case, since in the first two 'white' may be used only in contrast to black. In the third case, the reason for white is not clear, and we observe only that, when worn, it was worthy of note. Similarly, *Ta'anit* 4.8 says that on the 15th of Ab and the Day of Atonement the 'daughters of Jerusalem used to go forth in white raiments'. Again, the colour is noted as being special. Finally, during the eschatological war described in the Qumran *War Scroll*, at one point seven priests put on garments of white *byssos* (*shesh laban*). These are special garments for battle, not for the sanctuary, though they sound remarkably like the garments described in Exodus (there is also a decorated sash) – except for the word 'white' (1QM 7.8–10). Possibly the author thought that priests always wore white fine linen, and that these garments would only be a different set, but it is also possible that their whiteness would distinguish them.

In some instances 'white' is contrasted either to the priests' robes or to linen. At a crucial moment the high priest Jaddus, following a dream, had the people of Jerusalem dress in white, while he and the other priests dressed 'in the robes prescribed by law' (*Antiq.* 11.327). The Mishnah distinguishes between the high priests' garments of *byssos* (using the loan word *bûts*) and his white (*laban*) garments (*Yoma* 3.6; 7.1, 4). Further, in *Parah* 4.1 the priest who burns the red heifer is said to have dressed in white. Thus the rabbis thought that there was a distinction between *byssos* and white, and that priests wore white only on very exceptional occasions.

In view of all this, we must think that the fact that the Essenes dressed in white was not an imitation of the priesthood, though it probably had some other symbolic significance. White was even more special than the ordinary priestly garb, and it probably represented special purity, like the robe of the priest who burned the red heifer.

The Essenes may nevertheless have imitated another aspect of the priestly garments: they 'girded themselves with linen coverings', obviously around the loins (War 2.129). Possibly these were loincloths, and were not quite like the priests' breeches, but putting linen around the loins may nevertheless have been a priestly gesture.

Some scholars think that the ordinary priests had a separate set of garments, of *bad*, ordinary linen, rather than *shesh*, fine linen, and that the *bad* was worn by the priest who, first thing in the morning, went up to the altar to remove the ashes.[15] According to Lev. 6.10f. [Heb. 6.3f.], this priest put on his garments of *bad* and his breeches of *bad* to clean off the ashes, and then took them off and put on 'other garments' to take the ashes outside. These 'other garments', according to this view, were his regular priestly garb of *shesh*, distinguished from the garments of *bad*, which were used only for the especially holy task of collecting the ashes. This is possible, but it seems to me more likely that priests had only one set of linen clothes and that the 'other garments' were street clothes.

There are three arguments. (1) According to Ezek. 44.19, whenever the priests went into the outer court, they took off the garments that they wore while sacrificing, 'lest they sanctify the people with their garments' – that is, render them dedicated to the temple. In Ezekiel's view, the priests' sacrificial garments were not to be worn outside the Court of the Priests, and this would explain the change of garments required of the priest who removed the ashes in Lev. 6: he put on ordinary clothes. (2) Different words for the linen of the priests' vestments are used in different books of the Bible. For the priests' and the high priest's garments, Leviticus never uses the term *shesh*, 'fine linen', always *bad*, 'linen' (Lev. 6.3f.; 16.4, 23, 32). Exodus uniformly uses *shesh* for the priestly vestments, except in the two cases that we have seen, the breeches of *bad* (28.42), and the breeches that are said to be of both *bad* and *shesh* (39.28); but here the two terms refer to only one pair of breeches. Ezekiel uses *shesh*, but not of the priests' garments, and *bad*, of a man seen in a vision, while for the priests' clothes he uses *peshet* (Ezek. 44.17f.), a third word for linen. *Peshet* is used in Leviticus and Deuteronomy, but not of the priests' clothes. (The special problem of the high priest's clothes will occupy us just below.) These different terms for linen conceivably show divergent views or historical development, but they do not prove that priests had different sets of linen garments at any one time. (3) The *War Scroll* harmonizes the terms. The seven special priests noted above wear 'garments of white *shesh*', namely a tunic of *bad*, breeches of *bad*, a sash of *bad*, twined *shesh*, and a headgear whose cloth is not mentioned (1QM 7.8–10). This passage counts strongly against the view that the priests in Jerusalem had two sets of linen garments, one fine linen (*shesh*), the other ordinary linen (*bad*).

I shall deal very briefly with the high priest's clothes. Exodus, Ben Sira, and Josephus (in two separate descriptions) agree very closely.[16] The following description follows *Antiq.* 3.159–78, except where noted. The high priest wore as undergarments the four items worn by the priests (*Antiq.* 3.159). Over the linen tunic, he put a blue tunic (presumably of wool), which almost touched the floor. Around it was a second sash, 'with the same gay hues as adorned the first', but with gold thread added to the decoration. Golden bells, alternating with tassels that looked like pomegranates, were attached to the lower edge of the outer tunic. The bells really worked, and their ringing could be heard when he served in the temple (Ben Sira 45.9). The blue tunic was remarkable partly because it was made of one piece, which implies an extremely wide loom. It was slit in the middle to allow the head to go through, and the edges of the slit were covered with a border. The blue tunic did not have sleeves, but rather slits at each side. Over this went still a third tunic, 'which is called an *ephod* and resembles the Grecian *epōmis*'. An *epōmis* was the upper part of a woman's tunic; as Thackeray points out, it was therefore a kind of waistcoat (in American, a vest), but it covered only the chest and the top part of the back and did not go down as far as the waist.[17] The ephod was woven 'of all manner of colours along with gold embroidery'. There was an opening in the front centre. Into it was fitted another piece of cloth, called the *essēn*, 'breastplate', which was attached to the ephod with rings and secured with blue thread. At the shoulder, the ephod had two sardonyxes, with the names of the twelve tribes engraved into them, six on each stone. On the breastplate were four rows of three semi-precious stones each, attached to the cloth with gold wire. The breastplate was further secured at the top with rings and golden twine, and at the bottom by a band that was tied around the chest.

On top of the ordinary priestly head-gear, the high priest wore a 'crown of gold in three tiers'. For this Josephus gives a remarkable description, which I shall not try to summarize (*Antiq.* 3.172–8).

There are some questions about details, including the arrangement of the semi-precious stones, but the main outline is fairly clear. The high priest had three layers of clothing, both top and bottom. Bottom: breeches, full-length linen tunic, full-length blue tunic; Top: linen tunic, blue tunic, ephod (a very abbreviated tunic). The ephod had sardonyxes at the shoulder. Attached to it was a breastplate with semi-precious stones. He wore an enormously elaborate head-gear: a turban covered by plain cloth, on top of which went a three-tiered crown.

When he sacrificed, however, he did not wear this entire outfit all the time. Here we come to the only substantial question about his clothes. According to Lev. 16, which describes the Day of Atonement, the high priest started the day with only linen clothing on: the linen tunic, linen breeches, linen sash and linen head-gear. He bathed, put them on, and went to work. He sacrificed the bull as a sin offering for himself, one goat as a sin offering for the people, and he laid his hands on the second goat, confessed Israel's sins, and sent the goat off into the wilderness. All this, with only linen on. Then Leviticus ordains:

> [He] shall put off the linen garments which he put on when he went into the holy place, and shall leave them there; and he shall bathe his body in water in a holy place, and put on his garments, and come forth, and offer his burnt offering and the burnt offering of the people and make atonement for himself and for the people. (Lev. 16.23f.)

'Offer his burnt offering' means 'cut it open and burn the sacrificial parts'. At this point in the service, the high priest has killed the two sin offerings and has sprinkled the blood inside the Holy of Holies. Now he has to dispose of the bodies. The fatty pieces were burned on the altar and the carcasses were taken outside the temple and burned entirely (Lev. 16.27; *Yoma* 6.7). The verses just quoted may also be read as meaning that the high priest changed his clothes: he took off the linen garments, *left them*, bathed and put on his clothes. The same clothes or different clothes?

The rabbis concluded the second. Their description of the Day of Atonement begins earlier than Lev. 16, with the regular morning burnt offering, which preceded the special sacrifices. In their view, just after dawn the high priest slaughtered the morning burnt offering in 'raiments of gold', that is, in his full high-priestly attire. The incense was then offered (as usual). Next he bathed and put on *white* garments (*Yoma* 3.1–6). These were linen: according to R. Meir, he wore Pelusian linen (from lower Egypt) in the morning and Indian linen in the afternoon (3.7).[18] In this white linen he slaughtered the special sacrifices of the day and entered the Holy of Holies. Unlike Leviticus 16, the Mishnah does not provide for a change of clothes between sending out the scape-goat and offering the fatty parts on the altar. Rather, without changing clothes he performed these parts of the service and then read from the scripture. 'If he was minded to read in the linen [*bûts* = *byssos*] garments he could do so; otherwise he would read in his own white vestment' (7.1). After reading, he put on the 'vestments of gold', offered further sacrifices, bathed again, and put on 'the white vestments' so that he could retrieve the ladle and the fire-pan from the Holy of Holies (7.3f.).

The Mishnah, then, distinguishes 'linen' (*bûts*) from 'white vestments', which (according to 3.7) were also made of linen. Some scholars propose that he had two sets of linen, one ordinary and white, and one 'fine'. The ordinary white linen was holier. This is what the high priest wore each time he went into the Holy of Holies.[19] According to this view, Lev. 16.4, which says that the garments made of *bad* are the holy garments, means that they were made of ordinary rather than fine linen, and were therefore the most holy garments. When the high priest bathed and put on 'his clothes' again in 16.23f., he put on his usual linen garments, which (according to Exodus) were of *shesh*: *bad* for the Holy of Holies, *shesh* for other duties. We have already seen, however, that it is doubtful that we can distinguish *bad* in Leviticus from *shesh* in Exodus. I doubt, that is, that Lev. 16 intended to prescribe two sets of linen. The priest does take the clothes off and leave them while he bathes, but then he puts on 'his clothes', quite possibly the same ones.

Josephus intended to describe the Day of Atonement in a work that unfortunately he did not write. The consequence is that he skipped over it in the *War* and the *Antiquities*, and thus we do not have his account. Possibly, had he written it, he would have agreed with the Mishnah and with the scholarly reconstruction that we have just noted: the high priest had two sets of linen, one described as *shesh* (used outside the Holy of Holies), one called *bad* (used when he went into the Holy of Holies). In this case, 'his own white vestment' in *Yoma* is the *bad* of Leviticus, and the *bûts* (*byssos*) in *Yoma* is the *shesh* of Exodus. I do not wish to argue against this as a reasonable development, unmentioned by Josephus because he did not describe the rites of the Day of Atonement. I wish simply to mention another possibility: the distinction may be the rabbis' own exegetical work. They had *shesh* in Exodus and *bad* in Leviticus. *Shesh* is definitely *byssos*, for which they had a fairly recent transliteration, *bûts*. *Bad*, however, may mean 'white linen'. If there are two terms in the Bible, they may have reasoned, there must have been two sets of clothes. They could then have inserted various changes of clothing in order to give each set a different function.

I wish to emphasize that *anyone* might have studied Leviticus and Exodus and come to these conclusions; possibly here the rabbis, the Pharisees and the high priests all agreed. The exegesis is reasonable. Yet once we see that it *is* exegesis, we must wonder just who thought it up and when. We recall from above that the author of 1QM read both Leviticus and Exodus and described garments of *shesh*, that is, of *bad*. His exegesis led him to equate the terms.

7

Sacrifices

The Bible does not offer a single, clearly presented list of sacrifices. The legal books (Exodus, Leviticus, Numbers and Deuteronomy), we know now, incorporate various sources from different periods, and priestly practice evidently varied from time to time. There are three principal sources of information about sacrifices in the first century: Josephus, Philo and the Mishnah. On most points they agree among themselves and with Leviticus and Numbers; consequently the main outline of sacrifices is not in dispute. Josephus, in my judgment, is the best source. He knew what the common practice of the priesthood of his day was: he had learned it in school, as a boy he had watched and assisted, and as an adult he had worked in the temple. It is important for evaluating his evidence to note that his description of the sacrifices sometimes disagrees with Leviticus or goes beyond it. This is not an instance in which he is simply summarizing what is written in the Bible: he is almost certainly depending on what he had learned as a priest.

Though the Mishnah is often right with regard to pre-70 temple practice, many of the discussions are from the second century: the rabbis continued to debate rules of sacrifice long after living memory of how it had been done had vanished. Consequently, in reading the Mishnah one is sometimes reading second-century theory. Occasionally this can be seen clearly. For example, there is a debate about whether or not the priest who sacrificed an animal could keep its hide if for any reason the animal was made invalid (e.g. by touching something impure) after it was sacrificed but before it was flayed. The mishnah on this topic opens with an anonymous opinion, according to which the priest did not get the hide. R. Hanina the Prefect of the Priests disagreed: 'Never have I seen a hide taken out to the place of burning'; that is, the priests always kept the hides. R. Akiba (early second century) accepted this and was of the view that the priests could keep the hides of invalid sacrifices. 'The Sages', however, ruled the other way (*Zevahim* 12.4). R. Hanina the Prefect of the Priests apparently worked in the temple before 70, but survived its destruction and became part of the rabbinic movement; Akiba died c. 135; 'the sages' of this passage are probably his contemporaries or possibly the rabbis of the next generation. Here we see that second century rabbis were quite willing to vote against actual practice in discussing the behaviour of the priests and the rules they followed. The problem with using the Mishnah is that there is very seldom this sort of reference to pre-70 practice that allows us to make critical distinctions: not only are we often reading second-century discussions, we may be learning only second-century theory.[1]

Philo had visited the temple, and some of his statements about it (e.g. the guards) seem to be based on personal knowledge. But his discussion of the sacrifices is 'bookish', and at some important points it reveals that he is passing on information derived from the Greek translation of the Hebrew Bible (the Septuagint), not from observation. The following description basically follows the Hebrew Bible and Josephus, but it sometimes incorporates details from other sources.

One may make the following distinctions among sacrifices:

With regard to what was offered: meal, wine, birds (doves or pigeons) and quadrupeds (sheep, goats and cattle).

With regard to who provided the sacrifice: the community or an individual.

With regard to the purpose of the sacrifice: worship of and communion with God, glorification of him, thanksgiving, purification, atonement for sin, and feasting.

With regard to the disposition of the sacrifice: it was either burned or eaten. The priests got most of the food that sacrifices provided, though one of the categories of sacrifice provided food for the person who brought it and his family and friends. The Passover lambs were also eaten by the worshippers.

Sacrifices were conceived as meals, or, better, banquets. The full and ideal sacrificial offering consisted of meat, cereal, oil and wine (Num. 15.1–10; *Antiq.* 3.233f.; the menu was sometimes reduced: see below).

Community sacrifices

Every day, without exception, the community as a whole provided two male yearling lambs that were offered to God as burnt (that is, entirely burnt) sacrifices, along with flour, oil and wine (Ex. 29.40), one in the morning, to open the temple service, and one in the evening, just before its conclusion.

The wine was poured out as a libation around the altar, while the lamb and the mixture of flour and oil were burned. On the sabbath these sacrifices were doubled. The community offered additional sacrifices to mark each new moon (*Antiq.* 3.237f.: two oxen, seven yearling lambs, a ram, and a kid, which atoned for inadvertent sins). On the major festivals and the annual fast (the Day of Atonement) there were still further community sacrifices.

These were paid for by the temple tax of one-half shekel, contributed by adult male Jews all over the world. Besides the sacrifices, the tax paid for the general overhead cost of the temple (see Neh. 10.32–33 for a list of expenses charged to the tax).

The Bible does not specify the precise purpose of most of the community sacrifices. It would have been simple to interpret the daily burnt offerings as atoning, since the temple tax was called 'atonement money', and its purpose was 'to make atonement' (Ex. 30.16). These terms, however, were not applied specifically to the two lambs. Philo regarded thanksgiving as the purpose of the daily offerings, the morning sacrifice being made in thankfulness for the blessings of the night, the afternoon sacrifice for the blessings of the day (*Spec. Laws* 1.169). Josephus never comments on what function they served, but they were not atoning; he points out that at new moons and festivals, when there was a multitude of community sacrifices, a kid always served as the expiatory offering (*Antiq.* 3.238, 246, 247, 249, 253). We shall return to the purpose of burnt offerings below, in considering individual sacrifices.

The Mishnah has a description of the sacrifice of the daily burnt offering. The lamb was tied, 'with its head to the south and its face to the west'; that is, it was laid on a table on its left side. The priest who wielded the knife 'stood to the east with his face to the west', behind the animal. He slit the throat, and another priest received the blood in a vessel, then sprinkled part of it on the altar. The rest was poured out at the base of the altar, where it ran into a channel and was flushed out of the temple area. The carcass was hung up by its hind leg and partially flayed. Apparently it was then taken down and again laid on a table, where the priest removed the hide completely, slit the heart, and cut off the legs. He laid the underside open and removed the inwards, which another priest took and washed. The carcass was then carefully cut into parts, following the natural divisions so that the bones were not broken, and the parts were washed and salted. The entirety was burnt.[2] The description of the division of the lamb takes over a page of meticulous detail (*Tamid* 4.1–3). The general principles were the same as in Greek sacrifice.[3]

Individual sacrifices

Individuals presented a variety of sacrifices for a variety of reasons.

1. According to Lev. 1.4, the individual burnt offering, which had to be a quadruped (*Antiq.* 3.226), was for atonement. The Bible, however, never requires individuals to bring burnt offerings. It stipulates that they bring sin and guilt offerings, which are not burnt offerings, for shortcomings and transgressions. The result seems to have been that people did not think of burnt offerings as primarily atoning sacrifices. They thought of them more generally as being gifts to God: no one else benefitted from them. Josephus often specifies that a burnt offering is 'to God' (*Antiq.* 3.243, 251; 6.121; 7.389; 11.137; 15.419). He sometimes connects such an offering with thanksgiving (*Antiq.* 11.110f.), sometimes with placating God. Thus in the time of David God stopped a plague. David bought a threshing floor, built an altar, and offered burnt offerings. Josephus concludes the story, 'by these means the Deity was appeased and once more became gracious' (*Antiq.* 7.331–3; II Sam. 24.8–25). The plague had already stopped, and so the sacrifices did not 'purchase' God's favour; but, when offered, they made him feel even more kindly (so Josephus). Burnt offerings could also simply honour God, as did Solomon's (*Antiq.* 8.22), and God was prepared to grant favours in return (derived from II Chron. 1–2, but Josephus adds the statement that Solomon 'honoured' [*edoxe*] God).

Philo also emphasized that burnt sacrifices honoured God, and especially that they represented unselfish devotion.

> If anyone cares to examine closely the motives which led men of the earliest times to resort to sacrifices as a medium of prayer and thanksgiving, he will find that two hold the highest place. One is the rendering of honour [*timē*] to God for the sake of Him only and with no other motive, a thing both necessary and excellent . . . To the Godward motive which has Him alone in view he assigned the whole-burnt-offering, for, whole and complete in itself as it is, it . . . carries with it no element of self-interest . . . The whole-burnt-offering [has] no other in view but God Himself alone, Whom it is good to honour [*timasthai*]. (*Spec. Laws* 1.195–7)

Neither Josephus, Philo nor other first-century Jews thought that burnt offerings provided God with food (note the ancient title in Lev. 3.11 and elsewhere, 'food by fire for the Lord'), but they still thought that these sacrifices were in some sense 'given' to God, and their costliness paid him honour. It was all 'for God', including the hide, which went to his representative, the priest (Lev. 7.8).

According to Leviticus (1.5) the man who offered a burnt sacrifice killed the animal, while the priest did the rest. Josephus agreed:

An individual who offers a holocaust[4] kills an ox, a lamb, or a kid, these last being a year old; the slain oxen may be older than this; but all victims for the holocausts must be males. The beasts being slaughtered, the priests drench with the blood the circuit of the altar, and then, after cleansing them, dismember them, sprinkle them with salt, and lay them upon the altar, already laden with wood and alight. The feet and the inwards of the victims are carefully cleansed before being placed with the other portions for consecration in the flames; the skins are taken by the priests. (*Antiq.* 3.226f.)

Philo, on the other hand, was of the view that the sacrificer washed his hands and laid them on the head of the victim, while one priest cut the throat and another caught the blood (*Spec. Laws* 1.198f.). Here we should follow Leviticus and Josephus with regard to standard practice. I do not have an explanation of Philo's disagreement. He was firmly of the view, however, that, apart from Passover, only priests killed sacrificial animals (*Spec. Laws* 2.145f.).[5]

Here we should explain that pagan and Jewish methods of slaughtering were similar, and that all or most males would know how to do it. The animal's throat was cut, or the carotid arteries were opened, ordinarily while it was standing. In Jewish slaughter, because of the prohibition of consuming blood, one had to be especially careful to slit the throat in such a way that the animal lost most of its blood; that is, the windpipe was not to be cut through, lest the animal choke on its own blood. A deft stroke would sever the carotid arteries relatively painlessly, the blood would gush out, and the animal would soon lose consciousness.

I assume that, when the offerer slit the victim's throat, he reached over the parapet that separated the Priests' Court from the Israelites' Court. We recall that these two courts were separated only by 'a low stone parapet, fair and graceful, about a cubit high' (*War* 5.226), that is *c.* half a metre or 18–20 inches. Birds and yearlings could simply be handed over. The priest took care of the birds by himself. Two people, however, were required to kill a lamb, kid or calf. One person could pull the head back so as to expose the throat and wield the knife, while the second caught the blood. This could, of course, be done by two priests. In many cases, however, the offerer probably reached over the parapet, held the victim's head and cut the throat.[6]

2. Sin offerings and guilt offerings are closely related, and in Lev. 5 they intertwine. As we shall see below, it is possible to classify the guilt offering as a special category of sin offering. In both cases the priest received the meat and the hide of quadrupeds. The meat had to be eaten in the temple and on the same day (*Antiq.* 3.231; 4.75; not in the Bible); thus the sacrificing priest

shared it with others who were on duty (Lev. 6.29; 7.6f.). But since most sin offerings were birds (as will be explained below), only the priest who performed the sacrifice dined (Lev. 6.26). There were cooking vessels in the Priests' Court ('in a holy place'), and meat was boiled (Lev. 6.28).

The purposes for which sin offerings were required reveal that the term is no longer entirely satisfactory. In some cases the English word 'sin', which implies transgression, is inappropriate, and consequently some scholars prefer 'purification offering'. After childbirth, for example, a woman brought a 'sin offering' (Lev. 12.6), though she had done nothing wrong. The ancient Hebrew term reflects a conception of 'sin' as 'deviation from the norm'. A woman who had given birth was restored to 'normality' by a 'sin offering'. No moral or ethical issue was involved. On the other hand, a sin offering was required of a person who refused to come forward as a witness when he should have done so (5.1). This is a case that we should now consider a 'moral' fault. Despite its difficulties, I shall keep the traditional rendering 'sin offering', with the occasional reminder that there may have been no transgression.

Josephus (*Antiq.* 3.230–32) makes the sin offering a major category, and within it distinguishes between sacrifices for sins committed in ignorance (Lev. 4.27–35) and those for transgressions committed consciously (6.2–7; similarly Philo, *Spec. Laws* 1.226, 235). The latter are the biblical guilt offerings.[7] That is, he treats the sin offering of Leviticus as expiating an inadvertent sin and the guilt offering (to which he does not give a separate title) as being for a witting transgression. This is generally correct, but he does not explain that the 'sin offering' was sometimes not for 'sin', but for purification. That some impurities required sacrifice, of course, he knew perfectly well, but in outlining the sacrifices he did not give a full description of the purposes of each type.

The sin offering, according to Josephus, consisted of a lamb *and* a female kid (the Bible allows a lamb as an alternative to a kid), though he points out that people who could not afford the sacrifice could bring two birds. This agrees with Lev. 5.7; 5.11 permits grain to be substituted if the sacrificer cannot afford birds. Conscious transgressions, Josephus continues, require the sacrifice of a ram (so Lev. 6.6, on the guilt offering).

Philo also emphasizes the difference between involuntary and voluntary transgressions. He further distinguishes transgressions against what is sacred from those against other humans. In discussing voluntary transgressions against one's fellow, he follows Lev. 6 in pointing out that the offender must repay whatever he has taken wrongly, add a fifth of its value, and only then go to the temple to seek remission of his sin. Philo thinks the issue through from the standpoint of the transgressor: he is 'convicted inwardly by his conscience', 'makes a plain confession', 'asks for pardon', repays his fellow, adds a fifth, and then seeks God's forgiveness by the sacrifice of a ram (*Spec.Laws* 1.234–8). That the guilt offering implies inward conviction of transgression is also clear in Josephus' account: the person who brings a ram is 'conscious of sin, but has none to convict him of it' (*Antiq.* 3.232).[8]

The worshipper, if a male, put his hand on the head of the victim and told the priest what the sacrifice was; it was in this sense that the priests heard confession. Leviticus specifies confession only for the transgressions and impurities of 5.1–5, but Numbers requires it for guilt offerings in general (5.7). On the other hand, Lev. 26.40 is a general admonition to worshippers to 'confess their iniquity and the iniquity of their fathers', and confession probably accompanied any sacrifice that corrected a fault (whether moral or not). We do not know whether or not priests responded with any sort of formula. Probably not: they worked in silence, and the worshipper understood that, if the sacrifice was for a transgression, offering it was the final step in securing God's forgiveness. On the other hand, if the sacrificer were uncertain of what he should offer, he would have to explain the situation to the priest, and the priest would have to instruct him. Otherwise, the animal might be sacrificed under the wrong heading. The rabbis debated the question of the validity of sacrifices slaughtered under the wrong name (e.g. *Zevahim* 1.1f.); we cannot know precisely what the priests thought, but all would have agreed that it was preferable to get things straight.

According to Lev. 4.29, 33 the male who presented a sin offering killed the animal. Josephus does not specify, but says only that 'they' sacrifice on account of sins (*Antiq.* 3.230). Probably he means 'those who bring the animal' sacrifice.

When a woman brought a sacrifice, she told the Levite or priest who carried it to the altar what its purpose was. It is not certain, however, to whom she gave her lamb or basket of two birds. *Sheqalim* 5.1 gives a list of temple officers, as we noted above. It names Petahiah as being over the bird offerings, and Mazar infers from this that it was he, 'a kindly priest', who took the birds from the women and sacrificed them.[9] (Most women presumably accepted the option of two birds after childbirth.) Apart from the fact that this one priest was not always on duty, it is doubtful that priests conveyed women's sacrifices from the Women's Court to the Priests' Court, since *Arist.* 95 states that assistants, presumably Levites, brought animals forward. It is intrinsically likely that the priests stayed in their own court, thus not risking impurity, and that Levites did whatever was necessary beyond its bounds. There is also doubt as to whether or not the woman laid her hand on the victim's head (if it was a quadruped) and confessed, just as did men. The Mishnah says not (*Menahot* 9.8), but the Mishnah's view about where people laid hands on the sacrificial victim (at the very spot where the animal was killed, which, in its view, was out of reach of the Court of the Israelites) requires laymen to enter the Court of the Priests (n. 6 above). This is most dubious, and it may be that the Mishnah is equally wrong about whether or not women laid their hands on the heads of their sacrifices.

While the 'norm' for sacrifice was a quadruped, accompanied by flour, oil and wine, in many or even most cases birds were substituted. For the substitution of birds in sin offerings, see Lev. 5.7; 12.8; *Antiq.* 3.230.[10] Further, birds were required for the purification of a man or woman who had suffered from an abnormal 'discharge' (Lev. 15.14, 29). Whenever birds were sacrificed, a different set of rules applied: one bird was entirely burnt, the other was designated as a sin offering. The priest wrung the neck of the sin offering, sprinkled some of the blood on the side of the altar, drained the rest at its foot, cooked the bird and ate it (Lev. 5.8f.). Generally, then, the 'norm', (quadruped, flour, oil, wine) governed the community sacrifices but relatively few individual sacrifices. Only a well-to-do individual would offer a quadruped as a sin offering. (Shared sacrifices are another matter; see below.)

In case of severe financial hardship, flour could be brought as a sin offering. This flour was not mixed with oil; some was burnt, the rest went to the priest, who presumably turned it into bread (Lev. 5.11f.). Flour or meal, we have seen, accompanied quadrupeds, in which case it was mixed with oil. According to Josephus, some people offered flour, also mixed with oil, in fulfilment of a vow. When mixed with oil, the priest's portion of the flour could be boiled, probably along with meat; it would make a kind of dumpling (*Antiq.* 3.235).

3. The third individual sacrifice has traditionally been translated 'peace offering', since the Hebrew word is *shelem*, which is related to *shalôm*, 'peace' (so, for example, the RSV, e.g. Lev. 3.1). The precise meaning of *shelem* in this usage, however, cannot be determined. The Greek translators in the third or second century BCE sometimes chose a Greek word for 'peace' (so the translators of I and II Samuel, I and II Kings), but for the most part they preferred *sōtērion*, 'welfare'. The English translations also vary. The New Revised Standard Version has 'a sacrifice of well-being' (cf. the LXX), the Jerusalem Bible uses 'communion sacrifice', and the New English Bible has 'shared-offering'. The last two translations provide the best descriptive terms, and I shall follow the lead of the NEB and use 'shared sacrifice'.

The shared sacrifice had to be a quadruped (*Antiq.* 3.228;, implied by Lev. 3.1–16). It was apportioned between the altar, the priest and the offerer, who further shared it with family and friends. This is the sacrifice that Josephus has in mind when he says that some sacrifices were for feasts (*Antiq.* 3.225).

Priests on duty banqueted on sin and guilt offerings (cf. *Antiq.* 3.249), ordinary people, when they could afford it, on shared sacrifices. As always, the fat was burned and the blood was sprinkled and poured on or around the altar. The priest got the right thigh and the breast, which the sacrificer 'waved' before the altar (probably without stepping over the parapet). Instead of eating his portion in the temple, the priest took it home to share with his family; they too finally got red meat (Lev. 7.30–32; Num. 18.11). The sacrificer, however, retained the rest of the meat, neatly butchered by the priest, and he could carry it out of the temple.

The references to the priest's portion of the shared sacrifice provide an opportunity to comment on how first-century Jews dealt with competing biblical passages. According to Deut. 18.3, the priests received from any sacrifice 'the shoulder and the two cheeks and the stomach' ('stomach' is literally 'maw', the last of the ruminant's stomachs). Leviticus, we have seen, had different views: the priests got all of sin and guilt offerings, the breast and right thigh of shared sacrifices. This was the view that prevailed, and the parts specified in Deut. 18.3 were interpreted as referring to animals that were slaughtered by laymen away from the temple. On this, Josephus, Philo and the Mishnah agree (*Antiq.* 4.74; *Spec. Laws* 1.147; *Hullin* 10.1). This was almost certainly a very old way of harmonizing the biblical requirements. 'The law' that regulated sacrifices and related matters was principally that of Leviticus and Numbers (plus Nehemiah on some points), and various passages from Deuteronomy were incorporated in some way or other.

There were sub-divisions of the shared offering: the thank offering, which had to be eaten the same day (Lev. 7.12), the votive offering (to fulfil a vow) and the freewill offering, both of which could be eaten over two days (7.16f.; 22.21–3). It is worth pausing again over the terms. The Greek translation, we saw, chose 'welfare offering' as the name of the main category (our 'shared sacrifice'). The translators selected 'praise offering' for the Hebrew 'thank offering'. Josephus, writing in Greek, but remembering the Hebrew, once mentioned 'welfare sacrifices' (*Antiq.* 3.222), following the usual term of the Septuagint, but when he described them he used 'thank offerings', taking up the Hebrew term for the first sub-category. He did not use 'praise offerings', the Septuagint's term for the first sub-category, at all.[11] He derived 'thank offering' entirely from Hebrew; it does not appear in the Greek Bible. Philo used the two main Septuagintal terms, 'welfare offering' and 'praise offering' (*Spec. Laws* 1.212, 224). These terminological differences give us another chance to assess our sources. The explanation is this: In translating the principal word, *shelem*, into Greek, the scholars responsible for the legal books of the Bible not unreasonably chose 'welfare'; in translating its chief sub-category, they selected 'praise' (which is not the most obvious, but is a possible translation of the Hebrew *tôdah*). Josephus, who sometimes conformed his description of biblical law to the Greek version that was available to his readers, even when it departs from the Hebrew, in this case did not do so. He was a priest; he knew that the Greek did not properly convey the meaning of the Hebrew; in discussing his own specialist subject he would not use the wrong words.[12] He did not, however, try to say just what *shelem* means; he decided instead to replace the main category with the first sub-category, and so he called this sacrifice the 'thank offering'. Philo, on the other hand, was probably limited to Greek, and so he simply passed on the terms chosen by the Septuagint translators. Here we see his 'bookishness', which I mentioned above.

Philo's heart was in the right place, and he knew that some sacrifices must be for thanksgiving. But, reading the Greek Bible, he did not find any. This may be the reason why he interpreted the daily burnt offerings as thank offerings (p. 105).

Because of the confusion over terms, I give a chart:

Our translation	Hebrew Bible	LXX	Josephus	Philo
shared sacrifice	*shelem*, peace?	*sōtērion*, welfare	welfare (once)	welfare
thank offering	*tôdah*, thank	*ainesis*, praise	thank (main category)	praise

We have seen that there were sub-categories of the shared sacrifice and one distinction among them: the amount of time allowed for eating the meat. All other points were the same. The animals, as always, had to be unblemished (Lev. 3.6); we noted above that quadrupeds were required. They could be male or female, from the flock or the herd (Lev. 3.1). The Bible does not specify the age of the animal, but Josephus says that it should be one year old or older (3.228). Instead of the usual flour, oil and wine, the victim was to be accompanied by cakes and wafers, some leavened and some not (Lev. 7.12f.). The priest got one cake, the rest were taken out of the temple by the worshipper and eaten with his share of the meat.

Though both priest and sacrificer ate their portion of the shared offering at home, or at a camp site (in the case of pilgrims), they nevertheless had to eat it in purity (Lev. 7.19–21).

A family at the temple: an example

Below I shall describe some aspects of the three pilgrimage festivals, during which the temple did a very large percentage of its annual business. Let us now, however, imagine how a family sacrificed while present in Jerusalem on one of these occasions.

First of all, they had money set aside: the 'second tithe' money (the value of ten per cent of the year's crops) had to be spent in Jerusalem, and a pilgrimage festival was the obvious occasion. Let us say that during the year the wife had had a child, her uncle had died, and the husband had dishonestly appropriated a deposit that a neighbour had left with him to secure the loan of an animal. Some things had to be done in advance. The removal of corpse-impurity required seven days. To make matters easy, let us make several suppositions: (1) A priest had come to their village with the mixture of ashes and water and had removed corpse impurity before the pilgrimage. (If not, they would have to wait in Jerusalem for seven days, being sprinkled on the third and sixth, before they could enter the temple.) (2) The man had already repaid his neighbour and added a fifth of the value of what he had taken. (3) The child had been born three months before the pilgrimage. (4) The woman was not a menstruant.

They immersed in one of the public pools before nightfall and abstained from sex that night.[13] The next morning they went to the temple. Nearby they bought a ram (for the man's guilt offering) and a lamb (for a thank offering). They entered the temple by the eastern gate in the southern wall, assuring the gatekeeper that they were bringing in only sacrificial animals, and emerged into the Court of the Gentiles. They turned around and walked back to the Royal Portico. There they found baskets or bowls, each containing two inspected birds, and they bought one basket for the woman's offering after childbirth. They crossed the Court of the Gentiles and came to the balustrade that warned Gentiles to go no further. Here they assured one of the Levites on duty that they were pure. At some point, probably close to the barrier, they presented their ram and lamb for inspection. At the inner wall, they separated, the woman going off to the right or left to enter the Women's Court, the man walking straight through the first eastern gate. Near the entrance to the Court of the Women, the woman found a Levite and gave him her birds, explaining that they were a sin offering for childbirth. She then entered, went upstairs, into a gallery, and watched what happened to her birds. Her husband, however, went straight through, continuing past the second eastern gate. At some point on his way in, he found his own Levite, who took the lamb, later to be offered in thanks. The man then took the ram to a priest, explained that he had defrauded his neighbour but had made restitution and paid the penalty, and was now bringing his guilt offering. While saying this, he put his hands on the head of the ram. He and the Levite lifted the animal over the parapet, the priest put a basin beneath its throat and the man held back its head and slit the throat. The priest took the ram away to flay, butcher and cook. The man then took the lamb from the Levite and thanked him for his help. Another priest came up with a basin, and they slaughtered the lamb. Meanwhile, the woman's Levite had found a priest to sacrifice the two birds.

The man and the woman might watch for a while, at least until the priest who had taken the shared sacrifice (the thank offering) came back, approximately ten minutes later, with the results of his work. The man waved the lamb's breast in front of the altar and handed it and the right thigh to the priest. He then left with the rest of the butchered lamb in hand. His wife, watching, knew when to go to the eastern gate of the inner wall to meet him. They took the meat back to their campsite and joined their friends. The feast could begin.

The infant and the couple's toddlers would have been left with a friend or relative, but the other children could come along, the boys going with the husband and the girls with the wife. The children, awed, would be silent and obedient, though naturally curious.

What was sacrifice like as a religious activity? Although there are no absolutely certain answers, the question merits reflection. Most of the readers of this book, like its author, have no first-hand knowledge of sacrifice. To comprehend it, we must first recognize that sacrifice was a natural part of worship in the ancient world, as natural as singing hymns and saying prayers are today. People did not view it as a strange and barbaric way to worship God – not even philosophers, such as Socrates and Philo.

We should, however, start with basics. Most of us are not only far removed from the world of sacrifice, we are also unaccustomed to slaughter and butchery. We may assume that a functioning temple did not have the effect on ancient people that it would have on many today: queasy stomachs and possibly vomiting and fainting. The isolation of most individuals from slaughter is very recent. Even I know, on the basis of first-hand experience, the meaning of the phrase 'like a chicken with its head cut off'. My father understood 'squealing like a stuck pig', since he grew up on a small farm, where the family slaughtered a pig each autumn. Most males in the ancient world knew how to kill an animal with a knife, and most had done it. Further, they were accustomed from childhood to seeing it done and so did not feel the modern inhibition.[14]

On the other hand, slaughter was not an everyday experience. Many people ate fowl once a week, but red meat only a few times a year. Slaughter of a quadruped was significant from this point of view alone. The event was a special occasion: it was anticipated, the senses were sharpened, and the quick flood of blood evoked an emotional response. The secular slaughter of the family pig in the autumn, which was widely practised by rural and semi-rural families in the western world before World War I, produced all these responses. The emotional response (my father's autobiographical tale continues) was pleasure and even hilarity. The children played games, using the bladder as a football, and the only work done was the butchery of the animal.

For many ancient societies blood was more significant than it is in ours, and the shedding of it was important and meaningful. This was true not only of Judaism. The Greeks thought that the animal should nod its consent before being slaughtered, and often a tuft of hair was cut first, so that it was no longer inviolate, but was prepared for the ultimate violation. One can see Greek depictions of animals and their preparation, as well as butchery after the incision and bleeding, but there are no depictions of the crucial instant when the blood was let. It was a numinous moment, sacrosanct, not a subject for art.[15]

In Judaism, great significance attached to the blood. The blood belonged to the Lord. Preferably, the blood of domestic animals that were slaughtered for food should be sprinkled on the altar or poured around its base. If one had to slaughter away from the temple, the blood should go directly to the ground.

> The life of the flesh is in the blood; and I have given it for you upon the altar to make atonement for your souls; for it is the blood that makes atonement, by reason of the life. Therefore I have said to the people of Israel, No person among you shall eat blood, neither shall any stranger who sojourns among you . . . Any man also of the people of Israel, or of the strangers that sojourn among them, who takes in hunting any beast or bird that may be eaten shall pour out its blood and cover it with dust. (Lev. 17.11–13)

Deuteronomy offered it as a special concession, because of the enlargement of their territory, that Israelites could slaughter animals away from the temple, but it repeated the warning that the blood must be poured on the ground (Deut. 12.15–28). As I have more than once remarked, no one still held the ancient anthropomorphic theory that the sacrifice fed God (if that had ever been literally thought). Nevertheless, the rarity of slaughter, the strong prohibition against human consumption of blood, the common association of the slaughter of a quadruped with worship in the temple, the silence and sanctity of the setting, ensured that, when the man reached over and slit the animal's throat, he felt something, and so did those who watched. At the very least, they felt awe.

Although sacrifice was a normal and standard part of worship, it was not a routine activity. Most Jews resident in Palestine probably sacrificed on only a few occasions each year. The act was surrounded by mystery and awe, and in this respect the Jerusalem temple outdid its pagan counterparts. The days of purification in advance (seven days for corpse-impurity), the majesty of the setting, the physical actions – selecting fat, unblemished victims, seeing them inspected by experts, walking with them to within a few yards of the flaming altar, handing them over, laying hands on the head, confessing impurity or guilt, or otherwise dedicating the animal, slitting its throat, or even just holding it – these guaranteed the meaningfulness and awesomeness of the moment.

Actions, setting and physical contact helped create the worshippers' interior response. No one who believed that God had commanded the entire service (and who did not, therefore, view it as would a modern anthropologist) could go through it without being caught up in it.

Those who participated in the service felt awe, but did their response to the act of sacrifice vary according to its category? Did the man feel forgiven when he killed his guilt offering, thankful when the priest took his thank offering? Did the woman feel pure when she saw her sin offering dispatched? We can only guess, and perhaps we should fall back on the standard answer: some did and some did not attach the right feeling to each sacrifice. I incline to think they did. The worshipper had to name the sacrifice to the priest who accepted it, or the Levite who took it to the priest, and before the naming he or she had had to prepare (repayment of misappropriated property, immersion, selection of the victim). The act of sacrifice was always the last moment in the correction of either impurity or guilt. It is reasonable to assume that people felt it to be such, and also that they felt joy and thanksgiving when they were able to afford a thank offering and saw it sacrificed.

The daily temple routine

Let us now consider a day in the life of the temple. There were two principal periods of sacrifice each day: early in the morning and in the afternoon (*Apion* 2.105). The day lasted twelve hours; that is, the available daylight was divided into twelve parts, which meant that an hour in the summer was longer than an hour in the winter. The position of the sun was the main indicator of time, and in a large edifice like the temple the sun's progress was easy to mark by noting which part of the wall it was over.

For the daily routine, our best source, Josephus, deserts us. One may query some of the Mishnah's details, but it certainly gives an account of the main things that had to be done.[16] According to *Tamid*, some priests spent the night in the temple. Before dawn they rose, immersed and cast lots for some of the day's tasks. One was delegated to clear and tidy the altar. The previous evening, it had been left still burning, consuming the last burnt offering. The designated priest washed his hands and feet in the laver and cleared off the ashes. He pushed to one side the remaining pieces of meat. Other priests brought new wood, which caught fire from the embers, and they put the previous day's unburnt pieces on the fire. A second fire was started for the incense, to be offered on the altar in the first chamber of the sanctuary. The priests then withdrew to the Chamber of Hewn Stone, where they again cast lots to determine tasks. When daylight was announced, a lamb was brought; it was slaughtered, butchered, washed and salted (as described above). Meanwhile, other priests, chosen by lot, entered the first chamber of the sanctuary, cleared the altar of ashes and prepared the candelabrum. The priests returned to the Chamber of Hewn Stone to recite the *Shema'* and prayers. Again lots were drawn. Some priests went to the inner altar and burned the incense. They all then gathered at the front of the Court of the Priests and pronounced a blessing. Finally, the portions of the lamb were put on the fire. A libation of wine was poured out, and meal was also put on the fire. During this, the Levites clanged cymbals and sang a psalm. 'When they reached a break in the singing they blew upon the trumpets and the people prostrated themselves; at every break there was a blowing of the trumpet and at every blowing of the trumpet a prostration' (all from *Tamid*; quotation from 6.3).

During the opening service, the new watch of priests came in, and one of the prayers was for them (*Tamid* 5.1). The priests who had slept over presumably left after the trumpets and prostrations. It is possible that there was more going and coming of priests than I have described. It appears from *Tamid* that a new shift came on after the morning burnt offering, but we do not know that all of them stayed all day, nor whether or not they all slept over to begin work before dawn the next day. It is likely that there was a change of shifts at noon.[17]

After the opening whole-burnt offering, the temple was ready for any who wished to bring sacrifices. As we noted above, not all the priests sacrificed at once. According to *Pesahim* 5.1, individual sacrifices ceased at the eighth-and-a-half hour (mid-afternoon), and the afternoon burnt offering was sacrificed. The service concluded with scriptures, prayers and incense.[18] I am slightly suspicious about the time of the last sacrifice. According to the Bible, the last lamb was sacrificed 'between the two evenings' (Ex. 29.39; Num. 28.4), that is, at twilight. It may be, however, that in the first century the closing ceremonies took longer than in the biblical period, since prayer and scripture had been added. 'Between the two evenings' is also subject to more than one interpretation.

The flushing of blood through the channels deserves a special word. The temple was provided with a great supply of water. Ben Sira 50.3 refers to a 'reservoir like the sea in circumference'; Aristeas said that the supply of water was so great that it was as if there were a plentiful spring, and that there were underground reservoirs (*Arist.* 89f.). According to the Mishnah, there was a chamber in the Court of the Priests that enclosed a cistern that provided water for the temple court (*Middot* 5.4), and Josephus also mentions a huge reservoir for collecting rain (*War* 5.165). It is now known that two major aqueducts supplied Jerusalem with water, since the local springs were not adequate. The lower aqueduct entered the temple over Wilson's Arch and filled one or more cisterns inside the temple.[19] A great deal of water was required: the priests had to wash their hands and feet, and sometimes immerse, and the inwards of sacrificial animals were washed. Still more water was required to flush the blood down drains. At festivals, especially Passover, when thousands of lambs were slaughtered, there was a large quantity of blood. It was washed down into the brook Kidron, which ran through the deep valley to the east of the temple mount. According to the Mishnah, the water of the brook became so thickened that it was sold to farmers as fertilizer, but since it was sacred, the temple received the proceeds (*Yoma* 5.6; *Middot* 3.2; *Meilah* 3.3).

8

The Common People:
Daily Life and Annual Festivals

Ordinary life

We have seen how individual worshippers could participate in the temple cult, and now we shall consider the occasions when great throngs gathered for festivals. First, however, let us consider more generally who the ordinary people were and what they did.

The occupations of Palestinian Jews were the same, on average, as those in other Mediterranean countries. In discussing rules for the sabbath, the Mishnah very helpfully enumerates the thirty-nine main classes of work. The first seven have to do with agricultural work outside (down to cleansing the crops); the next four with preparation of food inside (from grinding to baking); the next thirteen with producing textiles; the next seven with hunting, slaughtering and butchering; two with writing; three with construction; two with fires; and one is general: carrying (*Shabbat* 7.2). The social and economic circumstances known by the Mishnaic rabbis cannot have been much different from those that prevailed before the destruction of the temple, and we may take this as an accurate depiction of what 'work' was.

Most people made their living by agriculture.[1] According to Aristeas, in Judaea 'the zeal of the farmers [was] indeed remarkable'.

> ... their land is thickly covered with large numbers of olive trees and cereal crops and pulse, and moreover with vines and abundant honey. As for the fruit trees and date palms which they have, no number can be given. They have many flocks and herds of various kinds. So they perceived clearly that the areas needed to be well populated, and designed the city and the villages accordingly. (*Arist.* 112f.)

Philo also commented on the prosperity of the country. The gift of first fruits to the priesthood gave them an abundance, since the nation was populous, and the people were especially noted as good 'graziers and stock-breeders, and [kept] flocks and herds of goats and oxen and sheep and of every kind of animal in vast numbers' (*Spec. Laws* 1.133, 136).[2] The most fertile parts of the country are Galilee and Jericho, and had the pious travellers gone that far, they would have remarked even more on the prosperity of the farms there. Josephus described Galilee as being

> everywhere so rich in soil and pasturage . . ., that even the most indolent are tempted . . . to devote themselves to agriculture. In fact, every inch of the soil has been cultivated by the inhabitants; there is not a parcel of waste land. (*War* 3.42f.)

He emphasized the variety of food-producing trees and vines, and especially the long growing season. Around the Sea of Galilee grew

> the walnut, a tree which delights in the most wintry climate . . ., palm-trees, which thrive on heat, and figs and olives, which require a milder atmosphere . . . Not only has the country this surprising merit of producing such diverse fruits, but it also preserves them: for ten months without intermission it supplies those kings of fruits, the grape and the fig . . . (*War* 3.517–519)

Jericho, warm even in winter (the inhabitants wore linen when it was snowing in the rest of Judaea, *War* 4.473) and watered by abundant springs, was more fertile yet. In an area 'seventy furlongs (*stadia*) in length and twenty in breadth' (8 miles × 2⅓; 12.8 km × 3.75) grew date-palms, which produced 'copious honey, not much inferior to that of bees'; the cypress and other rare and choice plants; and balsam, described as 'the most precious of all the local products' (*War* 4.459–75). Josephus' statement about balsam is modest compared to Pliny's, who said that the plant was very rare and its juice extremely valuable: from the time of Pompey, the trees 'figured among the captives in our triumphal processions'. The balsam tree is thought to have provided the famous balm of Gilead.[3]

We may suspect Aristeas, Philo and Josephus of exaggerating the prosperity of the country. Certainly they omitted descriptions of unemployment, landlessness, high taxes, poverty and begging. Detailed investigation of economic conditions lies beyond the scope of this book, though we shall consider a few points in the next chapter, in connection with the cost of maintaining the temple and the priesthood. Here I shall offer only a generalization. We do not know very much about poverty in the ancient world: how many people at any place and time had neither land nor employment. There is no reason to think that conditions in Palestine were on average worse or better than in Syria or Asia Minor. Few authors saw a need to discuss the poor: their presence could be assumed ('the poor you have always with you', Mark 14.7). The fact that there were beggars in Palestine does not disprove the claims that the country was prosperous. Even in some developed countries today prosperity and poverty live side-by-side.

These glowing reports may also be challenged from another point of view. The modern traveller to Judaea, especially the area around Jerusalem, is struck by the thinness of the soil, the rather small ratio of soil to rock, and the steepness of the hills – all of which make farming difficult and relatively unremunerative. The key word, of course, is 'relatively'. A lot of the land in countries around the Mediterranean is rocky, hilly and difficult, at least by the standards of northern Europe and North America.[4] People who visited Jerusalem had certainly seen worse and less rewarding countryside. We must also reckon with a deterioration of the land in the Judaean hills. During the siege of Jerusalem the Romans stripped the land around Jerusalem bare. In order to build earthworks, so that their catapults and battering rams could be brought up to the walls of the city, they levelled houses and filled in some of the valleys, using wood to support the fill. More wood went into the circumvallating palisade, built partly to prevent a Jewish military break-out, but also to keep as many people as possible in the city and thus exhaust the food supply.[5] Trees were felled for miles around: Josephus estimates ninety furlongs or eighteen kilometres (about eleven miles). 'Sites formerly beautified with trees and parks [were] now reduced to an utter desert' (*War* 6.5–8; cf. *War* 5.107, 130, 264). Subsequent invasions over the centuries, though the battles were not as prolonged and massive as the Roman siege of Jerusalem, also resulted in deforestation and consequently in erosion: the soil may be thinner now than it was. In any case, both Judaea and Galilee before the war appeared to travellers as fertile and well-to-do. Most people lived on the land and worked it, and so most 'common people' were small farmers or farm labourers. On the sea of Galilee and on the Mediterranean coast there were obviously fishermen, but most Jews outside the big cities were engaged in agriculture.

Clothing is next to food in importance in everyday life, and many Palestinians were engaged in the production of textiles. Wool was abundant in Palestine. We noted just above that ancient authors remarked on the size of the flocks and herds, and we may be confident that flocks were much larger and more numerous than herds. Palestine affords relatively little pasturage for cattle, but a lot for sheep and goats (see nn. 2 and 33). The temple and the festivals required both animals, especially lambs. We shall see below that each spring there had to be a surplus of some 30,000 male lambs to provide meat for the Passover meal. This implies very sizable flocks, and consequently a lot of wool.

Men, we may assume, sheared the sheep and carded the wool, as well as ploughing and harvesting, but much of the work involved in feeding and clothing the family was done by women. According to the Mishnah, 'these are works which the wife must perform for her husband':

> grinding flour and baking bread and washing clothes and cooking food and giving suck to her child and making ready his bed and working in wool. If she brought him in one bondwoman [as dowry] she need not grind or bake or wash; if two, she need not cook or give her child suck; if three, she need not make ready his bed or work in wool; if four she may sit [all the day] in a chair. R. Eliezer says: Even if she brought him in a hundred bondwomen he should compel her to work in wool, for idleness leads to unchastity. (*Ketuvot* 5.5)

We should not, however, think that it was the sages who dreamt up these tasks for women; this discussion simply reflects social reality, slightly schematized. On the whole, men worked in the fields and women did the rest, as has usually been the case in agricultural communities; their combined efforts produced food and clothing. When we consider the purity laws of the Pharisees, and the standard supposition that they did not allow menstruants to touch their food or garments, we shall have occasion to recall this passage and the enormous amount of work that the men would have had to take on if women were sequestered during menstruation.

Grinding, baking, washing and cooking are well-known activities. The only special word of explanation that is required about these aspects of life is that it appears from this passage that grain was often milled at home; it would take about three hours a day for a woman to grind the grain for the next day's bread for a small family.[6] Working in wool deserves a few more words.

Yigael Yadin and his team discovered in caves near the Dead Sea, in Wadi Nahal Hever, the remains of people who had fled the Romans at the time of the second revolt (which ended 135 CE), with many of their belongings. The textiles constitute one of the most important finds of ancient fabric, especially wool.[7] In first- and second-century Palestine,

> there was available a knowledge of the fine points of dyeing fast colours on wool which was essentially equal to the best which were known and used in the rest of the world until the middle of the nineteenth century.[8]

The dyeing was probably done by professionals.[9] There were also professional weavers and tailors,[10] but it is probable that most of the spinning and weaving was done by housewives, and they appear to have been expert at it. Yadin's evidence even confirms the rabbinic view that women of prosperous families worked with wool; there were balls of yarn 'among the belongings of women of the "upper class"'.[11]

Palestinians dressed as did other people in the Greek-speaking world. (See plates IV and V). In fact, third- and fourth-century portraits of Jews show that, at least at this later period, they looked the same in all respects. In terms of clothing, they wore tunics and mantles (Greek, *chitōn*, *himation*). A tunic is made by sewing two sheets of fabric together, one sheet covering the front and one the back, with a space left in the middle for the head and neck. Throughout the Mediterranean, and also in Palestine, tunics had a vertical stripe, running the length of the garment, over each shoulder. In general, the width of the stripe indicated age or prestige.[12] The length of the tunic is hard to determine. Those found in Palestine, Yadin estimated, would have fallen to a point just below the knee, but they were belted and the cloth was folded over the belt.[13] Thus they probably struck the wearers above the knee. In Greece, tunics not infrequently came to mid-thigh.[14] Over the tunic went a mantle, a long piece of cloth that was wrapped around the body. It could be worn in such a way that it fell off of one shoulder or both (thus exposing the stripes of the tunic), or the wearer could pull it up around the neck or even over the head for protection from the weather.

Yadin has shown that Palestinian women's mantles were more colourful than men's (on average), and also that the decoration was different. Men's mantles had a stripe with a notch cut out, women's an L shaped stripe at each corner[15] (called a *gamma*, because of the shape of the Greek letter of that name, which looks approximately like an upside-down L).[16] The background colour of men's mantles was usually yellowish or yellow-brown; that of women's sometimes fell into the same range, but sometimes was reddish or purplish.[17] In the decorative stripes and gammas the chemists whom Yadin consulted found red or blue dyes or both combined, which yielded a colour in the maroon to purple range.

We saw that Yadin's evidence dates from 135 CE and obviously contains textiles from a slightly earlier date. One assumes that colours and styles had not altered greatly in the preceeding few decades, and thus we may take these as typical of our period. Styles did not change very rapidly in the ancient world. The same clothes, with the same decoration, can be seen in art of various periods from Egypt and Dura-Europos,[18] and cloth with the same decoration has been found in a variety of sites.[19]

The surviving art also shows hair styles. Women ordinarily covered their hair with a net, sometimes with a cloth. So contained, it usually fell to the nape of the neck or just touched the shoulder. Men looked like Julius Caesar: short haircut, clean shaven. I exaggerate only slightly. The paintings from Dura, which are of Jews, show men with short hair and either no beards or very short beards, trimmed close to the face all around. The same holds true of paintings on Egyptian coffins, some of which are probably of Jews.[20] Paintings are often idealized; or, if realistic, they show people at their best. I do not suppose that Palestinian farmers actually shaved or made it to the barber every day, nor that their hair was always neatly trimmed. Shaving with an iron razor was something of a fine art, and in Rome a good barber was greatly prized.[21] Nevertheless, in Rome, and probably in other urban centres, no grown male except 'a soldier or a philosopher could decently have ventured . . . to shrink from the razor'.[22] If we combine the general style of the times with the realities of life in a village, we shall probably conclude that most men trimmed their beards close on occasion, perhaps once a week.

We should dismiss the view that Palestinian Jews wore Bedouin clothes and had beards that looked like Methuselah's. Graeco-Roman styles in both clothes and hair were pervasive: they penetrated even beyond the borders of the empire, and (as we noted above) they changed slowly. First-century Egypt, second-century Palestine, and third-century Mesopotamia (Dura-Europos) show the same styles of clothes. The treatment of men's hair changed very little. The style of women's hair and men's beards varied from time to time, but not by much. The hair of wealthy Roman matrons was piled higher and higher during the course of the Empire, and the style of men's facial hair was subject to slight changes (Hadrian, for example, had a short beard), but overall the styles were as persistent as they were pervasive.[23]

We turn now to Jerusalem, which was prosperous and bustling. The range of occupations went greatly beyond providing the necessities of life. According to Aristeas, Jerusalem was 'the home of many crafts', where there was 'no lack of goods imported from overseas' (*Arist.* 114). Besides the normal crafts and trades, there were those peculiar to the needs of the temple, which directly or indirectly generated most of the city's business. For example, since stone is not subject to impurity, a special industry arose to produce stone vessels, many of which have been found in the houses of the Upper City. They were made by being turned on enormous lathes. Large quantities of incense were used in the temple service, which gave work to those who imported, ground and mixed it. There was a brisk business in linen, used for the priests' robes. Then, of course, there was the 'tourist trade', since thousands of Jews came annually to the major festivals. They required doves, pigeons, lambs and goats in large numbers, and they doubtless found many things to buy in the shops.

The sacrifices also produced hides, most of which went to the priest, though the offerer of a Passover lamb or a shared sacrifice kept the hide. Tanning and working leather were well-developed skills, but because of the odour, tanners would not have been found in Jerusalem itself (see Acts 9.43).

The city's size, at least that of the area within the walls, can be estimated. When Jerusalem fell, there were three walls, built at different periods and enclosing different parts of the city (*War* 5.142–55; see the map, p. 306). Walls 1 and 2 enclosed the principal areas – the Lower City, physically below and to the south and southwest of the temple; the Upper City, on the hill west of the temple; the Tyropoean Valley, west and north of the temple; and the temple itself. Wall 3 enclosed the large 'suburban' area to the north. This third wall was started under Agrippa I (41–44 CE) and finished hastily during the revolt. Thus for most of the first century it was not there.

Pseudo-Hecataeus (second century BCE) estimated the circumference of the city at 50 stades (*c.* 10 km or 6.2 miles) (Josephus, *Apion* 1.197). He may have been including not only suburbs but also the farmland that led up to them. In any case the city was not that large. Aristeas said that 'as far as one can estimate' the city was 40 stades (8 km; 5 miles) (*Arist.* 105), but that is also too large. Josephus (*War* 5.159) fixed the circumference at 33 stades (6 km, 3.8 miles), and 'the land surveyor of Syria' put it at 27 stades (5.4 km, 3.35 miles) (Eusebius, *Praep. Evang.* 36). Archaeology now puts the circumference of the area enclosed by walls 1 and 2 at about 4.3 km or 2.67 miles, while the addition of wall 3 brought the total circumference to 5.4 km or 3.4 miles. Josephus' estimate, which included all three walls, turns out to be fairly accurate, doubtless because he had a good source – the Roman army.[24] We saw above that the circumference of the temple wall was 1.5 kilometres or nine-tenths of a mile. In terms of the area enclosed, the temple complex was about one-tenth of the city. (An area 1.1 km in each direction – that is, the area within walls one and two if they were squared off – is 1,210,000 square metres; the temple occupied 144,000 square metres.) For the sake of comparison, we may note that the area enclosed by the present (medieval) city wall is smaller than the area within walls 1 and 2: it is about 3.2 km (1.98 miles).

Population is much more difficult to estimate. Pseudo-Hecataeus proposed 120,000 (*Apion* 1.197), but the figure cannot be confirmed, since there is no guide to population density. The temple, at all periods, took up a lot of the city. In later years, the Hasmonean palace, Herod's palace, the palace of the high priest, and other large houses in the Upper City consumed space without contributing much to population. We can best consider population by moving to the major topic of the chapter, festivals.

People and festivals

In the first century, Jerusalem would hold a very large number of people. We have seen Herod's appreciable efforts to make the temple court, its porticoes and the streets around it adequate for large crowds. Josephus gives some fantastic figures for the number of people present at two different Passovers. Cestius, he says, ordered the chief priests to estimate the population, so that he could impress Nero (Cestius was the legate of Syria at the time of the revolt). The priests counted 255,600 Passover lambs as being slain. Josephus estimated that ten people shared each lamb, and, rounding the total up, concluded that there were 2,700,000 people at that Passover (*War* 6.420–427). He estimated the crowd at Passover in 65 CE as 3,000,000 (*War* 2.280). Speaking of the offerings of Jews in Babylon, Josephus says that they were stored in the two most easily defensible cities and taken to Jerusalem in convoy by 'many tens of thousands of Jews' to protect them against Parthian raids (*Antiq.* 17.313).

No one believes the largest of these figures, though other ancient writers also refer to enormous crowds. According to Philo, each feast attracted 'countless multitudes' (*Spec. Laws* 1.69), and Aristeas wrote that at Passover tens of thousands of lambs were slaughtered (*Arist.* 88), which would mean that there were hundreds of thousands of worshippers. Very large numbers also come from Josephus' descriptions of the siege of Jerusalem in 70 CE: a refugee who escaped said that 115,880 people from the lower class had already died of starvation and from the civil war in the city. The refugee had been in charge of public funds, which had provided for burials. A later refugee said that the corpses of 600,000 of the lower classes had been thrown out of the gates (*War* 5.567–569). The total number who died in the siege, according to Josephus, was 1,100,00 (*War* 6.420). Finally, the Roman historian Tacitus put the number besieged in Jerusalem at 600,000 (*History* 5.13).

These numbers obviously do not lead to accurate figures. It is in fact extremely difficult to enumerate a population and harder to estimate a crowd. Even today estimates of large gatherings vary enormously.[25] Accurate population figures require a census, while accurate crowd estimates require either aerial photography or automatic counters at gates. The Romans had evaluated Judaea for tax purposes in 6 CE (*Antiq.* 18.1–2; 20.102), which may have included some estimate of the population; but, as we saw above, less than sixty years later Cestius had to tell the chief priests to devise some means of counting. It is striking that Josephus, who had access to Roman records, does not give the population of Judaea.

There is no doubt, however, that the city of Jerusalem was populous in peacetime, that thousands of pilgrims came to the festivals, and that hundreds of thousands died in the war, many of them in Jerusalem. The number who died in Jerusalem during the war is of relevance to our topic, public participation in the religious rites, especially festivals, since it gives some idea of how many people could be crammed into the city. Let us suppose that Tacitus' figure for the number besieged, 600,000, is correct. We may then further suppose that, during festivals, fewer than that would find accommodation within the city walls. There would be many who brought their own tents and who camped outside the city (*Antiq.* 17.217). It seems to me not unreasonable to suppose that some hundreds of thousands celebrated Passover at Jerusalem.

There is one further way of estimating crowds. The Jewish population of Palestine, though sometimes put as high as 2,500,000, in addition to a Gentile population of a few hundred thousand,[26] is more reliably estimated as being less than a million, possibly only about half that (depending on the estimate of the non-Jewish population).[27] It is probable that most Palestinian Jews made at least one pilgrimage a year, the most popular festival being Passover (*Antiq.* 17.214).[28] The Jerusalemites, of course, were always there. If we assume fifty per cent attendance at Passover, there may have been 250,000 to 400,000 Palestinian Jews, plus a large number ('tens of thousands') of pilgrims from the Diaspora. Herod's temple, let it be noted, could accommodate 400,000 pilgrims. The Sacred Mosque at Mecca, with an area of 180,000 square metres, will hold 500,000 pilgrims at prayer;[29] we recall that Herod's temple was 144,000 square metres. In the case of Passover, not every pilgrim needed to be in the temple area at the same time (as we shall see below), though when they were there they occupied more space than a Muslim at prayer, since they sacrificed lambs. At other times during the festivals, especially the Feast of Booths, many or most of the pilgrims may have gone to the temple at the same time, and there would at least have been standing room in the outer court.

It may be helpful to consider two cases, one ancient and one modern, in which writers have estimated the number of pilgrims. Writing in the fifth century BCE, Herodotus enumerated five main Egyptian festivals. The largest, at Bubastis, held in honour of the goddess Pasht (whom Herodotus identified with Artemis), drew 700,000 men and women (Herodotus, *Histories* II.59–60). Herodotus' figure can no more be confirmed than can the numbers offered by Josephus, but we must note that his estimate of attendance at the biggest Egyptian festival is only one-fourth the number that Josephus claimed for Passover.

According to Mohamed Amin, before World War II the largest number of pilgrims to Mecca was 108,000, though with modern travel and greatly increased prosperity among many of the Arab nations this figure has now risen to over 2,000,000.[30] These numbers, I think, are fairly accurate. Before the airplane, pilgrimage to Mecca was more difficult than pilgrimage to Jerusalem, and the local population was also smaller than that of Jerusalem and its environs. Thus I think it safe to guess that attendance at festivals in Jerusalem exceeded that at pre-war Mecca by a substantial margin.[31]

Few aspects of ancient history are as uncertain as numbers. While we can never know how many people were present at one time, it seems to me reasonable to think of 300,000 to 500,000 people attending the festivals in Jerusalem, especially Passover: more than the number who gathered in Mecca before the War, but fewer than those who (we are told) flocked to Bubastis.

Festivals were very much a part of ancient life, and people were prepared to endure crowded conditions in order to participate. Herodotus described the pilgrims who travelled to Bubastis as coming by boat, drinking and singing, and not infrequently making rude gestures at those whom they passed. While we may assume more decorous behaviour on the part of most Jewish pilgrims, feasts were for festivities, and rejoicing may have started on the road. People travelled in groups. Large caravans, which protected the temple tax, came overland from Babylonia (*Antiq.* 17.313). Caravans and ships brought other groups of pilgrims from Syria, Asia Minor and North Africa (*Spec. Laws* 1.69). Galileans and Idumaeans also travelled in companies (e.g. *War* 2.232). Those who walked had songs to sing, the Psalms:

> How lovely is thy dwelling place, O Lord of Hosts!
> My soul longs, yea faints for the courts of the Lord;
> My heart and flesh sing for joy to the living God (Ps. 84.1f.)

> Oh send out thy light and thy truth;
>   let them lead me,
> let them bring me to thy holy hill
>   and to thy dwelling!
> Then I will go to the altar of God,
>   to God my exceeding joy;
> and I will praise thee with the lyre,
>   O God, my God. (43.3f.)

> I was glad when they said to me,
> 'Let us go to the house of the Lord!' (122.1)

There is no reason to exclude secular ditties, jokes, and more wine than usual at night. The Jewish festivals were like Christmas: a blend of piety, good cheer, hearty eating, making music, chatting with friends, drinking and dancing. While the festive atmosphere started on the road, the true feast came in Jerusalem. We recall that pilgrims had their 'second tithe' money to spend. According to Deuteronomy, as long as the money was spent in Jerusalem, it could be spent for whatever you desire, oxen, or sheep, or wine or strong drink, whatever your appetite craves; and you shall eat there before the Lord your God and rejoice, you and your household. (Deut. 14.26)

We may accept that the pilgrim families followed this advice; their trip to the temple was their main feast of the year and was an occasion for 'splurging'.

We cannot say precisely where the pilgrims found accommodation. An inscription from a synagogue in Jerusalem indicates that it contained rooms for foreign visitors,[32] and many inhabitants rented space to temporary lodgers. The villages nearby afforded some accommodation (Mark 11.11f.). According to the Tosefta, local residents did not precisely 'rent' rooms or beds; they gave them, but they received as gifts from their guests the hides of the animals that they sacrificed (*T. Ma'aser Sheni* 1.12f.). Barter is perfectly reasonable and many may have offered goods instead of coins. Many pilgrims, however, especially the prosperous ones, brought their own tents and stayed outside the city (*Antiq.* 17.217).

Above we briefly sketched the sacrifices that a small family might have made on one day during a festival, and we have seen that the shared sacrifice provided a banquet for family and friends. Most people ate red meat only a few times a year (*Hullin* 5.3 assumes four or five times), and fowl or fish only on other holy days – either on the sabbath or on the festival days which they did not spend in Jerusalem, or for which they could not afford a shared offering (though people who lived near the Sea of Galilee may have eaten fish more often). The essentials of life were wheat, milk, wine ('the blood of the grape'), and oil (Ben Sira 39.26). Grain constituted over fifty per cent of the average person's total caloric intake, followed by legumes (e.g. lentils), olive oil, and fruit, especially dried figs. Vines were abundant, and grapes provided food in various ways: fresh, dried (as raisins), and pressed as wine. Palestine, known as a 'land flowing with milk and honey', provided a good quantity of dairy products, for the most part butter and cheese made from the milk of sheep and goats. We noted above that Palestine affords little pasturage that is suitable for cattle, but that flocks were abundant. Honey, the only true sweet in the region, was apparently plentiful (*Arist.* 112, quoted above). We also noted above that dates, grown in Jericho, could be pressed to yield a substitute for bee's honey. Eggs and fowl provided further sources of protein, and various vegetables and seasonings were known, including onion and garlic.[33] There is nothing remarkable about this diet; the Greeks (for example) also relied heavily on grain, legumes, fish and wine. For Jew and Gentile alike, festivals were the time for a change of diet, and especially for feasting on red meat. The consumption of wine also went up.

There were three pilgrim festivals: Passover, Weeks and Booths. The

Bible requires all Israelite males to attend each of these festivals (Ex. 23.17; 34.23; Deut. 16.16). Josephus put it this way:

> Let them assemble in that city in which they shall establish the temple, three times in the year, from the ends of the land which the Hebrews shall conquer, in order to render thanks to God for benefits received, to intercede for future mercies, and to promote by thus meeting and feasting together feelings of mutual affection. (*Antiq.* 4.203)

Philo also emphasized the communal aspects of the pilgrimage festivals:

> Friendships are formed between those who hitherto knew not each other, and the sacrifices and libations are the occasion of reciprocity of feeling and constitute the surest pledge that all are of one mind. (*Spec. Laws* 1.70)

Josephus' summary of the Mosaic legislation reveals the obvious interpretation that Jews who resided abroad were exempt from the biblical requirement to attend three festivals each year (pilgrimage was required only from the land that the Hebrews conquered). Many Diaspora Jews, including women (*War* 5.199), did make the pilgrimage, but it is doubtful that many came more than once in their lifetime. Above I offered the guess that Palestinian Jews on average attended one of the three festivals each year. The requirement to attend three times each year was either ignored or evaded by exegesis; some laws became 'dead letters', though we cannot now establish just how or when. A man travelling alone can cover about fifteen miles each day. It is almost a hundred miles from Jerusalem to northern Galilee; let us say seven or eight days' journey. If the pilgrim stayed a week in Jerusalem, attending all three festivals would take a total of over nine weeks each year and would consume too much money as well as too much time. Further, two of the festivals fall in the spring; only those who lived near Jerusalem could attend both. The spread of the Jewish population throughout Palestine, which was basically achieved by the conquests of the Hasmoneans, required a certain amount of benign neglect of the festival laws.

The festivals were almost certainly family entertainments. Only males were required to attend, but the existence of the Court of the Women shows that numerous women also worshipped in the temple. Where women went, children also went (and vice-versa). An interesting mishnah reports a debate between the Hillelites and the Shammaites on the age at which males were required to make pilgrimage:

> Who is deemed a child [and is therefore not required to attend the festivals]? Any that cannot ride on his father's shoulders and go up from Jerusalem to the Temple Mount. So the School of Shammai. And the

School of Hillel say: Any that cannot hold his father's hand and go up [on his feet] from Jerusalem to the Temple Mount . . . (*Hagigah* 1.1).

Social reality was more important than Pharisaic debates about who attended the festivals. They were times for feasting and rejoicing, and men brought their families. At Passover, 'all the people streamed from their villages to the city and celebrated the festival in a state of purity with their wives and children, according to the law of their fathers' (*Antiq.* 11.109).

The festivals are tied both to specified days of certain months and to seasons. Passover begins on the fourteenth day of the seventh month[34] of the Jewish year and Weeks comes fifty days later. At the Festival of Weeks, the first fruits were presented (Lev. 23; Num. 28.16–31). Further, Deut. 16.1 and Ex. 13.4 require Passover to be 'in the month of Aviv', and Aviv means 'spring'. Both points require Passover to fall in the spring.

Calendars constitute a very complicated topic, and I shall offer only a partial explanation. The basic problem is that the obvious ways of marking time have no common denominator. Nature dictates that there are days, months, seasons and years, but these do not combine to make a neat system. Solar days cannot be multiplied by an even number to produce lunar months, nor lunar months to produce seasonal years. In the common western calendar, we make adjustments: some months have 30 days, some have 31 days, and one has 28 days. If February were lengthened to 30 days, and two of the 31-day months were also made 30 days long, there would be seven 30 day months and five 31 day months. There is a further variation every fourth year, when there are 366 days rather than 365. These adjustments are necessary so that any given month and day will always fall in the same season. Following the natural indicators of time, one would first try to correlate days with months, marked by the phases of the moon. An average lunar month is 29 days, 12 hours, 44 minutes and $3\frac{1}{3}$ seconds; that is, approximately 29½ days. One can keep months more-or-less in line with the phases of the moon by alternating between 29 and 30 days for each month. This, however, yields a year of 354 days, which is approximately 11 days shorter than a seasonal year. If this system is used (as it still is by Muslims), each year a specified day of a month will fall approximately 11 days earlier than the year before, and soon the springtime festivals will fall in the winter.

The modern western calendar meets this problem by breaking with the phases of the moon: months alternate (more or less) between 30 and 31 days, rather than between 29 and 30 days. Consequently the first day of the month does not necessarily coincide with the new moon. The ancient Jews, or at least most of them,[35] preferred to insert a thirteenth month every three years or so, rather than eleven extra days scattered throughout each year. Thus when it became visibly apparent that Passover would not fall in the spring, an extra month was added; each month, however, began and ended according to the phases of the moon.

When the Jewish calendar for a few successive years is laid side-by-side with the common western calendar, the feasts will be seen to come approximately eleven days earlier each year, until suddenly they are pushed down by approximately 19 days. (The calendar adds a full month of 29 or 30 days, but from this must be subtracted the annual loss of approximately 11 days.) The Christian Easter follows the same pattern, since it too depends on correlating the lunar month with the seasonal year (in the West, Easter is the first Sunday after the first full moon after the vernal equinox). The rhythm of the Jewish festivals and of many of the Christian festivals (Easter, Pentecost and others) is approximately the same.

	1991	1992	1993	1994	1995	1996	1997
Passover*	29 March	17 April	5 April	26 March	14 April	3 April	21 April
Booths**	23 Sept.	12 Oct.	30 Sept.	20 Sept.	9 Oct.	28 Sept.	16 Oct.

*14 Nisan[36] in the Jewish calendar   **15 Tishri

Passover (Hebrew, *Pesaḥ*), also called *Unleavened Bread* (*Maṣṣôt*), commemorates the exodus from Egypt. Passover comes in the spring, and the chart above indicates the general range of dates. The biblical story is that the Lord, in order to force the Egyptian Pharaoh to let the Israelites return to their own land, killed the first-born in each Egyptian house, as well as the first-born of the cattle (Ex. 12.29). He preserved the Israelites and, by the hand of Moses, led them out of Egypt. Passover celebrates this, the basic act of God's redemption in Israel's history.

Originally, there were two different festivals, Passover and Unleavened Bread. At one time in Israel's history, in fact, Passover was not a pilgrimage festival, but a domestic one; this is reflected in Ex. 12, where the temple is not mentioned.[37] Before our period the two festivals had been merged and had become, in effect, a single pilgrimage festival that lasted eight days (though those learned in the law, such as Philo and Josephus, knew that there were technically two festivals). The combination is clear in Lev. 23.4–8 and Deut. 16.1–8. The law that prevailed in Jerusalem, as usual, was that of Leviticus: Passover was on the 14th of the month; on the 15th came Unleavened Bread, which lasted seven days. The 14th, 15th and 21st of Nisan were days of 'holy convocation', when no work was done and when Jews were expected to be in Jerusalem if possible (so Lev. 23). Josephus agrees with Leviticus: on the 14th of Nisan they sacrificed the Passover lamb (or kid),[38] and 'on the fifteenth the Passover is followed up by the Feast of Unleavened Bread, lasting seven days' (*Antiq.* 3.248f.; so also Philo, *Spec. Laws* 2.149f., 155). Josephus frequently, however, described these feasts as one, in which case he sometimes called the entire festal period 'Unleavened Bread' rather than 'Passover'. This explains why he once wrote that Unleavened Bread lasted eight days.[39]

Deuteronomy forbids Israelites to celebrate Passover anywhere but Jerusalem (16.1–8). Numbers 9.10–12 provides a second Passover, a month after the first, for those who had corpse impurity or who were away on a journey on the 14th of Nisan. This also implies that Jews could celebrate Passover only in Jerusalem and only when they were pure. The removal of corpse impurity required a mixture of water and ashes that ran out fairly soon after the temple was destroyed. After the fall of the temple, therefore, those who interpreted these passages in their obvious sense no longer celebrated Passover, but only Unleavened Bread. In the course of history, however, the term 'Passover' prevailed, with the result that in the modern Jewish calendar Passover begins on the 15th of Nisan.

Despite the clear meaning of Deuteronomy and Numbers, some Jews, perhaps relying on Exodus, slaughtered the Passover lamb on the 14th of Nisan even when they could not do so in Jerusalem. In *Jubilees* there may be a clue that this was so in Palestine in the third or second century BCE. The author insists that the Passover sacrifice may be eaten only in Jerusalem and only in the temple precincts (possibly meaning in the open area in front of the temple before it was enclosed by a wall). The commandment is repeated so often (*Jub.* 49.16, 18, 20, 21) that one suspects that some people did not agree; we cannot tell, however, whether they observed Passover in other towns, or only in the wrong part of Jerusalem. Better evidence is provided by Philo. In his view, after the exodus from Egypt the people were so joyful that they 'sacrificed without waiting for their priest'. The law then sanctioned such sacrifices once each year. On the 14th of Nisan, 'every dwelling-house is invested with the outward semblance and dignity of a temple'. A victim is sacrificed. People are purified by sprinkling themselves from a basin; they then attend the banquet, at which there are also prayers and hymns (*Spec. Laws* 2.145–9).[40] Philo's other references to purification by sprinkling from a basin of water show that at least sometimes this was a domestic rite, invented by Diaspora Jews for their own use, and distinct from the purificatory sprinklings and bathing that removed corpse impurity at the temple.[41]

In and of itself, Philo's statement that 'the whole people . . . [were] raised for that particular day to the dignity of the priesthood' might mean only that laymen sacrificed the Passover lamb when they observed the festival at the temple.[42] The statement that every house became a temple is possibly exegetical and allegorical: the fact that the first Passover was observed before the appointment of priests and the construction of the tabernacle proves that *in spiritual/allegorical theory* 'the dwelling together of several good persons in the home was a temple and altar' (*Quest. Ex.* 1.10). Perceiving such points, most scholars, possibly all who have looked at the topic, have concluded that 'there is . . . no evidence to suggest that paschal sacrifices were made in Alexandria or that Philo would have sanctioned them'.[43] It is conceivable, barely, that Philo's reference to purification by sprinkling from a basin is short-hand for the seven-day purification that removed the corpse impurity of pilgrims in Jerusalem, a rite that he elsewhere discusses more fully.[44] The most natural reading of the whole passage, however, is that all Jews, whether in Jerusalem or not, could gather in companies and participate in the Passover sacrifice. The Bible ordains that this one time each year laymen may act as priests. Every house becomes a temple, 'the victim is then slaughtered', and the guests assemble, having first sprinkled themselves (*Spec. Laws* 2.146–8).

Supporting evidence that some Jews in the Diaspora sacrificed at Passover comes from Josephus' list of decrees issued by various cities in the Greek-speaking world, giving Jews new rights or confirming old ones. The city of Sardis (in Asia Minor) permitted local Jews to 'gather together with their wives and children and offer their ancestral prayers and sacrifices to God' (*Antiq.* 14.260). The city fathers, of course, may have used the word 'sacrifice' loosely. If, however, the word meant what it usually means, it could refer to the slaughter of Passover lambs (the most likely sacrifices to be made away from the temple, because of the domestic setting of Ex. 12). Finally, we note that after the destruction of the temple there was some disagreement about roasting a kid for Passover. Some rabbis allowed a kid to be roasted in such a way that it *looked like* a Passover sacrifice (Rabban Gamaliel 11 in *Betsah* 2.7; cf. *Betsah* 23a).[45]

Above, in envisaging part of the sacrificial routine of a small family (p. 113), I assumed that a local priest had purified the family and house of corpse impurity before the pilgrimage. If this was not done, however, the pilgrim had to come at least seven days early. Philo, probably reflecting his own experience as a pilgrim, observed that the law bids the worshipper

> stay outside [the temple] for seven days and be twice sprinkled on the third and seventh day, and after that, when he has bathed himself, it gives him full security to come within and offer his sacrifice. (*Spec. Laws* 1.261)

Josephus reflects the same waiting period. The people assembled for the feast of unleavened bread 'on the eighth of the month Xanthicus' (*War* 6.290). Xanthicus is the name of a Macedonian month that Josephus equated with Nisan. He is not here actually reckoning time according to the

Macedonian calendar, only using a Macedonian name.[46] If the people assembled on the 8th of Nisan, they came a week early, doubtless to be purified of corpse impurity. The seventh day of purification would have been the 14th. They would be sprinkled, then they would immerse, and afterwards they could enter the temple to sacrifice the Passover lamb.

When the day finally came, the evening burnt offering was sacrificed earlier than usual, and then the Passover service began. Between the ninth and eleventh hours of the day (approximately 4.00 to 6.00 p.m.), the lambs were sacrificed (*War* 6.423). The full priestly and Levitical contingent of thousands was in attendance. According to *T. Sukkah* 3.2, the Levites sang the Hallel, Psalms 113–118, whose main themes are praise and thanksgiving for deliverance, both national and personal:

Praise the Lord!

. . .

Who is like the Lord our God,
    who is seated on high, who looks far down upon the heavens and
        the earth?
He raises the poor from the dust,
    and lifts the needy from the ash heap,
to make them sit with princes,
    with the princes of his people.
He gives the barren woman a home . . . (Ps. 113)

Not to us, O Lord, not to us,
    but to thy name give glory,
for the sake of thy steadfast love and thy faithfulness . . . (115.1)

Gracious is the Lord, and righteous;
    our God is merciful.
The Lord preserves the simple;
    when I was brought low, he saved me. (116.5f.)

When Israel went forth from Egypt,
    the house of Jacob from a people of strange language,
Judah became his sanctuary,
    Israel his dominion. (114.1f.)

All nations surrounded me;
    in the name of the Lord I cut them off!
They surrounded me, surrounded me on every side;
    in the name of the Lord I cut them off! (118.10)

The last lines quoted show that freedom from bondage included military and political deliverance.

During the singing, worshippers came with their lambs. Since one lamb was adequate for a group of ten people (*War* 6.423), presumably only one of the ten brought the lamb to the temple. According to the Mishnah, the worshippers came in three separate groups, each time filling the inner courts.

> When the first group entered in and the Temple Court was filled, the gates of the Temple Court were closed. [On the *shofar*] a sustained, a quavering, and again a sustained blast were blown. The priests stood in rows and in their hands were basins of silver and basins of gold . . . (*Pesahim* 5.5)

The Mishnah continues: the man who had brought the animal slaughtered it, and the priest caught the blood. The basins were then passed from hand to hand, until the blood was tossed against the base of the altar (5.6). The first group left, and the court was washed down – even when Passover fell on the sabbath, though this work was performed 'not with the consent of the sages' (5.8). R. Judah (mid-second century) thought that before the court was washed, a cup of the blood was scooped up and thrown on the altar, but his contemporaries did not agree (5.8).

The Mishnah's description must be generally correct: not every one could sacrifice at once. But let us try to imagine the scene more concretely. There were, let us say, 300,000 present for Passover, and thus approximately 30,000 lambs to be slaughtered. There were at least 10,000 priests: enough for each lamb if the lambs were brought in three groups. Twenty thousand people (half worshippers and half priests), plus 10,000 lambs, however, would not fit inside the inner wall. The next larger area was that enclosed by the balustrade that warned Gentiles to go no further. In Busink's reconstruction, the total area enclosed by the balustrade (which included the sanctuary) was 254 metres $\times$ 151 = 38,354 square metres. One-and-a-half square metres might just suffice to hold two men and a lamb, but 20,000 men and 10,000 lambs would pack an open area of 38,000 square metres, and there would be no room to hang the animal up and flay it. Besides, by no means all the 38,000 square metre area was available: laymen did not take their lambs into the sanctuary, and there were also numerous rooms around the interior of the inner wall, further reducing the space available. Ten thousand lambs could not have been slaughtered inside the balustrade at the same time.

We must, then, consider other possibilities. Either each group spread out over the entire temple area, including the Court of the Gentiles, or people came forward to the inner courts continuously, rather than in three distinct groupings. I see no way of deciding definitively between these two possibilities. Let us consider the second. On this view, a contingent of priests stood spread around the area inside the balustrade, both between the balustrade and the inner wall and also inside the inner wall. The Court of the

Gentiles, outside the balustrade, was full of worshippers and lambs. The crowd slowly filed past the balustrade, each man taking his lamb to a priest. The man cut the throat and the priest caught the blood. The priest then passed the blood back towards the altar. He carried the lamb to a hook on one of the walls (*Pesahim* 5.9), hung it up and flayed it. He removed the principal fatty portions, returned the lamb and its hide to the owner, and took the fat to be burned on the altar. This would take about ten minutes if he did not have to wait for a hook. He was then ready for the next customer. After a few lambs he would retire to rest, and another priest would take his place.

Although the Mishnaic rabbis did not worry about how many lambs could be sacrificed at one time in the temple area, they did note the problem of hooks for hanging the carcasses.

> If any had no place where to hang and flay, there were thin smooth staves which a man could put on his own and his fellow's shoulder and so hang and flay. (*Pesahim* 5.9)

This means of supporting the carcasses would have allowed more lambs to be slaughtered at one time, and also a larger area of the temple complex to be used, possibly the entirety of the Court of the Gentiles. Use of the entire area would allow several thousand lambs to be sacrificed at the same time, though getting the blood to the altar would be extremely difficult. On the whole, I think it somewhat more likely that the priests stayed inside the balustrade (or possibly inside the inner wall), and that there was a continuous flow of people and animals, rather than the three distinct sessions proposed by the Mishnah. One cannot in any case accept both of the Mishnah's views: that there were three distinct sessions and that all the sacrifices took place inside the inner wall.

Though the priests flayed and partially eviscerated the animals, they did not butcher them. The worshipper carried out the whole lamb, which was roasted on a skewer and eaten after night fell (Ex. 12.8f.; cf. *Pesahim* 7.1f.).

Wherever it was held, the Passover meal consisted principally of a roasted lamb or kid, unleavened bread and bitter herbs (Ex. 12.8). The meal was eaten with loins girded, sandals on the feet, and staff in the hand to recall the haste in which the Israelites fled Egypt (Ex. 12.11).

The biblical story explicitly requires that the occasion be used for the instruction of the young.

> And when your children say to you, 'What do you mean by this service?' you shall say, 'It is the sacrifice of the Lord's passover, for he passed over the houses of the people of Israel in Egypt, when he slew the Egyptians but spared our houses'. (Ex. 12.26–27)

The Mishnah offers further information about instruction. The son asks his father, 'Why is this night different from other nights?' The father answers, '"A wandering Aramean was my father . . ."' until he finishes the whole section' (the avowal, Deut. 26.5–11). According to Rabban Gamaliel, at Passover a person should recite or recall the biblical verses dealing with Passover night, the unleavened bread and the bitter herbs – probably all of Ex. 12 (*Pesahim* 10.4f.).

Since the feast embodied the theme of national liberation, it is not surprising that it was sometimes an occasion when unrest at Israel's current state led to riot. In 4 CE, when Archelaus was ethnarch and ruler of Judaea, some men, standing in the temple court, took the opportunity to protest against the execution of the two teachers who had inspired their students to take down the eagle over the entrance to the temple (above, p. 38). Archelaus sent in a cohort (500 to 1,000 troops) to arrest the ringleaders. The crowd pelted them with stones, killing some. More troops were sent, and about 3,000 worshippers were killed, the rest dispersed, and the sacrifices cancelled (*War* 2.10–13). A few decades later, when Cumanus was procurator (48–52 CE), there was another riot. A cohort of Romans was on guard, watching the crowd from the roof of the portico of the temple. One of them 'stooped in an indecent attitude, so as to turn his backside to the Jews, and made a noise in keeping with his posture'. There was a fight, stones were hurled, and Cumanus sent in troops. Thousands were killed (*War* 2.224–227: 30,000; *Antiq.* 20.112: 20,000). We learn here that it was customary for the Roman prefect or procurator, with additional troops, to be in Jerusalem at Passover and for guards to be posted on the roofs of the porticoes.

We cannot be sure how long people stayed in Jerusalem. As we saw above, those who had corpse impurity had to come at least a week early in order to be purified, and the two festivals combined lasted eight days. Many pilgrims probably stayed for the entire two week period. They had other sacrifices to present; and, besides, once they had made the trip they naturally wanted to enjoy the benefits of the city.

The Feast of Weeks (Hebrew *Shavuʿot* or *ʿAtseret*, 'concluding feast'), also called 'Pentecost' or 'Day of First-Fruits', was an agricultural festival. It comes *fifty* days or seven *weeks* after Passover (whence 'Pentecost' and 'Weeks') – that is, in the late spring or early summer – and was principally distinguished by the offering of new wheat.[47] Two loaves of bread were made from the season's first wheat, and they were presented as 'first fruits' (Lev. 23.15–21; cf. Num. 28.26–31 for the new grain and accompanying sacrifices). Thereafter began the period during which individuals brought their offerings of first fruits to the temple.

This feast was the occasion to declare God's ownership of the land and his grace in causing it to bring forth food, but it also provided an opportunity to recall and give thanks for God's mighty acts on behalf of Israel: the election, the covenant and the exodus (see Deut. 26.1–15; further below, p. 154).

In 4 BCE the Feast of Weeks was the occasion of a fight between Romans and Jews. The story is a complicated one, having to do with the wish of Sabinus, the procurator (financial officer) of Syria, to claim for Rome (and himself) some of Herod's treasure after his death. At the Feast of Weeks 'tens of thousands' of Jews began an attack on Sabinus' troops, which resulted in considerable loss of life on both sides (*Antiq.* 17.221–268, quotation from 17.254; *War* 2.42–44). Even at this, the smallest of the pilgrimage festivals, there were large numbers, and consequently the possibility of tumult and violence.

The Feast of Booths (Heb., *Sukkot*) or Tabernacles is an autumn festival that begins five days after the Day of Atonement. (For the range of dates, see the chart above.) For seven days 'all that are native in Israel shall dwell in booths' (Lev. 23.42). A festival day (when work was prohibited) was added (Lev. 23.33–36), in effect extending the festal period to eight days.

The booths were made of 'branches of olive, wild olive, myrtle, palm, and other leafy trees' (Neh. 8.15). People who lived in Jerusalem probably built the booths on the roofs of their houses, while pilgrims built them outside the walls. According to Josephus, the festival was 'observed with special care' (*Antiq.* 15.50), and it is probable that most families built booths. One may imagine that children were especially enthusiastic in gathering branches and tying them together to make a booth.

This was also an agricultural festival, marking the conclusion of the season of harvest. It was a showy and happy occasion with something of a carnival spirit. Worshippers carried *lulavs*, made of branches from palm, willow and myrtle trees, to which a citron (a citrus fruit) was attached (Lev. 23.40; *Antiq.* 3.245). Priests carrying willow branches marched around the altar. There was flute playing and dancing by night. The Mishnah gives the flavour of the celebration:

> Men of piety and good works used to dance before them with burning torches in their hands, singing songs and praises. And countless Levites [played] on harps, lyres, cymbals and trumpets and instruments of music, on the fifteen steps leading down from the Court of the Israelites to the Court of the Women, corresponding to the Fifteen Songs of Ascent in the Psalms [Ps. 120–134]; upon them the Levites used to stand with instruments of music and make melody. (*Sukkah* 5.4)

According to the Mishnah, the Hallel was sung on each of the eight days (*Sukkah* 4.8), and during the singing the worshippers shook their *lulavs* (3.9). We know from a story about Alexander Jannaeus (cited below) that they did in fact bring their *lulavs* into the temple, and this may be one of the occasions when everybody crowded into the temple area. Even in the Court of the Gentiles, they could have heard the songs and participated by shaking their *lulavs*.

As at the other feasts all the priests were employed (see *Sukkah* 5.7), and sacrifices were offered in profusion. The community sacrifices deserve special mention: on the first day, thirteen oxen or bulls,[48] fourteen lambs, two rams and a kid (as a sin offering). On each successive day, the number of oxen was reduced by one, while the other burnt offerings remained the same (Num. 29.12–34; *Antiq.* 3.246). Large cattle were extremely valuable, yet during the festival seventy were slaughtered and burnt.

According to Neh. 8.17f. Ezra had read from the law on each day of the festival. Deuteronomy requires that the law be read every seventh year at the Feast of Booths (Deut. 31.10f.), and it is probable that study of scripture remained an important part of the festival.

Leviticus manages to connect even this festival with the exodus, the paradigmatic event that shows God's grace to Israel:

> You shall dwell in booths for seven days; all that are native in Israel shall dwell in booths, that your generations may know that I made the people of Israel dwell in booths when I brought them out of the land of Egypt . . . (Lev. 23.42f.)

. The Feast of Booths was second to Passover in terms of the number of pilgrims. At the beginning of the Jewish revolt, when Cestius, the legate of Syria, reached Lydda, he 'found the city deserted, for the whole population had gone up to Jerusalem for the Feast of Tabernacles' (*War* 2.515). It had the advantage of coming after the harvest, a time when people were both ready and able to have a few days' holiday, and the joyous celebration made it an attractive ceremony. A large crowd, however, also has the potential to create disturbance. One of the most famous riots of Jewish history took place during this festival. Alexander Jannaeus (103–76 BCE) was serving at the altar when the crowd began to pelt him with citrons. They further insulted him, by saying that he was descended from captives (and thus may have been a bastard and not eligible to serve as a priest). He called in the troops, and some 6,000 were killed (*Antiq.* 13.372f.).[49]

It was also at Booths that Jesus son of Ananias first created a public disturbance.

> Standing in the temple [he] suddenly began to cry out, 'A voice from the east, a voice from the west, a voice from the four winds; a voice against Jerusalem and the sanctuary, a voice against the bridegroom and the bride, a voice against all the people'. (*War* 6.301)

He was punished by the magistrates (*archontes*) and then scourged before the procurator, but he would only repeat his cry. He was finally released. He continued his lament for seven years and five months, crying most loudly at the festivals. Finally he was killed by a Roman missile (*War* 6.300–309).

The Day of Atonement. In counterpoint to the three great feasts was the fast of the Day of Atonement (Hebrew, *Yôm Kippûr*), the only fast prescribed by biblical law. It comes in the autumn, on the 10th day of Tishri, five days before Booths – thus in the first month of the year in the system that prevailed, which in the Bible is often called the seventh month.[50] The fast began at sunset on the 9th of the month and continued until sunset the next day. It was, and still is, 'day of solemn rest', on which participants are to 'afflict' themselves (Lev. 23.32). 'Affliction' means more than fasting; the Mishnah further specifies abstaining from 'washing, anointing, putting on sandals, and marital intercourse' (*Yoma* 8.1).[51] God had warned that he would destroy those who did not afflict themselves or who worked (Lev. 23.29–30). The Day was intended to be one of examination and confession of sins.

The day of fast, like the three great feasts, was a time of 'holy convocation' (Lev. 23.27). Josephus, remarkably, says virtually nothing about it, mentioning it only as the day on which first Pompey and then Herod took Jerusalem (though probably not accurately: see *Antiq.* 14.66; 14.487 and Marcus' notes in the Loeb edition). We do not learn, for example, that crowds gathered and that it was the occasion of riots. It was not a time of pilgrimage, and the 'holy convocation' for the Day of Atonement was probably only a convocation of those who lived in and near Jerusalem. It was, however, a communal day of worship. Moses had said, 'On this day shall atonement be made for you, to cleanse you; from all your sins you shall be clean before the Lord' (Lev. 16.30). The nation fasted together; what happened in the temple was for all.

The rites of atonement were elaborate and all-inclusive. The various sacrifices of the Day purified the altar, the sacred objects in the temple, and the sanctuary, as well as atoning for the sins of all Israel. According to the summary of *Shevu'ot* 1.6f., even sins punishable by 'cutting off' were atoned for. The high priest himself officiated. After sacrificing the regular daily burnt offering, he bathed and dressed in linen garments (Lev. 16.4). The distinctive sacrifices of the day – besides which there were many others – were a bull and two goats. Standing between the goats, he cast lots that designated one of them 'for the Lord' and the other 'for Azazel'. His first sacrifice was of the bull, the standard sin offering of the high priest (Lev. 16.11; 4.3). The Mishnah attributes to him this confession: 'O God, I have committed iniquity, transgressed, and sinned before thee, I and my house. O God, forgive the iniquities and transgressions and sins which I have committed . . .' (*Yoma* 3.8). The high priest slaughtered the bull. He then took a censer of coals and incense, entered the Holy of Holies, and put the incense on the fire. (There was a debate between Pharisees and Sadducees on when the incense was put on the fire; below pp. 396f.) This produced smoke, which was originally intended to keep him from seeing 'the mercy seat . . ., lest he die' (Lev. 16.11–14). The Ark of the Covenant and the mercy seat above it had long since disappeared, and inside the Holy of Holies was 'nothing whatsoever' (*War* 5.219), except the foundation stone on which they had once stood (*Yoma* 5.3). The censer with the smoking incense was put down on this stone. The high priest then went back through the veil that covered the entrance to the Holy of Holies and returned with some of the blood of the bull, which he sprinkled with his finger. He then went outside and sacrificed the goat which was 'for the Lord' as a sin offering, re-entered the Holy of Holies, and sprinkled some of the blood. He returned to the altar in the Court of the Priests and put some of the blood from each animal on the altar's 'horns', then sprinkled more blood on the altar. This sanctified the altar itself. The goat 'for Azazel' was then brought to him. He put his hands on it and confessed 'all the iniquities of the people of Israel'. A designated person took this goat, the scape-goat, which bore the sins of Israel, into the wilderness (Lev. 16.15–22). According to the Mishnah, the people cried 'Bear [our sins] and be gone!' as the goat was led out (*Yoma* 6.4).

The high priest then bathed again and put on his own garments – probably the glorious robe of the high priest.[52] He burned the fat of the two sin offerings on the altar, and the remaining carcases were taken outside the temple and burned entirely, including 'their skin and their flesh and their dung' (Lev. 16.23–28).

Leviticus does not describe the rest of the service, but the Mishnah has a fuller narrative, and we shall follow it. The high priest read Lev. 16 (the passage just summarized) and Lev. 23.26–32 (the passage that ordains the fast). He then recited by heart Num. 29.7–11 (which summarizes the sacrifices of the Day of Atonement). There followed prayers: 'for the Law, for the Temple-Service, for the Thanksgiving, for the Forgiveness of Sin, and for the Temple separately, and for the Israelites separately, and for the priests separately; and for the rest a [general] prayer' (*Yoma* 7.1). Some of these (for the temple service, for thanksgiving and for forgiveness) correspond, at least with regard to their main themes, to some of the prayers of the Eighteen Benedictions, which will be considered below. That the high priest prayed at some point in the service, however, is not in doubt. According to Ben Sira, the high priest Simon pronounced a blessing using the proper name of God, 'glory[ing] in his name' (Ben Sira 50.20). That is, he pronounced the otherwise unpronounced name that consists of four consonants, YHWH, called by Philo and others the 'tetragrammaton' (*Moses* 2.115), which modern scholars reconstruct as 'Yahweh'.

In the view of some rabbis, further washing, sacrifices, and a change of clothing came after the scriptural passages and blessings (*Yoma* 7.3). If so, when these last sacrifices were over, the high priest again washed and changed his clothing, putting back on the white linen garments in order to re-enter the Holy of Holies and retrieve the censer. Still again he washed, put on 'the golden garments' (the full regalia of the high priest) and burned the evening incense. After a final ablution he donned his own clothes, suitable for wearing outside the temple, went home, and 'made a feast for his friends for that he was come forth safely from the Sanctuary' (*Yoma* 7.4).

Ben Sira gives further information about the conclusion of the service, which deserves to be quoted in full:

> Finishing the service at the altars, and arranging the offering to the Most High, the Almighty, he reached out his hand to the cup and poured a libation of the blood of the grape; he poured it out at the foot of the altar, a pleasing odour to the Most High, the King of all.
>
> Then the sons of Aaron shouted, they sounded the trumpets of hammered work, they made a great noise to be heard for remembrance before the Most High.
>
> Then all the people together made haste and fell to the ground upon their faces to worship their Lord, the Almighty, God Most High. And the singers praised him with their voices in sweet and full-toned melody. And the people besought the Lord Most High in prayer before him who is merciful, till the order of worship of the Lord was ended; so they completed his service.
>
> Then Simon [the high priest] came down, and lifted up his hands over the whole congregation of the sons of Israel, to pronounce the blessing of the Lord with his lips, and to glory in his name; and they bowed down in worship a second time, to receive the blessing from the Most High (Ben Sira 50.14– 21)

Conclusion

The masses, we have seen, participated in the national religion. This generalization covers both Palestine and the Diaspora – Babylon, Egypt, Syria, Asia Minor, Italy and other parts of the world. We shall shortly see that the adherence of Jews to their ancestral faith drew the criticism of others and was exploited in various ways. Some scholars suppose that the common people were 'in general lukewarm about religion',[53] but few generalizations could be less true. We have seen throughout how intertwined were religion and patriotism: the God of Israel was God of the world, but he had chosen the nation of Israel. All who aspired to leadership spoke in his name. Loyalty to the community was inseparable from loyalty to the deity who called it into being; group identity and devotion to God went together. Nothing called forth Jewish passion as much as did a threat to a divine institution. Taxes were resented, but they were nothing compared to a threat to the sanctity of the temple – or even the lesser offence of bringing Roman standards into Jerusalem. A re-reading of our catalogue of tumults and outbreaks will provide ample illustration.

The temple was the visible, functioning symbol of God's presence with his people, and it was also the basic rallying point of Jewish loyalties. To it came the temple tax and other offerings from Jews throughout the world, as well as thousands of pilgrims. Caligula's threat to put up his statue in it not only led a mass of Jews to appear before Petronius, offering to die instead (above, p. 39), it also led Philo to threaten world-wide revolt. 'Everyone everywhere, even if he was not naturally well disposed to the Jews, was afraid to engage in destroying any of our institutions.' To protect these institutions, especially the temple, Jews would 'die and be no more, for the truly glorious death, met in defence of laws, might be called life'. Caligula's threat was against 'the corporate body of the Jews', all of whom were marked by zeal for the temple. Jews, numerous throughout the empire, posed a danger if outraged: 'Heaven forbid indeed that the Jews in every quarter should come by common agreement to the defence. The result would be something too stupendous to be combated' (*Embassy* 159–215).

We must always bear in mind that atheism was almost unknown in the ancient world. Virtually all believed that there really was a divine sphere and Jews believed that the God of their ancestors had given them his law, and that it was to be kept. God was one 'whose eye no criminal escapes' (*Antiq.* 4.286), and it was he who was to be thanked for every blessing of life.

There doubtless were exceptions to this general loyalty – people who, though perhaps with some fear and trepidation in the dark watches of the night, lived as if there were no God – but the adherence of most Jews to the national religion cannot be doubted. It repeatedly led to difficulties with the rest of the world. Besides the two massive revolts in Palestine, we may mention uprisings in Cyrene (*Life* 424) and a major attack by the other Alexandrians on the Jewish residents (the subject of Philo's *Against Flaccus*). Jews obviously rejected a good deal of the common culture, and just as obviously they kept their own. In later chapters we shall see which of their customs and observances were most irritating to others, which are thus singled out as major identity markers.

9

Tithes and Taxes

According to biblical law, the priests and Levites were to be supported by the people's offerings and sacrifices. We noted this at the beginning of ch. 6, and now we shall examine their income, as well as restrictions on income-producing activities, in more detail. In the second part of this chapter we shall consider the total financial cost of all forms of taxation.

Financial support of the priests and Levites

The basic biblical legislation governing feeding the priests, the Levites and their families is this:

> And the Lord said to Aaron, 'You shall have no inheritance in their land, neither shall you have any portion among them; I am your portion and your inheritance among the people of Israel'. (Num. 18.20)

> To the Levites I have given every tithe in Israel for an inheritance, in return for their service . . . (Num. 18.21). You may eat it in any place, you and your households (18.31).

> The Levitical priests, that is, all the tribe of Levi, shall have no portion or inheritance with Israel; they shall eat the offerings by fire to the Lord, and his rightful dues. They shall have no inheritance among their brethren; the Lord is their inheritance, as he promised them. (Deut. 18.1–2)

This legislation is not quite as clear as may at first appear. 'Portion' and 'inheritance' are a little vague, and Deuteronomy names first priests and then all the tribe of Levi (priests and Levites). Did the same rules apply to both? What was it that they could not have? What is clearest is that the focus is on food: the priests and Levites were to eat the offerings and other dues. 'Portion' and 'inheritance' presumably meant 'private means of food production'. Early in the second temple period Nehemiah found that the

Levites were not receiving their tithes and consequently had 'fled each to his field'. He required the tithes to be paid (Neh. 13.11f.).

Nehemiah does not say that he forbade the Levites to own fields; his concern was that they be supported by the temple so that they would keep to their posts. Evidence for the Levites disappears, but during the period of the second temple priests owned property. We know this directly from Josephus about himself. To indicate to the reader how much Titus appreciated his services, Josephus recalled that he was compensated for the loss of his property in Jerusalem (*Life* 422). It appears that he saw no difficulty about owning property, though he was a priest. We may be confident that other priests owned property as well. The priestly aristocracy was prominent throughout the second temple period, and in the ancient world aristocracy and wealth were usually inseparable from the ownership of land. In cities near ports, traders could amass fortunes, but Jerusalem was not a port, and we cannot suppose that the wealth of Jerusalem aristocrats derived entirely from trade and not from land, especially in view of Josephus' statement.

It does appear, however, that the priests (and presumably the Levites) did not *work* the land. That is, they seem to have interpreted the biblical passages as meaning that they could own land but could not produce food.

We have seen that animals and meal brought to the temple fed the priests who were on duty. Further, when people slaughtered an animal away from the temple they were supposed to give the shoulder, cheeks and maw to a priest, presumably one who resided locally (above, p. 111). He could share this non-sacrificial meat with his family. Similarly the agricultural offerings helped feed both the priests and their households.

The principal offering of agricultural produce was the *tithe*. The English word is now archaic and is used only for a gift of ten per cent for religious purposes. It does, however, mean 'tenth'. The Hebrew and Greek terms were not archaic and clearly said 'one-tenth' to the people who used them. Tithes provide us with an unusually good opportunity to study competing interpretations of biblical law. The legal books of the Bible offer different definitions of tithes, which in our period scholars conflated and harmonized in at least two different ways.

Deuteronomy requires tithes of farm produce ('all the yield of your seed', 14.22) every year except the seventh (sabbatical) year, when the land was to lie fallow. Most years the people who separated the tithe of their produce enjoyed its benefit: they ate it. The food was to be taken to Jerusalem and consumed there, or, which was the usual practice, converted into money to be spent in Jerusalem as the one who tithed wished: 'oxen, or sheep, or wine or strong drink . . .' (Deut. 14.22–7). The purpose of the provision was to support Jerusalem financially. Every third year (probably the third and sixth years of the seven year cycle) the tithe was to be given to support the Levites and the needy (Deut. 14.27–9; 26.12f.).

Leviticus, however, states that 'all the tithe of the land, whether of the seed of the land or of the fruit of the trees, is the Lord's' (27.30). 'The Lord's' most naturally means that it belongs to the priests. The only other way of giving something to the Lord was to burn it, and the tithe was not destined to be offered in this way. Leviticus proceeds to state that one of every ten animals owned 'shall be holy to the Lord' (27.32). In the first century, as we shall see below, 'holy to' was not taken to mean that the animal was given to the temple, but rather that it was eaten in purity.

In Numbers there is a still different understanding of the tithe. It went to the Levites, who in turn paid a tithe of the tithe to the priests. The Levitical tithe provided food for the Levites and their families: it was not eaten in the temple (Num. 18.21–32). Numbers mentions neither the poor nor the consumption of the tithe by those who produce it. The situation is the same in Nehemiah: the Levites receive the tithes, pay a tenth to the priests, and keep the rest (Neh. 10.37b–39; cf. 13.5).

The first-century scholar, who did not separate the various books in the Bible as belonging to different periods and thus as reflecting different customs, or different views of what customs *should* be, found that scripture required tithes for the priests, for the Levites, for the poor, and for the support of Jerusalem. It was quite simple to combine Leviticus ('to the Lord') with Numbers and Nehemiah (to the Levites, who in turn tithed to the priests): Leviticus was simply read in light of the other two books. Ten per cent of produce went to the Levites, who gave ten per cent to the priests. Every tenth animal, which was 'holy to the Lord', was to be eaten in a state of purity by the people who raised it.[1]

Deuteronomy, however, posed a different problem. It requires the farmer to spend a tithe in Jerusalem and to give a tithe to the Levites and the poor in years three and six of each seven year cycle. It was the integration of Deuteronomy into the laws of Numbers and Nehemiah that led to competing views of how many tithes were owed.

The older combination was probably that there were two tithes every year (except the sabbatical year, when the land rested): one for the Levites (who gave ten per cent to the priests), one to be spent in Jerusalem. In the third and sixth years there was still a third ten per cent for the poor. We may call this the fourteen tithe system: fourteen tithes in every seven years, two in years one, two, four and five; three in years three and six; none in year seven. The author of Tobit (third or second century BCE) has his hero describe himself as giving a tenth of his produce 'to the sons of Levi who ministered at Jerusalem'; he sold a second tenth and spent the money in Jerusalem; he gave a third tenth 'to those to whom it was [his] duty' (Tobit 1.7f.). This seems to mean that he gave three tithes every year, and thus followed an eighteen tithe system, but perhaps the author simply did not find it necessary to give further details. *Jubilees* (second century BCE) refers to 'the second tithe', which is to be eaten every year in Jerusalem (*Jub.* 32.10–14). This implies that there was a first tithe, given to the Levites, and that in at least some years a third tithe was given to the poor. *Jub.* 32.15 also prescribes that the tithe of cattle ('holy to the Lord', Lev. 27.32) be given to the priests. This would have been excruciatingly expensive. Finally, Josephus assumes that Moses required two tithes every year and a third tithe in years three and six (*Antiq.* 4.69, 205, 240). It is Josephus who provides the explicit statement of the fourteen tithe system.

The Mishnaic rabbis harmonized the biblical passages differently (tractates *Ma'aser* and *Ma'aser Sheni*).[2] (1) First tithe was given every year except the seventh to the Levites, who tithed it to the priests (so Numbers and Nehemiah). (2) Second tithe, sold for money that was spent in Jerusalem, was set aside in years one, two, four and five of each seven year cycle (so Deuteronomy). (3) Poor tithe replaced second tithe in years three and six (also Deuteronomy). The Mishnah represents a twelve tithe system: two in years one to six of every seven year cycle. It requires two fewer tithes to be spent in Jerusalem than does Josephus' fourteen tithe system. The Mishnah is thus easier on the farmer and less generous to Jerusalem, both the temple and the merchants. It is probable that here the Mishnah reflects Pharisaic interpretation, and that in our period some people followed a twelve tithe rather than a fourteen tithe rule.

We cannot, however, be sure who tithed what. We must take seriously Josephus' easy assurance that Moses required fourteen tithes in each cycle. It is very probable that he represents the standard priestly interpretation of the various biblical passages. Levites and priests collected the tithe in person (Neh. 10.37f.), and it may also be that Levites served as almoners and dispensed the poor tithe. Thus, every year farmers had officials of their religion knocking on the door and asking for tithes. That collection actually took place in the first century is indicated by several passages. Josephus relates that he and two other priests went to Galilee to assess the situation at the outbreak of revolt against Rome (*Life* 29). The other two priests collected tithes and returned with them to Jerusalem (*Life* 63). *T. Pe'ah* 4.3 depicts priests and Levites as standing by the threshing floor waiting to collect. Josephus also recounts two instances in which the system was abused: in one, the servants of the chief priests went to the threshing floors and took the tithes; in the other, the servants of the high priest did the same (*Antiq.* 20.181, 205f.).[3]

A farmer, faced by such requests from God's ordained clergy, would have difficulty refusing. Some, however, may have argued that another group of experts, the Pharisees, held that in years three and six they were not required to spend a tithe in Jerusalem; the Pharisees maintained that poor tithe replaced second tithe rather than being added to it. We saw above that spending second tithe in Jerusalem was an entertaining and popular thing to do. Nevertheless, people who gave poor tithe in years three and six may have felt unable to spend a third tithe in Jerusalem. In this case, they would have been grateful for the Mishnaic (presumably Pharisaic) interpretation.

We also know that some were reluctant to pay the Levites their portion of first tithe. When we discuss the Pharisees, we shall see that they debated what they should do if they bought produce from someone who may not have tithed it (that is, who may not have given first tithe). Most scholars miss the fact that the relevant passages assume that the ordinary people gave the priests their part; it was the Levites' share, nine-hundredths of the entire crop (nine-tenths of first tithe), which was imperilled. Even the Pharisees did not regard it as a transgression to eat the Levites' portion (below, pp. 429–31).

Josephus and the Mishnah agree that the tithe of cattle was not given to the temple or its employees. Josephus lists the entire revenue of the priests but does not mention an enormous tax of one of every ten animals owned (*Antiq.* 4.68–75; cf. Philo, *Spec. Laws* 1.132–57); we must assume that it was not collected. The Mishnah treats the tithe of cattle as 'holy to the Lord' in a different sense from 'given to the priests'. It interprets Lev. 27.32 as referring to second tithe: the worshippers could eat the animals in Jerusalem, or sell them and spend the money there. In the second case, the 'tithe of cattle' might end up as a shared sacrifice, an animal bought with second tithe money, sacrificed and then consumed by the offerer (except for the breast and right thigh, which went to the priest) (*Zevahim* 5.8; *Hagigah* 1.4; *Menahot* 7.5). In our period, the tithe given to the Levites and priests was agricultural produce, not animals.

According to Nehemiah, after the tithes were collected in the countryside, the priests' portion was brought to the temple and stored before being distributed (Neh. 10.38; 13.5). II Chronicles 31.11f. attributes this custom to the time of Hezekiah. Philo considered central storage and distribution worth a special comment: the priests could then receive the offerings as having come to them from God and did not need to feel shame because they were dependent on donations (*Spec. Laws* 1.152). This implies excellent facilities for storing grain, wine and oil. That the ancients knew how to keep grain for long periods is evident from the story of Joseph. Grain from seven good years was stored to meet the needs of seven years of famine (Gen. 41).

The second source of non-sacrificial food for priestly consumption was *first fruits*. First fruits constitute a large category that includes food (first produce and firstlings), money (redemption of non-edible firstlings) and fleece. Like the tithes, first fruits of food could be eaten by the priests' families, provided that they were pure.

The Bible defines *firstlings* as 'everything that opens the womb of all flesh, whether human or beast' (Num. 18.15; cf. Ex. 13.2). That is, the first time that a female bore young, the offspring, if male (Ex. 13.12f.), belonged to the Lord, and thus to the priests. Firstlings of pure animals (sheep, goats and cattle) provided red meat for priests and their families. Other firstlings were redeemed. To redeem the first-born son, the father paid five shekels; according to Josephus, impure animals (donkeys, horses, camels and the like) cost one and a half shekels (*Antiq.* 4.71). This is slightly cheaper than Num. 18.15f., which requires five shekels in both cases. It may be, however, that the firstborn of an ass was redeemed with a lamb rather than with money.[4]

As in the case of tithes, Deuteronomy has a cheaper law of firstlings: the people who raise them eat them in Jerusalem (Deut. 15.19f.). Exodus and Numbers prevailed: firstlings belonged to God, that is, to the priests. The rabbis agreed with this, but they nevertheless reduced the cost. They argued that Ex. 13.13; 34.20, by specifying that the firstling of an ass was to be redeemed by giving a lamb to the priests, meant that other impure firstlings need not be redeemed at all. The result is the same as in the case of tithes: Josephus' interpretation costs more money than does that of the rabbis (who probably inherited the Pharisees' view). Exegetically, the situation is a little different. Num. 18.15 reads literally, 'the first born of human and the first born of impure beast' in the singular. The obvious sense is that both singular nouns are used collectively, implying a plural: 'the first born of [every] impure beast'.[5] Because of the grammatical singular, however, the Pharisees or rabbis could argue that the ass of Exodus is the (one and only) impure beast of Num. 18.15. This is not a conflation of various laws (as in the case of tithes), but a simple interpretation of one law by another.[6] Again, we cannot know how many people followed each teaching, but the cheaper interpretation (assuming that it existed before 70) must have had some appeal. The total difference of cost, however, was not great, since the most common impure animal was the ass. Camels and horses were much rarer.

Presumably the redemption money for first-born sons and impure animals was evenly distributed among the priests; if so, this constituted a fairly small but nevertheless welcome cash payment. Though not a 'first', we should also list here *hides*. The hides of sin and guilt offerings went to the individual priest who presided at the sacrifice, and they too could be turned into cash (cf. *Spec. Laws* 1.151).

The *first fruits of produce* included 'the first ripe fruits of all that is in their land' (Num. 18.13) or 'of all the produce of the earth' (*Antiq.* 4.70). Further specifications are the first meal, made into a cake (Num. 15.20), and grain, fruit, wine, oil and fleece (cf. Num. 18.12; Neh. 10.35, 37; Deut. 18.4). That is, first fruits included primary and secondary produce: both raw food (grain, grapes, olives and the like) and the first things made from it (cakes, wine and oil); both the first-born lamb and the first of the year's wool.

With regard to agricultural produce, the rabbis required only the 'seven kinds' mentioned in Deut. 8.8 ('a land of wheat and barley, of vines and fig trees and pomegranates, a land of olive trees and honey'), and they further specified that dates were not brought from the hill country, that produce was not brought from the valleys and that only the choicest olives were eligible (*Bikkurim* 1.3). Josephus, on the other hand, maintained the biblical view: the first of everything that the land produced. The first fruits of agricultural produce, as we shall see immediately below, were very minor in quantity, and it is not clear that the rabbinic (possibly Pharisaic) interpretation was part of an attempt to save the small farmer money. On the other hand, the Mishnah also specifies that the law requiring the first of the fleece applies only when the farmer has many sheep (*Hullin* 11.1). Conceivably there is a moral point: keep the taxes as low as possible.

According to Exodus, the second of the three annual pilgrimage festivals (Weeks) was the 'feast of harvest, of the first fruits of your labour' (Ex. 23.16; cf. 34.22; Num. 28.26). Leviticus, however, distinguished between the offering of the first fruits of the harvest (when a sheaf of grain was waved before the Lord) and the Feast of Weeks, which was to come fifty days later and which was the time when the first cakes or loaves were brought (Lev. 23.10–17; cf. Deut. 16.9f.). Josephus follows Leviticus with regard to the separation of offerings. On the second day of Unleavened Bread (that is, early in Passover week), the first fruits of barley were offered. Josephus' details show that he is describing actual practice:

> After parching and crushing the little sheaf of ears and purifying the barley for grinding, they bring to the altar an *assarôn* [small measure] for God, and, having flung a handful thereof on the altar, they leave the rest for the use of the priests. (*Antiq.* 3.251)

This is not what Lev. 23 prescribes, which is that a sheaf (LXX *dragma*) of grain be waved before the Lord.[7] Josephus conflates Lev. 23 and 2.14, new grain 'parched with fire', and he also restricts the grain that was offered in Passover week to barley.[8] He continues: on the fiftieth day after this ceremony, at the Feast of Weeks, the loaves are presented (*Antiq.* 3.252). One assumes that the other firsts were due then as well.

Since Weeks, coming as it did just fifty days after Passover, was the least well attended festival, it is probable that only a few non-Judaeans brought their first fruits during the festival. Presumably the farmer set them aside and brought them to the temple when he had the opportunity. The Mishnah allows him any time up to Booths in the autumn (*Bikkurim* 1.10), and this is quite reasonable. A lot of people came to Booths, and many may have delayed the presentation of first fruits until then. That is, the Feast of Weeks, intended by Exodus to be the time when people presented first fruits, may have functioned in this way for a minority. The first grain (barley) was presented at Passover, and the other first fruits were presented at the farmer's convenience, often at the Feast of Booths.

For those in remote areas, who probably came only to Passover, we must consider other possibilities. Deuteronomy requires that farmers give first fruits of the harvest to a priest at the temple and make an avowal. Leviticus 23.10, in requiring that the first grain be offered during Passover, also uses the terms 'first fruits' and 'harvest'. Exegetically, then, one could link the avowal of first fruits in Deuteronomy with the presentation of first grain in Leviticus, and conceivably some people made this connection. This would have allowed those who made one annual trip to Jerusalem, at Passover, to fulfil the requirement to say the avowal before a priest. If they said the avowal at Passover, they might have given the bulk of the first fruits, when they were ready, to local priests, rather than bringing them to Jerusalem. The rabbis insist that the avowal be said at the Feast of Weeks or later, and they forbid saying it earlier (e.g. at Passover) (*Bikkurim* 1.3; cf. 1.1, 10; 3.2–6). The prohibition may show that some people thought that it could be said prior to the Feast of Weeks. The rabbinic discussion of the times when the avowal could be made supports the view that relatively few people outside of Judaea came to the Feast of Weeks; thus they needed to make the avowal at some other time.

This is an interesting question, though we cannot answer it definitively, because it shows how the ideal legislation had to be reconciled with social reality. Ideally, people went to the temple twice in the spring, offering first grain during Passover and the rest of first fruits during Weeks, at which time they said the avowal. Many Palestinian Jews could not have made both trips. Could they have fulfilled the main thrust of the biblical requirements? Possibly some said the avowal at Passover.

My basic assumption – here as throughout the book – is that other people besides the rabbis wanted to obey the law and that they considered how best to do so. A priest who lived in Upper Galilee would have seen the problem and offered some kind of advice. What we should not assume is what most scholars do assume: people either obeyed the rabbis (or Pharisees), or they were non-observant. We must always remember the very large number of people who, when push came to shove, were ready to die for the law, and who kept most of it in ordinary circumstances. Sadducees figured prominently in the great revolt and Essenes also took part. Most rebels, however, were 'ordinary people', the ʿammê ha-ʾarets of rabbinic literature, who are defined as being the people who did *not* obey all the Pharisaic/rabbinic rules. Just as later they would fight and die for Jerusalem, the temple and the law, so during the heyday of the temple they tried to fulfil their scriptural obligations. In the case of first fruits, we cannot know just how they did so. We should assume, however, intention and effort to observe the law.

First produce, first wine, first oil and first fleece were only nominal amounts, as Josephus' use of *assarōn* indicates. This is a Latinism, derived from the *assarius*, a small coin, which the RSV translates 'penny' in Matt. 10.29. It was about one-sixteenth of a denarius. Josephus uses the term to mean 'small quantity'; the Bible would lead one to think of a basketful (Deut. 26.2; cf. *Bikkurim* 3.4). It is probable that most people gave token amounts of their various 'firsts' to the priests in one way or another. The gift of firstlings and the redemption money for inedible firstlings was at least occasionally a more substantial donation than first produce and first fleece, but even rabbinic literature does not complain that people avoided these gifts.[9]

Those who took their first fruits to the temple had a prescribed avowal to say, one of the great passages of the Hebrew Bible, Deut. 26.1–11. The worshipper took his basket to the priest and said, 'I declare this day to the Lord your God that I have come into the land which the Lord swore to our fathers to give us' (26.2f.). The priest set the basket before the altar, and the worshipper continued,

> A wandering Aramaean was my father; and he went down into Egypt and sojourned there, few in number; and there he became a nation, great, mighty, and populous. And the Egyptians treated us harshly . . . Then we cried to the Lord the God of our fathers, and the Lord heard our voice, and saw our affliction . . .; and the Lord brought us out of Egypt with a mighty hand . . .; and he brought us into this place and gave us this land, a land flowing with milk and honey. And behold, now I bring the first of the fruit of the ground, which you, O Lord, have given me. (Deut. 26.3–10)

As we noted in discussing the Feast of Weeks, the avowal combines the themes of God's gift of the land and the exodus. In both cases the emphasis is on what theologians would later call the 'prevenient' grace of God. First he gives, then he requires a token back, with thanksgiving.

The third offering of food (in addition to the tithe and first fruits) was *heave offering*, Heb. *t'rûmah* (anglicized terumah). The word 'heave' would better be translated 'raised' or 'elevated', though I shall retain 'heave' because of its currency. Were it not for rabbinic literature, we could not be sure that this was a separate offering. Josephus never mentions it, nor does Philo.[10] In the Pentateuch offerings are sometimes said to be 'raised' or 'heaved up'. Thus Num. 18.11, referring to the priests' portion of the shared sacrifice (indicated by the word 'waved'), states that 'this is yours, the terumah of their gifts'. Presumably the worshipper lifted up the breast and thigh. Numbers 15.20 calls the first fruits of meal, offered as a cake or loaf, terumah. In both passages the noun terumah and cognate words (see Num. 15.20) are used to refer to offerings that have other primary names: the shared sacrifice and first fruits. 'Give your first fruits as terumah' thus means simply 'as something "offered up" to God.' In lists of sacrifices and offerings in Deut. 12.6, 17, terumah appears separately, but first fruits are not mentioned; probably it was used as an alternative term.[11]

Terumah may be a separate offering in Neh. 10.37, 39 [Heb. vv. 38, 40], though this is not entirely clear. In any case, the rabbis regarded it as a fully separate agricultural offering. Doubtless finding it referred to in the verses that we have mentioned,[12] they understood it to be a small offering of produce, not altogether unlike first fruits. 'If a man is liberal, [heave offering] is one-fortieth part (the School of Shammai say: One-thirtieth); if he is liberal in medium degree, one-fiftieth part; if he is mean, one-sixtieth part' (*Terumot* 4.3).

Did the priests, like the Pharisees and rabbis, find a distinct agricultural 'heave offering' in the Bible, and did they tell the ordinary people that they owed it? Josephus' list of priestly and temple revenues (*Antiq.* 4.68–75) counts against it. He knew what the priests received as a rule and there is no Greek term in his list that might represent the Hebrew terumah. Against this is to be set the fact that in *Antiq.* 4 he is summarizing the biblical legislation, and he may simply be listing the terms that appear in the Septuagint. As I have pointed out elsewhere, the Septuagintal translators did not regard heave offering as separate, but usually translated it 'first fruits'.[13] If Josephus' list is literary, then 'heave offering' would not appear.

The rabbis assumed not only that they should give heave offering, but that other people gave it. As we noted above, they worried about people not giving the Levites' portion of the tithe, but thought that they could be relied on to give the priests' portion. Similarly they did not worry about heave offering, which went to the priests. The lack of controversy about heave offering in rabbinic literature leads me to think that it was in fact given and received in the late second temple period, and that Josephus' list does not provide a full account of first-century practice.

The amount was not too burdensome, though even one-sixtieth would have been more produce than first fruits provided.

Finally, we note briefly the *temple tax*, which did not support the priesthood, but rather paid the temple's overhead, especially the community sacrifices (above, p. 105). Exodus 30.13–16 requires every male twenty years old or older to pay a tax of a half shekel to support the tabernacle (which preceeded the temple), apparently meaning this to be a tax that was for one time only. Nehemiah 10.32 [Heb. v. 33] levies an annual tax of one third shekel. In our period, these passages were interpreted as requiring an annual tax of one half shekel (= two drachmas), to be paid by every adult Jewish male. This is not a large sum: approximately two days' pay for a day labourer, a man at the bottom of the pay scale.[14] That it was paid is one of the things about first-century Judaism that is most certain. Aristeas referred to 'one hundred talents of silver for sacrifices and the other requirements' being sent from Alexandria to Jerusalem (*Arist.* 40).[15] Josephus and Philo agree that the sum was paid by Jews all over the world, and Josephus claimed that huge convoys brought the tax from the Jews of Babylonia. Successive Roman emperors explicitly permitted the money to be exported from other provinces to Jerusalem. As we saw above, despite this it was occasionally confiscated. After the revolt, Vespasian ordered that the same tax be paid, but that the tax base be broadened to include children and women, and that the money be paid to the temple of Jupiter Capitolinus in Rome. Receipts found in Egypt show that the tax was collected from all Jews.[16]

The entire system of sacrifices, offerings, charity, purity and consumption of food was backed up by the sternest warnings from God himself. The priests' food, for example, was sacred. Whenever the priests ate tithe, first fruits and heave offering, they had to be pure, even though these foods were eaten at home. Their families had to be pure as well in order to eat their share (Lev. 22.4–7; Num. 18.13). That is, they had to be free of corpse impurity, semen impurity and menstrual impurity, as well as the rarer conditions, leprosy and genital 'discharge' (Lev. 22.4). This is the warning that accompanies the requirement that the priests' families must eat the holy food in purity: 'They shall therefore keep my charge, lest they bear sin for it and die thereby when they profane it: I am the Lord who sanctify them' (Lev. 22.9). Not only the people but also their houses had to be free of 'leprosy' and corpse impurity ('in any pure place', Lev. 10.14).

It was a major offence for a lay person to eat the priests' holy food. Even unwitting consumption of what should go to the priests required that the same amount, plus a fifth, be given to them (Lev. 22.14). The rabbis prescribed death for intentionally consuming first fruits and heave offering (probably including 'heave offering of tithe'; that is, the priests' share of first tithe) (*Bikkurim* 2.1). They could not enforce this, but the passage points to the sacredness of the priests' food.

Ordinary Israelites had to eat and handle second tithe in purity. Worshippers were to say in the temple, and thus in the presence of God,

> I have removed the sacred portion out of my house, and moreover I have given it to the Levite, the sojourner, the fatherless, and the widow, according to all thy commandments . . . I have not eaten of the tithe while I was mourning, or removed any of it while I was unclean . . . (Deut. 26.13–14)

Most people believed in and followed these commandments. Relatively few people were brave enough to eat what belonged to the priests. Many would not eat the food that was to be given to the Levites and the poor. The ideal of the biblical legislation was not achieved, and there were inequities, but the system worked well enough to be maintained. Sacrifices, tithes and offerings were brought, food was distributed to the priests and the Levites, and some went to the poor as charity.

Cost

How burdensome were the various taxes and dues? To see this in full context, we should have to know what the situation was in other parts of the empire, what taxes were levied by successive heads of state in Palestine, and what tribute went to Rome. On many of these points our information is inadequate. We do know that in the Palestine of our period conditions varied from time to time and area to area. For part of the period Judaea was governed by a native ruler (Herod and then Archelaus; from 41 to 44 by Agrippa I), while for part of the period it was a Roman province. Galilee remained under Herodian rule longer, but after the death of Agrippa I the situation became more fluid. We can be sure that the government always demanded and received taxes. What this meant to the small but independent farmer, trader or craftsman is an extremely difficult question, and one to which there is no single answer.

There are, to be sure, long-standing and strongly held scholarly traditions about both the level of taxation and the general plight of Jewish peasants (labourers and small landowners). According to Applebaum, the Jewish peasantry was

> crushed with merciless exactions under Pompey and his successors and no less under Herod. In the latter's reign, indeed, they had to bear the double

yoke of Roman tribute and the taxation required to finance Herod's ambitious programme of internal public works and aid to Greek cities outside his kingdom.

Between 37 and 4 BCE, 'the combination of Roman tribute and Herodian taxation, with religious dues, would have been extremely oppressive'.[17] Applebaum further states that Herod's annual revenue of 900 talents would have required 'an average yearly payment per head of 3.3 drachmae, not counting religious dues' (on the optimistic assumption of a population of three million).[18] A per capita tax of that amount (had it been levied) would have been a substantial tax on a family. Further, the Jewish population was much smaller than three million, probably less than one million; the hypothetical per capita tax would thus have been much greater.

For decades, New Testament scholars have depicted the Palestinian peasantry as being in a worse plight than that described by Applebaum. Richard Horsley speaks of 'the tightening noose of institutionalized injustices such as double taxation, heavy indebtedness, and loss of land'.[19] Peasant families 'fell ever more heavily into debt under the steady economic pressures of double taxation' (p. 232), the wealthy lent them money that they could not repay, charged very high rates of interest,[20] and then foreclosed on the property, so that estates became larger and larger while more and more people were forced off the land.[21] Everything became progressively worse: society was in a downward spiral, with the number of landless people increasing every year and more smallholdings falling into the hands of creditors every year. There was 'rising indebtedness' (p. 11) and a 'declining peasantry' (p. 13); the 'social-economic infrastructure' was 'in decline' and poverty was 'worsening' (pp. 29f.). The author gives a few details about taxes: 'Roman tribute was superimposed on the tithes and other taxes'. He concludes, 'The Jewish agricultural producers were now subject to a double taxation, probably amounting to well over 40 per cent of their production' (p. 56).

According to Marcus Borg, in another recent book on Jesus, 'the various tithes[22] added up to slightly over 20 per cent per year'. Then Rome added its taxes: 'the land tax (1 per cent of its value) and crop tax (12.5 per cent of the produce)'. 'There were other Roman taxes as well (customs, toll, and tribute): but even without them, the combined total of Jewish and Roman taxes on farmers amounted to about 35 per cent. This was a crushing amount, and would be even today'.[23]

The scholars who cite percentages do not reveal how they arrived at them. My guess is that they depend, possibly indirectly, on the pioneering essay by F. C. Grant, *The Economic Background of the Gospels* (1926), who estimated that in the second year of each seven year cycle taxes amounted to thirty-five per cent in addition to the tithe for 'Hyrcanus and his sons' (that is, the high priest Hyrcanus II), which Grant incorrectly thought was different from the tithe that supported the priesthood.[24]

The views of Grant, Horsley and Borg are based on erroneous assumptions; parts of Applebaum's essay (the parts cited above) are also misleading. The common perception of the economic situation should be moderated; the situation was bad enough, and it does not need to be exaggerated. The general assessment of economic conditions lies outside the range of this book, but I shall discuss taxes, since otherwise we misunderstand the place of religious dues in the entire system. There are numerous errors in the above accounts, and the figures are overstated. I shall try to give a more accurate set. This can be done fairly successfully for the Jewish taxes, though for Roman taxes we must base assumptions on very incomplete evidence. The discussion of Herod's taxes will lead us to an observation about unemployment, both in his lifetime and earlier.

1. It is misleading to speak of the double or (in the case of Applebaum) triple taxation (Herod, Rome and the temple). I shall return to Herod, and first consider the taxation policies of Rome and the Jewish religious establishment. According to Grant, each of the two systems 'had been designed without regard to the other, and therefore could not be modified in its favour' (p. 89). In his view, the Jewish taxes had been originally intended to 'support the Government' and to 'equip and pay armies and build navies' (p. 93). While Applebaum, Horsley, Borg and others are not this explicit, the discussion of 'double' taxes implies this understanding.[25] If Roman tribute and Jewish taxes were always understood to have two different purposes, and if each system took the other into account, one could not say that Palestinian Jews paid *double* taxes. We shall see that the two systems did, in effect, take each other into account.

(a) The Jewish part of the tax system of first-century Palestine was basically post-exilic, and it had been first put into effect when Palestine was under Persia, was paying Persian tribute, and was not equipping an independent army and navy out of the temple revenue. There was no Jewish navy, just as there was no Jewish seacoast. Unfortunately, there were no ports either, and Jerusalem under the Persians did not have what Herodian Palestine had, rich duties from goods in transit. After the defeat of Persia, Palestine continued to pay tribute to the Seleucids or Ptolemies, and still did not equip its own army and navy out of temple revenue.

According to Applebaum, 'the Jewish peasantry' was 'virtually free of fiscal exactions' between the time of Simon the Hasmonean and Pompey.[26] He must base this on the assumption that the Hasmoneans' only revenue was the biblical tithe and the minor offerings. It is a comparison with the supposed Hasmonean system that leads him to speak of 'double taxation' under Herod and Rome. Under the Hasmoneans the biblical offerings paid for everything.

This is virtually impossible. The Hasmoneans had very considerable expenses, since they fought numerous wars. Possibly some, such as Jannaeus, who conquered Hellenistic cities, took a lot of booty, but booty never pays the daily bills. It satisfies the troops and the conqueror. Some of the spoils of war adorned the temple walls (*Antiq.* 15.402). Deuteronomy, Leviticus, Numbers and Nehemiah, the books that discuss the tithes and other offerings, envisage *no national army*, and they dispose of all the holy food and money by assigning it elsewhere (to be eaten in purity in Jerusalem; to support the Levites and the priests). The Hasmoneans would have had to break these biblical laws if they did not tax the people independently of the temple revenue. Ninety per cent of the only substantial agricultural offering, first tithe, went to the Levites. If they did not receive it, we cannot explain how they lived; why they continued to serve in the temple, instead of fleeing to their own fields (Neh. 13.11f.); or why the pietist literature of the period does not criticize the Hasmoneans for robbing the Levites. If the Levites did receive the tithe, the Hasmonean ruler would have had only the priests' portion of the offerings and sacrifices. Even if he appropriated all of these for himself, leaving the other priests to starve, he could not have financed his government.

The polemic against the priest/kings requires a few extra words. The pietists complained that the Hasmoneans robbed the temple treasury (*Ps. Sol.* 8.11). Whether this accusation was well founded or not, it implies that there were two pockets: one for holy money, one for the king's other expenses. The pietists did not complain that the Hasmoneans starved the Levites and priests, but that they paid for other things out of temple money. The Hasmoneans, however, could not have covered all their military and other expenses out of the temple's stored wealth, or there would have been even more complaints. Besides, the accumulated wealth would have been exhausted after a hundred years of such a policy, and it would not still have been there to be stolen by Crassus (pp. 83f. above). The accusation of theft from the temple probably referred to some occasion on which one of the Hasmoneans felt in need of extra money, as did two of the later Roman administrators. (See the comments on Pilate and Florus below.)

It is likely that when they escaped foreign tribute, the Hasmoneans reduced 'secular' taxes, though they could not have eliminated them. In this case, Judaea paid taxes to support the temple and its staff, as well as foreign tribute, for some centuries, from 515 BCE to approximately 164. The farmers then paid the temple dues and Hasmonean taxes from 164 to 63 BCE. The Roman conquest did not create a novel situation.

In short, the Jewish tax system of the second-temple period was always one part of a dual system. It never supported both the priests and the Levites as well as the needs of an army and a court.

(*b*) It is not true that Roman tribute was a fixed and inflexible system that nothing could alter,[27] nor was it imposed on any and all without regard to ability to pay. After he defeated Pompey, Julius Caesar revised or restated the financial obligations of Jewish Palestine to Rome, although unfortunately the text in Josephus does not allow us to calculate sums. The context, however, is clear: gratitude for Jewish support during his recent war with Pompey. He accordingly imposed only selective taxes, waived all tribute in the seventh year, and excused Jews in Palestine from expenses borne by residents of other parts of the empire, such as being required to billet Roman troops (*Antiq.* 14.202–10). These are not the actions of an empire that has inflexible tax rules, nor of an empire that levies the same tribute no matter what the local conditions. We must assume that when Caesar revised Palestine's liability for tribute, he levied an amount that was payable. His attitude was quite different from that of Vespasian after the great revolt, who did punish the Jewish people by taxes, as well as in other ways.

The exemption of Jewish Palestine from special imposts is very important.[28] This is Rostovtzeff's comment on taxes in the early empire: taxation was 'highly differentiated . . . and based on the traditions prevailing in the various parts of the Empire'. It was 'not very oppressive'. Rostovtzeff continues:

> The direct taxes – the land-tax and the poll-tax – were paid in the various provinces in accordance with their traditions . . . If the provinces complained of their burdens, it was not because of the taxes. What bore heavily on them was the extraordinary payments, the provisioning of the armies and of the officials by means of compulsory deliveries, the war requisitions, the spasmodic confiscations, and the forced work. The responsibility for the assessment and the collection of the taxes was not resented as a very heavy burden by the municipal aristocracy. What they complained of was the responsibility for the extraordinary burdens imposed on the population . . .[29]

It was precisely these extraordinary burdens from which Caesar exempted Palestine, and there is no indication in Josephus that the exemption was removed at any time before the outbreak of the revolt. We hear of two cases in which the Roman administrator ignored the exemption and levied special charges: Pilate confiscated some of the temple's funds for a very good civic purpose, the water supply, and Florus took money from the same source for 'the imperial service'. In both cases the resentment was so great, and the demonstrations were so loud, that we may be sure that it was very rare for a Roman official to meet special needs in this way.[30] Josephus is silent about other extraordinary charges, such as a special tax on produce, though he was eager to list Roman provocations in order to explain Jewish outbursts. We may be confident that some of the traditional 'rights' of empires were not exercised in Jewish Palestine. Certainly Roman troops were never billeted on the population of Jerusalem. My guess is that most of the time Roman taxes were limited to the standard tribute.

(c) Applebaum states that under Herod Palestinian Jews paid triple taxes: they 'had to bear the double yoke of Roman tribute and the taxation required to finance Herod's ambitious programme . . .', in addition to the religious taxes.[31] We shall see below that Herod's buildings were not financed entirely by taxes. Here we note that he paid Roman tribute out of his total income. One cannot add tribute to his total expenses, as if not part of them. Everyone recognizes that Rome levied tribute by requiring local leaders to pay it.[32] They could, of course, turn to the people and collect it from them (so the members of the Jerusalem council in 66 CE: *War* 2.405). Herod, however, had several sources of income, and tribute was simply one expense among others, all of which he paid from his total revenue. Rome's taxes were not added to his.

(d) It is not true that only Palestine had two levels of taxes, imperial and local. Most areas did. Further, more-or-less everyone had had dual taxes from time immemorial. Rostovtzeff pointed out that Rome charged tribute in accordance with local traditions (quoted above). Asia Minor, for example, had the same history as Palestine: first it was under the Persians, then under Alexander, then under one of his successors, then under Rome. New imperial powers did not suddenly and drastically change the level of tribute.[33] Rather, in cases of need they made special demands, as Rostovtzeff pointed out.

Thus we may conclude that the dual taxation that so many believe was especially oppressive in Palestine was standard in the Roman empire, as in other empires, and that Rome's requirement of tribute took into account the local conditions. It is especially noteworthy that Caesar's decree refers to the obligation to pay the Levitical tithe and also acknowledges that no tribute could be collected in the seventh year, when the land lay fallow (*Antiq.* 14.202f.). I do not mean that imperial bureaucrats annually surveyed agricultural productivity and sympathetically adjusted the tribute when necessary. But the initial tribute set by Caesar took local conditions into account, and a drastic revision would have left a mark in Josephus' history. As we noted above, he was keen to cite individual examples of Roman mismanagement, since they served to explain the revolt and to shift the blame off the Jewish people. A major new tax probably would have provoked some sort of protest, and Josephus would have mentioned it.

A last word with regard to the supposed 'double' taxes of the Roman period. Scholarly criticisms of Rome, Herod and the chief priests for their heavy taxation are based on comparison with another system, whether it is expressed or implied. Both Applebaum and Horsley compare the expenses of farmers in our period to costs in other periods. Both of them romanticize the other period. We saw above that Applebaum compares the situation under Rome and Herod to the Hasmonean period, when the farmers were 'virtually free of fiscal exactions'. Horsley writes more vaguely about the 'earlier' biblical legislation, when taxes benefitted the farmer instead of supporting a centralized temple and priesthood.[34] Just as I do not believe that the Hasmoneans left the people untaxed, I do not believe that, after the time of David, there was a period with no taxes to support centralized institutions. Under Solomon, the temple probably had no distinct power of taxation, but Solomon did, and he paid for the temple and its upkeep. Ever after, taxes were paid to a central Jewish government, except during the Babylonian exile. Deuteronomy (which Horsley seems to have in mind) does not describe the exilic period, nor does it give a full account of any historical period. It is idealistic; and its idealism is the basis of Horsley's judgment that things were much worse in the first century.[35]

2. The local 'religious' taxes of Jewish Palestine did not make it unique in the ancient world, and special features moderated the cost. Although the expense of the Jewish temple was higher than that of the average temple in the empire (above, pp. 49f.), other countries had more than one temple. In any case, all cities had temples and local expenses of all sorts. Support of the Jerusalem temple also supported local government, since the temple guards served as the 'police force', and the priests fulfilled many administrative and juridical functions (see ch. 10).

Further, in Jerusalem the heaviest cost of the sacrifices themselves, the burnt offerings (two six days a week, four on sabbaths, many more on New Moons, festivals and the Day of Atonement), was defrayed by non-Palestinians. Community sacrifices were paid for by the two-drachma temple tax, donated by Jews throughout the world. It was probably foreign money, not local, that largely accounted for the temple's wealth. In one of the moderate portions of his essay, Applebaum takes this into account, and he quite reasonably finds it impossible to decide whether or not Jewish Palestine had a net foreign exchange surplus. That is, the temple's income from abroad may have been as great as the entire nation's foreign expenditures (the purchase of imported goods; Herod's gifts to foreign cities). Applebaum even points out that the payments of Mesopotamian Jews to the temple helped to offset the *empire*'s imports of spices and other luxury items from the east.[36] The cost of the temple lay less heavily on the shoulders of Palestinians than most people recognize. I should emphasize that in Applebaum's essay the taxes for the temple and priesthood do not loom large; his essay in some ways counts against a substantial part of the position of Grant, Horsley and Borg.

3. Applebaum's statements about Herod's taxes ('crushing', 3.3 drachmas a head) are, as several parts of his own essay show, dubious. Herod *created* a lot of new wealth. To mention two prominent examples: he developed Jericho (both industry and agricultural goods) and Caesarea, including especially the port. These and some other parts of the country were crown lands. Herod had received Jericho as a gift from Augustus; it had previously belonged to Cleopatra. It had always produced wealth for its owner; under Herod its productivity was increased.[37] Caesarea, which Herod built from almost nothing, may not have turned much of a profit during his lifetime, since it was not complete until about six years before his death, though he would not have had to wait that long before using the harbour. Applebaum points out, however, that Herod controlled several trade routes from the Orient to the empire, not just the port at Caesarea; thus he earned revenue from customs and transit charges. Applebaum reasonably suggests that the control of this trade may have been one of the factors that led Herod to give benefactions to Greek cities in Asia Minor, whose citizens consumed some of the eastern luxury goods that passed through his ports.[38]

Herod's income, from which he financed his grandiose building schemes, then, was by no means derived entirely from the labour of Palestinian peasants. Applebaum points this out; therefore his estimate of how much money Herod would have had to raise in taxes in order to meet his total expenditure is misleading. We cannot give figures or percentages, but it is entirely conceivable that Herod's revenue from crown lands, ports and enterprises exceeded his tax revenue. Applebaum[39] proposes that he spent more than he earned, which may be true, but a lot of the money was new wealth, and a fair amount came from abroad (charges for goods in transit; profits derived from exports from the crown holdings).

Moreover, a lot of Herod's expenditure was ploughed back into the local economy. Applebaum calls many of his building schemes 'unproductive monuments'.[40] The temple, however, was not unproductive; Herod's expansion, which included additional space for shops, served pilgrims, who brought a lot of money, a good deal of which came from other countries. Moreover, Herod's projects provided employment for thousands. According to Josephus, when the temple was finally completed, long after Herod's death, 18,000 people were thrown out of work, and Agrippa II had to find a new project to employ some of them (*Antiq.* 20.219). During Herod's lifetime, the number of labourers must have been much larger, since he carried out numerous massive building projects, some of which ran concurrently (the temple, Caesarea, a series of palaces at Jericho, fort-palaces at Matsada and the Herodium, Sebaste (Samaria), and others).

4. This last point suggests that scholars tend to exaggerate the number of the unemployed. Applebaum finds references to them in various places, such as *War* 1.153, where they are not mentioned,[41] but more importantly in Josephus' reports of 'bandits' or 'brigands'. According to Applebaum, there was a vast increase of such people, especially in the years from 40 to 66; the bandits were 'the landless tenantry and labouring class'.[42] This is a common view,[43] but again we need to be cautious. The people whom Josephus termed 'bandits' or 'brigands' may have been impoverished, but not necessarily. We saw above a 'brigand' who objected to Herod while he was campaigning in Galilee.[44] There is no reason to think that his protest was socio-economic; Herod at the time did not control the economy of the country. When used in describing the events of 40–66, the term 'brigand' allows Josephus to present his own (apologetic) case to Rome: the only rebellious Jews were brigands; every insurrection was just the act of bandits; Jews were otherwise easy to govern and respected Rome's authority.[45] It is, to be sure, reasonable for us to think that few of the well-to-do engaged in insurrections,[46] but we cannot know that the issues were always landlessness and unemployment, and so we should not claim to have proved the hypothesis that the country was impoverished when we point out that there were insurgents. There were poor people and there were rebels; some people were doubtless both. But Josephus' use of 'brigand' or 'bandit' does not prove that the rebels were landless and unemployed.

Nor does Josephus' account prove that poverty was *increasing* all the time. The assumption that it was is based on combining the theory that the rebels were the landless and unemployed with the view that there were more and more insurrections, involving larger and larger numbers, as the great revolt neared. This second view corresponds to Josephus' own presentation, which most scholars have accepted. But, as we saw above, this aspect of his narrative reveals dramatic art.[47] Further, some of the tumults demonstrably had nothing to do with poverty. When a Galilean was killed during a conflict between the Samaritans and a group of Galilean pilgrims passing through their country, there was a major disturbance. The Syrian legate had to be called in. Some of the notables were sent to Rome for trial.[48] It is quite wrong to interpret such incidents as proving that greater and greater poverty led to more and more insurrections, which is what happens when one counts conflicts between 40 and 66 and attributes upheavals in general to increasing poverty. (This event took place when Cumanus was procurator, between 48 and 52 CE.)

We cannot estimate total unemployment at any given time, since joblessness
has numerous causes. I have been concerned here to make two limited points:
First, from the time of Herod until the outbreak of the revolt, construction
projects greatly reduced the number of the unemployed; the story about the
appeal to Agrippa II, and his partial agreement, shows that people were aware
of the value of this policy. Therefore it worked; to what extent we cannot know.
Secondly, Josephus' references to brigands – cited in favour of the view that
there was mass unemployment – are apologetic and thus may be misleading.
The wealthy seldom engaged in insurrections, but the less well off sometimes
did and sometimes did not. Further, occasionally even the aristocrats were
ready to take up arms (as the revolt shows). Even if we had statistics about how
many people demonstrated in the streets, or how many clashes there were
between Jews and Romans, we still would not know how bad unemployment
was.

5. The estimates of the total percentage of earnings that went to taxes,
which are offered by Grant, Horsley, Borg and others – Applebaum, wisely,
offers none – are in part wrong and in part sheer guesswork. We do not know
what Roman tribute was at any given time. Borg offers two figures: a land tax of
1 per cent of the capital value and a crop tax of 12.5 per cent. The second of
these is taken from Stern, who cites *Antiq.* 14.203.[49] That passage, however, is
not clear. Josephus wrote that Caesar decreed that 'in the second year they shall
pay the tribute at Sidon, consisting of one fourth of the produce sown'. Stern
does not give his reasoning, but it appears that he took 'in the second year' to
mean 'every other year', and so he put the crop tax at 12.5 per cent. Neither
Stern nor Josephus says anything about a capital tax on land. Caesar's decree in
Antiq. 14, by not mentioning a land tax, seems to exclude it. Borg apparently
takes that tax from information about Syria in the days of Appian (second
century).[50] Borg further increases Roman taxes by writing that tribute was in
addition to these taxes. But the produce tax *was* tribute, the only tribute
mentioned in our sources that was paid by the ordinary Jewish citizens.[51]

The amount of the Roman produce tax, as levied by Caesar, is uncertain.
About Roman tribute in subsequent periods we are entirely ignorant. Stern's
guess that Caesar required 12.5 per cent is not unreasonable, but Stern also
wrote that 'we have no information on the total sum collected [by Rome] in
taxes in Judaea, or whether the Roman government of the province enjoyed a
surplus of revenue over expenditure'.[52]

Borg is equally wrong about tithes. He thinks that there were two, totalling
20 per cent. We have seen, however, that in most years the second tithe was
consumed by those who produced it. It was given away only two years in each
seven year cycle: the outlay was eight tithes in the six productive years of the
seven year cycle, or 13.33 per cent on average.

Let us try to estimate the size of a farmer's payments to the temple, the priests and the Levites. In order to have figures to work with, we shall imagine a farmer at the very bottom, earning a bare subsistence, whose crops were worth 500 drachmas. (I assume that a day-labourer, at the bottom of the economic ladder, earned a drachma for a day's work,[53] and I put the annual income of a small farmer somewhat higher.) For the purpose of this exercise I shall also assume that the farmer had neither a flock nor a herd, but only a pair of asses. His taxes were as follows (costs are in drachmas):

first tithe	50.00
poor tithe (avg: 500 − 50 × 10% ÷ 3)	15.00
first fruits	nominal
heave offering (450 ÷ 50)	9.00
temple tax	2.00
TOTAL	76.00
Percentage	15.2%

Let us say that our farmer had a bad year: one first-born son, one first-born male donkey. These cost him 6.5 shekels, 26 drachmas. This would be pretty well the worst possible case – his wife and his female ass would each have a first-born male offspring only once. In such an exceptional year his total taxes would be 102 drachmas, 20.4 per cent. Since two of the taxes are flat rate (temple tax and first-borns), they would be a smaller percentage of the income of anyone more prosperous. With regard to Roman taxes, I shall follow Stern, who, in trying to make sense of the passage in Josephus, guessed that farmers paid 12.5 per cent of their crops to Rome. Since no other tribute is mentioned, and since we receive no news about dramatic tax increases, I shall use this figure for both the Roman and the Herodian period. On this assumption, our hypothetical farmer's total taxes in most years would be under 28 per cent; in the worst possible case they would be 33 per cent, a good deal less than Borg's estimate of 35 per cent *in addition to* customs, tolls and tribute, and also less than Horsley's 'well over 40 per cent'.

Jews who made the full contributions to the temple and charity paid a lot in taxes and dues. Second tithe counted as festival and holiday money, and it was probably not felt to be a tax. People who observed Josephus' fourteen tithe system paid a further 10 per cent every three or four years to the poor. Those who observed the Mishnah's twelve tithe system gave money to charity instead of going to a festival two years out of seven. First tithe was a substantial impost, and we have noted that many people tried to avoid paying it in full. They probably would rather have given it to the Levites than to Herod or Rome, but about these they had no choice. The gifts that went to the priests, as distinct from the Levites, seem to have been paid by most. This judgment is based on rabbinic literature, and we shall see the passages when we discuss the Pharisees. The priestly gifts, however, were fairly light: one hundredth of the crops as first tithe; a firstling once during the lifetime of each ewe, cow and nanny goat, one and a half shekels for other firstlings; five shekels for the first-born son; token amounts of first fruits of produce, wine, oil and fleece; one thirtieth to one sixtieth of agricultural produce as heave offering. One half shekel went towards the temple's overhead. These offerings and dues are not terribly burdensome, and probably most people paid them fairly cheerfully. The failure of the rabbis to complain that the priests' dues were not paid is striking.

Nevertheless, the people were hard pressed. Modern scholars are in one sense right to speak of their 'oppression'. The wealthy did not sit down each night and try to devise ways of making the peasantry more comfortable. The populace was a resource to be utilized. Not all rulers managed their greatest natural resource with equal wisdom and moderation. No ruler wanted a tax revolt, but the general tendency was to press the populace as hard as possible without causing one. Both Syria and Judaea complained of heavy Roman tribute in 17 CE (Tacitus, *Annals* 2.42),[54] but they did not revolt, as did several of the states in Gaul two years later (according to Tacitus, because of heavy debts: *Annals* 3.40–6). Suppression of the uprising in Gaul required only small forces in one area but the deployment of two legions in another, though the actual battle seems to have been minor. Economic conditions in Egypt were especially severe.[55]

Financial hardship has more often than not been the fate of small farmers. In our own time, we have seen the widespread impoverishment of farmers in Mexico and, most recently, in parts of the United States. Small farmers in the Judaean hills today do little more than eke out a living. The lot of first-century Palestinian farmers was doubtless difficult, but they had enough money to attend the festivals, and most seem to have been able to survive the sabbatical years. Things could have been worse, and in some places they were.

The central importance of first-century Jewish Palestine as the cradle of two great religions has the effect of making people today think that what was going on there was extraordinary. One of the manifestations of that view is the feeling that it was a society in *crisis*. Things were desperate. Something had to give. The system could not continue. After all, it did not continue. In historical perspective, however, the social and economic situation was not very remarkable. The Jewish peasants acted very much like the peasants of Syria or Anatolia; Herod acted very much like a minor king (although more so); Rome played the part of a great empire to perfection. What was *peculiar* to the situation was not taxation and a hard-pressed peasantry, but the Jewish combination of theology and patriotism. Any disregard of national tradition was offensive to God, and people loyal to God knew that he would save them. I have, however, digressed. The full unfolding of this theme lies ahead, in ch. 14 and in Part III.

10

The Priests and Levites Outside the Temple

Jobs and responsibilities

When not serving in the temple (which required one week in every twenty-four, plus the pilgrimage festivals), the priests and Levites could see to their private affairs. Many lived in Jerusalem, not all, though we cannot say much more about the density and distribution of the clerical population. According to Nehemiah 11.18, at that time 284 Levites lived in Jerusalem. Previous verses number 1,192 priests (Neh. 11.10–14), and this may be the number of priests in Jerusalem. Above we noted that Hecataeus said that there were 1,500 men who received tithes and were responsible for administration. It seems from these bits of information that, about 450–300 BCE, there were approximately 1,500 priests and Levites who resided in Jerusalem. We have also seen that the total number of priests and Levites rose by the first century. It is not unreasonable to suppose that a few thousand priests and Levites lived in Jerusalem in Josephus' day. The rest lived in the cities of Judaea and Galilee, but we have no idea of their distribution. It has sometimes been suggested that Sepphoris in Galilee, a wealthy city, and one that stayed pro-Roman in the revolt, was the home of a high priestly family.[1] Although the evidence is not entirely convincing,[2] it is suggestive. If aristocratic priests lived anywhere other than Jerusalem, Sepphoris is the most probable city. We may assume, in any case, that the ordinary priests were scattered through the main parts of the country.

It is very probable that in their towns and villages they were teachers and magistrates. Tiberias, which was contaminated by corpse-impurity, presumably made do without priests. In most parts of Palestine, however, the priests probably assumed the leadership roles that were traditional to them. These included teaching the law and serving as judges; in both tasks, at least in the late biblical period, they were assisted by the Levites (e.g. Neh. 8.7–9; I Chron. 23.3–6; II Chron. 17.7–9; 19.8–11). Priests and Levites were often scribes, a title that covers a range of activities: copying texts, drawing up legal documents and serving as experts on the law. The precedent was set by Ezra (fifth century BCE). He was a priest, but equally he was a 'scribe skilled in the law of Moses' (Ezra 7.6). When he expounded the law in Jerusalem, attempting to establish or re-establish certain practices, he was assisted by the Levites (Neh. 8.9–12). Similarly one of the treasurers appointed by Nehemiah was 'Zadok the scribe' (Neh. 13.13), whose name marks him as being also a priest. The post-exilic biblical evidence uniformly points to the fact that the priests (and Levites, at least a few of them) were 'scribes' in the sense of studying, teaching and enforcing the law. One assumes that they could read and write and that some of them were able to draw up documents and copy texts. II Chronicles 19.5–11, purporting to describe an earlier time, but reflecting post-exilic practice, names 'certain Levites and priests and heads of families' as being the magistrates.

Deuteronomy places the law in the hands of the priests: Moses consigned his books to the priests 'and to all the elders of Israel' (Deut. 31.9), and the king was instructed to write out for himself a copy of the law that was 'in [the] charge of the Levitical priests' (17.18).

This situation continued in the post-biblical period and into the first century, if anything becoming more pronounced rather than less. Ben Sira regarded the priests as the nation's teachers (Ben Sira 45.17), a position that he does not accord the elders. The Dead Sea community expected the King-Messiah to defer to the priests in all legal matters (4QpIsa),[3] which goes beyond Deut. 17.18. Josephus also surpassed Deut. 17.18: he attributed to Moses the commandment 'to let [the king] do nothing without the high priest and the council of elders' (*Antiq.* 4.24). In summarizing Deut. 31, in which Moses consigns the law to the priests and the elders, Josephus left out the elders (*Antiq.* 4.304). In general, Josephus regarded the priests as the nation's rulers and judges: God assigned administration to 'the whole body of priests', who exercised 'general supervision' and also tried cases and punished malefactors (*Apion* 2.165, a 'theocracy'; 2.184–7). Later he states that the high priest governed 'with his colleagues' (*Apion* 2.194), and on another occasion he attributes to the nation the view that it was 'the custom of the country' to be ruled by priests (*Antiq.* 14.41).

Other evidence in Josephus reveals the priests' role as expert interpreters of the Bible. In one interesting passage this is conveyed indirectly, which makes it all the more convincing. During the revolt, the Pharisee Simeon b. Gamaliel persuaded the revolutionary council in Jerusalem to investigate Josephus' conduct of the war in Galilee. Everyone assumed that what was required was *biblical* expertise; as we shall see more fully immediately below, knowledge was not divided into sub-categories. An expert in the Bible was an expert in everything, including war. The investigating committee consisted of four men, 'of different classes of society but of equal standing in education'. Two members were 'from the lower ranks and adherents of the Pharisees'; the third was both a priest and a Pharisee; the fourth was 'descended from high priests'. Since they were all expert, they could stand up to Josephus and not be put to rout by his superior knowledge of the Bible and the ancestral customs (*Life* 196–8). What is interesting about this is that Josephus assumes that the reader will know that the priests knew the law; he has to explain that the two non-priestly Pharisees, even though they were from the ordinary people, nevertheless knew the law.

The next evidence is slightly more complicated. Josephus regarded himself as a great expert on the law (*Life* 9), and his work bears out this self-appraisal. He was also competent to understand prophecy, as this description of himself shows: 'a priest himself, and of priestly descent, he was not ignorant of the prophecies in the sacred books' (*War* 3.252). At this point in his narrative, he is explaining how he came to the view that God had foreordained that Rome would and should win the war and that Vespasian would be emperor. This had been partially revealed to him in dreams, and he was an expert interpreter of those as well. He combined the two sources of information – dreams and scripture – in coming to his new view of the will of God (*War* 3.350–54).[4] This is all, of course, self-serving. He is arguing that in going over to the Roman side he was not a traitor, but that he acted in accordance with the will of God as he deduced it from dreams and scripture. What is of interest in this argument is that he simply assumes that, as a priest, he was expert. As an individual, he was more expert than most, but interpretation of scripture was, in his view, a priestly function. Later he describes 'sacred scribes' as rightly reading portents of Jerusalem's destruction (*War* 6.291). The term *hierogrammateus* is more literally translated 'priestly scribe'. Most of his other uses of the term refer to priests who were advisors to the Egyptian Pharaoh (*Antiq.* 2.205, 209, 234, 255).

Expertise was expertise. Specialization of knowledge was not as fully developed as it is in modern universities. Experts in the Bible were not an entirely separate group from experts in astronomy, esoteric lore, interpreting dreams and waging war. We should not, however, make one-to-one equations. There were other biblical experts besides priests, and Josephus singles out the Pharisees in this regard. There could also be non-priestly interpreters of dreams and non-priestly soothsayers. Conversely, not all priests were equally adept at everything. Most modern scholars, however, think that in the Judaism of Josephus' day the priests had *surrendered* their traditional role as biblical experts and magistrates (judging cases on the basis of biblical law), and that the Pharisees or lay scribes had taken over these roles. Some scholars tend to equate Pharisees with lay scribes, some to keep them formally separate, while allowing for a large overlap; most assume the dominance of lay Pharisaic or scribal experts over the priesthood. The present argument is that priests maintained their traditional responsibilities, though they did not have a monopoly of them.

We have not yet discussed the Pharisees, and so it is premature to try to decide how to balance their claims to authority against those of the non-Pharisaic priests. I do wish, however, to let the reader know the degree to which my description of the priests as teachers and magistrates differs from that of most scholars. The standard view that the priests withdrew from study, teaching, judging, and serving as legal experts is part of a complex myth about late second-temple Judaism. Chronologically the myth runs like this: At an early date, at least by 200 BCE, lay scribes (scribes in the sense of biblical experts) began to be very influential. The high priests moved towards Hellenization, and the law fell into the hands of the laity. These lay scribes were on the whole Pharisees. Their titles changed: from 'scribe' to 'sage' to 'rabbi', but there was a continuing succession of people who led the religious life of the nation, who were not priests, who were Pharisees or close to the Pharisees, and whose ultimate successors were the rabbis of the Mishnah. These scribes developed 'oral law', later written down in rabbinic literature. This law governed the country. By the New Testament period, the transfer of learning, knowledge and spiritual leadership from the priesthood to the laity was 'fully completed'.[5]

Meanwhile, the Pharisees (whose leaders were scribes) were taking control directly. There was a central legislative and judicial body, called the Sanhedrin, which governed Palestinian and, to some degree, Diaspora Judaism. From the time of Salome Alexandra the Pharisees were in the majority. Rulers governed in collaboration with the Sanhedrin, but it was the Sanhedrin that passed legislation, ruled on the interpretation of biblical law and judged serious cases. Thus on two fronts the Pharisees won: they controlled the legislative/judicial body, and as the principal experts on the law they controlled religious life and worship.

Here we are considering only one part of this reconstruction: the priests no longer served as legal experts, teachers and magistrates, but had turned these duties over to the laity, led by the Pharisees. I have thus far proposed that some priests and Levites, when not on duty in the temple, continued their traditional roles as scribes (in the various meanings of the term) and magistrates. We shall note below that many had some other occupation when not in the temple; just now I wish to pursue the question of priests and Levites as scribes and magistrates.

This topic requires careful consideration, since it is not possible to settle it by quoting passages. There is very little positive evidence about the identity of scribes and magistrates in our period. The handbooks on Jewish history, however, say that there is conclusive evidence about *scribes*, and they further claim that the evidence proves the reconstruction that I above labelled a 'myth': scribes were laymen and were led by Pharisees. Unfortunately I shall have to spend a few pages on these claims. I shall take Jeremias as an example, because his treatment is more compact than that of Schürer, though much of what follows could be exemplified from Schürer.

Jeremias made the standard claim that the important posts in Jewish public life had, by the first century, passed out of the hands of the priestly aristocracy and into the hands of lay scribes, most of whom he identified as Pharisees. Lay scribes, he said, far outnumbered priestly scribes.[6] Scribes were called 'Rabbi', and 'only [these] ordained teachers transmitted and created the tradition derived from the Torah which, according to Pharisaic teaching which the mass of the people respected, was regarded as equal to . . ., and indeed above the Torah . . .'[7] The view that 'Pharisaic teaching' was 'above the Torah' is directly contrary to the rabbis' opinion of non-biblical traditions, which presumably continues the Pharisaic view.[8]

Jeremias then claims to give the result of plebiscites:

> When a community was faced with a choice between a layman and a scribe for nomination to the office of elder to a community, of 'ruler of the synagogue', or of judge, it invariably preferred the scribe. This means that a large number of important posts hitherto held by priests and laymen of high rank, had, in the first century AD passed entirely, or predominantly into the hands of scribes.[9]

He gives no evidence for the first sentence, about nominations and elections, which is understandable, since there is no evidence and there were, as far as we know, no elections. There are of course a lot of passages about priests and laymen of high rank. Subsequently Jeremias states that 'Pharisaic scribes were by far the most numerous' and that 'it was a fact . . . that even before the destruction of the Temple the Sadducean scribes exercised in public life a very much less important role than the Pharisaic scribes', citing *Antiq.* 18.17, which does not mention scribes. We shall eventually study what it says about Pharisees and Sadducees. Finally, he proposes that not all Pharisees were scribes, but only the leading Pharisees. He gives names of people from rabbinic literature as scribes, though the term is missing from the texts.[10]

These assertions come in the midst of evidence that shows that the priests were traditionally the teachers and magistrates, which he cites. Then he simply says that in the first century it was no longer true. The 'no longer true' part, like the claims that most scribes were Pharisees and that communities held elections and always voted for scribes, rests on no evidence at all.

The lack of evidence requires a few more words. At two different points Jeremias lists the names of people whom he calls 'scribes'. In the early days, he writes, some scribes were priests, such as R. Hananiah (*Avot* 3.2) and the chief priest Simon (*Life* 197). These passages, however, contain the names but not the title 'scribe'. This is generally the case in Jeremias' passages.[11] After listing a few priests whom he has decided to call scribes, Jeremias, for the most part citing rabbinic passages, lists other people, whom he also calls scribes, but to whom the title is not given in the literature. He occasionally digresses to Christian literature and writes that Paul was a scribe (though we know that Paul needed a secretary). He then states that the non-priestly scribes 'far outnumbered the rest'.[12] In a subsequent passage, arguing that Pharisaic leaders were scribes, he again lists names, such as Jose b. Joezer (*Hagigah* 2.7) and Abtalion and Shemaiah, whom he calls scribes. After giving a substantial list, he states that there were many more Pharisaic scribes than he is able to name.[13] But he named none. In listing scribes he failed to mention the most obvious single case, Nahum the 'Scrivener' (*Pe'ah* 2.6), as Danby translates *liblar*, a loan word from the Latin *librarius*, used in rabbinic Hebrew to mean a clerk, copyist or scribe. From Josephus, he might have mentioned the scribe (secretary or assistant) of Eleazar, the aristocratic priest who helped inspire the revolt (*Antiq.* 20.208f.). These two men are actually called 'scribes'.

In Jeremias' two lists, there is virtually no evidence about scribes at all. (That is, there is none as far as I have noted.) Why he chose some people and not others for the title I do not know. I have looked at his comprehensive list of the scribes of Jerusalem[14] without discovering the common denominator. But once he starts identifying individuals named in rabbinic literature as 'scribes', the conclusion that there were many more Pharisaic than priestly scribes is inevitable. Rabbinic literature names a lot of Pharisees, many more rabbis, no Sadducees and not many priests. This kind of 'proof' is rather like opening the volume of the Manhattan phone directory that covers A to E and concluding that in New York there are more people named Cohen than Weiss and Weissmann combined.

Students and other scholars, of course, suppose that Jeremias' claims are supported by evidence and that a study of the passages that he cites has shown that the Pharisees came to dominate the ranks of the scribes and that the priests dropped out. In fact, he produced no evidence. The influence of the phrase 'scribes and Pharisees' in Matt. 23 probably lies behind it all.

Jeremias' overall view about Pharisees and priests (leaving aside his 'proof' from 'scribes') is held by most scholars. According to Hyam Maccoby, the Priests, as such, had no teaching role and had no power to pronounce on matters of religious doctrine or practice. This was the province of the Wise Men, or Rabbis, who, for their part, had no role in the service of the Temple.[15]

He continues by stating that 'the priests not only lacked teaching authority; they never even claimed it', and that the division between priest and teacher was old and standard in Judaism. He cites Moses, who was not a priest,[16] overlooking the passages, cited above, that indicate that Moses turned the law over to the priests, the fact that Ezra was a priest, Ben Sira's statement that priests were teachers, and so on.

Tessa Rajak similarly states that 'by far the greatest number of educational institutions . . . were certainly under the auspices of the sages . . .' The sages, in turn, were 'the creators and transmitters of the Rabbinic tradition', and they are to be identified as Pharisees.[17] The truth is that it is impossible to count schools. We shall elsewhere consider the view that 'rabbinic tradition' existed throughout the period, having been formed by the earliest sages.[18] Further, Rajak held that 'priests were not especially renowned in Jewish tradition for their interpretation of the Holy Scriptures' and that 'from the time of Ezra, this had been the province of the scribes'. This is a worse error than Maccoby's. Maccoby left Ezra out, Rajak claimed that he was not a priest, though he was, and a Zadokite at that (Neh. 7.1–6). Supposing that he was not a priest, Rajak uses this 'fact' to count against Josephus' claim that his expertise in biblical interpretation was connected with his being a priest. Against his self-description, she states that the priests did not claim 'any special relationship with the Torah'[19] – though the two people whom she cites, Ezra and Josephus, quite clearly did.

I offer one more example of the assumption that only Pharisees cared about the law and teaching. An inscription found in Jerusalem gives some information about a Greek-speaking synagogue dedicated to the study of the law:

Theodotus the son of Vettenus, priest and ruler of the synagogue, son of a ruler of the synagogue, son's son of a ruler of the synagogue, built the synagogue for reading of the law and for teaching of the commandments, also the strangers' lodging and the chambers and the conveniencies of waters for an inn for them that need it from abroad, of which (synagogue) his fathers and the elders and Simonides did lay the foundation.[20]

Hengel says that Theodotus was a Pharisee.[21] What is clear here is that the rulers of the synagogue were priests, three generations of them, and very prosperous priests at that. If we must assign them to a party, the Sadducean would be the most likely guess, but there is no reason to think that they represented a party. What we learn from the inscription is that a family of wealthy priests who could speak Greek built and maintained a synagogue for Greek-speaking pilgrims, and that the synagogue had the dual purpose of serving as a guest house and a place of instruction. The inscription supports the evidence of the literature: it was the priests who taught the law. I assume that Hengel identified the priest as a Pharisee because of the assumption that *only* Pharisees taught.

This is an assumption that has endured over decades and has been accepted by scholars on all sides, both Christian and Jewish. Of the scholars cited here, only Jeremias and the original Schürer thought that evidence needed to be given. We have examined Jeremias' evidence, which is not greatly different from Schürer's.[22] On inspection, it turns out to be worthless. Everybody else, however, has simply inherited a view of first-century Palestine that can be shown to be in error; but that is because they supposed that the experts had done their home work.

Contrary to the standard claims, then, there is relatively little positive evidence of the identity of 'scribes' in the sense of legal experts and teachers of the law. What there is points towards the conclusion that priests had not vacated the field. Besides the literature summarized above (pp. 170–2), we have also just seen the single piece of inscriptional evidence from Palestine, which says that a priestly family headed a synagogue and taught the law. From the Diaspora comes slight and indirect evidence. According to Philo, sabbath instruction was led by a priest or elder, and a later inscription from a synagogue in Asia Minor refers to a priest who was also a sage or wise man.[23]

That priests served as *magistrates* and judges, those who applied the law, besides being directly stated by Josephus (*Apion* 2.187), is confirmed by the story of the healing of a leper in Mark 1.40–45. Jesus cured him, and then told him to show himself to the priest, who alone could determine whether or not the former leper was now cleansed.

Pharisees did, to be sure, teach in Jerusalem, as did Essenes,[24] and I do not wish for a moment to suggest that there were not lay teachers who had their own followings. Such there clearly were. Some people in need of a legal decision, a 'judgment', might have asked a Pharisee. This does not mean, however, that priests no longer served as judges and advisers on the law.

Rabbinic literature, of course, gives the impression that rabbis knew things and decided everything and that the priests were ignorant and had to be constantly tutored by Pharisaic sages. The reader of the tractate *Nega'im*, on the identification of 'leprosy', might well conclude that Pharisees or rabbis had to stand beside the priest to tell him how to judge each case. It was, however, the priest who had the legal responsibility of deciding when skin disease constituted 'leprosy' and when a person was cleansed of it, and it is doubtful that priests ran to the nearest Pharisee to bring him out of his shop or field to examine the case. Priests, after all, were professionals, non-priestly Pharisees were amateurs.

In the battle between rabbinic literature, which implies that priests needed non-priests to tell them what to do, and Josephus, who states that priests served as teachers and judges, I prefer Josephus.[25] One of the reasons is chronological. By the time rabbinic literature was written, the lay teachers had in fact become ascendant. The Mishnah faithfully reflects a social setting, namely, its own. Josephus' praise of the excellence of priestly rule is biased, but it nevertheless reflects *a* social setting in which priests played a leading part, namely, his own experience in Jerusalem. Besides his summaries, Josephus' narratives of concrete events show the prominent role of priests, a point that weighs quite heavily with me, though it bears more directly on the chief priests than on the ordinary priests.[26] Because of the amount of narrative detail in Josephus and detailed legal debate in the Mishnah, I find it difficult to think that either of these settings was created from nothing. I am sure that even before 70 the Pharisees sat together and studied and debated. They decided things such as that the temple courts could not be washed after the Passover slaughter if Passover fell on a sabbath. The priests, however, carried on flushing away the blood (*Pesahim* 5.8). As the decades after 70 passed, the sages had to pay less and less attention to priests, and they began to treat them as if they had never mattered: that is the overall impression of the Mishnah. This social setting came to exist, but not until after the temple was destroyed. If it were, however, a question of inventing a purely imaginary world, the rabbis of the Mishnah show themselves to be much abler than Josephus, which again counts in his favour.

I attach at least equal weight to general considerations, which I shall now spell out more fully. We have seen that priests were educated, and this was especially true of the aristocratic priests, such as Josephus himself. Since he states that at the age of nineteen he began to follow the rules of the Pharisees, some scholars attribute his evident command of the Bible to his Pharisaism.[27] But at nineteen, he had already finished his education and was ready to take his place in the world. He claims that he was an acknowledged expert at the age of fourteen; he studied the different parties between the ages of sixteen and nineteen, but for most of this period he was a disciple of Bannus, who apparently was not a Pharisee (*Life* 7–12). Josephus' education, then, was partly the standard education of a priest of good family, partly his own special effort to learn more widely. But he was

not the only well-educated aristocratic priest. It is reasonable to think that
some of these men put their learning to good use, by teaching and judging.

The second general consideration bears on the non-aristocratic priests
and the Levites, and this will lead us to a discussion of scribes. Since
Josephus was an aristocrat and owned property, he did not have to earn
money. It is probable that most priests and Levites did. The temple provided
Levites with no cash, though a lot of food. We must doubt that the priests'
revenue from hides and from redeemed firstlings and first sons gave them
enough money. They were not to grow their own food, but there is no reason
why they could not have done other work.[28] Some priests and Levites may
have worked at fairly lowly jobs. They could have been masons or
ironmongers. They could also have been scribes. The first requirement of a
scribe of any sort is literacy. The Levites could read the Psalms, and the long
association of priests and Levites with both teaching and learning the temple
routine means that many of them were literate. We recall from above that
Josephus had to explain that two lay Pharisees knew the law. The explanation
was not needed for the priests. Not everyone who could read and write,
however, could serve as a professional, fee-earning scribe; that required
special training, in part to learn the professional script.

The ancient world required scribes in vast numbers. A great deal is known
about their work, thanks especially to Yadin's discoveries of material from the
time of the second revolt (ended 135 CE). Among the finds was a bundle of
thirty-five documents, mostly legal, belonging to a woman named Babata.[29]
The documents range in date from 93 to 132 CE, and they relate to property
situated in Maoza (or Mahoza) (in Nabataea, at the southern end of the Dead
Sea) and in En-Gedi (in Judaea, on the western shore of the Dead Sea). The
earlier documents in the collection come from a time when Nabataea was a
semi-independent state, while the later ones (after 106 CE) are from the time
after Trajan made Nabataea part of the Roman Province of Arabia. Thus the
early documents reflect Nabataean laws and scribal practice, the latter ones
Roman laws. Since Babata was Jewish, her marriage documents had to
conform to parts of Jewish law as well.

While legally the documents are 'Nabataean' or 'Roman', scribally they
follow the form of composition, witnessing and sealing that are known from
the Mishnah. This does not prove that Pharisees had imposed their laws on
Nabataea, but rather that the Mishnah codifies common civil practice.[30]
Babata's papers reveal both expert legal advice and professional preparation:
two kinds of scribal work.

There are several aspects of these documents that are relevant for our topic
– priests, Levites, literacy and scribes. In the first place, we see that even in a
backwater town legal paperwork flourished. Babata had married twice, and

her life was complicated. One of the trustees of a child by the first marriage had not lived up to his obligations. Her second husband left a large estate, divided among several heirs. Most families did not require thirty-five documents to keep their legal affairs straight, but all except the poorest had legal affairs, if only the papers for a marriage and a small inheritance. Babata's case gives us a glimpse of the paperwork, which was detailed and meticulous.

This means, secondly, that there was a professional cadre. There were lawyers or solicitors in the modern sense: people who gave legal advice. One document 'must have been drafted by a clever lawyer who was conversant with both Roman and Jewish law concerning "gift deeds."'[31] There were also scribes in the sense of 'clerks' or 'copyists', people who wrote a neat, small and precise hand. It is not possible to be certain whether or not the legal expert also wrote the document. One would think that in a small town the same person might well do both. Babata's documents also testify to the existence of magistrates.

We may assume that the situation was the same in Judaea and Galilee. In small villages there may have been only one magistrate and one legal expert who also drew up documents. In larger and more populous areas we may imagine a small number of magistrates, three or more, depending on the population, and several legal experts/scribes. In main centres, we may suppose that specialization developed; perhaps those who gave legal advice had clerks to prepare documents. These are guesses based on the general tendency to multiply offices and to introduce distinctions of rank and status.

If every community had its own scribe or scribes (who may also have been legal experts), how many were there altogether? According to Josephus, there were 204 towns and villages in Galilee alone (*Life* 235). Dio Cassius claimed that during the second revolt the Romans destroyed 50 forts and 985 of 'their most famous villages' (*Roman History* 69.14.1).

The temple also required a lot of scribes, and one assumes that many of them were priests and Levites. Some worked as copyists, since the temple needed copies of the Bible, especially the Psalms, which were the Levites' song books. Others were *especially* expert in the laws and customs (so *War* 2.417). What a person did depended on ability and status, economic and otherwise. Two references in Josephus make us think that some temple scribes were Levites rather than priests, though in both cases the scribes were probably mere copyists. The two passages, both referring to the pre-Hasmonean period, list people connected with the temple who received special benefits. Both texts distinguish the 'scribes of the temple' from priests. One of them names Levites as well as priests, temple-musicians, porters, temple-servants and scribes of the sanctuary (*Antiq.* 11.128, Persian period, the time of Ezra); that is, there were temple scribes who were neither priests nor Levites, and who seem to have been on the level of porters and cleaners. In the second list, a letter from Antiochus III, the beneficiaries are 'the council of elders, the priests, the scribes of the temple, and the temple-singers' (*Antiq.* 12.142). The Levites are not separately named, and they seem to be covered under the terms 'scribes' and 'singers'.

Once there was an adequate supply of Levites and priests who could serve as 'scribes of the temple' (as there may not have been when the temple was first rebuilt in the sixth century BCE), I see no reason for the temple authorities to have gone outside their own ranks in order to recruit the large number of copyists and legal experts that the temple required. Probably some Levites, when not serving in their weekly courses, were otherwise employed by the temple as 'scribes', that is, copyists. In any case, in calculating Palestine's need of scribes, we must include the temple as a large employer.

We shall not be able to arrive at definite numbers, but we may assume that there were some thousands of scribes in Jewish Palestine in our period: legal advisors in each locality, people who could draft documents, and legal experts and copyists in the employ of the temple. At the time of Herod, according to Josephus, there were about 6,000 Pharisees. We have seen that there were 18,000 to 20,000 priests and Levites. We now note that the Mishnah largely legislates for small farmers, and it gives very few rules that would govern the actual work of scribes, though some scribal practices are accurately described (as comparison with the documents discovered by Yadin shows). Finally, let us recall that priests and Levites were forbidden to work the land and that they were on duty only one week in twenty-four, plus the three pilgrimage festivals, a total of five or six weeks every year. They were not tied to farms, as many Pharisees were, and they could take other employment.

As Ben Sira wrote, in a passage that some believe to prove that ordinary lay people were taking over scribal tasks in his day,

> The wisdom of the scribe depends on the opportunity of leisure; and he who has little business may become wise. How can he become wise who handles the plow . . .? (Ben Sira 38.24f.)

In this section Ben Sira is describing himself, a sage and a biblical expert. To be a scribe in that sense one must be rich or a priest or Levite, living off the tithes and offerings. Ben Sira was rich, and he may have been a priest.[32] He hardly proves that ordinary lay people, the assumed ancestors of the Pharisees, were taking over.[33]

I think that it is unreasonable to suppose that the small number of Pharisees, most of whom probably worked from dawn to dusk six days a week, also served their communities as lawyers and scribes, while the large number of priests and Levites, who were on duty in the temple only a few weeks a year, who could not farm, and who were educated in the law, did nothing. It is much more likely that many ordinary priests and many of the Levites put their learning to good use and served as scribes and legal experts.

Josephus explicitly wrote that priests were judges (*Apion* 2.187). I believe that we should accept this, while noting that in villages minor judicial duties were also performed by the heads of major families, village elders who were not priests. Priests and Levites were the employees of the nation for the purposes of maintaining the worship of God in the temple, and teaching and judging the people. They continued to fulfil those roles in the first century. There is no reason to think that they lacked interest in the law and voluntarily handed over their traditional tasks to lay Pharisees, nor is it possible that there were enough Pharisees who had the time needed to supplant the priests and Levites as teachers, scribes and magistrates.

In subsequent chapters, we shall see that, however many people found the teaching of the Pharisees Shemaiah, Abtalion and their successors popular, the 'chief priests', assisted by 'the powerful' laymen, held real power and used it as they wished. In my judgment we shall never know how many priestly and lay teachers there were, nor who more greatly influenced the private opinions of the populace. Here I wish only to show that the nation's official teachers and magistrates were the priests, and that a good number of them spent their time on these tasks when they were not on duty at the temple.

Sincerity, hypocrisy and greed

There were numerous criticisms of the priesthood in the Roman era. In many cases, perhaps most, they were aimed chiefly against the aristocratic priests, whom we shall consider in ch. 15. For two reasons I wish to take them up here. First, it would be reasonable to think that the priests as a whole followed the example of their leaders, so that allegations of immorality and impurity against the chief priests would also apply, to some degree, to all priests. Secondly, I shall argue that the priesthood maintained its integrity. I do not want to sweep charges that may have included the ordinary priests under the rug, nor even delay discussing them for five chapters. I shall, however, reserve for ch. 15 Josephus' stories about scandalous and dishonest behaviour on the part of named aristocratic priests, since in these cases it is beyond doubt that the charges are specific.

Around 63 BCE the author of *Ps. Sol.* 8 accused 'them', obviously priests, of incest, adultery, making agreements to trade wives, bringing menstrual blood into the sanctuary and plundering the temple treasury. Jesus, according to Mark 11.17, accused the priests of operating a 'den of thieves'. The Dead

Sea Commentary on Habbakuk condemned 'the Wicked Priest' for committing abominable deeds and defiling the temple (1QpHab 12.8). The community of the *Covenant of Damascus* charged that the priests had intercourse with their wives when they were suffering from 'discharge' (non-menstrual bleeding, Lev. 15.25) and also that they were guilty of incest and theft (CD 4.17–5.11; 6.15–16). *T. Moses* 6.1 accused the Hasmonean priest/kings of performing 'great impiety in the Holy of Holies'.

This all sounds quite devastating, and many scholars, both Christian and Jewish, have accepted the polemic against the priesthood as generally true and as indicating its immorality. One now reads that the priests 'misuse[d] their calling . . . by carrying on business to make profit',[34] or that they 'abused their position . . . through nepotism and oppression'.[35] The people 'and their Pharisaic representatives' harboured 'bitter hostility' against 'the venal priesthood'.[36] The aristocratic Sadducean priests were held in contempt by the populace.[37] The elegant houses in the Upper City attest to the 'nepotism, cruelty and corruption' of the chief priests, who oppressed the people.[38]

The poor priests, especially the chief priests, condemned by all generations! In evaluating the polemic, we need to consider three possibilities: the charges may have rested on only one case; they reflect legal disputes; they are typical of religio-political debates and should not be taken at face value.

To give something of the flavour of the invective, to show continuity, and to indicate how a general charge might rest on an individual transgression, I shall quote a passage from the *Testament of Levi* that attacks the priests or aristocratic priests of a period before the Roman conquest:

You plunder the Lord's offerings; from his share you steal choice parts, contemptuously eating them with whores. You teach the Lord's commands out of greed for gain; married women you profane; [you defile the virgins of Jerusalem];[39] you have intercourse with whores and adulteresses. You take gentile women for your wives and your sexual relations will become like Sodom and Gomorrah. (*T. Levi.* 14.5f.)

These accusations belong to the Hellenistic or, more likely, the Hasmonean period.[40] I quote the passage here because, if the passage is from *c.* 80 BCE, we can identify the culprit. Alexander Jannaeus, we know, had concubines (*Antiq.* 13.380). Possibly he let them share his portion of the offerings. He did not marry a Gentile, but perhaps some of the priests of his day did. Accusations of adultery and homosexuality cannot now be proved or disproved; but, human nature being what it is, there must have been some adulterous and homosexual priests.

Accusations, that is, though often couched in general terms, may be specific. Let us say that, when Jannaeus feasted with his concubines on his balcony, looking at the agony of eight hundred of his enemies hanging on crosses, he and his companions were eating first fruits.[41] Let us further say that the attack in the *Testament of Levi* is against him and his subordinate priests. If these hypothetical assumptions were true, the charge would be accurate, but it would not be generally revealing about the priesthood.

Most of the charges against the priests, however, rest on legal disputes. The accusations of contact with female blood, either menstruation or non-menstrual 'discharge', are not the result of installing cameras in the priests' bedrooms. They might be no more than general slander, but more likely they reflect differences of opinion about precisely when a woman was impure. Without more details, we cannot say just what each disagreement was, but I shall give an example to illustrate legal debate about female blood. The Pharisees were of the view that a woman's menstrual period began with the first show of blood and lasted for seven days, even if the flow stopped before then. After these seven days, there came eleven days when vaginal blood could not be menstruation. If during these eleven days there was a flow of blood that lasted two consecutive days (as they interpreted the biblical 'many days'), it was non-menstrual discharge (Lev. 15.25). If in the middle of the eleven day period the woman found blood, the couple could not have intercourse until the end of the *next* day; that is, they had to wait to see if the discharge would last 'many' days (two). If it did, then the rules of Lev. 15.25–30 applied (seven days impurity, sacrifices, etc.). If bleeding did not continue, the first show of blood was meaningless. It was neither menstruation nor discharge.[42]

We do not know just how early the Pharisees came up with these specifications of how to define 'menstruation' and 'discharge'. It is easy to imagine, however, that not every one agreed. Some might think that after the end of the menstrual period there were fifteen days, rather than eleven, during which blood could not be menstrual. Or they could take 'many days' to mean three, or they might rule that the couple could engage in intercourse while they counted the days – and so on. We do not know what the actual disputes were; we only see that pietists accused the priests of not following the right rules. They graphically wrote that the priests brought menstrual blood into the temple, but this should not be taken as a literal description.

The charge of theft in CD has partly to do with the use of vows: property that may have been stolen was vowed to the altar, with the result that it could not be recovered. The *Covenant of Damascus* accuses the priests of accepting such property, not of being the original thieves (see 16.13–16).

The accusation of incest also rested on legal disagreement. The Bible has a list of 'forbidden degrees', relatives by blood or law with whom sexual intercourse is forbidden (Lev. 18.6–18). The pious forbade some marriages that the Bible allows. Moses forbade a man to marry his mother's sister, while, according to CD 5.8–11, the forbidden degrees should be extended to prohibit analogous marriages between uncle and niece. The author of CD regarded such a marriage as 'incest'. Josephus tells one story of a pre-Hasmonean Zadokite priest who married his niece (he had intercourse with her, not knowing that she was his niece, and married her when he learned her identity; *Antiq.* 12.185–9). Among the Hasmoneans, a son of Aristobulus II married his cousin, a daughter of Hyrcanus II (*Antiq.* 15.23). Possibly there were other cases. If so, they were all allowed by the biblical law, but opposed by some pietists.[43]

The charges of plundering the sanctuary and of accepting ill-gotten gains are harder to evaluate. There must have been some dishonest priests, but that many stole from the temple must be doubted. Actual theft would have been difficult, because of the number and zeal of the guards; and had theft been committed and become known, there would have been public demonstrations, which would have made the pages of Josephus. In the previous chapter (p. 160), I suggested that one of the accusations of plundering the temple, *Ps. Sol.* 8, referred to a specific act by one of the Hasmoneans. In any case, it is doubtful that ordinary priests were in a position to take the temple's money. The charge of theft in CD may rest entirely on legal disputes about gifts vowed to the altar (cf. Mark 7.11).

Though it is not a disagreement about interpretation of the law, we should consider here the accusation that 'you have made [the temple] a den of robbers' (Mark 11.17). The phrase probably does not reveal what Jesus himself thought about the temple and the priests. I shall not, however, repeat the arguments that several people have brought forward with regard to these words, which are quoted from Jer. 7.11.[44] Here I note, instead, that the saying does not accuse priests of being robbers, but rather says that the temple was a den of robbers. The reference is to the bird-sellers and money-changers. As far as we know, these were not priests, though the temple officials provided them with space. As I indicated above, bird-selling was subject to the law of supply and demand (pp. 85–9). Moreover, none of the temple traders had a monopoly. The law requires that birds be sacrificed and that they be unblemished. People could buy them in the Royal Portico as a convenience, but they were not forced to do so. The same is true of the half shekel cash contribution. It could be sent in from abroad, and there was no way of compelling pilgrims to change money at the temple. Thus I think that the phrase 'den of robbers' does not prove that priests cheated, stole or robbed, nor does it show that the priests gave a small number of traders a monopoly that allowed them to cheat and steal.

We now move to the third point, the nature of religio-political debate. In evaluating any polemic, one should always consider its normal characteristics and also the source of the accusations. Polemic is stylized. People who are out of power not infrequently accuse those who are in power of dishonesty, corruption and favouritism; sweeping charges are common. In religious polemic, charges of sexual or cultic misbehaviour are also fairly frequent. Thus, for example, in Rom. 1 Paul accused Gentiles in general of committing homosexual acts, while in Rom. 2 he charged that Jews robbed temples. He also hurled serious charges at his opponents within the Christian movement. The other apostles who came to Corinth were servants of Satan, masquerading as 'servants of righteousness' (II Cor. 11.14f.). In Galatia, his opponents were motivated by fear and a desire for 'glory' (Gal. 6.12f.). In turn, Paul's enemies accused him of being a man-pleaser (Gal. 1.10), as well as being inferior in general qualities (II Cor. 11.5). In the view of the Essenes the Pharisees were 'lying interpreters' (1QH 2.31f.), traitors (4QpNah 7), people who 'justified the wicked and condemned the just', 'caused others to transgress', and persecuted the upright 'with the sword' (CD 1.18–21).[45] Charges of sexual immorality are missing in the Essene attacks on the Pharisees. This could be accidental, though it may also be that the Pharisees' sexual code was almost as strict as the Essenes'. The accusations in CD and *Ps. Sol.* against the priests are stronger, and they include charges of sexual immorality, but they are of the same genre: religious polemic.

These broad accusations were for 'in-group' consumption, and they did not have to be substantiated in public. Thus they could be sweeping and general. We note that the critics of the priesthood were out-of-power pietists, some of whom had suffered at the hands of the dominant group. The Essenes in large part owed their existence to a dispute over the high priesthood, and the Teacher of Righteousness had been persecuted by the 'Wicked Priest' in Jerusalem. The final author of the gospel of Mark was probably not himself a Jew who had been persecuted by the priests; but he spoke for the Christian movement, which in its early days had been harassed by the chief priests. Accusing the priests of allowing the operation of 'a den of thieves' probably seemed like perfectly reasonable retaliation. The authors of the *Psalms of Solomon* belonged to a pious group that was out of power and deeply resented the Hasmonean government. In *Ps. Sol.* 17.6–8 for example, the Jewish leaders are accused of casting 'us' out and of establishing a worldly monarchy. As Gray put it, 'we are dealing with a strongly partisan work. Neither the righteousness of the righteous, nor the sinfulness of the sinful, must be accepted too literally'.[46] We do not expect entirely impartial reporting from such sources. I am not, however, accusing the pietists of blatant dishonesty. By their own lights, they were right. Priests who did not follow their rules really were bringing menstrual blood into the sanctuary. The sweeping generalizations – 'you all do it!' – while not literally true, are typical of the genre. The priests who were being attacked probably thought of pietists in general as self-righteous prigs – which only some of them were.

From ancient literature we know of only one true champion of the priests, and from modern scholarship even fewer! Josephus admired the priesthood and praised it warmly. The government of Judaea was an 'aristocracy' (*Antiq.* 20.251) or a 'theocracy' (*Apion* 2.165); that is, the priests, especially the aristocratic priests, were in charge. He asked, rhetorically, whether there could be a finer constitution than government by the priests: he thought that there could not be and that the priests were fair, honest, decent and motivated by piety (*Apion* 2.185).[47]

Josephus' voice is that of an aristocratic priest. Just as the accusations of gross immorality are polemical and come from enemies of the priesthood, those who felt that they had suffered at their hands, Josephus' praise is apologetic and comes from a member of the privileged class.

Informed only by biased witnesses, can we come to fair generalizations? I think that it is possible to penetrate behind the generalized and sweeping condemnation and praise. There is, in the first place, the inference to be drawn from Josephus' own theology, which is succinctly presented in *Antiq.* 4 and *Apion* 2. The chief points of that theology will emerge in the discussion of the law (chs 11–12) and common theology (ch. 13), and here I wish only to indicate its general character. The world is under God's providence, and he bestows blessings on all (*Apion* 2.166), though Israel is the object of his special care (*Antiq.* 4.213, 242f.). Worshippers should thank him for past blessings and pray that they continue (*Antiq.* 4.242f.). They should not, however, primarily ask for blessings, since God has already bestowed them, but rather for 'capacity to receive' and keep them (*Apion* 2.197). In such passages as these, a priest explains the theology that he was taught. Josephus was not a creative theologian, and profundity is lacking. His theology is simple and straightforward; the grace of God is one of its prominent themes. The human response should be thanksgiving. It is almost certain that Josephus learned this theology in school, as part of his training for the priesthood. Not all priests lived up to the ideal, but they were at least taught it.

The best method of getting past Josephus' bias, as we have seen in other sections, and shall demonstrate more fully in later chapters, is to analyse individual narratives. He may offer false generalizations, but he did not beat each individual story into a pre-determined shape. Against his own view that the chief priests were perfectly reliable leaders and rulers of the nation, he tells stories that discredit some of them. These all have to do with named aristocratic priests, and I shall not narrate them here. I only note that Josephus' undoubted bias did not keep negative stories about other aristocratic priests out of his history. A majority of the stories about the priests, though, show them as acting in accord with what they saw as the welfare of the Jewish nation as a whole, explicitly including the general populace.

Other stories show that many or most of the ordinary priests kept the commandments strictly. We recall that it was the priesthood at the time of Pompey's conquest of Palestine (63 BCE) that is maligned in the *Psalms of Solomon*. The main target is a Hasmonean, but possibly an avaricious high priest or chief priest led the ordinary priests to be more concerned about money and comfort than about the worship of God. Josephus described the behaviour of some of the ordinary priests of this same generation. Those who were serving in the temple at the time of Pompey's assault on Jerusalem were directly attacked, first being bombarded by missiles and then struck down by the swords of their enemies. Nevertheless, they continued their service and died at their posts.[48]

It may be helpful to compare the Jerusalem priests with those of Babylonia at the time of Alexander's conquest of the Persian empire. The Persians had destroyed some of the Babylonian temples in retaliation for revolt, and the priests had become accustomed to drawing their tithes but not spending the money on temple worship. When Alexander took the city, he commanded that the great temple of E-sagila be rebuilt. When he was next in Babylon, after his campaign in India, he found that the work had not been done.

> The priests of Babylon had preferred their own finances, for as long as the temples were incomplete, they could spend the income from sacred land on more congenial goods than sacrifice and silver-polish, and they had delayed the building plans to suit themselves.[49]

I think that all students of second-temple Judaism will agree that no parallel can be found to this sort of behaviour. The temple service never suffered from neglect, and its rites were meticulously observed. This, in turn, implies the devotion of the priesthood and, in fact, of Jews generally, who faithfully brought their sacrifices and paid most of the temple dues. While there are stories of wicked individual priests, there are no accounts indicating that the priests in general failed in their commitment to the worship of God.

Thus not only Josephus' idealized generalizations, but also his stories of particular people and events point to the general piety of the priesthood, both the aristocratic and the ordinary priests. One sees not insincere abusers of office and callous usurpers who cynically milked the people, but earnest and devoted servants of the Lord and his temple who sought the welfare of the people and who were faithful to their commission and ordination, even to death.

The priests' first concern was the sacrificial system. The sacrifices were required by God, and they atoned for the sins of Israel. The priests who continued serving at the altar while they were being cut down by enemy swords show their attitude clearly enough: manning the gates and walls were secondary activities. What mattered were the sacrifices. Thus they were as a class 'pacifist'. They favoured smooth relations with Rome, relations that allowed their services to continue. Military and political independence were secondary. To this extent they were like some of the pietist movements: any political arrangement that did not transgress what they regarded as most important was satisfactory, though doubtless they preferred some arrangements to others.

Despite this, they were not immune from the feeling of nationalism. It was the ordinary priests who finally 'declared war' on Rome. During the late stages of the tumult under Florus that led to the revolt (pp. 485f.), Eleazar, a member of a high priestly family (his father was Ananias), persuaded the priests serving in the temple 'to accept no gift or sacrifice from a foreigner'. Rome had not attempted to make the Jews sacrifice to Rome, representing the state, but the Jews did sacrifice on behalf of the nation and Caesar.[50] The priests now rejected those sacrifices and allegiance to Rome along with them. The chief priests appealed to the serving priests, but the latter 'remained obdurate', and the die was cast (*War* 2.409f.). The priests, teachers of the nation, had decided to fight for independence.

11

Observing the Law of God I: General Characteristics, Worship and Sabbath

We now move outside the temple to consider religion in the routine lives of ordinary people. We shall shortly take up worship in the home and synagogue, but first I wish to develop more fully the description of the distinctiveness of Judaism and its law that we began in ch. 5.

In our account thus far, we have seen Judaism as a religion of things that are done, especially in the cult. This emphasis is in part intended to correct most portrayals of Judaism, which focus either on politics or on theology. The temple service is today little understood, and some people shrink from it as something alien and unpalatable. The act of historical understanding requires that this alienation be overcome and that the ancient religion be seen as it really was. But, more important, this mode of description corresponds to how religion was viewed in the ancient world. 'Religion' (which went by such terms as 'piety', 'worship' or 'service') was defined primarily as cultic worship. What was the worship of Zeus? Temples, purifications, sacrifices and festivals. The same is true of all the other gods of antiquity. In paganism there were numerous different cults, and it is hard to offer generalizations that hold good in every case, but we may say that not infrequently the rules and rituals were difficult and, to many, bewildering. In Rome, where some of the major priestly offices accompanied success in the political sphere, the elite holders of these positions prided themselves on their ability to perform all the rites correctly and rehearsed tirelessly in order to get them right.[1] At some pagan shrines, however, enthusiasm for maintaining all the inherited rituals flagged, and temple service became debased. Periodically there were reforms that aimed at salvaging old routines. Apollonius of Tyana, for example, a first-century sage and miracle worker, was also a reformer and corrector of cult, who attempted to restore neglected rituals (*Life of Apollonius of Tyana* I.16).

Judaism, by comparison, was simple and straightforward. Most Jews probably did know their own laws better than did most pagans (as Josephus claimed, *Apion* 2.175–8). Jewish sacrificial and temple ritual was not especially difficult, and in any case the principal responsibility for doing it right fell on the shoulders of the hereditary priests, who had been educated for the job since childhood. In comparison with other religions, Jewish cultic ritual did not stand out as being excessive, burdensome and anxiety-producing.

Judaism's most distinctive point, however, was the extension of divine law to all the areas of life, as we noted at the outset. As Josephus put it, in Judaism virtue was a sub-category under piety, rather than piety a sub-category under virtue (*Apion* 2.170; p. 51 above). Religion – 'piety', devotion to God – was the all-embracing category, within which everything else came.

As such it embraced what people *did* more than what they thought. As we shall eventually see, there were theological convictions that were common, but agreement about speculative theology was not a requirement that was imposed on Jews. Though Judaism went beyond the general ancient concentration on cultic activity, it did not break with the ancient view that religion requires certain *behaviour*. 'Piety governs all our actions and occupations and speech; none of these things did our lawgiver leave unexamined or indeterminate' (*Apion* 2.171). This emphasis on correct action in every sphere of life, technically called 'orthopraxy', is a hallmark of Judaism. Judaism, that is, required obedience to the law, which includes the sacrifices and the offerings, but also much more.

As Morton Smith has pointed out, one of results of the fact that Judaism became a religion of 'the book', which in theory covered all of life, is that lay people could study it.[2] They seized the opportunity, as we shall see below. They could study laws of sacrifice and develop theories about them, and some did so. This was rather like doing theoretical engineering without a consultancy or a contract: they fashioned theories in case they could find a pliant priest to apply them. But the laity could also study aspects of divine law that they themselves could control: prayer, sabbath, some of the sub-categories of purity, planting, sexual relations and the like. Priests were the official authorities on even these domestic rules, but they could not *do* anything about the way most people kept them. Consequently the possibility of lay leaders arose, non-priestly teachers of the law. We have seen them before and we shall see them again. Just now I want to emphasize the degree to which ordinary people were responsible for knowing and observing the law in their private lives, so that they had a degree of control over it. Lay people could make private decisions about divine law; this was quite exceptional. Few individuals, to be sure, would make decisions that went very much against the norm, but it is nevertheless important that the Jewish law was

internalized and individualized to a degree that sets Judaism apart from
Graeco-Roman paganism. The distinction is not absolute, but it is important:
Judaism could survive and, it turned out, even flourish when the cult
disappeared. The groundwork was laid earlier; in the period that we study,
progress towards the capability of maintaining indefinitely a non-cultic
religion was far advanced.

The law: basic distinctions

Two distinctions will help us understand the law as a whole:
1. Laws govern either (*a*) relations between humans and God or (*b*)
   relations among humans (with implications for the human-divine
   relationship).
2. Transgressions of the law are either (*a*) involuntary or (*b*) intentional.

These divisions are quite clear in Lev. 5–6. There a distinction is made
between the person who 'commits a breach of faith and sins unwittingly in
any of the holy things of the Lord' (5.15) and the one who 'sins and commits a
breach of faith against the Lord by deceiving his neighbour' (6.1). In these
lines we see the differentiations between unwitting and intentional transgression, and between sins against God (the holy things of the Lord) and those
against both God and the neighbour (against the Lord by deceiving the
neighbour).

Philo, with his eye on this passage, pointed out the legal categories.
Unwitting sins against God that involve the 'holy things' (for example
accidentally eating first fruits) require repayment, the addition of a fifth (paid
to the priests), and the offering of a ram (*Spec. Laws* 1.234; Lev. 5.14–19).
Voluntary offences against a fellow human require inward conviction of the
sin, a confession, restoration of what was taken, an added fifth, and a
sacrifice, which shows that the sin was also against God (*Spec. Laws* 1.235–8;
Lev. 6.1–7). These acts resulted in forgiveness (*Spec. Laws* 1.235; Lev. 6.7).
Redress of the wrong was to precede the sacrifice (*Spec. Laws* 1.235; cf. Matt.
5.23–4).

Some crimes required more compensation than the added fifth: theft of an
ox or sheep must be repaid fivefold or fourfold respectively if the animal had
been sold or killed, double if the thief still had it (Ex. 22.1; slightly different in
Antiq. 4.272).

Philo emphasized that the Bible required equal penalties for unwitting
transgression against God and intentional transgression against others (the
added fifth, *Spec. Laws* 1.238); that is, offences against God were punished
more severely. While inadvertent transgression against God requires an
added fifth, the Bible considers intentional transgression against God to be

punishable by death (e.g. in the case of the sabbath, Num. 15.32–6) or by 'cutting off' – extirpation of the person and his or her descendants from the people of Israel. An example of intentional transgression against the holy things of God would be deliberately and wilfully eating holy food while in a state of impurity, or consuming the blood of animals: Lev. 7.20f., 25f. Many rabbis, living after the time when 'holy things' were a live issue, reversed the order of severity. Sins against God alone – such as taking the name of the Lord in vain, which the Bible specifies as not being forgivable (Ex. 20.7) – were sometimes regarded as the more easily atoned for, requiring only repentance, while transgressions against one's fellow required both repentance and restitution. This was not a uniform doctrine, but it was a noticeable tendency.[3]

The division of the law into two parts, sometimes called 'two tables' (one governing human relations with God and the other relationships among humans), was widely recognized in the first century, and it will enhance our understanding of Judaism if we consider the two tables more fully and note the terminology in the Greek-writing authors. This will aid us when we inquire into Jewish treatment of other Jews and of Gentiles.

Philo discusses two sets of five commandments each in *Who is the Heir of Divine Things*, one set consisting of right behaviour towards God, the second set of responsibilities towards other humans (*Heir* 168).[4] These ten general commandments, he wrote, covered almost all possible cases (173). He and others who wrote in Greek often used 'piety' (*eusebeia*) and 'justice' or 'righteousness' (*dikaiosynē*) as words that encapsulated the two parts of the law. Thus Philo wrote that the first set of commandments governed 'piety', while the second set prohibited 'injustice' (*Heir* 172) and that on the sabbath Jews throughout the world gathered in synagogues, where they learned their ancestral philosophy, which fell under two headings, 'One of duty to God as shown by piety and holiness, one of duty to humans as shown by love of humanity and justice' (*Special Laws* 2.63).[5] Or, as he put it elsewhere, 'God asks nothing of you that is heavy or complicated or difficult, but only something quite simple and easy. And this is just to love him . . ., to serve him . . . with your whole soul . . . and to cling to his commandments'. He then remarked that 'the law stands pre-eminent in enjoining fellowship (*koinōnia*) and love of humanity' (*philanthrōpia*) (*Special Laws* 1.299f., 324). The two-fold division of the law into 'justice' and 'piety' also appears in *Virtues* 175 and *Rewards and Punishments* 162. We note that, in accord with Deut. 6.4–6 and Lev. 19.18, 34, piety towards God includes love of God and justice towards other people includes loving them.[6]

'Justice' and 'piety' served as the two key words governing Jewish behaviour before Philo (*Arist.* 24, 131) and also in other Diaspora literature (*Sib. Or.* 5.142). Josephus also used this terminology, as, for example, in explaining the preaching of John the Baptist, who exhorted the Jews 'to practise justice towards their fellows and piety towards God' (*Antiq.* 18.117; cf. also 6.265; 8.121, 134; 9.16; 10.50; 12.56; 14.283; 15.375; *War* 2.139, on the Essenes).[7]

As did Philo, Josephus sometimes used two words to describe the treatment of other humans, *philanthrōpia*, love of humanity, and *koinōnia*, fellowship. In *Apion* 2.146 he distinguishes them: 'fellowship' (or 'commonality') governs relations with other Jews, 'love of humanity' relations with non-Jews.[8] Both were to be treated decently, even if they were enemies and even in warfare. (On enemies, see further pp. 233–5).

Modern scholars often try to divide the law into 'ritual' and 'ethical' categories, but this is an anachronistic and misleading division.[9] In such analyses the 'moral law' is often considered to be embodied in the Ten Commandments, but this puts the commandments governing use of the Lord's name and graven images into the 'ethical' division, where they do not belong. Similarly some say that the 'Noachian' commandments – those thought to have been given to all the descendants of Noah, and therefore to be required of Gentiles – are 'moral' commandments.[10] But these, too, include idolatry and blasphemy. It is noteworthy that the list of core commandments that, according to Acts, the Jerusalem church wished to impose on Gentile converts, included the prohibitions against idolatry and eating meat with the blood in it – neither one 'moral' (Acts 15.20). Many Christians define their own stance towards the Jewish law as acceptance of the 'moral' code and rejection of the 'cultic', and so they naturally see this division as existing in the first century, and often as determining the views of Jesus and Paul, but both are incorrect. When Jews – including Jewish Christians – offered a list of 'core' commandments, they usually included some laws that cannot be defined as 'ethical' or 'moral' (e.g. I Cor. 6.9–10). Jesus and Paul both accepted the top commandment on the first table: to worship only the God of Israel. This is not a 'moral' law.

The anachronism of this distinction is seen in another way: 'ritual' commandments not infrequently have an 'ethical' aspect. Thus tithing (a 'ritual' requirement) included charity (a 'moral' duty), and the laws of the sabbath provided rest for labourers and even for animals (Deut. 5.14). There are certain overlaps between the ancient category of 'commandments that govern relations with God' and the modern one of 'ritual law', and also between the ancient 'commandments that govern relations with fellow humans' and the modern 'ethical law', but no more than overlaps.

In the eyes of first-century Jews the same God gave all the commandments, and loyalty to him required obedience of them equally. Modern objectors to ancient Judaism regard it as regrettable that first-century Jews did not see that the cultic laws were trivial, man-made affairs that have no place in true religion. This misses the ancient perspective. From that point of view (to reiterate) the peculiarity of Judaism was to bring all of life under divine law, to treat deceiving one's neighbour as being just as serious as accidentally eating food that should have gone to the priests or the altar. That is, ancients generally thought that cultic worship was in accord with divine intention. Even ancient Christians did not criticize non-Christian Jews for engaging in temple worship, but rather for not accepting the death of Christ as the true atoning sacrifice. Judaism maintained temple worship but greatly expanded the areas covered by explicit commandments from God. Its fundamental moral and humane direction is best seen precisely in its refusal to separate cult from other aspects of behaviour. Scholars not infrequently attribute the desire to bring all of life under the law just to the Pharisees,[11] but it is central to biblical law itself and was common to all forms of Judaism.

We shall now expand consideration of laws generally kept to include those that were not primarily connected with the temple, but were daily or weekly obligations, and thus a very important part of communal and private life. Most of the evidence that will be cited in the following sections is literary and, moreover, comes from pietists. How do we know that it represents 'common' Judaism, especially when we ask about practices that were private? Proof, obviously, cannot be absolute, but I shall mention three points: (1) On one topic, immersion, there is excellent archaeological evidence of general observance; one case counts in favour of others. (2) When our literary sources, which often disagree with one another, sometimes violently, all agree on a given point, they probably reflect general acceptance. (3) This is especially the case when they reveal that people *believed* that God had commanded a certain practice. Ancient Jews believed in God, and if they thought that he required them to pray every morning, they probably prayed every morning. How do we know they generally believed that? When diverse sources take it for granted that God commanded it, and even insert it into their descriptions of (for example) the Ten Commandments: that is, when our sources *presuppose* rather than *argue* that such-and-such a practice is desired by God. The more strenuous the argument, the more we doubt common practice; in all probability, we are reading an attempt to convince people who do not agree.

Worship of the one God in synagogue and home

Fundamental to Jewish life and worship was the Shema', the biblical passage that begins 'Hear [*sh*e*ma*'], O Israel, the Lord our God, the Lord is one; and you shall love the Lord your God with all your heart, and with all your soul, and with all your might' (Deut. 6.4–5). The passage continues by saying that the commandments are to be 'upon the heart', taught to children, spoken of at home and abroad, and remembered before sleep and upon waking. They are to be bound upon the hand, placed 'as frontlets' between the eyes, and put on the doorpost of the house and on the gate (vv. 6–9).

The plain meaning of the text is that all of the commandments are to be remembered in these ways, especially those that immediately precede the Shemaʿ: the Ten Commandments of Deut. 5. This was generally understood and widely observed. The opening verses of the Shemaʿ ('hear . . . love') and other passages were written and posted in the doorway, bound between the eyes and on the hand, and recited morning and evening. The Shemaʿ and the Ten Commandments served as a kind of core that was often written and repeated. They appear together on the Nash Papyrus, a single sheet of the second or first century BCE emanating from Egypt. The importance of its being a single sheet, not part of a scroll, is that this makes it likely that it was used for devotional or educational purposes.

According to the Mishnah the Shemaʿ, along with the Ten Commandments and a few other passages, was recited by heart by the priests after the sacrifice of the daily burnt offering (*Tamid* 4.3; 5.1; *Taʿanit* 4.3). Further, the mishnaic rabbis simply took it for granted, as something that did not require debate or proof, that every Jew said the Shemaʿ (along with daily prayers) twice a day, morning and evening (*Berakhot* 1.1–3). The Dead Sea Scrolls shows that the Sectarians understood and observed the plain sense of Deut. 6. One author wrote that 'With the coming of day and night I will enter the Covenant of God' (1QS 10.10). 'Entering the covenant' morning and evening probably refers to saying the Shemaʿ. This practice seems to have been very widespread.

The centrality of the Shemaʿ is also confirmed by the evidence for the use of *mᵉzûzôt* and *tᵉphîllîn*. Mezuzah (plural -ot) is the word now used for the small containers holding biblical passages that are attached to the doorway of many Jewish homes. Tefillin are the devices used to strap key portions of the Bible to the arms and forehead. These practices, which are prescribed in Deut. 6.6–9, are well attested for the ancient world. Matthew 23.5 criticizes the Pharisees for making their tefillin (called 'phylacteries' in Greek) too broad, but not for wearing them, which shows that others wore them as well. Aristeas states that 'the Words' are posted on gates and doors and that a sign is worn on the hands (*Arist.* 158f.). Josephus refers both to inscribing the blessings of God on the doors and displaying them on the arms. All who wished to show the power of God and his goodwill towards his followers should 'bear a record thereof written on the head and on the arm' (*Antiq.* 4.213). The observance was also kept at Qumran, where texts from mezuzot and tefillin have been found.[12]

Accompanying the saying of the Shemaʿ were *daily prayers*.[13] The Qumran Community Rule prescribes prayer ('blessing God') 'at the times ordained by

Him', which include 'the beginning of the dominion of light' and 'its end when it retires to its appointed place' (1QS 9.26–10.1). According to Josephus Moses himself required prayers of thanksgiving at rising up and going to bed (*Antiq.* 4.212). He probably found this requirement, as did others, in Deut. 6.6–9, since he joins it to the commandment to post mezuzot and to wear tefillin. Prayers of thanksgiving are not actually required in the law; Josephus' putting them in that category shows that they were a standard part of Jewish practice. The rabbis so took the daily prayers for granted that they debated only whether or not one should say the Eighteen Benedictions or just their substance (*Berakhot* 4.3; these prayers are described below). One passage in the Mishnah, in fact, prescribes saying the prayers three times a day (*Berakhot* 4.1), but this was probably a sign of extraordinary piety even within the pietist groups. Praying twice a day was the common practice.

Although Josephus and the Rabbis put the evening prayer at bedtime, others offered it at the time of the last sacrifice in the temple, that is, just before sunset. This may have been the case at Qumran (see the passage quoted just above). Judith is depicted as praying 'at the very time when that evening's incense was being offered' at the temple (Judith 9.1).

It seems then, that Jews generally accepted the biblical requirement to bear in mind the laws of God, and they fulfilled it by saying the Shema^c, posting mezuzot and wearing tefillin. We should assume that for some this was mere routine, but we may also think that a lot of Jews really believed in recalling the passages contained in their tefillin, and that they recalled them. In this case they reviewed for themselves both the blessings of God and his commandments. They also prayed twice a day. Scholars sometimes imagine that Jews went to the synagogue to say their daily prayers. While they may have prayed when they assembled in the synagogues (discussed below), it is evident in all the discussions that they ordinarily said the Shema^c and prayed at home ('when you lie down and when you rise up', Deut. 6.7). The rabbis and Josephus alike assume that morning and evening worship took place at home. In the *Sibylline Oracles*, from the Greek-speaking Diaspora, there is also a reference to morning prayer while still in bed (3.591–3). The monastic community at Qumran, which we shall discuss below, offers the only evidence of a regular system of daily community prayers. For most Jews, however, the home was a primary place of worship – in fact, the one used most frequently.

Further *study of the scripture* was for most people probably confined to the sabbath, but then it did take place. Jews were generally well educated in the Bible, and this is attributable to the practice of attending the synagogue, where the scripture was read and expounded. As Philo put it, on the seventh day Jews gave 'their time to the one sole object of philosophy with a view to the improvement of character and submission to the scrutiny of conscience'. He saw the pursuit of the Jewish 'philosophy' on the sabbath as being a Mosaic commandment (*On the Creation of the World* 128). Josephus was of the same view: Moses had decreed that once every week people should 'assemble to listen to the Law and to obtain a thorough and accurate knowledge of it' (*Apion* 2.175). In Pseudo-Philo's *Biblical Antiquities* (first century CE), the requirement to assemble on the sabbath 'to praise the Lord' and 'to glorify the Mighty One' is made part of the Ten Commandments (*Bibl. Antiq.* 11.8). The assumption that Moses ordained sabbath assembly, like Josephus' view that he commanded twice-daily prayers, shows how common the practice was – as common as if it had been in the written law. The Bible (Deut. 31.10) requires the public reading of the law once every seven years, at the Feast of Booths, but by the first century the practice was to read portions of it weekly in the synagogue. It was there that people assembled to hear it read and expounded.

We do not know the history of the *synagogue* or *house of prayer*, either its age or the degree to which practice varied from one synagogue to another.[14] The basic question with regard to its origin is whether it was seen as a substitute for the temple service, an alternative to it, or a supplement to it. One possibility is that the synagogue arose among Jews cut off from the temple, for example in Mesopotamia during the exile or in the western Diaspora. Secondly, the practice of weekly gatherings might have begun among people who were not physically, but rather spiritually cut off from the temple – those who wanted a more informal and easily accessible form of public worship. Thirdly, some people may have felt that attendance at the temple service simply could not be frequent enough and needed to be supplemented. Synagogues probably played all these roles from time to time and place to place, and we cannot assign their origin to just one of the possible causes.

Despite uncertainty about the history of the institution, there is no doubt that synagogues were important in Jewish life and worship in the first century. The New Testament routinely places some of the teaching of both Jesus and Paul in synagogues (e.g. Mark 1.21; Acts 13.15). Our other first-century authors, Josephus and Philo, similarly take them for granted. No one argues for them, everybody assumes them. Josephus discusses at some length events that centred around the synagogue in Caesarea. The building adjoined a plot owned by a Gentile, and Jews had access to it only through 'a narrow and extremely awkward passage'. This led to trouble, which was initiated by Jewish hot-heads. A Gentile, however, raised the stakes by putting 'beside the entrance a pot, turned bottom upwards, on which he was sacrificing birds'. This spectacle confronted the Jews on the sabbath, when they assembled according to their custom (*War* 2.285–290). In this narrative, sabbath assembly at the synagogue is taken for granted.

Josephus discusses the 'house of prayer' in Tiberias as a place that would accommodate large crowds (*Life* 277, 280, 290–303). That is where the populace met to discuss the revolt. On at least one occasion, while he was there Josephus fulfilled the 'requirements' (*nomina*) concerning prayer (295). This took place before a meeting that was held first thing in the morning, and it is probable that in this case Josephus had omitted his morning worship at home and so was conducting it in the house of prayer. If there was a large building for prayer and study in Tiberias – a city that was permanently impure – we may assume that there were such buildings elsewhere in Palestine.

We noted that Philo wrote that Jews spent the sabbath studying their 'philosophy' (*Creation* 128). He described sabbath study as taking place in specially designated buildings: they assembled 'in the same place on these seventh days', sitting together and hearing the laws read and expounded 'so that none should be ignorant of them'. A priest or an elder read and commented on the law, and most people sat silent 'except when it is the practice to add something to signify approval of what is read'. The session continued until late afternoon (*Hypothetica* 7.12f.). Philo uses different terms for the buildings where Jews assembled on the sabbath. 'On each seventh day there stand wide open in every city thousands of schools of good sense.' In these 'schools' (*didaskaleia*), Jews heard the law expounded under two main heads: duty to God and duty to fellow humans (*Spec. Laws* 2.62f.). These are the main categories of the Jewish law, as we saw above. The Essenes, Philo also wrote, were instructed in the law at all times, 'but particularly on the seventh day'. Then 'they abstain[ed] from all other work and proceed[ed] to sacred spots which they call synagogues' (*Every Good Man is Free* 81). Most often Philo used the term that Josephus used in discussing the building in Tiberias, *proseuchē*, 'house of prayer'.[15] There were, according to Philo, 'many in each section of [Alexandria]' (*Embassy* 132; cf. 134, 152 and elsewhere). Houses of prayer were even allowed in Rome, since the Romans did not require the Jews 'to violate any of their native institutions'. Jews were accustomed to gather in these houses of prayer 'particularly on the sacred sabbaths when they receive as a body a training in their ancestral philosophy' (*Embassy* 155f.).

We may infer from Philo's usage that in the Diaspora the standard name for a synagogue was 'house of prayer', though he also used 'schools' in describing their function, and he knew that some people called them 'synagogues'. These were not different institutions. Philo assigns to them all the very same role: they were buildings where on the sabbath Jews gathered to study.

Since Judaism as a religion included rules for daily behaviour as well as sacrifice, Philo called it a '*philosophy*'. Josephus also chose to describe the parties in Jerusalem as 'schools' within a 'philosophy' (*War* 2.119). We may now think that this term was not entirely appropriate, since few Jews engaged in abstract or metaphysical speculation (as far as we know), and we call Judaism a 'religion'; but for a Greek writer in the first century 'philosophy' was the best word to describe an all-inclusive way of life that was inculcated by regular instruction.[16] Although, when he discussed sabbath assemblies, Philo emphasized the 'philosophical' study of the law, the term that he preferred, 'house of prayer', also points towards what we would now call 'worship'.

Only a few pre-70 synagogues have thus far been discovered in Palestine, but that is probably because they were demolished in favour of later ones, whose ruins are abundant. The three pre-70 synagogues that have been found are at sites where habitation ended at the time of the first revolt. Only a few such sites exist in Palestine, since towns and villages were almost always resettled. It is remarkable that in three cases where there was no resettlement synagogues have been found. Only one is in a town, Gamla, which is in the Golan Heights, north-east of the Sea of Galilee. This is also the only one of the three that was originally built to be a synagogue.

An illuminating and convincing reconstruction of the Gamla synagogue has been offered by Zvi Ma'oz. The building was about 16 × 20 metres overall. Columns divided the interior into a central nave and tiered aisles that ran around all four sides. The nave was 9.30 × 13.40 metres (30 ft × 44). There were four tiers, each one consisting of a row of stone benches, with areas for walking at the foot of the bottom row and above the top row. The top row of benches, if laid end to end, would be about 50 metres long and would seat about one hundred people. The lower rows would seat fewer; together the four rows would seat approximately three hundred people. Though the benches and walkways were stone, as were the columns, the floor of the nave was earthen. Ma'oz points out that in Palestine the main rooms in houses and other buildings were earthen and were covered with rugs; the same was probably true of the central floor of the synagogue. This floor plan, with a public area built of stone for heavy traffic, and with seats on all sides, facing the centre, which was covered with rugs, indicates that only a few people used the central area. The arrangement would 'allow free discussion among the seated public and enable them to hear speeches delivered from the center of the hall and the lowest tier of seats'. In a synagogue of this construction, 'the most important element was the *congregation*, which assembled to worship, listen to the scriptural readings, and participate in instruction and prayer'.[17]

The other two pre-70 Palestinian synagogues have been found in two of Herod's fortress/palace complexes, Matsada and the Herodium. In these cases, the synagogues were built by the Jewish rebels during the war with Rome. Herod, that is, though he built immersion pools for himself and his court (below, p. 223), did not build synagogues, at least not of the Gamla type. The rebels made synagogues within pre-existing buildings by constructing rows of benches around all the walls, very much like those at Gamla.[18]

If Herod did not build synagogues at all, we would have to assume that he and his advisers did not consider them necessary for the observance of the Jewish law. Herod did not intentionally trangress major aspects of the law (except, of course, when required to do so by political or military expediency). If he did not provide synagogues for himself and his entourage, he and his advisers did not share the view that Moses himself had decreed sabbath assembly. Yet we cannot be certain that his palaces did not contain rooms that functioned as synagogues. It is possible that at Matsada and the Herodium one of the halls served for gatherings on the sabbath, and that the defenders modified it to their type of synagogue by adding rows of benches around the room. While this is conceivable, we must also remain open to the possibility that, although many or most Jews thought that sabbath assembly was an integral part of their religion, and although towns and villages had synagogues, not everyone shared this opinion and not everyone attended synagogue.

Though only three pre-70 synagogues have thus far been found in Palestine, there is archaeological evidence for another. Above we noted the discovery in Jerusalem of a synagogue inscription that informs us that the priest Theodotus and his ancestors led a Greek-speaking synagogue that was dedicated to teaching the law and that could accommodate visitors. This reveals both that Diaspora Jews who came to Jerusalem expected to attend a synagogue and also that Jews in Jerusalem, including a wealthy priestly family, thought it proper to provide for them. It thus supports the other evidence for the common practice of attending synagogues, both in Palestine and elsewhere.[19]

The Theodotus inscription is graphic evidence of the role of priests in synagogues, a role that some of them retained in the Diaspora. We recall that according to Philo a priest or elder was responsible for sabbath instruction (*Hypothetica* 7.13). At the synagogue in Sardis an inscription was found that refers to a man who was a 'priest and teacher of wisdom'.[20] This is from the fourth century CE. Its relevance is that it shows continuity with the passage in Philo and the Theodotus inscription. In neither Palestine nor the Diaspora did priests withdraw from public life and community study and worship. By our period, prayer and reading of the Bible had already been incorporated in the temple service (above, pp. 80, 116f.). It was a natural development for priests to perform both functions in synagogues as well.

Just as the synagogues at Gamla, Matsada and the Herodium were arranged to allow and even encourage participation by the congregation, the New Testament assumes that anyone with something important to say would be allowed to speak: thus Jesus and Paul could use the synagogue service for their message (Mark 1.14–15; 6.1–5; Acts 13.15: 'Brethren, if you have any word of

exhortation for the people, say it.'). Paul gave instructions about prophesying and exhorting in the Christian worship services, and he supposed that
first one then another participant would speak (I Cor. 14.26–33). His
assumption of active participation by many probably reflects synagogue
practice as he knew it. Philo's description, on the other hand, assumes less
informality and spontaneity. The priest or elder read and interpreted the
Bible, and others for the most part remained silent (*Hypothetica* 7.13).

In I Cor. 14 Paul also refers to hymns and lessons. Since his view of
group worship was almost certainly influenced by the synagogue services
that he had attended, we may add singing to prayers and the reading and
exposition of scripture as possible synagogal activities.

Paul's discussion of the Lord's supper offers yet another. He urged that
food should be shared (I Cor. 11.21f.), a view that may have depended on
what he knew of meals at synagogues. Two passages in Josephus refer to
meals or 'sacrifices' in the Diaspora (*Antiq.* 14.216, 260). Whether or not
Diaspora Jews observed Passover (as I suggested above), at least some
communities assembled for communal meals.

We shall now consider *prayer* more closely. The desire to communicate
with a higher power runs deep in humanity, and to many first-century Jews
prayer must have been the most important religious activity. It was almost
certainly the most frequent. The pseudepigraphical books that purport to
describe the lives or deaths of biblical characters have a paradigmatic and
exhortative function: one should live like the hero or heroine. Adam and
Eve, Moses, Abraham, Job, Daniel, the twelve patriarchs, the scribe
Baruch, and many others are depicted as praying often. The same is true of
other heroes and heroines of the faith, such as Tobit and Judith. These
people were models to be emulated. According to *The Life of Adam and Eve*,
Eve, before dying, 'looked up to heaven, rose, beat her breast, and said,
"God of all, receive my spirit"' (*Apocalypse* 42.8): one should die with a
prayer on one's lips. In the *Testament of Abraham*, the patriarch is depicted
as customarily praying after the evening meal (*T. Abraham* A. 5.2): one
should pray every evening. Baruch, seeking illumination from God, prayed
for forty days (*III Baruch* 4.14). Job prayed by singing 'praises to the Father'
(*T. Job* 40.2f.). Levi prayed for deliverance (*T. Levi* 2.4). Judith prayed every
morning and evening (Judith 12.5–8; 13.3, 10). In Tobit the characters pray
on every occasion: when in despair (Tobit 3.1–6), even when feeling
suicidal (3.10–16); before consummating marriage (8.5–9); when thankful
(8.15–17; 11.14) and when rejoicing (13.1–18). In the *Letter of Aristeas* a
visiting Jewish expert recommends 'continual prayer to God' to king
Ptolemy (*Arist.* 196; 248), and the Jews are said to pray every morning
(305f.).

At the great crisis of his life, when Josephus decided to surrender to the Romans, he silently prayed (or so he later reported):

> Since it pleases thee, who didst create the Jewish nation, to break thy work, since fortune has wholly passed to the Romans, and since thou hast made choice of my spirit to announce the things that are to come, I willingly surrender to the Romans and consent to live; but I take thee to witness that I go, not as a traitor, but as thy minister. (*War* 3.354)

Individual prayer constitutes an aspect of worship that has changed little in the last twenty centuries. People prayed then as people who pray do now, to offer thanks and to present petitions to God: for health and happiness; for a good mate and worthy progeny; for strength in facing the vicissitudes of life; for prosperity and good fortune; for favourable weather; for blessings to be bestowed upon the community; for forgiveness and acceptance; for comfort in bereavement.

In discussing the temple and sacrifices, especially the Day of Atonement, we saw that the priests blessed the people and asked God for forgiveness. It is possible that individuals also went to the temple to pray (so Luke 2.37). Besides praying privately and at the temple, many Jews prayed when they attended their synagogues or houses of prayer. Josephus quotes Agatharchides, a critic of Judaism, as saying that on the sabbath the Jews 'pray with outstretched hands in the temples until the evening' (*Apion* 1.209). The reference is especially to the temple in Jerusalem, and the point is that the Jews would not fight on the sabbath because they were otherwise engaged; the plural 'temples', however, may show that the author also had synagogues in mind. In any case, the term 'house of prayer' is probably to be taken as descriptive of one of the main activities.

We cannot know to what extent there were set prayers or set themes for prayer at the synagogue. Many scholars have thought that the Christian work *The Apostolic Constitutions* contains synagogal prayers, reworked to include distinctively Christian themes, but even if so they are probably later than our period.[21] The rabbinic discussions of the group of prayers called the 'Eighteen Benedictions' indicate that they were not prayed as set texts, but rather as set themes (*Berakhot* 4.3). Some rabbis may have had set texts, but there was some sentiment against a rigidly prescribed form (*Berakhot* 4.4), and we should think in terms of established topics rather than a memorized text. We recall that the early rabbis linked prayer with saying the Shemaʿ, and consequently they thought of the morning and evening prayers as being said privately at home. They allowed, however, a good deal of leeway with regard to times (*Berakhot* 1.1–4; 4.1–7).

To understand daily piety, we must understand prayer, preferably including common themes. The Eighteen Benedictions offer the best chance of doing this. Although we cannot assume that they have come down to us as they were said, nor even that non-rabbis or non-Pharisees prayed according to their main themes, it is worthwhile to summarize them as probably indicating the themes of the prayers of a leading pietist group, the Pharisees, and as illustrating the sorts of prayers that people of the day offered. I have used a medieval text of the Eighteen Benedictions that was found in the Cairo Genizah.[22]

First, to give something of the flavour of the prayers, I shall quote in full Benedictions 4, 7, 14, 16, 17 and 18:

4. Graciously favour us, our Father, with understanding from thee,
   And discernment and insight out of thy Torah.
   Blessed art thou, O Lord, gracious bestower of understanding.

7. Behold our afflictions and defend our cause,
   And redeem us for thy name's sake
   Blessed art thou, O Lord, Redeemer of Israel.

14. Have compassion, O Lord our God, in thine abundant mercy,
        on Israel thy people,
    And on Jerusalem thy city,
    And on Zion, the abode of thy glory,
    And upon the royal seed of David, thy justly anointed.
    Blessed art thou, O Lord, God of David, Rebuilder of Jerusalem.

16. May it be thy will, O Lord our God, to dwell in Zion,
    And may thy servants worship thee in Jerusalem.
    Blessed art thou, O Lord, for it is thou whom we worship in
        reverence.

17. We thank thee, Our God and God of our fathers,
    For all the goodness, the lovingkindness, and the mercies
    With which thou hast requited us, and our fathers before us.
    For when we say, 'our foot slips',
    Thy mercy, O Lord, holds us up.
    Blessed art thou, O Lord, to whom it is good to give thanks.

18. Bestow thy peace
    Upon Israel thy people,
    And upon thy city,
    And upon thine inheritance,
    And bless us all, together.
    Blessed art thou, O Lord, Maker of peace.

The other prayers bless God for one or more of his attributes. He is the one

1. Who is creator of heaven and earth, our shield and shield of our fathers.
2. Who resurrects the dead.
3. Who is the only true God.
5. Who desires repentance.
6. Who forgives readily.
8. Who heals the sick.
9. Who grants abundant harvest.
10. Who gathers the dispersed.
11. Who loves justice.
12. Who curses the apostates.
13. Who shows mercy to converts.
15. Who hears prayer.

As we have them, the Eighteen Benedictions are communal in nature: God is blessed for encouraging *people to repent* and *forgiving those who do*. This is formally different from individual confession of sins and petition for forgiveness. We see here synagogal shaping that may have come after our period. Individuals may have followed these themes, but cast their prayers in a more personal form. Perhaps we get a better idea of what individual prayers were like from the Dead Sea Scrolls. I quote here some of the lines from the prayer that concludes the *Community Rule* and also one of the prayers from the *Thanksgiving Hymns*:

> I will declare His judgment concerning my sins,
> > and my transgressions shall be before my eyes . . .
> I will say to God, 'My Righteousness'
> > and 'Author of my Goodness' to the Most High . . .
> I will meditate on His power
> > and will lean on His mercies all day long.
> . . .
> As for me,
> > my justification is with God.
> In His hand are the perfection of my way
> > and the uprightness of my heart.
> He will wipe out my transgression
> > through his mercy.[23]
> . . .
> As for me,
> > if I stumble, the mercies of God

shall be my eternal salvation.
If I stagger because of the sin of the flesh,
    my justification shall be by the mercy of God . . . (1QS 10–11)[24]

I [thank Thee, O Lord],
    for Thou has enlightened me through Thy Truth.
In Thy marvellous mysteries,
    and in thy lovingkindness to a man [of vanity,
    and] in the greatness of Thy mercy to a perverse heart,
    Thou has granted me knowledge.
Who is like Thee among the gods, O Lord,
    and who is according to Thy truth?
Who, when he is judged,
    shall be righteous before Thee?
For no spirit can reply to Thy rebuke
    nor can any withstand Thy wrath.
Yet Thou bringest all the sons of Thy truth
    in forgiveness before Thee,
[to cleanse] them of their faults
    through Thy great goodness,
and to establish them before Thee
    through the multitude of Thy mercies for ever and ever.[25]

The prayers from Qumran are marked by the special piety of the group, which among other things greatly emphasized the inability of humans to be righteous and which correspondingly dwelt on the mercy and righteousness of God. Jews in general knew that they transgressed and therefore had to appeal to God's mercy for forgiveness, but we cannot attribute to them quite the same degree of consciousness of human nothingness before God. The Qumran prayers are extreme, but when this is granted they may be read as reflecting some of the main themes of Jewish prayer in general. Thanksgiving for God's mercy was a major aspect of first-century Jewish prayer.[26]

The prayers of the Hymn Scroll may represent individual or collective piety; we do not know how they were used. We do know, however, that at Qumran there were communal prayers. A very fragmentary text of morning and evening blessings has been found (4Q503).[27] Josephus singled out the Essenes as having inherited prayers from previous generations which they said each morning (War 2.128), and this statement is confirmed by 4Q503. The fact that Josephus said this about the Essenes makes it all the more likely that other Jews did not have set texts. Thus, while we cannot know just how ordinary Jews prayed, we may be sure that they did pray, and the material that has been quoted above gives some idea of the nature of first-century Jewish prayers.[28]

We have seen that most Jews worshipped God every day by recalling the commandments or saying the Shemaʿ and praying privately. On the sabbath, they studied the Bible and, at least in some synagogues, they prayed, but probably they did not all pray the same prayer in unison. As Lee Levine has remarked, it is probable that the range of activities in synagogues increased with distance from Jerusalem.[29] The evidence indicates that study of the law was standard in all synagogues and that prayer was common.[30] For hymns and meals we have pre-70 evidence only from the Diaspora. This does not prove that Palestinian Jews did not sing, nor that they did not share meals at the synagogue. Those who could sometimes attend the temple, however, had many of their religious needs fulfilled in that way.

To conclude our discussion of worship, let us ask whether or not Jews had worship services of the type familiar to millions of Jews and Christians: set times, set scripture, set texts (whether prayers, hymns or creeds), and recitation or singing in unison. The available evidence suggests the following conclusions:

1. Privately, Jews repeated the Shemaʿ at set times, and they also prayed according to a regular schedule: either when going to bed and rising, or at the times of prayer in the temple, or some combination of the two. Publicly, they met at set times on the sabbath.

2. Since the main point of sabbath assembly was study of the law, it is reasonable to think that the various synagogues studied passages of scripture in some order or other, quite possibly an order determined locally. We do not have good evidence that standard lectionaries – lists of scriptural passages to be read sabbath by sabbath – had developed by our period. It is, in fact, possible that the selection of passages was made on the spot (see point 4).

3. The monastic community at Qumran had at least some set prayers to be said at set times. Rabbinic discussions make it likely that the Pharisees had standard themes for the morning and evening prayers, but we do not know how widely these were accepted. The term 'house of prayer' for synagogues, especially used in the Diaspora, shows that many Jews prayed during sabbath assembly, but there is no evidence in favour of the recitation of prayers from a fixed text.

4. In fact, first-century Jews probably did not do anything in unison. Possibly the Qumran community prayed their set prayers together; there is no evidence one way or another. If Jews were in a synagogue at a time for prayer (e.g. first thing in the morning or at the time of the evening sacrifice in the temple), they may all have prayed, but not necessarily precisely the same prayer, and probably not in unison. While Josephus was making his morning devotions in the synagogue in Tiberias, someone addressed him. People were in the synagogue, and it was time for prayer, but they were not all doing

the same thing at the same instant.[31] Paul, our best single witness to what went on in Diaspora synagogues, wrote this about the worship services of his converts in Corinth: 'When you come together, *each one* has a hymn, a lesson, a revelation, a tongue, or an interpretation' (I Cor. 14.26). His discussion implies that people should take turns. Although spontaneity was especially prized in the Christian movement as evidence of the presence of the Spirit, it is nevertheless probable that it did not cross Paul's mind that the congregation might sing a hymn in unison. In a synagogue of long standing, to be sure, certain routines would have been established, but our scanty evidence is against congregational participation in unison.

We have found the recitation of a semi-credal passage (the Shemaʿ), prayers, hymns, and study of the scripture; but these had not yet come together to make up a standard worship service.

The sabbath

Besides attendance at the synagogue, what else characterized observance of the sabbath? The Jewish sabbath, the seventh and last day of the week, like all other days in the calendar, begins at sundown, not sunrise. The general requirement to keep it as a day of rest is one of the Ten Commandments (Ex. 20.8–11; Deut. 5.12–15). The rationale is slightly different in the two passages. According to Exodus, the seventh day was to be observed because God himself had rested on the seventh day of creation, while according to Deuteronomy it commemorates the exodus from Egypt. In both lists it includes not only Israelites (adult males and, in this case, females) but also children, servants, foreigners and animals. Short forms of the sabbath requirement appear in Ex. 34.21 and Lev. 19.3. In subsequent Israelite history the sabbath laws were elaborated. Jeremiah forbade carrying burdens in or out of the city, and even in or out of the house (Jer. 17.19–27). According to Neh. 10.31 the Israelites pledged themselves not to buy things from Gentiles or dubious Jews ('the peoples of the land') on the sabbath, as well as to let the land lie fallow and not to claim debts in the seventh year. Nehemiah 13.15–22 narrates Nehemiah's strong measures to prevent trading on the sabbath, both by Jews and Gentiles. To do this he shut the gates of Jerusalem and posted Levites as guards. According to this narrative the commandment that non-Jews who lived in the land of Israel must also rest was enforced by keeping them outside the city gates, which is what a strict reading of the text requires ('the sojourner who is within your gates', Ex. 20.10).

The Bible prescribes death by stoning as the punishment for deliberate transgression (Num. 15.32–6). Unwitting or inadvertent transgression required a sin offering (Lev. 4.27–31).

Both insiders and outsiders singled out observance of the sabbath as the most unusual aspect of standard Jewish practice. Many pages ago we saw that, during the Hasmonean revolt, some of the pious were killed because they would not defend themselves when attacked on the sabbath. This led to the resolution to fight in self-defence, but not otherwise (I Macc. 2.29–41). This resolution was kept – not just by the specially pious, but generally. Thus, for example, when the Roman general Pompey had hemmed up the followers of Aristobulus II in the temple, he took advantage of Jewish adherence to the law by raising earthworks on the sabbath, while refraining from firing missiles. The Jews could have responded to missiles, a direct attack, but not to the building of earthworks. Thus the battering rams could be brought into service in perfect safety (*War* 1.145–7; Dio Cassius 37.16.2f.). Aristobulus was an ally of the eminent against the Pharisees (*Antiq.* 13.411), and nothing that is known about him marks him as super-pious; he was simply following standard Jewish law. His grandfather, John Hyrcanus, had once broken off an important siege because of the coming of the sabbath year (*War* 1.157–60): all the laws governing days, years and seasons seem to have been faithfully kept. It accords with this that Julius Caesar exempted Judaea from tribute in the seventh year (*Antiq.* 14.202).

The same picture emerges from the Diaspora. Gentiles could exploit Jewish obedience to the sabbath laws. In Ionia, we are told, they took Jews to court on holy days in order to outrage their religion – and possibly to tie the Jews' hands, since some of them may have refused to appear in court on the sabbath (*Antiq.* 16.45–46). Many Gentile authors ridiculed the sabbath, while some seriously criticized it. Seneca (to illustrate the second point) wrote that the gods do not need lamps to be lit on the sabbath, since they do not need lights, while people should 'find no pleasure in soot' (Seneca, *Moral Letters* 95.47). This example, and many others, occupy ten usefully arranged and annotated pages of pagan comments on Jewish sabbath observance in Molly Whittaker's collection.[32] The comments come from a wide range, both chronologically and geographically, and they show that Gentiles viewed sabbath observance as a chief characteristic of the Jews.

Keeping the law in the Diaspora was sometimes a struggle, as the previous paragraph indicates. Thanks to the adroit political and military manoeuvring of Antipater, Herod's father, however, the problem was eased. In gratitude for Jewish support during the Roman civil wars, Julius Caesar bestowed numerous favours on Jews, both in Palestine and in the Diaspora. To show their loyalty to Caesar, the Greek-speaking cities of Asia Minor passed decrees that granted Jewish rights. Ephesus decreed that 'no one shall be prevented from keeping the Sabbath days nor be fined for so doing' (*Antiq.* 14.264). Several of the decrees exempt the Jews from military service. This was directly connected to their right to keep the sabbath, as a letter from a Roman official to Ephesus makes clear: since Jews 'may not bear arms or march on the days of the Sabbath', they 'cannot undertake military service' (14.226).

Positively, as we have seen, the sabbath day was an occasion for special sacrifices in the temple and for prayer and study in the synagogue. Pagan authors not infrequently referred to the sabbath as a fast, perhaps because Jews did not cook, which made it seem like a fast to outsiders (see Whittaker, as above). The sabbath in fact was not a fast, but rather a joyous occasion. Fires could not be lit on the sabbath itself, but food was left to cook or keep warm on a fire lit before sunset on Friday. The Friday evening meal was as festive as people could afford to make it. The Pharisees devised special rules that allowed near neighbours to carry food and dishes from one house to another, and dining with friends or relatives was a sign of festivity. We may also assume that the sabbath meal included a special dish, probably fowl or fish; that is, not red meat, as at a full festival, but something better than ordinary. The Pharisees debated whether or not on a festival day one could move the ladder to take down a pigeon or dove from the dovecote (*Betsah* 1.3).[33] We have this debate only because the biblical law governing working on festival days is subject to more than one interpretation. Moving the ladder on the sabbath would be clearly against the law, and thus there is no comparable debate. It seems likely, however, that the meals were similar, since festival days were semi-sabbaths. It is also intrinsically likely that the sabbath was an occasion for intermediate meals, not a full banquet, as at festivals, but more than the usual bread, lentils and cheese.

The criticism and ridicule of learned pagans may have been especially sharp because of the attractiveness of the Jewish sabbath in the eyes of many Gentiles. Josephus claimed that in all countries and cities there were some who imitated the Jewish abstinence from work and marked the day, as did the Jews, by having lamps burning (*Apion* 2.282). He elsewhere stated that the Jewish rites and celebrations attracted many (*War* 7.45, Syria; cf. *War* 2.560; Acts 10.2).[34] Many years later, John Chrysostom, a Christian priest in Antioch at the end of the fourth century, would attack the Jews, whose attractive ceremonies were proving enticing to many of his parishioners. Marcel Simon, commenting on this situation, pointed out that 'even the more troublesome obligations of Jewish observance found a large public willing to comply with them'.[35] These 'troublesome obligations' included sabbath observance as a main feature, but Jews did not consider it 'troublesome' (except when Gentiles took advantage of it), and apparently neither did the pagans who adopted the custom.

In discussing the sabbath, I have left rabbinic literature and the Dead Sea

Scrolls out of account, since we shall examine the practice of the Pharisees and Essenes separately. They will in no way alter the impression given by the rest of the literature, which is unanimous with regard to the sabbath. The gospels, Josephus, Philo, apocryphal and pseudepigraphical writings, pagan literature, and the decrees of Roman rulers and Hellenistic city councils all attest to the fact that Jews kept the sabbath. We may be sure that they did not work in any ordinary sense of the term and that they would not fight unless directly attacked. Exterior jobs (farming, selling and the like) and domestic work (such as baking and cooking) were treated alike: all were forbidden, and the Bible's basic prohibition of work was observed.

We have firm evidence that most Jews went beyond the biblical specifications for sabbath observance in two ways. They attended the synagogue for part of the sabbath, and they all agreed the fighting was prohibited. The Bible nowhere explicitly applies the sabbath law to warfare, and this seems to have been a post-exilic development. It was, however, universally accepted, both in Palestine and the Diaspora, and both by Jews and by Gentiles, who, because of it (as we just saw), did not conscript Jews (*Antiq.* 14.226).[36]

What the details and modifications were in private observance of the sabbath we cannot know. We shall later see that the two main pietist groups modified the sabbath law in various ways, sometimes making it stricter, sometimes more lenient. We may imagine all kinds of private or family variations on the part of others: the equivalent of 'It will not hurt anything if I just darn this sock', or 'We never brush the crumbs off the table'. Whatever their individual or group variations, virtually all Jews abstained from the most obvious forms of work, had a special meal and went to synagogue. It later became almost a rule that married couples should have intercourse on Friday night, and this may very well have been part of ordinary sabbath observance in the first century.

The right to observe the law in the Diaspora

It was not especially difficult in Jewish Palestine to follow the laws and to maintain the practices that we have considered in this chapter – worshipping the one God in home and synagogue and keeping the sabbath. These observances were of vital importance, but they were also matters of community routine. Buying something on the sabbath would have been harder than not buying it. We have seen that it was otherwise in the Diaspora, and that Jews needed legal permission to practise their religion, and sometimes protection as well. I wish now to indicate what rights were most important to Diaspora Jews.

We have made extensive use of a set of decrees and letters in *Antiq.* 14. As I explained above, Julius Caesar, in gratitude for Jewish support during his war with Pompey, bestowed benefits on both Palestinian and Diaspora Jews, and various cities in the empire followed suit by giving the Jews certain rights. Josephus quotes these decrees as well as letters from Roman officials relating to the same issues. The rights most frequently mentioned are these:

1. The right to assemble or to have a place of assembly: 5 times
   (*Antiq.* 14.214–16, 227, 235, 257f., 260f.)

2. The right to keep the sabbath: 5 times
   (14. 226, 242, 245, 258, 263f.)

3. The right to have their 'ancestral' food: 3 times
   (14.226, 245, 261)

4. The right to decide their own affairs: 2 times
   (14.235, 260)

5. The right to contribute money: 2 times
   (14.214, 227)[37]

There are, in addition, numerous general references to the right to follow their 'customs' (*ethē,*) or to keep their 'holy rites' or 'regulations' (*ta hiera, nomima*) (14.213–16, 223, 227, 242, 245f., 258, 260, 263).

These rights doubtless covered aspects of Jewish practice that Jews themselves thought were basic. The right of assembly, now taken for granted in the western democracies, but one of the main points of the American Bill of Rights, was crucial. Caesar's decree claims that other religious societies were forbidden to assemble in the city of Rome, but that the Jews were allowed to do so (*Antiq.* 14.215f.). According to Suetonius, Caesar himself 'dissolved all guilds, except those of ancient foundation' (*Julius Caesar* 42.3).[38] Philo praised Augustus for permitting 'Jews alone' to assemble in synagogues (*Embassy* 311). The question of foreign ethnic or religious assemblies in the city of Rome is a complicated one, but we may accept the implication of our text, that Caesar conferred a special privilege on the Jews. The right to gather to worship the one God, and the freedom to observe the sabbath, without penalty (14.264), meant that a Jewish way of life could be maintained. Worship and sabbath observance were central to Jewish practice.

12

Observing the Law of God II: Circumcision, Purity, Food, Charity and Love

Circumcision and identity

Jewish families circumcised their sons. It is a slightly curious fact that even though Jews were not the only circumcised males in the Mediterranean world,[1] nevertheless both insiders and outsiders regarded circumcision as distinctively Jewish.[2] Josephus defended the Jews against Apion's criticism, that they would not eat pork but did require circumcision, by replying that both points were true of the Egyptian priests (*Apion* 2.137–42). This illustrates the fact that many people, both pagan and Jewish, regarded circumcision as 'Jewish', though more-or-less everyone knew that others observed it as well.

In discussing the period of Antiochus IV Epiphanes, we saw the cultural conflict between the Greek view that circumcision was mutilation and the view of most Jews that disguising circumcision was rank apostasy (p. 17). This issue arose again after our period, when Hadrian proscribed circumcision.[3] During the early Roman period, Jews circumcised their sons, and others commented on it but did not, as far as we know, harass them about it.

The standard theological interpretation of circumcision was that it was a sign of the election of Israel and the covenant with Abraham (Gen. 17). The direct commandment that on the eighth day after birth sons be circumcised appears in Gen. 17.12f. Those not circumcised will be 'cut off' (17.14). The commandment to circumcise on the eighth day is repeated in Lev. 12.3.

As on every point, there was some variety of interpretation and practice. Mendelson has pointed out that Philo saw circumcision not as a rite 'whereby a male child gains entry into the congregation of Israel', but rather a sign of 'the spirit of compliance or non-compliance in the parents'.[4] The allegorizers to whom Philo refers, but whose position he does not fully describe, may have

wished to surrender circumcision as a sign of being Jewish.[5] Further, it is not
certain that all Jewish communities required circumcision of adult males who
converted to Judaism. Despite some diversity in interpretation and a few
exceptions to the rule, circumcision of males was commonly regarded as an
essential part of Jewish practice.

Purity

Purity regulations were the next most obvious and universally kept set of
laws. We have seen that most impurities were not forbidden and that a
majority of purity laws affected only entrance to the temple and handling or
eating 'holy things'. It was not wrong to contact semen, bury the dead, have a
child or menstruate. These caused impurity, which one must not convey to
the sanctuary, but in and of themselves they were right, good and proper. We
return to these below.

Purity of food

Food is different from the purity laws of Lev. 12, 15; Num. 19. Law
regulates what Jews can eat, and some possible foods are completely
prohibited, being labelled not only 'impure' but also 'abominable' (Lev. 11;
Deut. 14). Intentional transgression of the prohibitions constitutes a serious
offence. The Bible makes two major restrictions: it allows Jews to eat only a
few living creatures; it forbids them to consume the main fatty parts of an
animal and its blood. These rules, together with a few others, constitute what
are now called the laws of 'kashrut'. Only certain food is 'kosher', suitable for
Jews to eat.

Edible quadrupeds are those that chew the cud and have cloven hoofs
(Lev. 11.3–7; Deut. 14.6–8). This means that cattle, sheep and goats are
permitted, as well as a few other animals, such as wild goats and deer. Fish
that have fins and scales may be eaten (Lev. 11.9), as may many birds –
notably excluding birds of prey (Lev. 11.13–17). Insects and other 'swarming
things' (serpents, lizards, weasels and the like) are forbidden, but some forms
of life that fly and that 'have legs above their feet' are permitted (locusts,
crickets and grasshoppers) (Lev. 11.20–45).

The animal whose absence from the Jewish diet attracted most attention
was the pig, and pagan authors sometimes discussed whether Jews honoured
pigs or abominated them.[6] The Jewish restrictions were frequently a point of
fun or ridicule. Macrobius attributed to Augustus Caesar the statement that
he would rather have been Herod's pig than his son; Herod kept the Jewish
law and thus did not eat pork, but he had three of his sons executed.[7] Some

Gentiles, though, found abstinence from many forms of food to be a good thing, and Seneca indicated that a period of vegetarianism in his own life was encouraged by 'foreign rites' which required 'abstinence from certain animals'.[8] Seneca may have been following not the Jews, but the Pythagoreans, who were vegetarians, but in any case we see that abstemiousness could be attractive.

The laws governing what foods may be eaten are so explicit in the Bible that they were subject to only the most minor modifications. When Jews came across animals or birds that the biblical classifiers had not discussed, they examined them and established whether or not they were suitable for food. Thus the Greek translation of the Hebrew Bible explicitly mentions and allows the buffalo (that is, the water buffalo of Egypt) and the giraffe (LXX Deut. 14.4f.). Philo adds cranes and geese to edible fowl (*Spec. Laws* 4.117). No one, to my knowledge, tampered with the prohibitions.

In the Jewish areas of Palestine it would have been difficult or impossible to eat prohibited animals, and we may assume general compliance. Keeping pigs would attract a good deal of attention and would amount to a public statement that the family was not observant. There may have been some temptation to trap and eat the hare and the badger (forbidden by Deut. 14.7), which would provide free meat; but, again, setting traps cannot be kept secret, and the Jew who did it would face disapproval and perhaps ostracism. It was simpler and better to build a dovecote, which also provided free food, since doves and pigeons feed themselves (preferably on the neighbour's grain rather than one's own!).

Jews who lived in the pagan world had to be concerned about their food supply, as we saw at the end of the previous chapter. In some places they had to request the authorities to require the market managers to provide them with food that they could eat. A Roman proconsul wrote to Miletus, instructing the city to give the Jews permission to 'manage' or 'handle' their produce (*Antiq.* 14.245).[9] The decree of Sardis claimed that the Jews there had previously been given many privileges, while tacitly admitting that this had not been true lately. The Jews had recently petitioned the council concerning their laws, pointing out that the Roman Senate had restored them. The Sardis council hastened to put itself on the same side as Rome. It ordered, among other things, that 'the market-officials of the city shall be charged with the duty of having suitable food for [Jews] brought in' (*Antiq.* 14.259–61). Unfortunately we do not know just what the special food was, and consequently we cannot know what sort of difficulties the Jews of Sardis had been experiencing. I would guess that the problem was not that of obtaining red meat from a suitable animal. In Palestine the principal red meat was lamb or kid; in the pagan Mediterranean it was pork, lamb or kid. Jews need only have avoided the pork.

There were, of course, two other potential problems. I shall mention them very briefly.[10] An animal might have been sacrificed to a pagan deity, or it might have been slaughtered in such a way as still to have blood in it (for the prohibition of blood, see e.g. Lev. 3.17). The first was frequently true of the red meat available in Gentile cities. As in Judaism, slaughter was usually sacrificial; animals did double duty. The second possible problem (that blood was still in the meat) need not have been true. Pagan slaughter was not precisely like Jewish; the animal was not hung up by the leg after the throat was cut. By the time the Greek or Roman priest or butcher was through, however, there was no blood left, since he both eviscerated the animal and boned the meat. Yet not all Gentile slaughter followed Greek sacrificial technique, and Jews especially feared eating meat from an animal that was literally strangled. They may also have *suspected* pagan slaughter of leaving blood in the meat, and there seems to have been some fear that a pagan butcher might cut an animal's throat in such a way as to make it choke on its own blood.[11] Though Jews might have been legally justified in accepting some Gentile meat as bloodless, they may not have been willing to do so.

There are possible problems with other foods, especially the main liquids, oil and wine. A libation to a pagan deity might have been offered from wine before it was sold; oil also might have an idolatrous connection. Perhaps, for example, the olive grove belonged to a pagan temple, as many did. (On reluctance to use Gentile oil, see *War* 2.591; *Life* 74; *Antiq.* 12.120.)[12]

Finally, some Jews were *generally* unwilling to eat pagan food, even when there might be no legal objection to it. Some, if they had to eat Gentile food, would eat only vegetables and drink only water; some would eat nothing cooked at all.[13] That is, some Diaspora Jews responded to their pagan environment, full of idolatry and sexual immorality (from their perspective), by cutting themselves off from too much contact with Gentiles. In such families, there was a desire to control their food supply entirely. Other Jews, it must be emphasized, participated in numerous aspects of pagan culture, such as the theatre and games, quite cheerfully. All civic ceremonies included acknowledgment of one or more pagan deities, but some Jews were willing to overlook this (as today some will without protest sit through prayers that end 'through Jesus Christ our Lord'), and these people may have felt less queasy about Gentile food.[14] In I Cor. 10.27, Paul advises Christians not to ask about the source of food when in someone else's house, and it is most likely that in the Diaspora some Jewish families followed the same practice.

Thus we cannot say just what it was about the food in the public market to which the Jews of Sardis objected. We do see, both from this decree and from numerous pagan comments about the Jews' dietary restrictions, that in general they tried to keep the food laws and that even in the Diaspora they kept the major ones.

Finally, we note one further possible food restriction. In three different passages the Bible prohibits 'seething a kid in its mother's milk' (Ex. 23.19; 34.27; Deut. 14.21). We now attribute such repetitions to overlapping sources, but in the first century a thrice-repeated prohibition was considered to be an especially strict one. At some point the commandment not to seethe a kid in its mother's milk was elaborated to mean that meat and dairy products should not come into contact with each other. The earliest text that reveals this restriction is *Hullin* 8.1f. The Houses of Hillel and Shammai debated the topic, the Shammaites holding that a fowl could be served with cheese provided that the two were not eaten together, the Hillelites that fowl and cheese could be neither served nor eaten together. Subsequent rules offer further modifications: some rabbis held that fowl and cheese could be put on the same serving table or buffet and that the Houses had debated only what was permitted at a table where people ate (8.1). Rabban Simeon b. Gamaliel maintained that two strangers could eat at a table where both meat and cheese were served if one ate cheese and the other meat (8.2). The last stage in the argument is probably represented by the rule that now comes first, at the beginning of 8.1: 'No flesh may be cooked in milk excepting the flesh of fish and locusts; and no flesh may be served up on the table together with cheese excepting the flesh of fish and locusts' (8.1).

The Houses debate presupposes that red meat and cheese may not be served together, and also that flesh, even of fowl, may not be cooked together with a dairy product. These presuppositions probably represent pre-70 Pharisaic law. Although we cannot know whether or not other people accepted restrictions on mixing meat and dairy products, I think it quite likely that many people would not cook meat and milk or cheese together.

Other principal purity laws

In discussing the temple we saw that several impurities had to be kept away from the realm of the sacred: the impurities that arise from death, childbirth, menstruation, semen, and other discharges from the vagina or penis. People affected by these major *changes of status*, which have to do with life, death and reproduction, were to stay away from what was holy (above, pp. 70–72). We shall now consider these and a few other impurities in more detail, as well as the means of purification.

Corpse impurity is the subject of Numbers 19, which prescribes an elaborate ritual for purification. A priest slaughtered a red heifer outside the temple and burnt it. The ashes were kept and were mixed with water. The mixture was sprinkled on impure people on the third day and the seventh; they then washed their clothes and bathed, and the impurity was removed. Not only people who had been near the corpse, but also the room where it had lain and the contents of the room had to be sprinkled.

The study of corpse impurity reveals a very important aspect of second-temple Judaism. Many people considered purity to be a positive good, the proper state to be in, *whether or not* one was about to enter the temple. We see this, for example, in Philo's discussions of corpse impurity. From the point of view of biblical law, there was nothing that he and other Diaspora Jews could do about it: they all had it all the time, and they could remove it only when they made pilgrimage to Jerusalem. Nevertheless, Philo thought that, after mourning the dead, people should go home and splash themselves from a basin of water, thus becoming 'really pure' – for all purposes except entering the temple (*Spec. Laws* 3.205f.). He and other Diaspora Jews made up new, readily observable, purity rites, so that they could feel pure (other examples will be seen below).

The view that one should remove impurity, whether or not one was about to enter the temple, may lie behind a difficult passage in Josephus. A person who remains corpse-impure for more than seven days 'is required to sacrifice two lambs, of which one must be devoted to the flames and the other is taken by the priests' (*Antiq.* 3.262). This is not actually required by the Bible. Nor could the new law have been followed by people who lived a long way from Jerusalem, since the mixture of ashes and water that removed corpse impurity was kept at the temple (though the priesthood may have organized occasional missions to purify houses outside of Jerusalem). It is impossible to be certain of the practical import of Josephus' 'law', but a speculation may suggest how laws were interpreted. According to Num. 19.13, 20, the person who is not purified 'shall be cut off from the midst of the assembly', that is, be executed. Numbers 19.20 continues, however, by explaining that such a person has 'defiled the sanctuary of the Lord'. In context, it is only entering the temple while corpse-impure that is a capital offence. Josephus' statement seems to reflect the following interpretation: the first part of Num. 19.20 (before the words about the sanctuary) has independent status and is the equivalent of a positive commandment, 'remove corpse impurity'. Failure to fulfil this commandment is a lighter transgression than breaking the negative commandment, 'do not enter the temple while corpse-impure'. Therefore the penalty is only a sacrifice, not death. Alternatively, the ancient interpreters supposed that failure to remove corpse impurity was 'inadvertent', since people who lived away from the temple could not readily do so. Inadvertent transgression of a purity law requires a sin offering (Lev. 4.27–35),[15] which should be presented the next time the person was in Jerusalem.

It may be that the non-biblical law, cited by Josephus as if it were a Mosaic decree, was a priestly rule that constituted an extra tax on pilgrims. Presumably if a person confessed to (say) Josephus, while he was serving in the temple, that he had been corpse-impure for six months, but said that he could not afford two animals, Josephus would have allowed him to substitute birds or meal (cf. Lev. 5.7–13).

But whatever be the explanation of *Antiq.* 3.262, the existence of the sentence shows the tendency to make purity a positive commandment, with the consequence that remaining impure was regarded as a transgression.

Childbirth, another major change of status, resulted in lengthy impurity that was divided into two stages. During stage one, which lasted for one week if the child was a boy, two weeks if a girl, the mother was impure as if she were menstruating; that is, she could not have sexual relations. Stage two lasted for thirty-three or sixty-six days, depending on the sex of the child. During it the woman could not touch 'anything holy' (Lev. 12.4). The period concluded with the presentation of offerings: either a lamb as a burnt offering and a bird (pigeon or dove) as a sin offering, or two birds if she could not afford a lamb (Lev. 12.1–8).

Menstruation resulted in seven days impurity for the woman. In the first century, she then bathed (see below). Her bed and anything on which she sat also became impure. Thus there would be a large washing to be done at the end of the seven days. Anyone who touched her bed or chair had to bathe and wash his clothes; he was impure until sunset (Lev. 15.19–23). Intercourse with a menstruant was strictly forbidden. If it was inadvertent, which would be the case if the couple saw blood only afterwards, the man was also impure for seven days (15.24), and both parties owed a sin offering (4.27–5.13; on blood found after intercourse, see also *Niddah* 2.4). If the act was intentional, both parties were to be executed ('cut off') (Lev. 18.19; 20.18). In the nature of the case, conviction for intentional transgression of this law would have been impossible, but the theoretical penalty drives home the point that menstruation (and stage one of childbirth impurity) interrupt normal domestic relations, as well as access to the temple.

Irregular discharges from the genital areas also created impurity (Lev. 15.1–15, 25–30). The principal cause of discharge in women was miscarriage. Male spermatorrhoea (irregular emission of semen) can have various causes, the most serious being gonorrhoea. These impurities functioned as did menstruation: the afflicted person rendered impure what he or she lay or sat on, and others who touched their beds or chairs had to bathe and wash their clothes. Discharge impurity, however, was more severe than menstruation; therefore, after the discharge ceased, purification required sacrifices as well as the passing of seven pure days and bathing.

A man who had a *nocturnal emission* was to bathe his whole body and wash anything that the semen had touched. Impurity lasted until sunset (Lev. 15.16f.). Contact with semen as a result of *sexual intercourse* rendered both parties impure. Purification required bathing and sunset (15.18).

Carcasses could also render one impure. Touching the carcass of either an impure animal (one forbidden as food) or a forbidden 'swarming thing' (rodents, weasels, lizards, crocodiles and the like) also resulted in impurity, which passed away at sunset without bathing (Lev. 11.29f.). Carrying the carcass of an impure animal, however, required that one's clothes also be washed (Lev. 11.8, 24f., 27, 31).[16]

Dead swarming things also rendered moist food, liquids, vessels and ovens impure (Lev. 11.32–8).[17]

The principal remaining impurity is '*leprosy*', not necessarily clinical leprosy as now defined, but various kinds of spots or irruptions on the skin. The leprosy laws comprise two full chapters of Leviticus (13–14), and the procedure for purification was elaborate. It included both inspection by a priest and sacrifices. Leprosy is not covered by the general rule that impurity consists of a 'change of status', and it may be better described as an 'improper mixture' (i.e., of unhealthy skin with normal skin).[18] Leprosy shows the degree to which the ancient idea of purity was different from modern notions of health and sanitation. 'If the leprosy has covered all his body, [the priest] shall pronounce [the leper] pure' (Lev. 13.13). The person whose skin turned entirely white no longer suffered an improper mixture.

Things as well as people could become impure. Everything in the room with a corpse, except stoppered vessels and their contents, was impure and had to be sprinkled with the mixture of ashes and water that was used for people (Num. 19.15–18). Carcass impurity and the emission impurities sometimes required the garments and bed-coverings be washed. 'Leprosy' could beset clothes and houses (Lev. 13.47–59; 14.33–53). We noted just above that the carcasses of 'swarming things' could render vessels, moist food and liquid impure. Garments, skins, sacks and wooden utensils were purified by washing, but earthenware vessels had to be broken.

One of the principal modifications of the purity laws between the time of Leviticus and our period affected *women*. Leviticus prescribes only the passage of time for the purification of women (except in the case of contact with semen), while it requires both bathing and the passing of time for the purification of men. In late second-temple Jewish Palestine it was agreed on all hands that women, like men, bathed for purification. The explanation of this development is probably the expansion of the temple complex and the admission of women. When women did not in any case enter the temple area, but handed the priest their sacrifices at the gate (cf. Lev. 12.6, 'at the door of

I Remains of the synagogue at Gamla.

II An immersion pool at Gamla.

III Steps leading into an immersion
pool at Qumran, divided into sections.

IV Young Jewish females, showing hair coverings and notched gammas on the lower right side of the mantles.

V Young Jewish males, showing notched decoration on mantle,
  which covers a tunic with stripes over the shoulder.

VI An ordinary *frigidarium* (cold bath) in a bath area at one
of the palaces at Jericho.

VII An immersion pool at a palace at Jericho, which serves as
the *frigidarium* in a Hellenistic/Roman bath area.

the tent of meeting'), they did not need to bathe. By our period, however, the practice of admitting women to their own special court was established, and so bathing was required. We may assume that women bathed after menstruation and stage one of childbirth impurity. Bathing, we shall see more fully below, meant immersion.

These regular forms of impurity imposed only a few restrictions according to biblical law. No one could enter the temple while impure (Lev. 15.31); intercourse was forbidden during the seven-day menstrual period and stage one of childbirth impurity; the woman with childbirth impurity was forbidden to touch holy things – food destined for the temple.[19]

By our period a further restriction had developed: impure people should not handle the priests' food. This is a complex topic, and we cannot be sure about the precise limitations that most people accepted. There were two aspects of handling priests' food in which there was variation of practice: not everyone kept the same impurities away from the priesthood; not everyone started handling the priests' food in purity at the same point in the food chain. One person might keep only corpse impurity away from the priests' food, while another might protect it from lesser impurities as well. Some people handled the priests' food in purity only after it had been set aside, but others began handling food in purity earlier. It should be borne in mind that it was not possible to keep all impurities away from food all the time. A farmer was often impure, either from intercourse or from touching a menstruant's bed. Someone might die in the middle of the harvest, thus making all the mourners corpse-impure. They had to bring in the crops anyway. People who say that the Pharisees handled all food in purity have not paid attention to the realities of life. We shall now look at the evidence to learn when rules about handling developed and to discover, as best we can, what practices were commonly accepted.

The Pentateuch requires priests and their families to be pure when they eat first fruits and other holy food (e.g. Num. 18.11), but it says nothing about keeping the food away from impurities while it is still in the hands of those who produced it. There is, however, early evidence that indicates that purity was applied to the priests' food before it reached them. According to Isa. 66.20 the cereal offerings were to be *brought to the temple* in pure vessels. Presumably the grain had not been harvested by pure people. According to Judith 11.13 it was against the law for ordinary people to touch the first fruits and tithes *after they had been sanctified* and set apart. Judith is probably to be dated *c.* 150–125 BCE. The town-dwelling Essenes held that only pure people should take offerings to the temple (CD 11.19–21). This evidence shows that handling the priests' food in purity at some point in the food chain was pre-Pharisaic and was accepted by many pietists. We shall discuss the Pharisees' own rules in ch. 19.

What is most striking is that Pharisaic or early rabbinic passages show that the Pharisees trusted the ordinary people to protect the priests' food from corpse impurity after it was harvested; a priest's vessels left with an ordinary person would not, in the sages' view, contract corpse impurity (*Tohorot* 8.2).[20] This means that the ordinary person would prevent them from doing so. We may assume that a lot of people tried to ward off *some* impurities *at some point* in the process of getting food from the fields to the priests, even though the legal books of the Bible do not require this. Probably it was *common* to keep the vessels in which the priests' food was sent to the temple pure (so Isaiah) and also for it to be carried to them by pure people (Judith, CD). Even people who ignored some impurities would keep holy food and vessels free of corpse impurity (*Tohorot* 8.2).

Means of purification

General description (see plates II-III and VI-VII)

Water was essential to purification. Most impurities required bathing, and some necessitated washing the clothes and other objects. Water and ashes helped purge corpse impurity, but bathing was also necessary. At least as early as the Hasmonean period Palestinian Jews began to define 'bathing' and the water used for it. By our period, 'bathing' meant 'immersion'. Quite remarkably, Palestinian Jews seem all to have agreed. There was an exegetical basis for this view. According to Lev. 15.16 a man who has a nocturnal emission should bathe 'his whole body'. It was probably obvious to later interpreters that 'whole body' should be understood in other verses that require bathing, and 'whole body' was taken to mean 'all at once'. Where should this be done? Exegesis supplied the answer: even a dead swarming thing cannot render impure a 'spring or a cistern holding water' (Lev. 11.36). Lev. 15.13 requires that a man with a discharge bathe in 'living', that is, 'running' water. These verses, when combined with 15.16, led to the view that one should immerse in spring water or in a large pool, large enough for the entire body; if the water was not actually running, it should originally have been running water, and therefore it should have collected in the pool naturally.

In Palestine, few people lived near a spring or river, and those who did not do so dug deep pools and channelled rain water into them. The pools were cut into bedrock. This method of construction reflects the view that purifying water should not be carried in anything that a person built. In rabbinic parlance, it should not be 'drawn water'. Preferably, there should be a natural pool of water. Since large natural pools were in inadequate supply, people imitated nature by making pools in rock. Building a pool above ground would not do.

Thus far, all Jews in Palestine seem to have agreed. Archaeology proves the general agreement. Numerous types of pools have been found, but they share these points in common: cut into bedrock, deep enough for complete immersion, steps leading to the bottom, filled by means of channels that carried rain or spring water. Stepped pools large enough for full immersion have been found in numerous areas: the palaces of the Hasmonean priest-kings (Jericho), Herod's palaces (Jericho, the Herodium, Matsada), the houses of the aristocrats who lived in the Upper City, the houses of the ordinary people in Jerusalem, Sepphoris (one of the major cities of Galilee), remote Gamla (in the Golan Heights, northwest of the Sea of Galilee), Qumran and many other places. At Matsada, not only did Herod's palace have an immersion pool, so did the bathhouse that he built for his retinue. There were also pools near the temple that were for public use,[21] presumably that of pilgrims (though at least one Greek-speaking synagogue also provided pools for pilgrims).[22] There were public pools in villages and towns; Gamla, our one example of a pre-70 town, had at least one public immersion pool, which was almost adjacent to the synagogue. The use of immersion pools was common to one and all: aristocrats, priests, the laity, the rich, the poor, the Qumran sectarians, the Pharisees and the Sadducees. The evidence in favour of general observance could not be more impressive.

Practice in the Diaspora was not nearly so uniform. Philo discusses ablutions numerous times, always referring either to splashing with water from a waist-high basin or to bathing, but never to immersion.[23] The *Letter of Aristeas* and the *Sibylline Oracles* mention handwashing but not immersion (*Arist.* 305f.; *Sib. Or.* 3.591–3). One passage in Justin Martyr refers to the Jewish use of 'cisterns' for purification, which shows that the custom was known outside Palestine (*Dialogue with Trypho* 14.1). Although the identification of the building as a synagogue has been disputed, it appears likely that there was a synagogue on the Greek island of Delos that contained an immersion pool.[24] While immersion may have been more widely practised than present evidence indicates, it seems not to have had the status in the Diaspora that it had in Palestine.

Diaspora Jews, like their Gentile neighbours and their Palestinian compatriots, believed that it was a good thing to be pure: all of the purifications mentioned in the previous paragraph are extra-biblical. To satisfy their desire to be pure, they invented purifications. For example, instead of the biblical requirement not to enter the temple when semen-impure, Philo has 'not to touch anything'; instead of the biblical bathing after sexual relations, he has splashing or sprinkling (*Spec. Laws* 3.63). For corpse impurity he requires both sprinkling and bathing *in the Diaspora*, which he distinguishes from the rite of purification that pilgrims went through at the temple (*Spec. Laws* 3.205f.; cf. 1.261).

The reference in *Aristeas* to washing hands in the sea may explain the fact that several Diaspora synagogues were near water.[25] According to Acts 16.13, Paul and his companions went to the riverside near Philippi, expecting to find a synagogue there. It is quite likely that, before the synagogue service, many Diaspora Jews walked down to the shore and washed their hands, and probably their feet as well.

We see that some Diaspora Jews immersed (so Justin), some washed their hands in the sea or in rivers (*Aristeas*; synagogues near water); some sprinkled or splashed (Philo). Possibly these purifications overlapped. What was common was the desire to be pure and to signify purity by a rite.

Immersion: detailed description[26]

The Palestinian immersion pools provide us with very interesting evidence about religious practice, and so we shall look at them in more detail. First of all, immersion pools are distinctive.[27] They are neither bathtubs nor storage cisterns, as we shall see below. Immersion pools (Hebrew, *miqva'ot*, sing. *miqveh*) were fairly large, but not large enough to store a family's water supply. Miqva'ot vary in size, but they share general characteristics: (1) They are deep, often 2 metres or 7 feet, but sometimes deeper. (2) They have a large surface area, often two metres or so in one direction, three metres or so in another (*c.* 7–10 ft), though, again, many are larger. (3) Consequently they held a lot of water. A pool with a surface area of 3.6 × 2 metres and a depth of 2 metres would hold 14,400 litres of water (3,170 Imperial gallons, 3,800 US gallons). (4) A lot of the interior space is taken up by steps, which go all the way to the bottom. (5) Frequently there is some sort of mark that divides left from right on each step; sometimes there is no mark, but there are two sets of steps. (6) They cannot be drained: there is no plug at the bottom.

These pools are not bathtubs. They are far too large, the water could not be heated, and it could be changed only with a great deal of effort. Nor are miqva'ot cisterns for storing drinking water. Cisterns are common in Palestine; they are often found beside miqva'ot, and the cisterns are much the larger. Much of the space of a miqveh was taken up by steps that allowed the immerser to descend until water came over his or her head. Cisterns, by contrast, either have no steps at all (the water being hauled up by a bucket) or steps that take up a small percentage of the space. Cisterns have a small opening at the top, and they expand underground. The sides of immersion pools are straight up and down.

Though the rulers in Palestine had swimming pools, and the recreational use of water was well known, the pools identified as miqva'ot were not for pleasure. They were in the basement of the house or in a small separate structure with a low roof (sometimes the roof itself was bedrock, and the pool was entered from the side). In short, they had no conceivable purpose except religious purification. Once this is seen, all of their characteristics are explained. They were moderately unsanitary, but their purpose was not personal hygiene. They were uncomfortable, but they were not for pleasure. Even the practice of dividing the steps, or cutting a second set, is explained: one descends impure, comes out pure, and the difference is marked by a physical division. In the case of public miqva'ot, physical contact between the pure and the impure was avoided by dividing the steps.

Rulers and aristocrats could make the miqveh-experience (as it might now be called) not unpleasant. In Herod's bathhouses, the miqveh served as the cold bath in his Hellenistic-Roman style bathing quarters, where there was also a hot room and sometimes a tepid room. An aristocrat in the Upper City could have a miqveh dug as part of a bathing complex in the basement, with tiled floors, changing room, sometimes a separate footbath, and usually a bathtub. The water in the miqveh would still be stagnant and cold, but the bather did not have to stay in it, and there was relief near by. A bathtub was fairly small; the bather could not stretch out and lie down, and the tub held very little water. After immersion, a member of the privileged few could sit in the bathtub, while someone, doubtless a servant, poured warm, clean water over him or her.

Most people, however, entered a very small area, disrobed, walked down the steps until full immersion was achieved, came back up, towelled off (probably using their garments), and dressed.[28] In some cases the changing room would have been quite dark, and in all cases the miqveh area itself was cold and dark. Even in a hot climate, and even in the summer, a large pool of water in bedrock, covered by a roof, is cold.

We know that in Palestine there was substantial disagreement about religious practice. We have direct evidence that shows that pietists criticized priests (e.g. *Psalms of Solomon*), that the Pharisees criticized both the common people and the Sadducees (rabbinic literature) and that the Essenes criticized everybody (the Dead Sea Scrolls, including the *Covenant of Damascus*). What, then, are we to make of the happy harmony on immersion and pools?

They provide us with the best physical evidence on 'unity and diversity'. The basic decisions about miqva'ot, as we saw, were exegetical. The Bible, to be sure, does not explicitly say 'dig pools in bedrock four cubits deep and fill them with rain or spring water', but that is not an unreasonable interpretation of Lev. 11.36; 15.13 and 15.16. Palestinian Jews agreed with one another on this exegesis, and consequently there were no party disputes. But if we dig deeper (pun intended), we find disagreements. I shall mention a total of three, one disclosed by archaeology, the other two by literature. I think that it may be possible to derive from the study of miqva'ot socio-religious data and also information that bears on the question of Pharisaic influence. Therefore we shall consider them carefully.

1. There are many sub-categories of immersion pools, but they all fall into one of two basic types: the miqveh proper is either beside an unstepped pool of a similar size or it has no adjacent pool. A minority of the stepped pools (miqva'ot) that have been found thus far have a companion pool without steps, in later Hebrew called an 'ôtsar, storage pool, which is joined to the stepped pool by a pipe at the top. A Mishnaic passage clarifies the function of the second pool. When it rained, both pools were filled with water. During the long dry seasons, the miqveh lost water to evaporation, and possibly some of it was removed by a bucket to allow the introduction of fresh water. The new water would have to be 'drawn': carried in a bucket from a nearby source, or hauled up from a cistern. Pharisees regarded 'drawn' water as invalid for purification. They thought, however, that the drawn water could be purified by contact with the water in the 'otsar, the unstepped pool. The pipe was briefly opened, the water mingled, and the transfer of purity was achieved. Pharisees, that is, thought that one could immerse *only* in rain or spring water that collected naturally, by the force of gravity, but that if such water ran out it could be *recreated* by bringing together drawn and 'natural' water. There are a few such pools in Palestine, and they are explained by a passage in the Mishnah (*Miqva'ot* 6.8). The passage cannot be definitely atributed to pre-70 Pharisees, but the pools themselves, at least those in Jericho and Jerusalem, are pre-70.[29]

Since this rule about the use of an 'otsar is found in rabbinic literature, and since archaeology shows that someone followed it before 70, we may attribute it to the Pharisees. The revolutionaries who defended Matsada after the destruction of the temple also accepted it; they built miqveh + 'otsar complexes, despite having Herod's capacious single miqva'ot to hand. The defenders of Matsada were Sicarii, and probably very few Pharisees were Sicarii. The inference is that the Pharisaic rule was accepted by at least some other pietists (though not the Qumranians). The distribution of miqveh + 'otsar complexes in Jerusalem is interesting from this point of view: one such complex has been found in the aristocratic Upper City, a good number in the poorer Lower City. There is also one in a Hasmonean palace at Jericho. At least some of the Hasmoneans had accepted the (apparently) Pharisaic theory, as did some of the die-hard revolutionaries and some of the people in the Lower City.

Herod, the aristocrats, the Qumran sect, the residents of Gamla, and some of the residents of Sepphoris used miqva'ot with no storage pool beside them. A lot of work is required to dig the second pool, yet those who could best afford it did not have one dug. They obviously accepted different rules about water and its validation. They dug their pools in bedrock, and they channelled rainwater into them. Thereafter, however, practice diverged. My guess is that between rainy seasons they had the pools partially emptied by bucket and fresh water added in the same way, without validating it by contact with water in a second pool. It is possible that the Pharisees would have approved of these miqva'ot, although I doubt it.[30]

The socio-religious point is this: Herod and the Jerusalem aristocrats, many of whose houses have been excavated, had only single pools (with one exception). Some of the smaller houses of Jerusalem and Sepphoris also had single pools, but double ones are, with only the one exception, in smaller houses. The revolutionary defenders of Matsada also built double immersion pools. Thus I think it likely that *most people*, including the aristocrats, did not follow Pharisaic views about immersion pools, although other pietists (such as the defenders at Matsada) may have shared the Pharisees' definition of valid water.

2. That some people added 'drawn' water to their pools, and that the Pharisees and early rabbis objected, is proved by rabbinic passages. According to one, the Pharisees, down to the time of Shammai and Hillel, carried on a running dispute among themselves about how much drawn water could be added to a miqveh. They agreed that not much was allowed; proposals ranged from 0.9 to 10.8 litres in a pool that contained thousands of litres (*Eduyot* 1.3). Presumably non-Pharisees would allow more.

3. The second passage is even more interesting. According to *Shabbat* 13b, the House of Shammai (one of the main wings of the Pharisaic party, obviously after the time of Shammai and Hillel themselves) 'decreed' that people who immersed in drawn water, or who had drawn water poured on them, made heave offering unfit to eat. This seems to be directed against the practice of the aristocratic priests, who did not use the Pharisaic second pool, but probably added fresh 'drawn' water to the miqveh, and who bathed afterwards by sitting in a tub while a servant poured warm water over them. The Shammaites ruled that they rendered their own food (heave offering) unfit and that they should not eat it. The aristocratic priests doubtless continued to do as they wished.

Whether or not I have correctly interpreted this passage, we see that, within general uniformity (miqva'ot in bedrock, seasonally filled with rain water) there were disagreements. Some people used water that other people considered invalid.

We do not know how often people immersed. The priests and their immediate families – everyone who shared their holy food – probably immersed every day. Since holy food is to be eaten in purity, and since purity requires bathing/immersion and sunset, the priestly routine was probably immersion just before sunset and the main meal after night fell.[31] Possibly the priests did not eat during the day (three meals a day is a fairly modern invention), possibly they ate non-holy food in the course of the day. Lay people who followed the biblical law did not need to immerse very often: only before entering the temple and before eating holy food (second tithe, Passover and the shared sacrifice). A *possible* annual routine for ordinary people would have been to visit Jerusalem during Passover week, to eat second tithe while there, and to offer whatever scrifices were required. This would allow them to eat their year's supply of holy food during Passover week. Biblical law, strictly followed, would require ordinary people to be pure for only one week each year, more only if they attended more than one festival.

The existence of immersion pools in remote areas, however, shows that people immersed more often than they went to the temple. If immersion after menstruation and childbirth was generally accepted, as is almost certain, women would have immersed more frequently. Men who touched menstruants, their beds or chairs probably also immersed. Men and women both *may* have immersed after intercourse. We have already noted that many people shared the view that purity was a positive good and that it should not be limited to just those occasions required by the Bible. The Essenes and the Pharisees observed special purity rules (chs 16 and 19). There were doubtless some who lived at the other extreme, and who purified themselves as seldom as the law allowed. We may imagine a whole range of practices, from immersion only when required by the Bible (cf. the Tiberians, who accepted being corpse-impure except when they went to the temple) to immersion every day.

Many Jews thought that they should be pure. Because of semen impurity and menstrual impurity (both direct and indirect), most adults were impure a lot of the time. How was the conflict resolved? How often did the *average* person immerse? The reader's guess is as good as mine (almost), but I shall offer mine anyway. Most people probably ignored semen impurity completely and immersed once a month, after the woman's menstrual period ended. Since women were frequently pregnant, however, those who followed this rule would not actually have to immerse every month. They would immerse after stage one of childbirth impurity but not again until the wife's menstrual periods returned or they went to the temple.

Since not only people but also things could become impure, things were immersed. Some objects that were immersed slipped and fell to the bottom of the pool, where modern archaeologists can find them. Pharisees and priests probably immersed their garments. An early Mishnaic passage discusses whose garments were most likely to be pure. A Pharisee's clothing was more likely than a priest's to be impure, but the garments of the ordinary person were regarded as always impure (*Hagigah* 2.7). Garments acquired secondary impurity from coming into contact with the impurities of Lev. 15. Consequently not only other members of the family, but also their garments were made impure by contact with a menstruant, her bed or her chair. It is then not surprising that a rabbinic discussion refers to the immersion of a bed (*Miqva'ot* 7.7). The Pharisees may well have immersed garments, bedding and chairs after the woman's menstrual period and stage one of childbirth impurity. Most people ignored some of the secondary impurities, especially of clothing.[32]

Purity and the ordinary person

In Palestine Jews kept most of the biblical purity laws. Neusner has recently exclaimed, 'as if the masses kept the purity laws!',[33] as if he knows that they did not. Apart from the customary admonition to remember that ancient Jews believed in God and thought that he had given the biblical laws, I shall here summarize the evidence that indicates general observance. One point was noted above and will be explored in the chapter on the Pharisees: the rabbinic material shows that even the Pharisees thought that ordinary people kept many of the purity laws. They were not entirely reliable about protecting wet foodstuff from becoming impure, and they did not avoid *midras* impurity (the secondary impurity that is contracted by touching certain impure things, such as a menstruant's bed). They were, however, trustworthy to keep liquids (wine and oil) pure and to handle second tithe in purity (biblical requirements), and they exceeded biblical law by keeping some impurities away from the priests' food.[34]

The very wide distribution of immersion pools, so strikingly demonstrated by archaeology, shows that the purity laws were generally obeyed. It should be especially emphasized that archaeologists have found miqva'ot *wherever* they have explored substantial remains from the late second temple period. We should not go beyond the Pharisees and rabbis and accuse the ordinary people of not obeying the purity laws. On the contrary, a lot of Palestinian Jews accepted more purity rules than the Bible requires, as we saw when we discussed handling the priests' food.

Modern critics of ancient Judaism often find all this objectionable. Often it is said that only the Pharisees developed and cared about purity laws, a supposition that assists the criticism of Pharisaism as being externalistic and trivial. In fact, purifications were common to all ancient religions. Pagans washed their hands before sacrificing and dipped their hands or sprinkled themselves before entering a temple.[35] All groups within Judaism purified themselves in various ways; there was also a distinct tendency to invent new purifications or to extend the biblical laws beyond their original sphere. We see again that the Judaism of our period was an ancient religion. Its external observances were different from those of other religions in detail, not in kind. Jews and Gentiles disagreed about a lot of things: about pork, but not about whether or not dietary laws were appropriate;[36] about the sabbath, but not about the importance of holy days. Had they debated it, pagans would have argued against Palestinian Jews that immersion was stupid: one should sprinkle and dip.

Thoughtful ancient people, however, whether Jew or Gentile, interpreted their rituals as the external expression of piety, not as a substitute for it. A rite was a rite and what mattered was what it stood for. According to Aristeas, the 'custom of all the Jews', to wash their hands in the sea while praying, was evidence that they had done no evil (*Arist.* 305f.). Philo, noting that his purificatory rites were the same as those of pagans (he sprinkled rather than immersed), criticized them for entering their temples after washing their bodies but not their souls. It was the latter that needed to be 'subjected to sprinkling-basins and cleansing purifications' (*Unchangeableness of God* 7f.). This is, of course, only religious polemic. The present point is that it shows that Philo knew that 'real' purification is inner, though he thought that outer purification should also be practised. Philo spent a lot of energy instructing his readers in such points, and so did other Jewish teachers. The custom of gathering on the sabbath for study meant that such instruction could be conveyed in person, not just in writing.

Charity and love

The final set of laws that we shall consider governs charity and love of neighbour. We saw above that the laws of tithing include charity, since the tithes were intended to support not only the Levites and priests but also the poor. The Bible contains one other principal provision for charity: not harvesting the fields too carefully, but leaving some for the poor:

> When you reap the harvest of your land, you shall not reap your field to its very border, neither shall you gather the gleanings after your harvest. And you shall not strip your vineyard bare, neither shall you gather the fallen grapes of your vineyard; you shall leave them for the poor and for the sojourner: I am the Lord your God. (Lev. 19.9.f; cf. 23.22)

The parallel passage in Deuteronomy also contains the commandment not to go back to retrieve a sheaf that was forgotten in the field, but to leave it 'for the sojourner, the fatherless, and the widow'. The passage concludes by reminding the Israelites that once they were slaves in Egypt (Deut. 24.19–22).

The Mishnah shows the way in which the pious could specify and elaborate the laws of charity. The amount left in the field should never be less than one-sixtieth of the harvest, and the harvesters should leave more in hard times (*Pe'ah* 1.2). Further, all foods that grow from the ground should be included, not just those specified in the Bible (grain, olives and grapes) (*Pe'ah* 1.4). The discussion of the 'forgotten sheaf' is based on the assumption that the householder should be sure to forget a sheaf (*Pe'ah* ch. 6).

Where the reader of the Bible first meets these laws of charity, Lev. 19, there are numerous other laws dealing with 'relations between human and human' (see above, pp. 192–5). These laws command Jews not to steal, deal falsely or lie, especially not to lie by using the name of God (19.11–12). Although this is an offence against God, it is also against one's fellow, since false oaths can be used to defraud. These verses constitute the priestly law's summary of some of the ten commandments. Readers are also commanded not to oppress others, nor to be slow to pay labourers, nor to be unjust in judgment, nor to favour the prosperous to the disadvantage of the poor, nor to slander, nor to hate one's brother, nor to bear a grudge (Lev. 19.13–18a). The commandments governing relations among Jews are then summarized: 'you shall love your neighbour as yourself: I am the Lord' (Lev. 19.18).

Just as Jesus' citation of the Shema᾿ ('love God', Deut. 6.4f.) as the greatest commandment would have caused no surprise, neither would this quotation of Lev. 19.18 as the second greatest commandment (Mark 12.28–34). Both these passages are presented in the Bible itself as summarizing the two aspects of the law: the commandments that govern relations with God and those which govern relations with others.

We should note especially that 'love of the neighbour' and 'of the stranger' in Leviticus is quite specific. It is not just a vague feeling (though a right feeling in the heart is commanded in 19.17), but rather it is to be expressed through concrete and definable actions: not to slander, not to oppress, not to rob, and the like. We see again the genius of Jewish law, which not only embraced all of life, but which also gave specific and achievable instructions about how to fulfil it.

The law was meant to be interiorized, taken into the heart and observed naturally because one's heart is right. That is the plain intention both of the command not to 'hate your brother in your heart' (Lev. 19.17) and also of the provisions in the Shema᾿ that require the constant reminders of principal aspects of the law. In accord with the general development of life and thought in the Mediterranean, Judaism had become increasingly individualized and interiorized.[37] As we shall shortly see, the idea of God's covenant with a group, the people of Israel, was very strong in the first century, but individuals were increasingly expected to accept the spirit of the law within and to orientate their own lives in accord with it.

On the other hand, doing good to others was not to be postponed until one's heart commanded it. In Jewish scripture and tradition, the commandment to love is inseparable from the commandments to act. Love may include feeling, but in law it involves concrete and specific actions. How does one love the neighbour? We have seen the answer of Leviticus and Deuteronomy: First, be charitable; that is, in an agricultural environment, do not reap your field to its borders; leave a sheaf behind for the poor. Secondly, be honest: use just weights and measures. Philo got the point. 'What a person would hate to suffer he or she must not do to others.' After that summary, he continued: do not pick up what you have not laid down; do not filch; do not grudge giving fire or food; do not worsen the plight of a person who is in hard straits; do not maltreat animals; 'no unjust scales, no false measurements, no fraudulent coinage'. Thus one fulfils the basic summary of the law, 'What a person would hate to suffer he or she must not do to others' (*Hypothetica* 7.6–8).

It is almost as if the ancient Hebrew legislators and their first-century commentators knew a great secret of human psychology, one that was explained centuries later and several decades ago by Ryle and James. External actions can create feelings. Go by yourself into a dark room, sit down, hug your arms to your body, glance around with widened eyes; soon you will start to feel fear. Of course it works the other way, as the lyricist of 'The King and I' pointed out:

> Whenever you feel afraid,/hold your head erect/and whistle a happy tune,/so no one will suspect/you're afraid.

Not only can one fool others by this rather simple device, one may also persuade one's heart not to thump; the feeling of fear can be partially controlled by outward behaviour. As Anna put it, 'When I fool the people I fear, I fool myself as well'.

With regard to our topic, charity, love and honesty, the moral is clear. One who treats one's neighbour well also feels better towards the other person. A story about Abraham Lincoln served, at least in the small Texas town in which I grew up, as a paradigmatic tale that implied a law. When a young man, Lincoln once gave incorrect change, a minor amount. Realizing it, after work he walked for hours to repay the sum. This was a merchant's law in my childhood. I can attest that many merchants observed it (though it did not require them to walk miles), and one could even say that more-or-less everybody kept it, merchant and customer alike. Whenever the occasion arose to correct overpayment or underpayment, everyone felt good about it and about one another. I wish that it had happened more often. In the Britain that I first knew, in the early 60s, similar rules prevailed. Umbrellas left in a train could be reclaimed. Honest citizens turned them in, and they ended up in a central office. Often lost items were not reclaimed, and after a certain period they would be sold. The large quantity of goods (especially umbrellas) that were for sale attested to the general honesty of the populace. I dare say that every time someone turned in an umbrella, especially an expensive one, that person felt good, not just self-righteous, but good towards the unknown stranger who could get the umbrella back.

Sadly, neither the merchant's law of my childhood nor the umbrella law of my early adult years has endured.

These homely examples are intended to illustrate the way the equally homely Jewish laws of honesty and charity and fair treatment operated. Keeping the law *was* loving the neighbour or the stranger, but it also *helped create* the feeling of love.

'Love' in the sense of 'decent treatment' was also supposed to govern relations with *Gentiles* and even with *enemies*. Numerous Christian scholars have canvassed Jewish literature in order to prove that the Jewish attitude towards Gentiles was uniformly harsh, a criticism that has been answered by the quotation of an even larger number of passages that are favourable towards Gentiles.[38] This is a question that requires more common sense and less prooftexting.* In the years 69 and 70 CE, it would have been difficult to find any resident of Jerusalem who would speak very favourably about Gentiles – possibly even harder than to find an American who would speak kindly even about Japanese gardens in 1942, or a Londoner who praised German philosophy and music in 1941. I believe that to this day the survivors of Mai Lai do not pen paeans of praise to Americans – and so on, as long as one wishes. In 66, a Jerusalemite might have been able to say, 'Oh, the Romans haven't been so bad' and live, but not in 69. Probably the Jews in Sardis felt more kindly towards Gentiles after the city council required the market manager to supply Jewish food than they had when they were living on vegetables, bread and water. It is not reasonable to speak about 'the Jewish attitude towards Gentiles in the late second-temple period'. It varied.

We can be sure of a few points. The Greek-writing authors, as we saw above, were most emphatic that Jews believed in *philanthrōpia*, 'love of humanity', most definitely including Greeks and Romans. They were defensive about the topic: some pagans accused Jews of being misanthropic. This charge arose from the fact that they would not share in many aspects of

*'Prooftexting': attempting to settle an issue by quoting one-line statements out of context.

common life – those tainted (in Jewish eyes) by idolatry. We shall consider separatism in the next chapter. Here I note only that thoughtful Jews, the leaders of their communities, favoured cordial relations with Gentiles. This was true both in Palestine and in the Diaspora. The harshest biblical statements about idols were even modified, and the Bible was construed as prohibiting attacks on 'the gods', thus discouraging hotblooded monotheists from defacing pagan temples or statues.[39]

The claims of 'love of humanity' by Josephus, Philo and others do not prove that all Jews 'loved' Gentiles, any more than the statements by anti-Jewish pagans, that Jews were misanthropes, prove that all Jews hated Gentiles. What we can *know* is what the best Jewish teachers taught: they taught honest, decent treatment of one and all: 'love' in that sense.

What about enemies? Partly in agreement with biblical law on the treatment of enemies, but partly going beyond it, Josephus wrote that even in warfare Jews were forbidden to burn the enemies' fields and houses, cut down food-producing trees, despoil fallen combatants, or rape women (*Apion* 2.212; cf. Deut. 20.19f.; 21.10–14). Numerous other Jewish texts pick up the prohibition of retaliation against enemies from Prov. 20.22, 'do not say, "I will repay evil"'. One instance is found in *Joseph and Aseneth*, a first-century Jewish romance, written in Egypt. In the story, some Gentiles are out to get the Jews, and the Jews fight back. One Jew has just wounded Pharaoh's son, and intends to finish him, when his colleague says,

> By no means, brother, will you do this deed, because we are men who worship God, and it does not befit a man who worships God to repay evil for evil nor to trample underfoot a fallen (man) nor to oppress his enemy till death. And now, put your sword back into its place, and come, help me, and we will heal him of his wound . . . (29.3f.)

In real life, we may be sure, these noble admonitions about treatment of enemies were not always achieved, any more than they were by Christians, who had before them not only Paul's similar exhortations, based on Prov. 20.22 and related passages (Rom. 12.17–21), but also Jesus' admonition to love enemies and pray for persecutors (Matt. 5.44). Religions, however, must be assessed on the basis of their highest ideals, not the failures of individuals. Judaism espoused the ideal of piety towards God and kindness and justice to all, Jew and non-Jew alike. Both attitudes it called 'love'.[40]

For our study, it is important to see that this was not a pious wish, but law. Restraint even in war and fair treatment of Gentiles are required by the Bible, and their status was recognized in the period of our study. By assigning these laws to God, Judaism made them as important in his sight as were sacrifices and purity. In the ancient world, that elevated them rather than debased them. Judaism's achievement will be better recognized if we consider how long it took the countries of the Christian West to require *in law* that people whom the majority considered 'aliens' be treated equally. This was not true in the USA until the Supreme Court rulings and the civil rights legislation of the 1950s and 1960s. Jews were not given full rights in Great Britain until 1890.[41] Social reality, of course, drags behind the law, but Judaism at least came up with the right law and had the wisdom to attribute it to God.

The law: conclusion

I have not intended these two chapters to constitute an encyclopaedic account of each biblical law and how it was viewed by various Jews in the late second-temple period. It would be useful to have such an encyclopaedia, and the need is not and has never been met by the general encyclopaedias of the Bible and of Judaism. The Judaica encyclopaedias, where one expects to find such information, pay too little attention to Josephus, and usually less yet to Philo and other Diaspora sources; and many of their articles treat rabbinic material of all periods as representing post-biblical Judaism in general. The Talmuds have views on everything, and anyone who uses them as the main source for second-temple Judaism has the advantage of being able to canvass all the laws. The problem is that one then has a seriously distorted view of actual practice in the period of our survey.

A critical treatment of each law or category of law would result in many question marks. On some points we would have only Diaspora evidence, on some only Palestinian, and on all only selective information that *might* reveal the practice or preference of a small group or an eccentric individual. Careful study could sometimes discover common practice (as I have attempted to do on these few topics), but doubts and uncertainties would remain. This would, however, be preferable to the present state of affairs, in which one has the choice of accepting the Talmuds of late antiquity as representing the Judaism of middle antiquity, or of thinking that nothing can be known about anything. A careful sifting of the evidence, both literary and archaeological, will result in good knowledge on many topics.

In these chapters I have discussed worship, many aspects of which are not governed by direct biblical laws, and only a few specific laws: sabbath, circumcision, food, purity, charity, and treatment of friend and foe. Of the specific laws, the first four serve as main identifying marks of Jews, and details of sabbath and purity practices also identify different groups within Judaism (as we shall see more fully in the following chapters).

The laws of charity and love occupy a special place within Judaism, since they are attached to cultic law and have the same divine origin. The opening

verses of Lev. 19 ground the commandments in holiness: 'You shall be holy;
for I the Lord your God am holy' (19.2). The concluding verses base the
commandments on salvation history: 'I am the Lord your God, who brought
you out of the land of Egypt' (19.36). The appeal to the exodus was standard
by the time Leviticus was compiled. One of the achievements of the priestly
authors was to tie human-human commandments to human-God commandments. The holiness or sanctity of God required that he be approached
in purity and that his priests eat in purity. Such rules were common in the
ancient world, and they were highly regarded. Leviticus goes further. We
may paraphrase: I am holy; you also are to be holy. In emulation of my sanctity
love your neighbour and the stranger as yourself.

Divine law covered many topics not mentioned here at all, neither in these
chapters nor in those on the temple and offerings. I have discussed a few
more topics in *JLJM* (oaths and vows, blasphemy and fasting). To give just
an example of the range of law, we may note here the rules on mixtures. They
were generally forbidden, whether of crops, cloth or animals (Lev. 19.19;
Deut. 22.9–11). Such laws had to be commented on and modified. The
prohibition of mixing two kinds of seed in the same field, for example,
required a definition of 'field' that would not make farmers depend on only
one crop. Information on these matters is not thick, and often one has only
rabbinic literature. While the reader of this book has not seen anything like a
full itemization, he or she has covered the points that are treated in most
detail in non-rabbinic sources, especially Josephus and Philo's *Special Laws*.

We have seen that the law was studied and followed by most Jews, and also
that the study of it did not lead them all to the same conclusions. At a general
level there was wide agreement: the biblical law should be known and
followed. But 'following' did not mean the same thing to all the people all the
time. Even the most basic commandments, such as the prohibition of
idolatry, as we shall see in the next chapter, were subject to varying
interpretations. The attempt to apply the law to all of life, however, seems to
have been widespread.

In this and the previous chapter we have paid attention to laws that were
generally and commonly observed, both in Palestine and in the Diaspora. In
many large areas of life Jews all over the world did much the same things:

1. They worshipped God daily and weekly, saying the Shemaʿ, recalling
the ten commandments and praying. On sabbaths they studied the law by
hearing it read and expounded. I do not think that it is idealistic to suppose
that most Jews did all these things. To some, sabbath attendance at the
synagogue may have been largely a matter of social conformity, and some may
not have prayed wholeheartedly. But simple unbelief, which has turned many
people in the modern West away from regular religious observance, was

virtually non-existent in the ancient world (to repeat the point still one more time). Most Jews believed in God and in the Bible, and they prayed to the one and studied the other.

2. Similarly they kept the sabbath. Here pious groups elaborated sabbath observance, but the day was kept as a day of rest by most Jews – virtually all. Most forms of transgressing the sabbath are publicly obvious – the open shop, the smoking hearth – and that there were many who defied the sabbath laws is unlikely.

3. With few or no exceptions (depending on precisely what the allegorizers did: n. 5 above), Jews circumcised their sons.

4. Some purity observations were also general. The peculiarity of the Jewish diet was almost as famous as observance of the sabbath. In Palestine there was agreement on immersion, though we can only guess about the frequency with which ordinary people immersed. The practice of ablutions in the Diaspora is much less certain. Philo's references to purificatory washing make it doubtful that he had recourse to an immersion pool, and it is unlikely that special pools – which are not, after all, required by the Bible – were a common feature of Diaspora life. How far handwashing had spread we do not know. The explanation in Mark 7.3 that 'the Pharisees and all the Jews' wash their hands seems to indicate that the author could not expect all his readers to know of the practice.

5. As we saw in an earlier chapter, there was another large area where most Jews agreed: support of the temple. From Palestine and the Diaspora alike the temple tax was brought. Many Diaspora Jews made supplementary gifts. Palestinian Jews paid tithes, first fruits, firstlings and probably heave offering. We may here think of more people seeking to evade at least some of these expenses; and Philo, as we saw, once hinted that such was the case. Nevertheless, we should think of compliance as common, especially with regard to the temple tax. The temple did in fact have great wealth, as the stories of taking it illegally show. Further, in this area social pressure could readily be brought to bear.

Our ability to specify general compliance with other parts of the law is not very great, due to lack of information. How many practised love of the neighbour in ways that would matter we cannot know. One trusts that the admonitions in the synagogue did some good.

We have seen enough to justify speaking of orthopraxy in worldwide Judaism. The five areas of law just enumerated establish it, even while no one of them shows absolute uniformity. All over the world Jewish practice was based on the Bible, which constituted common ground. Further, representative Jews from a vast area met one another in Jerusalem, and this too helped to promote certain forms of agreement. A Jew could travel from the westernmost part of the empire to Mesopotamia, go to the synagogue, recognize at least aspects of the service, and perhaps even find a common language. If invited to a meal, he might find the combination of foods and the spices to be entirely new, but there would be no pork and the meat would not be bloody. On the sabbath a few customs might be strange, but the constantly burning lamps, the absence of toil, and the service of prayer and study would be, at least in general terms, the same as the customs which he left so many miles to the west.

Even when Jews disagreed vociferously, it seems usually to have been the law about which they disagreed; this implies the important agreement that living by the law was what mattered. Josephus represents knowledge of the law as being of prime importance for Jews, even in circumstances that seem strange to pragmatic moderns. We have noted that those who examined his conduct of preparations for war in Galilee had to be *biblical* experts (*Life* 198). Knowledge of the law was a prime consideration in estimating anyone's ability.

However they interpreted the law, Jews were zealous in keeping it. As I pointed out in ch. 8, some scholars, possibly thinking of our own day, have proposed that most Jews were 'lukewarm'.[42] Few statements could less adequately reflect the impression gained from reading ancient literature, whether Jewish, Christian or pagan. Paul, in the course of lamenting the fact that his 'kin by race' had not accepted Jesus as the Messiah, granted to them, in their favour, that they had zeal for God (Rom. 10.2).

The willingness of Jews to die for their faith and their law is a prominent theme in this book, having already come up more than once. This is suitable, since it is a prominent theme in several of our sources, and it was a very important aspect of first-century Judaism. In ch. 14 we shall see the relationship between this willingness and various hopes for the future, and when discussing the Pharisees (ch. 18), we shall have to analyse their view and compare it with that of others. Here I wish to give a fairly full collection of passages that deal with common, ordinary Jews, not the fanatics, and not the super-pious.

With regard to the importance of controlling the temple, Josephus writes that Jews 'would rather give up their lives than the worship which they are accustomed to offer God' (*Antiq.* 15.248). The point is expanded in *Apion*. Even the Spartans, Josephus points out, surrendered their laws when they lost their liberty and independence, while Jews remained loyal to theirs 'notwithstanding the countless calamities in which changes of rulers in Asia have involved us' (*Apion* 2.227f.). 'Has anyone', he asks, 'ever heard of a case of our people, not I mean, in such large numbers [as the Spartans], but merely two or three, proving traitors to their laws or afraid of death', even when faced with death by torture? (2.232f.). His answer is 'no': Jews face 'death on behalf of [their] laws with a courage which no other nation can equal' (2.234). Later he returns to the theme: 'And from these laws of ours nothing has had power to deflect us, neither fear of our masters, nor envy of the institutions esteemed by other nations' (2.271). 'Robbed though we be of wealth, of cities, of all good things, our Law at least remains immortal; and there is not a Jew so distant from his country, so much in awe of a cruel despot, but has more fear of the law than of him' (2.277). Philo also claimed that Jews 'would even endure to die a thousand deaths sooner than accept anything contrary to the laws and customs which [God] had ordained' (*Hypothetica* 6.9).

Some of these claims are, to be sure, exaggerated. There were some Jews who preferred surrender to death. Nevertheless, the claim of Jewish willingness to die is true. This was noted by pagans. Sextus Empiricus (second century CE) wrote that 'A Jew or an Egyptian priest would prefer to die instantly rather than eat pork'.[43] No other nation can be shown to have fought so often in defence of its own way of life, and the readiness of Jews to die for their cause is proved by example after example. While Josephus' summary is exaggerated, individual instances which he gives here and there in his history are probably correct, at least in general. The numbers may be doubted ('tens of thousands'), but we cannot deny that many Jews were prepared to die rather than have a statue of Caligula erected in the temple (*Antiq.* 18.262). This threat moved Philo to write that 'we will die and be no more, for the truly glorious death, met in defence of laws, might be called life' (Philo, *Embassy* 192). Similarly many were prepared to die rather than have Roman standards in Jerusalem (*War* 2.169–174). The repeated insurrections and revolts show the point clearly (above, ch. 4). We have also seen that dedication to keeping the sabbath led to defeat and death. The point is made not only by I Maccabees and Josephus (above, p. 209), but also by the pagan author Dio Cassius:

> If they [the Jerusalemites] had put up a similar resistance every day, he [Pompey] would not have taken the Temple. As it was, they used to let pass the days called Saturn's without any action at all and so gave the Romans the opportunity of damaging the wall in these intervals. (Dio Cassius, *History of Rome* 37.16.2)

Elsewhere Dio Cassius wrote that when Jerusalem fell, its defenders counted it 'victory and salvation and happiness' 'that they perished along with the temple' (66.6.3). He regarded the 'passionate fervour' that they felt for God as well known (37.17.4).[44]

The Jews, then, were zealous for God and his law. They argued fiercely with one another about its precise meaning and how best to fulfil it. Against outside threats they were prepared to fight to the death. It is now time to look at the theological understanding that lies behind and is implied by Jewish adherence to the law.

13

Common Theology

The history of Israel in general, and of our period in particular, shows that Jews believed that the one God of the universe had given them his law and that they were to obey it. This basic and fundamental doctrine also implies belief in the election: God chose Israel to do his will. Jews understood the election to lay upon them the obligation of obedience, but also to involve promises on God's part: that he would save and protect them. One of the fundamental factors that contributed to their willingness to fight, and if need be die, was the conviction that God would save those who were loyal to him. This confidence endured right to the end of the great revolt. Despite the crushing defeat that concluded the war, the same conviction revived and helped to fuel a second revolt.

Belief that their God was the only true God, that he had chosen them and had given them his law, and that they were required to obey it are basic to Jewish theology, and they are found in all the sources. These points are often stated explicitly, but they are also implied in a multitude of ways. Rather than canvassing the literature for prooftexts to illustrate each point, however, I shall present Jewish theology in an analytic way, beginning with the commandment to worship God, and proceeding through the various forms of worship. We shall also take into account Jewish attempts to analyse and summarize the law. The main headings of the analytical discussion are these: (1) the theology implied by the Shema' and the first two of the Ten Commandments; this leads to (2) the view of God as creator of the world and controller of history; we shall then consider (3) the theology behind the sacrifical system; (4) the theological implications of attempts to summarize the law: (5) the theology of prayer. Finally we shall consider 'covenantal nomism' as a summary of some of the main aspects of Jewish theology.

Worship of the one God

The most important theological point that is conveyed by the Shema᷎ and the Ten Commandments is that Israel should worship only the one true God. Originally, the commandment to worship only the God of Israel did not constitute a denial that there were other gods. By our period, however, Jews had come to the view that the other gods were not real gods. In technical terms, Judaism progressed from *henotheism* (our God is God number one) and *monolatry* (we worship him alone) to *monotheism* (our God is the only real God; him alone we worship).

The first of the Ten Commandments forbids the worship of other gods, the second the making of 'graven images', or, indeed, 'any likeness of anything that is in heaven above, or that is in the earth beneath, or that is in the water under the earth' (Ex. 20.3–4; Deut. 5.7–8). The Shema᷎ specifies that the Lord God is *one*, which in the first century implied strict monotheism: the one Lord is the *only* Lord. Jewish sensitivity to these commandments was high.

Sensitivity increased as one got closer to the temple. The world was densely populated with statues of various gods, and Jews did not go around the world trying to pull them down. Fortunately, the translators of the Septuagint provided Greek-speaking Jews with a biblical justification for tolerance of Gentile gods. The Hebrew of Ex. 22.27 means 'you shall not revile God', but 'God' is plural, as is usually the case: Hebrew distinguished the God of Israel from any other god by using the plural for the singular Israelite deity. In this particular verse (LXX and ET 22.28), the Septuagint kept the plural, so that in Greek the commandment read, 'you shall not revile the gods'. Both Philo and Josephus interpreted this to mean that Jews were forbidden to blaspheme other people's gods, and Josephus extended the law, so that it prohibited them from robbing foreign temples and taking treasure (for example, in war) that had been dedicated to other gods. Philo also construed Lev. 24.15 (do not curse God) to mean do not curse the gods of the cities.[1] Jews tolerated temples built for other gods, both outside Palestine and in the cities of Palestine where Gentiles lived (e.g. Caesarea).

They were extremely sensitive, however, about Jerusalem. Some people objected to Herod's theatre, since they feared that it was decorated with human busts (*Antiq.* 15.277–9). We have already seen the tumult touched off when Pilate introduced Roman standards into Jerusalem (*War* 2.169–74). And, of course, they were more sensitive yet about improper images in the temple (Herod's eagle).

This all seems clear and straightforward, but as always there was variety of interpretation and practice. During the exile, Ezekiel thought that the temple should be decorated with depictions of palm trees and cherubim (angels) with two faces, one a human's and one a lion's (Ezek. 41.18–20, 25). By the first century, views of graven images were stricter. Even Herod, despite his placement of the eagle, generally avoided images of people or animals. His coins did not have his image on them, nor that of Augustus, but rather such devices as wreaths, palm branches, anchors and cornucopias. It is noteworthy that the most rigorous Jews did not take 'any likeness of anything' quite literally. No one protested against Herod's coins; some of his designs, in fact, were borrowed from Hasmonean coins.[2] Herod's descendants sometimes used images of people. Philip the Tetrarch, whose realm was largely populated by Gentiles, minted coins depicting first Augustus and then Tiberius Caesar. He even struck coins bearing his own image,[3] as did Agrippa I early in his reign. After Judaea was added to Agrippa's domain, however, he struck coins in Jerusalem that did not have a human portrait.[4] When Antipas built Tiberias as his new capital, siting it partially over a burial area, perhaps to make sure priests left him alone, he also decorated his palace with representations of animals (*Life* 65). He may have thought that his palace was his private business; he did not put offensive images on his coins, but used plants typical of the region he governed.[5]

Despite the general Herodian caution not to flout Jewish sensibilities too much, coinage that portrayed humans or even pagan deities circulated in Jewish Palestine. Herod, for example, did not mint his own silver coins, but relied on the Tyrian shekel and half-shekel, which constituted the principal silver coinage in circulation.[6] The Tyrian coins had a graven image: the head of a god, Melqart (equated with the Greek Herakles). Despite this, they circulated freely and, according to the Mishnah, were the coinage demanded by the temple (*Berakhot* 8.7).[7] The silver content of the Tyrian coins was high (ninety to ninety-two per cent) and consistent. The Roman silver provincial tetradrachmas, for example, were only eighty per cent pure,[8] and this probably accounts for the temple's preference for Tyrian coins. The widespread use of the Tyrian coinage in Palestine shows that the temple's requirement reversed the doctrine that bad money drives out good[9] and also overcame the general dislike of coins with images of people or deities. This gives a good idea of the temple's 'clout'.

In any case, coinage bearing graven images – both of people and of pagan deities – circulated in Palestine (cf. Mark 12.13–17), but these images did not lead to riots. As is always the case, those who followed the Bible literally had to decide when to do so: large-scale offences in Jerusalem drew people's wrath, and lesser ones were allowed to pass, and some images were not regarded as offences at all. Even the coins struck by the Jews during the revolts used such figures as vines, vessels and lulavs. Common opinion accepted these depictions as not breaking the commandment not to make 'any likeness of anything'. This commandment might have been construed quite differently. The present-day traveller to the Arab countries of the Near East readily sees what strict observance could mean. Decorations in mosques include only geometric designs and passages from the Quran in the flowing Arabic script: no wreaths, anchors or conucopias, much less eagles, and certainly not human faces. During the period of the second temple, Jews did not interpret the commandment this strictly.

Just as 'graven images' on coins were acceptable to most Jews (though many frowned on the depiction of faces), so were other decorations in the home and even in the temple. The recent excavations in Jerusalem have revealed one house that had 'depictions of birds in the style of Pompeii', though most houses had geometric designs.[10] The front of the sanctuary was adorned with 'golden vines, from which depended grape-clusters as tall as a man' (*War* 5.210). This led some Gentiles to think that the Jews worshipped Bacchus, the Roman god of vineyards (see Thackeray's note in the LCL). The Jerusalemites were apparently willing to run the risk of misunderstanding in order to have on the entrance to the sanctuary a symbol of the abundance of the land and a reminder of the enormous cluster of grapes brought back by those who 'spied out the land' at the time of Moses (Num. 13.21–7). The vine and grape clusters recalled a glorious moment in Israel's history, unlike Herod's golden eagle, which reminded people of Roman domination.

Comments by Philo and Josephus show how Jews could interpret other objects symbolically, and thus make physical depictions acceptable, so that they were seen not as transgressions of one of the Ten Commandments, but as symbols of the glory of the God who gave them. For example, the veil in front of the doors of the sanctuary portrayed 'a panorama of the heavens, the signs of the Zodiac excepted' (*War* 5.214). This seems to mean that the stars were depicted, but that the lines connecting them, which make the signs of the zodiac, had not been woven into the fabric. Josephus, as did Philo, found astral and other symbolism in many other things connected with the temple (below). The important point here, however, is that the stars could be actually depicted without causing offence. This is significant in light of the large role played by astrology in pagan religion of the time. Jews, of course, thought of themselves as worshipping not the astral deities, the different gods represented by each planet, but rather the one God who made the heavens and the earth.

The birds used as decoration in one house, the stars on the temple veil and the golden cluster of grapes in the temple were not regarded as pagan. They simply show that there was some freedom of interpretation with regard to what did and did not count as a forbidden 'likeness of anything'. The house decorated with birds is the only one found thus far in Jerusalem, but it is dubious that it was completely aberrant: the owners were responsible, but artisans had to be found who could and would do the work. If there were such artisans, they may have decorated more than one house.

We have seen Josephus' reservation that the signs of the zodiac themselves were not woven into the veil. In later synagogues this restriction was sometimes dropped. In Hammath, just south of Tiberias, there is a third- or fourth-century synagogue with a beautiful mosaic floor, depicted on which, along with the scroll of the law, are the signs of the zodiac and the Greek god Helios ('Sun') in the centre of them.[11] We may pause for a moment to consider the importance of the sun god in Jewish Palestine, which will help us better to understand the meaning of 'monotheism' in first-century Judaism.

The sun was personified and worshipped in much of the ancient world. I do not wish to attempt to trace the history of the worship of the sun in Palestine and among Israelites, or of the various ways in which people could include aspects of sun worship within the worship of God. It should be noted, however, that there is an important distinction between 'worshipping the sun' and 'incorporating elements of sun worship into the worship of God'. Israelite reformers opposed both. The most important instance was when Josiah, who became king of Judaea in about 624 BCE, instituted a reform of worship, during which 'vessels made for Baal, for Asherah, and for all the host of heaven', doubtless including the sun, were taken out of the temple, and priests of other gods were deposed (II Kings 23.4f.).

This is usually regarded as having been a decisive rejection of other deities, but elements derived from sun worship continued. Subsequently Ezekiel attacked those who turned 'their backs to the temple of the Lord, and their faces toward the east, worshipping the sun toward the east' (Ezek. 8.16). According to the Mishnah, at one point during the feast of Booths priests 'turned their faces to the west', recalling that their predecessors had faced east and worshipped the sun, and proclaimed that 'our eyes are turned toward the Lord' (*Sukkah* 5.4).

Despite this, the practice that Ezekiel condemned was continued by some. Josephus wrote that the Essenes 'are particularly reverent towards the divinity [*to theion*] for, before the Sun rises, they say nothing of profane things, but [only] certain ancestral prayers to him, as beseeching [him] to rise' (*War* 2.128).[12] By using the term *to theion* rather than *ho theos* – 'the divinity' rather than 'God himself' – Josephus may have intended to indicate that the Essenes regarded the sun as a divine being below God, rather than as a symbol or aspect of the one God, though perhaps we should not press his wording too hard. In any case he depicted the Essenes as directing worship towards the sun, rather than simply using sunrise as a chronological marker indicating the time for prayer. Josephus further wrote that, when going to stool, the Essenes wrapped their mantles about them, 'so as not to offend the rays of God' (*War* 2.148). In this instance 'God himself' seems to be represented by the sun, and his all-seeing eye by its rays. These passages come in the course of a long discussion of the Essenes, one that is full of praise for them. Josephus himself – a priest, a Pharisee, and a convinced Jew – was a monotheist. He did not see the Essenes' practice as constituting a denial of monotheism, or he could not have included it in his panegyric on them. The passage alerts the reader to the fact that practices and beliefs that later would be regarded as pagan were in the first century followed by people who regarded themselves as true to the God of Israel.

That the Essenes really offered prayer to the sun is made more probable by a passage in the Qumran *Temple Scroll* (30.3–31.9). In its description of the new temple that the sect would build, the scroll describes a tower that would be most appropriate for worship of the sun, as Morton Smith has shown. The tower was intended for the sole purpose of enclosing a staircase to the roof, and it was to be plated with gold. Thus it had a special importance, and Josephus' reference to praying to the sun may tell us what that importance was. Other descriptions of the real or longed-for temple do not include such a tower.[13]

Above we noted the floor of a synagogue at Hammath that had as its main decoration the signs of the zodiac in a circle, with the god Helios in the middle. This synagogue floor, with its blatant pagan decoration, was built at the time when rabbinic Judaism was strong in Galilee – after the redaction and publication of the Mishnah, during the years when the material in the Tosefta and the Palestinian Talmud was being produced and edited. According to the Tosefta, Rabbi Judah, who flourished in the middle of the second century, said that 'If anyone says a blessing over the sun – this is a heterodox practice' (*T. Berakhot* 6[7].6).[14] In light of the floor, it seems that he was opposing contemporary practice.

It is generally thought, however, that during the second, third and fourth centuries synagogue worship became more eclectic, more accepting of alien influences. Certainly there is a lot more evidence of apparently pagan decoration in fourth-century sites than in pre-70 sites. We cannot say that the special Essene interest in the sun represents common piety, nor that the fourth-century synagogues, with pagan decoration, represent pre-70 attitudes. Yet even in the first century monotheism was thought to be compatible with representations of the stars and planets. If, before 70, the heavens were portrayed on the veil of the temple, it is entirely reasonable to think that what was omitted there – the signs of the zodiac themselves – appeared elsewhere.

Intermediate between worshipping the sun and using it as a chronological marker indicating the time for prayer was thinking of it as an emanation or representation of the power of God, and worshipping it in that sense. Helios himself might be portrayed with such an intention. As Goodenough has shown, many religious values and symbols were more or less universal in the Mediterranean world of our period. Vines and the rays of the sun indicated life in all its fullness, including life eternal. Jews accepted that ideal and the symbols that pointed to it. They thought, of course, that only their God truly gave life, but the symbols were often the same as in pagan culture.[15] Christians also adopted the same values and symbols, as the references to Christ as the 'true light' and the 'true vine' in the gospel of John show (John 1.9; 15.1). He is the true vine, and the vine of Bacchus is false, but the vine and what it symbolized were the same: life.

Finally, we may note that for few Jews did the confession of 'one God' mean the complete denial of the existence of other supernatural beings. The point is most easily illustrated from Paul, who, before becoming an apostle of Christ, was a zealous Pharisee (Phil. 3.2–6).[16] He wrote that the Galatians had been 'in bondage to beings that by nature are no gods' – but that were, nevertheless, 'beings' (Gal. 4.8). To the Corinthians he wrote that there are 'so-called gods in heaven or on earth' – beings incorrectly called gods, but nevertheless populating both heaven and earth (I Cor. 8.5). He looked forward to the time when Christ would triumph over 'every ruler and every authority and power' (I Cor. 15.24), when 'every knee should bow' at the name of Jesus, whether in heaven, on earth, or under the earth (Phil. 2.10). Paul, that is, accepted that the pagan deities existed, but he did not wish to call them real gods. In I Cor. 10.20 he settled on 'demons' (the wording is based on LXX Deut. 32.17; Isa. 65.11). This reservation allows us to call him, and thousands of other Jews of his time, a 'monotheist', one who thought that there was only one real God.

Jews, then, who frequently said the Shemaʿ and recalled the Ten Commandments, believed that there was only one true Lord, and they intended to worship only him. The meaning of monotheism, however, was flexible, and Jews were by no means completely isolated from the pervasive influence of the rich and variegated religious world of their environment.

Creation, providence and history

Jews believed that all of life was governed by God's will. God created and rules over the entire world. The doctrine of creation – that this world was made by God, is good, and is to be cared for as his – is perhaps Judaism's most important single contribution to civilization. Most Jews also thought that God controlled history. We shall observe how these ideas were worked out in first-century Judaism.

We take first the *created order* and the theology derived from the commandment to observe *the sabbath*. The need to care for the universe was not seen as clearly in the first century as it is now, but it was taken account of as part and parcel of the general theme that God cares for what may appear to humans as of small importance or even trivial. Since the creator had rested on the sabbath, he ordained that humans should do the same. Thoughtful Jews saw that the sabbath rest was beneficial, and they pointed out that it applied to slaves, animals, and the land itself. With regard to the land, which was allowed to lie fallow in the seventh year, Philo observed that 'monotony without a break, particularly in work, is always seen to be injurious'. He emphasized that the sabbatical year for the land was not observed in order to save its owners and tillers work, since it could be let and farmed, but rather was kept 'out of consideration for the land' itself: the rest was good for it (*Hypothetica* 7.15–18).

The animals were also granted sabbath rest (Ex. 20.10; Deut. 5.14). Josephus remarked pointedly on other biblical laws regarding animals: not to muzzle the oxen that tread out the grain (*Antiq.* 4.233; Deut. 25.4) and to help another's beast out of the mire (*Antiq.* 4.275; Deut. 22.4). Both Philo and Josephus (the latter possibly in dependence on the former) maintained that Jews followed other laws of kindness to animals. 'There must be no maltreatment of animals contrary to [the use allowed] by God . . .; no destroying of their seed . . .' (*Hypothetica* 7.7). As Josephus put it, God authorized 'their use only in accordance with the law' (*Apion* 2.213). Both authors add a curious point: 'Creatures which take refuge in our houses like suppliants we are forbidden to kill' (*Apion* 2.213; *Hypothetica* 7.9). Further, when at war in a foreign country Jewish troops were forbidden to kill the beasts of labour (*Apion* 2.213).

Philo recognized that many readers (who did not know about ecology and animal rights) would find all this trivial, and he replied: 'These things are of nothing worth, you may say, yet great is the law which ordains them and ever watchful is the care which it demands' (*Hypothetica* 7.9). The greatness of the law, in Jewish eyes, lay in part in the very fact that it covers all the trivia of life and of the creation. Josephus also thought that Moses had been correct in leaving 'nothing, however insignificant, to the discretion and caprice of the individual' (*Apion* 2.173). Rabbis remarked on the same point, though not in connection with animals:

Ben Azzai said: Run to fulfil the lightest duty even as the weightiest, and flee from transgression; for one duty draws another duty in its train, and one transgression draws another transgression in its train. (*Avot* 4.2)

Here life is seen as a seamless whole. In every aspect one may either fulfil or transgress God's will, and one thing leads to another. The universe is God's garden; humans are not his only creatures.

Josephus and Philo, as we saw, found symbolism in many aspects of the temple, often cosmic symbolism. This corresponds to seeing God as creator of the entire universe and also as its ruler: it continues to run as he intends. Philo regarded the high priest's robe as 'a likeness and copy of the universe'. It was circular, thus symbolizing the air, while other aspects represented the hemispheres and the zodiac (*Spec. Laws* 1.84–7). In Josephus' eyes the seven-branched lampstand represented the planets and the twelve loaves on the altar stood for the zodiac and the year, while the spices symbolized sea, inhabited land and desert (*War* 5.216–18).[17]

All this shows, stated Josephus, that 'all things are of God and for God' (*War* 5.218). As he put it elsewhere, God 'is the beginning, the middle, and the end of all things' (*Apion* 2.190). These phrases remind one of Paul's slightly earlier formulation: 'for us there is one God, the Father, from whom are all things and for whom we exist'. Paul then included Christ: 'one Lord, Jesus Christ, through whom are all things and through whom we exist' (I Cor. 8.6). One guesses that, before his call to be an apostle, Paul would have assigned to God mediation (through whom) as well as origin and destination (from whom, unto whom). It was common Jewish opinion that, just as God had brought the world into being, he controlled its destiny and its end. 'The whole universe is governed by providence' (*pronoia*) (*Arist.* 201). 'He that runs away from God declares Him to be the cause of nothing', whereas one should refer 'everything to God' (Philo, *Alleg. Interp.* 3.29f.).[18]

This has brought us to our second point under the present heading, the belief that *God controlled history*. A lot of unfortunate and evil things happen in the world, and all philosophies and religions face the problem of explaining them. In our period, Jews were torn between a straight monotheistic explanation of evil – God intends it – and a dualistic explanation – there is another power (Satan) or a congeries of other powers (demons). I shall not go very far into the topic of dualism[19] in Jewish literature. Many aspects of Persian religion (Zoroastrianism) had penetrated the West, and had influenced Judaism in particular. Jews had met Persian beliefs while in exile in Babylonia, and for some centuries Palestine had been part of the Persian empire. Angelology, demonology, belief in the resurrection, and dualism are some of the main areas of theology where Iranian influence is visible.[20] Even where we see dualism most clearly, however, we also see that Jewish theologians simultaneously maintained monotheism. Two brief examples: The Qumran sectarians described 'the war of the sons of light against the sons of darkness' (1QM) and discussed 'the ways of the spirit of falsehood'

(1QS 4.9). They thought that most people were 'ruled by the Angel of Darkness' (1QS 3.21). It is perfectly clear, however, that in their view there was only one real God. Paul (whose views on these points seem not to have been altered by his call to be an apostle of Christ) wrote that Satan (standing in for the angel of darkness) could disguise himself as the 'angel of light' (II Cor. 11.14) and that 'this age' is governed by another 'god' (II Cor. 4.4) or by other 'rulers' (I Cor. 2.6).[21] But for him too there was only one true God (I Cor. 8.6). Jewish theologians sometimes had recourse to a form of dualism to explain evil, but (not being speculative philosophers) they did not think that this involved the denial of monotheism.

For our present purposes, it is most instructive to see the degree to which some Jews attributed evil directly to God. This is the natural consequence of monotheism, and in the period that we study many Jews were sufficiently brave monotheists to lay evil at God's door. Tessa Rajak has succinctly stated one of Josephus' main doctrines,

> that of the divinely planned transference of power to the Roman side. God, or the Deity, or Fate, or Destiny, or Providence, or Chance had decided that the Romans should be victorious . . . Vespasian was the chosen agent . . . In the furtherance of this objective, specific Roman successes and Jewish disasters had been arranged, and the Jews rendered blind. The destruction of Jerusalem, with the Temple, was but a part of this pattern.[22]

Josephus thought that, since God controls history, whatever in fact happened was in accord with his will. Roman troops had destroyed the temple, therefore God had intended them to do so. Josephus interpreted the destruction as punishment for Israel's sins.

Paul shared this theology. From his Christian perspective, he thought that Christ saved and the law condemned. He was then pushed, by the same force that led Josephus to ascribe Roman victory to God's will, to the remarkable conclusion that God had given the law with the express intention that it condemn (Gal. 3.22; Rom. 5.20; cf. Rom. 11.32). Similarly Paul originally assumed that God would save first the Jew and then the Greek (see e.g. Rom. 1.16). As he surveyed the scene late in his career, however, he realized that the mission to the Gentiles was more successful than the mission to the Jews, and so concluded that God had intended to reverse the sequence, saving first the Gentiles, then the Jews through jealousy of them (Rom. 11.11f., 14, 25f., 30f.). No matter what happened, God planned it and would use it to further his ultimate purpose.

In discussing the Jewish parties Josephus often comments on their view of 'fate', one of the principal words that he employed to convey Jewish views about God's providence to his Greek-speaking audience. The Pharisees 'attribute everything to Fate and to God' (*War* 2.162). The Sadducees denied Fate (2.164), but the Essenes fully accepted it, leaving 'everything in the hands of God' (*Antiq.* 18.18). The Pharisees combined belief in fate (God's providence or predestination) and free will (*War* 2.163), as indeed did Josephus himself. God planned the transfer of power to the Roman side (Rajak, above), but the Jews deserved what happened. They had broken the sabbath and assassins had spilled blood in the temple. Its fiery destruction served as just punishment, necessary in order to purge it (*War* 4.323; 6.110; *Antiq.* 20.166).

Paul could also discuss the history of salvation in terms of both predestination and free will: God foreordained that Gentiles would be saved by faith, apart from law (Gal. 3.8). In former times he had chosen some but rejected others, quite apart from their individual merits (Rom. 9.15f., 22f.). Despite this, people needed actively 'to call on the name of the Lord' and to 'confess with the lips' in order to be saved (Rom. 10.10–13). And, further, all were responsible for their own deeds and would be judged for them (e.g. Rom. 2.13; I Cor. 5.10). Free will and predestination were also combined in Qumran. Despite Josephus' view that the Essenes rejected free will, the Dead Sea Scrolls show that they regarded individuals as free to accept the true covenant or not, and to obey its regulations or not. This they combined with the view that God had placed people in either the realm of darkness or of light.[23]

Jews who combined God's providence and human free will did not work them out philosophically, just as they did not worry about combining monotheism and dualism. They did not see the need to solve the problem of the incompatibility between God's providence and human free will, and they simply asserted both. One statement would apply to one case, another to another. Thus, for example, confessions that everything is in the hands of God come when people consider the whole sweep of history; statements of free will appear when they think of individual human behaviour.[24]

Generally Jews believed that God, creator of the world, cared for it all and ruled over what happened in it, including the march of human history. (On the last point the Sadducees may have disagreed.) Nevertheless, individuals were free to follow his way or not. The doctrine of God the creator and ruler did not lead to 'hard' predestination, but it did have to accommodate itself to whatever actually happened in history.

The theology of offerings and sacrifices

Since offerings and sacrifice were such large parts of ancient religion, thoughtful people reflected on their value and meaning. The avowal in Deut.

26, said when bringing first fruits, guaranteed that this offering was seen as a token given back to God in thanks for his great bounty. It is possible that the other agricultural offerings were seen in the same light.

A good deal more can be said about the theological interpretation of the various sacrifices.

1. Before sacrificing, people had to be purified. Most pilgrims waited outside the temple for seven days, being cleansed of corpse impurity, while others had to immerse to remove semen impurity, menstrual impurity and the like. Outer purification brought to mind inner purification. I think it safe to say that everyone knew that those who went up to the temple should have 'clean hands and a pure heart' (Ps. 24.4), and that they saw a connection between inner and outer purity. Philo made a great deal of the superiority of being sprinkled with the mixture of ashes and water that removed corpse impurity over pagan lustrations, which used water alone: ashes and water represent the substances of which humans are made, and being sprinkled with them reminds the worshippers who they are, whence they come, and to whom they owe their existence (*Spec. Laws* 1.263–6). The seven-day wait induced thoughtfulness.[25] Not many, to be sure, had Philo's intellect, sophistication or ability to allegorize. On the other hand, purification was a standard metaphor in Judaism for the elimination of evil or unworthy thoughts and desires, and we may assume that many pilgrims took the opportunity to purify their hearts as well as their bodies. While the festivals themselves were joyous, the period of preparation beforehand was a time for self-examination.

2. Sacrifices atone for sins. The notion that atonement and purification require the shedding of blood was widespread, and in the Jewish sacrificial system the guilt offering, the sin offering and the sacrifices of the Day of Atonement provided for cleansing of impurity and expiation of sin. This part of Jewish theology was given a prominent place in Christianity, and early Christian literature offers a great number of quotations that show the connection. Most famous is Heb. 9.22: 'Indeed, under the law almost everything is purified with blood, and without the shedding of blood there is no forgiveness of sins'. The chapter is a prolonged discussion of the theme. That the blood of Christ brings atonement or cleansing is also stated, for example, in Rom. 3.25; 5.9; Eph. 1.7; I John 1.7. Paul's use of the theme shows that it goes back to the earliest Christian community, and thus to those who had grown up in first-century Jewish Palestine. The theology of animal sacrifice was employed in the earliest christological formulations. This simply shows that the theology of atonement by the shedding of blood was common.

Non-Christian Jewish authors emphasized that sacrifice provides the occasion for repentance and confession of sin. This agrees with the interiorization of religion to which we earlier referred. Blood does not atone automatically. Those who bring sacrifices should 'ask for pardon and forgiveness for their sins' (*Spec. Laws* 1.67). As we saw on pp. 108f., Philo elaborates on the inner stance of the offerer. The sinner is 'convicted inwardly by his conscience', 'reproaches himself', repays the one whom he has injured plus an added fifth, and 'makes a plain confession of the wrong he has committed'. The true advocate for forgiveness is 'soul-felt conviction' on the part of the worshipper (*Spec. Laws* 1.235–237). Atonement requires both 'prayers and sacrifices to propitiate the Deity' (*Moses* 2.147). The sacrifice represents the sanctification of 'the mind of the worshipper' (*Spec. Laws* 1.203). Those who participate are thus 'changing their way for the better' (1.227). In short, Moses 'holds the sacrifice to consist not in the victims but in the offerer's intention and his zeal' (1.290). God so values repentance that he gave to it 'the same honour as to innocence from sin' (1.187).

Rabbinic literature offers a rich harvest of passages on the importance of inward intention and of repentance.[26] With regard to sacrifices, it is said that the size of the offering does not matter; the Bible calls even a bird offering or a meal offering 'an odour of sweet savour'. This is 'to teach that it is all one whether a man offers much or little, if only he directs his mind towards Heaven' (*Menahot* 13.11). The rabbis expended considerable argument to show that, even though the Bible says simply that the Day of Atonement atones, it means that it atones for those who repent (*Sifra Emor*, pereq 14.1–2; on Lev. 23.27). This is, in fact, pretty good exegesis of Leviticus. The passage on the Day of Atonement requires self-affliction, probably as penance for transgression (Lev. 23.26–32), and Leviticus subsequently requires confession of iniquity and humbling of the heart on the part of sinful Israel (Lev. 26.40–42).

Ben Sira emphasized the atoning power of kindness and charity (Ben Sira 3.14, 30; 29.12; 35.3), urged people to confess (4.26), warned them not to count on abundance of sacrifices to wipe out bad deeds (7.9), and said that the gifts that lawbreakers gave to God were worthless (34.18f.; 35.12). Yet he thought that the sacrifices should be offered (7.29–31), and he admonished the reader not to 'appear before the Lord empty-handed', since God desired 'the sacrifice of a righteous person' (35.4–7). This is, in effect, the view that inner and outer should be aligned: one should confess, pray for forgiveness *and* bring a sacrifice. Thus when Philo emphasized the interior aspect of sacrifice, he was not simply indulging his penchant for allegory, but rather was in agreement with common Jewish views.

3. Sacrifices show thanks to God and praise him. We recall that one of the major categories of offerings is the shared sacrifice, of which a principal sub-category is the 'thank offering'.[27] Leviticus does not offer illustrations of occasions that called forth thank offerings, but they may readily be imagined.

Happy events and success of various kinds led to the desire for a celebratory meal, and the thank offering allowed this universal human desire to be combined with thanksgiving to God.

We also saw above that Philo, reading the Greek translation of the Bible, did not find 'shared sacrifice' and 'thank offering', but rather 'preservation (or 'welfare') offering' and 'praise offering'. This did not, however, prevent him from finding offerings of thanksgiving. He regarded thanks to God as one of the basic motives for sacrifices in general (*Spec. Laws* 1.67), and so he needed a prominent sacrifice that expressed it. This he found in the daily community burnt sacrifices, which he interpreted as thank offerings, one for the blessings of the night, the other for the blessings of the day (*Spec. Laws* 1.169).

More generally, Philo interpreted all burnt offerings as being for 'the rendering of honour to God for the sake of Him only and with no other motive' (*Spec. Laws* 1.195); that is, the worshipper sought nothing for himself or herself. Thanksgiving is, of course, a main example of sacrifices that are motivated only by the desire to honour God (ibid.).

Ben Sira characterized the songs that accompanied the sacrifices as being songs of praise (Ben Sira 50.18), and this shows that the theme was connected with the temple service at an early date (*c.* 200 BCE).

4. Sacrifices allow for communion with God. This idea is almost demanded by the shared sacrifice, which was divided in three ways. The blood was poured out 'to the Lord', and the fat was offered to him by fire; the priest received part of the slaughtered animal and also part of the meal offering that accompanied it; most of the meat was taken outside the temple and eaten by the offerer and those whom he or she invited (Lev. 10.14; 7.11–18). This division may itself point to communion: God, the priests and the worshipper share in the same sacrifice.

Partnership with God was not, in Philo's view, the chief aim of the shared sacrifice (following the Greek translation of Leviticus, he called it a 'preservation' or 'welfare' sacrifice). Its principal point was 'the safe preserving and bettering of human affairs' (*Spec. Laws* 1.197). He also saw, however, that in eating their portion of this sacrifice the worshippers shared what was basically God's: they entered into a 'partnership' (*koinōnon*) with the altar (*Spec. Laws* 1.221).

Paul was also of the view that sacrifices provide communion with God: 'Consider the people of Israel; are not those who eat the sacrifices partners (*koinōnoi*, 'participants' or 'communicants') in the altar?' (I Cor. 10.18). In I Corinthians, this statement illustrates the point that participating in rites involving eating and drinking results in participation with the God or demon whose rites are being observed. Jewish cultic theology serves only to prove his case. This indicates that he took for granted the view that sharing a sacrifice provides communion with the deity. We may conclude that Jews commonly regarded the shared sacrifices in this way.

5. As we have just seen, Philo interpreted the shared sacrifice, for which he had the Greek word *sōtērion* – 'welfare', 'safety' or 'preservation' – as having the goal of 'participation in good things' (*Spec. Laws* 1.196) or of 'bettering of human affairs' (1.197). To some degree, the sacrifice constituted participation in good things: it provided a banquet. It is likely, however, that Philo saw it also as a *petition* for good things, especially since he thought that it benefitted or 'preserved' both soul and body (1.222).

Since biblical law does not specify prayer in connection with the temple service, petition for blessings is not part of the Bible's sacrificial theory. Yet it was a natural development, one that we find as early as Ben Sira. He describes the prayers of non-priestly worshippers in the temple as being 'supplications' or 'requests' (*deomai*; Ben Sira 50.19). Since the service that the author describes is the Day of Atonement (see 50.5), he may have had in mind principally petitions for forgiveness. Ben Sira concludes, however, by offering a prayer in which he asks God to bestow gladness of heart, peace, mercy and deliverance (50.22–24). It is likely that Ben Sira regarded the sacrifical service as being an occasion to request God's blessings in general.

Finally, we note that Josephus wrote that at the sacrifices prayers were offered 'for the welfare (*sotēria*) of the community' (*Apion* 2.196) and that at the festivals people prayed 'for future mercies' (*Antiq.* 4.203).

6. Some of the sacrifices were offered for the good of the whole world. Again, this is not a biblical category, but we find it in first-century literature. Philo interpreted the community sacrifices as being 'for the whole nation', and then corrected himself: 'rather, . . . for all humanity' (*Spec. Laws* 1.168). He contrasted Jewish practice with pagan:

> Among the other nations the priests are accustomed to offer prayers and sacrifices for their kinsmen and friends and fellow-countrymen only, but the high priest of the Jews makes prayers and gives thanks not only on behalf of the whole human race but also for the parts of nature, earth, water, air, fire. For he holds the world to be, as in very truth it is, his country, and in its behalf he is wont to propitiate the Ruler with supplication and intercession, beseeching Him to make His creature a partaker of His own kindly and merciful nature. (*Spec. Laws* 1.97)

It is not certain just which sacrifices Philo here had in mind. The Jews offered sacrifices on behalf of (that is, in intercession for the welfare of) Caesar and the people of Rome (*War* 2.197, 409; *Apion* 2.77), and Philo may have been thinking of these.[28] In any case the sacrifices on behalf of Rome show that the general notion of intercession for others was not absent from the common understanding of the meaning of sacrifices.

7. Sacrifices, especially at festivals, provided for the feeling of community among all Jews. Philo wrote that when the multitudes of worshippers came together in Jerusalem they formed new friendships, 'and the sacrifices and libations are the occasion of reciprocity of feeling and constitute the surest pledge that all are of one mind' (*Spec. Laws* 1.70). Similarly Josephus: 'meeting and feasting together' created 'feelings of mutual affection' (*Antiq.* 4.203).

Of these seven theological interpretations, which were common? Philo held that there were three principal reasons for sacrifice: to honour God (the burnt offering), to gain blessings (the shared sacrifice) and to atone for trespasses (the sin offering, under which he included the guilt offering) (*Spec. Laws* 1.197). He also dwelt long and lovingly on the connection between inner and outer purification (e.g. *Spec. Laws* 1.261–72), and we have been able to cite him under the other headings as well (communion with God, intercession for the whole world, and harmony among Jews). I think it likely, however, that he overstated intercession when he included the whole world. Certainly all Jews knew that sacrifices were offered on behalf of Rome; and Rome, to many, must have appeared to be 'the whole world'. But sacrifices were offered for the whole world only in this restricted sense.

That is the only one that I would rule out as 'common'. It is doubtful that all Jews who feasted on a shared sacrifice had the same theology of participation in God that Paul had, but it seems likely that they at least knew that they were participating in a very personal way in the divine service. The crude idea, that they shared God's food, had passed into history; just how they interpreted sharing we cannot know. But the idea of participation was built into the sacrifice, and most people probably grasped it in one way or another.

The other strictly theological ideas – inner purification, atonement, thanksgiving and petition – need very little comment. These were all part of standard Jewish belief. We do not know that Jews sacrificed *in order* to petition God; but, by our period, prayers of petition were common and the temple service was an occasion on which they would be said.

That the festivals were occasions that partly reflected, partly created the feeling of solidarity is a very important point. Even apart from the festivals, the temple served this function. The annual collection of the temple tax and its delivery reinforced Jewish solidarity both in Palestine and in the Diaspora. The act of giving, by its very nature, created community spirit. Not all Jews had 'reciprocity of feeling' for all other Jews, nor were they all quite 'of one mind' (Philo's phrases), but those who sent the tax, and especially those who made the pilgrimage, showed that they had something in common with other

Jews. Let us imagine the situation concretely. Of a few dozen Jewish families in a city in Asia Minor, let us say that five had been to Jerusalem at least once. While there, they had made friends, some with Jews from North Africa, some with Jews from Mesopotamia, some with Judaeans. When they returned home, they would remember their friends and be conscious of how much they had in common. This feeling, in turn, would be communicated to the other members of their synagogue. Jewish solidarity became a great socio-religious fact, one that endured after the temple was destroyed. It was expressed through attending the synagogue and keeping the same laws, especially those of sabbath, food and circumcision. While the temple stood, however, it was a focal point of Jewish loyalty, and participation in its service, even when minor and remote (sending the temple tax), expressed commitment to the God of Israel and thus to other Jews as well.

The theology of the summaries of the law

We saw above that the legal books offer their own summaries or epitomes of the major categories of the law – commandments that govern relations between humans and God and those that govern relations among humans. The Deuteronomist seems to have intended the Shema᷄ (Deut. 6.4–9) to be a partial summary of the laws that had just been given. It urges Israel to hear and love the Lord who had just spoken, to bear the commandments always in mind, and to do them. Similarly the priestly author of Lev. 19 grouped together several commandments that govern relations among humans and then concluded with a statement that encapsulated them: 'you shall love your neighbour as yourself' (Lev. 19.18).

We also saw that it was widely recognized that love of God and love of humanity were the two main aspects of the law. Both Jesus and Philo cited them as such (Mark 12.29–31; *Spec. Laws* 1.299f., 324), and numerous authors regarded 'righteousness' (towards humans) and 'piety' (towards God) as summarizing the proper religious life.[29]

Here I wish to focus on epigrams and other one-line epitomes of the law, which were generally based not on the Shema᷄ (love God), but on Lev. 19.18 (love neighbours) and 19.34 (love strangers). The one-line epitomes include both 'neighbour' and 'stranger', since they speak of 'people' or 'others'.[30] Most famous is the 'golden rule', 'Whatever you wish that people would do to you, do so to them, for this is the law and the prophets' (Matt. 7.12). The conclusion shows that this is meant to epitomize the whole law, though in terms of contents it summarizes only the second table. In negative form, the epigram appears in other literature. Tobit 4.15 has 'what you hate, do not do to any one', though in Tobit this is one admonition among many rather than an epitome of the whole law. In Philo, however, the epigram 'what a person would hate to suffer he or she must not do to others' comes at the head of a list of commandments, some of which are also recast as epigrams, such as 'What he or she has not laid down he or she must not pick up' (*Hypothetica* 7.6; the same epigram appears in *Apion* 2.208, though it is not visible in Thackeray's translation).

The best-known instance of the epigrammatic epitome occurs in a story told of Hillel, the great Pharisee who was Jesus' older contemporary:

> On another occasion it happened that a certain heathen came before Shammai and said to him, 'Make me a proselyte, on condition that you teach me the whole Torah while I stand on one foot'. Thereupon he repulsed him with the builder's cubit which was in his hand. When he went before Hillel, he said to him, 'What is hateful to you, do not to your neighbour: that is the whole Torah, while the rest is commentary thereof; go and learn it'. (*Shabbat* 31a)

Since this appears for the first time in a late source, and since other sources attribute epigrammatic sayings to Hillel, but not this one (e.g. *Avot* 2.5–7), we cannot attribute it to him with confidence. Finally, we note that Paul twice summarized the law by quoting Lev. 19.18: Gal. 5.14; Rom. 13.8–10. In the second instance he also cited the commandments not to commit adultery, not to kill, not to steal and not to covet. Interestingly, he then explained that since 'love does no wrong to a neighbour' it 'is the fulfilling of the law' (Rom. 13.10). That is, Paul knew the negative form of the saying and found it useful.

Two remarks are necessary about the epigrammatic epitome of the law, 'do to others . . .' or 'do not do to others . . .' One has to do with the difference between the positive form (Jesus) and the negative form (Tobit, Philo, Paul and the Talmud). 'Do not do what you would hate' prohibits transgression and corresponds to the way in which laws are usually formulated: do not murder, do not steal, do not exceed the speed limit. Even in Lev. 19 the commandments 'love your neighbour' and 'love the stranger' summarize laws that are themselves often expressed negatively: do not reap your field to its very borders; do not pick up what falls on the ground, but leave it for the poor. Negative and positive are two sides of the same coin, but the negative is clearer and more law-like. 'Feed the poor' is not nearly so explicit as 'do not pick up food that falls to the ground'.'Do to others what you yourself would like' is open-ended and requires creative thinking in order to give it content. In terms of rhetorical force, it is more challenging. We should not think, however, that people who used the negative form intended only to prohibit bad actions, not to encourage good ones. Philo followed his version of the negative epitome with positive commandments, such as that a person must give food to the poor and the disabled (*Hypothetica* 7.6). In Paul's longer summary of the law, Rom. 13.8–10, the basic commandment is positive ('love your neighbour'), but the others are negative, including Paul's own reformulation, 'Love does no wrong to a neighbour, therefore love is the fulfilling of the law'. We should not take this to mean that he wished to discourage positive good deeds.

Secondly, we should emphasize that one cannot determine the full contents of a teacher's ethics or theology from the teacher's own epitome. Scholars sometimes think that, since Paul gave Lev. 19.18 as 'the whole law', he intended to exclude from 'the law' what they call the 'ritual' commandments. This does not follow.[31] We noted that two different summaries are attributed to Jesus, one in the passage about the greatest commandments, where he gives the basic commandment under each of the law's two heads, the other the 'golden rule', where he says that only the second of these is 'the law and the prophets'. This does not mean that he wished to retract the commandment to love God. The same is true of Paul. His one-line summary does not mean that he intended to oppose the laws on the first table. He was not in favour of idolatry, and he did believe in 'serving' only the God of Israel, which is what the second commandment requires (by implication). In Rom. 9.4 Paul lists as one of Israel's advantages that to them belonged 'the service' (*latreia*, RSV 'worship'), that is, the temple service. Paul accepted the so-called 'ritual' commandments, those on the first table (though he did not believe that his Gentile converts had to keep the sabbath). Similarly Philo, who employed the 'negative golden rule', fully believed in the commandments on the first table. Hillel – or whatever rabbi should get the credit for his one-line summary of the law – can hardly be suspected of opposing sacrifice, though it is not logically included in 'do not do to others what you do not want them to do to you'.

Put another way, several people might agree that Lev. 19.18 is 'the whole law', while disagreeing about a lot of things. Epitomes are not logically precise summaries, and we should not expect too much of them. They aim at catching the spirit of the law, not at summarizing all of its parts.

The rabbis subsequently offered numerous summaries or cores of the law:

> If one is honest in his business dealings and the spirit of his fellow creatures takes delight in him, it is accounted to him as though he had fulfilled the whole Torah. (*Mekilta Vayassa* 1; Lauterbach II, p. 96)

> Charity and deeds of loving-kindness are equal to all the commandments [*mitsvot*] in the Torah. (*T. Pe'ah* 4.19)

> '[If you turn aside] from the way which I command you this day to go after other gods . . .' (Deut. 11.28). On the basis of this passage they said:

everyone who confesses to idolatry denies the entire Torah, and everyone
who denies idolatry confesses to the entire Torah. (*Sifre Deut.* 54 end)

Only in the last instance is the first table explicitly in mind. The others are
basically derived from considering Lev. 19.18 (plus 19.34) as the summary of
the law. These passages further help make clear that, to ancient Jews, love of
the neighbour and of the stranger was to be expressed in concrete actions,
such as honesty and charity.

Did Jews in general think that the 'whole law' was fulfilled by loving God
and loving the neighbour? Did they know that one implied the other, that to
love God meant to obey his commandments, including the command to love
other people? We may confidently say that this is what their teachers taught.
We have more than once noted Philo's statement that every sabbath in the
synagogues the Jewish 'philosophy' was expounded under two heads, duty to
God (*eusebeia*, 'piety') and duty to other people (*dikaiosynē* 'justice') (*Spec.
Laws* 2.63). Similarly Aristeas wrote that Moses gave commandments about
'piety' and 'justice' (*Arist.* 131). The author depicted Jewish sages as teaching
King Ptolemy that a ruler should imitate God, who treats people more
leniently than they deserve, and who thereby leads them to repentance (188);
if he would consider God, who is the source of blessings and mercy, he would
be inclined to mercy (208). That is, God's love for humans should create
their love for God and for one another. The person who governs his actions
by 'piety' will uphold 'virtue' and will never transgress 'justice' (215). Love of
God and of neighbour were seen as inseparable; so Jews taught one another
and, when they had the chance, others who would listen.

Aristeas and Philo represent Diaspora synagogal instruction at its best.
The great thing about education is that people who themselves cannot see the
forest for the trees can be taught to do so. We do not have to imagine every
individual Jew as sorting through the laws and coming up with Deut. 6.4f. and
Lev. 19.18 as the two greatest, nor attribute to them all the insight that Lev.
19.18, 34 epitomize the entire law, since love of other humans depends
ultimately on loving God and what he created. Aristeas, Philo, Jesus, Paul,
various rabbis – they all saw it, and we must assume that so did others, and
that it was taught. Since I intend to deal with real life, I hasten to add that the
percentage of the population that lived up to this ideal was probably the same
then as now.

The theology of the prayers

We first need to recall several points about prayer from ch. 11 above. The
custom of praying morning and evening was widespread. The Pharisees

probably used the themes that now appear in the Eighteen Benedictions. When texts of these prayers finally come to light, we can see that some of them are post-70 or contain post-70 motifs (such as the petition for the rebuilding of Jerusalem). The text quoted above (pp. 204f.) also reveals synagogal shaping, since the phrasing is communal rather than individual.

Even taking account of all these points, as well as of our uncertainty as to whether or not non-Pharisees accepted the themes of the Eighteen Benedictions, I think that it is possible to turn to the surviving Jewish liturgy to gain information about common theology. There are three reasons. First, it is doubtful that the Pharisees in enclave sat down and worked out themes all on their own. We could believe this of the Qumran sect, isolated from other Jews, but not of the Pharisees. They tried to teach their views – with some success. Secondly, other parts of subsequent Jewish liturgy share the same themes. This makes it all the more likely that the basic elements were not solely Pharisaic. Finally, we shall see that the theology of the later 'statutory' prayers agrees with what we have found in other sources.

Joseph Heinemann, in his classic study of prayer, in which he argued against the early existence of set texts, said of the Eighteen Benedictions and other 'statutory' prayers (such as the blessing at the end of the sabbath), that their content 'clearly reflects the basic beliefs and tenets of faith of the Jewish people at the time of the Second Temple and during the Tannaitic period, their outlook on life and their aspirations'.[32] I think that on the whole this is correct, though we must always bear in mind that there was no standard worship service in the synagogues that would guarantee that the same liturgical themes would spread throughout world-wide Judaism (above, pp. 207f.). Nevertheless, it will be useful to see what the main topics of the later synagogal liturgy are, for the reasons indicated above:

1. God as creator
2. The unity of God
3. His 'providential concern for the world that he has created – and particularly for his people Israel'
4. Israel's chosenness
5. The hope for redemption[33]

Heinemann also pointed out the basic structure of Creation-Revelation-Redemption. This is seen in the prayers summarized above (pp. 264f.). It would be helpful to the reader to turn back to those pages and to review the summary of the Eighteen Benedictions. No. 1 declares God to be creator; 4 thanks him for giving 'understanding', which is connected with the Torah; and 7, 10 and 14 emphasize the hope for redemption. One also sees these themes in the rabbinic Grace after Meals. In the first benediction God is praised for providing 'food for all of the creatures whom he has fashioned', and in the second for bringing Israel out of Egypt and bestowing on them the Torah. The third benediction appeals for compassion on Israel, Jerusalem, and the line of David.[34]

We have seen these three main themes in our other sources. The belief that the one God is *creator* of the world and cares for the whole creation emerged from our discussion of the Shemaʿ and the first two commandments. The insistence on orthopraxy, which we discussed in chs 11 and 12, reflects the basic belief that God *revealed* the law to Israel and required obedience to it. That *redemption* is possible for individuals is seen in the study of sacrifices of intercession and atonement. In the next chapter we shall summarize the diverse Jewish hopes for collective redemption. We have, then, a basic theological framework for common and general Judaism, based on the analytic study of the Shemaʿ, the first two of the Ten Commandments, sacrifices, epitomes of the law, and prayers: The one God of heaven and earth chose Israel; he alone is to be worshipped; his people are to obey his law; they are therefore a people apart; they are to show love to one and all; God will remain true to the election and will redeem his people.

Covenantal nomism

This analysis shows that, in the Jewish view, God's grace precedes and is wider than the election of Israel: it includes the entire created order. Yet in another sense Jewish theology begins with the election. Jews believed that the God who chose them was creator of the world, but it was the election that set Israel apart and gave to the Jewish people their particular character. The proper response was to obey his law. Fixing on these two points, I previously gave the name 'covenantal nomism' to the *common* Jewish understanding of 'getting in and staying in' the people of God. In this term 'covenant' stands for God's grace in election ('getting in'), 'nomism' for the requirement of obedience to the law (*nomos* in Greek; 'staying in').

Covenantal nomism does not cover the entirety of Jewish theology, much less the entirety of Judaism.[35] It deals with the theological understanding of the constitution of God's people: how they get that way, how they stay that way. In terms of Judaism as a religion, this leaves out a lot of details of what people did, though it requires analysis of why they thought that they *should* do what they did: not the details of sacrifice, but how they explained the requirement to sacrifice. Theologically, it leaves out creation (considered above) and the future (ch. 14). What it covers, however, is crucial for understanding Judaism, which is a national religion and way of life, focused on the God of Israel and the people of Israel: God called them; being Jewish consists in responding to that call.

I shall now summarize the principal aspects of covenantal nomism, citing a few examples from pre-70 literature under each point, occasionally using an illustration from second-century rabbinic material, and for the most part making use of material that I did *not* use in *Paul and Palestinian Judaism*. There I argued that these beliefs constitute a theological common denominator in a wide range of Jewish material, running from Ben Sira to the Tannaitic rabbis, that is, from 200 BCE to 200 CE, including the Dead Sea Scrolls, some of the other pietist literature, and the major apocalypses.[36] No one who has discussed this argument has challenged it, and numerous scholars, when dealing with parts of the literature, have confirmed aspects of it. I remain persuaded that the theological common denominator was really there, but here I shall not repeat the actual argument, which was that the common view was *presupposed* as well as stated explicitly. Proving presupposition requires lengthy analysis, which I shall here refrain from.[37] In the present section, I shall quote individual statements for the purpose of illustration. They do not, in my judgment, have the probative force of my earlier argument about what was common and presupposed, but they can be succinctly presented, and they show the currency of the theological ideas that constitute 'covenantal nomism'.

1. *The election and the covenant.* God, though sovereign of the world, chose Israel especially and gave them the law.[38]

Philo stated the doctrine directly:

Yet out of the whole human race He chose as of special merit and judged worthy of pre-eminence over all, those who are in a true sense men, and called them to the service of Himself, the perennial fountain of things excellent . . . (*Spec. Laws* 1.303)

In the *Psalms of Solomon* several statements are equally direct. The author of *Ps. Sol.* 9 wrote a moving appeal to God not to remove his mercy from the house of Israel, and the ground of the appeal was that

. . . you chose the descendants of Abraham above all the nations, and you put your name upon us, Lord,
and it will not cease forever.
You made a covenant with our ancestors concerning us . . . (*Ps. Sol.* 9.9–10)

Similarly the law codes from Qumran – both those that were intended to govern the sect and the *Messianic Rule*, which looks forward to the new age – are explicitly covenantal. The members of the sect could say either that they belonged to 'the new covenant' (CD 6.19; 1QpHab 2.3–4), or to 'the covenant for all Israel' (CD 15.5), or to the covenant with the Zadokite priests (1QS 5.8–9; 6.19), or to God's covenant (IQSa 1.2). The sectarians regarded their covenant, which was in some sense 'new', as identical with 'God's covenant'. That is, they saw their separation from the rest of Israel as being a matter of having the right covenant, the one that contained some of their own rules. The way in which they argued their case (for their own consumption) presupposes the common view that being in the covenant was what mattered.

In the *Biblical Antiquities*, Pseudo-Philo takes God's initiation of the covenant as a major theme, working explicit statements into its summary of the biblical narrative. Between quotations of Ex. 19.1 ('they came to the wilderness of Sinai') and 19.15 ('be ready' to receive the law), the author puts this in the mouth of God:

> I will give a light to the world and illumine their dwelling places and establish my covenant with the sons of men and glorify my people above all nations. (*Bibl. Antiq.* 11.1f.)

In a later passage God's mercy is motivated by the covenant 'and the oath that he has sworn not to abandon you forever' (30.7), and there are many similar statements.

Paul provides excellent evidence of the assumption of a covenantal relationship between God and Israel. He wrote that to the Israelites belong 'the sonship, the glory, the covenants, the giving of the law, the worship and the promises; to them belong the patriarchs, and of their race, according to the flesh, is the Christ' (Rom. 9.4f.). Further, he thought that these gifts and the calling of Israel were 'irrevocable' (Rom. 11.29). 'As regards election they are beloved for the sake of their forefathers' (Rom. 11.28). In some ways even more telling is the fact that in Galatians Paul argues against the view that Israel is elect: the blessing of Abraham, he claims, 'skipped' from Abraham to Christ, and now passes to those who are in Christ, who become 'Abraham's offspring' (Gal. 3.15–18, 29). Here he opposes what was essential to Judaism – the election of the physical descendants of Abraham – and simultaneously tries to appropriate the category 'Abraham's chosen offspring' for those in Christ.

Finally, we note the criticism of the Jews for holding to the election and relying on it in Matt. 3.9, where John the Baptist is said to have warned Israel not to have confidence in their descent from Abraham (cf. also John 8.39).

The doctrine of the election is the theological expression of the feeling of community that bound together the Jews of the ancient world. We noted this feeling above, in discussing sacrifices (p. 256). It is expressed often and in a variety of ways. Thus Josephus spoke of the 'mutual harmony' that prevailed among 'the members of the community' (*Apion* 2.170). This comes in a list of virtues that is modelled on the Platonic school, except that 'harmony' replaces 'wisdom' (the other three are justice, temperance and fortitude; see *Apion* 2.170 and Thackeray's note).

Mutual harmony did not in fact always prevail, and the history of the time is full of internecine strife. Yet community spirit was real. Jews in one part of the empire were affected by events in another; both Jews and Gentiles saw world-wide Jewry as constituting a single group. Jews throughout the world paid the temple tax. Jewish solidarity is most graphically illustrated, however, by noting certain military and political events. When Hyrcanus II and Antipater (Herod's father) decided to help Julius Caesar in the Roman civil wars, they dispatched an army to Egypt. It became necessary to persuade the Egyptian Jews to co-operate, and Antipater did so by appealing to 'their common nationality' and by showing them a letter from Hyrcanus, the high priest (*Antiq.* 14.127–32). The appeal was effective, and the Egyptian Jews supported Palestinian military action in Caesar's cause. Caesar responded by conferring favours not only on Antipater, Hyrcanus and the Palestinian Jews, but also on Jews in all parts of the Diaspora, not just Egypt. Further, he encouraged the semi-independent cities to do the same (*Antiq.* 14.137, 143–8; various decrees follow). Herod later helped the Jews of Ionia (in Asia Minor) gain redress for wrongs (*Antiq.* 16.27–61). Jews all over the world were alarmed by Caligula's threat to have his statue put up in the temple, and Philo threatened *worldwide* revolt (above, p. 144). Agrippa II and Herod of Chalcis urged Claudius to act favourably on behalf of Alexandrian and other Jews (*Antiq.* 19.279, 288). After the first revolt, Vespasian imposed a tax (replacing the temple tax) on all Jews in the empire, not just Palestinians. This all corresponds to the Jewish self-perception of being a people set apart by God's choice.

One of the sides of the doctrine of election is exclusivism.[39] Christian scholars sometimes say that purity laws meant that Jews would not mingle with Gentiles at all. This is not true, as consideration of elementary facts will make clear. Jews travelled, many lived in pagan cities, and many lived in mixed cities even within Palestine; the idea of completely self-enclosed ghettos had not yet arisen. Jews were happy when Gentiles attended synagogue, and they warmly welcomed 'God-fearers' or 'sympathizers'. Jewish leaders, up to and including the high priest and, in the Diaspora, the most respected members of the community, had to negotiate with Roman officials. In Palestine the high priest sometimes consulted with the prefect or procurator. Philo led a delegation to petition the emperor. Josephus called on Nero's wife, Poppaea, when he travelled to Rome to try to secure the release of imprisoned priests (*Life* 16). One doubts that Jews conducted these

negotiations by standing in specially purified rooms and yelling.[40] Ancient
literature that urges exclusivism also, in most cases, supports cordial social
relationships. Aristeas, who wrote that Jews were surrounded by palisades 'to
prevent our mixing with any of the other peoples' (*Arist.* 139), thought that it
would be a very good thing for Jews to dine with a pagan monarch (180 and
following). The author of *Joseph and Aseneth*, who opposed not only
intermarriage but also eating at the same table, nevertheless depicted his
hero, Joseph, as visiting an Egyptian priest in his home and having warm
relations with him and his family, based on mutual respect (chs 3–7).

Although Jews maintained various kinds of relations with Gentiles,
exclusivism was part and parcel of Judaism. Breaking down all the barriers
would have finally meant accepting idolatry, and this was strongly resisted.
The surest way of coming into contact with paganism would be to marry a
pagan, someone who ate food offered to idols, preferred pork to lamb, and
offered a libation from each flagon of wine. Thus it is not surprising that Jews
generally opposed intermarriage. One sees this not only in sectarian or
semi-sectarian books, such as *Jubilees* (*Jub.* 30.7, 14–17), but in many other
works as well, such as Pseudo-Philo's *Biblical Antiquities* (9.5 and elsewhere)
and Tobit (4.12). The apocryphal Addition to Esther 14.15 (LXX 4.17u)
indicates that Jewish women should avoid intercourse with uncircumcised
males. Most striking, Josephus wrote that it was 'not in accord with the
[Jewish] laws' to take a Gentile wife (*Antiq.* 18.345). In Josephus' view
Solomon had transgressed the law of Moses when he married Gentile
women (*Antiq.* 8.191).[41] Philo too attributed to Moses the prohibition of
marriage with a person of another nationality (*Spec. Laws* 3.29). Even less
pious Jews – if sufficiently prominent – observed the prohibition: When
Drusilla, daughter of Agrippa I, married a Gentile king, he accepted
circumcision (*Antiq.* 20.139).

The *theology* of exclusivism was not that snobbery was good, but that God
set Israel apart so that they would be 'preserved from false beliefs' and
worship 'the only God' (*Arist.* 139f.) This might help others 'rise above
ignorance and achieve progress in life' (130). As Philo put it, Jews do not mix
with others 'to depart from the ways of their fathers' (*Spec. Laws* 1.324).
Josephus pointed out that, while Jews welcomed converts, they did not admit
'casual visitors' to 'the intimacies of our daily life' (*Apion* 2.210). All these
authors urged *philanthrōpia*, love of humanity, and 'equal treatment of
everyone', including Gentiles (*Arist.* 257; Josephus and Philo above, pp.
194, 233f.). Monotheism, however, required some degree of exclusivism.
Later, Christians would make the same discovery, and many cut themselves
off from pagans altogether, though others participated in some aspects of
common civil life.[42]

The flip side of the doctrine of the election and obedience to the law was that other people singled the Jews out for special treatment, which was sometimes favourable (as in the case of Julius Caesar), but sometimes hostile. I shall not discuss anti-Judaism in the ancient world, but only point out that pagans noted Jews' persistent loyalty to their own way of life and sometimes resented the fact that they would not merge into the common culture. The numerous criticisms of Jews in pagan literature show that they were recognized as a people apart.

2. *The gift of the law and obedience to it.* That God gave the law and that Jews were to obey it is implied by the entirety of the ancient literature and has been seen throughout the present study. Temple, sacrifices, offerings, sabbath, purity and every other point of law – Jews thought that all these laws were given by God, and most of them obeyed most of the laws. No more need be said on these topics here.

There is, however, a question about the law to consider in the present context. The covenantal idea led Jews to accept the fact that their law separated them from others. The law as given to Moses applied only to Jews. Did these two facts lead Jews to think that Gentiles were completely outside the law and the scope of God's grace? Could they be in any way part of the people of God? This question is related to, but it is not the same as, the question of Jewish attitudes towards Gentiles (ch. 12). The current question is a legal/theological one: could Gentiles participate in covenantal nomism without converting? In the Jewish view, could they be the recipients of God's grace while they remained Gentiles? We saw one aspect of this topic when we discussed Gentiles and the temple: the Jewish purity laws did not apply to Gentiles. If Gentiles were impure, it was not because of Lev. 11, 15 and Num. 19. Consequently they did not need to purify themselves in the same way that Jews did. What about the rest of the law? Were Gentiles *guilty* for not keeping parts of it?

Pseudo-Philo gives a clear answer: yes.

I have given an everlasting Law into your hands and by this I will judge the whole world . . . For even if men say, 'We have not known you, and so we have not served you,' therefore I will make a claim upon them because they have not learned my Law. (*Bibl. Antiq.* 11.2)

Other Jewish writers also thought that Gentiles were guilty, principally because of idolatry, but also because of sexual practices. Philo's criticism was scathing, and he seems to have thought that Gentiles who engaged in homosexual relations (forbidden by Jewish law, Lev. 18.22) should be executed (*Spec. Laws* 3.37–42). Aristeas, also commenting on sexual behaviour, claimed that Jews were distinct and that Gentiles, who had relations with males and even defiled mothers and daughters, 'commit a great sin' (*adikia*, 'injustice') (*Arist.* 152). In Paul's vice lists, idolatry and sexual immorality are first and foremost (Rom. 1.18–32; I Cor. 5.11; 6.9–11; Gal. 5.19–21); these passages reflect Diaspora Jewish views of Gentiles.

With regard to idolatry, the author of the Wisdom of Solomon had a hierarchy of fault. He had some sympathy with those who, amazed by the elements of nature or the heavenly bodies, revered them.

> If through delight in the beauty of these things people assumed them to be gods, let them know how much better than these is their Lord, for the author of beauty created them. (Wisd. Sol. 13.2f.)

These people were 'little to be blamed', but nevertheless they were wrong, since they should have inferred the creator from the created. The verdict is 'guilty' (13.6–9). Other forms of idolatry were worse: 'But miserable, with their hopes set on dead things, are the people who give the name 'gods' to the works of men's hands . . .' (13.10). Making an idol and then worshipping it was stupid, and it led to all kinds of other sins, especially sexual immorality (14.12). Yet the author could see a rationale for worshipping idols in human form. Someone, he proposed, made an image of a dead human being, or of a distant monarch, and over time these images came to be worshipped, especially because they were so beautiful (14.15–21). This was worse than worshipping the elements of the cosmos, but still comprehensible; the depths of degradation had not yet been reached. That was the achievement of the Egyptians, who worshipped not just animals, but even those that were so ugly that no one wanted them (15.18f.). The Egyptians were duly punished at the time of the Exodus (18.7f.; 19.1–5). Punishment, in fact, will generally be the lot of the ungodly (3.10–13).

Diaspora Jews accepted the view, common in their cultural environment, that life should be in accord with 'nature'. Greek and Roman philosophers had differences of opinion about what nature requires, but Jews disagreed with the vast majority of pagans on two points: idolatry and sex. We have just seen the author of the Wisdom of Solomon arguing that, while Greek and Roman idolatry is comprehensible, it shows a failure to understand *nature*: they mistake creatures for the creator (13.1). Paul argued precisely the same way: that God is creator has been revealed to Gentiles, not by Jewish prophets, but by nature: 'his eternal power and deity' have 'been clearly perceived in the things that have been made'. Gentiles 'exchanged the glory of the immortal God for images . . .' (Rom. 1.18–23). Gentile sexual practices were also 'against nature' (1.26f.). Paul delivered the same verdict as did the author of the Wisdom of Solomon: guilty. 'They are without excuse' (Rom. 1.20); 'all who have sinned without the law will also perish without the law', where 'perish' means not just die, but also be found guilty at the judgment (Rom. 2.12f.). Some Gentiles will keep the law 'written on their hearts' and thus be found innocent (2.14–16). Here we have not Paul the Apostle, arguing that all people, Jew and Greek alike, can be saved only by faith in Christ, but Paul the Diaspora Jew, arguing that Gentiles are just as guilty in God's sight as are Jews, because they should have learned from nature some of the things that Jews learned by revelation.[43]

The rabbis developed the category of 'righteous Gentiles'.[44] There is no single definition, but there are sporadic comments to the effect that all people should keep the 'Noachian' or 'Noahide' commandments, those given before the flood. An early list of the Noachian commandments comprises one requirement, to establish courts, and five prohibitions: of idolatry, 'cursing the name' (of God), incest, bloodshed and robbery (*T. Avodah Zarah* 8.4). The 'Apostolic Decree' in Acts 15.19f. points in a similar direction, and thus dates this kind of list to the first century. The 'Decree' prohibits idolatry, sexual immorality, meat from animals that were 'strangled',[45] and the consumption of blood.

The argument from 'nature', which we know from Diaspora literature, was not primarily exegetical. The rabbis show a tendency, though not a powerful and consistent effort, to find a biblical basis for defining the requirements that a Gentile should keep. What was common? It seems that Jews in general regarded the characteristic Gentile sins as being idolatry and sexual immorality, especially homosexual relations. How they reached those conclusions we cannot be sure. Both the appeal to nature and to 'Noachian' commandments were probably secondary rationalizations. They 'knew' that idolatry and homosexual practices were wrong. Both are condemned in the Mosaic law. Yet the great majority of Jews (Pseudo-Philo is an exception) granted that the law of Moses does not govern Gentiles. Could they then do anything they liked and still be guiltless? Jews did not think this. *Some* laws must apply to Gentiles. I think that the practices that end up on various lists of things that make Gentiles guilty in God's eyes – rather than just not Jewish – were largely instinctive. Jews found some things repugnant. Idolatry is obvious. Sex and food come next, for the normal cultural reasons. A lot of societies have strong views about sex and food, and these views usually seem obvious and natural. Many people today find the idea of homosexual activity repulsive. The point is even easier to illustrate if we use food: few of the readers of this book wish to contemplate eating insects and rodents.

Those Jews who thought about a final judgment – perhaps not very many – probably thought that Gentiles would be condemned and punished for idolatry and sexual immorality.[46] Jews may have thought that Gentiles deserved punishment for these offences in this world, but they left it to God.

Philo may have favoured execution, but even in Palestine Gentile practice was tolerated, and there is no evidence that Jews anywhere tried to punish Gentiles for idolatry and sexual offences. Those who thought that there were 'righteous Gentiles' probably thought that they avoided idolatry, sexual immorality, and possibly one or two further transgressions.

Such Gentiles (according to the Jews who held this view) would have a share in the world to come (*T. Sanh.* 13.2; cf. Rom. 2.14f.). That is, even though they were not in *the* covenant or covenants to which Jews belonged (with Abraham and Moses), they were in *a* covenant, the covenant with Noah, or the covenant implied in the creation and written 'on their hearts'. They would be saved. 'Covenantal nomism' was thus potentially expansive. God had made promises to humanity before he had made them to Abraham. The promises entailed obligations; those who accepted them were 'in'.

How many Gentiles accepted the laws that, in the Jewish view, should be followed even by non-Jews? We cannot know, but I shall guess: very, very few. There were probably a lot of 'sympathizers' with Judaism, people attracted by its monotheism and high ethical standards.[47] But it is unlikely that sympathizers actually gave up idolatry without converting fully to Judaism. This would have made them nothing at all. Religiously they would have been neither pagan nor Jewish, and legally their position would have been shaky: they could not have participated fully in the civic religion, and non-participation might draw the charge 'atheism', which could be a capital crime.[48] The existence of the category, 'the righteous of the nations of the world', shows generosity of spirit, but it also follows logically from the way Jews thought about their own relation with God. They were in a covenant, and they had obligations. Their God, however, had created the world and had made a covenant with humanity. It must be at least theoretically possible for Gentiles to be in it.

3. *Reward and punishment, justice and mercy.*[49] Jews believed that God was just, and that consequently he would reward obedience and punish transgression. The main lesson to be learned from Jewish history, according to Josephus, was that

> people who conform to the will of God, and do not venture to transgress laws that have been excellently laid down, prosper in all things beyond belief, and for their reward are offered by God felicity; whereas, in proportion as they depart from the strict observance of these laws, things (else) practicable become impracticable, and whatever imaginary good thing they strive to do ends in irretrievable disasters. (*Antiq.* 1.14)

No evil-doer can escape: God knows everything and punishment is sure (*Antiq.* 3.321; 4.286).

Philo wrote an entire treatise on *Rewards and Punishments*. General consent that evil would be punished and good rewarded need not be proved by adducing a list of passages; this view accompanies the idea that God is just. If he did not reward and punish appropriately and reliably, he would be capricious and unfair.

It is more interesting to consider how this view was combined with others: that God is merciful; that sinners may repent and atone for their transgressions; that membership in the covenant is by God's grace and does not depend strictly on behaviour.

Repentance is straightforward: God will forgive those who repent of their sins and who make restitution (if the sin is against another human). Repentance works for one and all, not only for those in the covenant but also for others. Outsiders repent by turning away from idolatry and 'embrac[ing] the creed of one instead of a multiplicity of sovereigns' (Philo, *Virtues*, 179). In this case, there is 'reciprocation of choice': the former idolater chooses God, and God makes him or her one of the chosen; the God-loving is also the God-loved (*Virtues* 184f.). The author of *Joseph and Aseneth* also called Aseneth's decision to convert to Judaism 'repentance' (*Jos. & Asen.* 15.7).

Josephus, as we saw, wrote that his history would demonstrate the reliability of reward and punishment. His history also shows that he thought that repentance would avert punishment. The prophetess Hulda, in Josephus' revision of the story of Josiah, told the king that since Israel had not repented, though given a long time to do so, the nation would be driven out of their country after his death (*Antiq.* 10.59–61). Earlier, God had accepted Jehoahaz's prayer of repentance, admonished the powerful rather than destroyed them, and restored the country to prosperity (*Antiq.* 9.175f.). Similarly Philo thought that God would restore the nation of Israel if they would 'make a full confession and acknowledgment of all their sin', first in their minds and then with their tongues; they would 'find favour with God the Saviour, the Merciful (*Rewards* 163). According to the Prayer of Azariah, an apocryphal addition to Daniel, God saved the young men who were thrown into the fiery furnace (Dan. 3.23) because Azariah offered a moving prayer of repentance:

We have sinfully and lawlessly departed from thee, and have sinned in all things and have not obeyed thy commandments . . .

. . .

Yet with a contrite heart and a humble spirit may we be accepted, as though it were with burnt offerings of rams and bulls, and with tens of thousands of fat lambs . . .; and may we wholly follow thee, for there will be no shame for those who trust in thee. (Prayer of Azariah 6, 16f.)

Similarly the apocryphal Prayer of Manasseh depicts the wicked king
(II Kings 21.1–17) as repenting in prayer and appealing to God's compassion
and mercy. The efficacy of repentance is clear in virtually all the literature of
our period.[50]

God's election of his people meant that he would be merciful to them; this
view either guaranteed forgiveness if they repented, or meant that he would
overlook some trespasses, or that he would postpone punishment in order to
encourage repentance – or all of these things. Jews who sinned had
'intercessors' with the Father, one being that he preferred forgiveness to
punishment, another that he would remember 'the founders of the race'
(*Rewards* 166). According to Pseudo-Philo, even though the people sinned,
God would have mercy on them; he would pity them because of the 'covenant
that he established with [their] fathers and the oath that he [had] sworn not to
abandon [them] forever' (*Bibl. Antiq.* 31.2; 30.7). The author of the Wisdom
of Solomon held that God overlooked sins in order to lead people to
repentance (Wisd. Sol. 11.24), a theme that is echoed in Paul (Rom. 2.4).
Philo wrote that God in his mercy would take the initiative in bringing back
'the mind which has strayed everywhere in prolonged vagrancy' (*Rewards*
117). According to Aristeas, the Jewish sages urged Ptolemy to imitate God,
who was longsuffering and who treated people more leniently than they
deserved, so that he could 'convert them from evil and bring them to
repentance' (*Arist.* 188).

It was, then, well known that mercy and leniency *led to* repentance. This
insight appears even in such an unlikely place as one of Josephus' stories of
Herod and his sons. Herod accused two of his sons of conspiring against him
(*Antiq.* 16.91). Augustus, to whom the accusation was made, was convinced
that they were innocent. He urged Herod 'to put away all suspicion'; a change
of heart on his part would 'stimulate their goodwill to each other' and lead
them to apologize. The entire rift was healed, at least for the present
(16.124–6). People knew that clemency encourages contrition, and Jews
ascribed this insight to God as well as to wise sovereigns. He did not punish
strictly, and his forbearance led to repentance.

When Christian scholars discuss Judaism they usually think of reward and
punishment as 'soteriology': God rewards those who do good by giving them
eternal life, but he condemns those who do evil. Many scholars then work this
out mechanically: God counts deeds and saves those who have more good
deeds than bad. Repentance serves to eliminate only one evil action, and thus
it is the same as a good work in God's system of counting.

This is a gross perversion of the evidence. In most discussions in the
Jewish literature of our period, reward and punishment function within this
world; life after death is not a major theme, and Christian scholars often

impose soteriology on the material. Further, when Jews thought about salvation beyond this world, they did not suppose that fifty-one per cent of one's total deeds would determine the issue. God's grace always emerges as the most important point. Finally, repentance was comprehensive in scope. Philo thought that people who had gone astray should repent and turn back to the right path – all at once, not one item at a time. Even if Jews came to disregard the laws of piety and justice altogether, had 'been seduced by the polytheistic creeds which finally lead to atheism' and had 'forgotten the teaching of their race and of their fathers', they could make 'a full confession and acknowledgment of all their sin' (*Rewards* 162f.). In rabbinic parlance, a person who was completely wicked could repent at the end and be saved (e.g. *T. Qiddushin* 1.15f.). Azariah is depicted as confessing that he and his colleagues had 'sinned in all things and [had] not obeyed [the] commandments' (above).

God had another way of wiping out the sins of people who were basically loyal to him: punishment. Paul shared a common view, that punishment in this world is adequate; one is not punished both in this world and in the world to come; there is no 'double jeopardy'. In theological language, suffering and death atone. People in Corinth who ate and drank unworthily became ill or died; they did not go to hell (I Cor. 11.30). The man in the Corinthian church who committed incest deserved death, but his spirit would be saved (I Cor. 5.1–5). The second-century rabbis elaborated on the point: one should worry about *not* suffering in this world, since it might mean that punishment was still in store. The righteous suffer in this world for their (few) sins.[51] The idea that suffering was God's punishment or chastisement was very common in our period, as well as before and afterwards,[52] and with this went the view that justice had been done when a person had suffered. Further punishment would be unjust, but God was righteous. The punishment for sin was not damnation, but suffering and, at worst, death.

If this did not work, reward and punishment could be shifted to the world to come. Paul thought that Christians ('we') would all appear 'at the judgment seat of Christ, so that each one may receive good or evil, according to what he or she has done in the body' (II Cor. 5.10). This is not a threat that some Christians will be destroyed, only that they may be punished. Thus, speaking of himself and Apollos, he wrote that the work of a not-very-good apostle would be burned up and that the apostle himself would be saved 'only as through fire', that is, singed (I Cor. 3.15). In the same context, Paul claimed that he knew nothing that might count against himself at the judgment, but that God might think of something and, one presumes, punish him for it (as if he had not already suffered enough!). When the Lord comes, Paul continued, God will give each person an appropriate 'commendation' or 'approval' (I Cor. 4.4f.). In these cases reward is not heaven and punishment is not hell. Paul is discussing people who will be saved, but they will be 'commended' or lightly punished at the judgment, depending on their deeds.

During times of persecution, Jews had to think of other explanations of suffering and flourishing in this world, since it was precisely those who were most loyal to God who suffered most. Persecutions preceded and followed our period, but I shall say a few words just to indicate the ways in which Jewish theologians could cope when the standard view ran into difficulty. After the persecutions under Antiochus IV Epiphanes, for example, some people interpreted the deaths of righteous martyrs as vicarious, and they pointed out that the martyrs had not died in vain, since their cause was later vindicated: the Jews won that revolt.[53] After the second revolt against Rome, which was preceded by Hadrian's proscription of circumcision, it was again the most righteous who suffered most. In this case the rabbis transferred reward and punishment to the world to come. 'The payment of the reward of the righteous is for the time to come.' God is 'a God of faithfulness' (Deut. 32.4); therefore, just as he

> pays the completely righteous the reward of a commandment that he fulfilled in this world [after he is] in the world to come, so he pays the completely wicked the reward of a commandment that he fulfilled in this world [while he is in] this world . . . (*Sifre Deut.* 307).

This passage, like II Cor. 5.10 and I Cor. 4.4f., has the judgment explicitly in view: 'In the future, when he sits on the throne of justice, he will sit in judgment . . . and give each person what is appropriate.'[54]

I do not propose that in our period it was *common* to transfer reward and punishment to the world to come. On the contrary, most Jews seem to have accepted the view of Deuteronomy, that God's justice is administered within this world (though moderated by his mercy). Josephus, contemplating the horror of the first revolt, still clung to the view that his people had deserved what they got. I have been arguing, rather, that reward and punishment are not 'Jewish soteriology'. Even when they are shifted to the world to come, as in the case of Paul and some post-135 rabbis, they are still not soteriology. If justice is not administered *in* this world, it will be administered *in* the world to come. Salvation depends on overall stance, whether or not one is 'in'; for non-Christian Jews, salvation depended on being in *the* covenant (with Moses) or, in the case of Gentiles, in *a* covenant (with humanity or with Noah). For Paul, of course, the question was whether or not one was in the body of Christ. In the view of all Jews, including Paul, reward and punishment depend on deeds. Paul and the rabbis did not work these principles out in precisely the same way. The rabbis held that the punishment of the righteous is completed in this world, while their reward is delayed; Paul envisaged the possibility that the righteous would be slightly punished in the world to come. We find what was common by discovering the underlying principles, that God saves according to his mercy and the basic stance of the individual, but rewards and punishes according to his justice, thereby taking account of particular good and bad deeds.

Jews did, of course, think that there was a general correlation between good people and those who were saved, and between bad people and those who did not gain eternal felicity. This is not 'works righteousness', but only common sense, as anyone will see who imagines the reverse. 'By their fruits you will know them', as Jesus put it (Matt. 7.16). It would be preposterous to think that people who loved God and wished to be members of the covenant in good standing would not try to keep his laws – at least most of them most of the time. Similarly Paul could not imagine that those who lived by the Spirit would bear the fruit of the 'Flesh' (e.g. Gal. 5.16–24), and he was always amazed when they did. In normal Judaism, a person who systematically and regularly ignored the commandments would be regarded as an apostate, and people would expect God to deal with him or her accordingly. Intentionally and deliberately sinning, 'with malice aforethought', and refusing to repent, cut one off from the covenantal blessings.

There was a general tendency to divide the world into the 'wicked' and the 'righteous', but these were not water-tight compartments. In particular, it was well known that the righteous could sin. That is why they suffered; God chastised them. The chastisement was not in proportion to the sin, as we saw above. Those who trespassed were corrected 'little by little', punished with 'great care and indulgence' (Wisd. Sol. 12.2, 20). God corrects transgressors only temporarily and 'not in anger' (*Bibl. Antiq.* 19.9). He does not punish people 'in proportion to their offences nor by the greatness of his strength, but exercises clemency' (*Arist.* 192). This is a main theme of the *Psalms of Solomon*, which are to be dated at the beginning of our period, about the time of Pompey's invasion. God will distinguish between the righteous and the wicked, delivering the former but punishing the latter 'forever' (*Ps. Sol.* 2.34f.). The righteous, to be sure, do suffer, but they accept it as chastisement (3.3f.; 8.26; 10.1f.). 'Not alike are the chastening of the righteous (for sins done) in ignorance, and the overthrow of the sinners' (13.7).

A religion of grace

Fundamental to Jewish piety was the view that God's grace preceded the requirement of obedience and undergirds both the life of Israel and also the

entire universe. The themes of creation and election show this especially:
God created the world and blessed its produce, declaring it good, before he
gave commandments; and he chose Israel and redeemed the people from
Egypt before giving the law. God's prior grace underlies human existence:
'let your mercy sustain us until the end, and your fidelity for length of days;
for unless you had mercy, who would ever be born?' (Pseudo-Philo, *Bibl.
Antiq.* 15.7). Another author asked,

> How would anything have endured if thou hadst not willed it? Or how
> would anything not called forth by thee have been preserved? Thou sparest
> all things, for they are thine, O Lord who lovest the living. (Wisd. Sol.
> 11.25f.)

Not only life, but food and clothing were the gift of God. We recall the avowal
(Deut. 26), said when handing over the first fruits. In Josephus' rewording,
the Jewish farmer was to give 'thanks to God for having delivered his race
from the insolence of the Egyptians and given them a good land and spacious
to enjoy the fruits thereof'. The worshipper then declared that he had
separated the tithes, and asked

> God ever to be favourable and gracious to himself and to continue such
> favour towards all Hebrews in common, preserving to them the good
> things that He had given them and adding thereto all else that He could
> bestow. (*Antiq.* 4.242f.)

The daily prayers that Moses required were (according to Josephus)
thanksgiving:

> Let all acknowledge before God the bounties which He has bestowed on
> them through their deliverance from the land of Egypt: thanksgiving is a
> natural duty, and is rendered alike in gratitude for past mercies and to
> incline the giver to others yet to come. They shall inscribe also on their
> doors the greatest of the benefits which they have received from God and
> each shall display them on his arms; and all that can show forth the power
> of God and His goodwill towards them, let them bear a record thereof
> written on the head and on the arm, so that men may see on every side *the
> loving care with which God surrounds them*. (*Antiq.* 4.212f.; emphasis mine)

According to this passage, fulfilling the commandments to wear tefillin and
post mezuzot did not earn merits, but attested to the all-encompassing 'loving
care' of God.

The same theology is found in Josephus' discussion of prayer in the
temple. Whether this reflects priestly prayers, or is a more general indication
of how Josephus thought all Jews should pray when at worship, cannot be

determined with certainty. In any case the passage shows the theology of one pre-70 priest and Pharisee:

> At [the] sacrifices prayers for the welfare of the community must take precedence of those for ourselves; for we are born for fellowship, and he who sets its claims above his private interests is specially acceptable to God. We should beseech God not to give us blessings, for He has given them spontaneously and put them at the disposal of all, but for capacity to receive, and, having received, to keep them. (*Apion* 2.196f.)

Even people's good actions are not entirely their own: 'God brings to completion the affairs of all people and guides (them) with (his) sovereign power' (*Arist.* 195). Likewise fame and riches come not through people's merits, but are bestowed as gifts by God (*Arist.* 196).

The general Jewish understanding of religion, then, had at its centre the prior grace of God – what Christian theologians later would call 'prevenient grace' – and the subsequent command of obedience. Discussions of New Testament theology have often contrasted Christian theology, in which 'indicative' precedes 'imperative', with Jewish theology, which (it is believed) works the other way around. That is, whereas Christianity says 'God loves you; therefore love one another', Judaism is believed to say: 'love one another and thereby earn God's love'. Christianity is a religion of grace, Judaism a religion of merit and works-righteousness, in which people must strive to purchase God's favour, and in which they are always anxious that they have not done enough to earn it. In favour of this distinction, Christians can quote John 1.17: 'The law was given through Moses; grace and truth came through Jesus Christ.' This proves that Christianity was the first religion of grace.

Historically, that is not so. It is of course true that many of those who found God through Jesus saw him as the one and only mediator of God's grace. But as a matter of historical record, pre-Christian and non-Christian Jewish theologians held that God's grace underlay all of life, that God chose and redeemed Israel from bondage before requiring obedience to the law, and that God would remain true to his promises *despite* disobedience. They understood obeying the law as the Jews' appropriate response to the prior grace of God.

Perceiving, quite correctly, that in describing Judaism in this way I sometimes used terms from Christian theology ('gift precedes demand' and the like),[55] some people have claimed that I *imposed* this theology on Jewish literature, where in fact it is not to be found.[56] All I can do is to urge such readers to study the passages that I have quoted above, as well as the passages in *Paul and Palestinian Judaism* that I have not quoted here (see nn. 51, 54,

55). I think that it would be impossible to state the priority of grace any more clearly than did these ancient Jewish theologians.

As David Daube has pointed out, 'the abstract or general goes on unremarked for very long where the concrete or specific monopolizes attention . . .'[57] The generalizing terms 'prevenient grace', 'the priority of gift to demand', and 'the indicative precedes the imperative' reveal theological abstraction based on concrete points. The story that God redeemed Israel from Egypt before requiring obedience to the law is in Exodus, but Exodus does not use these or similar phrases. Even Paul did not coin the generalization 'grace precedes demand'. But that idea is as clear in non-Christian Jewish literature as it is in the letters of Paul. Rabbis urged that the Jews in Egypt merited extinction, but that God saved them instead.[58] Why did God wait until Ex. 20 before giving the Ten Commandments? Because he chose to redeem his people first, and only then to require them to obey his law.[59] Why do Jews bring first fruits and say the avowal? In thanks to God for delivering his people and giving them a land to farm. What do Jews pray in the temple? They offer thanks to God for his mercies. Why do Jews post mezuzot and wear tefillin? To display the loving care with which God surrounds them (all from Josephus).

Thus far we have seen that, in the common Jewish view, God graciously chose Israel and gave them his law; that they were to obey it; that transgression was punished and obedience rewarded; that God's grace modified punishment in several ways, since God wished not to condemn and destroy; that he displayed mercy so as to lead people to repentance; that they could repent and atone; that God could also effect atonement by punishing those who were basically loyal to him; that obedience and atonement kept people in the covenant of grace.

We have thus far, however, said little about the ultimate outcome of human life. What did the future hold?

14

Hopes for the Future

Judaism was not primarily a religion of individual salvation. An abiding concern was that God should maintain his covenant with the Jewish *people* and that the *nation* be preserved. One of Josephus' strongest and most convincing claims was that Jews had remained true to the election and the law through thick and thin. No other nation showed such commitment to its constitution (e.g. *Apion* 2.234). National survival looms much larger than does individual life after death, and so we shall begin with hopes for the nation's future.

The future of Israel

Most Jews in Palestine in the Roman period longed for 'freedom'. It is doubtful that even the chief priests and the 'powerful', the principal beneficiaries of direct Roman rule in Judaea, truly liked having to answer to Rome. Herod enjoyed autonomy in internal affairs, but he must at times have wished that Rome did not look over his shoulder. Herod's descendants were prevented from warring on each other because they were all answerable to Rome, and this was doubtless of benefit to them; but some of them would have liked to have been independent kings. 'Freedom', as long as it remained undefined, was something Jews could agree on, rich and poor alike, though they may have hesitated to use the word. The Romans knew perfectly well one of the things it meant.

There agreement stopped: it did not run very far. One person's freedom was another's bondage. The Hasmoneans, descendants of the family that liberated Israel from the Seleucid yoke, were seen by many as imposing a worse one. Direct rule by Rome would be better. Open the gates to Pompey! (*War* 1.142f.). Later, some wanted the gates to be opened to Herod rather than to be ruled by Antigonus (*Antiq.* 15.3). There were periods when the only ones at peace were those who so defined their desire for freedom that it did not conflict with others' desire for domination. The Pharisees, it seems, finally mastered this art (ch. 18). They caused the aristocrats to flee Jerusalem during their tenure of power under Salome Alexandra (76–67); but when Aristobulus II, the supporter of the aristocrats, seized the throne and the high priesthood after his mother's death (*War* 1.117–21), the Pharisees obviously lay low. We do not hear of wholesale executions. Decades later (*c.* 20 BCE) they refused Herod's loyalty oath, fifteen years later two of their teachers urged young men to take down Herod's golden eagle from the temple (5–4 BCE), and after one more decade some supported Judas the Galilean (CE 6); but mostly they kept their discontent to themselves. We may suppose that they were free to do what they thought most important: worship God and live by the law. But we may be sure that they continued to hope for something other than the alliance between the Roman administrators and the chief priests.

Hope for the future ran the full gamut from plotting revolt and storing arms to praying quietly that God would do something to change things. In theory, we might distinguish the goal – a longed-for better time – from the means – prayer, bearing arms and the like. Some people had very modest hopes, such as a better high priest or greater prosperity, while others had grandiose dreams, such as the subjugation or conversion of the Gentiles. Some were willing, some unwilling to countenance or participate in violence in order to accomplish what they wanted. Our information, however, is sketchy, and we cannot always describe both means and ends. There is more evidence about what people were willing to do to hasten a better day than there is about what it would be like, but in both cases we can discern a wide variety. It is this range that I wish to exemplify here. It may be that the Sadducean aristocrats did not hope for much in the future. The best hoped that nothing would go wrong, that the Roman administrators would be fair and decent, that the crops would not fail and that the people would not revolt. The worst wanted to get richer. Yet some, I shall show, would have liked change, as did most people.

War and resistance

Hope for the future often expresses itself in negative ways: complaints, protests, insurrections. We shall consider these means first.

1. There were those who were ready, given any reasonable opportunity, to take up arms. Josephus attributes this view to the 'fourth philosophy', founded by Judas the Galilean and Saddok the Pharisee in 6 CE (*Antiq.* 18.3–10., 23–5; *War* 2.117f.). In that year Archelaus was deposed, Rome sent its first prefect to govern directly, and there was a census for tax purposes.

The Jews had been accustomed to pay taxes indirectly to Rome, since Rome levied tribute on Herod and his descendants. Judas the Galilean and his followers chose to fight to resist the significant further imposition of foreign rule that direct taxation represented (this is the motive assigned them in *Antiq.* 18.4).

In the *War* Josephus wrote that Judas' party had nothing in common with the others, while in the *Antiquities* he said that it was in full agreement with the Pharisees, except that its members loved freedom more than life. These are two different attempts to deny that Jews in general wanted political freedom and were prepared to fight for it and if need be to die. In fact, as we saw in ch. 4, the uprising led by Judas the Galilean was preceded by similar incidents, as it was followed by them; the fourth philosophy was not entirely new. In ch. 18 we shall explore more fully the relationship between the fourth philosophy and the Pharisees; here we note only the alliance.

A long-standing scholarly convention has been to identify the 'fourth philosophy' as a party or sect, to call its members 'the Zealots', and to think that the Zealot party was the freedom movement that eventually took Israel into war against Rome. On this view, a single party endured from 6 CE until the fall of Matsada, championing revolution throughout the entire period. The Zealot party had a radical wing, called 'the Sicarii', 'assassins'.

There are two faults with this view. Terminologically, the title 'the Zealots' (with a capital Z) is best used as Josephus used it: the name of a group that emerged part of the way through the great revolt, attacked and defeated the aristocratic leaders, executed some of the remaining aristocrats, and defended Jerusalem to the bitter end (*War* 2.651; 4.160–6.148; 7.268). The Sicarii were not a branch of this group; they arose earlier and had a separate history. It is, I realize, convenient to have a blanket name for insurgents, and 'Zealots' seems like a good one, since the ideal of zeal for the law was well established. Nevertheless, it would be better if we did not use a single name, and especially if we did not call all insurgents 'Zealots'. (1) That name refers to a specific group at a specific period. (2) The use of one party label to cover diverse movements over a long period incorrectly implies that the motive and rationale for uprisings remained constant.[1] There was, of course, the general issue of freedom: freedom to live according to the law as *we* see it; freedom from the Hasmoneans, from Rome, from Herod – and so on. It is, however, misleading to think that there was a single overarching concern that triggered every insurgency.

The more important issue is whether or not there was a continuing *party* with a consistent philosophy: armed revolt. By naming the fourth philosophy along with the other parties (Pharisees, Sadducees and Essenes), Josephus implies that there was. Many scholars, even some who know that Judas the

Galilean should not be called a Zealot, and who do not merge all the different protesters into one party, accept Josephus' implication and speak of Judas as founding a continuing 'sect'. The difficulty with this is that the party disappears from Josephus' account for sixty years (6–66 CE). If throughout this period a significant party championed armed revolt, why do we not hear more about it? There were lots of occasions during those sixty years that a party committed to revolution could have used to foment open revolt. Rhoads attempts to do justice to this fact, while still accepting Josephus' statement that Judas founded a 'philosophy'; he concludes that Judas founded a sect (though it was not called 'Zealot'), but that it was quiescent for a full generation, from 6 to 44 CE, and that even after 44 it was too minor to deserve separate mention.[2] It would be better to admit that there is no evidence of a continuing party. Judas inspired one revolutionary outburst among many. Josephus wanted to isolate rebels, and he did this in part by relegating them to a separate 'philosophy'.

The philosophy that Josephus ascribes to Judas the Galilean is 'no master but God' (to use the common paraphrase of Josephus' various phrases: *War* 2.118; *Antiq.* 18.23). The determination to be ruled by God alone is also ascribed to the Sicarii, who defended Matsada (*War* 7.323; that these rebels were Sicarii: *War* 4.516), and who killed themselves rather than submit to Rome. Other Sicarii escaped to Egypt (*War* 7.410f.), where they were eventually captured. 'Under every form of torture and laceration of body, devised for the sole object of making them acknowledge Caesar as master, not one submitted . . .' (7.418). Does 'no master but God' prove that Judas the Galilean founded a party, later called 'the Sicarii', that was comparable to the Essenes, Sadducees and Pharisees?

The fact that this slogan comes up twice does not prove that Judas founded a 'party'. I offer an analogy. Addressing the Virginia House of Burgesses, in the period leading up to the American Revolution, Patrick Henry proclaimed, 'I know not what course others may take, but as for me, give me liberty or give me death'. Today, New Hampshire puts on its automobile licence plates 'live free or die'. This does not prove that Patrick Henry founded a party, the remnants of which are now to be found in New Hampshire. In between, lots of Americans fought and died for freedom, though they did not necessarily chant the slogan. Did the soldiers from the Midwest and Northeast, whom Grant hurled against the Army of Northern Virginia, with the intention, among others, of crushing slavery, think of themselves as belonging to the party of the Virginian Patrick Henry? Were they all from New Hampshire? The answers are obvious.

Let us pose another question: just what did 'no master but God' mean? Apparently not anarchy. The holders of this philosophy seem to have applied it principally against being ruled by Rome, usually not against native rulers, and never against their own leaders.[3] This observation, together with our analogy with Patrick Henry, help us to see the 'fourth philosophy' for what it was. It was a radical religio-political ideal that could be called forth by various people to justify extreme action at what they regarded as moments of crisis, and that they could thus apply selectively. 'No master but God' goes only a step beyond the common view, 'die rather than tolerate heinous transgression'. The question is when one applies one of these principles. Once articulated, they are available to be used or exploited.

This gives us a better notion of 'the fourth philosophy' than does the idea of a party that had a constant platform in favour of revolt, but that was inactive for decades. There was, however, a connection between Judas the Galilean and the Sicarii besides the slogan: there was a family relationship. Menahem, a son of Judas, set himself up as a tyrant in the early stages of revolt. He was overthrown and killed. It was some of his followers, led now by Eleazar, a relative, who escaped to Matsada (*War* 2.433–48); these people were Sicarii, as we noted above. Thus while Judas did not found a party, he did have an heir, who was connected with the Sicarii, the group that used Judas' slogan.

The slogan may have been used by relatively few, but many Jews over the years were ready to bear arms and risk death whenever there seemed a fair opportunity to rouse the populace against the Romans. Although a party founded by Judas is not likely, a recurring spirit of readiness to fight and die is certain.

Many hard-nosed revolutionaries thought concretely and hoped for practical results.[4] When the great revolt began, the Roman empire looked shaky. Nero had been emperor for fourteen years, and he had deteriorated as a ruler. He sought prizes as a performing artist while the business of empire languished. He would last only three more years, and when he was forced to commit suicide confusion reigned: in 69 there were four emperors. The situation in Rome was stabilized only when Vespasian left the campaign in Palestine in the hands of his son, Titus, and returned to Rome to take control. The Jewish rebels had the misfortune to face the general who turned out to be the man capable of saving the empire. They did not know this in advance. At first, they could hope that, just as internal confusion in Syria had allowed the Hasmoneans to establish an independent state, Rome's instability would give them the chance of victory. As we shall see more fully below, Rome's opening moves were clumsy and ineffectual. This induced others to join the rebel cause. They did not know that Rome was only pausing for breath and that its greatest period lay ahead.

There is not enough evidence to say how concretely the insurgents of 6 CE (Judas the Galilean) had thought. Probably they calculated their chances and decided that they might have limited but useful success. At that point, Rome had not ruled any of Palestine directly, but rather had relied on Hyrcanus II,

Antipater, Herod and Herod's sons. When Archelaus was deposed, some thought that they might get rid of the Herodians and either establish an independent state or a client state that was more to their liking.

2. Over the years many other Jews had shown themselves ready to die passively rather than to transgress the law or to have it transgressed. We cited instances above of people who, insisting that they did not intend to fight, asked to be killed rather than have an atrocity continue. One of the principal instances came early in Pilate's prefecture, after he introduced Roman standards into Jerusalem (*c.* 26 CE; *War* 2.169–174), another when Caligula ordered Petronius to set up his statue in the temple (*c.* 41; *Antiq.* 18.261–278). Josephus attributes to the latter group of protesters such statements as these: 'slay us first before you carry out these resolutions' (18.264); 'we will sooner die than violate our laws' (18.271). In the *Testament of Moses* (first century CE) there is a sentence that serves to sum up an attitude that runs unchecked from Antiochus IV to Hadrian – that is, from Mattathias and his sons to Bar Kokhba: 'Let us die rather than transgress the commandments of the Lord of lords, the God of our fathers' (*T. Moses* 9.6).

We may put into this category those who were guilty of pulling down the eagle and the teachers who inspired young men to do the deed. These men did not intend warfare; rather they carried out a single, non-military act of protest against transgression of the sanctity of the temple, especially against profaning it with a symbol that reminded people of Rome.

What such people as these hoped for, at least in the first instance, was simply for the Romans – or the Hasmoneans or Herod – to leave Jerusalem, and especially the temple, alone. If this were granted, they could tolerate more-or-less anything else.

It would seem, however, that those who wanted to be allowed to worship and live in their own way had a second hope if the first, modest hope was disappointed. According to Josephus, the men who faced Petronius, at the time of the crisis precipitated by Caligula, reasoned that, for those who were determined to take the risk, 'there is hope even of prevailing; for God will stand by us if we welcome danger for His glory' (*Antiq.* 18.267). They hoped, that is, that if reason did not prevail God would intercede, either fighting on their side (on which, see 3 below), or producing a miracle that would confound the enemies of his temple.

In the case of the teachers who inspired some of the young to take down the offending eagle, they first of all hoped that Herod was too near death to do anything. Their second hope, in case that turned out not to be true, was personal life after death: 'immortality and an eternally abiding sense of felicity' (*War* 1.650).

It does not matter whether or not the participants in these two events actually reasoned in these ways. Josephus, as a good Hellenistic historian, attributed to them sentiments appropriate to the occasion. The thoughts that God might directly intervene, or that he would give eternal life to those who served him, were current in his day and were relied on by those who risked their lives for a different future.

3. Intermediate between these two types were those who looked forward to a great war, one in which God, either directly or by proxy, would play the crucial role, but in which they too would bear arms. Some of these wrote up their visions of the future. The principal two documents are *Ps. Sol.* 17 and the *War Rule* from Qumran. According to the former the Davidic Messiah will enter Jerusalem, banish the Gentiles and also Jewish sinners (especially the Hasmonean priests), and establish the new Israel, with the tribes reassembled, as an ideal kingdom. Though the son of David will not trust in arms and numbers, but in God alone, one supposes that the author of the psalm thought that he would spill some blood. According to the *War Rule* the sectarians – who will have become a full true Israel, with all twelve tribes represented – will first destroy the sinful Israelites and then the Gentiles, with God himself striking the decisive blows.[5]

The pious of the *Psalms of Solomon* and the Qumran sectarians were not the only ones who harboured the hope that God would fight on their side. When Felix was procurator (52–59 CE), a man known only as 'the Egyptian' gathered a multitude and marched on Jerusalem. (The multitude was put by Josephus, *War* 2.261, at 30,000; by Acts 21.38 at 4,000.) According to one of Josephus' accounts, the Egyptian marched from the desert to the Mount of Olives. He intended to 'force an entrance into Jerusalem and, after overpowering the Roman garrison, to set himself up as tyrant of the people' (*War* 2.261–263). According to the other, the Egyptian rallied 'the masses of the common people' to join him on the Mount of Olives. He claimed that 'at his command Jerusalem's walls would fall down' (*Antiq.* 20.169–172). In either case heavily armed Roman troops put an end to his hopes, killing many of his followers, though he himself escaped.

That the Egyptian seriously thought that his rabble could conquer Jerusalem by conventional means must be doubted. The statement in the *Antiquities*, that he and his followers expected the walls to fall down, probably points in the right direction, at least in part. His followers had not counted swords, spears and armour, and concluded that they could outman and outfight the Romans; they thought, rather, that if they would take the first step, if putting their lives at risk they would strike the first blow, God himself would see to the rest.

Earlier, when Fadus was procurator (44–46), an apparently even less militaristic prophet, Theudas, had assembled 'the majority of the masses' in the desert (400 according to Acts 5.36), persuaded them to bring along their possessions, and promised that when they reached the Jordan the river would part. Fadus sent cavalry, and many were killed, including Theudas, whose head was brought to Jerusalem (*Antiq.* 20.97–98).

In summaries Josephus points towards other such instances. In the time of Felix various 'deceivers' persuaded crowds to follow them to the desert 'under the belief that God would there give them tokens of deliverance' (*War* 2.258–260; *Antiq.* 20.167–168).

It seems that, apart from the mob led by the Egyptian, none of these groups intended to fight, or at least not much. The people who followed other prophets in the wilderness expected God to give 'tokens of deliverance', such as those that had accompanied the Exodus and the conquest of Canaan (parting of the water, collapse of the walls). They probably thought that, by stepping boldly forth and risking their lives, they would hasten the day of their deliverance, but they looked to God as the commander-in-chief who would strike the decisive blow. Their vision of the future probably differed from that of the readers of the *War Rule* only in degree. They would have to fight less hard than the Qumran sectarians thought. In all these instances redemption was basically up to God.

This hope never entirely vanished. When the Roman troops set fire to the last temple portico, 'poor women and children of the populace and a mixed multitude' – the same sort of people who followed earlier prophets of salvation – were burned alive, having followed a prophet who said that God commanded them to go to the temple, there to receive 'the tokens of their deliverance'. Josephus adds that this prophet was not alone and that others had bidden people to 'await help from God' (*War* 6.283–7; cf. 1.347).

It should be emphasized that most ancients expected God (or one of the gods) to take a direct hand in human affairs; and, in fact, they saw him as having done so no matter what the outcome. If failure and death were the result, it was because God willed it. As we saw in ch. 13, Josephus thought that God intended the Jews to lose their war against Rome. The temple had been fouled by the assassinations of the Sicarii, and there were other transgressions. The result was that God 'brought the Romans upon us and purification by fire upon the city, while He inflicted slavery upon us together with our wives and children; for He wished to chasten us by these calamities' (*Antiq.* 20.166).

From the point of view of ancient thinkers, matters could just as easily have gone the other way. It was not a question of calculating military strength, but rather of what God chose. Jews of all persuasions kept hoping that he would choose to back them. Josephus describes the 'impostors and deceivers' who promised the people signs of salvation as thinking that these would be 'in harmony with God's design' or 'providence' (*Antiq.* 20.168).[6]

Josephus attributes belief in 'free will' to the Sadducees, and it is conceivable (barely) that they did not think that God controlled history. But everyone else did. God was thought to make all the real decisions. Those who hoped to trigger divine intervention in the cause of freedom were not, by the standards of the time, members of the lunatic fringe. The real question was whether Israel had suffered enough – as the second Isaiah had long since proclaimed (Isa. 40.2) – or whether the sins of the people required still further punishment at the hands of the Gentiles. Many people thought that the time was right for God to free his people from their bondage. They thought that they did not have to do much, but rather just to provide the right occasion and encourage God's action by demonstrating their trust in him. Their trust, after all, was based on the assurance of God's own word, as reported by Isaiah: 'I myself will fight against those who fight you' (Isa. 49.25; see more fully below, p. 297).

It seems likely, as I just hinted, that at least some Sadducees thought that God might take a hand directly. We may consider the career of the aristocratic priest, Ananus son of Annas. He was a Sadducee and had been high priest for a short time (*Antiq.* 20.199–202). In 66 CE he favoured reconciliation with Rome, as did the other aristocratic priests, but he finally joined the war party and became one of the leaders of the revolt (*War* 2.647–651; 563). When he fell, defending the temple against the Zealots and the Idumaeans, Josephus lamented him, saying among other things that

> to maintain peace was his supreme object. He knew that the Roman power was irresistible, but, when driven to provide for a state of war, he endeavoured to secure that, if the Jews would not come to terms, the struggle should at least be skilfully conducted. In a word, had Ananus lived, they would undoubtedly either have arranged terms . . . or else, had hostilities continued, they would have greatly retarded the victory of the Romans . . . (*War* 4.320f.)

This gives a credible picture of a noble man: he led the fight in order to drag the war out and secure better terms.

There is, however, a further, supplementary possibility. After the opening stages of the revolt, the Syrian legate, Cestius, advanced on Jerusalem. His army suffered a minor defeat but still threatened the city. Cestius unexpectedly withdrew his troops from the siege, and as they retreated they were successfully attacked by Jewish insurgents (*War* 2.499–555). 'Many distinguished Jews' now fled Jerusalem, knowing that Rome would retaliate (2.556). It was immediately after this that Joseph son of Gorion and Ananus the former high priest were elected by a mass meeting in the temple to head the revolutionary government (2.562f.). It seems to me quite possible that the aristocrats who stayed, including the Sadducee Ananus, saw in Cestius' retreat a *sign* that God was with the Jews. I think that we should not rule out entirely the possibililty that even the Sadducees, who did not believe in 'fate', still thought that God could intervene to save his people. They had, after all, read the Bible.

This intermediate category – ready to fight, but hoping for miraculous intervention – was probably a large one and included a range of views. According to I Maccabees, Judas Maccabeus had reminded his followers of how their ancestors were saved at the Red Sea and urged them to 'cry to Heaven, to see whether he will favour us and remember his covenant with our fathers and crush this army before us today' (I Macc. 4.8–11). Yet, we know, the Maccabees were very good practical planners and knew how to organize guerilla warfare, as well as how to exploit the divisions within the Seleucid empire. If we knew enough, we would probably see that the militaristic or practical wing of our 'intermediate' group would embrace those in category 1, the hardcore, calculating revolutionaries. They too doubtless trusted in God. Our intermediate group also had a pacifist wing, those who would not plan and calculate revolt, but who would join in if the signs looked right.

4. Some quietly prayed for God to liberate his people. Their attitude is perhaps best conveyed by the end of the *Testament of Moses*. In ch. 12 God suddenly transports Israel to heaven. Others may have prayed for different kinds of miracles and different kinds of escape, but we may be sure that many people wished to do nothing except to wait and pray. They would not bare their necks to Roman swords in order to protest against transgression. They hid instead. The 'weaker' elements of the Jerusalem populace (as Josephus called them, *War* 1.347) tended to gather around the temple in time of trouble (see above), probably thinking that God's redemptive activity would begin there. As did everyone else, the meek (as we might better call them) had some kind of theology. If God wanted things to change, he would see to it. If he did not, there was no point in doing anything.

It is interesting to speculate on Josephus' own position. He was one of the aristocratic priests who joined the war, and he had responsibility for Galilee. Sometime during the early part of the war, he became persuaded that God intended Rome to win, and he found a new task, that of conveying to Jew and Roman alike the solemn truth: fortune had passed to the Romans. God, he felt, had chosen him to 'announce the things that are to come', including the fact that the Roman general Vespasian would become emperor (*War* 3.350–4, 401). This does not mean that he lost all hope for Jewish revival. Though writing under Roman patronage and largely for a pagan audience, and though he wished to argue that Jews were law-abiding members of the empire, he still slipped in some sly remarks that show that he hoped for change in the future. God, he explained, 'who went the round of the nations, bringing to each in turn the rod of empire, now rested over Italy' (*War* 5.367): now rested, would not rest there in the future. Josephus noted that the prophet Daniel had predicted the profanation of the temple by Antiochus IV Epiphanes and its restoration, and he pointed out that both came to pass. Daniel, he wrote, also predicted the coming of the Roman empire. Here he broke off, and commented generally on God's providence, which governs human affairs (*Antiq.* 10.276–81). I do not doubt that he felt constrained from saying that the Roman empire too would come to an end and that Jerusalem would be restored; he could not say it, but he probably did think it. Earlier about Daniel he had written this:

> And Daniel also revealed to the king [Nebuchadnezzar] the meaning of the stone, but I have not thought it proper to relate this, since I am expected to write of what is past and done and not of what is to be; if, however, there is anyone who has so keen a desire for exact information that he will not stop short of inquiring more closely but wishes to learn about the hidden things that are to come, let him take the trouble to read the Book of Daniel, which he will find among the sacred writings. (*Antiq.* 10.210)

Even the present-day reader of Daniel can see that the stone that breaks all other kingdoms is the kingdom of God, Israel (Dan. 2.34, 44f.). This is a broad hint of what Josephus thought would come: something that he could not write.

Josephus seems to have moved from our no. 3 (let us fight as best we can; perhaps God will help) to no. 4 (wait, pray and hope for the best). Even he, who came to think that God desired Roman victory, did not relinquish the hope that one day God would choose otherwise.

Positive hopes

I have been dealing largely with negative actions and with the means that people chose to accomplish what they wanted: war, 'passive resistance', symbolic acts of defiance and the like. Those who were ready to risk their lives, of course, often were filled with visions of a new and better age. In general, the visionaries looked forward to the full restoration of Israel. Just what that meant would have varied from group to group and even from person to person, but there was a lot of common ground, and the main lines can be clearly discerned. The chief hopes were for the re-establishment of the twelve tribes; for the subjugation or conversion of the Gentiles; for a new, purified, or renewed and glorious temple; and for purity and righteousness in both worship and morals.

These hopes go back to the biblical prophets, and for convenience I shall illustrate the four points by quoting Isaiah.

1. The whole people of Israel will be reassembled. In particular, the ten tribes scattered by the Assyrians will be brought back to the land. This hope is expressed by speaking of 'Jacob', the father of the twelve tribes. The prophet depicts God as saying to his servant,

> It is too light a thing that you should be my servant
>> to raise up the tribes of Jacob
>> and to restore the preserved of Israel . . . (Isa. 49.6a)

2. The passage just quoted continues by saying that the servant of the Lord will be 'a light to the Gentiles', so that salvation 'may reach to the end of the earth' (49.6b). In other passages there is the hope that the Gentiles will be subjugated and will pay tribute to Jerusalem.

> They shall bring gold and frankincense,
>> and shall proclaim the praise of the Lord. (60.6b)

> Those who do not submit will be destroyed. (60.12)

3. In 'the latter days' God will make Mount Zion, the site of the temple, 'the highest of the mountains', and the Gentiles will come to worship (Isa. 2.1–3). Jerusalem will be built as never before:

> I will make your pinnacles of agate,
>> your gates of carbuncles,
>> and all your wall of precious stones. (54.12)

Lebanon will supply 'the cypress, the plane, and the pine', and the temple ('the place of my feet') will be made glorious. (60.13)

4. The kingdom that will be established, since it will be God's, will be pure and righteous.

> Your people shall all be righteous;
>> they shall possess the land for ever,
>> the shoot of my planting, the work of my hands,
>> that I might be glorified. (60.21)

These hopes, fostered by reading the scripture, were widely held among Jews. That is so to such an extent that we can speak of common Jewish hopes for the future. For the sake of clarity and succinctness I shall present the evidence in outline form. The four themes (the gathering of the whole people; subjugation, destruction or conversion of the Gentiles; Jerusalem and the temple rebuilt, renewed or purified; purity and righteousness) will be presented in that order, and passages from the surviving literature will be cited, divided into three sections: (*a*) non-biblical literature from the pre-Roman period that continued to be used and read; (*b*) Palestinian literature of the Roman era; (*c*) Diaspora Jewish literature.

1. The twelve tribes of Israel will be assembled.

(*a*) Pre-Roman era literature:

God will 'gather all the tribes of Jacob' (Ben Sira 35.11); Elijah will 'restore the tribes of Jacob' (48.10) (Palestine, pre-Hasmonean).

Israel will be regathered 'from east and west' (Baruch 4.37; 5.5) (Palestine, *c.* 150 BCE).

Jonathan (the Hasmonean) prays that God will gather 'our scattered people' (II Macc. 1.27f.; cf. 2.18).

God will gather his people from among the Gentiles (*Jub.* 1.15) (Palestine, pre-Hasmonean or early Hasmonean).

(*b*) Palestinian literature of the Roman era:

Jerusalem's children will come from east and west, north and south, as well as from 'the islands far away': *Ps. Sol.* 11.2f..

The people will be divided 'according to their tribes upon the land': *Ps. Sol.* 17.28–31; cf. 17.50; 8.34.

The twelve tribes will be represented in the temple service: 1QM 2.2f.; cf. 2.7f.; 3.13; 5.1.

The *Temple Scroll* also envisages the restoration of the twelve tribes: 11QT 8.14–16; 57.5f..

(*c*) Diaspora literature:

Philo does not mention the number 12, but he does look forward to the return of the Diaspora Jews to Palestine: *Rewards* 164f. (Alexandrian Jew, early to middle of the first century CE).

2. The Gentiles will be converted, destroyed or subjugated.

(*a*) Pre-Roman era literature:

Ben Sira calls on God to lift up his hand 'against foreign nations', to 'destroy the adversary and wipe out the enemy'; and he prays that 'those who harm thy people' will meet destruction (Ben Sira 36.1–9).

The author of *Jubilees* looks forward to the time when 'the righteous nation' will eliminate the Gentiles; 'no remnant shall be left them, nor shall there be one that shall be saved on the

day of the wrath of judgment' (*Jub.* 24.29f.). In the repetition
of biblical history in *Jubilees*, this is directed against the
Philistines, but in the author's day it was probably meant more
generally.

According to *I Enoch* 90.19 'the sheep' (=Israel) will kill the wild
animals (=Gentiles).

(*b*) Palestinian literature of the Roman era:

The Davidic king will 'destroy the lawless nations by the word of
his mouth': *Ps. Sol.* 17.24.

After the Davidic king purifies Jerusalem, 'the nations shall come
from the ends of the earth to see his glory': *Ps. Sol.* 17.31.
(Thus not quite all the Gentiles were destroyed.)

In the endtime God will punish the Gentiles and destroy their idols:
T. Moses 10.7.

In the endtime the Gentiles will be destroyed: 1QM.

The *Covenant of Damascus* allowed for proselytes (CD 14.6), and
so we cannot attribute the hope for destruction of the Gentiles
to all the Essenes.

(*c*) Diaspora literature

Sib. Or. 3 (the third *Sibylline Oracle* is Egyptian Jewish, 160–150
BCE) has a rich store of literature on the Gentiles, some
looking forward to their defeat and destruction, some to their
conversion. Some examples: All people will 'bend a white
knee . . . to God the great immortal king' (3.616f.); those who
attack the temple will be destroyed by 'the hand of the
Immortal' (3.670–2); the Gentiles will be defeated by God
himself (3.709), but then, not all destroyed, they will recognize
the one God, send gifts to the temple, and study God's law
(3.710–20); 'from every land' will be brought 'incense and gifts
to the house of the great God' (3.772f.).

The Gentiles will come to recognize the virtue of the Israelites
among them and let them return to their own land. The
Gentiles will fare well if they do not try to stop the
resettlement and rebuilding of Palestine, but if they do they will
meet defeat: Philo, *Rewards* 93–7, 164.

3. Jerusalem will be made glorious; the temple will be rebuilt, made more
glorious or purified.

(*a*) Pre-Roman era literature:

Jerusalem will be built with precious stones and metals, and the
temple will also be rebuilt: Tobit 13.16–18; 14.5.

The temple will be rebuilt: *I Enoch* 90.28f.

In the end time (the 'eighth week') the temple 'for all generations forever' will be built: *I Enoch* 91.13.

God will build his own sanctuary: *Jub.* 1.17; cf. 1.27.

In the time to come the sanctuary of the Lord will be created on Mount Zion: *Jub.* 1.29

God's people will build his sanctuary 'unto all the ages': *Jub.* 25.21.

(*b*) Palestinian literature of the Roman era:

On 'the day of blessing', God promises, 'I will create my temple and establish it for myself for all times': 11QT 29.8–10.

From protests against impurity within the temple or the city, and against desecration of the temple, we may infer that many wished to see the temple and, indeed, Jerusalem purified, though perhaps not rebuilt: Herod's golden eagle was pulled down from the temple; many demonstrated against Pilate's introduction of Roman standards into the city; the 'pious' of the *Psalms of Solomon* objected to the impurity of the Hasmonean priests (8.12) and looked for the son of David to purify Jerusalem (17.30).

(*c*) Diaspora literature:

In the last days 'the Temple of the great God (will be) laden with very beautiful wealth', and the kings of the Gentiles will want to destroy it. They will attack the sanctuary, but 'the sons of the great God will all live peacefully around the Temple', defended by God himself: *Sib. Or.* 3.657–709. Here the temple is not rebuilt as part of the endtime, but has already been made glorious and is defended by God.

God will rebuild Jerusalem so that it will be 'more brilliant than stars and sun and moon', and the temple will be 'exceedingly beautiful in its fair shrine'; there will be 'a great and immense tower over many stadia touching even the clouds and visible to all': *Sib. Or.* 5.420–5 (*Sib. Or.* 5 is Egyptian Jewish, from the end of the first century CE).

When the captive Israelites are released they will rebuild the cities of Palestine and will have great wealth: Philo, *Rewards*, 168.

4. In the time to come worship will be pure and the people will be righteous. This more or less goes without saying, but I give a few examples. (The theme of purity of people and worship partly overlaps with purity of temple, the previous category).

(*a*) Pre-Roman era literature:

Placing the commandment in the time of Jacob, but thinking of his own period, the author of *Jubilees* wrote that 'there shall be nothing unclean before our God in the nation which he has chosen for himself as a possession' (33.11), and that 'Israel is a holy nation unto the Lord its God . . ., and a priestly and royal nation . . .; and there shall no such uncleanness appear in the midst of the holy nation' (33.20).

(*b*) Palestinian literature of the Roman era:

Those who mourned the deaths of the teachers of golden eagle fame urged Archelaus to depose the high priest and appoint a man 'of greater piety and purity' (*War* 2.7).

In the congregation of the last days no person who is impure will enter, 'for the angels of Holiness' will be present: 1QSa 2.3–10.

In the *War Rule* the impure are excluded from the battle, again because holy angels are present: 1QM 7.5f.

The *Temple Scroll* excludes the impure from Jerusalem: 11QT 45.11–17.

The Davidic king will gather 'a holy people, whom he shall lead in righteousness . . . and he shall not permit unrighteousness to lodge any more in their midst': *Ps. Sol.* 17.26f.

(*c*) Diaspora literature:

In the time to come there will be 'a common law . . . throughout the whole earth'; Gentiles are to worship God, avoid adultery, refrain from homosexual practices, and not expose their children; even wealth will be 'righteous': *Sib. Or.* 3.756–81.

These four elements of the future hope were very common, but it is obvious that there was nothing like uniformity of expectation. The general hope for the restoration of the people of Israel is the most ubiquitous hope of all. The twelve tribes are sometimes explicitly mentioned and often indirectly referred to (e.g. by use of the name 'Jacob'), but sometimes the hope is stated more vaguely: the children of Israel will be gathered from throughout the world. In such instances we cannot be sure that the lost ten tribes were explicitly in mind, though it seems likely enough; in any case the reassembly of the people of Israel was generally expected.

'Reassembly' implies a focal point, and hopes for the future of the Jewish people often explicitly included the free possession of Palestine. Philo, who, in accord with his philosophical and mystical outlook, defined 'Israel' as 'the one who sees God', and who thought that the mystical vision of God was the true goal of religion,[7] nevertheless looked forward to the time when Jews would return to Palestine and rebuild its cities (1(*c*) above).[8] More particularly, Jerusalem was the focal point, and thus its rebuilding, improvement or purification is usually implied even when it is not directly mentioned. This holds true of the temple as well. Not everyone who looked forward to the worship of God in the Land thought that a new or more glorious temple must be provided. Expectation ran the range from 'this temple will do' to 'God will build his own, the most glorious building the world has ever seen'. In the period that we study, it seems that virtually no Jews wished to exclude worship at the temple when they envisaged an ideal future. How common the expectation was can be seen when we note that in the New Testament Apocalypse, when the seer has a vision of the new Jerusalem descending from heaven, he explicitly excludes the temple, since there was only one Lamb of God (Rev. 21.22). This is a Christian adaptation of the Jewish theme of a new Jerusalem. Non-Christian Jews expected sacrifices to continue.

There was wide variety in views about what would happen to the Gentiles. The Qumran sect was hardline: Gentiles will be destroyed. Others could envisage their conversion, though when they thought of Gentiles as God's enemies they predicted their subjugation or destruction. Both views are found in the biblical prophets, and so they are both echoed in later literature (e.g. the *Psalms of Solomon*; *Sib. Or.* 3). Philo exhibits a nice balance: the Gentiles will be left alone if they do not hinder the return of the scattered Jews and the rebuilding of the cities. They will be defeated if they do.

That in the future Israel would be pure and righteous was the general expectation. The Qumran sectarians thought concretely and in terms of the biblical law: those ritually impure by reason of bodily blemishes (blindness and the like) will be excluded. Further, they applied the exclusion to the city of Jerusalem, not just to the priests who ministered in the temple (as was the case in the Bible). Other authors spoke more generally of 'purification' and 'righteousness' (e.g. *Ps. Sol.* 17).

The expectation of a messiah was not the rule. It is hard to discuss messianism in general terms that are satisfactory to all. It was once the scholarly custom to talk about the hope for a Davidic king as a standard expectation of first-century Jews. Then scholars, recognizing that there are relatively few passages that attest to this expectation, began to play it down.[9] Now, as is to be expected, there are reassertions of the importance of the longing and hope for a return of Davidic rule.[10] There are a few clear biblical passages, of which these are the most famous:

> Behold, the days are coming, says the Lord, when I will raise up for David a righteous Branch, and he shall reign as king and deal wisely, and shall execute justice and righteousness in the land. (Jer. 23.5f.)

> Of the increase of his government and of peace there will be no end, upon

the throne of David, and over his kingdom, to establish it, and to uphold it with justice and with righteousness from this time forth and for evermore. (Isa. 9.7).

The hope is missing from important sections of the prophetic corpus (such as Isa. 40–66), but with such clear statements as these in the Bible it could not be completely surrendered by first-century Jews.

Despite this, there are relatively few – strikingly few – references to a Davidic king in the literature of our period. He plays the key role only in *Ps. Sol.* 17. In Qumran, there was belief in two messiahs, a priestly messiah ('the Messiah of Aaron') and a secular messiah ('the Messiah of Israel') (1QS 9.11).[11] The priestly messiah was the more important. According to the *Messianic Rule*, when the messiahs arrive there will be an assembly, into which members will enter in order: first the priestly messiah, then the priests, only then the messiah of Israel, and finally the rest. There will be a messianic banquet, with rank properly respected: the priestly messiah takes the lead (1QSa 2.; *DSSE³*, p. 102).

We cannot trace in much more detail what the messiahs and the prophet (also mentioned in 1QS 9.11) were supposed to do. It appears that the sect expected the priestly messiah to run the new community and to teach its members how to live. The *Midrash on the Last Days*[12] refers to 'the Interpreter of the Law', who will arise in the last days, and the *Covenant of Damascus* looks forward to the one who 'teaches righteousness in the end of days' (CD 6.11). This person repeats, in perfect form, the role of the original Teacher of Righeousness. In accord with the general view of the Scrolls, and the importance of the sons of Zadok to the community, the end-time teacher is probably the messiah of Aaron the priest.

We would expect the secular messiah to be a descendant of David and also to be a great warrior. One can see traces of this view in the surviving Scrolls. According to the *Midrash on the Last Days* the 'Branch of David', who will be accompanied by the 'Interpreter of the Law', will 'arise to save Israel'.[13] The *Blessings of Jacob* maintains that the 'covenant of kingship' was granted to the Branch of David 'for everlasting generations'.[14] 'The Prince of the Congregation' is given a war-like role in the *Blessings*, a work that seems to refer to the age-to-come, but the Zadokite priests play an even more prominent part.[15] What is most striking about the sect's 'messianic expectation' is that there is no Davidic messiah in the *War Rule*, where one would expect him to take the leading role. In the war against the forces of darkness, the chosen priest does his part by urging the troops on, but the Branch of David does not put in an appearance. Angels, especially the archangel Michael, the 'Prince of Light', play a major role, but God himself steps in to bring about the final victory of 'the Sons of Light'. 'Truly the battle is Thine!', proclaims the author (1QM 11.1). God will raise up 'the kingdom of Michael' (17.7), not of David, and God will strike the last blow: the victory of the Sons of Light comes 'when the great hand of God is raised in an everlasting blow against Satan and all the hosts of his kingdom' (18.1).[16]

I believe that there are two explanations of these aspects of Qumran's hope for the future (the superiority of the priestly messiah and the non-appearance of a Davidic messiah in the *War Rule*). First, the Bible is by no means entirely in favour of kings, not even Davidic kings. There are two main theories of government in the Bible. One is that a Davidic king rules, but the other is that the priests rule. Moses handed the law to the priests to administer, not to a king (Deut. 31.9). Government in the second-temple period was priestly, though the Hasmoneans took also the title 'king'. Some people protested and wanted to be ruled by non-kingly priests instead (*Antiq.* 14.41). The Qumran sect was founded by overthrown Zadokite priests, who believed that priests were the people who knew things and who should run things. Qumran is a special case; no other group, to our knowledge, emphasized priesthood to the same degree. Nevertheless, the Qumran sectarians were not the only ones who thought that the proper order of things was for priests to be in charge, as we shall see in ch. 21.

The second explanation is less certain, though it seems to me probable. I suspect that the *War Rule* not only reveals *that* the climactic battle can be imagined without mentioning David, but also hints why that is so. The scale had become too large for a mere king. The Qumran sectarians knew about the biblical promises to David and his line, but they contemplated fighting Rome, and they knew that they needed divine help. Once God is thought of as doing the main fighting anyway, the need for a warrior-king is reduced. The sectarians did not invent the theory that God would fight on behalf of his people. Above (p. 287) we quoted Isa. 49.25, 'I will fight those who fight you'. Subsequent writers, not just at Qumran, often saw God as their warrior. This view governs, for example, *T. Moses* 10.7: God himself will wreak vengeance on the Gentiles and destroy their idols (though 10.2 looks forward to the coming of an avenging angel); and *Sib. Or.* 3.708f.: 'No hand of evil war, but rather the Immortal himself and the hand of the Holy One will be fighting for them'. Even in *Ps. Sol.* 17, where the son of David is expected to do a lot of kingly things, he will not 'rely on horse and rider and bow', because 'the Lord himself is his king, the hope of the one who has a strong hope in God' (17.33f.).

According to the gospels, Jesus was hailed as 'son of David' (Matt. 21.9), and descent from David is a main feature of the genealogies in Matthew and Luke, as well as being mentioned by Paul (Rom. 1.3). The importance of

David in Christian messianic thinking[17] has led to the view that all Jews hoped for a son of David. That is misleading; Jewish hope for the future took many forms. Since there are biblical prophecies about the house of David, few Jews would have wanted to say outright, 'our ancestors were warned against kings (I Sam. 8.10–18), and we don't want one either, Davidic or not', but some were not enthusiastic about kings. They thought, as did the author of Deuteronomy, that kings needed to be controlled by priests, the guardians of the law (Deut. 17.18–20). More to the present point, when Jews who thought about the future concretely sat down to describe it, they did not have only one model to follow. They all trusted in God. *That* is common. There seems to have been no overwhelming consensus about what people he would use, and what their descent would be; and indeed some thought that he would do everything himself.

To conclude: many Jews looked forward to a new and better age. This applies very widely. The same hopes are seen in literature from the time of the Maccabees to the destruction of Jerusalem, and in the Greek-speaking Diaspora as well as in Palestine. The hopes centred on the restoration of the people, the building or purification of the temple and Jerusalem, the defeat or conversion of the Gentiles, and the establishment of purity and righteousness.

Life after death

Individual immortality or resurrection is not a major topic of our literature, but it is probable that most Jews expected death not to be the end, though they may have conceived the future quite vaguely. Many were influenced by Greek thought – often remotely, to be sure. The spread of Hellenistic culture meant, among other things, that acceptance of immortality was easy and, to many, self-evident. I do not mean that life after death was a major topic in the Greek-speaking world, but it was generally supposed that each person had an immortal element. In traditional mythology, the shades wandered down to Hades, where they had a weakened and not very satisfactory existence. There were, however, many different opinions about the soul, and there was no Hellenistic orthodoxy.[18] Nevertheless, that death was final would have been a view that was against the spirit of the age. Persian influence, acquired during the exile and the long suzerainty of Persia after the return to Palestine, was perhaps even more important than Greek. From Persian Zoroastrianism came such ideas as the resurrection of everyone, the last judgment, destruction of the wicked and eternal happiness for the righteous.[19]

Philo had imbibed a major Greek philosophical view: God made the world partly of the immortal, partly of the mortal (*Rewards* 1). These two natures mixed in individual humans as well. This is Philo's description of Moses' death:

> The time came when he had to make his pilgrimage from earth to heaven, and leave this mortal life for immortality, summoned thither by the Father Who resolved his twofold nature of body and soul (*sōma kai psychē*) into a single unity, transforming his whole being into mind (*nous*), pure as the sunlight. (*Moses* 2.288)

Moses, whose two-fold nature was resolved into 'mind' at death, was a special case. But everyone, in Philo's view, had these two component parts while alive, one immortal, usually called either 'soul' or 'mind'.

The immortal part could sometimes escape the body even while the latter still lived, and look directly on the immortal world, or at least something closer to it than the world that is perceived by the five senses. The mind can 'come to a point at which it reaches out after the intelligible world' (higher than the world of sense-perception), and it 'seems to be on its way to the Great King Himself', though it cannot quite make it (*Creation* 70f.).[20] In any case this escape was accomplished at death. Philo does not give a picture of heaven: no harps, angels or clouds. Just what happens to the soul is not entirely clear.[21] It is, however, immortal.

Philo, perhaps needless to say, is an extreme case. While the broad spread of Hellenistic culture may have helped incline Jews towards taking some kind of future existence for granted, the full acceptance of the soul's immortality (which implies pre-existence in some form or other, e.g. *Heir* 274) seems to have been fairly rare.

Josephus distinguished the Pharisees and Essenes from the Sadducees partly on the question of 'Fate', partly on that of the afterlife. We shall consider his passages on the latter.

1. The Pharisees:
   (a) Every soul, [the Pharisees] maintain, is imperishable, but the souls of the good alone pass into another body, while the souls of the wicked suffer eternal punishment. (*War* 2.164)
   (b) [The Pharisees] believe that souls have power to survive death and that there are rewards and punishments under the earth for those who have led lives of virtue or vice: eternal imprisonment is the lot of evil souls, while the good souls receive an easy passage to a new life. (*Antiq.* 18.14)

2. The Sadducees:
   (a) As for the persistence of the soul after death, penalties in the underworld, and rewards, [the Sadducees] will have none of them. (*War* 2.165)

(*b*) The Sadducees hold that the soul perishes along with the body. (*Antiq.* 18.16)

3. The Essenes:
   (*a*) It is a fixed belief of [the Essenes] that the body is corruptible . . ., but that the soul is immortal and imperishable. Emanating from the finest ether, these souls become entangled, as it were, in the prison-house of the body, to which they are dragged down by a sort of natural spell; but when once they are released from the bonds of the flesh, then, as though liberated from a long servitude, they rejoice and are borne aloft. Sharing the belief of the sons of Greece, they maintain that for virtuous souls there is reserved an abode beyond the ocean . . .; while they relegate base souls to a murky and tempestuous dungeon, big with never-ending punishments. (*War* 2.154f.)
   (*b*) [The Essenes] regard the soul as immortal. (*Antiq.* 18.18)

It will be worthwhile here to give other passages in which Josephus ascribes similar views to himself, to other specific Jews, or to Jews in general.

4. Judas and Matthias (the golden eagle teachers) taught that
   it was a noble deed to die for the law of one's country; for the souls of those who came to such an end attained immortality and an eternally abiding sense of felicity. (*War* 1.650)

5. Josephus ascribes to himself the view that those
   who depart this life in accordance with the law of nature and repay the loan which they received from God, when He who lent is pleased to reclaim it, win eternal renown; . . . their houses and families are secure; . . . their souls, remaining spotless and obedient, are allotted the most holy place in heaven, whence, in the revolution of the ages, they return to find in chaste bodies a new habitation. But as for those who have laid mad hands upon themselves, the darker regions of the nether world receive their souls, and God, their father, visits upon the posterity the outrageous acts of the parents. (*War* 3.374f.)

6. Josephus composed for Eleazar, leader of the last defenders of Matsada, a lengthy speech on the immortality of the soul, in which he said that
   life, not death, is a person's misfortune. For it is death which gives liberty to the soul and permits it to depart to its own pure abode . . . It is not until, freed from the weight that drags it down to earth and clings about it, the soul is restored to its proper sphere, that it enjoys a blessed energy and a power untrammelled on every side, remaining, like God Himself, invisible to human eyes. (*War* 7.343–6)

7. Finally, he ascribes to Jews in general the following view:
> Each individual . . . is firmly persuaded that to those who observe the laws and, if they must needs die for them, willingly meet death, God has granted a renewed existence and in the revolution [of the ages] the gift of a better life. (*Apion* 2.218)

One may make a few distinctions among these passages. The last two do not say that punishment is in store for some; since dying for the law was the topic, however, the question of punishment did not arise. Passage 1(*a*) implies transmigration of the soul, which is different from a happy existence under the earth (1(*b*)). In 5 souls wait in heaven until they migrate to another person. The phrase 'revolution of the ages' (5; a short form in 7) may point towards transmigration (souls return to chaste bodies), though perhaps it reflects the Stoic idea that periodically the world is consumed with fire and starts all over again.

It is not wise to make too much of the details of these passages. Josephus wanted to present the Jewish 'schools' in Greek dress, as is clearest when he compares the future state for which the Essenes hoped to the Greek Isles of the Blessed (*War* 2.156).[22] Belief in the transmigration (or reincarnation) of souls also crops up in various Greek thinkers.[23] In some of the passages above Josephus depicts all souls as basically immortal but as retaining the individuality of a single human being, rather than as migrating from one to the other: some live forever in bliss, some in torment (1(*b*); 3(*a*)). Long-enduring individual bliss or suffering is more likely to be a Palestinian conception than is transmigration, since it is closer to Persian thought than to the Greek schools that influenced Josephus' description of the parties, and it also corresponds to Judaism's natural drive to distinguish the wicked from the righteous and to maintain that God punishes each person justly. Josephus' attempt to use Greek categories is so thoroughgoing, however, that we cannot confidently say just what the Pharisees and Essenes thought – nor even, in the speech that Josephus attributes to himself, just what he thought.

At another level, we can probably rely on what his discussions imply: it was not just the Pharisees, but most Jews, perhaps all but the Sadducees, who thought that there was an afterlife, though often they may have conceived it very vaguely.

The other primary literature is of some help with regard to the Pharisees and Essenes. The rabbis, as we saw above (pp. 274f.), believed in reward and punishment after death, but they were reluctant to discuss details.

> All Israel gathered together before Moses and said to him, 'Our master Moses, tell us what good things the Holy One, blessed be He, has in

store for us in the future'. He replied, 'I do not know what to tell you. Happy are you with that which is prepared for you'. (*Sifre Deut.* 356, trans. Hammer).

The Qumran literature provides very little about resurrection or immortality. Resurrection seems to be in mind in 1QH 6.29f.

> And then at the time of Judgment
>   the Sword of God shall hasten,
> and all the sons of His truth shall awake
>   to [overthrow] wickedness;
> all the sons of iniquity shall be no more.

Here as generally in the Scrolls the author's eye is fixed on the destruction of the wicked and the victory of the Sons of Light, but he may include among the latter those who were 'asleep'. The expectation that the 'wicked' (that is, non-sectarians) will be severely afflicted and destroyed is quite common. The opening curses of the *Community Rule* provide lush examples:

> Be cursed because of all your guilty wickedness! May He deliver you up for torture at the hands of the vengeful Avengers! May He visit you with destruction by the hand of all the Wreakers of Revenge! Be cursed without mercy because of the darkness of your deeds! Be damned in the shadowy place of everlasting fire! May God not heed you when you call on him . . .![24]

This refers to Jews who did not join the sect. The subsequent curses, which are directed against apostate sectarians, are *really* severe. Such passages seem close enough to one of Josephus' statements, that the Essenes relegated 'base souls to a murky and tempestuous dungeon'. What is hard to find is a statement in the Scrolls that is parallel to the passages in Josephus about the joys of the righteous in heaven and the Isles of the Blessed. The positive Qumran hope was strongly communitarian: they would fight a great battle and win; all of God's adversaries would be destroyed; they would rebuild the temple and run it correctly; they would observe the right calendar; they would live in peace, love and joy (especially 1QM and 11QT; cf. 1QSa). We do not learn just what happened to dead sectarians.

If we leave the literature that has provided most of the material for our study thus far, and look through the apocalypses, we can find lots of visionary material about the judgment and the other world. This material especially collected around the name of Enoch, the original man who ascended bodily into heaven. *II Enoch* provides descriptions of various layers of heaven. In the third heaven, for example, Enoch found trees that emitted pleasant fragrances and provided abundant fruit (*II Enoch* 8). To the north, he found a place of cruel darkness, raging fire, pitiless angels, and all the trappings of the mediaeval Christian hell (*II Enoch* 10). I do not propose to survey the heavenly visions and tours.[25] It is sufficient to know that some people tried to envisage the next world.

What we would most like to know is how representative such material is. Unfortunately, we cannot know. The rabbis tried to discourage speculation about what was in the heavenly places,[26] which may show that a lot of people engaged in it. If they did, did they take it seriously, or did it function like fairy tales and ghost stories? Probably it varied from time to time and place to place. Fabulous visions of heaven and hell have had a very diverse history within Christianity. Hell, in particular, has fluctuated from being a main theme of a high percentage of sermons to being not mentioned at all. Perhaps this gives us a way of thinking about detailed descriptions of the next world in Judaism.

Josephus, unfortunately, does not provide much help. He does not describe directly what the masses thought about religion, much less their opinions about abstruse subjects like the afterlife. And his comments on the Essenes and Pharisees are not especially helpful, since we have to discount the Isles of the Blessed and transmigration as being Greek motifs, introduced to impress his audience. When we add everything together, including the esoteric literature, we are left knowing that Jews – certainly a lot, probably most – believed in an afterlife and in individual reward and punishment. I think that this was common as a general view. We cannot, however, go much beyond this somewhat vague generalization, except to say that at some times some people engaged in detailed fantasies about the other world.

What is much clearer is the widespread hope of a *new age* on this earth, one in which the God of Israel will reign supreme, being served by loyal Jews, and possibly by converted Gentiles, in purity and obedience. This is a main theme, which runs from the biblical prophets to such diverse later sources as the Qumran Scrolls and Philo. The hope that God would fundamentally change things was a perfectly reasonable hope for people to hold who read the Bible and who believed that God had created the world and had sometimes intervened dramatically to save his people.

Temple Plans

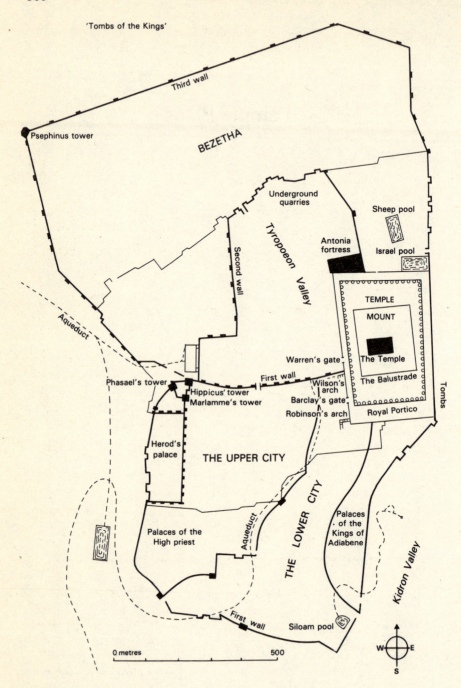

'Tombs of the Kings'

Third wall

Psephinus tower

BEZETHA

Underground
quarries

Sheep pool

Tyropoeon Valley

Antonia
fortress

Israel pool

Second wall

TEMPLE

MOUNT

The Temple

Warren's gate

The Balustrade

First wall

Wilson's
arch

Phasael's tower

Hippicus' tower

Barclay's gate

Marlamme's tower

Robinson's arch

Royal Portico

Tombs

Aqueduct

Herod's
palace

THE UPPER CITY

Palaces
of the
Kings of
Adiabene

Palaces of the
High priest

Aqueduct

THE LOWER CITY

Kidron Valley

First wall

Siloam pool

0 metres   500

W ⊕ E
S

3 Jerusalem in Second-Temple Times

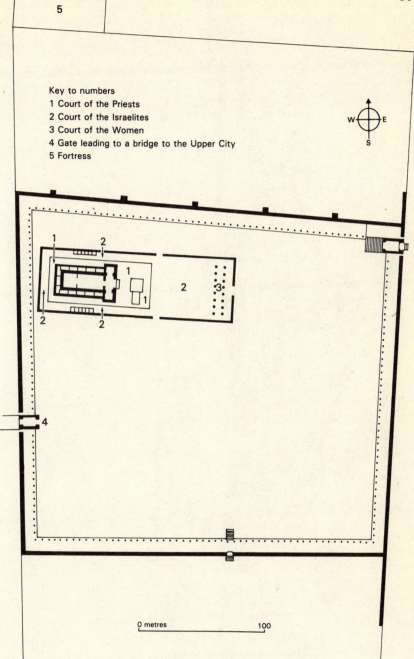

Key to numbers
1 Court of the Priests
2 Court of the Israelites
3 Court of the Women
4 Gate leading to a bridge to the Upper City
5 Fortress

4 The Pre-Herodian Temple

5 The Temple Mount 70 CE (elevation viewed from the south-west)

Key to the Plans of Herod's Temple (Plans 5–9)

1 The Antonia fortress.
2 Retaining wall.
3 'West Wall Street'.
4 'Wilson's Arch', spanning the Tyropoeon Valley.
5 'Robinson's Arch', which leads to the street below.
6 Shops.
7 Porticoes (stoas).
8 The Royal Portico.
9 The exit gate.
10 The entrance gate.
11 'Solomon's Portico' (pre-Herodian).
12 The Mount of Olives.
13 The Court of the Gentiles.
14 The entrance to the platform, connected by a tunnel to no. 10.
15 The exit from the platform, connected by a tunnel to no. 9.
16 Steps and balustrade prohibiting Gentiles.

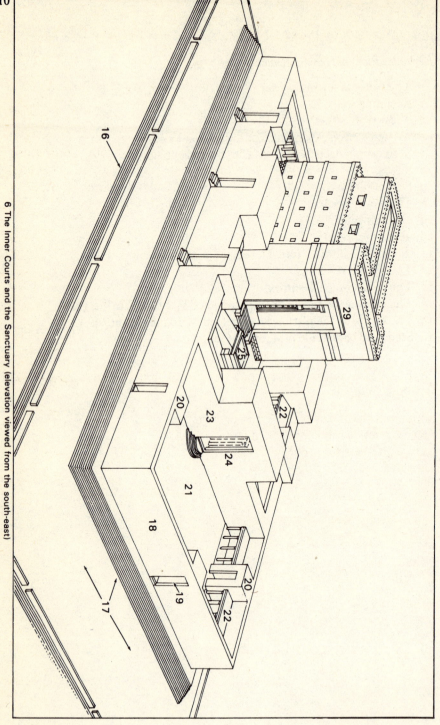

6 The Inner Courts and the Sanctuary (elevation viewed from the south-east)

17 Inner platform and steps.
18 Inner wall.
19 First eastern gate, through which male Israelites entered.
20 Southern and northern gates, through which female Israelites entered.
21 Court of the Women.
22 Inner porticoes (stoas).
23 Wall separating Court of the Women from the male area.
24 Second eastern gate, through which male Israelites entered. I believe that there may have been a barrier from 19 to 24, preventing men and women from mingling in the Women's Court, and that there may have been a gallery on top of 23, allowing women to see the priests at work.
25 The altar for burnt sacrifices.
26 Court of the (ordinary, male) Israelites.
27 Parapet separating priests from ordinary Israelites.
28 Court of the Priests.
29 The façade and entrance to the sanctuary.
30 The first chamber (with incense altar and candelabrum).
31 The Holy of Holies.
32 Upper floors.

Supplementary Key to Plan 9, the Inner Courts and Sanctuary according to Mishnah Middot

Numbers are the same as in plans 5 and 6.
16 Balustrade prohibiting Gentiles (no steps).
21a Chambers for various purposes.
[22 Inner porticoes: missing (as are outer porticoes).]
[27 Parapet separating priests from ordinary Israelites: missing.]
33 Shambles.
34 Chambers for various purposes.

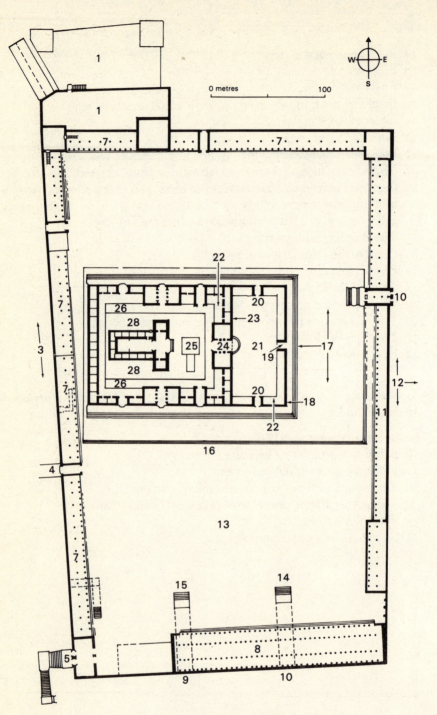

7 The Herodian Temple Area

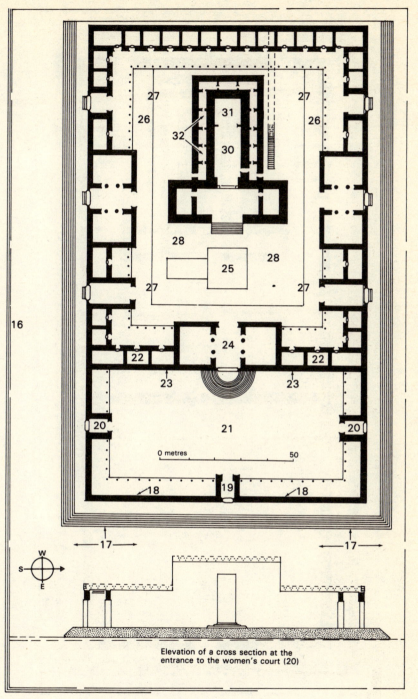

Elevation of a cross section at the
entrance to the women's court (20)

8 The Inner Courts and the Sanctuary

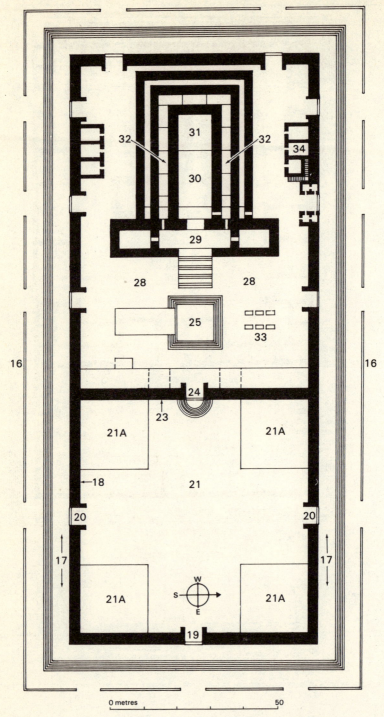

9 The Inner Courts and the Sanctuary according to Mishnah *Middot*

PART III
Groups and Parties

15

Aristocrats and Sadducees

We now return to where we were in chs 2–4, to the history of the late second-temple period, and in particular to the parties that became prominent during the rule of the Hasmoneans. We shall go back over some of the same ground, sometimes giving more detail, sometimes simply repeating. I assume that relatively few readers carry the history of the period in their heads, particularly since it sometimes seems that everyone had the same name. Thus in the chapters that follow I shall say enough about Aristobulus II to distinguish him from other people named Aristobulus, and also from the various Agrippas and Antipaters.

In ch. 2 we saw that the parties as we know them grew out of the turmoil of Palestine in the Seleucid and Hasmonean periods. Of the surviving groups, all except some of the Essenes backed the Hasmonean settlement: the agreement that Simon would be high priest and also 'leader', a title that his successors soon grew out of and exchanged for 'king'. When the external enemies were driven out, and the extreme Jewish Hellenizers were defeated, other internal divisions appeared. Not every shade of opinion resulted in a distinct group, but we know of three named parties: Sadducees, Pharisees and Essenes. In discussing the reign of the Hasmonean Jonathan (161–143 BCE), Josephus wrote that 'at that time' there were three parties (*Antiq.* 13.171). He ascribes no actions to any of the parties that early, however, and it is possible that he knew that they arose in the Hasmonean period and arbitrarily assigned them to the time of Jonathan.

We shall now examine first the history and then the characteristics of each party in some detail. An actual history cannot be written, and especially not for the Sadducees. The named parties and other identifiable groups (such as the chief priests) appear only sporadically in the pages of Josephus, and the other sources provide more information about their characteristics than about their development. We shall, however, do as much of a history as is possible. The aim is to learn about the viewpoints and influence of the parties during our period.

We shall consider Sadducees and aristocrats together. The common assumption, which I share, is that there was a high degree of correspondence between them. Not all aristocrats were Sadducees, but it may be that all Sadducees were aristocrats. We can say very little about the Sadducees as a 'party', but quite a lot about the aristocrats in general. The following discussion will focus first on the aristocracy, and our few facts about the Sadducees will appear in the second part of the chapter.

As Martin Goodman has pointed out to me, lumping Sadducees and aristocrats together might be misleading, and the question requires consideration. The evidence that the Sadducees were aristocrats (not that the aristocrats were Sadducees) is this: (1) According to Josephus the Sadducean 'doctrine' (*logos*) was made known 'only to a few males', but they were 'foremost in worthiness' (*Antiq.* 18.16f.). (2) The one person during our period whom Josephus names as a Sadducee is Ananus, an aristocratic priest. (Earlier, Hyrcanus I had allied himself with the Sadducees.)[1] (3) The Book of Acts links the high priest *c.* 30–33 CE (Caiaphas) with the Sadducean party (Acts 5.17). (4) It is possible that the term 'Sadducee' was derived from 'Zadok' (above, pp. 25f.). If this etymology is correct, the original Sadducees were aristocratic priests. (5) By the time of the Mishnah (*c.* 220 CE), both the old aristocracy and the Sadducean party belonged to the past and were regarded as insignificant. The Mishnah treats the high priest like an incompetent dunce, and the rabbis only occasionally regard the Sadducees as worthy sparring partners.[2] Put another way, after the destruction of Jerusalem the aristocracy began to decline, the priestly aristocracy soon disappeared, and the Sadducees dropped from sight. These facts are probably interrelated.

We should always query Josephus' summaries and can never consider them to be true of all times and places. The authors of the gospels and Acts had imperfect knowledge of Jewish parties. The case of Ananus may have been the exception rather than the rule. The etymology of 'Sadducee' may be incorrect. Thus most of the above points are subject to doubt. The most general evidence is the best: the simultaneous decline of the aristocracy and the Sadducees. Taking it all together, I shall accept the general view that the Sadducees were aristocrats.

It must again be emphasized that we cannot assume the reverse, that aristocrats were Sadducees. We can enumerate and name neither the class nor the party (with a few exceptions), and so we cannot say that the authority of the aristocrats proves the predominance of the Sadducees. In what follows, I shall give a brief history of the aristocracy, then comment on Sadducean 'doctrine', then consider the overall piety of the aristocrats and the question of their morality. The evidence allows the discussion of these three topics, but not others (such as the history of the Sadducean party).

The high priest[3]

In the pre-Hasmonean period, Jewish government – in effect, local government, whatever was not decided by the foreign empire that had ultimate control – was in the hands of the high priest, who was head of the *gerousia*, 'council of elders'. We do not know the history of the council; here it need be said only that in the early period there was one. Its existence during the Persian period and the early years of the Hasmoneans is shown by the references to it in both Josephus and I and II Maccabees (II Macc. 1.10; 4.44; 11.27; *Antiq.* 13.166, 169). The last attested use of gerousia is at the time of Jonathan; that is, before 143 BCE. I Macc. 12.6 (= *Antiq.* 13.166) gives this as the salutation of a letter to Sparta:

> Jonathan the high priest, the gerousia of the nation, the priests and the rest of the Jewish people to the Spartans their brothers, greetings . . .

That is the correct form of letters at the time, and we may take it that there was a gerousia. Rule by the high priest, assisted by the gerousia, is reflected also in Judith, written during the Hasmonean period or somewhat earlier (Judith 4.8; 11.14; 15.8).

The coins struck by Hasmonean rulers were often inscribed 'X the high priest and the *ḥever* of the Jews'.[4] The precise significance of the phrase is disputed.[5] The simplest meaning of *ḥever* is 'association', and the simplest assumption is that the term applies to the council that (one further assumes) succeeded the gerousia. For the present, I shall take it that all the Hasmonean high priests ruled with the aid of a council.

We recall that the Hasmonean period ended in a shambles. Hyrcanus II and Aristobulus II contested for the high priesthood, and each held it for a fairly brief period. After the death of Aristobulus II, his son, Antigonus, aided by the Parthians, gained control of Jerusalem and became ruler and high priest. He mutilated his uncle, Hyrcanus II, so that he was ineligible to serve as high priest.[6]

After Herod conquered Jerusalem and sent Antigonus to be executed, he had to appoint a new high priest. He chose Ananel. Josephus describes him as 'a rather undistinguished priest from Babylon' (*Antiq.* 15.22) and also as a member of 'a high-priestly family', a descendant of the Jews taken to Babylon centuries before and also a long-time, valued friend of Herod (15.39–41). It makes sense for Herod's first appointee to have been both of an old

aristocratic family, presumably at least remotely Zadokite, and also to have
been undistinguished. The crown was not yet secure on Herod's head, and
he did not want competition. On the other hand, he may have wanted to
upstage the upstart Hasmoneans by appointing a man from the older
aristocratic family.

A few years later (36 BCE), Herod deposed Ananel and appointed
Aristobulus III, a Hasmonean, and, further, Herod's brother-in-law, the
brother of his wife Mariamme. Aristobulus III was eye-catching, as was
Mariamme, and mentioning this allows Josephus to pass on a bit of salacious
gossip. Marc Antony, who saw a picture of the boy, wanted Herod to send
him to Egypt, presumably for the boy's 'education'. Herod saw through the
plan and knew that Antony, 'who was more powerful than any Roman of his
time', was 'ready to use [Aristobulus] for erotic purposes'. Herod put off the
request, saying that Aristobulus was too popular at home. He then decided to
appoint the boy high priest. This kept him at home, safe from moral
depravity, but simultaneously under Herod's watchful eye. It had the further
advantage of partially satisfying the ambitions of his wife and his
mother-in-law. So Herod deposed Ananel and appointed Aristobulus III
high priest (*Antiq.* 15.23–41).

Herod's good intentions went awry. The young man, still in his teens,
handsome, a Hasmonean, brother-in-law of the king, who could wear the
diadem and magnificent regalia of the high priest, had an appreciable
following. The crowd 'called out to him good wishes mingled with prayers, so
that [their] affection became evident' (*Antiq.* 15.52). Herod, understandably,
was alarmed. After the Feast of Booths, the extended family took a holiday at
Jericho, at the Hasmonean palace, where there were swimming pools.
Aristobulus went for a swim with some of Herod's other friends and servants,
and in play they held him under the water. Quite by accident, no doubt, they
held him under too long (15.50–56). Before too many years passed, there
were no Hasmoneans left. Meanwhile, Ananel was reappointed high priest
(15.56).

The high priesthood was an office greatly to be desired, and the high priest
was the natural leader of the people. Save for the years 76–67 BCE, when
Salome Alexandra was queen, the high priest had been the chief figure in
Judaea since sometime early in the Persian period: in round numbers, 500
years. Aristobulus III, of course, was a special case. He was the scion of the
House of Hashmon, and his mother and others may well have hoped that
eventually he could overthrow Herod. The office of high priest, however, had
its own importance. Even Aristobulus III was more important if he was high
priest than if he was not; as high priest, he posed a threat to Herod. Herod
had already had one high priest executed (Antigonus, who was killed on

Roman orders, therefore only indirectly by Herod). He had an army. One would think that he need not fear a high priest. Nevertheless, he had to be careful who held the office. Fortunately, the good Ananel, loyal friend, of old family, was around.

The story of Aristobulus III and Ananel is interesting from another point of view. The tradition had been that the high priest, once appointed, served for life. When Josephus narrated the deposition of Ananel, he wrote that 'never had anyone been deprived of this office when once he had assumed it', a statement that he had immediately to retract, since there had been changes of the high priest late in the Seleucid period, and Aristobulus II had deposed his brother, Hyrcanus II, after the death of their mother the Queen (*Antiq.* 15.40f.). Pompey reappointed Hyrcanus II, who was later deposed by his nephew Antigonus. Nevertheless, the statement that no one had ever been deposed reflects the standard expectation before Herod became king. From the time of Herod on the office became a kind of political football. The secular ruler controlled it and appointed whom he wished.

High priests were appointed by Herod (until his death in 4 BCE), by his son Archelaus (4 BCE to 6 CE), and then by Roman legates or prefects during the first period of direct Roman government of Judaea, 6–41 CE. In 41, when Agrippa I became king over Herod's former kingdom, he was allowed to appoint the high priest, and he exercised the authority three times during his brief reign (died 44). Since his son, Agrippa II, was too young to rule, Rome again appointed military and fiscal governors. The Jews, however, successfully petitioned Rome to allow a Jewish ruler to appoint the high priest. Authority was given first to Herod of Chalcis (44–48) and then to Agrippa II, who retained it until the outbreak of the revolt in 66. During the last two years of the war the Zealots chose by lot a non-aristocratic high priest.[7]

The standing of the high priest during the Roman period (including the Herodian) was a curious one. On the one hand, it might be thought that the office fell into disrepute. On the other, it is clear that successive high priests maintained not only power but also influence with the masses. Conceivably, both things could be true simultaneously. People might realize that a given high priest had obtained his office by bribery or flattery and was morally unworthy of it, while also thinking that he was ordained as God's spokesman and thus should be respected and obeyed. People today sometimes view their leaders and rulers in both ways, even when they do not think that the office includes mediation between people and God. It is not difficult for us to imagine that people respected the office and the man who held it, either only when he was fulfilling his divine duties, or also when he was not, depending on his personal worth.

We may exemplify this point by considering the career of Joazar son of

Boethus, who was not one of the more successful high priests. The story spans the period of change from Herodian to direct Roman rule of Judaea. When, in the last year of Herod's life, the young men tore down the golden eagle from the temple, Herod not only had the malefactors executed, he held the high priest partly responsible, deposed him and appointed Joazar (*Antiq.* 17.164). When Herod died, shortly thereafter, a group of people (according to Josephus, 'bent on revolution') began to lament the loss of those who had been executed for taking down the eagle. The protesters thought that reform should start with the removal of Joazar, since 'they had a right to select a man of greater piety and purity' (*War* 2.5–7). This movement did not succeed. Archelaus kept Joazar and then went to Rome to be confirmed in his office. When he returned from Rome as ethnarch rather than king (as he had hoped), he deposed Joazar for having supported those who objected to him (*Antiq.* 17.339). In 6 CE, however, Archelaus reappointed Joazar. Archelaus himself was then deposed, and Quirinius, legate of Syria, was sent to take a census of Judaea. There was naturally opposition to registration of property for tax purposes, but Joazar persuaded many of the people to comply with Roman wishes (*Antiq.* 18.3). Despite his efforts, however, there were uprisings, and Quirinius deposed Joazar because he had been 'overpowered by a popular faction' (*Antiq.* 18.26).

This is a very instructive career. (1) We see that the high priest was expected by the secular power to be in control and not to let things get out of hand. One high priest failed to prevent the removal of the eagle, one failed to prevent some uprisings, and both were deposed. (2) The willingness of the secular authority to change high priests, searching for an effective one, is evident. (3) The pious and zealous (those who lamented the execution of the men who took down the eagle) wanted the high priest to be on their side and also to be as pious and zealous as they. (4) Even a high priest who was basically loyal to the secular ruler could join in agitation against the man to whom he owed his office. (This assumes that there was some foundation to Archelaus' suspicions.) (5) Many people could be persuaded by the high priest even when he championed an unpopular cause (the registration of property). With regard to points (4) and (5), we do not know who Joazar's allies were, and thus we cannot know that he sided only with 'the populace' in protesting against Archelaus, nor that he single-handedly persuaded the majority of the people to submit to the Roman census. Possibly a lot of people saw that the issue was not worth armed revolt. Nevertheless, we see the position that the high priest was supposed to occupy and the potential range of his responsibilities.[8]

During the years of direct Roman rule, and to a lesser degree during rule by one of Herod's descendants, the high priest was the man in the middle, between the secular ruler and the people. His responsibilities included representing the people to the ruler and the ruler to the people. To this end he formed alliances with other leading figures, gathered around him a council of advisors, and employed the usual means of diplomacy: often private meetings but sometimes public appeals. His success in preventing serious disturbances depended on several factors, some of which were out of his control. Some high priests were abler than others, and some more generally respected than others. All had a certain amount of authority by virtue of their office. Several holders of the office sought diligently to satisfy both the secular ruler and the desires of the populace, though in a pinch they almost always urged the crowd to submit and so to maintain the peace.

The high priests had to be able to get along with the secular power, whether Herodian or Roman: this was not an option, but a necessary condition for holding the office. The high priest's character mattered little while Herod was king, since he made all the important decisions. He could have a high priest who was a nonentity, and in fact preferred it, though even he expected the high priest to do rather obvious things like keeping the temple from being vandalized. After Herod's death and the deposition of Archelaus, however, the office again became an important one, both in terms of influence and in actual authority. The Roman prefects and procurators usually stayed, with most of their troops, in Caesarea; and the high priest, his council, and their armed guards administered Jerusalem. This is shown both by numerous passages in Josephus and also by the stories of trials in the gospels and Acts (Mark 14.53–15.1 and parallels; John 18.12–32; Acts 5.17–42; 7.1; 23.2–5). Under Rome, the situation was basically the same as it was in the days of the Persian empire and the Hellenistic kingdoms: the high priest governed the temple and Jerusalem, and it is probable that he effectively governed Judaea. Towns and villages had their own magistrates to handle minor cases, and probably small councils.[9] A difference between the earlier empires and Rome, however, which especially affected Jerusalem, was that Rome breathed more heavily down the necks of the local Jewish rulers.

Of the high priests during the period 6–66 CE, some were corrupt, out for their own gain and that of their sycophants, while some used their power and influence to protect the people from direct intervention by Rome: that is, they sincerely attempted to administer Jerusalem in such a way as to preserve a measure of independence, while not offending Rome. To complicate our assessment still further, one person could fall in both camps, a point that we shall explore later in this chapter. Prominent and generally effective was the family of Annas (*Antiq.* 20.198).[10] He was high priest from 6 to 15, and five of his sons were high priests subsequently. The most successful high priest during the Roman period was Joseph Caiaphas, who held the office from 18 to 36. According to the New Testament, he was Annas' son-in-law (John 18.13).

In ch. 10 we noted that Josephus recounted stories that discredit some of the high priests. These are intimately connected with stories that depict other aristocrats (chief priests and Herodians) as engaging in shameless and illegal activity, and we should look at these narratives as a group. There are six principal passages, which I shall summarize in chronological sequence. (1) At the time of the high priest Ishmael son of Phabi (*c.* 59–61 CE), there was enmity among the chief priests 'against one another', and strife between the chief priests and 'the priests and prominent members of the populace of Jerusalem' (*Antiq.* 20.180).[11] (2) The servants of some of the chief priests collected tithes from the threshing floors, with the result that some of the ordinary priests starved (*Antiq.* 20.181). (3) The chief priest Ananias allowed his servants to steal tithes, and they were joined by other chief priests. When the farmers resisted, wishing to save the tithes for the ordinary priests, they were beaten. Again, some priests starved (*Antiq.* 20.206f.). (4) When Agrippa II replaced the high priest Jesus son of Damnaeus with Jesus son of Gamaliel (*c.* 63 CE), there was a feud, and the followers of the two priests resorted to street fighting (*Antiq.* 20.213). (5) During the strife between these two priests, Ananias 'kept the upper hand by using his wealth to attract those who were willing to receive bribes'. (6) Two descendants of Herod, Costobar and Saul, 'collected gangs of villains' and plundered the property of people who were weaker than they (*Antiq.* 20.214).

These stories all come from the period when Agrippa II had the power to appoint the high priest, which he exercised six times in about seven years (*c.* 59–65 CE). They reveal factional strife primarily *within* the aristocracy.[12] High priest fought former high priest; chief priests opposed not only ordinary priests but also the leaders (*prōtoi*, 'first people') of the populace; Ananias used his wealth to maintain his influence with more important people (the procurator and the serving high priest, *Antiq.* 20.205), doubtless at the expense of other aristocrats.

We shall come back to these stories after we have surveyed the other groups of aristocrats. Here we note that high priests such as these clearly demeaned the office. One would have thought that it would have lost credibility entirely, and these stories give some modern readers that impression. Many scholars say that the high priests were corrupt; those who held the office used bribery to get their way. Inevitably, such generalizations refer to one passage, Josephus' description of how Ananias retained influence after he was deposed (*Antiq.* 20.205).[13] This conduct is then attributed to the high priests in general.

This is misleading. One should also remember those who, at the time of the revolt, were chosen to lead the people, apparently by popular acclaim (*War* 2.562f.); who stayed, fought and died; and who seem to have behaved nobly. The warmest praise in Josephus is reserved for a high priest, Ananus son of Annas. He served only a few months in 62, being deposed because he convened a *synedrion* (court) and had James the brother of Jesus executed without Roman authorization (*Antiq.* 20.199–203). He remained prominent, and he was one of those chosen to lead the war effort (along with Joseph son of Gorion, also an aristocrat) (*War* 2.563f.). The same popular assembly appointed several other priests to places of command (*War* 2.566–8). In the dreadful civil war that marked the last stage of the revolt, the two leaders who tried to withstand the efforts of the Zealots and Idumaeans to gain control were the chief priests Jesus son of Gamalas and Ananus. Several thousand Jews (Josephus says 8,500) died defending them (*War* 4.238, 305–18), and it is on Ananus that Josephus bestows the most glowing tribute in his pages (*War* 4.319–25). Here I quote Josephus' general assessment of him:

> A man on every ground revered and of the highest integrity, Ananus, with all the distinction of his birth, his rank and the honours to which he had attained, yet delighted to treat the very humblest as his equals. Unique in his love of liberty and an enthusiast for democracy, he on all occasions put the public welfare above his private interests. (*War* 4.319–320)

That is only part; the praise goes on. It is of course a set piece, full of conventional phrases, some fitting and some not ('enthusiast for democracy'). Further, Josephus' own position with regard to the revolt was the same as that of Ananus: he at first favoured conciliation and wanted to yield when the Syrian legate brought an army against Jerusalem, but he decided on revolt when the Romans withdrew. Thus we must suspect Josephus' panegyric of being exaggerated. Nevertheless, Ananus acted in what he perceived to be the best interests of the people. They sometimes coincided with his own, but almost all public figures manage to identify self-interest and public interest in some way or other. Had he and his principal priestly ally been motivated only by self-interest, they could have fled, finding refuge with the legate of Syria, as did some aristocrats (*War* 2.556f.). Agrippa II stayed safely on the side of Rome. Ananus and his colleague Jesus, along with other eminent men, such as Zacharias son of Baris (*War* 4.335), fought for what they believed in, and they died for their cause. Part of 'their cause' was that *they* should remain in control of the war, not the Zealots and the Idumaeans. Josephus' judgment was that, had Ananus lived, he would have come to terms with Rome (*War* 4.321). This does not, in my judgment, make him either corrupt, cowardly, selfish or power-mad.

Josephus distinguished his characters one from another: the behaviour of some high priests was scandalous, that of others admirable. But even within each of these broad types, he makes further distinctions. His hero, Ananus, was harsh in judgment (*Antiq.* 20.199f.). This seems to be a mild criticism.

Just how many of each sort there were is hard to say; few were at either extreme. On the whole, the impression given by Josephus is that during the periods of direct Roman rule the high priests tried to be honest brokers, mediating between the prefect or procurator and the people. This was apparently true even of Ananias, as we shall see below. It is clear that Ananus and Jesus son of Gamalas had the welfare of the people at heart and were respected by many. We cannot read these stories and conclude that the aristocratic priesthood was entirely corrupt. Most important, not only Josephus, but also the populace could distinguish; they killed Ananias (*War* 2.441f.) and followed Ananus.

A different kind of anecdote is the best evidence of the prestige of the office, whatever the worthiness of the occupant. It is the running story of the high priest's vestments.[14] Herod locked them up in the citadel in the northwest corner of the temple area, allowing the high priest to have them only when he had to sacrifice – at the three pilgrimage festivals and on the Day of Atonement. They remained guarded after Herod's death, throughout Archelaus' reign, and during the first thirty years of direct Roman government. When Vitellius, the legate of Syria, visited Jerusalem in 36 CE, he asked what return he could make for his kind reception. The Jews asked to have the vestments under their own authority, and Vitellius obtained this favour from Tiberius (*Antiq.* 15.403–5; 18.90–95). They remained in Jewish control until the death of Agrippa I in 44. Fadus, the procurator who was then assigned to Judaea, demanded that the vestments be given into his custody. The Jews asked permission to petition the emperor Claudius, which was granted, and a delegation went to Rome, leaving their children in the hands of the Romans as hostages. Claudius granted the request and gave authority over the vestments to Herod of Chalcis (who then also obtained authority to appoint the high priest). The same authority passed to Agrippa II and thus remained in Jewish hands until the temple was destroyed (*Antiq.* 20.6–16).

This is an extremely revealing sequence of events. Control of the vestments was important, so important that two Roman emperors concerned themselves directly with it, important enough that people who had absolute military power worried about letting these garments out of their control. Herod could appoint and depose high priests; so could Archelaus; so could the legate of Syria. Why, then, worry about who controlled the vestments? Why would Fadus, freshly arrived from Rome after the death of Agrippa I, make it one of his first concerns, especially since he also had a military conflict between two cities to worry about (*Antiq.* 20.1–5)? The answer is clear: With his sacred vestments on, the high priest spoke for Israel to God, and for God to Israel. The office, symbolized by the vestments, was not just respected, it was revered.

Goodman has argued, partly in agreement with earlier scholars, that from the time of the Herodian appointments on, Jews were conscious that the high priests were illegitimate. The leading families were neither Zadokites nor Hasmoneans; they were upstarts, brought to the fore by the Romans' need to have a local aristocracy to whom to relate, and they never gained the full confidence and support of the people. I think that there is something to this, and we should also grant that the custom of deposing and appointing downgraded the office. On the other hand, I remain impressed with how often the high priest or the chief priests (see below) effectively interceded, and the various indications that the office was still revered. I doubt that the post-Herodian priestly aristocrats were all 'despised by the very populace that they were meant to lead'.[15] I have argued this anecdotally, by telling the stories of Joazar, Ananus, Ananias and the vestments. Further evidence would also be anecdotal: one would simply tell all the stories about the high priests or chief priests. I shall not do this here, though a few more stories will be cited below or in the chapter on self-government. The general impression given by all the stories, to repeat, is that the high priest retained a lot of influence with the people, by virtue of his office, though it is true that the high priests of the Roman period did not have the status of the Hasmoneans or Zadokites before them.

We should now recall a point from the history of the Hasmoneans. The objections to them had to do with their being high priests, not secular rulers. Some people did not like the combination – as if the king came from battle with defiled hands and sacrificed to God – but at its heart the objection was based on respect for the high priesthood. After Pompey's conquest, Hyrcanus II was not allowed the title 'king', but only 'ethnarch'; yet he was high priest. The Jews naturally then thought that Antipater the Idumaean and his sons Phasael and Herod should be subordinate to him (below, p. 479). To many, many Jews the office of high priest was the one that really counted. In the absence of a Davidic king the natural assumption was that the high priest was ordained by God to lead the people. The vestments were sacred, and they symbolized his holy office – whether or not the wearer was worthy of them.

The chief priests

In some respects the high priest was only 'first among equals'. In everyday dealings with the Romans and the populace 'the chief priests' often acted collectively and effectively. They are prominent in governmental matters throughout the pages of Josephus (except during the time of Herod), and also in the trial scenes in the gospels and Acts. We do not know just how one qualified to be a 'chief priest'. The designation was not an official one; there was no election to it, and no higher ordination made one a chief priest. In this study I try to maintain a distinction between 'high' for the serving high priest and 'chief' for the others, but there is no distinction in Greek between the two adjectives. The serving high priest, in our Greek sources, is called the *archiereus*; the collective chief priests are called the *archiereis*, which is the plural form of the same noun. Ananus when serving as high priest was *archiereus*; after he was deposed, he was still *archiereus*. We cannot be sure whether the title was kept as an honorific (as a former US President is sometimes addressed as 'Mr President', though he would not be called 'the President'), or whether the meaning has undergone a subtle shift, for which we conveniently have a separate English term, from 'high' to 'chief'. Further, we do not know what a former high priest or the collective chief priests were called in spoken Hebrew or Aramaic. In the *War Rule* the same adjective (*r'ôsh*, head, not *gadôl*, 'great') is used in both the singular and the plural.[16] The official term for the high priest was *kôhen gadôl*, as the Hasmonean coins prove. It would be possible in either Hebrew or Greek to distinguish the chief priests terminologically from the serving high priest. There is, however, no evidence for a consistent terminological distinction in any language, and the Greek evidence points towards no such distinction.[17] The reason for wondering about terminology is this: if the adjective for the chief priests was the same as that for the high priest (as seems likely), it is probable that the chief priests were very closely tied to the office of high priest. Different adjectives would favour a more general definition of 'chief priests'.

These observations bear on the two principal proposals for defining the 'chief priests': that they were men who belonged to the four or five families from whom the high priests were drawn,[18] or that they were priests who held one of the special offices (e.g. treasurer).[19] Following Schürer, Vermes, Millar and Goodman, I think it better to accept the former meaning: men who belonged to the high priestly families.[20] This means that there were a good number of chief priests, since a few families, even in one or two generations, would have produced a lot of males, especially if the brothers of a man who served as high priest also qualified as chief priests.

In describing the leaders of the revolt, Josephus makes distinctions of status among the chief priests. He calls Ananus 'the senior chief priest', which denotes either rank or age or both (*War* 4.151). According to *War* 4.160 Ananus and Jesus son of Gamalas were 'the best regarded' of the chief priests. It seems probable that such descriptions reflect only Josephus' estimate of the leadership and influence of individuals.

In discussing the high priests, we have already seen some of the evidence that indicates the status of the chief priests, especially of the men who had once served as high priest. Two of them, Ananus and Jesus son of Gamalas, we noted, were leaders of the first phase of the revolt. There was animosity against the aristocrats in some quarters, which erupted when the Zealots took Jerusalem. Most of the early leaders of the war, not just Ananus and Jesus, were aristocratic priests. The commanders dispatched to Idumaea were Jesus son of Sapphas and Eleazar son of Ananias, both of high priestly families (*War* 2.566). To Galilee were sent three aristocratic priests: Joazar, Judas and Josephus himself (*Life* 29). The Joseph son of Simon who was given command of Jericho may be the same as the Joseph son of Simon who was high priest from 60 to 62 (*War* 2.567; see Feldman's note to *Antiq.* 20.196). We can hardly maintain that the entirety of the common people disliked or distrusted the chief priests. They followed them into war.

Not every chief priest fought to the bitter end, though many stayed until there was no more hope. When the Romans had invested Jerusalem, Josephus, standing outside the wall of the city, made a speech urging capitulation, and many of the aristocrats fled the city (*War* 6.114). Yet it is noteworthy that these aristocrats, mostly priests, had remained loyalists during most of the revolt, and they had not been executed by the Zealots when they overthrew Ananus and his supporters. Just as only one was killed by the mob when the revolt began to erupt, only some were killed by fanatics in its late stages. This means that some aristocrats, both priest and lay, could pass the most rigorous test of loyalty and were not suspected of being self-serving.

In ordinary times, the precise role that the chief priests played depended on circumstances, and in particular on the personality and character of the high priest. We shall return to more detailed consideration of their role in ch. 21, having said enough here to indicate that it might be appreciable.

There were also aristocratic lay people, who are covered by terms such as 'the powerful' (*dynatoi*) or 'the best known' (*gnōrimoi*) in Josephus and 'the elders' (*presbyteroi*) in the New Testament. Other terms appear to include both priestly and lay leaders: 'the first (leading) people' (*prōtoi*), 'the rulers' or 'magistrates' (*archontes*), 'the leaders' or 'eminent' (*hoi en telei*). The 'powerful' are generally lumped together with the chief priests when Josephus describes events in which the leading citizens play a role. I shall summarize just one incident that shows how he used various terms.

About the year 50 CE, during a clash between Samaritans and Galilean pilgrims passing through Samaria, one of the pilgrims was killed. A crowd came from Galilee, bent on revenge, but 'the best known' (*gnōrimoi*) went to the Roman procurator, Cumanus, to urge him to send troops and punish the murderers, thus putting an end to the matter. He did not do so. News reached Jerusalem, and many of the people there rushed to Samaria, though 'the magistrates' or 'rulers' (*archontes*) tried to restrain them. The magistrates, however, did not give up; and, clad in sackcloth, and with ashes on their heads, they went after the hotheads and tried to persuade them not to do anything rash, since a battle would surely lead Rome to intervene with a heavy hand. This appeal was effective, and the Jewish mob dispersed (though some smaller bands stayed on for pillage). 'The powerful' (*dynatoi*) Samaritans went to Syria to lay their case before the Roman legate, and 'the best known' Jews, including the high priest, did the same. The legate went to Caesarea and Lydda, in each place ordering executions of some of the guilty parties. He sent others to Rome to be tried by Claudius: two men of the 'highest power' (*dynatōtatoi*), namely, the chief priest Jonathan and the serving high priest Ananias, as well as Ananias' son, other 'best known' Jews and 'the most distinguished' Samaritans (*War* 2.232–44).[21]

This is a very typical narrative. Aristocratic priests are sometimes named, but sometimes lumped together; important laymen are seldom named. One has the impression of leading citizens, both chief priests and prominent laymen, who co-operated in trying to restrain people, thus also protecting them from Rome. They were not always effective: the mob in Jerusalem went to Samaria despite the appeals of the rulers. Often, however, they were effective: the rulers finally got the mob to disperse, at least partially without major bloodshed. In the end, the eminent had to answer to Rome. They were responsible for good order.

In general, the prominent lay people acted as did the chief priests. During the revolt, they displayed the same range of behaviour. With most of the chief priests, they tried to nip the revolt in the bud (*War* 2.301–422);[22] some (including Costobar and Saul, on whom see p. 324) fled Jerusalem as soon as it was certain that there would be war (*War* 2.556); some stayed and fought, as did some of the chief priests; when the Zealots and Idumaeans captured the city and killed the leading chief priests, they also executed prominent lay people; at each new stage of fanaticism, more of the eminent were brought forward to be tortured or executed; at each appeal from the Roman side, some of the aristocracy left the city. Yet, many stayed. One might have thought that the Zealot's purge of the aristocracy was complete, but it was not. Some of the formerly 'powerful' lived through it, stayed on to fight, and were later killed in further purges.[23]

It is quite reasonable to reproject information gained from the behaviour of the aristocracy during the revolt to earlier periods. Some aristocrats were greedy and self-seeking, but some tried to use their money and influence in what they perceived to be good causes, which ordinarily included keeping the Jewish populace and Roman soldiers apart; this, in turn, mostly required persuading people not to yield to the impulse to protest, yell insults, throw stones and the like. The aristocrats also, however, tried to present the people's side of a dispute to the procurator or prefect, and to urge him to be moderate in dealing with the populace. Some were prepared to lay their lives on the line in this cause, and to accept partial responsibility for the behaviour of the mob (as we saw in the story of the Galileans and Samaritans above). We can put this another way. Rome was going to hold *someone* responsible for the good behaviour of the populace. The people who accepted that responsibility were not simply public-spirited citizens motivated by the desire to risk their lives for the general welfare. People who seek authority have diverse and complicated motives. But once a wealthy priest became high priest, he was virtually *compelled* to do his best to mediate between the populace and the Roman official in Caesarea or Syria. The same is true of the chief priests and prominent lay people who took a role in public affairs. By far the greatest number of the aristocrats who accepted responsibility tried diligently to fulfil their obligations.

One of the things that is hardest to assess is the degree to which the aristocracy maltreated the ordinary people. Let us return to the list of six unfavourable stories above (p. 324). These mostly deal with *infighting* among the aristocracy. The hoodlums who acted for Saul and Costobar plundered the property of weaker people, but not of poor people, who did not have enough to make plunder worthwhile. Even the people who stole the tithes stole from the priests, not from the farmers, and they beat the farmers to make them turn over their tithes, not to coerce extra contributions (so Josephus). There is a lament in the Babylonian Talmud that refers to the same situation:

> Abba Saul b. Bothnith said in the name of Abba Joseph b. Hanin: 'Woe is me because of the house of Boethus; woe is me because of the staves! Woe is me because of the house of Hanin, woe is me because of their whisperings! Woe is me because of the house of Kathros, woe is me because of their pens! Woe is me because of the house of Ishmael the son of Phabi, woe is me because of their fists! For they are High Priests and their sons are [Temple] treasurers and their sons-in-law are trustees and their servants beat the people with staves.' (*Pesahim* 57a)

The chief priests of this generation – 59–66 CE – were not well-loved. They were harsh, they were callous, and they allowed their greed to get the better of them. I nevertheless note that many of them tried to fulfil the public responsibilities that their birth laid upon them, by keeping the Jewish citizenry and the Roman troops apart.

I have no wish to challenge the dictum of Lord Acton, that power corrupts and absolute power corrupts absolutely. We should, however, see the aristocrats in context. This is what Philo wrote about a man who was not born an aristocrat but who was in a position of power:

> Capito is the tax-collector for Judaea and cherishes a spite against the population. When he came there he was a poor man but by his rapacity and peculation he has amassed much wealth in various forms. (*Embassy* 199)

John the Baptist is reported to have urged the tax collectors to 'collect no more than is appointed you' (Luke 3.21). In the numerous stories told about the Jerusalem aristocracy, we do not find this sort of accusation: that they used the office of high priest, or their status as chief priests, in order to steal from the people. Even the pietist critics accused the holders of high priestly positions of plundering the sanctuary, not extorting money from farmers (and the like).[24] Modern scholars say that one or more of the chief priests had a monopoly on sacrificial victims, but we saw above that there is no evidence in favour of this and several considerations that count against it – one of them being that the sale of sacrificial animals was not a monopoly.[25] The silence of our sources *may* be only an accident. Perhaps someone extorted money from the common people. Certainly the Jerusalem aristocrats were not wise kings, concerned with the prosperity of the peasantry. But the general impression is that they used their inherited wealth to jockey for position rather than using their positions to squeeze additional money out of the peasants.

Sadducean religious principles

Only occasionally are we told that a given individual was a Sadducee (above, p. 318). As I explained above, I do not assume that all aristocrats were Sadducees, but I do assume that all or almost all Sadducees were aristocrats. Thus this is the most appropriate place to discuss the points that distinguished Sadducees from common Judaism. It should first be said, however, that they shared the essential points of common Jewish theology: God had chosen Israel, and Israelites were to obey the law. They should love God, thank him for his blessings, and treat other people decently, as the law requires. The Sadducees were less lenient than the Pharisees, but there is no reason to think that they were routinely vicious. They were, on the whole, good Jews.

Their 'doctrine' was defined by two principal and, some think, overlapping beliefs: (1) they accepted only the written law; (2) they denied the resurrection. Josephus also reports that they believed in free will (*War* 2.164f.; *Antiq.* 13.173); that is, they denied that God always controlled what happened. He offers two other generalizations about them: they were harsh in judgment and 'rather boorish in their behaviour', being rude even to their peers (*War* 2.166; *Antiq.* 20.199).

The New Testament confirms that they denied the resurrection (Mark 12.18 and parr.), and Acts depicts them as being the chief persecutors of the early Christian movement, while the Pharisee, Gamaliel, argued for leniency (Acts 4.1–6; 5.17, 33–39). Both points support Josephus' description.

The principal reason for thinking that not all the aristocrats were Sadducees is that some aristocrats believed in the resurrection (or some other form of 'renewed existence', to use Josephus' general term: *Apion* 2.218). Josephus, in the passage just cited and elsewhere, represents this belief as common to Jews, and he accepted it himself. He professed himself to be a Pharisee (*Life* 12), possibly for this reason, though by birth he was an aristocratic priest (an ancestor had married the daughter of the Hasmonean Jonathan). There is no way of knowing how many members of the aristocracy shared belief in an afterlife, but it was a common and popular belief, and some held it.

It is generally supposed that the Sadducees denied the afterlife because they accepted only the biblical text, not further 'traditions'. The Bible contains the sentence 'many of those who sleep in the dust of the earth shall awake, some to everlasting life, and some to shame and everlasting contempt' (Dan. 12.2), but resurrection and immortality are not prominent in it. Further, Daniel is a very late book, dating from approximately 165 BCE, and the idea of resurrection cannot be found clearly in the earlier biblical books. Isa. 26.19, 'the dead shall live', is metaphorical. Possibly Sadducees, like modern biblical critics, distinguished dates and recognized metaphors. Or, more plausibly, perhaps they accepted only what was in the Pentateuch. In any case, scholars usually connect their literalism with their rejection of life after death.

Things cannot have been quite this simple; strict adherence to the written law is not an adequate explanation of the Sadducees' views.[26] As Daube put it, that the Sadducees are to be explained as 'literalists' 'is a myth'.[27] What is in the Bible partially depends on what spectacles one wears. Later, the rabbis wished to argue that the doctrine of the resurrection is in the law (*Sanhedrin* 10.1),[28] and so they found it there. According to Matt. 22.32, Jesus 'proved' the resurrection by quoting Ex. 3.6. We may be certain that the Sadducees accepted at least some practices that are not in the law. I do not mean that the Pharisees forced them to follow their views, but that the Bible does not give enough detail about various matters to allow anyone to follow it without supplementing it. It seldom, for example, correlates crimes and punishments.[29] 'Whoever strikes a man so that he dies shall be put to death' (Ex. 21.12). How? When it came to the actual execution, the guilty party had to be killed in some particular way. The Bible mentions various modes of execution (stoning, burning and so on), but these are only sometimes related to particular crimes. The Mishnah tries to straighten all this out (tractate *Sanhedrin*). The present point is that anyone who was actually in power had to decide one thing rather than another. Since some people who followed the Sadducees had authority over life and death before Pompey's conquest (e.g. Hyrcanus I), they must have had non-biblical rules about execution.

Similarly the Sadducean high priests had to accept some calendar or other. The Bible gives hints about calendar arrangement, but it does not prescribe a calendar. The Sadducees must have been conscious of this fact, since the Qumranians, and possibly others, had a calendar different from the one accepted in Jerusalem. Again, the Sadducees had to follow a particular practice that was not explicitly prescribed in the Pentateuch. It cannot be the case that they accepted no non-biblical practices and beliefs at all.

We need to look more carefully at precisely what Josephus wrote about the Sadducees, Pharisees and non-biblical traditions:

> The Pharisees handed down [*paredosan*] to the populace certain regulations [*nomina*] from [their] forebears [*ek paterōn diadochēs*], which are not written in the laws of Moses, and which on this account are rejected by the Sadducean group, who hold that only those regulations should be considered valid which are written down, and that those which are from the tradition of the fathers (*ek paradoseōs tōn paterōn*) do not need to be kept. (*Antiq.* 13.297)

My guess is that Josephus' implication that the Sadducees rejected *anything* that was not written in the laws of Moses (that is, from Ex. 12 to the end of Deuteronomy) is an overstatement, and that in fact they rejected the Pharisaic 'traditions of the fathers', as well as, of course, the special Essene revelations. Put another way, they rejected non-biblical traditions of which they did not approve, especially those that *characterized* the other parties.[30]

They may well have engaged in creative exegesis in order to base customs of which they approved on the Bible. Possibly they argued that the calendar was based on biblical interpretation. One cannot reasonably find the requirement to intercalate a month in the Bible,[31] but they may have managed to do so. We must always remember that interpretation is a very flexible tool. Since the Sadducees' literature did not survive, we do not have an example that shows how they derived something from the Bible even though we would now judge that it is not there, but we can give examples from the Dead Sea Scrolls and rabbinic literature. I shall offer just one. Lev. 23.37f. states that at the 'appointed feasts' the priests are to offer sacrifices 'apart from sabbath offerings', 'apart from votive offerings', and 'apart from freewill offerings'. That is, on these occasions the special offerings are in addition to any other offerings, such as sabbath offerings and freewill offerings. The *Covenant of Damascus* reverses the evident meaning of the text: 'Let no one offer on the altar on the Sabbath [any offering] except the burnt-offering of the Sabbath; for thus it is written, "apart from your Sabbath-offerings"' (CD 11.17f.). By simply prefacing 'apart from sabbath offerings' with 'let no one offer . . . except', CD rules that when sabbath and festival overlapped, only the sabbath offerings were to be made. This opens up endless possibilities. If the Sadducees engaged in equivalent exegesis, they could have proved that numerous things were in the Bible that we no longer find there.

In studying the few cases in which we have probably reliable remembrance of Sadducean interpretation, we can find an instance in which the Sadducees were closer to the biblical text than the Pharisees, and one that goes the other way. (1) They opposed the Pharisaic practice of joining house to house in order to permit vessels to be carried from one house to the other on the sabbath (*Eruvin* 6.2). Since this is one of the Pharisaic traditions that has not a particle of biblical support, the Sadducees who argued against it had the Bible on their side. (2) The Sadducees thought that when the high priest enters the Holy of Holies on the Day of Atonement, he should put incense on the coals before he opens the curtain. The Pharisees thought that he should hold the censer in one hand and the incense in the other, somehow managing to carry them separately past the curtain (perhaps by going past it backwards, hoping that the heavy folds would not knock the censer and incense out of his hands.)[32] Here the Pharisees are closer to the text of Leviticus, while the Sadducees show prudent common sense.[33] They, after all, supplied some of the high priests.

We cannot, unfortunately, go much further than this in understanding how and why they differed from the Pharisees. It seems that, against the Pharisees, they *claimed* to follow only the biblical law. This cannot, however, have been entirely true, since the Bible requires not only interpretation but also supplementation. It may be that they had their own body of additional rules and rejected only those that the Pharisees called 'the traditions of the fathers'. This possibility is supported by rabbinic references to a Sadducean book of decrees.[34] Even so, we do not know how they decided what the correct interpretations and supplements were, nor how they justified them. *Possibly* the Sadducees practised very creative exegesis and found all sorts of things in the Bible. Perhaps they were content to follow the Bible approximately, staying as close to the text as seemed reasonable at the time. If the Sadducees debated other groups, they would have had to engage in exegesis of the scriptural text. It may be, however, that they did not bother to debate, but simply followed their own views whenever they were in a position to do so – which was a lot of the time. However they derived and justified them, they had their own rules and rejected the traditions that characterized the Pharisees.

Hostility and polemic

Various pious groups regarded the aristocratic priests, some of whom were Sadducees, as not sufficiently strict in keeping the law. In ch. 10 we saw several charges against the priests, many of which were directed especially against the leading priests.[35] The *Psalms of Solomon* accuse the priests of impurity and various kinds of immorality. That the targets of attack were the Hasmoneans is clear in *Ps. Sol.* 17.6–8: the Jewish leaders cast 'us' out and established a worldly monarchy. The original author(s) of the *Covenant of Damascus* probably also opposed the Hasmoneans, but later readers may have understood its accusations as being appropriate to subsequent ruling priesthoods. One of the criticisms of these two documents, lack of strictness with regard to avoiding female impurity, appears in the Mishnah as a criticism of the Sadducees (*Niddah* 4.1f.). I do not suppose that the author of this mishnah had in mind the same people as the authors of *Ps. Sol.* and CD, but we see continuity of polemic by pietists against others, especially against priests and aristocrats.

If it is true, as I suspect, that the accusations against the priests cited above were mostly against the aristocratic priests, we learn that they had enemies. This is inevitable; leaders and rulers always do. What is surprising is that so many contemporary attacks against the priesthood, especially against its leading members, survived. The Essenes doubtless kept their bitterest and least temperate accusations private; they may have carried on public or quasi-public debate in more courteous terms.[36] The gospels circulated after the destruction of Jerusalem, and for the most part outside of Palestine, and the authors were free to criticize priests and Pharisees as they wished. The *Psalms of Solomon* seem to have circulated more widely. They come from a time of tumult, however, and possibly there was no opportunity for retaliation. It is still noteworthy that there are more contemporary accusations of the aristocratic priests than there are of Herod (for example). One suspects that the priests were less ruthless towards those who criticized them. Mostly, despite criticisms, the aristocrats went about their business. They held actual power: the temple, wealth and armed guards; they could shrug off polemical accusations. Further, they did not agree that they were impious or unworthy. Most of them were, by their own lights, devout Jews, pious in the ways required by the Bible.

Morality and public responsibility

We historians make moral judgments about the people we study all the time, and sometimes we even admit it. These moral judgments are especially clear in the present chapter. I have been arguing that the Sadducees were on average upright Jews; and, against the general opinion, I think that this is true of the aristocracy as well. What we need to do is to avoid thinking of and portraying rich first-century Jews as if they were wealthy cattlemen in a B Western. Even the better Westerns do not portray all cattle barons as wicked and all sheep ranchers as good. With regard to the people considered in this chapter, I have thus far argued that the charges of immorality, which are true in some cases, should not be considered to be altogether true in all cases over a period of decades. I wish now to take up three topics in order to give more nuance to our understanding of the Jerusalem aristocracy.

First, individual immorality, such as greed or sexual promiscuity, does not necessarily make a person a bad leader. In the modern democracies, such flaws, if made public at the right time, may cost a politician an election or an office; but, looking back, few historians will think that the fact that Roosevelt had a mistress, or that Kennedy had affairs, proves that they were bad presidents. We can readily apply this to the first century. A given aristocratic priest may have committed adultery or engaged in homosexual activity. In ancient eyes, if it was known, this rendered him completely unfit. But he may have kept his sexual life private and have been honest, decent and kind, solicitous of the welfare of his parents, wife, children and the public. Even a person who was greedy and avaricious, who tried to beat down tradesmen and who left his bills unpaid for as long as possible, might have been perfectly trustworthy in public affairs. And so on. Human nature has not changed much. Such things are possible now, and they were possible then.

We may even have, in the person of Ananias, an example of personal immorality and reasonable diligence when in office. He was the high priest who was sent to Rome, to answer for his conduct before Claudius, after the strife between Jews and Samaritans (above, pp. 329f.). We do not know precisely what role he had played. Was he one of those who displayed the signs of mourning and who rushed to Samaria? This is, in my judgment, only a question of how *active* he was. Surely his position on the issue was that of the rest of the aristocracy: to prevent the clash from spreading; to persuade the procurator, the legate and finally Claudius that the Samaritans were the trouble-makers; to reduce the number of Jews who were executed; and to keep Roman troops and a violent Jewish mob apart. In the end, he had to answer for his behaviour and for the conduct of a lot of people whom he could not directly control. He may have been personally dishonest. This does not prove that he did not try to be a good middle-man.

Secondly, when we are considering a remote time or place, we tend to make simple equations between rich and bad, and between poor and good. People who live in the country not infrequently think of 'rich city folk' as being also morally depraved. We do the same sort of thing when we look back. According to Horsley, rich people in first-century Palestine were rich because they robbed poor people: 'the rich man's wealth was, almost by definition, gained by "unrighteous mammon"'.[37] Rajak assumed that the wealth of the wealthy proves their iniquity and supports the idea of class war.[38] Certainly the aristocrats were rich. Since the ideal of equal distribution of goods had not yet arisen, it is a bit hard on the Jerusalem aristocracy to say that their wealth proves dishonesty. There is no reason to think that the members of Jerusalem's oligarchy were worse than the wealthy of other cities. The prominent people who used their money and influence for the common weal were appreciated, as they always have been. That high rank and office were accompanied by a large house and servants is true. To this day, leading churchmen (e.g. the Archbishop of Canterbury, the Methodist Bishop of the Dallas area) have offices, staffs and nice houses. Such privileges, even today, when egalitarianism is at least a known ideal, are not taken to prove dishonesty. Looking back, it is easy to say that the rich should have shared their surplus with the poor. But today, many of us – not just bishops – have spare bedrooms in our houses, while others are homeless. Those of us with spare rooms should do more. I am still unwilling to say, however, that people who have big houses are necessarily wicked.

That rich people were wicked seems not to have been what average first-century Jews thought. The crowd asked Archelaus for a purer high priest, not a poorer one. We do not know that the reason they killed Ananias and followed Ananus – to stay with my favourite example – was that Ananias was richer. Rajak and others exaggerate the degree to which the civil war that accompanied the revolt against the Romans was a class war. While many aristocrats favoured peace, one of the first instigators of revolt was an aristocratic priest, Eleazar, son of the infamous Ananias. Other aristocratic priests, as we have noted several times, led the revolt and served as generals. They had the backing of the Jerusalemites. Goodman shows that members of the 'ruling class' 'remained actively involved in the revolt right up to the destruction of the city in AD 70'. Even those who were responsible for the overthrow of Ananus were themselves members of the elite.[39] They also carried out, as we saw, a purge of the aristocrats – that is, of some of the aristocrats. During the civil conflict in Jerusalem, being an aristocrat seems to have been almost a necessary condition for being executed, but it was not a sufficient condition. There were aristocrats among the purgers and many whom the purgers did not touch. Many aristocrats lived through it and continued to fight (above at n. 23).

Thirdly, for the general purposes of this study, there is more at stake than our approval or disapproval of a small group of rich people. The habit of accusing the aristocracy of immorality supports the view that the wealthy had no following, and may have helped create it. Scholars who accept the standard view of the aristocracy – that they were *both* wicked and hated – give the wrong overall impression of the period: the populace sided with 'their representatives', the Pharisees, against the aristocratic priests (or, in some scholarly reconstructions, against all the priests), whom they despised. They would not co-operate with the priests, who were morally bankrupt and who got their way only by coercion and oppression. An alternative is that the populace hated the chief priests and admired the Pharisees, but the Pharisees were in their way even worse than the aristocrats, and they despised the populace for not being sufficiently pure. We here leave the Pharisees out of account and emphasize that in both these views the relationship between the general public, especially in Jerusalem, and the aristocracy is misrepresented.

With regard to the *personal qualities* of the aristocrats: anyone who gives more-or-less equal weight to Josephus' various narratives about aristocrats – leaving completely aside his glowing generalizations – will conclude that some aristocrats were admirable, while others were despicable. He excoriates some and praises others. With regard to *standing with the populace* and *leadership*, the same applies: admirable and admired; despicable and despised. So many individual stories show the aristocrats as influencing the populace, and doing so in a good cause – especially protecting them from getting into trouble with Roman troops – that we must accept that many of the aristocrats in fact behaved in this way.

It is commonly said that the aristocrats disappeared as a class after the destruction of Jerusalem. By the time of the Mishnah, the Sadducees and other aristocrats were regarded as insignificant and as having been dominated by the lay 'sages'. Josephus' history, however, shows that they maintained their position until the fall of Jerusalem. Even then, some escaped, and after the war they played a role in community life. Rajak has proposed, I think correctly, that Josephus' *Life* was written in the context of criticism of his behaviour by other surviving aristocrats.[40] Descendants of the one known aristocratic Pharisee, Simon son of Gamaliel, survived and greatly influenced the rabbinic movement. The dominance of the aristocratic priesthood, however, was decisively broken by the revolt, never to revive.

To summarize: Our evidence for the Sadducees is very slight, and for the aristocrats it is sporadic. We know a few points about disagreements between the Sadducees and other parties (fate, non-biblical traditions, and life after death), but even on these we do not know precisely what the Sadducees believed, since we have no Sadducean sources. We can offer very good generalizations about the role and behaviour of the aristocrats during the Roman period narrowly defined (6–41, 44–66 CE), and Josephus' description of the period of revolt allows us to describe a range of aristocratic behaviour. I assume that what is generally true of the aristocrats is generally true of the Sadducees: some were self-seeking, some were motivated by concern for the public welfare.

Josephus and the New Testament both show that the high priest was the leading person in Jerusalem during the years of the Roman prefects and procurators. At least some high priests were Sadducees. The Romans expected not only the high priest, but also the aristocrats in general to control the populace and to maintain order. The aristocrats did this with fair success, and the populace was generally willing to heed them.

16

The Essenes and the Dead Sea Sect I: Origins, History, Membership and Organization

The Essenes, once the object of fanciful speculation, are now the best-known Jewish group of our period. Thanks to the discovery of manuscripts and a settlement near the Dead Sea, we could discuss their institutions and beliefs in considerable detail. In this case, however, I shall present the material in less detail than I have in previous chapters. There are four reasons for this. First, I wish to keep the description of a small group short. It is misleading to say that one is writing about 'Judaism' and then to write more pages on a tiny and fairly marginal sect than on 'most people'. Secondly, there are very good brief accounts of the Essenes, but relatively little on common Judaism.[1] Thirdly, both the aristocrats and the Pharisees (in my view) need to be saved from misinterpretation, while this is not true of the Essenes. They were not major players in politics and society, and no one says they were; they had complicated theological views about grace and perfection, and everyone acknowledges this. The evidence is excellent, and consequently central issues of identity and basic principles are not subject to the same range of academic disagreement as is the case in the discussion of the Pharisees, the aristocrats, and ordinary people. Finally, the major disputed point has to do primarily with the origin and early years of the party, which fall outside our main period.

Origins and sub-groups

We saw in ch. 2 the prevailing consensus, which is attractively and conveniently presented in books by Geza Vermes and Michael Knibb (n. 1 above). In approximately 152 BCE a group of pietists (often equated with some of the Hasideans of I Maccabees) was joined by 'the Teacher of Righteousness', a Zadokite priest, possibly the unnamed high priest who immediately preceded the Hasmonean Jonathan. Thus was formed the Essene party or one branch of it. The question is whether or not we should use the word 'Essene' before the Teacher joined the group or begin to use it only from that point on. In either case, the party came to be composed of at least two branches, one a monastic and fully separatist sect that lived near the Dead Sea (from about 140BCE), the other a group that married and did not entirely separate from common Jewish religious practice (on 'monastic', see n. 6). The *Community Rule* (1QS) and some of the other Scrolls found near Wadi Qumran speak for the monastic group, while the *Covenant of Damascus* (CD) speaks for the town-dwelling group. Some scholars take one of the groups, usually the Qumranian, to be the parent of the other. Others propose, more plausibly, that the Qumran sect was a splinter movement.[2]

This overall view rests on identifying characters in the Essene literature, who are generally designated by nicknames, such as the Wicked Priest and the Spouter of Lies, with one another and with known personages. Further, it rests on harmonizing a wide range of evidence: the biblical commentaries found at Qumran; the *Covenant of Damascus* (fragments of which were found at Qumran, but which circulated more widely and which was first discovered in medieval manuscripts found in Egypt); archaeology; Josephus; the elder Pliny (who refers to the Essenes as living near the Dead Sea); and Philo. One of the problems that historians regularly face is when to harmonize fragments of evidence and when to segregate them. In the case of the Essenes, the evidence does not fit together completely smoothly, but it fits well enough to allow most scholars to be content with harmonization.

I shall mention just one point that has to do with the origin of the party to show both how evidence is fitted together and also some of the questions that harmonization raises. The Teacher of Righteousness is mentioned in CD, the *Commentary on Habakkuk* (1QpHab), and apparently in the *Commentary on Psalm 37* (4QpPs37) (in a line that is only partially preserved). In 4QpPs37 3.15 he is called 'the priest', which probably should be read as *the* priest, that is, the high priest, and in 1QpHab 11.5, 12 he also seems to be equated with 'the priest'. In 1QpHab 2.2; 5.10 he is contrasted with 'the Liar', and in 11.4f. we learn that he was persecuted by 'the Wicked Priest'. In the list of high priests in I Maccabees, no one is named for the years 159–152 BCE (see I Macc. 9.56; 10.18–21), while according to Josephus for seven years there was no high priest (*Antiq.* 20.237). Putting these pieces together, and sometimes preferring one bit of evidence to another, numerous scholars have concluded that there was a high priest from 159–152, that he was a Zadokite, that Jonathan deposed him, and that he became the Teacher of Righteousness.[3] One may cite two further passages to support the view that the Teacher was a Zadokite priest. The Teacher was the one 'to whom God made known all the mysteries of the words of his servants the prophets' (1QpHab 7.4f.); the covenant to which the Qumran sect was loyal was the Zadokite priests' covenant (e.g. 1QS 5.2). Both passages refer to mediators of the correct understanding of scripture and God's will, the Teacher of Righteousness and the Zadokite priests; the similarity of role argues in favour of identifying the Teacher as a Zadokite. One can then either equate the Liar and the Wicked Priest, or propose that the Teacher had two different enemies. In either case, Jonathan was the Wicked Priest. Further, the *Covenant of Damascus*, apparently speaking of the Wicked Priest and his followers, says that 'the chief of the kings of the Greeks' wreaked vengeance on them (CD 8.11). Jonathan was killed by the Greek-speaking Syrians, while Simon was killed by his own brother-in-law. Thus this reference fits Jonathan. Finally, the date of the Teacher is approximately confirmed by references to 390 years and 20 years in CD 1.5–10: 390 years after the exile marks the beginning of the sect; the Teacher joined it 20 years later. A handbook of dates will now give 196–191 as being 390 years after the exile, but since errors about the length of the Persian period were often made, that date can be shifted down by several years: the party started *c.* 175 and the teacher joined it *c.* 152.

This combination of evidence to make a total picture can be challenged.[4] (1) The line that is usually read as saying 390 years *after* Nebuchadnezzar (CD 1.5) does not contain the word 'after'; and, besides, Jewish knowledge of the length of the Persian period was so slight that any date that refers to it must be looked at with extreme scepticism. Moreover, the references to years in CD 1 appear to be later glosses, added to the text by a reviser. (2) It is possible that the various enemies, to whom different Scrolls give nicknames, lived at different periods. The Scrolls were not all written at the same time, and it may be an error to suppose that several of them refer to the same enemies and events; the use of nicknames means that general characterizations could disguise different people. In CD 20.14f. the 'unique Teacher' is contrasted with the 'man of Lying'. Is this the same as the contrast of the Teacher of Righteousness and the Liar in 1QpHab? That is possible, but not certain.

My intention here is neither to prove nor disprove the dominant hypothesis (the party as we know it originated about the year 152; the Teacher of Righteousness was a Zadokite priest of that period). I wish rather to illustrate the fact that, even when we have a lot of evidence – much more evidence than exists for the origins of the Sadducees and Pharisees – there are problems. While not all the evidence fits into a single view without a rub, the convergences are greater than one ordinarily finds in the study of ancient religion. I am happy enough with the harmonization proposed by Geza Vermes and others, which has been accepted by numerous scholars, of whom the most recent leading spokesman in the English-speaking world is Michael Knibb. The question of Essene origins, which leads also to the assessment of other early Jewish documents, especially *Jubilees*, is still a fertile field for research, as will be readily granted by those who support the dominant hypothesis. The origin and early years of the Essenes, however, fall outside the main interest of the present study.

What is necessary here is for me to make clear how I propose to use the sources that describe Essene religious practice and theology: principally Josephus, CD, the *Community Rule* (1QS), the *Thanksgiving Hymns* (1QH), the *Temple Scroll* (11QT), and Philo. I take it that these all do describe *the Essenes* (that is, various branches of the Essenes at various times, not all of them all the time), although that party label occurs only in Philo and Josephus. There are numerous overlaps among these sources, both in practice and theology, and that they all refer to the same *general* party or movement can hardly be doubted.[5] There are also, however, substantial differences. 1QS is a law code for the Qumran sect, a separatist community that rejected common Judaism as represented by the Jerusalem priests. 1QS does not mention women, though it gives numerous special purity rules, and so we may take the Qumran sect to have been monastic.[6] Part of CD is also a law code, but the laws are quite different from those of 1QS; among other things, its members married and sacrificed at the temple.

The question of marriage allows us to illustrate the information on the Essenes provided by Josephus and Philo. They both understood celibacy to have been the Essene norm. According to Philo, 'no Essene takes a wife' (*Hypothetica* 11.14). Josephus wrote that the Essenes did not marry (*War* 2.120; cf. *Antiq*.18.21), but then he added that marriage was practised by 'another order', which engaged in sex only for the sake of procreation (*War* 2.160f.). Thus he seems to refer to both the Essenes of CD and those of 1QS. He does not, however, separate his general description of Essene religious practice according to these two groups. Some of his statements can be paralleled in 1QS, some in CD; but some have no parallel. Further, he does not say anything about Qumran: he wrote, instead, that the Essenes settled 'in large numbers in every [city]' (*War* 2.124). He did not describe precisely what we have in 1QS and CD combined.[7] Thus on this point his information is both very good (some married and some did not) and inadequate (he does not mention the isolated community on the shores of the Dead Sea). We may assume that his evidence on other points also varies in quality, but we cannot always know what is high quality and what is not.

In this discussion, I shall usually suppose that Josephus' comments describe *some* Essene practice. Perhaps on some point or points he was completely in error, but for the sake of the present description I shall assume not. There may have been more sub-groups than are reflected in our two principal legal documents, and some of Josephus' unparalleled evidence might apply to a branch of the party about which we otherwise know nothing. Philo I shall treat more cursorily, citing him primarily when there is a strong parallel with Josephus or one of the legal documents. I suspect, here as elsewhere, that Josephus had read Philo, at least the *Hypothetica*, though it is possible that the two authors had a common source. In any case, there are some striking parallels between their accounts.[8]

History

We know nothing about historical developments within the Essene party (though there are hypotheses based on attempts to stratify the literature, which I regard as too speculative to be helpful) and very little about the history of its relations with other Jews. I shall, however, summarize the available evidence.

The archaeology of the settlement at Qumran, especially the discovery of coins, shows that a small group inhabited the site from about 150 or 140 BCE until approximately the death of John Hyrcanus (104 BCE). The community was enlarged in a second stage of its occupation, which extended from the end of phase one to the early years of Herod (beginning 37 BCE). It was destroyed by an earthquake, possibly one that is known to have occurred in 31 BCE, which tallies with the datings derived from coins. After some decades, it was rebuilt and was inhabited until it was destroyed by the Romans in 68 CE. Study of the handwriting of the Scrolls shows that they were copied (not necessarily composed)[9] during this same period, except for a few biblical manuscripts, which may be older.

Immediately below we shall see literary evidence that indicates that Herod was favourably disposed to the Essenes and also that they may have lived in one area in Jerusalem. Possibly this evidence fits into the outline provided by archaeology: when the settlement at Qumran was destroyed by earthquake, Herod was king. He was friendly towards all the Essenes, and even the most radical group felt comfortable living in Jerusalem while he ruled. They had, after all, a common enemy: the Hasmoneans.

The earliest reference to the Essenes in literature is Josephus' story of an individual, Judas the Essene, who is said to have predicted the assassination of Antigonus I by his brother Aristobulus I in 104 BCE (*War* 1.78–81; *Antiq.* 13.311–13). We may assume that Judas did not have a solitary mission, and thus that at this time there was an Essene community in Jerusalem. According to the account in the *Antiquities*, Judas was instructing his followers in foretelling the future. Further, all the sources emphasize that community was important to the Essenes, a point that we shall take up below.

The next reference is to another prophet, Manaêmus, who, when he saw Herod as a boy, predicted that he would be king, and further that he would forget piety and justice. Josephus comments that many Essenes 'have indeed been vouchsafed a knowledge of divine things because of their virtue' (*Antiq.* 15.373–9).

When Herod demanded an oath of loyalty from his subjects (*c.* 20 BCE), he excused the Essenes (*Antiq.* 15.371). According to Josephus, Herod held them in honour (15.372). Subsequently he remarks that they refused to take oaths (*War* 2.135), except, of course, the oaths taken on entry to the community (see below; *War* 2.139–42).

Josephus mentions yet another Essene prophet, Simon. He interpreted a dream of Archelaus to mean that his situation would change for the worse. Within five days the prediction began to be fulfilled (*Antiq.* 17.346–8).

The Essenes, like the Pharisees (as we shall see), now disappear from Josephus' history for several decades. Josephus, of course, wrote primarily the history of rulers, wars and public tumults; groups are not mentioned unless they have an effect on a ruler or play a substantial role in a military adventure or other notable public activity. This explains why the chief priests disappear when Herod is king: he dominated public action, and the priestly aristocracy had little to do except sacrifice. The Essenes and Pharisees played a role in Herod's affairs only a few times, and so Josephus seldom mentioned them. After Archelaus, Rome governed Judaea directly, and the prefect or procurator related to the populace primarily through the high priest and his associates. Thus Josephus does not mention the parties during this period. Once one understands this aspect of Josephus' history, it is predictable that the Essenes will reappear at the time of the revolt, and so they do. John the Essene was one of the commanders appointed by the common (revolutionary) council or assembly, being given responsibility for Lydda, Joppa and nearby areas in the northwest of Judaea (*War* 2.567). He died during an attack on Ascalon (*War* 3.11–19). After the Roman victory, the Essenes showed great endurance under torture, refusing 'to blaspheme their lawgiver or to eat some forbidden thing' (*War* 2.152f.).

It is likely that the Essenes who fought alongside other Jews were from the town-dwelling branch (or branches), while the Qumranians did not fight until their settlement was attacked *c.* 68 CE. They probably remained separate to the end. It would be helpful to know how the Essenes thought about the revolt. According to Philo, they were completely pacifist and did not even own weapons (*Every Good Man is Free* 78). We know from the Scrolls that at least some of them thought that there would be a great war, 'the war of the Sons of Light against the Sons of Darkness', in which the Angels and God himself would fight on their side, and which would end with the destruction of the wicked and the victory of the sect, who would then take over Jerusalem (the *War Rule*, 1QM). Possibly they identified the actual revolt with the ultimate war against the wicked. This would have justified their willingness to fight, even though they may have declined to participate in earlier uprisings, thus earning the reputation of pacifism.

The community resident at Qumran was never larger than a few hundred.[10] According to Philo and Josephus, the Essene party numbered about 4,000 (*Good Man* 75; *Antiq.* 18.20). If that is anywhere near correct, most members lived in ordinary settled areas. We saw above that Josephus wrote that they occupied not just one city, but that many lived in each city (*War* 2.124).[11] In one of his accounts, Philo wrote that they 'live in villages and avoid the cities' as being impure (*Good Man* 76), while in the other that they live 'in many cities . . . and in many villages' (*Hypoth.* 11.1). It may well have been an issue for Essenes whether or not to live in Jerusalem. Josephus' individual stories about Essene prophets indicate that some could be found near the court, which implies that they did not always avoid Jerusalem; Josephus also mentions a 'gate of the Essenes' in Jerusalem, which makes it likely that some Essenes lived there, at least some of the time, perhaps especially during the reign of Herod.[12] CD forbids its members to have sexual relations in Jerusalem (12.1f.), which may imply that its readers went to Jerusalem to sacrifice but did not ordinarily live there. We may conclude that most Essenes lived in towns and villages, and that at least sometimes an appreciable number lived in Jerusalem, though we do not know what sexual rules Essenes who lived in Jerusalem followed, whether those of CD and the *Temple Scroll*, which prohibit sex in Jerusalem, or a less restrictive code.[13] If married Essenes had sex only for the sake of procreation, they could have lived in Jerusalem and spent only enough time outside it for the woman to conceive each year.

Essenes engaged in the normal occupations. Most, including those at Qumran, worked the land. The Judaean wilderness near the Dead Sea is extremely arid, and the group that lived there relied on being able to fill large pools when it rained in the hills above. This took care of water for drinking and bathing. Below the settled area, however, nearer the sea, there is a spring that permits crops to be grown. The Qumranians could also have kept sheep and goats. The other occupation of which Qumran gives us knowledge is the production of scrolls. The sect's scribes were very skilled, but probably their work was for internal consumption only and did not bring cash into the community.

Philo emphasized that the Essenes lived a life of voluntary poverty, growing just enough food and making just enough of the other necessities to support life (*Good Man* 76f.; *Hypoth.* 11.8f.). He added that they had a single treasury, into which all revenue went, and that even their clothes were held in common (*Good Man* 86f.; *Hypoth.* 11.10–12). They also lived together, 'formed into clubs, bands of comradeship with common meals' (*Hypoth.* 11.5). Josephus wrote that they practised community of goods, and that in every town one of their number was appointed to provide travelling members with food and clothing (*War* 2.122, 125; cf. *Antiq.* 18.20).

The surrender of private property is a main feature of 1QS. It figures in the preamble, which deals with membership (1.11f.). Subsequently we learn how this requirement was applied: after an extensive probationary period the new sectarian's private goods were handed over to the Bursar (6.19f.). Only after a further trial period, however, were they mingled with the community property (6.22). Lying about property resulted in exclusion from the common meal for one year (6.24f.).

Josephus' second point, that travelling Essenes were provided for, seems to be matched in the *Covenant of Damascus*. According to it the members gave two days' wages each month to the overseer, who used the money to provide for the needy, presumably the needy members of the party (CD 14.12–16).

The kind of information that Josephus and Philo provide is noteworthy: they tell us that the Essenes practised community of goods and charity. From the legal documents, we learn that the monastic wing of the party practised complete community of goods, while the town-dwellers made monthly donations to a central treasury that provided charity. It is reasonable to think that married, town-dwelling Essenes contributed two days' pay per month (CD), while Philo's view that all members of the party contributed their entire income to the central treasury is unrealistic, as is Josephus' statement that the entire property of all members was given to the community (*War* 2.122). We probably find here only the normal sort of exaggeration to which strange practices lead. The Essene documents allow us to make distinctions that Philo and Josephus do not provide.

We shall now describe some of the major characteristics of the Essenes, focusing especially on what distinguished them from other Jews. A partial outline of the theology of the Scrolls will conclude the discussion. The general picture that will emerge will be this: a group of dedicated people who lived under an extraordinarily strict regimen, who surrendered most personal freedoms to the community, and who were subject to a strict hierarchy. They waited for the war of the endtime, when they would destroy first their Israelite enemies, then the Gentiles, and take control of Jerusalem. They would construct the temple to suit themselves and continue their lives of piety and purity. The discipline of the monastic group was stricter than that of the married group, but the latter was still quite strict.

Membership

One did not become an Essene overnight. Josephus describes a two-stage novitiate. During the first year, the would-be Essene began to observe some of the rules, but in important ways he remained an outsider. After a year, if worthy, he could 'share the purer water that was used for purification' but could not attend meetings. After two years in this stage, he had to swear 'tremendous oaths', and only then could he touch 'the common food' (*War* 2.137–9). The *Community Rule* also has a two-stage novitiate, though the details are different. A person who volunteered for membership was examined by 'the Guardian' and then admitted to the covenant and instructed in the rules. He had to stand public scrutiny before his admission was confirmed (1QS 6.13–16). Apparently at this stage, when he 'entered the covenant', he took the oath of membership, to observe the laws of Moses as revealed to the Zadokite priests (1.18–2.10; 5.7–11). He was then on probation for a year. If he passed, he could eat the Pure Meal (discussed below). After a further one-year probation he was again examined. If he was once more successful, he could share the Drink of the congregation and his property was mingled with that of the community. He was then also allowed to attend meetings and speak (6.18–23).

Since lying about one's property was a serious offence, it is probable that the oath (or one of the oaths; possibly there was one at each stage) included a declaration of possessions. Josephus gives a substantial list of things covered by the oath: piety, justice, hatred of the unjust, defence of the just, truthfulness and fidelity, kindness to inferiors, hatred of lies and love of truth, not to keep secrets from the other members, nor to disclose theirs to non-members, and so on (*War* 2.139–42). In the *Community Rule* (1QS 5.7–11) and the *Covenant of Damascus* (CD 15.5–16.6) the main content of the oath is the pledge 'to return to the law of Moses', and 1QS immediately adds 'in accordance with all that has been revealed of it to the sons of Zadok, the Keepers of the covenant . . . and to the multitude of the men of *their* covenant'. The general context in CD implies very much the same thing: the oath was to obey the law as the group interpreted it. Some of their interpretations cut them off from the rest of Judaism, either partially (CD) or completely (1QS). After the oath was taken, disobedience was severely punished.

1QS does not mention the major transgressions of the biblical law. One may only imagine what the Qumranians would have done if a member committed a serious offence, such as stealing, murdering or engaging in homosexual

relations with another member. They lived in a self-enclosed world, outside
the common law, and presumably they would try criminals and, if need be,
execute them. The offences that are actually mentioned are lying with regard to
property, answering impatiently, swearing 'when frightened by affliction'
while reading the Bible or praying, speaking angrily to a priest, insulting a
companion, bearing malice, speaking foolishly, falling asleep during a public
meeting, spitting in an assembly – and so on. The monastic sect, that is, had
monastic rules. One is only surprised that there is no prohibition of having
special friends, since special friendships disrupt community life and
sometimes create moral problems. Perhaps this was not necessary, since
members sat in prescribed places, depending on their rank.

A monastic order with monastic rules naturally applied monastic penalties to
those who transgressed. Offenders were either excluded from the Pure Meal,
or they suffered a reduction in their food allowance, or both. (For offences and
punishments, see 1QS 6.24–7.25; 8.16–9.2).[14]

The *Covenant of Damascus* reckons with the possibility of capital offences. A
witness to a capital crime should tell the Guardian, who wrote it down; if a
second witness saw the same kind of transgression on another occasion, the
case was considered proved. Two witnesses to a single offence, apparently a
capital offence, sufficed to have the sinner excluded from the Pure Meal. In
case of an offence about property, one witness provided adequate proof for the
same penalty (CD 9.17–23). CD also envisages imprisonment, which in
15.12–15 seems to apply to any transgression after the oath of membership.
Infringement of laws prohibiting work on sabbaths or festivals was to be
punished by imprisonment for seven years, though the biblical penalty is death,
which CD explicitly rules out (12.3–6).[15]

As we shall see more fully when we discuss theology, the Dead Sea sect
thought that only members of their community were destined for salvation. It
agrees with this that complete and permanent exclusion was the sect's most
severe penalty, a penalty that befell those who betrayed the community and
refused to accept its authority (1QS 7.16f., 22–4). On entry to the community,
members had heard the priests and Levites call on God to curse the backslider:

> Cursed be the man who enters this Covenant while walking among the idols
> of his heart, who sets up before himself his stumbling-block of sin so that he
> may backslide! . . . God's wrath . . . shall consume him in everlasting
> destruction . . . He shall be cut off from the midst of all the sons of light,
> and . . . his lot shall be among those who are cursed for ever. (1QS 1.11–18)

After hearing this awful curse, the entering members had affirmed it: 'Amen,
amen!' They believed in the power of oaths, vows and curses. Probably not
many denied the covenant after joining.

Josephus says that, since the Essenes had sworn not to eat others' food, members who were expelled often starved to death, though sometimes they were readmitted out of compassion (*War* 2.143f.). If true, this shows that a member could transgress severely enough to be expelled, but not reach the point of unbelief: he still regarded the oaths as binding. The member had sworn to forsake all else and feared to eat any other food. The Essenes believed that God would punish trangression with a penalty worse than death.

Worship

I wish here only to remind the reader of two topics discussed in earlier chapters. One is prayer. Josephus wrote that the Essenes offered ancestral prayers (*War* 2.128). According to 1QS 6.3, 8 the Qumran sect prayed together, and a very fragmentary scroll containing daily blessings has been found (4Q503). Communal prayer was distinctive. Other Jews prayed twice a day, and some may have followed set themes, but recitation of the same prayers by a community is not otherwise securely attested in Palestine, and Paul's evidence made us doubt that Diaspora Jews prayed (or sang) in unison (above, pp. 196f., 202–8). We cannot be sure what the practice of town-dwelling Essenes was. CD mentions meetings and discussion but does not describe a service (20.3–5; 14.3–12). The 'house of prostration', where one might go to pray (11.22), to enter which one should have washed, might be a synagogue, but it is more likely to be the temple, especially in view of the context.[16] If Josephus' view of Essene worship was basically derived from Qumran practice, we cannot say that other Essenes prayed together every day. They could well have done so, since they are said to have lived in certain 'quarters' of a city or town (*Hypoth.* 11.5; the Gate of the Essenes in Jerusalem; Josephus' statement, that 'they live by themselves', *Antiq.* 18.22, seems to refer to the monastic group).

The second topic under 'worship' is the special role that the sun played.

Their piety towards the Deity takes a peculiar form. Before the sun is up they utter no word on mundane matters, but offer to him certain prayers, which have been handed down from their forefathers, as though entreating him to rise. (*War* 2.128)

I proposed above that this meant not that they worshipped the sun, but that in facing the sun they maintained an old priestly practice, criticized in Ezekiel and the Mishnah (Ezek. 8.16 and *Sukkah* 5.2–4), and that they prayed to God, whose power was manifested in the sun (pp. 245f.).

Exclusivism

The Qumran sectarians were fully separate from the rest of Judaism, though the CD community was less so. The question of Essene exclusivism and separatism is an important one, not only for understanding this group, but for understanding first-century Judaism in general. When did differences of practice or belief amount to schism? In discussing this topic, I find it useful to distinguish between a 'sect' and a 'party'. A sect considers itself to be the only true Israel and all other Jews to be apostates. The boundary lines are rigid and impermeable. The members of a sect do not share the common religious life, which in Palestine would mean that they avoided the temple. A party, on the other hand, has distinctive views and practices, but it does not define itself as being all Israel, and its members constitute a party *within* common Judaism rather than being an alternative to it. We shall see that 1QS and related documents represent a sect, while CD represents an extremist party.

Given our general knowledge of Judaism and Jewish law, we know in advance that three overlapping topics were likely to determine full sectarianism: food, purity and temple. Different sabbath laws, for example, no matter how divergent from the norm, would not, by themselves, make a group a sect, nor would different rules about sowing more than one crop. If a group would not sell, buy or eat other people's food, or not associate with them for fear of impurity, or would not share in temple worship, we are justified in saying that the group was a sect. I shall propose below that temple worship was the central point, but we shall begin with the other two topics.

Exclusivism: food and purity

According to Josephus, the Essenes' daily routine consisted of work, a meal at the fifth hour (approximately noon), more work, and an evening meal. Before each meal, they 'girded their loins with linen cloths' and bathed in cold water. They entered a room that was forbidden to non-members. 'Pure now themselves, they repair[ed] to the refectory, as to some sacred shrine'. The priest said a blessing, and then they ate. After a closing prayer, they 'laid aside their raiment, as holy vestments' and went back to work. They followed the same routine in the evening (*War* 2.129–32). This apparently means that they worked in tunics and put on linen loincloths in order to bathe; since they immersed in a common pool, they probably put on the loincloth for modesty's sake. One assumes that after the meal they took off the linen cloth and put on a tunic that was reserved for eating. This then was discarded in favour of work clothes after the first meal, and put back on after bathing before the evening meal.

Bathing before a meal is, in general, 'priestly'. The lay Essenes did not think that they were priests, but they followed some of the purity rules that were regularly observed by priests, or by lay people before eating second tithe and other holy food. I shall enumerate some major points below. Just now we note that Josephus was well aware of the significance of the Essenes' purifications: they went to the dining hall 'as to some sacred shrine'. They also kept special clothes for their meals, since there would be no point in immersing if they then put on impure garments. The wearing of linen loincloths when immersing may also have been 'priestly'. Priests, we saw above, wore linen breeches, and when they immersed in other peoples' presence, for example in the temple itself, they may have kept their breeches on, or put on a separate pair.

As did other Palestinian Jews, when the Essenes 'bathed' for purification they immersed. At Qumran, there were large pools in which water was collected. It rains but seldom near the Dead Sea; but when it does rain, water pours down the wadis in great abundance. The sect built channels to bring the water into deep pits within the community area. Some of these were used for immersion.

In CD the concern for purity is seen especially in the prohibition of sexual relations in Jerusalem (12.1f.). Semen is a source of impurity, and according to biblical law one must bathe after emission and before entering the temple. CD extends the holy area to cover the entire city.[17] For purificatory baths, CD explicitly requires pools large enough to permit complete immersion (10.10–13). When the groups from various cities met together, they were concerned 'to distinguish between the unclean and the clean, and to make known the distinction between the holy and the profane' (12.19f.).

The *Community Rule* frequently refers to 'the Purity', which included food (and possibly also the vessels and dishes used to prepare and serve it). Scholars generally think that the Purity was the daily common meal,[18] and thus they equate it with Josephus' description of bathing and eating. They further interpet 1QS 6.2–5 (quoted below) as giving the rite for eating the daily meal. When 1QS 7.24f. forbids a member to share 'his *Purity*' with someone who has been expelled, Vermes translates 'Purity' as 'food', and this seems to constitute a parallel to Josephus' statement that expelled Essenes starved to death: other members would not give them *food*, and they could eat no other. Similarly Vermes wrote that the daily meal and the messianic meal were the same.[19] This rests on an equation of the meal in 1QS 6.4f. with the daily meal. This is, I believe, in error: the daily meals of 1QS may not have been 'the Purity'; but in any case, the rite described in 1QS 6.4f. is not the rule for daily meals.

· Most references to the Pure Meal (as I shall now translate 'the Purity') come in the section on punishments, where exclusion from the Pure Meal is distinguished from a reduction in the ordinary food allowance. Lying with

regard to property resulted in exclusion from the Pure Meal for one year and
the loss of one-quarter of the transgressor's 'bread', that is, his basic daily
sustenance (1QS 6.24f.). Other misdeeds also resulted in exclusion from the
Pure Meal, but not in expulsion from the order; that is, the person could
continue to live at Qumran, and not starve to death, though he was excluded
from the Pure Meal (7.3; 7.16f., distinguished from expulsion; 7.19; 8.17f.,
someone lives through exclusion from the Pure Meal; 8.24–6). It agrees with
this that novices were 'admitted to the covenant' but not allowed to touch the
Pure Meal for a year (6.16f.). The Pure Meal was distinguished from 'the
Drink' of the congregation, which a novice could not touch until a second
year had passed (6.20), and from which a straying member might be excluded
for two years (7.19f.). We then note that 1QS 5.13 specifies 'entering the
water' only before eating the Pure Meal. Were there, as Josephus claimed,
two immersions and thus two Pure Meals a day? This seems not to be the
meaning of 1QS, which distinguishes daily sustenance from the Pure Meal
and which has a still higher category, 'the Drink'.

It is possible to note these distinctions and still maintain that the Pure Meal
was held daily: it was Pure because everybody immersed and ate it together;
exclusion from it meant that the offending member had to eat alone; he ate
the same food (the daily portion of bread), reduced by the amount of his
fine.[20] On the basis of the passages just cited, this seems unlikely. If the
common meals were all Pure Meals, one would have to suppose that novices
ate alone for an entire year, and that after the year's probation, when they
joined the Pure Common Meals, they still could not drink what everyone else
drank. This is possible, but in that case one would expect rules for the
novice's meals, especially in 1QS, where novices are a major topic. I think it
more likely that the Pure Meal and the twice-daily meals were not identical.

Let us now look at the passage mentioned above, which Vermes and Knibb
(for example) take to describe the daily common meal.

> They shall eat in common and [3]pray in common and deliberate in
> common.
>
> Wherever there are ten men of the Council of the Community there
> shall not lack a [4]Priest among them. And they shall all sit before him
> according to their rank and shall be asked their counsel in all things in that
> order. ///And when the table has been prepared for eating, *or* the new
> wine [5]for drinking, the Priest shall be the first to stretch out his hand to
> bless the first-fruits of the bread *or* the new wine. (1QS 6.2–5)

The italicized *or* in lines 4 and 6 is my slight alteration of Vermes' translation.
He understood 'ô, literally 'or', to mean 'and', which is possible, but I think
incorrect in this case. Approximately the same regulations appear in the

Messianic Rule, which looks forward to a new age. There the text apparently does have *and* between the bread and wine.[21] A second difference is that after the priest blesses the bread and wine, the Messiah of Israel extends his hand over the bread, and the other members offer a prayer (1QSa 2.17–21). This certainly is a meal, with both bread and wine. The passage in 1QS, however, is another matter.

At first glance, 1QS 6.2–5 seems to say that every time ten men gather all these rules apply (first they confer, then the priest blesses, and then they have a meal), but probably the subject changes, a new topic beginning with 'when the table has been prepared', since it would not be possible to have the *first* of the bread or the *new* wine at every gathering, and certainly not at every meal. Schiffman also points out that the various activities of 1QS 6.2–5 did not necessarily take place at the same time. The sectarians ate together, and they prayed together, and they took counsel together, but they did not do all three every time they met.[22] Thus, in the text quoted above, I have marked a probable change of topic with ///. Whenever ten met for counsel, they sat before the priest in order. /// New topic: When they prepared the table for eating . . .

With regard to the new topic, the passage does not say 'every time anyone prepared a table to eat any food'. Schiffman points out that there is 'no obligation that all meals be communal'.[23] The *or* is probably important: this is not every meal, but a rite for certain occasions, times when a group of sectarians ate the first fruits of bread *or* drank the new wine. The definition of these terms is crucial. They ate *re'shît ha-leḥem*, 'first fruits of bread' and drank *tîrôsh*, 'new wine'. Thus the sentence reads, 'when they prepared the table for eating first fruits of bread . . .' As Yadin proposed, this is probably a first-fruits festival, or, more accurately, the rule about how to celebrate the first fruits of bread or the first fruits of wine.[24] Schiffman translates *re'shît ha-leḥem* 'first (portion) of the bread', and he understands *tîrôsh* as 'a weak, diluted, and often unfermented grape wine, similar to modern grape juice', though he also cites Licht, who argued that the Hebrew of 1QS is biblical, and that in biblical Hebrew *tîrôsh* meant 'new wine', rather than 'grape juice' (which is its usual meaning in rabbinic Hebrew).[25] The terminology of our passage recalls Num. 15.19–21 (whenever you eat of your *leḥem*, you shall give *re'shît* of your coarse meal); 18.12 (the best of your *tîrôsh* and grain, their *re'shît*); Deut. 18.4 (the *re'shît* of your grain, your *tîrôsh*). These passages refer to first fruits, and that is the best interpretation of the rite described in 1QS 6.4f.[26]

In Jerusalem, first fruits were given to the priests, who could share them with everyone in their house who was pure. At Qumran, it appears, all the members were included among those who could share the first fruits. Since the *Temple Scroll* has four first-fruits festivals (barley, wheat, wine and oil), instead of one, it is possible that there was more than one annual first-fruits feast at Qumran.[27] The sect presumably observed all the festivals with special meals, and it may be that these constitute the Pure Meal.

We do not know, however, that the Pure Meal had to coincide with a festival, and it may be that such meals were more frequent and that they followed the ritual cited just above (except that 'first' and 'new' would not apply). A compromise solution would be that Pure Meals accompanied all solemn gatherings such as are described after the first fruits passage:

> This is the rule for a session of the many. Each (shall sit) according to his rank. The priests shall sit in the first seats . . . In the same order they shall be asked for judgment, or concerning any counsel or matter which has to do with the many . . . (6.8f., trans. Knibb)

To summarize: The standard view is that one combines the general rule that 'they shall eat in common' (1QS 6.2), the term 'the Purity', the description of the first fruits meal (or rite), and Josephus' statements about food and purity: all the members of the Qumran community bathed twice a day, before every meal; they entered the refectory as if it were the temple; a priest always presided; the name of every meal was 'the Purity'. I think that we should make distinctions. At Qumran there was food apart from the Pure Meal, namely, the daily basic provision. It seems to me likely that this was eaten in common: 1QS 6.2 refers to the universal rule; everything was done in common. 1QS 6.4f. governs only the eating and drinking of first fruits, and not every common meal was a first fruits feast. Moreover, every common meal may not have been 'the Purity'. That term, and immersion, certainly applied to the festival meals, and perhaps also to numerous other gatherings of the congregation.

If it is correct to distinguish the daily meals from the Pure Meal, Josephus' report is exaggerated, not wrong. 1QS confirms bathing before some meals and eating in common. I have argued that there is room to doubt that the sectarians regarded all the meals, fourteen each week, as Pure Meals that required immersion.

What, then, about Josephus' statement that expelled members starved to death? Possibly he exaggerated, but it is more likely that there was an oath to eat only the sect's food, perhaps after the novice's probation, when his possessions became common property. Josephus says that it was at that point that the new member swore 'tremendous oaths' (*War* 2.139), and also that the former members who starved were bound by their oaths (2.143). That is, an oath could cover the food, whether or not every meal was 'the Pure Meal'.

While on food, we may note two other comments by Josephus, that the Essenes were always sober and that they 'allotted portions of meat and drink [according] to the demands of nature' (*War* 2.133). The second point is confirmed by 1QS, which requires a reduction in the food allowance for minor offences, thus proving that there was a standard allotment. The first point, sobriety, has proved more puzzling. Vermes and others (Schiffman, for example) have suggested that the 'new wine' of the Scrolls was unfermented grape juice, pointing out that Lev. 10.9 and Ezek. 44.21 prohibit priests from imbibing alcohol when serving in the temple. If the sectarians treated the community as a temple – which in some ways they did, as we shall see – they would not have drunk wine. I argued above, however (following Yadin), that *tîrôsh* in the Scrolls means 'new wine'. Yadin proposed that Josephus' statement that the Essenes did not drink wine described their daily 'simple sober meals', while the meal described in the *Community Rule* was an annual meal to celebrate the first fruits, a meal that included wine.[28] This seems to me likely: usually the sectarians did not drink wine, occasionally they did. Though they considered the community to be a substitute temple, they could not have maintained temple rules consistently and also have observed all the other biblical laws. Numbers 18.12, for example, requires people to give the priests the best of the wine. This implies that they should drink it – not in the temple, but outside. If sectarians lived in the community as if they were in the temple, the sectarian priests could not obey both rules. As Vermes suggests, they could have circumvented this by interpreting 'new wine' as unfermented, and thus drunk the first of the 'wine' without consuming alcohol, but it is more likely that they did not consistently apply temple rules to the community. Mostly they did not drink wine, sometimes they did.

Josephus mentions other purity rules.

Oil they consider defiling, and anyone who accidentally comes in contact with it scours his person; for they make a point of keeping a dry skin and of always being dressed in white. (*War* 2.123)

They are divided, according to the duration of their discipline, into four grades; and so far are the junior members inferior to the seniors, that a senior if but touched by a junior, must take a bath, as after contact with an alien. (2.150)

The avoidance of oil could be solely for reasons of purity. Oil, as a liquid, is more susceptible to impurity than is dry foodstuff (because of Lev. 11.34, 38), and Jews were generally reluctant to use other people's oil (*Antiq.* 12.120; *War* 2.591; *Life* 74).[29] On the other hand, oil is no more susceptible to impurity than is drink, and if the Essenes made their own oil they could have

kept the olives and the oil pure as easily as grapes and wine or grape juice –
which they permitted. Yadin offers a different solution. One of the new
festivals of the *Temple Scroll* is the feast of the first of the oil, and he suggests
that the Essenes considered oil 'impure and "defiling" because they were
unable to observe the first fruits ritual of "purification", complete with the
sacrifice of the new oil on the altar of the Temple'.[30] If this is correct, oil was
impure because it could not be sanctified as long as the wrong priests
governed the temple. This solution, however, has the same flaw as the
explanation that liquids were more susceptible to impurity than solids: it does
not explain the distinction between wine and oil. If the sectarians could not
use oil until the first oil had been sanctified by the correct rite at the temple,
they should have made a similar rule about wine, for which they also required
a special festival.

J. Baumgarten's explanation is the best yet offered. In the Essene view,
even wood, stones or dust become susceptible to impurity if they have oil on
them (CD 12.16). Following this logic, so does the skin. Even with dry skin, if
a sectarian touched another sectarian of lower rank he had to bathe (*War*
2.150), and oil on the skin may have made it susceptible to a higher degree of
impurity.[31]

The Scrolls themselves do not say that members should not anoint
themselves, and possibly Josephus' information was in error. I am inclined,
however, to accept his statement, and to think that the Essenes considered oil
on the skin to make them especially subject to impurity, or subject to a more
severe degree of impurity than they otherwise were.

The Scrolls also do not say that the sectarians dressed in white, but, again,
Josephus may be correct. White clothing, as I suggested above (pp. 96–8) was
a sign of special sanctity and, probably, of purity.

Bathing after contact with even an inferior member of the order (*War*
2.150) is especially striking. Several impurities are conveyed by contact (for
example, by touching a menstruant), and such contact rendered clothing
impure as well (Lev. 15.22). Priests probably immersed shortly before eating
their main meal, since they might have touched an impure person or impure
clothing.[32] The Pharisees also worried about touching the garments of an
ordinary person, which might have picked up secondary impurity, though I
think that they did not immerse every day.[33] In any case, Essenes seem to
have followed a priestly rule if they touched an impure person.

In some respects the Qumran community served in place of the temple.
Special purity rules are only one example. We shall see below that prayers
substituted for sacrifices (pp. 376f.). Outside the community's area of sanctity
and communion with the deity lay only darkness and death. The force of the
threat of expulsion comes from considering the community's priests the only

true priests, and its festivals the only true feasts (in the interim period, until the sect could take control of Jerusalem and run the temple correctly). In the messianic era, the sect expected priestly rules to apply more widely. People with blemishes or disabilities would be banned from office and from participating in meetings of the congregation (1QSa 2.3–11), just as in the present blemished priests were not allowed to sacrifice (Lev. 21.21–3). The entirety of Jerusalem would be treated like the temple, and its residents like worshippers in the court of the Israelites: only males, no emission of semen.[34]

We shall consider the *degree* of purity a little more closely. Did the Qumranians live like priests *in* the temple, like priests at home, like laymen in the temple, or like laymen when eating second tithe or the shared offering?

1. It was priestly to bathe after touching anyone less pure, or at least to do so before eating.

2. If the Qumranians immersed before every meal, they treated all their meals as equivalent to holy food eaten outside the temple by priests, their families, or ordinary Jews during the festivals.

3. If they did not drink wine, they behaved as if they were in the temple. No one drank wine in the temple.

4. If their avoidance of sexual intercourse was governed by the desire for freedom from semen impurity (as seems likely in view of 11QT),[35] they again behaved as if they were in the temple (or getting ready to enter it).

5. Bathing immediately after defecation (*War* 2.149) is behaving like a priest in the temple.[36] Priests outside the temple would take care of such impurities all at once, immediately before sunset and the evening meal.

6. We must note a purity rule that is absent from the main surviving documents: avoiding corpse impurity. Priests were to avoid corpse impurity all the time, and no one was permitted to take it into the temple. A priestly sect should have rules about not acquiring corpse impurity, and a group of people who regarded their community as the temple should have a way to rid themselves of it. The Qumranians probably did have their own rite for removing corpse impurity,[37] but until we have better knowledge we should be cautious about saying that the sectarians lived like priests.

No one could be as pure as priests in the temple, or as laymen in the temple, all the time. It *is* possible once a day, immediately after immersion and sunset, to be free of all impurities except corpse impurity. This achievable standard of purity was typical of priests and their families when they ate tithes at home, or of pilgrims when they enjoyed a festival meal or ate second tithe. The Qumranians may have aimed at this level of purity: immersing before sunset, eating the main meal after sunset. In the nature of the case, however, they could not avoid corpse impurity. They all had it, and thus they were not like priests, nor even like lay people when they worshipped in the temple or ate the Passover lamb.

On the other hand, the sectarians added one or two temple rules to their daily lives: immersing after defecating and avoiding wine (except first fruits of wine). These are, respectively, priest-in-the-temple and anyone-in-the-temple rules. Seeking a higher level of purity than that attained by anyone else, the Essenes, especially the Qumran branch, assembled a collection of additional purity laws, laws that the Bible applies either to priests, the temple, second-tithe meals or festivals (or some combination thereof). The ones that they assembled, of course, were ones that they could conceivably keep. They could not precisely duplicate the purity laws that governed any one of the domains just listed, but they were as pure as possible.

Exclusivism: calendar, secrecy, view of outsiders

While living in purity, awaiting fulfilment of its hopes, the Dead Sea group secured its isolation from the temple, and thus from the common religious life, by adherence to a different calendar from the one used by the Jerusalem priesthood. This meant that the holy days were never the same. The force of having a different calendar is clear in a story from the early days of the sect. On the sectarian Day of Atonement the 'Wicked Priest' 'pursued the Teacher of Righteousness to the house of his exile . . . He appeared before them to confuse them, and to cause them to stumble on the Day of Fasting . . .' (1QpHab 11.4–7). We do not know the result of this visit, neither whether the sectarians fought even on their Day of Atonement, nor whether the Teacher of Righteousness was killed, but the importance of the calendar is evident.

The calendar that the sect accepted is also known from *Jubilees* and *I Enoch*. We saw above that the calendar followed in the temple was luni-solar; that is, its months were lunar months, and occasionally a thirteenth month was added in order to adjust the calendar to the solar or seasonal year. The calendar of *Jubilees* and the Scrolls was solar: the lunar months were ignored, and the year consisted of 364 days: 52 weeks precisely. The months were 30 days long, except for the third, sixth, ninth and twelfth months, which were 31 days.[38]

It is probable that the Zadokites and their followers, when they withdrew from Jerusalem, merged with a pre-existing pious group (Essenes or proto-Essenes) that had already rejected the Jerusalem calendar, or else had already campaigned to have it revised. *Jubilees* is extremist in numerous respects, and it is unlikely that it represents common practice. It is perhaps conceivable that when the Zadokites left Jerusalem they brought their calendar with them, and that the Hasmoneans then changed the temple calendar, but it is much more likely that the calendar of *Jubilees*, *I Enoch* and the Dead Sea Scrolls was revisionist before the Zadokite adoption of it. In this case, the Zadokites intentionally chose a calendar that cut their sect off from the Jerusalem temple. It was 'a sign and symbol' of 'their dissidence from the body politic'.[39]

There are further points about the sect's exclusivisim to be noted. One is the command to *secrecy*. Josephus noted that the Essenes took an oath to conceal 'nothing from the members of the sect', and to reveal 'none of their secrets to others' (*War* 2.141). According to 1QS the Master was instructed to 'conceal the teaching of the Law from men of falsehood' (9.17), and the members were to practise 'faithful concealment of the mysteries of God' (4.6). They thought that other Israelites should seek to know their secrets (1QS 5.11–12), but apparently not that they should themselves conduct teaching missions. Here the Dead Sea sect is to be distinguished sharply from the Pharisees, who had special traditions, but not secret ones. They would have been glad to teach them to anyone and debate them in public.

Josephus emphasized that the Essenes practised *love of one another* and vowed to wrong no one, whether Essene or not. They 'show[ed] a greater attachment to each other than [did] the other sects' (*War* 2.119). This theme is echoed in the Scrolls. According to CD 13.9 the overseer shall '"take pity upon them [the members] like a father upon his sons", and "shall bring back all them that have strayed . . . like a shepherd his flock"' (quoting the Bible). The members of the monastic community were exhorted to rebuke one another only 'in truth, humility, and charity', not with 'anger, or ill-temper, or obduracy, or with envy prompted by the spirit of wickedness' (1QS 5.24–26).

On the other hand, they *hated 'the unjust'* and exposed 'liars' (*War* 2.139–141). They might show charity and goodness to one another (1QS 4.3), and possibly they really did treat non-sectarians decently, but in their enclaves they cultivated another attitude towards outsiders: 'everlasting hatred' (1QS 9.21). 'The unjust' whom they hated turn out to be the rest of humanity, especially other Israelites. People who joined devoted themselves not only to 'love all the sons of light', but also to 'hate all the sons of darkness' (1QS 1.9–10). The opening lines of the *War Rule* look forward to the destruction of other Jews before the showdown with the Gentiles. The *Messianic Rule*, however, is more optimistic and anticipates the conversion of other Israelites (1QSa 1.1–2).

Exclusivism in CD

The other branch of the Essenes was less exclusivist though by no means an open community. The *Covenant of Damascus* indicates that an offender should be 'set apart from the Purity', that is, the Pure Meal (CD 9.21), but the common meal does not loom as large as it does in 1QS. We do not know how often town-dwelling Essenes ate together. CD also knows of 'hidden things' (CD 3.14), it puts a restriction on when the full terms of the covenant can be revealed to a prospective member (only after a preliminary oath to the covenant has been taken, 15.10–13), and it threatens backsliders with expulsion (20.2–8) or imprisonment (15.14f.). It does not, however, require members to shun the temple, and it presupposes that they went to Jerusalem and sacrificed (9.13f.; 11.17–21; 12.1f.; cf. 16.14–19 on vows to give things to the temple).[40] Members were told to trade with 'the Children of the Pit' only in cash (CD 13.14–15), but they could trade with them. They were to limit contact with Gentiles in several ways (e.g. not to spend a sabbath near them: 11.14–15), but CD makes allowance for proselytes (14.3–6), which shows that contacts with Gentiles were allowed.

Exclusivism and the temple

While exclusivism and sectarianism have partially to do with theology (only we are members of the true covenant) and partially with general social behaviour (we avoid mingling with other people and deal with them as little as possible), acceptance or rejection of the temple and its sacrifices finally determined whether a group was 'sectarian' or not. 1QS offers the community as a temporary substitute for the temple, CD does not. It is not the case that CD entirely approves of the Jerusalem temple, priests and calendar. One sees a calendar complaint in a passage previously discussed, which states that when a festival and the sabbath overlap, only the sabbath sacrifices should be offered (CD 11.17f.). A properly arranged calendar would avoid the overlap, and in the 364 day calendar of *I Enoch, Jubilees* and the Dead Sea Scrolls, festivals never fall on the sabbath.[41] CD grants that the overlap will occur, thus conceding that the Jerusalem priests do not follow the Essene calendar, but it disagrees with them.[42] As P. Davies has remarked, disapproval does not necessarily mean full separation,[43] and we shall see the same situation when we consider Pharisaism, where objections accompanied continued worship in common with others.

When combined with sharing the temple, disagreements point to a 'party'. CD reflects an extreme party, more extreme than the Pharisees, with stricter laws and more cautions about relations with other people, but not completely sectarian. The Qumran sectarians, however, thought that their priests were the true priests, their calendar the true calendar, and their community the true temple, until they could take control of Jerusalem, at which time they would not only re-organize the year and the priesthood, but also rebuild the temple and impose new purity and sabbath rules. Meanwhile, in Jerusalem, a false priesthood served in the midst of an impure city, offering festival sacrifices on the wrong days. The Qumranians wished to have nothing to do with any of this. At one level, CD does not disagree. But its members were not completely cut off from common religious life, and this is a substantial difference.

The formation of parties and sects

People formed a party when they studied enough topics to have their own views that were different from others', especially from the majority's. Party implies study, at least on the part of the originators and the subsequent leaders.[44] The secrets of the Essenes, both legal and esoteric, were the result of study, and they were taught to new members.

Josephus noted that studies in 'the writings of the ancients' were especially important (*War* 2.136). This trait of the sect has been richly confirmed. Archaeologists discovered writing tables, ink wells and even ink, and the existence of the Scrolls proves the interest in study. The library included copies of biblical books, other works that were known outside of Qumran (such as *I Enoch* and *Jubilees*), and some of the special sectarian literature – though probably not all the most secret literature. 1QS is a rule partly for novices, and there were probably more difficult and possibly esoteric works for members of long standing. 1QS suffices, however, to show the necessity of study. Candidates for admission had to prepare, and they were examined (1QS 5.20f.). 'Knowledge' is a major theme of the sectarian Scrolls (e.g. 1QS 1.12; 3.13f.). The *Community Rule* requires that wherever ten gathered, 'there shall never lack a man among them who shall study the Law continually, day and night . . .' (6.6). The entire congregation was to 'watch in community for a third of every night of the year, to read the Book and to study law and to pray together' (6.7f.). Teaching also figures in CD (13.5–9). The *Messianic Rule* prescribes that children be taught for ten years (1QSa 1.6–8). Much of this study, we may assume, was specifically Essene. That is, members needed to learn the correct interpretation of the Bible, as well as the secrets and special rules.

In our period, as in others, Judaism tended to produce parties and sects (or at least one full sect). In the second and first centuries BCE, this tendency sprang from two characteristics of Judaism as a whole: the law covered all of life, and study was encouraged (largely by the development of synagogues). Getting together to study meant that people could come to interpretations that were different from others', and the range of the law meant that these differences could cover most aspects of life. Had Judaism been only a cultic religion, disagreements would have been possible only with regard to sacrifice and the temple, and they would have developed only among priests, at least at first. These aspects – cultic disagreements and teachers who were priests – were by no means absent from disputes in our period, but the arguments could range more widely and lay people could play leading roles. A party could survive because members could meet on the sabbath (at Qumran, every day), when teaching and learning could reinforce and develop the group's distinctiveness.

Priests and lay leaders

Who the continuing leaders of the Essenes were is an interesting question. We have seen the fundamental role of Zadokite priests, in the plural (e.g. 1QS 5.2, 9; 1QSa 1.2, 24; 2.3; 1QSb 3.22, CD 3.21–4.5); priests who are not called 'sons of Zadok' also figure prominently (e.g. 1QS 1–2; 5.21; 9.7; 1QSa 1.15, 23). 1QS and related Scrolls assume the continuing presence of a lot of priests, including Zadokites. Priests and Levites say the curses and blessings when new members join (1QS 1–2); the community lives 'under the authority of the sons of Zadok' (5.1f.); priests always enter first when the congregation gathers (6.8).

If the community of 1QS was always monastic, however, the Zadokite priests died off, and more would have had to be recruited from the broader Essene community, or from Zadokites who were not Essenes. I think that it would have been difficult for the monastic group to recruit new generations of Zadokites. When the Zadokite establishment was broken up by the Hasmoneans, the deposed aristocrats all had to go somewhere, and some ended up among the Essenes. By the next generation, however, there was no longer a large pool of unconnected Zadokite priests. I suspect that the *Community Rule* reflects their original contribution – the full covenant was revealed to the sons of Zadok (1QS 5.9) – more than their continuing role, though, to be sure, it sounds as if they continued. It is noteworthy that both 1QS and CD require that a priest be present when there is a formal gathering. 1QS follows this with the prescription that a priest must bless the first fruits of bread and new wine (1QS 6.4f.). These lines reveal no doubt that a suitable priest will be present. CD requires the priest among a group of ten to be 'learned in the Book of Meditation'. It continues, however, by saying that if the priest is not properly educated, and a Levite is, the Levite should rule, with one exception. Only a priest can inspect a person for leprosy, but 'the Guardian' may instruct him. Further, only the priest can require a leper to be locked up, 'even if the priest is a simpleton' (CD 13.2–7).

CD reveals, I suspect, that the aristocratic and well-educated Zadokites, who played such an important role in establishing the Essenes as we know them, had for the most part gone to Qumran – where, however, they had died out. Both CD and 1QS refer to leaders or officials who are not called priests, and who therefore were probably laymen. We have just seen 'the Guardian' in CD instructing a priest. The Guardian appears very often in that document (see also, for example, 9.18–22) and twice in 1QS (6.12, 20), where he has a good deal of authority. A man called 'the Master' (Vermes) or 'the wise leader' (Knibb), which may be simply another title for 'the Guardian', also plays an important role in 1QS (3.13; 9.12–21; cf. CD 12.21). Whether the Master was the same as the Guardian or not, presumably both words refer to a layman.[45]

I do not have a precise proposal. I shall, however, clarify my suspicion. CD reveals that, in the non-monastic branches of the Essenes, there had been a decline in the number of learned priests, and this was probably also true at Qumran. Their apparent continuation in 1QS is misleading; either the rule was not revised, or its presentation is idealistic. The references to a lay leader may show the true situation.

Obedience and democracy

The strict rules of the sect required equally strict governance. According to Josephus, the Essenes were obedient to superiors in the hierarchy, doing 'nothing without orders from their superiors'. On their own initiative members could do charitable deeds, but nothing else (*War* 2.134). We have also seen that in theory the Qumran community was governed by Zadokite priests, but that there were other leaders, probably lay, who exercised authority. Further, members were supposed to obey those who had joined the order before them: a seniority not of age but of membership (1QS 6.26). On the other hand, according to Josephus, their leaders were elected by the whole group (*War* 2.123; cf. *Antiq.* 18.22), and they showed democracy in trials, 'never passing sentence in a court of less than a hundred members' (*War* 2.145).

There is no sign in the *Community Rule* that the leaders were elected, though they may have been. But the other two points, which on the surface appear to be contradictory – that a hierarchy was strictly obeyed and that judgment was the responsibility of a large group – both appear in 1QS. At the annual renewal of the covenant, the members enter with the priests first, 'ranked one after another according to the perfection of their spirit'; the Levites second; and everyone else third, but apparently also ranked, so that 'every Israelite may know his place . . .' No one could move down or up (1QS 2.19–23). There was a chain of command: everyone had to know who was above and below him, so that he could 'obey his companion, the man of lesser rank obeying his superior'. The rankings were adjusted once each year in accordance with 'perfection of way' and offences (5.23–24). In work and money each man had to obey his superior (6.2), and when they assembled for debate or discussion they had to sit in order: priests first, then elders, then 'all the rest ... according to their rank' (6.8–9). Nothing could be more authoritarian.

On the other hand, another note is struck. Members are not only 'under the authority of the sons of Zadok, the Priests who keep the covenant', but also under 'the multitude of the men of the Community'. 'Every decision concerning doctrine, property, and justice shall be determined by them', where 'them' probably refers to the entire community (1QS 5.1–3). Thus it appears that the authoritarianism of the leaders was subject to the control of democracy. As did Josephus, the *Community Rule* assigns to a large number (Josephus, at least 100; the *Rule*, all the full members) the responsibility for trying cases. The entire congregation must decide on admission (1QS 7.20–21; 8.18–19); after members join, they may then take part in the 'trial and judgment and condemnation' of transgressors (1QS 5.6–7).

Probably in practice these two principles (absolute hierarchy and total democracy) did not conflict often. In day-to-day life the hierarchy was observed and obeyed, while big decisions – entrance, changes of the rules, expulsions and food limitations – were referred to the community as a whole. Josephus' statement that they obey both their elders and a majority (*War* 2.146) seems to have been correct.

Josephus also attributes to the Essenes great care in speaking: if, in a group of ten, nine desire silence, the tenth must also be silent (2.146). According to 1QS members were asked their opinions in the order of their rank (6.4). Interruptions were not allowed (and were punished by a reduction of food for ten days: 1QS 7.9–10), each could speak only in turn, and in a full assembly permission of the Congregation had to be obtained before speaking, though this may have meant permission of the Guardian (6.10–12).

17

The Essenes and the Dead Sea Sect II:
Further Aspects of Practice and Belief

Sabbath

The Essenes were stricter than other Jews 'in abstaining from work on the seventh day'; they would not light a fire, remove a vessel 'or even go to stool' (*War* 2.147). The *Covenant of Damascus* contains a long list of special sabbath laws: the sectarian sabbath began early, 'when the sun's orb is distant by its own fullness from the gate' behind which it would set. Speaking about work was forbidden, as well as conduct of business. Their limit of a sabbath day's journey was 1,000 cubits (*c.* 500 metres or yards). The rabbis, and probably many others before them, accepted a limit of 2,000 cubits. The Bible restricts travel on the sabbath (Ex. 16.29), but it does not specify a limit. The Essenes and rabbis derived limits from Num. 35.4f., where 1,000 cubits and 2,000 cubits appear, though not with regard to the sabbath. Given these verses, however, the Essenes chose the stricter limit.

Other prohibitions include these: picking up food that had fallen in a field, drawing water into a vessel to drink, carrying anything into or out of a house, opening a sealed vessel, assisting a beast that was giving birth, lifting a new-born animal out of a pit, cleaning the house, carrying a child, or wearing medicaments (including perfumes). Essenes should also not cause Gentiles to work on the sabbath, nor were they to spend the sabbath near them. The only exception to the prohibition of work was that they could save human life (CD 10.14–11.18).[1]

These are the rules of CD. We may imagine that the Qumranians were at least as strict, but no code of sabbath law has been found. It is striking, however, that the penalty for breaking these strict rules was relatively light. CD 12.3–6 reduces the penalty for transgression, apparently even conscious transgression, from death (required by the Bible) to seven years imprisonment.

Eschatology

We have seen that most Jews looked forward to a better future. These hopes were often vague, as is quite suitable. In the modern West, people have looked forward to peace, prosperity, freedom and democracy. They have fairly seldom been explicit about what prosperity, for example, would mean: more cars than the roads will accommodate, air pollution, acid rain, skin cancer and toxic waste. The Dead Sea sectarians, however, were made of sterner stuff. They sometimes described the future concretely and did not shrink from spelling out the harsh implications.

Josephus does not mention the Essenes' eschatological hope. We cannot consider his silence to be other than intentional. The fervent desire for Israel's liberation was an embarrassment to his apologetic aims, which included convincing his audience that, now that the Zealots and Sicarii had been destroyed, the Jews were obedient and reliable subjects. He probably did not succeed in his effort, but at any rate we can understand why he wished to circumscribe the desire for national freedom and to assign it to only a few.

From the Scrolls, we learn that the sect looked forward to a dramatic change in the future, which modern scholars often call 'the eschaton', 'the last [event]', which is slightly misleading, since like other Jews the Essenes did not think that the world would end. Rather, other Israelites would either join the movement (so 1QSa) or be destroyed (so 1QM). There would be a great war (1QM) that would destroy the Gentile oppressors. It would be followed by an ordered community, led by two messiahs. The superior would be the Messiah of Aaron, the inferior the Messiah of Israel: the priests would be in charge. The messiahs are discussed above, pp. 296f.

The sect would occupy Jerusalem (1QM) and rebuild the temple according to their own plans (11QT). Purity would descend like an all-encompassing cloud. Jerusalem would be kept entirely pure, with sexual relations forbidden, women banned (except for short visits), and privies built outside the walls (privies: 11QT 46.13–16). Men could have sexual relations with their wives outside Jerusalem, but then they could not enter the city for three days (45.11f.). Outside Jerusalem would be three encampment areas, to house male Jerusalemites who became impure because of 'leprosy', genital discharge (e.g. gonorrhoea) or even nocturnal emission, which would require three days expulsion from the city (11QT 46.16–18). Elsewhere only slightly less strict rules would apply. Lepers, people with genital discharge, menstruants, and women after childbirth were all to be housed in camps outside the other cities (48.14–17).[2] The day would eventually come when God himself would descend and create his own sanctuary (11QT 29.9f.), but meanwhile the sect expected war and rigorous discipline.

As is generally the case with visions, the future hopes expressed in various Scrolls do not make up a perfectly neat scheme. They were penned by different authors and at different times. The *War Rule* envisages the sect as occupying Jerusalem and using the temple, while the war is fought outside the gates. When the formations of the Sons of Light confront their enemy, seven priests will leave the city by 'the middle gates' and stand between the opposing formations. They shall be clothed

> in garments of white byssus: a linen tunic and linen breeches, and girt with a linen sash of twined byssus, blue, purple and scarlet, and a brocaded pattern, cunningly wrought, and turbaned headdresses upon their heads, *these being* garments for battle, and they shall not bring them into the sanctuary. (1QM 7.9–11)

The select priests, suitably turbaned and garbed, cheer on the fighters, periodically sounding trumpets to direct the troops (e.g. 1QM 7.16; cols 8–9). This passage implies that when not required on the battlefield the priests serve in the temple. Nothing has been said in the Scroll about rebuilding it.

In the *Temple Scroll*, however, the correct design, which differs considerably from both the pre-Herodian and the Herodian temple, occupies a good deal of space. It may be that this all fits into a harmonious whole: they would first occupy and use the existing temple, then build their own; but it is better to see the documents as offering vignettes of the longed-for future, not every one of which fits into a single overall design. This is to be expected of descriptions of the ideal future.

Life after death

The Essenes, according to Josephus, believed in immortality of the soul (above, pp. 300–2). We shall look at this topic a little more closely. According to Josephus, they regarded the body as the prison of the soul and shared the belief of the Greeks, 'that for virtuous souls there is reserved an abode beyond the ocean' (*War* 2.154–157; cf. *Antiq.* 18.18). This is a good deal more explicit than one finds in the Scrolls. Scholars have debated whether 'immortality' (the soul never dies) or 'resurrection' (people, body and soul, rise from the dead) is the better word for their belief,[3] but 'vague and general expectation' is probably the best description. One finds such passages as this: there will be

> great peace in a long life, and fruitfulness, together with every everlasting blessing and eternal joy in life without end, a crown of glory and a garment of majesty in unending light. (1QS 4.7f.)

Other passages seem to predict that the entire congregation will possess not only Palestine but the whole world forever ('for a thousand generations'), while the wicked will be cut off (4Q171 3.1, 10–13; 4QAmram),[4] though the texts are fragmentary and not entirely clear.

To some degree it is even correct to say that the sectarians had a 'realized eschatology'; that is, that some of the benefits of the new age had already been realized in the community. Thus one of the hymns is a paean of thanks to God for what he has already done:

Thou hast redeemed my soul from the Pit,
and . . .
Thou hast raised me up to everlasting height.
I walk on limitless level ground . . .
. . .
Thou hast cleansed a perverse spirit of great sin
   that it may stand with the host of the Holy Ones,
and that it may enter into community
   with the congregation of the Sons of Heaven. (1QH 3.20–2)

Here the boundary between the blessings that God had already bestowed, in granting admission into the elect group, and the blessings of the future, seems very thin. To some degree the members already dwelt with the angels or the 'host of the Holy Ones', whose presence in the community would become more pronounced and important in the future (see immediately below). But precisely what the sectarians expected for the individual after death is difficult to say. There is no clear reference to a bodily resurrection, which would allow dead saints to join the Sons of Light when the messiahs come; but equally is there no clear expression of the immortality of the individual soul. The sectarians were not Sadducees: they did not think that it all ended with death. But they seem to have been content with a hope for the individual's future that remained shadowy and vague. The hope for the community's ultimate triumph, though not always crystal clear, was more concrete, and it may have included eternal life in a restored world for the victors.

Angels

Qumran shares with many of the books of the Apocrypha and Pseudepigrapha an elaborate angelology. During the exile, Jewish views of angels developed and became more concrete. Angels acquired distinctive names and tasks. Raphael was the angel of healing, for example, and the idea of a 'heavenly host' of warriors developed, often headed by Michael.[5] It is commonly said that angelology became more important because Jews increasingly thought of God as remote. He was exalted, people thought that he was too far away to care for them, and so they started thinking of angels as being closer to them.[6] I am completely unpersuaded by this explanation, partly because the evidence is against the notion that Jews perceived God as remote and inaccessible,[7] partly because angels play diverse roles in the literature of our period. Some angels were thought of as hostile, for example. If the only angels were messengers from God to earth and intercessors who pleaded with God on behalf of humans, this might be a reasonable suggestion; but as it is, I think that God's supposed remoteness does not explain angelology. That proposal is too determined by the notion that theology governs religion: first Jews began thinking of God as more transcendent; this led to his becoming remote and inaccessible; and therefore they started giving more importance to angels as mediators. It is more likely that during the exile they encountered attractive depictions of angels and learned how handy and convenient it is to know the names of angels and their functions. Once people see angels in action (verbally and pictorially), they can begin to attribute different kinds of deeds to different angels or spirits, and thus they avoid having God come into conflict with himself. This becomes clearest when we consider the problem of evil,[8] but belief in angels and spirits of different kinds helps explain all sorts of things, which some cultures put down to 'chance'. I do not believe that Jews saw God as remote – they prayed to him directly – but I do think that strict monotheism, especially the view that God controls history, is sometimes difficult to live with, and that it is lightened by having lesser spiritual beings who can share some of the responsibility for what happens. The history of the development of angelology, however, is a question that lies well beyond the scope of this book; it belongs to studies of the Babylonian exile and the Persian era.

In Qumran we see some differentiation among angels. As we noted in ch. 14 (pp. 296f.), they were expected to help in the final battle against the 'sons of darkness' (1QM 15.14). The 'war of the heavenly warriors shall scourge the earth; and it shall not end before the appointed destruction which shall be for ever and without compare' (1QH 3.35f.).

The recently published *Songs for the Holocaust of the Sabbath*[9] reveals angels, often called 'gods', as 'prie[sts] of the inner Temple, ministers of the Presence of the [most] holy King', that is, as beings that offer heavenly worship to God. 'Their expiations shall obtain his good will for all those who repent from sin'.[10] This seems to complement the sectarian view that their own prayers substitute for the sacrifices of the temple (p. 376 below): so do the prayers of the angels.

These songs also depict the angels as blessing 'the image of the throne-chariot'. 'When the wheels advance, angels of holiness come and go. From between his glorious wheels there is as it were a fiery vision of most holy spirits.'[11] This is speculation on the wheels that Ezekiel saw (Ezek. 1.15–21), described by Ben Sira as a vision of 'the chariots of the cherubim' (Ben Sira 49.8),[12] which will become one of the major themes of Jewish mystical literature. Here we see *apocalypticism*, the effort to envisage the divine realm.

Two of the most interesting parts of sectarian angelology are that angels require purity and that the members of the community in some sense dwell in the presence of angels. These ideas usually apply to an anticipated future state. In the time of the war against the sons of darkness, the sons of light must be 'pure with regard to [their] sexual organs . . ., for holy angels are in communion with their hosts' (1QM 7.6). The *Messianic Rule* similarly ordains that people who are impure cannot 'enter the assembly of God'; the blemished cannot 'hold office among the congregation of the men of renown'. The explanation is that 'the Angels of Holiness' will be with them (1QSa 2.3–9). Similarly, in the *Blessings* we read this petition: 'May you be as an angel of the Presence in the Abode of Holiness . . . May you attend upon the service in the Temple of the Kingdom and decree destiny in company with the Angels of the Presence' (1QSb 4.24–6). This is, apparently, the future temple.

Communion with the angels, however, has already begun. Just above we quoted 1QH 3.20–2.: God has purified the members of the community so that they 'may stand with the host of the Holy Ones, and . . . enter into community with the congregation of the Sons of Heaven'. They have 'an everlasting lot amidst the spirits of knowledge' (3.22). Similarly 1QH 6.12f. speaks of those who 'share a common lot' with the Angels of the Presence'; apparently this 'lot' is already in existence in Qumran. The hymn at the end of the *Community Rule* states that God has caused 'his chosen ones' to 'inherit the lot of the Holy Ones'. 'He has joined their assembly to the Sons of Heaven', and it will endure forever (see also 1QS 11.7–9).

As far as I can tell, the idea that the Qumran sectarians already lived in the presence of the holy angels reveals something of their spirituality, but it had no *legal* implications in the life of the community. In the future, at the time of the war, or at the messianic banquet, the presence of angels will limit the role of blemished or impure sectarians, but that seems not to be the case in the present.

Finally, we may note that in the hymns and prayers of the sectarians themselves, they do not pray to angels, nor do they ask angels to pray for them, they pray directly to God.

Predestination and freewill

In one of Josephus' accounts of the parties he focuses on Fate, ascribing belief in free will to the Sadducees, belief in Fate to the Essenes, and both to the Pharisees (*Antiq.* 13.171–173). It is certainly true that no other Jewish literature emphasizes God's sovereign determination of all things more than do the Scrolls. On the other hand, no literature expresses more forcefully the need for individual choice and commitment. This at first seems contradictory, and some scholars have attributed these two views to different schools or periods. The two beliefs, however, stand side-by-side and cannot be assigned to different people. Further, the supposed contradiction between predestination and freewill does not accord with the common ancient view, which held them together quite happily. Josephus himself thought both that God determined the outcome of the Jewish revolt and that the nation had failed to heed warnings and read signs, and so deserved to be punished.[13]

The members of the Qumran sect thought that God had chosen them:

I know that the inclination of every spirit [is in Thy hand];
Thou didst establish [all] its [ways] before ever creating it,
   and how can any man change Thy words?
Thou alone didst [create] the just
   and establish him from the womb
   for the time of goodwill,
that he might be preserved in Thy Covenant.
. . .
But the wicked Thou didst create
   for [the time] of Thy [wrath]. (1QH 15.13–19)

Thou, [O God], didst redeem us for Thyself as an eternal people,
and into the lot of light didst Thou cast us for Thy truth.
Thou didst appoint from of old the Prince of light, to assist
us . . . (1QM 13.9–11)

Similarly we read that the Angel of Light governs the children of righteousness, that the Angel of Darkness rules the men of falsehood, and that God 'established their whole design' (1QS 3.13–4.1). We seem to have in these passages direct statements of double predestination: some to good, some to evil. One of the words that designates the sectarians is 'the elect', those chosen by God (e.g. 1QS 9.14).

But another term is 'the volunteers', those who commit themselves to follow the sectarian covenant (e.g. 1QS 1.7). And we have seen in considering the regimen of the sect that people were considered able to transgress or to refrain from transgression, as they were able to join or not to join the sect.

Both predestination and free choice, depending on the circumstances, were considered to be true and could be stated by the same person. The electing grace of God that chooses some and rejects others was emphasized when the author was thinking primarily of himself or of his colleagues within the sect, especially vis à vis God. In such a context, gratitude is the appropriate response, accompanied by wonder at being chosen, a feeling of personal unworthiness and an intense perception of God's graciousness. When compared to God, no one can be righteous or worthy:

> As for me,
>   my justification is with God.
> In His hand are the perfection of my way
>   and the uprightness of my heart.
> He will wipe out my transgression
>   through His righteousness. (1QS 11.2f.)

It follows that membership in the community must be attributed to God's choice, not to human effort or merit:

> What am I, that thou shouldst [teach] me
>   the counsel of Thy truth,
>   and give me understanding
>   of Thy marvellous works . . .? (1QH 11.3f.)

It is not surprising that this attitude is found primarily in the hymnic material. The hymns are in the general category of prayers or blessings, and it is natural for one in the attitude of prayer to feel unworthy before God's grace, and thus to emphasize God's initiative and choice.

When considering community life, however, or outsiders, or those trying to enter the covenant, or the backsliders within the sect, and in giving rules for dealing with these people, the authors naturally wrote as if all were at the disposal of the individual. The same assumption will be found in all Jewish legal material, whether in the Scrolls or elsewhere, and in passages condemning those who are outside.[14]

The strong emphasis on both predestination and freedom of choice is to be attributed largely to the intensity of the sectarian life: their gratitude to God for putting them in the 'lot of light', and their insistence that they are fully committed to his way and obey him out of choice, thus justifying their superior position to the rest of humanity. Their consciousness of election was acute, since they thought that they had been selected from within a group, the Jews, who in general thought that they were the chosen of God. This gave rise to wonder and gratitude.

Grace and works

Accompanying these expressions of both predestining grace and freely offered commitment is an extreme emphasis on both grace and good deeds as necessary for salvation. The sectarians counted themselves both as worth nothing, capable of no good deed, and also as perfect or nearly perfect.

> What is a creature of clay
>   for such great marvels to be done,
> whereas he is iniquity from the womb
>   and in guilty unfaithfulness until his old age? (1QH 4.29f.)

> Who can endure Thy glory,
>   and what is the son of man
>   in the midst of Thy wonderful deeds?
> What shall one born of woman
>   be accounted before Thee?
> Kneaded from the dust,
>   his abode is the nourishment of worms. (1QS 11.20f.)

The legal material, however, shows that the sectarians were expected to live perfect lives. The penal code of the *Community Rule* is concerned with extremely minor matters – such as guffawing at the wrong time – and it appears that more substantial transgressions were not much of a problem. Further, the demand for 'perfection of way' is repeatedly made. 'The perfect of way' is one of the names that the sectarians had for themselves, along with other titles such as 'children of righteousness', 'the upright' and 'the righteous' (e.g. 1QS 4.22; 1QH 1.36). The members were required to 'walk perfectly together in all that has been revealed to them' (1QS 9.19).

The explanation of the feelings of both 'nothingness' and 'perfection of way' is similar to that just offered in discussing predestination and free will. Humans compared to God are imperfect, in fact hopelessly wicked and incapable, and they can be saved only by his grace. But compared to one another, or judged by the standard of an objective law, they may be perfect or nearly so. Happily, one of the Hymns says this explicitly:

> For no man can be just in Thy judgment
>   or [righteous in] Thy trial
> Though one man be more just than another ... (1QH 9.14–17)

This theology, which combines the feeling of complete worthlessness and total reliance on God's grace with the belief that members can lead virtually spotless lives, is not unique. It can be seen, for example, in rabbinic literature and in the Pauline letters. The notion that Paul devalued 'good works' is a straightforward academic error, readily visible to anyone who will read his letters without wearing glasses that filter out selected passages. The notion that 'works' and 'grace' are opposed to each other, like the supposed opposition of fate and freewill, is contrary to the ancient Jewish view. Reliance on grace and the requirement of works are, however, expressed in the Scrolls with unusual intensity, and each one is stated with a remarkable degree of extremism: the sectarians are worthless and can do nothing; they are quite capable of perfection.[15]

The community as temple

The radicalness of sectarian theology is seen when we consider the theme of the sect as temple. The sectarians thought that, while they were cut off from Jerusalem, their own community functioned as the true temple. In the previous chapter, we saw one of the component parts of this view: the sectarians applied to themselves extra purity laws, derived either from priestly practice or from the laws governing lay people when they ate holy food or entered the temple. The Qumran sectarians immersed before eating (at least before some of their meals), wore linen loincloths when they immersed (possibly like the priests), usually abstained from alcohol (like people in the temple), and bathed after touching someone less pure (possibly a priestly rule). In the messianic age the community would become more priestly yet: the blemished would be excluded from public meetings and all residents of Jerusalem would live as if they were in the temple: men who had nocturnal emissions would leave the city until they were purified.

The sectarians did not fantasize that laymen were priests. On the contrary, they were highly conscious of the distinction, and priests were invariably given pride of place in their rules and expectations. Rather, lay Essenes aspired to a higher degree of purity than the law requires. Jewish society already had a set of higher purity laws: those governing the priesthood, admission to the temple, and sacred meals (e.g. the shared sacrifice). The Essenes regarded these laws as stating an ideal of purity for one and all, and even lay Essenes, particularly the Qumran sect, tried to live by some of them some of the time.

The Qumranians, however, considered the community to substitute for the temple in a more radical way than we have yet seen. The existence of the community was regarded as atoning for 'the land' (1QSa 1.3), which probably means preserving its purity for their eventual habitation. More particularly, the sectarians atoned 'without the flesh of holocausts and the fat of sacrifice'; in their stead were 'prayer rightly offered' and 'perfection of way' (1QS 9.4–5).

The sectarians were neither the first nor the last Jews to find themselves forced to do without the rites of the Jerusalem temple, which God had appointed for atonement; the path they chose was a natural one, and it would be followed by others. 'Community as temple', for example, is a theme known from Paul (II Cor. 6.16; cf. I Cor. 3.16). 'Atonement without sacrifice' is common in rabbinic literature.[16] The priestly founders of the sect had to think seriously about the loss of the sacrificial system, and they came up with a good solution: prayer and obedience to the law.

There is, however, one curious omission. 'Repentance' (in Hebrew, 'return' rather than 'rethink') does not serve to repair intra-covenantal transgression. The word is used for those who enter the sect: they 'turn from transgression' (1QS 10.20), but not for those who subsequently break one of the community's rules (unless 1QH 14.24 is an exception). One supposes that transgressors within the covenant were meant to regret their slips, but 'repentance' does not count as atonement. Atonement required acceptance of punishment (reduction of food, exclusion from the Pure Meal) and sometimes a new probationary period. Purely internal repentance did not suffice, and punishment was also required.

The *Covenant of Damascus*, we saw above, did not exclude presenting sacrifices at the temple in Jerusalem. Josephus, in his second principal summary of Essene practice, said that members of the party sent 'votive offerings' to the temple, but performed sacrifices according to their own 'ritual of purification' (*Antiq.* 18.19). The difficulties of the text are discussed by Feldman in his note to the translation. Josephus seems to be describing a third practice: neither complete shunning of the temple (as the Qumran documents), nor acceptance of sacrifice in Jerusalem (as the *Covenant of Damascus*), but something in between: gifts that were set up in the temple area (votives),[17] rather than animal or cereal sacrifices. We noted above that Josephus may have information derived from Essene sub-groups other than the two of which we have direct knowledge, and the practice described in *Antiq.* 18.19 may have been observed by one or more such groups.[18]

Covenantal nomism

The Essene literature perfectly exhibits the underlying structure of covenantal nomism: prior grace, election, the covenant and the law, the requirement of obedience, reward and punishment, atonement. The Essenes' definitions of all these were partly different from those of other Jews, but the scheme is explicitly present.

The contents of the covenant and the law require one more word. According to both 1QS and CD, those who joined the Essenes 'returned' to the 'law of Moses', which, however, contained secrets that they could not have known until they joined.[19] The Essene formulation, 'return', shows that they thought that God really had revealed their version of the covenant and the law to Moses, and then to the Zadokite priests. They do not explicitly explain this: how the law could have been given to Moses and yet contain secrets that were later revealed to the Zadokite priests. But, in their view, Israelites who did not seek for and discover the secret revelations broke the law, and people who joined 'returned' to it. That is to say, in real terms the Essenes had a partly different covenant, a partly different law. Sometimes they used the term 'new covenant', which does justice to this aspect of their theology (CD 6.19; 8.21; 20.12; 1QpHab 2.3f.).

We considered above the problem of whether or not the Sadducees had non-biblical rules that they admitted to be such, or whether they claimed to base everything on the biblical text (pp. 333–5). Below we shall discuss the Pharisees' supposed view of 'oral law'. The Essene position is clear in general terms. Their covenant and their laws were partly different from those commonly known, but they had been revealed to Moses, and they had the very same status as what we now call the Bible. The *Temple Rule* is written in the first person, as if God speaks, and it revises aspects of the Pentateuch. The author, as Yadin makes clear, worked exegetically, basing the revision on phrases in the common Bible.[20] Thus the ancient learned sectarian would object to the way I am describing this; he did not write a 'revision', but a clarification of what God had really meant. We do not know the precise status of every Essene rule. It seems to me doubtful that they thought that the transgressions and penalties of 1QS 7 were secret parts of the Mosaic law, and more likely that they recognized them as simply community rules, decided by the Zadokites or by the majority of the sect and enforced by officers. Probably they regarded only such documents as 11QT, and possibly *Jubilees*, as well as books of which we know nothing, as belonging to the 'secrets' of the revelation to Moses.[21]

Conclusion

The Dead Sea branch of the Essene party left hidden in caves documents that allow us a first-hand examination of the thought of one of the parties of first-century Judaism. There is no known Sadducean literature. Pharisaic material must be painstakingly extracted from later rabbinic literature, and then never with complete certainty. The thought, practice and organization of a zealous – even fanatic – group stand sharply before us in manuscripts that are intense with fervour, determination, severity and hope.

Everything about the sectarians requires the use of superlatives: the most pious, the most rigorous and legalistic, the most conscious of human failings, the most reliant on the grace of God, the most radical, the most exclusive. The sectarian literature serves as a paradigm, showing us how to find the religious commitment behind sometimes arcane practices and beliefs, and how to understand theological views that at first sight do not cohere.

The Scrolls allow us to comment on Josephus and also on the relationship between primary sources and secondary description. Josephus was quite a good historian; that is, he had good sources plus some personal knowledge, and he got a remarkable number of things right. Some distinctions between the married and the celibate group he did not know or chose not to mention, and he gave no hint of the importance of Zadokite descent. When it comes to theology we find him a little less trustworthy. Certainly his description does not convey adequately the flavour of Scrolls. His bland statement that the Essenes hated 'the unjust' is a good example of the inadequacy of a second-hand summary to convey the passion and intensity of zealous believers. To catch this, one must read the Scrolls themselves, especially 1QS and some of the hymns (1QS 10.5–11.22; 1QH). There one will fully see the combination of internal self-absorption, fanaticism, vitriol and hatred of others, trust in God's grace, and love and devotion to him and his elect. No summary can do justice to the spirit of the Scrolls.

18

The Pharisees I: History

Survey

The Pharisees, like the other two parties, are mentioned at the time of Jonathan (161–143 BCE; *Antiq.* 13.171). The earliest event in which Pharisees figure comes a few decades later, early in the reign of Hyrcanus I (135–104). It shows that conflict with the Sadducees was already well established and thus supports the view that the parties originated earlier. A Pharisee, Eleazar, told Hyrcanus that he should surrender the high priesthood, and Hyrcanus then allied himself with the Sadducees (*Antiq.* 13.288–98). At the conclusion of this anecdote Josephus wrote that Hyrcanus 'quieted the outbreak [*stasis*] and lived happily thereafter' (*Antiq.* 13.299). An 'outbreak' or 'uprising' (a better translation of *stasis*) sounds more serious than the story of the Pharisee Eleazar had led us to expect, and one immediately thinks of icebergs and their tips. Perhaps there was more to it than a single rebuke by a single Pharisee. When we turn to the parallel account in *War* 1.67–9 we find the story of an uprising at the beginning of Hyrcanus' reign. Large numbers held meetings to oppose him and his sons, and finally a war erupted. Hyrcanus put down the revolt, and only then could he lead a quiet life. The account in the *War* does not mention Pharisees – neither one nor many – but we shall see that Josephus tried to play down or even eliminate the possibility that they were prone to revolt. It is by no means farfetched to think that there was a revolt (as in the *War*) and that Pharisees played an appreciable part in it (hinted at in the *Antiquities*), which led Hyrcanus to ally himself with the Sadducees. The story about Eleazar's rebuke puts into the terms of personal drama what was more likely serious religio-political opposition. It may even tell us one of the things that the party held against Hyrcanus: his combining the offices of high priest and king.

Hyrcanus was succeeded by his son Aristobulus I, who ruled for only one year (104–103). His brief reign was marked by suspicion of his brothers, one of whom he killed, while imprisoning others. When he died, his widow, Salome Alexandra, released the imprisoned brothers and saw to it that one of them, Alexander Jannaeus, became the next king. Apparently they also married.

The Pharisees are not explicitly mentioned during the bloody reign of Jannaeus (103–76). It seems, however, that they continued the hostility that they had shown to his father. Jannaeus certainly had serious internal opposition. In the midst of wars against enemies on his borders, he was also faced with civil disruptions. One year at the Feast of Booths his Jewish opponents (unnamed) began to revile him and to throw citrons at him (the citrus fruit that features in the festival). The result was that six thousand were executed (*War* 1.89; *Antiq.* 13.372–373). External wars and civil dissent continued to go hand in hand. At one point in the civil war, having put most of his enemies to flight, Jannaeus brought eight hundred of them as captives back to Jerusalem. There he had them crucified, apparently in the city itself; and while they still lived he had 'their wives and children butchered before their eyes, while he looked on, drinking, with his concubines reclining beside him' (*War* 1.97; cf. *Antiq.* 13.380).

Many scholars, with good cause, believe that these internal opponents were Pharisees or were led by Pharisees. There are three reasons for this view: (1) In discussing Hyrcanus Josephus mentioned animosity towards him 'and his sons', and then immediately referred to the hostility of the Pharisees (*Antiq.* 13.288). He added that Hyrcanus' break with the Pharisees led to the 'hatred of the masses for him and his sons' (13.296). Since Jannaeus was the son of Hyrcanus who reigned for a substantial period of time, it is reasonable to see the Pharisees as playing a major role in the internal opposition to him. (2) On his deathbed, Jannaeus (according to Josephus) counselled Salome Alexandra to 'yield a certain amount of power to the Pharisees', since they could 'dispose the nation favourably towards her' (*Antiq.* 13.401). This seems to show that it was the Pharisees who had caused Jannaeus trouble. (3) The story of Salome Alexandra's reign also points towards the Pharisees as the leaders of opposition to Jannaeus. We now turn directly to that account.

Salome Alexandra, who had put Jannaeus in power, survived him and took the throne for herself, becoming Israel's only reigning Queen (76–67). The Pharisees now had a period of power:

Beside Alexandra, and growing as she grew, arose the Pharisees, a body of Jews with the reputation of excelling the rest of the nation in the observances of religion, and as exact exponents of the laws. To them, being herself intensely religious, she listened with too great deference; while they, gradually taking advantage of an ingenuous woman, became at length the real administrators of the state . . . (*War* 1.110f.)

The Pharisees used their power to the limit, killing some of their enemies and causing others to flee Jerusalem (*War* 1.111–13; *Antiq.* 13.408–15). We discover who the Pharisees' enemies were: 'the eminent' (*War* 1.114) or 'the powerful' (*Antiq.* 13.411). These had recourse to one of the Queen's sons, Aristobulus II, who interceded for them, apparently with partial success, though the Pharisees continued to dominate during Alexandra's reign. According to *War* 1.114 'the eminent' were allowed to leave Jerusalem in peace; according to *Antiq.* 13.417 Alexandra's sons and 'the powerful' were entrusted with some of the fortresses in the country, but not in Jerusalem.

In the midst of the narrative of the Pharisees' persecution of their enemies, Josephus writes that what they were urging on Alexandra was revenge against those who had earlier persuaded Jannaeus to kill the eight hundred (*Antiq.* 13.410). Thus we learn that it was 'the powerful' or 'the eminent' who had supported Jannaeus' policy, including the brutal execution of his internal opponents, and that the Pharisees wanted to execute the 'powerful' in retaliation. This is the third point that leads us to think that the opponents of Jannaeus had included the Pharisees, probably as their leaders.

The identification of the Pharisees as the opponents of Jannaeus is also supported by one of the Dead Sea Scrolls, the *Commentary on Nahum*. It contains a reference to 'the furious young lion' who '[hanged] men alive, [a thing never done] formerly in Israel' (1.6–8). Those who were treated in this way are called 'the seekers of smooth things', apparently a punning reference to the Pharisees.[1]

Thus it appears that the Pharisees led very substantial opposition against Jannaeus, that many of them were executed, and that they retaliated when they had the chance to do so during the reign of Salome Alexandra, executing or banishing their enemies, 'the eminent' – who may reasonably be seen as including the Sadducees. This picture of internecine bloodshed is not pretty, but it is recognizable. One thinks of the exchanges of executions by Protestants and Catholics when power in England shifted from one party to the other after the death of Henry VIII.

It has long been scholarly convention to say that under Salome Alexandra the Pharisees became a majority in the Sanhedrin, believed to be the Jewish governing body. Lohse presents a slight variation. He read the stories of the execution and exile of the eminent when the Pharisees had the upper hand and concluded that Sadducean influence 'significantly declined'. He went further: the Sadducees still held a majority in the Sanhedrin, but now at least they 'were compelled constantly to give attention to Pharisaic views'.[2] I shall later discuss more fully the theory that there was a fixed governing body, called the Sanhedrin, which was composed of representatives of the two parties, and that changes of government brought only shifts from majority to minority positions. Here we need only note that Josephus did not intend to say that 'the eminent' became a minority, or a smaller majority, in a representative assembly. He wrote that the aristocrats lost control entirely. Some were executed and the rest were exiled from Jerusalem.

At this stage of history it is clear, within broad terms, who the Pharisees were. They were committed to interpreting the law accurately and obeying it precisely. They were not aristocrats, but they nevertheless wished to have governmental power for themselves. In the ancient world this was a rare ambition for those who were not wealthy and of prominent families. We shall eventually see that as long as the Jewish state endured the Pharisees never again came close to the kind of power that they exercised during the reign of Salome Alexandra. This is what we should expect. In the Hasmonean and Roman periods Judaism for the most part remained what it had been since the return from exile: an aristocratic oligarchy, headed by the high priest whenever there was no king.

After Salome Alexandra's death, her sons, Hyrcanus II and Aristobulus II, struggled for power. When Aristobulus died, the struggle continued between his son, Antigonus (supported by the Parthians), and Hyrcanus II (backed by Antipater and his sons). During this important contest, the Pharisees are not mentioned. We shall see below that we can infer that on the whole they sided with Hyrcanus II.

The Pharisees certainly played a role early in the reign of Herod. To rehearse the history: Antigonus and his Parthian allies seized power from Hyrcanus II, imprisoned him, and mutilated him, to disqualify him from serving as high priest.[3] Antigonus would have been wiser to have no allies than to seize power with the support of Rome's chief enemy. Rome backed Herod and named him king, thus formally deposing Hyrcanus II (40 BCE). Three years later the new king conquered his capital city. During the siege of Jerusalem, Pollion the Pharisee and Samaias his disciple urged the citizens to open the gates to Herod (*Antiq*. 15.3). This is entirely believable as the continuation of their policy, as we shall see when we discuss the Pharisees and Herod in more detail.

We are now at a crucial stage in our account. The Pharisees played a major role during the period from 135 to 63 BCE; they could affect public events very substantially when everything was intra-Jewish. But in 63 Rome entered the scene, then the Parthians, then Herod, backed by Rome. After Herod came into his own, and no longer needed Roman troops, his army was overwhelmingly strong within Palestine. For one thing, some of his soldiers were Idumaeans, who were probably less influenced by the party squabbles than were the Judaeans and Galileans. For another, he was abler than his predecessors. Things were never the same again. The role that the

Pharisees played at the time of Jannaeus and Salome Alexandra could not be repeated.

In these changed circumstances, we must work a little harder to understand the role of the Pharisees. We shall consider mild resistance, uprisings, official control of the mechanics of government, indirect influence, and popularity. The remaining few stories in Josephus are relevant to each point. Some of them will by now be familiar. I shall go over them again, this time numbering them to make reference more convenient, beginning with the event we just narrated.

1. When Herod besieged Antigonus in Jerusalem, Pollion and Samaias urged that the gates be opened to him (*Antiq.* 15.3).

2. According to one account, the Pharisees' support of Herod later stood them in good stead, since the party subsequently offended the king. About 20 BCE Herod demanded a loyalty oath from his subjects, but 'Pollion the Pharisee and Samaias and most of their disciples would not agree' (*Antiq.* 15.370). According to this account they escaped punishment because of their earlier service to Herod's cause.

There is, however, a second account, one probably derived from a better source. According to it, the Pharisees, who prided themselves on 'adherence to ancestral custom' and who claimed 'to observe the laws of which the Deity approves', over six thousand in number, refused to take the oath and were fined. A patroness paid the fine on their behalf, since the women of the court were in general ruled by the Pharisees (*Antiq.* 17.41f.).

3. Near the end of Herod's life, as his potential heirs jockeyed for position, this same patronness (the wife of Pheroras, Herod's younger brother) became involved in an intrigue. Herod's sister, Salome, disclosed the plot to the king, and he 'put to death those of the Pharisees who were most to blame'. He also executed 'all those of his household who approved of what the Pharisee said',[4] which included the prediction that royal power would be transferred to Pheroras, his wife and their children (*Antiq.* 17.43f.; cf. *War* 1.571).[5]

4. At the very end of Herod's life (*c.* 4 BCE), when it appeared that he was too sick to take effective action, two teachers (*sophistai*), Judas and Matthias, encouraged the young men who listened to their lectures to pull down the golden eagle that Herod had erected over the gate of the temple. They miscalculated Herod's condition, however, and the offenders were arrested. The king convened a public assembly in the amphitheatre at Jericho and asked the crowd what should be done.

The people, apprehensive of wholesale prosecutions, besought him to confine the punishment to the instigators of the deed and to those who had been arrested in the perpetration of it, and to forgo his anger against the rest. The king grudgingly consented; those who had let themselves down from the roof together with the doctors, he had burnt alive; the remainder of those arrested he handed over to his executioners. (*War* 1.648–55; cf.*Antiq.* 17.149–67)

I share the common view that these teachers were Pharisees. Josephus describes them as 'experts in the laws of their country' who 'enjoyed the highest esteem of the whole nation' (*War* 1.648). 'Experts' translates the verb *akriboun*, 'to be precise' or 'strict', and is the word that most often occurs when the Pharisees are discussed. [6] According to the parallel, *Antiq.* 17.149, the two teachers were the 'most learned of the Jews and unrivalled interpreters of the ancestral laws'. 'Precise' teachers of the 'ancestral laws' (*hoi patriōn nomoi*) who were esteemed by 'the whole nation' were, in all probability, Pharisees.

5. That at least some Pharisees were willing to participate in uprisings is shown by the next event in which Josephus mentioned them. After Herod's death, his kingdom was divided, and Judaea (as well as Idumaea and Samaria) fell to Archelaus. Ten years later, however, Archelaus was deposed and exiled, and Rome began to govern Judaea directly. One of the first steps was to take a census, a task that fell to Quirinius, the legate of Syria (6 CE). An insurgency (*apostasis*) was led by Judas the Galilean. According to the first account, he was a teacher or 'doctor' (*sophistēs*) who 'founded a sect of his own, having nothing in common with the others' (*War* 2.117f.). The parallel passage in the *Antiquities* gives a quite different depiction: Judas was aided by Saddok, a Pharisee (*Antiq.* 18.4), and Judas' new party 'agreed in all other respects with the opinions of the Pharisees, except that they had a passion for liberty that was almost unconquerable, since they were convinced that God alone was their leader and master' (*Antiq.* 18.23).[7] The common assumption is that in *Antiq.* 18.4, 23 Josephus has been a little less thorough in distinguishing rebels from other Jews, and from the major parties, than he was in *War* 2.117f. The statements that the rebels agreed with no one (*War*), and that the revolutionary part of their teaching distinguished them from the Pharisees (*Antiq.*) are apologetic; they support Josephus' argument that Jews as such were not inclined to rebellion, and that only a few brigands or eccentrics were willing to take up arms. Therefore the less extreme statement of the uniqueness of the 'fourth philosophy' is to be preferred: Judas was close to the Pharisees, and his main ally was a Pharisee (*Antiq.* 18). Judas' uprising may not have been very substantial, though he was remembered by later revolutionaries, the Sicarii (above, p. 283).

6. Pharisees do not appear again in Josephus' history for sixty years. They figure near the end of the negotiations between Florus, the last Roman procurator, and the chief priests, just before the outbreak of revolt in 66 CE. They seem to have been completely outside the counsels of the Jewish leaders until a very late date, when the strife between Roman soldiers and the Jerusalem populace had gone too far to be checked. Finally the chief priests consulted the 'leading Pharisees', probably seeking a common front in order to quiet the populace and to persuade Florus to remain calm (*War* 2.411). This depiction of consultation between the chief priests and the leading Pharisees, at the very brink of war, is confirmed by Josephus' later account of his own activities at that point. He had urged moderation, which was resented, and he had been compelled to find sanctuary in the Court of the Priests. When the situation calmed, he re-emerged and 'consorted with the chief priests and the leading Pharisees', who were considering what to do (*Life* 20–3). This was a time when all cool heads in the capital put aside other differences. In other terms, the leading Pharisees were co-opted by the chief priests. We shall analyse this crucial stage of history more fully in ch. 21.

7. After the revolt started there was a 'common council' (or possibly 'common assembly'), led by the former high priest Ananus and Joseph son of Gorion (*War* 2.563).[8] Allied with them was Simon son of Gamaliel, a member of the leading Pharisaic family (*War* 4.159, where his name is 'Symeon'). The chief priests and 'the powerful' obviously realized that a revolutionary government needed the co-operation of the leader of a more broadly based party than their own.[9]

8. The prominence of the Pharisees during the revolt is confirmed by Josephus' account of his own life when he commanded the Jewish forces in Galilee. I previously used this story to show that it was commonly assumed that priests, especially high ranking priests, were educated; now we shall note that it indicates two things about the Pharisees: even if they were 'from the lower ranks' (*dēmotikoi*), they were also educated; they were active in the revolt. The Jerusalem council sent a committee to investigate Josephus' handling of the defence of Galilee. Of the four delegates, three were Pharisees (one of them was also a priest) and one a member of a high priestly family (*Life* 189–98). Even the non-priestly Pharisees were 'of equal standing in education' with the priestly aristocrat, despite their lower social and economic status. The social standing of the Pharisaic priest is not given.

It was Simon son of Gamaliel who persuaded the council to send this investigating committee. This is Josephus' account of his enemy:

This Simon was a native of Jerusalem, of a very illustrious family, and of the sect of the Pharisees, who have the reputation of being unrivalled experts in their country's laws. A man highly gifted with intelligence and judgment, he could by sheer genius retrieve an unfortunate situation in affairs of state. (*Life* 191f.)

A good man to lead the Pharisees, a bad man to have for an enemy. Josephus' extreme praise for his former enemy, however, may have a concrete historical explanation. By the time he wrote the *Life*, in the 90s, Josephus had almost certainly been reconciled to the descendants of Simon son of Gamaliel. They led the rabbinic movement that eventually emerged as the leading force in Judaism; its coming predominance may have been clear by the 90s. We shall see just below that this also helps to account for Josephus' treatment of the Pharisees in his later works.

We have now concluded our historical survey based on Josephus. It is clear that we do not have a history of the party from the inside. We do not know for certain why they crop up here and there. A prominent explanation is that of Jacob Neusner. Noting the sixty years of silence from Judas the Galilean to the revolt, Neusner argued that, after the advent of Herod, 'the group [ended] its political life as a sect'.[10] He observed that only individuals figure during the time of Herod and later, and argued that the party as such had dropped out of 'politics'. Under the influence of Hillel, they became a 'pure food club', focused only on their own internal affairs, the principal concern of which was eating ordinary food in priestly purity.

We shall discuss the Pharisees and priestly purity laws below. I wish to propose here, however, a different explanation of why they seem to drop out of 'political' life after the time of Salome Alexandra. In part, they simply lost influence, in part they learned – though not perfectly – when to act and when not. They resisted the oath to Herod (no. 2 in the list above), but for most of his reign they remained quiet. Many people around Herod thought that it was safe to begin intrigues to secure the succession as he neared the end of his life, and the Pharisees joined one of these – some paying for it with their lives (no. 3). The Pharisees continued to have a hard time being silent about offences against the law, as they saw them. The learned teachers thought that Herod was too ill to retaliate for the destruction of the golden eagle, and they too were wrong (no. 4). While the Pharisees had learned caution, they were not always quite cautious enough, as no. 5 shows as well. This sequence of events does not indicate withdrawal, but rather normal prudence, which conflicted with zeal to obey the law and the desire to control public policy.

Put another way, if the Pharisees withdrew from public life, it was not voluntarily. Under Herod there were secret police, and meetings were forbidden (*Antiq.* 15.365f.). No one had much influence, or had it for long, neither the chief priests nor the Pharisees. The former play as little role as the latter in public life under Herod, but we cannot think that the aristocrats also renounced the desire to be active in society.[11] Herod's fears for his safety and jealousy were fatal to the ambitions of others. Thus Josephus' silence about the Pharisees during most of Herod's reign should occasion no surprise.

Once Rome came into direct control of Judaea, rebellions were almost equally hopeless. Further, Rome paid less attention to the internal Jewish parties than had Herod. For the most part, Roman authority was channelled through the high priest and his allies and friends – the chief priests and 'the powerful'. It was to them that the Romans looked for the maintenance of order and the collection of tribute. The Pharisees on the whole were not in this category, as we shall see more fully below. Thus the threat of military reprisal suppressed active dissent, while Rome's policy of ruling through the local aristocracy – a policy common to ancient empires – excluded most of the Pharisees from positions of influence. Rather than being pacifists during the Herodian and Roman years, however, they were as active as they could be without being crushed. The Pharisees seem to have stood for dissent in both periods. They were not in power, nor were they close to those who were. Yet when the time looked ripe, they offered resistance or even engaged in insurrection (nos. 5, 6, 7 and 8). It seems that they could always raise a fair following – though not so massive a following that they could either embroil the nation in an all-out war or prevent one.

The previous theory, which Neusner opposed, was that the Pharisees governed indirectly. Everyone did what they said. We shall look into this possibility – or, rather, begin to do so. Aspects of it will come back up in ch. 21.

Influence and control

The person who reads most scholarly accounts of the Judaism of our period finds lurking everywhere two ghostly figures, not only omnipresent but also all-controlling: the Pharisees and the Sanhedrin. In Josephus the reader discovers 'Mosaic' commandments that are not in fact in the Bible; the usual scholarly reconstruction is that he got them from the Pharisees, who singlehandedly created all extra-biblical laws. The priests had all sorts of rules governing sacrifice and temple procedure: at each step, they followed the Pharisees. There were synagogues in every community: they were run by the Pharisees. There were scribes, thousands of them in Palestine, copying scrolls of the Bible and other books, but mostly drawing up legal documents: they were Pharisees or led by Pharisees. Cities and towns had legal experts: they were Pharisees. There were schools: the teachers were Pharisees; courts: the judges were Pharisees; Diaspora Jews had various purity practices: travelling Pharisees instructed them. And so on, almost forever.[12] Very few people have been troubled by the fact that these Pharisees *are* ghostly and that their constant presence is not mentioned in ancient sources, but is inserted at each point by modern scholarship.

We have before us two extreme positions: that the Pharisees exercised general supervision of all aspects of life and Neusner's counter-proposal, that they dropped out of society altogether to form private eating clubs. Both extremes are unrealistic and can readily be shown to be so. The history that we have just surveyed shows that the Pharisees did not withdraw from society. We have already seen a good deal of evidence that counts against the view that they ran everything, but because of the strength and durability of that opinion, we shall consider it further.

It is important to distinguish between the popularity of the Pharisees and their ability to control official and public events. We shall begin with the latter topic.

1. Official or public control. The relatively minor incidents of Herod's reign and of 6 CE (nos. 1–5) point to the lack of institutional authority. The Pharisees would have liked to have more influence, but, being up against first Herod and then the native aristocracy backed by Rome, they were almost impotent. When they tried to intervene in public affairs by plotting, protesting or joining an uprising, their efforts were ineffective because of the power of the secular government. Josephus' long silences about them complement the accounts of sporadic attempts that failed: they were powerless. The actors who made it into the history were Herod, his descendants, the Jerusalem aristocracy, and of course the Romans themselves.

2. Despite all this, in summary statements Josephus attributes to the Pharisees great authority and *indirect power*. According to these passages, the Pharisees controlled the masses, with the result that others were only apparently in power, while actually they had to follow the Pharisees' rules. Two of these statements come in the discussion of the Pharisees during the early part of the reign of John Hyrcanus (*c.* 134 BCE).

> Particularly hostile to [Hyrcanus] were the Pharisees . . . And so great is their influence with the masses that even when they speak against a king or high priest, they immediately gain credence. (*Antiq.* 13.288)
>
> . . . the Sadducees [have] the confidence of the wealthy alone but no following among the populace, while the Pharisees have the support of the masses. (*Antiq.* 13.298)

The third passage appears in the account of the uprising led by Judas the Galilean:

There are but a few men to whom this doctrine [the Sadducean] has been made known, but these are men of the highest standing. They accomplish practically nothing, however, for whenever they assume some office, though they submit unwillingly and perforce, yet submit they do to the formulas of the Pharisees, since otherwise the masses would not tolerate them. (*Antiq.* 18.17)

It has long been observed that the first passage, *Antiq.* 13.288, does not actually relate to the reign of Hyrcanus I. It comes from some other period. Either Josephus took it from a source and simply inserted it into the earliest substantial discussion of the Pharisees, or his source (see immediately below) had already put it there, at *his* first discussion of the Pharisees. The separation of 'king' and 'high priest' indicates that the passage refers to a time when the two offices were separate – under Herod or Agrippa I – not to the time of Hyrcanus I, who was both.[13] It should be noted that in any case the Pharisees did not manage to get their way in the time of John Hyrcanus. There was an early uprising, but then Hyrcanus allied himself with the Sadducees and governed excellently and in tranquillity for thirty-one years (*Antiq.* 13.296–9). The long and peaceful reign of a Sadducean adherent, who explicitly rejected the Pharisees, does not agree with the summary that he had to follow them.

Josephus probably took both *Antiq.* 13.288 and 298 from the history written by Nicolaus of Damascus, Herod's courtier, spokesman and historian,[14] and thus these two paragraphs may throw light on the period of Herod's reign. Nicolaus' view of the Pharisees was shaped by his own experience of them. On this assumption, which the following discussion will help confirm, we shall look a little more closely at the Pharisees and Herod. There are aspects of their relationship that have often been overlooked or incorrectly assessed.

Both of the main pietist parties started out on Herod's good side. An Essene had made a favourable prediction about the young Herod; during his reign, it appears, the Qumran site was abandoned, and some Essenes lived in Jerusalem. Herod excused them entirely from the requirement to take the loyalty oath, probably because he respected their general refusal to take oaths.[15] He also had the support of the Pharisees when he was appointed king. We should recall the alliances and inherited enmities that explain this fact, which is at first surprising. Jannaeus executed 800 of his opponents; under Salome Alexandra the Pharisees retaliated against 'the eminent'; Aristobulus II backed the eminent; after Salome Alexandra's death, Aristobulus II seized the throne and the high priesthood from Hyrcanus II; Herod's family (led by his father) supported Hyrcanus II; Aristobulus II's son, Antigonus, had some role in the death of Herod's brother; Herod attacked Antigonus.[16] Josephus does not give the loyalties of the various parties during the strife between Hyrcanus II and Herod's family, on the one hand, and Aristobulus II and his son, on the other. His sporadic remarks on the Pharisees' allegiance skip from Salome Alexandra to Herod. I propose that we can understand why the Pharisees at first supported Herod, and consequently better comprehend the nature of the party at the time, if we note that Aristobulus II had opposed their measures during the reign of Salome Alexandra and that her preferred heir was Hyrcanus II, who was later supported by Antipater, Phasael and Herod. On one side we have Alexander Jannaeus, the eminent, Aristobulus II and Antigonus; on the other, the Pharisees, Salome Alexandra, Hyrcanus II, and Herod's family.

One story from the time of Hyrcanus II would lead us to expect hostility between the Pharisees and Herod: when Hyrcanus II called the young Herod to account for his actions in Galilee (he had executed some 'brigands' without authorization from Jerusalem), the Pharisee Samaias spoke against Herod (*Antiq.* 14.172). Because the account of Herod's trial in the *Antiquities* (14.168–80) disagrees so markedly with the parallel in the *War* (1.208–11), where Samaias does not appear, we cannot put too much weight on this story.[17] I shall assume, however, that even if Samaias did offend Herod on this occasion, he more than made up for it later, when he and Pollion wished to admit Herod to Jerusalem (no. 1 above).

Thus at the beginning of his reign Herod and the Pharisees were on good terms. They seem to have assisted him by foretelling the future (*Antiq.* 17.41). During the first dozen years (37 BCE to 25), Herod was heavily occupied establishing and consolidating his rule over the entire area allowed him by Rome. He settled down to enjoy kingship *c.* 25 BCE.[18] Approximately five years later, he demanded the oath of loyalty, which the Pharisees, as well as the Essenes, refused (no. 3). We may imagine that before then the Pharisees were already disenchanted, but we have no definite information. According to one section of *HJP*, during the first part of Herod's reign they had exercised their influence with the people to persuade them to put up with Herod, since 'subjection to a foreigner' was 'a divine punishment which should be borne willingly'.[19] According to another part of *HJP*, the Pharisees' popularity with the people was so great that they were 'best able to restrain' Herod.[20] The passages cited in the notes do not actually support these statements. *Antiq.* 15.176 says that when Samaias urged the Jerusalemites to admit Herod to the city, his advice was based on the view that 'on account of their sins they would not be able to escape him'. This does not say that the Pharisees for the next dozen years kept the populace in line behind Herod because they thought that punishment was needed.

The passage cited in favour of the view that the Pharisees restrained Herod is *Antiq.* 17.41. Jeremias went much further. He understood this passage to say that Herod had to tolerate the Pharisees because of 'their power'. Herod 'had to keep continually before him[self] the fact that the Pharisees had the support of the people'. The Pharisees were even ready 'to declare war on the king and to do him injury'. Fearful, Herod left them 'entirely undisturbed'.[21] The passage says nothing of the sort, neither that Herod feared them because of their popularity, which was so great that they could declare war, nor that they 'restrained' him, presumably from even more ferocious policies. It states that, though they had helped Herod with their predictions, they combatted and hindered him. The 'combat' was not the threat of open war, nor was the 'hindrance' amelioration of his policies; the topic is involvement in *secret plots* against Herod, which his sister Salome disclosed to him and which led to executions (no. 3). The question of the Pharisees' popularity with the people does not arise, nor is there any hint that they restrained him from doing anything he wanted to do.

This passage, like *Antiq.* 13.288 and probably 13.298, is almost certainly from Nicolaus of Damascus. *Antiq.* 13.288 ('when they speak against a king or high priest . . .') and 17.41 (the Pharisees 'combatted and hindered' Herod by engaging in plots) reflect the same period (Herod's reign) and the same point of view (the Pharisees were trouble-makers). When we add the facts that Nicolaus wrote a history that included the reign of Herod, that Josephus' narrative of Herod's reign gives details about what was going on at court, and that in general Josephus used Nicolaus in his account of both Herod and the Hasmoneans (n. 14), we must conclude that these two passages are from Nicolaus. On general grounds – Josephus' use of Nicolaus in this section – it is probable that *Antiq.* 13.298 ('the Pharisees have the support of the masses') is also from Nicolaus.

Once we perceive the source of these passages in Josephus, and the point of view from which they come, we see the situation clearly. Herod ruled to suit himself. He controlled the Pharisees as he controlled every one else. They made a brave show of resistance in refusing the loyalty oath, and they were let off very lightly because of their early alliance. Later, near the end of his life, some Pharisees joined in secret conspiracies. Moreover, in Herod's day memories of the Pharisees as being able to make a great deal of trouble were still strong. If we are correct in thinking that they led an insurrection against John Hyrcanus, and that they played an important part in the civil strife during the time of Alexander Jannaeus, Nicolaus' view that they could create serious difficulty is easy to understand. These considerations adequately account for Nicolaus' view, and they explain what two of the passages in Josephus (*Antiq.* 13.288; 17.41) originally meant. They are carping complaints made by Herod's courtier, who regarded the Pharisees as obstreperous and underhanded. Having written the history of the Hasmoneans, he knew that they might be able to cause serious trouble. These passages do not show that the Pharisees *controlled or strongly influenced public policy* because rulers, such as Herod, were afraid of the masses. They do show that Herod's true supporters distrusted the Pharisees and watched them carefully.[22]

Nicolaus' complaint that the Pharisees had popular support (*Antiq.* 13.288, 298) was probably true. Herod was not universally loved, and many would have applauded the Pharisees' minor resistance to him. Nevertheless, the summary statements that the Pharisees *governed indirectly because of their popularity* cannot stand. John Hyrcanus, Alexander Jannaeus and Herod ruled as they wished and did not pay much attention to public opinion polls (as related to them by the Pharisees). Later, the Roman prefects, procurators and legates did not march to the Pharisees' beat. Caiaphas and some other high priests may have balanced competing opinions and avoided giving offence if they could, but not a single story in Josephus can serve to back up the remarkable generalizations quoted above. Herod, like any autocrat, was wary of grossly and unnecessarily offending the entire populace. He did not put his own image on his coins or profane the temple; on the contrary, in most respects he observed the Jewish law and supported its institutions. He did not, however, kowtow to the Pharisees and obey their special rules. He took some trouble persuading the pious that his theatre in Jerusalem did not contain human images, and thus that it did not constitute a gross violation of the written law. It offended them in other ways as well, but it remained.[23] He did not wish to offend all his subjects at once, and so he generally observed the biblical law. He did not, however, fear the populace and consequently obey the Pharisees. The populace feared him, and the Pharisees mostly stayed out of his way (see also the discussion of *Antiq.* 17.206–18 below, pp. 402f.).[24]

The same general observations apply to *Antiq.* 18.17 (p. 390): the Sadducees, though 'men of the highest standing', had to submit to the Pharisees and could accomplish nothing. This passage, like the others, is a summary and does not necessarily belong where it is inserted, which is in the story of Judas the Galilean. It does not, however, describe any period after Salome Alexandra. We have seen that this was not true in Herod's day. In the post-Herodian period, individual case after individual case shows that the Pharisees did not control anyone. Archelaus used his soldiers when the crowd complained at him too much. After Archelaus was deposed, the chief priests and 'the powerful' ran things as they wished, as far as the Romans – not the Pharisees – allowed. Every example turned up by *case study* –

indispensable in the analysis of Josephus – shows that after Archelaus the high priest and his associates governed with the consent of the Roman overlord and that they served as mediators between the populace and the Romans.

In Jerusalem, the Pharisees' lack of power – both direct and indirect – is confirmed by the accounts of Jesus' trial in all four gospels and by the stories of the harassment of the apostles in the early chapters of Acts, in all of which the chief priest and those close to him are the chief actors. We shall see the very same situation when we consider the execution of James the brother of Jesus and the massacres and attempts at conciliation when Florus was procurator (see ch. 21). The reader of Josephus and the New Testament can find only a single account in which Pharisaic influence made a ruler or leader modify his behaviour. Gamaliel persuaded the council not to execute the early Christians, and so they were only scourged and admonished (Acts 5.33–42). Nevertheless, Stephen was killed, later James the brother of John, and finally James the brother of Jesus.[25]

The parts of the gospels that describe Jesus in Galilee give no comfort to those who maintain that the Pharisees controlled society and government. The synoptic gospels represent the Pharisees as Jesus' principal opponents in Galilee, along with the scribes. They accused him of allowing his disciples to work on the sabbath, but nothing happened. He moved about freely, and crowds, unhindered by the Pharisees' disapproval, sought him out – so Mark.[26] Furthermore, nothing is known of Antipas' reign that could lead to the view that the Pharisees secretly governed Galilee. Antipas built a new capital on a graveyard, decorated his palace with 'images', dismissed his wife and took his half-brother's wife, executed John the Baptist, fought a war against his first wife's father, sought the title king, and was exiled for storing arms – all without the benefit of the Pharisees' advice.[27]

The Herodians, the Roman administrators and the high priests, far from being guided by the Pharisees, were from first to last wilful. The inclination of Herod, Archelaus and the procurators, when faced with public dissent, was not to seek the Pharisees' advice about how to mollify the populace, but to send in troops, which sometimes led to a massacre, and to carry out exemplary executions, sometimes in large numbers.[28] In their one period of power, under Salome Alexandra, the Pharisees had behaved not much differently. They did not simply outvote the Sadducees in the supposed Sanhedrin. They executed and exiled. In so acting they were following the practice of the day. When they were out of power they did not govern indirectly by stirring up the crowd – though at the time of Jannaeus they seem to have tried. After that they finally learned *not* to excite the crowd, since doing so led to executions, but rather to muffle their dissent and await a propitious moment.

When they found what they thought was a good time to strike, and backed Judas the Galilean, they seem no longer to have been able to create a really serious uprising. Despite the prominence that Josephus gives to Judas, by ascribing to him a new philosophy, the insurrection that he expoused seems not to have amounted to much.[29]

The last point helps us to see that scholars who think that rulers obeyed the Pharisees because they controlled the masses misconstrue the way in which popular support functions in an autocratic society. The majority of the populace was not going to follow the Pharisees in an insurrection simply because the Pharisees wanted them to do so. The populace would have to be persuaded that the cause was right and the chances for success were good. Rulers knew this perfectly well. They were not afraid of the populace on a day-to-day basis. Moreover, they did not have good means of sampling public opinion. Rulers did want to avoid mass uprisings, and so they watched large gatherings closely. The general public had only one way of influencing government: taking to the streets *en masse*. If the Pharisees (or any other group) had a good enough issue, and convinced enough people to take to the streets, there would be a reaction, either concessions or military suppression, or first one and then the other. If, as seems likely, the Pharisees joined the opposition to direct Roman rule when Archelaus was deposed, most people thought that the issue was not important enough, or the alternatives not good enough, or the chances of success too slim, and they declined to go along.

Thus in place of Josephus' statements that the Pharisees were indirectly powerful, I propose that, after the reign of Salome, they were in moderate but usually ineffective opposition, and that those who spoke out too loudly, or acted rashly, were executed or killed during the futile uprisings.

3. Did the Pharisees have power and influence in other aspects of life than the 'governmental' control of courts, taxes and foreign affairs? Here we have another glowing summary from Josephus:

> [The Pharisees] are . . . extremely influential among the townsfolk; and all prayers and sacred rites of divine worship are performed according to their exposition. This is the great tribute that the inhabitants of the cities, by practising the highest ideals both in their way of living and in their discourse, have paid to the excellence of the Pharisees. (*Antiq.* 18.15)

Mishnah *Yoma* (on the Day of Atonement) and other tractates support this depiction. *Yoma* portrays the 'elders of the court', doubtless thinking of them as Pharisaic sages, as controlling the activities of the high priest for seven days before the Day of Atonement: making him recite the service so that he would know what to do; making sure he recognized the physical features of oxen, rams and sheep, so that he could sacrifice correctly; and allowing him as much to eat and drink as he wished, until the last night before the service, when he was not given much food and was kept awake. (*Yoma* 1.3–7)

This rather charming and fanciful story is just that – fanciful. Of course some scholars believe such things really happened, since 'it is laid down' in the Mishnah.[30] Here we may ask a simple question: Which of the high priests allowed himself to be treated in such a way, as if he were a complete incompetent? Annas? Ananias? Ananus? Caiphas? Certainly not. These men were tough, shrewd and competent – and very likely arrogant. 'Sages' did not lead them around by their noses. Further, virtually all the high priests of our periods (the Herodian and Roman), who belonged to a small number of families, were brought up to serve in the temple and to be ready to hold high office there. The priests in general were expert butchers, and it is very likely that boys and youths learned by watching their fathers work. Certainly the chief priests did not need sages to teach them about oxen and rams at the last minute before the Day of Atonement.[31]

The Mishnah elsewhere discusses the high priest who is an ʿ*am ha-ʾarets* (meaning, in this instance, unlearned), as if there were a lot who fell into that category (*Horayot* 3.8; cf. *Yoma* 1.6). We in fact know of one. During the last two years of the war with Rome the Zealots chose a high priest who, far from being an aristocrat, was a country bumpkin and did not know how to fulfil the office (*War* 4.155–57). Josephus' disapproval shows not only that he thought that aristocrats should hold the office, but also that this really was an exceptional case. High priests otherwise were of families that routinely prepared their sons for service in the temple.

Granted that the Mishnah waxes fanciful about the need to tutor ignorant high priests, is it nevertheless true that, when in office, the high priests officiated according to the rules of the Pharisees? We know of a substantial dispute between the Pharisees and Sadducees on sacrificial ritual: the Sadducees held that, on the Day of Atonement, before the high priest entered the Holy of Holies, he should first put the incense on the coals, so that smoke would precede him into the inner sanctum. The Pharisees held that the incense should be put on the coals inside the Holy of Holies (see e.g. *Yoma* 5.1).[32] In the Babylonian Talmud appears this story:

There was a Sadducee who had arranged the incense without, and then brought it inside. As he left he was exceedingly glad. On his coming out his father met him and said to him: My son, although we are Sadducees, we are afraid of the Pharisees. He replied: All my life I was aggrieved because of this scriptural verse: 'For I appear in the cloud upon the ark-cover'. I would say: When shall the opportunity come to my hand so that I might fulfil it? Now that such opportunity has come to my hand, should I not have fulfilled it? It is reported that it took only a few days until he died and was thrown on the dungheap and worms came forth from his nose. Some say: He was smitten as he came out [of the Holy of Holies]. (*Yoma* 19b)[33]

This seems to support Josephus' summary: the Sadducees were required to sacrifice according to Pharisaic rites. The Talmud draws the moral: and when they did not, they died.

The story must be considered further fancifulness: no one can identify the high priest who died and who was tossed on to a dungheap shortly after the Day of Atonement. But even if the story were true, it would show that the Sadducean high priests sacrificed to suit themselves.

In most aspects of temple service and worship, issues were not so clear-cut. The temple service followed the scripture and the long tradition of the Zadokites and Hasmoneans. While new disagreements about interpretation and implementation might have arisen after John Hyrcanus (who followed the Sadducees), they seem not to have defined the parties. Early rabbinic literature contains extremely few instances in which a Pharisee (or the House of Hillel or of Shammai) gives a ruling about what the priests should do. Most of the material is focused on aspects of worship and observance that lay in the power of the individual, and very few bear on public practice. I shall not elaborate here on the Mishnah and the Pharisees, but only note the fact (which Neusner has already noted) that the public cult does not loom large in the earliest layers of rabbinic literature.[34]

It may be useful to give an illustration of the degree to which major aspects of the temple service were not debatable. *Zevahim* 2.1 (which may or may not be Pharisaic) states conditions that render an animal sacrifice invalid: if the man who received the blood was not a priest, or was in mourning, or had entered the temple in a state of impurity, or had not washed his hands and feet, or was uncircumcised – and so on. It would have taken considerable effort to find much disagreement. Passages such as this, even if we knew that they are Pharisaic rather than rabbinic, would not prove that priests followed these rules *because* the Pharisees decreed them. Some are in the Bible, some are self-evident (the priest should be Jewish).

Our observations about rabbinic rules do not prove that the leading priests never accepted Pharisaic ideas. Probably at various periods different preferences that had popular support, or were sponsored by a special group, were incorporated by this or that high priest, especially at the large festivals. Thus on some occasion or other it might be possible to say that the Pharisees 'forced' the Sadducees to follow their rules of ritual. But consideration of the

general character of the high priesthood (above, pp. 321–7) will show that the
high priests and their close associates did not work according to Pharisaic
dictation. In other aspects of worship the Pharisees may have been more
influential. We shall consider the significance of their financial rules on tithes
and firstlings below, pp. 405f.

It is almost universally supposed that Pharisees controlled synagogues.
Above we noted the existence of a large synagogue in Jerusalem that was
headed by a prosperous priest – not, to our knowledge, also a Pharisee
(pp. 176f.). Further, Pharisees presumably did not control the synagogues in
Antipas' capital, Tiberias, which had been built on a graveyard – nor, for that
matter, did priests. Neusner has pointed out that in the rabbinic passages that
refer to Pharisees, there are 'no rules about synagogue life', nor about
'reading the Torah and preaching in synagogues'. He proposes, on the basis
of this evidence (or lack of it), that the Pharisees did not claim to 'exercise
influence in the life of synagogues' that they did not control. That is, they may
have had their own, rather than serving as teachers in synagogues generally.[35]
The gospels, however, depict Pharisees as being *present* in the synagogues of
Galilee, but not running them: Jairus is not called a Pharisee (Mark 5.21–4,
35–43), nor is the ruler of the synagogue in Luke 13.14; in another story,
Pharisees gather at a synagogue, along with others (Mark 3.1–6).

The issue of the control of synagogues (or of schools or courts) is in part a
question of numbers. We do not know the geographical spread of Pharisees,
nor of priests and Levites. We can be confident, however, that there were
many more priests and Levites than Pharisees. Based on Josephus' figures,
the ratio was more than three to one (20,000 clergy, 6000 Pharisees).[36] We
may assume that virtually all of these people were literate and thus able to
read the scripture and serve the community in various ways. I argued above
that the priesthood did not give up its ancient prerogative of teaching, and
also that there were enough priests to do the job (pp. 180–2). We cannot say
this of the Pharisees, especially since most of them, unlike the priests, had to
work full time at jobs that tied them down, such as shopkeeping or farming
(below, pp. 404f.). Some priests were also Pharisees, but this overlap was not
so large that Pharisaic priests could have filled all the necessary positions.

Finally, Josephus not only attributed great influence to the Pharisees, he
also wrote that the priests were the teachers and rulers of the nation (ch. 10).
As Mason has pointed out, he maintained the latter view consistently in all his
works, while his statements about the Pharisees vary.[37] We may even say that
Josephus presupposes that the priests were the official teachers of the nation,
though he also depicts lay Pharisees and Essenes as public teachers.[38] I think
that we cannot safely generalize about who dominated how many synagogues,
but we must doubt the general view that the Pharisees ran all of them.

The more extreme exponents of Pharisaic control of worship and private religious practice have held that they also taught Diaspora Jews how to live, what laws to obey and how to obey them. Diaspora Jews, beginning before the rise of the Pharisees, sent gifts to the temple; the Pharisees told them what they should be. Diaspora Jews followed food and purity rules; the Pharisees decided them. I have elsewhere shown that the Diaspora Jews loved God, studied the Bible, and came to their own decisions, which are sometimes prior to and other times completely different from the views of the Pharisees.[39] This subject allows me to exemplify how deeply scholars believe that the Pharisees governed Jewish life and worship, which I shall do anecdotally.

I once pointed out to another scholar that the purity practices known from the Diaspora do not reveal Pharisaic influence. Pharisees did not wash their hands in the sea while praying, as did 'all Jews' according to Aristeas. Pharisees did not keep basins in their bedrooms and splash themselves after intercourse, as did Philo.[40] The reply was that it was the Pharisees who had persuaded Diaspora Jews to adopt purity practices, but Philo and others had changed some of the details, or else the Palestinian Pharisees had voted in favour of a different set of purity rites, but for some reason the decree had not reached Alexandria.

The insertion of Pharisaic determination of what people did at every single point produces a coherent picture. It is, of course, based on a circular argument. This view of the Pharisees is very much like Josephus' belief in 'providence': if it happened, God planned it, since he plans everything. The extreme view of Pharisaic control is equally consistent and equally rests on a dogmatic conviction: only the Pharisees cared about the law and only they decided on how it should be observed; whatever rules people observed attest to the Pharisees' influence, since they made all the rules.

Pharisaic control and popularity: views of apologists

Traditionally both Jewish and Christian scholars have held that the Pharisees really controlled the only parts of religious life that people cared about. Many Jewish scholars, finding their own religious roots in the rabbinic movement, and correctly seeing in it the continuation of many Pharisaic traits and traditions, have held the Pharisees to have been the true religious leaders of their time. Thus, for example, Alexander Guttmann thinks that in the second century BCE the Pharisees 'came to power'. Among other things they opposed animal sacrifice and created instead synagogues as 'the unique Pharisaic institutions' where individual Jews affirmed their loyalty 'to the two-fold Pharisaic law'.[41] One supposes that the populace, controlled by the Pharisees, did not participate in the festivals and other sacrifices. Hyam

Maccoby, discussing Jesus' death (a topic that always comes up when people consider who led the nation), points out that the instigators were the priests, and proposes that the populace, led by the Pharisees, wanted Jesus to be acquitted.[42] Jesus himself was a Pharisee, and his views on love, mercy and grace were Pharisaic; the Pharisees led Israel; and thus on specifically religious questions Jesus, the Pharisees and the ordinary people were in agreement. The Hasidim (at the time of the Hasmonean revolt) were Pharisees, and the post-70 rabbis were Pharisees; throughout the whole period 175 BCE to 135 CE the populace basically followed the Pharisees.[43]

Christian scholars have also seen the rabbinic movement as heir to Pharisaism, and the more anti-Jewish of them have been especially keen to maintain that Judaism in Jesus' day was dominated by the Pharisees. If the Pharisees were in charge, they were at least indirectly responsible for Jesus' death. Jesus was killed because he believed in grace and mercy. Therefore he was opposed by people who opposed those qualities; these were the Pharisees. Their form of Judaism, which continues to this very day, was wretched, being based on self-righteousness and the petty bookkeeping of small merchants.[44]

These competing apologetic positions – (1) the Pharisees ran Judaism and were full of love for one and all; (2) the Pharisees ran Judaism and were awful – are both influenced by the need to explain Christianity's break with Judaism. Jewish scholars have generally seen Jesus as a good Jew who had few serious theological or legal debates with his contemporaries. Christianity was founded by Paul, not Jesus. It was Paul who exalted Jesus to such a degree that Christians broke with Jewish monotheism. That is, Jewish scholars have generally seen the break as *credal* and as being based on the doctrine that Jesus was divine. For a long time Christians agreed: what was wrong with Jews was that they denied the divinity of Christ. But in the eighteenth and nineteenth centuries many Christians began to lose confidence in the creeds. They defined Christianity humanistically, not by the creeds, but by religious and ethical virtues. They then needed a contrasting religion, one that denied what Christians believed in. A Christianity that is defined by love of neighbour, belief in God's grace, and good works that do not earn merit, but rather flow naturally from a person's basic religious orientation, needs a Jewish opponent, a religion that denies these views. Christian scholars found their opponent in rabbinic literature and concluded that the Pharisees opposed love, mercy and grace; they were legalistic, regarding good deeds not as response to God's love, but as items in an account book that force God to save them, quite apart from his mercy. Jewish heirs of the Pharisees, quite naturally, replied that Pharisaism was the champion of love, mercy and grace.

In terms of the Pharisees' ideals, there is no doubt that the Jewish apologists are correct. But casting the debate into these terms is historically misleading. It makes no more sense to say that the Pharisees were hypocritical and legalistic during the two hundred or so years of their history than it would to say that Christians were charitable and always loved their enemies during an equivalent period in their history. One gains no historical understanding by using such terms as 'hypocrisy' and 'charitableness' to cover the actual practice of a sizable group over a long period. This is to write history by using catchwords and slogans, and it is one of the main things wrong with a large number of books written by New Testament scholars that include a section on 'the Jewish background'.

This war of apologists has left numerous important topics inadequately considered. Apologists on both sides assumed that the Pharisees were what Jeremias called 'the new ruling class', and the debate proceeded from there. In fact, as I have tried to show, their role and influence in society varied and was only once as dominant as most people have assumed it generally was. Several other assumptions have accompanied the view of Pharisaic dominance. With regard to the apologetic dispute that has often focused on the death of Jesus, I agree with two of Maccoby's points: Jesus was executed at the behest of the high priest; the Pharisees, at least on average, favoured love, mercy and grace (though they were quite capable of retaliating against their enemies). But I must part company from him on the relative influence of the Pharisees and the priests, and from many others on most of the topics mentioned above: I do not think that the priests were entirely corrupt, that they were despised by the people, that the Pharisees and the populace opposed the temple service, that the Pharisees invented the synagogue and dominated all synagogues, that only they cared for and studied the law, that they dictated policy to Herod, Antipas, Pilate and Caiaphas, that they told the priests how to sacrifice, that they despised ordinary people, or that they pressed for the death sentence of people who believed in repentance. Especially I think that it is incorrect that they really governed 'Judaism' in the time of Jesus.

This 'low' view of the authority of the Pharisees is supported, as far as I know, only by Morton Smith, Jacob Neusner, Shaye Cohen and Martin Goodman. It will soon appear that I regard the Pharisees as more popular than does Neusner, and I disagree very substantially with him about their principal areas of legal concern. But Smith's basic insight has been accepted by all four of us: if one *studies cases* – reads Josephus' accounts of individual events – one can and must correct his often misleading summaries.[45] Summaries can be created by a few strokes of the pen. It is much harder to rewrite hundreds of individual events, and Josephus obviously did not do it.

The disappearance of the Pharisees from the history of the period 63 BCE to 66 CE, except for a few rebellious acts in 20 and 4 BCE and 6 CE, cannot be entirely accidental. The outbursts show that they were present, that they continued teaching, that they had influence, and that sometimes they could raise, or help raise, a mob.

These outbursts count against Neusner's view that the Pharisees withdrew from public life, but they simultaneously confirm that they were not in control, whether direct or indirect, of either 'government' or 'religion'. If they already ran everything, why did they continue to resist, protest, and join insurgencies? Why did they not persuade Herod to take down his eagle – or not to put it up in the first place? If the Pharisees through public teaching actually controlled the populace, why did not those who had military power come down harder on them and hold the party accountable when the crowd caused trouble?

Popularity

When, however, we turn from control of the state and of public worship, to the more general topic of whether or not the Pharisees were respected and often followed in private and semi-private ways, we come a little closer to Josephus' glowing summaries. I do not doubt that the Pharisees were admired and respected and in that sense 'popular'. Further, if one asks which of the three parties had the most popular support, the answer will be the Pharisees. The Essenes were too exclusivist and the Sadducees were too aristocratic. But the notion that the population had to line up behind one of these parties is wrong. Most aspects of religious practice were common. Within common practice, the Pharisees (as we shall see) made numerous, usually minor adjustments. There is no reason for us to suppose that at every step of each festival the ordinary person was conscious of complying with or opposing the views of the Pharisees.

That the Pharisees *could* muster popular support is evident. The case is not proved by Josephus' summaries, but rather by individual events that he narrates. We can assess the Pharisees' popularity in positive terms by using the very same method that leads us to reject the view that they were in control. For the reasons stated above (pp. 383f.), I start with the period after Salome Alexandra. No one disputes their influence prior to and during her reign. Numbers refer to the list on pp. 384–7.

4. The deaths of Judas, Matthias and their followers (of golden eagle fame) had large ramifications. Herod died shortly after the execution of these teachers and their young disciples; and Archelaus, his heir in Judaea, was soon faced by a crowd, who 'made a great outcry and wailing, and even flung

abuse' at him because of the executions. The crowd, significantly, demanded that Archelaus remove the last high priest appointed by Herod 'and choose another man who would serve as high priest more in accordance with the law and purity'. Archelaus sent a representative to try to calm the people, but he and others were unsuccessful. The crowd stoned some of his troops. Finally a riot broke out that Archelaus put down by using 'his whole army, including the cavalry'. According to Josephus, 3,000 were killed (*Antiq.* 17.206–18).

At the 'trial' of the teachers and their followers, in the theatre at Jericho, the populace had decided to support Herod by demanding executions. According to Josephus, the people were motivated by fear. They bravely besought the king to execute only the people directly involved, not others, but that was as far as they felt able to go when personally confronted by Herod (*War* 1.655, quoted above). When a crowd challenged Archelaus on the very same issue, the deaths of the teachers, they probably assumed quite correctly, that he was less formidable than his father; but he was nevertheless prepared to be ruthless when his small effort towards conciliation did not work.

This entire story (the golden eagle and its aftermath) is the best evidence we have for the place of popular opinion in the administration of Palestine under Herod and his sons. (The second best, Antipas' execution of John the Baptist *because* he was so popular, does not relate to the Pharisees. See *Antiq.* 18.116–19.) Popular opinion, loudly and forcibly expressed, would very likely result in a lot of deaths. Under Herod, people had no doubt about this, and so they kept quiet or cheered him on. The Pharisees were popular with the crowd, but this did not give them power.

6, 7 and 8. When the chief priests for the first and last time lost control of relations between the Romans and the crowd, the Pharisees were brought into consultation (6), and finally into the revolutionary government, where at least one was prominent (7). Other Pharisees were trusted and respected by the council (8).

We may add to these points a postscript: At the end of the war, when the policy of the aristocrats had been discredited, the Pharisees managed to survive as a coherent group.

One cannot consider these axial points of the history without seeing that the Pharisees had popular support. The summaries of Josephus are exaggerated: they did not really govern indirectly; the priesthood did not really dance to their tune. Nevertheless, some truth lies behind the summaries. The Pharisees had popular views, and people respected their learning and piety.

The course that the Pharisees were forced to follow, which they did not like at the time, led them to ultimate success. By not themselves being directly implicated in the day-to-day exercise of power, they avoided the animosity that is naturally directed towards the powerful. For one hundred and twenty-three

years, from the death of Salome Alexandra to the beginning of the revolt
(67 BCE–66 CE), they were there, but not in actual control. The Essenes, or
rather a group of them, withdrew completely from Jerusalem for most of the
period. The Hasmoneans and Herodians ruled with cunning, brutality, and
sometimes incompetence. The Roman administrators were a mixed lot,
some fairly honest and capable, but they were necessarily resented. The chief
priests again were mixed: some awful, some noble. In any case many people
doubtless saw them as involved in compromise with Rome. The Pharisees
studied and taught, did their jobs, waited for their chances, acted for the most
part with prudence, and occasionally went too far. These miscalculations
probably made them all the more popular, since they created martyrs. Given
the chance, the Pharisees would have run the country. They were not given it,
and they benefitted thereby.

Social and economic status

The question of the Pharisees' popularity with 'the masses' naturally raises
the question of how close to them they were. We have seen evidence that
indicates that they were not, on the whole, aristocrats, and now we shall draw
together the information that bears on their status in socio-economic terms.

The party seems to have been mostly composed of laymen. Josephus
mentions one Pharisee who was a priest, and rabbinic literature indicates that
there were a few more, one of whom had had an important position (Hanina
the Prefect of the Priests, *Pesahim* 1.6 and elsewhere). As we noted above,
there are relatively few traditions in the earlier layers of rabbinic literature
about the temple service (p. 397), but there are a lot about agriculture, and
priests were not farmers. All the leading members of the party appear to have
been laymen: some are explicitly described as laymen, and not one is called a
priest (Shemaiah and Abtalion, Hillel and Shammai, Gamaliel and Simon his
son). The Pharisees, then, are to be understood as basically a party of laymen
who followed the path opened to them by the fact that Judaism was a religion
of the Book. They studied it and formed their own views, as did some other
laymen of the period.[46]

There is a long scholarly tradition, which seems to me to be at least
partially correct, of identifying the Pharisees as (fairly small) merchants and
traders.[47] Neusner has pointed out that the assumed normal status in the
Mishnah is that of the small but independent landowner.[48] It is possible that
this assumed status in the Mishnah owes something to the work's Pharisaic
heritage. How many lived on the land and how many were urban merchants
we now cannot know. In very general terms, it is probable that most Pharisees
were people of modest means but with a regular income. The references in

Josephus, which contrast them with 'the eminent', which single out Simon son of Gamaliel as being of a notable family, and which describe two important Pharisees at the time of the revolt as being 'of the people' (*dēmotikoi*) constitute good enough evidence for this conclusion, and it gains some support from the more difficult analysis of social and economic presuppositions in early rabbininc literature.

This does not, however, mean that they were part of 'the masses' in the sense of 'the mob' – the large number of labourers who made up so much of ancient society. The Mishnah legislates for small landowners, not for those with no property at all. The disagreement on tithing also supports the view that many Pharisees were landowners. Further, the Pharisees were well-educated in the law, which presupposes that they could find some time to study. We should think of them as being neither leisured nor desitute.

There are two rabbinic passages that may throw some light on the Pharisee's economic status. One we quoted above, *Keritot* 1.7, on the price of doves for sacrifice: Rabban Simeon b. Gamaliel pushed the cost down to a quarter-denar (p. 89). According to *Hagigah* 1.2 the Houses of Hillel and Shammai debated how much should be spent on sacrifices that are brought on the first festival day of each of the pilgrimage festivals. The House of Shammai proposed that the burnt offering should cost at least two maahs of silver and the shared sacrifice at least one maah. The House of Hillel proposed the reverse. We recall that most of the food from the shared sacrifice was taken out of the temple and feasted on, while the burnt offering did not serve as food. Thus the House of Hillel wished the larger expense to be for the animal that served as food. The sums of money are quite small: one maah of silver is one-sixth of a denarius, and a denarius was a day's wage for casual labour (Matt. 20.2). The Houses agreed that three maahs altogether should be spent on these two sacrifices: thus one-half day's work for those near the bottom of the social scale. Although passages such as these do not reveal the relative prosperity of the Pharisees, they show that they were willing to consider the problems that even small sums could pose.

Whether or not the Pharisees themselves were economically well off, were they the people's party? Their rules of tithes and firstlings were cheaper than Josephus'. The Pharisees also sometimes opposed the 'powerful' and the 'eminent'. Were they, then, populists, the leaders of the poor and their consistent champion against the rich? The evidence does not show this. First, their opposition to the 'eminent' reveals that few Pharisees were rich, but it does not prove that they were populists. They did not, as far as we know, establish a popular assembly during their one period of power. They wanted people to follow *their* rules, not to organize and establish their own.

Secondly, their rule about tithes, if followed, would not result in farmers' giving less food to the Levites, since the Pharisees did not reduce first tithe. On the contrary, they upheld it vigorously. They did 'permit' farmers not to take second-tithe money to Jerusalem in years three and six of the seven year cycle; instead of adding poor tithe to second title, they allowed a substitution. Thus they did not favour charity over support of the temple establishment, but they urged their followers to prefer charity to their annual holiday. Some of the Pharisees' other rules saved farmers a little money. Those fortunate enough to own horses and camels saved 1½ shekels during the lifetime of each female, and everyone who grew minor crops (in addition to the 'seven kinds') saved a handful each year.[49] These rules do not lead us to think that the Pharisees' programme for Israel consisted of a series of measures to ameliorate the social and economic conditions of the poorer members of society. They were more interested in seeing their interpretation of the law followed than in promoting the interests of the 'working class'.

In the modern democracies, a politician running for election who championed tax reductions equivalent to the Pharisees' rules about firstlings and first fruits (which amounted to nothing for most taxpayers, to perhaps one-thousandth of their obligations for a few) would trumpet these policies on television. It is possible that the Pharisees used them in a similar way. When they wanted the crowd to do something, they may have cited their record on taxes. The aristocrats also knew how to appeal to the masses when they needed to do so. It was an aristocratic priest who persuaded the ordinary priests to cease the sacrifices on behalf of Rome (*War* 2.409), and he roused the crowd by urging that public records of debts be burnt (*War* 2.427).[50] The Pharisees might have used the slogan, 'lower taxes'. I do not imply that Pharisees were cynical. They doubtless sincerely thought that their rules were right. One of the common modern views of them, however, is that they championed the cause of the ordinary people against the aristocrats. This was, I assume, sometimes the case, but we misunderstand their position if we think that their overriding concern was to pass legislation in favour of the weaker members of society, and that this explains the peculiarities of Pharisaic rules. The modern notion of class antagonism does not provide a good basis for understanding first-century Judaism. Nevertheless, everyone knew that it was sometimes important to appeal to the populace. When an issue arose on which the Pharisaic party or some Pharisees wanted popular support, they would have been remiss not to put their best foot forward.

The last defence of those who wish to maintain that the Pharisees *really* ran first-century Judaism is that they were 'populist' in a more profound way than we have yet considered. Inwardly everybody agreed with them. Pharisees did not have to control anything, neither synagogues, the temple service, schools nor courts. They did not have to be able to rouse the crowd to support them.

They were the heart and soul of the nation, its true spirit, and thus the people lived Pharisaism, whether they belonged to the party or consciously followed it or not. We shall discuss this view in ch. 19, in connection with the Pharisees' distinctive rules.

Dying for their cause

Three of the events discussed above are especially noteworthy examples of dying for God, for the law, or for the participants' own cause (these being indistinguishable to most Jews): the golden eagle incident (4), the uprising of Judas the Galilean (5), and the revolt itself (7 and 8). There are connections among these events that place the Pharisees, or at least some Pharisees, very close to the Sicarii, who took as their slogan 'no master but God'. Josephus brings them together in *Antiq.* 18.4, 23. Saddok the Pharisee was the main ally of Judas the Galilean, who founded the 'fourth philosophy' in 6 CE. This philosophy agreed with the Pharisees, except that those who held it would rather be tortured and executed than 'call any man master' (*Antiq.* 18.23, above, p. 282). We now go forward almost 70 years. The revolt has come and almost gone. A group of the Sicarii are holding out against the Romans in Matsada, Herod's fortress. They have refused to use Herod's immersion pools, and instead have cut two sets of their own out of bedrock. Each set consists of a small stepped pool with a storage pool beside it, rather than being a single large stepped pool. The miqveh + 'otsar arrangement is recommended in the Mishnah.

Let us now consider the speeches that Josephus wrote for Judas and Matthias in urging that the eagle come down and for Eleazar on Matsada, when contemplating the imminent Roman victory. The golden eagle teachers said that

> it was a noble deed to die for the law of one's country; for the souls of those who came to such an end attained immortality and an eternally abiding sense of felicity; it was only the ignoble, uninitiated in their philosophy, who clung in their ignorance to life and preferred death on a sick-bed to that of a hero. (*War* 1.650).

Eleazar said, among many other things,

> that life, not death, is man's misfortune. For it is death which gives liberty to the soul and permits it to depart to its own pure abode (*War* 7.343f.). Unenslaved by the foe let us die, as free men with our children and wives let us quit this life together! This our laws enjoin, this our wives and

children implore of us. The need for this is of God's sending . . . (*War* 7.386f.)

Eleazar's speech had opened with the right slogan, 'we determined neither to serve the Romans nor any other save God' (7.323). Apart from this and the different practical issue – to commit suicide rather than to risk their lives – Eleazar's speech could have been spoken by the two teachers, or theirs by him.

Josephus, of course, wrote both speeches, but nevertheless the sentiments that he attributed to the Sicarii are very close to those attributed to the probably Pharisaic teachers. He consistently attributes the slogan 'no master but God' only to the representatives of the fourth philosophy, but they could be Pharisees in terms of piety and theology.

Lots of Jews, including many aristocrats, were prepared to die for God and the law if things got bad enough. Early there were the pietists who would not fight on the sabbath even though it meant their death. One man killed his family and then took his own life rather than submit to the young Herod.[51] The Pharisees (always assuming that Judas and Matthias were Pharisees), however, are depicted as going beyond that and voluntarily risking their lives, while the followers of Judas and the Sicarii took a striking slogan as encapsulating their resolve. Both the Pharisees and the Sicarii, however, calculated their chances. They did not seize every possible opportunity to die for the law.

I am not suggesting that the Pharisees were Sicarii. Pharisees did not carry out assassinations, as did some of the Sicarii (*War* 2.254–7). Nor do I think that in the 60s CE they were consciously allies, nor that they liked one another, nor even that they could have co-operated together in a common cause. The Sicarii seem to have gotten along with no one, and their tactics were probably reprehensible to most Jews.

I am, however, suggesting an ideological and historical connection. The pious practices of the Sicarii, as indicated by the miqva'ot, were sometimes the same as those of the Pharisees. It is true that sometimes different pious groups applied the law in the same way. Still, the miqva'ot of the Sicarii are noticeably different from those of Herod, the aristocrats in the Upper City, *and* the Qumran sectarians; and they agree so strikingly with the prescriptions of rabbinic law that they were the first pools to be decisively identified as miqva'ot.[52] When one adds to this the greater than average readiness to die for the law, bolstered by confidence in a happy afterlife, one will see that there was some sort of ideological connection. Finally, we return to the point at which we started: in one passage on the fourth philosophy, Josephus says that those who held it disagreed with the Pharisees on only one point. Based on the two issues that we can examine, this seems to be closer to the truth than his statement in *War* 2.118, that the fourth philosophy had 'nothing in common' with the other groups.

During the years since the reciprocal executions under Alexander Jannaeus and Salome Alexandra, most Pharisees had been cautious, and if they held views close to those of the fourth philosophy, they held them prudently. They would *rather* live for the law than die for it. A lot of the inner-Jewish strife from the time of the Seleucids (*c.* 200–175 BCE) to the conclusion of the second revolt (135 CE) had to do precisely with when to live for the law and when to die for it. The Pharisees in general were moderates on the issue, being neither the most hot-headed nor the most conciliatory. They would risk their lives when they thought they had a good chance of winning. Like George Patton, they would rather have the enemy die for *his* country.

Although Josephus' statement in *Antiq.* 18.23 and the miqva'ot point to a fairly close historical connection between holders of the fourth philosophy and the Pharisees, perhaps the most important point to see, and therefore the point with which to conclude this sub-topic, is that *most* Jews thought that God, the law and their way of life were *worth* dying for. This includes even those who, like Josephus, in the end chose not to die; he clearly admired the spirit of Judas, Matthias and even Eleazar, as shown by the speeches that he wrote for them. Pharisaic opinion did not determine at what point other members of the populace would start risking their lives. When external events increased the number, the Pharisees were among those who were ready to take the lead.

Josephus' biases

We now return to two of the peculiarities of Josephus' accounts that mention the Pharisees: (1) the initial denial that Judas the Galilean had anything to do with the three main parties; (2) the summaries in the *Antiquities* that assign so much power to the Pharisees, more than they had.

1. Josephus wished to isolate the revolt as an aberration and to claim that only 'brigands' and the like, or holders of some strange fourth philosophy, opposed peaceful existence under the rule of Rome. As a Jewish apologist he saw that it was advantageous for his nation if Rome could be convinced that the rebels were a minor radical fringe. Scholars generally accept this explanation of some of the peculiarities and contradictions of his narrative. He suppressed references to the Pharisees that would connect them with insurrection in several instances, not just his first account of Judas the Galilean:

a. The report in the *War* of an uprising against Hyrcanus; the Pharisees' involvement is indicated in the *Antiquities* (p. 380).

b. The stories in both the *War* and the *Antiquities* about civil war against Alexander Jannaeus. The inference that the Pharisees were involved is very strong (p. 381).

c. The account in the *War* of the execution of some Pharisees who were involved in an intrigue against Herod; the story is in the *Antiquities* (no. 3 above, p. 384).

d. The narratives about Judas and Matthias, who incited youths to take down the golden eagle and who were probably Pharisees (no. 4, pp. 384f.). This is a less secure inference than point b.

e. The *War* version of the uprising of Judas the Galilean; the Pharisees are connected with him in the *Antiquities* (no. 5, p. 385).

Josephus' desire to separate influential Jewish parties from sedition and revolt was very fully carried through in his first work, *War*, less consistently in the *Antiquities*, though he still did not directly mention the Pharisees' role in the rebellion against Jannaeus, perhaps because it was such a serious civil war. This indicates that he remained partially concerned to minimize the tendency of major groups to revolt and to protect the Pharisees from this charge.

(2) By the 90s, when Josephus wrote the *Antiquities*, it may have been apparent that the Pharisees held the future of Israel in their hands, and possibly Josephus wanted to bolster their standing. This would account for the summaries that attribute to them long-standing though indirect rule, which have no parallel in the *War*. This general explanation was offered by Morton Smith, and it has been accepted or partially accepted by the scholars listed in n. 45 above. The explanation is, I think, too simple, though it is partly correct. Josephus' editorial motives in the *Antiquities* were probably more complex than in the *War*, and the significance of the additional passages on the Pharisees is difficult to assess. I think it likely that, in the parts of the *Antiquities* that describe the Hasmonean and Herodian periods, he simply quoted more of Nicolaus of Damascus than he did in the *War*, including Nicolaus' complaints about the Pharisees and their influence (certainly *Antiq.* 13.288, probably 13.298). As Mason has pointed out (n. 22), the statements of Pharisaic influence are not necessarily favourable: the author deplores it. His attitude is especially clear when he emphasizes that it was through women that the Pharisees exercised influence (Salome Alexandra: *Antiq.* 13.417 [cf. *War* 1.110f.]; the women of Herod's court: *Antiq.* 17.41–3). I do not agree with Mason, however, that it was Josephus who so carefully crafted these sections of the *Antiquities*. We may safely attribute to Nicolaus the

subtle denigration of the Pharisees and their supporters.[53] Josephus probably read the summaries as do most modern scholars: the Pharisees were popular and therefore dominant. If so, he found the summaries agreeable because, in the 90s, he was glad to espouse Pharisaic influence, even when doing so meant connecting the Pharisees with revolt and dissension.

Josephus' generally favourable view of the Pharisees is proved by the previous point: he dissociated them from rebellion. In the *Antiquities* he changed tactics, using Nicolaus' summaries and adding his own (*Antiq.* 18.17) in order to enhance their prestige in post-war Judaism.

It is noteworthy that these two biases are ultimately at odds with each other. The more Josephus builds up the dominance of the Pharisees over the populace, the more difficult it is to maintain that they had no connection with rebellion. It cannot be true both that the populace always followed the Pharisees and that the Pharisees were pacifists. The pacifism of the Pharisees is not directly argued by Josephus: he simply eliminated references to them in several of his accounts of insurrections. This sort of editorial work does not immediately seem to be in conflict with the summaries that say that the Pharisees controlled the populace. But, once we see that it is, we should conclude that both biases resulted in exaggeration: the Pharisees were less dominant than the summaries state and more inclined to revolt than Josephus' silence suggests.

I should emphasize that I am by no means the only person to discover the role of the Pharisees in the uprisings listed above: on the contrary, this is commonly recognized. Nor am I the one who discovered that the summaries of Pharisaic control do not square with concrete events. These observations have not, however, been thoroughly worked out in such a way as to explain the standing of the Pharisees in the Herodian and Roman periods: they were popular, but not so popular that they decided when there were and were not uprisings, nor so popular that they forced Herod, Archelaus, Antipas, the Roman administrators and the chief priests to follow their interpretation of Jewish law. I have also tried to situate the Pharisees at the right point on the scale that measures readiness to revolt. They were a little left of centre, readier to take risks than were most people, not as prone to violent solutions as others.

These views of the Pharisees – popular, not in control of government, not able to determine how many people would join an insurrection or a protest, moderately ready to take action, but usually prudent – save all the evidence (except, of course, the statement that everyone always did what the Pharisees said). Given the right issue and the right circumstances, they could lead a substantial part of the populace. They hoped for freedom, and so did many others. They could not always be overtly vocal, for fear of mass executions, but their basic sympathy was doubtless widely known.

We conclude: the Pharisees were a substantial group, the largest and most influential group that is identifiable in pre-70 Judaism, except for the priesthood, headed by the chief priests. Altogether the priesthood was larger than the Pharisaic party. Josephus' figures (20,000 priests, 6,000 Pharisees (at the time of Herod) and 4,000 Essenes; p. 14) are of course round numbers, but they probably reflect relative size. There was only a small overlap: a few priests and Levites were Pharisees. During most of their history the Pharisees were out of power, though they desired it. They were thus a focal point for anti-establishment sentiment. When the time seemed right they, or at least some of them, were willing to take up arms against the government.

Some of the Pharisees were eminent in social and economic terms, but for the most part they were not an aristocratic group. Many people respected their piety, learning and scrupulousness with regard to the law, and many applauded them for their relative political independence and their hope for full independence. They did not, however, control any aspect of Judaism before 70, except during the reign of Salome Alexandra.[54] During the revolt they achieved a position of leadership, having been called in by the chief priests in order to broaden their base of support. After the destruction of Jerusalem, they led the reconstruction of Judaism, giving up their party name, becoming more catholic, and taking the title 'rabbis', 'teachers'.

19

The Pharisees II: Theology and Practice

Introduction

In describing Pharisaic practice and belief, scholars have traditionally had recourse to three sources: (1) summaries in Josephus; (2) the New Testament, especially the synoptic gospels; (3) rabbinic literature. Since most have thought that rabbinic literature repeated the views of the Pharisees, and that Pharisaism dominated pre-70 Judaism, they have often made few distinctions between what pre-70 Pharisees, post-70 rabbis, and Jews in general thought and did. Thanks largely to the work of Jacob Neusner, many scholars have now come to see that rabbinic literature must be used as evidence for pre-70 Judaism with extreme caution. It does contain pre-70 material, but one must stratify it to see what makes up the oldest layer. Even when this is accomplished, one may not assume that the earliest material represents common practice. I agree entirely with both these points.

Neusner has become reluctant to attribute even the earliest stratum of rabbinic literature to the Pharisees,[1] but in many respects the old arguments for linking Pharisaism and rabbinism still hold. There are substantial continuities between the two, such as the emphasis on non-biblical traditions. It is also important that the rabbis of the late first century and the second century regarded themselves as heirs of the Pharisees. In studying Pharisaism, we should, wherever possible, correlate different sources and not rely on only one. For details, however, we must go to rabbinic literature, since Josephus and the New Testament provide very few. It is much to be regretted that Josephus, who wrote extensively about the Essenes, said so little about the other two parties. A description of Pharisaism by Paul would be even more helpful, since we would discover what counted as Pharisaism in the Diaspora. The only direct information that Paul gives is that Pharisees were zealous for the law (implied in Gal. 1.14), which coincides perfectly with what we learn from Josephus, but it does not get us far.[2] In most of the following sections I shall make appreciable use of rabbinic literature, especially of passages identified as Pharisaic in Neusner's *Rabbinic Traditions about the Pharisees before 70*. This remains the best single body of evidence, but as yet it has been inadequately studied and utilized.[3] The present chapter by no means corrects that situation; we shall do no more than look briefly at a few points.

The discussion of Pharisaic theology will not take very long, partly because of the nature of the evidence, partly because so many aspects have already been discussed. Both these points require elaboration.

1. We have seen that, for details, we must have recourse to rabbinic literature, especially to the passages that we can attribute to the earliest layer. Early rabbinic literature, however, is largely legal; one can derive from it general theological beliefs, such as that charity is important, but nothing like the rich substance that the Dead Sea Scrolls provide for the Essenes. If all we had from Qumran were the *Community Rule*, without its concluding hymn, the evidence would be analogous to what the Mishnah tells us about the Pharisees: the Dead Sea sect would look like a religion in which nothing mattered but rules. Neusner, in fact, has proposed that this was true of the early rabbis.[4] This shows a lack of imagination and a failure to consider the accident of survival. If we had a collection of private Pharisaic prayers, we would find them as deeply devotional as are the hymns from Qumran. Since they did not survive, it will be important to reconsider the main themes of the Eighteen Benedictions, which probably show something of Pharisaic piety.

The accident of survival poses a further problem. If the earliest rabbinic literature tells us too little about Pharisaic theology and piety, it tells us too much about their legal interpretation; that is, too much to be adequately covered in the present chapter. The required stratification is, in the first place, very difficult to achieve.[5] The earliest rabbinic document, the Mishnah, is usually dated *c*. 200–220 CE. Much of the material is anonymous, while other passages are attributed to named sages. Of the attributed material, the bulk is second century rather than first (even assuming that all attributions are accurate). Separating the possibly first-century material from later passages in the Mishnah and other rabbinic sources is slow, difficult work, and categorizing it is almost equally hard. Neusner spent three volumes at the second task, but he mis-categorized the passages, and the entire job needs to be done again. I have attempted to do it for Purity (see n. 5), but the analysis of rabbinic legal debates is not really my métier, and I wanted to do just enough of it to see whether or not Neusner's passages support his conclusions. They do not.

The task of studying Pharisaic views, however, requires more than just stratifying and categorizing passages. Most of the early passages are *debates*, not rules, and one would have to probe behind each debate to see what the Pharisees agreed on. A lot of work is yet to be done.[6]

The problem in using the New Testament and Josephus to explore Pharisaic theology is simply that we cannot derive enough information from them. The fact that Josephus was biased in favour of the Pharisees,[7] and that the authors of the gospels were biased against them, would aid investigation rather than hinder it, if they addressed the same points. We could examine what is common to friend and foe. On a few legal topics, we can, in fact, make use of the gospels and the Mishnah in this way, but it is more difficult to do on theological issues. From the New Testament we learn very little specifically about Pharisaic theology. Josephus' reports on the Pharisees' beliefs are very brief, and he mentions only two theological points: belief in the resurrection and in the 'co-operation' of divine providence ('fate') and human free will. We have discussed both already,[8] though we can add a little information about providence. This leads to the second point.

2. The Pharisees shared the beliefs common to Jews, beliefs that we considered in ch. 13. Yet, not having the type of material that we have for the Qumran sect, we cannot give the sort of nuance to the Pharisees' beliefs that is possible in dealing with the Essenes. We may be certain, for example, *that* the Pharisees believed in both providence and free will, as did the sectarians, but we cannot describe *what* they specifically said and *how* they thought about these topics. We miss their passion, their depth, their insight. We are left with propositions, theological opinions, which are quite important, but which are a long way from what we would like to have. I am sure that Paul was not the only first-century Pharisee with driving commitment, quick intelligence, and passionate devotion. If, by an act of creative reading, we could apply these qualities to the Pharisees' views, we would probably be closer to the essence of Pharisaism. I shall not attempt to write in this way, because I do not have the skill; perhaps the reader will make good the deficit.

The theology that they shared was this: The Pharisees believed that God was good, that he created the world, that he governed it, and that it would turn out as he wished. God chose Israel: he called Abraham, made with him a covenant, and laid on him a few obligations. He redeemed Israel from Egypt; and, having saved his people, gave them the law and charged them to observe it. God is perfectly reliable and will keep all his promises. Among these are that he will act in the future as he has acted in the past: he will save his people, even though they are disobedient. He can be relied on to punish disobedience and reward obedience. He is just; therefore he never does the reverse. When it comes to punishment, however, his justice is moderated by mercy and by his promises. He does not punish as he might, or who could live? He does not retract his commitment to his people. He holds out his arms to the disobedient, urging them to repent and return. It is never too late for repentance and atonement, which wipe out all transgressions. When God punishes disobedience, or when the transgressor repents in the ways required by the law, all is forgiven. Transgressions against other humans require compensation as well as repentance; people who owe sacrifices should present them. Just as God maintains the people of Israel, so he supports individuals, and in the end he will give eternal felicity to every member of the covenant who has intended to live in accord with the divine will.

This is 'covenantal nomism'. How do I know that the Pharisees shared it? Partly because it was common to virtually all Jews and is to be found in all the main bodies of Jewish material. Partly because it is *presupposed* in the earliest rabbinic material that discusses these themes. In saying that it is presupposed, I do not mean that the rabbis do not provide explicit statements of these theological views. On the contrary, I can quote explicit statements in abundance. Establishing presupposition is, in my view, much stronger than quoting isolated texts. I shall give two examples, after I say a word about dates.

The rabbinic expression of the theology that I call 'covenantal nomism' appears most fully in the non-legal sections of the tannaitic midrashim (commentaries on the Bible that are attributed to first- and second-century Rabbis). The bulk of the material is in the name of rabbis of the period 135–200 CE. It was in the schools of R. Akiba and R. Ishmael that non-legal exegesis first flourished – at least as far as we can prove.[9] The points that these schools agree on are incontestably earlier. How much earlier? Here we must apply common sense. Akiba was and still is famous as a master halakhist, the best at fine legal argument. Did he also invent rabbinic theology? It is not likely; the competing schools, after all, agree. Then we note that many of the same theological points do appear here and there in early material – although, since so much of it is legal, they are not frequently repeated. We next observe that in general Jews whom we *know* lived before the year 70 held approximately the same theological views.

The first example is the election of Israel, which the rabbis assumed. They discussed the possible explanations of why God chose Israel.[10] This assumption appears in pre-70 Jewish authors. Who can read Rom. 9–11 and doubt that Paul *assumes* and cannot relinquish the view that 'the gifts and call of God are irrevocable'? That God will not renounce the election of Israel poses a problem for Paul, which confirms that this was for him self-evident.

To take another case. The rabbis of the high period of theological interpretation of the Pentateuch (not homiletical interpretation of the Psalms and Prophets, for which the evidence is later) discussed how to co-ordinate the various means of atonement with various transgressions. Precisely which sins were wiped out by each of the sacrifices on the Day of Atonement?

Which sins, if any, require only repentance? Since God sends punishment if sins are not voluntarily wiped out, how does it work? Are there degrees of punishment corresponding to the seriousness of sin? Such discussions as these *presuppose* that for every sin there is a means of atonement, and this includes the one sin that, according to the Bible, cannot be forgiven. 'You shall not make wrongful use of the name of the Lord your God, for the Lord will not acquit anyone who misuses his name' (Ex. 20.7, NRSV). This caused the rabbis a little trouble; that is, it called forth their ingenuity. 'R. Eleazar says: It is impossible to say, "he will not acquit", since [elsewhere the Bible] says, "and he will acquit" (Ex. 34.7) . . . He acquits those who repent but does not acquit those who do not repent"'.[11] Other rabbis made other proposals; they all agreed that even this sin could be forgiven. The R. Eleazar quoted above is probably Eleazar b. Azariah, late first century – early second. I would not attribute to the Pharisees his particular exegesis, in which he juxtaposes two biblical passages and applies each to a different situation. But it does seem reasonable to ascribe his concern to the Pharisees and to think that they too thought that God had appointed a means of atonement for every transgression. There are no dissenting voices in rabbinic literature, only different ways of arriving at the same result.

The general view that God will find a means of forgiving every transgression by a member of the 'in' group, even heinous sins, can be found, again, in Paul. The man who committed incest in the church at Corinth, he said, should be expelled; his body would be destroyed, but his soul would be saved (I Cor. 5.5). This is the view that suffering and death atone, a view richly represented in second-century rabbinic literature.

I shall not here try to prove in the same way that Pharisees held the theological beliefs that I sketched above (which in fact were common to most Jews), but it can be done. I am repeating the argument of *Paul and Palestinian Judaism*, with one modification. There I argued only that covenantal nomism is presupposed in first- and second-century rabbinic material and in all the other main bodies of material from 200 BCE to 200 CE. I have here proposed that we can say that this overall theology can be ascribed to the pre-70 Pharisees, and I have given a couple of examples from Paul. For the purpose of this book I shall refer the reader to the description of common theology (ch. 13), to the sketch of covenantal nomism in the Dead Sea Scrolls (ch. 17), and to the discussion of 'other pietists' in ch. 20. The same underlying view is seen throughout, and it is also assumed in the theological exegesis of second-century rabbis. This is adequate proof that the Pharisees held it. I only wish that we could discover just how they expressed themselves and what nuances they gave to their various theological convictions. We can do this, to some degree, in one case, devotion to and trust in God (below, p. 421).

With regard to the Pharisees' *legal* views, I am more hesitant to use second-century discussions and to infer backwards from them. The world had changed quite a lot; the destruction of the temple, the decline of the priestly aristocracy, and the loss of most of the wealth that was based on Jerusalem, meant that the social conditions were quite different, and consequently that the legal situation had changed. In ch. 21 I shall give an example of how the use of passages from the second to the fourth century gives a completely unrealistic view of laws governing shepherds and sheep raising in pre-70 Palestine. The fall of the temple mattered. Were we to try to explore Pharisaic legal traditions on some topics, this would become a major problem. For present purposes, I shall be content to discuss a few of the major Pharisaic positions on topics that are relatively uncomplicated.

I shall now present very briefly the evidence that we have on some *distinctive* or *partially distinctive* Pharisaic views, drawing on Josephus, the New Testament and the earliest layer of rabbinic literature; that is, leaving aside the material ascribed to second-century rabbis (except for illustrative purposes). We shall consider first a few theological topics, then a small selection of legal topics, and finally the character and some of the major concerns of the party.

Providence and freewill

Josephus attributes to the Pharisees belief in both providence ('fate') and freewill. Above I proposed that Jews generally (with the possible exception of the Sadducees) believed in divine Providence, and I discussed Josephus' own theology as exemplifying this more-or-less common theological belief.[12] Here I wish only to cite a few passages that bear directly on the Pharisees. According to Josephus, they

> attribute everything to Fate and to God; they hold that to act rightly or otherwise rests, indeed, for the most part with men, but that in each action Fate co-operates. (*War* 2.162–163)

In *Antiq.* 13.172 he reformulates this belief: 'they say that certain events are the work of Fate, but not all'; in *Antiq.* 18.13 there is a third effort to combine predestination and freewill. In each case he uses 'fate', *heimarmenē*, doubtless again casting the discussing in Greek (especially Stoic) terms for the sake of his audience. Elsewhere he explicitly wrote that between the Pharisees and the Stoics there were 'points of resemblance' (*Life* 12).

Paul, a former Pharisee, asserted both providence and individual free will. In Rom. 8.29f. he wrote of God's 'foreknowing' and 'predestining' some to be 'conformed to the image of his Son', and Rom. 9 is based on the assumption that God predetermined who would be elect and who not. On the other hand Paul obviously thought that individuals exercised free choice both in their behaviour and in their fundamental stance towards God, either rejecting or accepting his will. In Rom. 10.14–17 he makes acceptance of faith depend on a series of volitional acts by humans: 'How are they to believe in him of whom they have never heard?', and so on. All his ethical exhortation is based on the assumption of the freedom of the will.

It is striking that the Mishnah attributes to R. Akiba this same combination of views: 'All is foreseen, but freedom of choice is given' (*Avot* 3.16). Here we see that at least some rabbis continued the Pharisaic combination of fate and freewill.

Since fortunately they were not philosophers, Josephus, Paul and Akiba did not explain how to hold these two views together. The religious conscience readily finds occasion for expression of both complete determination by God and individual responsibility. Belief in God's sovereignty and grace leads to expressions of divine providence and foreknowledge, while belief in his commandments requires the assumption of individual choice. The Pharisees accepted both: election by grace, obedience by free will. They were not alone in combining the two, as we saw when we discussed the Essenes. The combination of these theological views is so basic to Josephus' own thought – God determined the defeat of the Jews; they deserved it – that we must suppose that this union of apparent opposites is more common-Jewish than distinctively Pharisaic, but doubtless it is Pharisaic.

Leniency

Josephus attributes leniency to the Pharisees and its opposite, harshness in judgment, to the Sadducees. He states this directly in discussing two cases. When Eleazar opposed John Hyrcanus, and Hyrcanus asked the Pharisees what the punishment should be, they prescribed only flogging and chains, 'for they did not think it right to sentence a man to death for calumny, and anyway the Pharisees are naturally lenient in the matter of punishments' (*Antiq.* 13.294). In discussing Ananus' execution of James the brother of Jesus, Josephus comments that Ananus was a Sadducee, and thus belonged to the group that was 'more heartless than any of the other Jews . . . when they sit in judgment' (*Antiq.* 20.199). Some opposed the execution, and these may have been Pharisees. They are described as 'those of the inhabitants of the city who were considered the most fair-minded and who were strict in observance of the law' (20.201). (On the Pharisees as 'strict' with regard to the law, see below.)[13]

Acts describes Gamaliel as taking a stand on the side of leniency when the Sanhedrin was considering what to do with Peter and John. The persecutors were the high priest 'and all who were with him, that is, the party of the Sadducees' (Acts 5.17; cf. 5.21), while the Pharisee Gamaliel urged his colleagues to let the Christians alone (Acts 5.33–40).

The Mishnah tractate *Sanhedrin*, which deals with courts and offences, especially those for which the Bible prescribes death, is remarkably lenient. According to its rules, it is most unlikely that anyone could be executed. Not only does it require more elaborate procedures before declaring for guilt than for innocence; not only does it state that the court may reverse itself in favour of acquittal but not in favour of guilt; not only does divided testimony lead to acquittal: the tractate also requires judges to ask witnesses whether or not they warned the accused in advance (5.1). *Sanhedrin* and the following tractate, *Makkot* ('stripes'), which discusses cases for which the penalty was thirty-nine lashes, contain so many rules requiring accusations to be thrown out of court that it is difficult to imagine a conviction.

Some of the rules for the definition of crimes and for the modes of execution may go back to actual court practices in the Hasmonean period,[14] but the courts of Mishnah *Sanhedrin* are to a considerable degree fantasy courts. The Great Sanhedrin is said to consist of sages, and the high priest is notable by his absence. In the world of the Mishnah, 'the king can neither judge nor be judged' (*Sanhedrin* 2.2), and courts of twenty-three try wild animals (1.4). Its authors considered that a court of seventy-one must declare war (1.4). This is not the real world, in which Alexander Jannaeus, Herod and other kings executed whom they would and waged war when they would. Nor does the tractate reflect the world of the high priests Caiaphas and Ananus – both of whom arranged for executions without consulting the laws that are now in the Mishnah.[15] Only occasionally does the real world penetrate the discussion. The rabbis first describe how people are executed by burning: the convicted are choked until they open their mouths and then are 'burnt' by forcing a flaming wick down their throats. There follows a comment by R. Eliezer b. Zadok: once a priest's daughter who committed adultery was burnt at the stake. 'They said to him: Because the court at that time had not right knowledge' (7.2). 'The court at that time' was probably a real court.

The fantasy of the Mishnah, however, mostly points in one direction: leniency. This fundamental element characterized the rabbis' Pharisaic predecessors.

Strictness and precision

The Pharisees were, according to Josephus', 'strict' or 'precise' with regard to the law. The Greek word *akribeia* (and cognates), which may be rendered in either of these ways, is regularly used by Josephus when he discusses the Pharisees, and it is probable that the word has both meanings: they were 'precise' in defining the law and 'strict' in keeping it. Josephus' statements, however, refer mostly to 'precision' of interpretation. Thus he wrote that the Pharisees were 'considered the most accurate interpreters of the laws' (*War* 2.162; cf. 1.108–109; *Life* 191). Acts uses the same word for the Pharisees (26.5), and the author also has Paul, who was a Pharisee, use this word of himself (Acts 22.3, 'educated according to the strict [or precise] manner of the law of our fathers').[16]

Rabbinic literature as a whole shows continuity with Pharisaism on this point. The Mishnah is a very large work, and the bulk of it consists of precise and meticulous discussion of laws. The Pharisaic legacy is clear.

Devotion to God

We should put together the last major point of the section on the history of the Pharisees, 'Dying for the law' (pp. 407–9), belief in the resurrection (pp. 299–302), and 'strictness'. The statement about resurrection (depicted as transmigration of the soul) that Josephus attributes to himself, and the similar statements attributed to the rebel leader Eleazar at Matsada and to the teachers Judas and Matthias (of golden eagle fame), closely tie together belief in an afterlife, the desire to live by the law, and the willingness to die for it. All Jews wished to be allowed to live in accord with God's will; if that was not possible, many of them were willing to die for their cause, trusting God to give them a renewed existence. The prominence of Pharisees in the repeated uprisings indicates that, as a group, they held these views. They may not have been alone in holding them, but hold them they did. We may combine these convictions and call them 'devotion to God'.

This shows, among other things, the application of covenantal principles to the individual's life after death. The covenantal agreement was that God would preserve his people as a whole and the nation would obey his law. Jews, including Pharisees, still believed that. By our period most Jews, prominently including the Pharisees, now added personal life after death: individuals should obey the law no matter what, confident that God would save them.

Traditions

One of the main distinguishing marks of the Pharisaic party was commitment to 'the traditions of the elders' as supplementing or amending biblical law. Josephus explains that the Pharisees had passed on to the people certain regulations handed down by former generations and not recorded in the Laws of Moses, for which reason they are rejected by the Sadduceaean group . . . (*Antiq.* 13.297)

The New Testament confirms the importance that the Pharisees attached to 'tradition' by having Jesus criticize them on that very point. It even names two of these traditions: handwashing, which is not a biblical requirement (Mark 7.1–8), and the practice of declaring property or goods *korban* (Mark 7.11). A man could declare something *korban*, 'an offering', dedicated to God, but maintain the use of it during his own life. Jesus is said to rebuke the Pharisees for abusing this device by using it to shelter goods or money from other claims while retaining it for their own use (Mark 7.12f.).

Rabbinic literature richly attests to extra-biblical traditions, and the Mishnah tractate *Avot* ('Fathers') gives a chain of transmission that presents in detail what Josephus had said in summary: they 'observed regulations handed down by former generations'. The chain of 'fathers' who transmitted the traditions runs from Moses to the great Pharisees of Herod's early rule, Shemaiah and Abtalion (probably the Samaias and Pollion mentioned by Josephus), and to their successors Hillel and Shammai. Hillel and Shammai lived later in Herod's reign and were older contemporaries of Jesus. The claim that their tradition goes back to Moses is not a theme in early rabbinic literature, but the implicit appeal to tradition is seen throughout.

The precise chain of tradition in *Avot* may not originate with pre-70 Pharisees, but the notion of following and building on traditional rules does. It will be of some interest to consider the 'genealogical tables' in *Avot*. After Hillel and Shammai, there are two lists of successors. One list runs through Hillel's physical descendants – Gamaliel, Simeon his son, and their later descendants. Gamaliel and Simeon were pre-70 Pharisees, and their descendants ended up at the head of rabbinnic Judaism. *Avot* traces them down as far as the son of Judah the Patriarch (ha-Nasi), who edited the Mishnah *c.* 200–220 CE. The other list runs from Hillel and Shammai through their student, Johanan b. Zakkai, who lived at the time of the revolt, to his five principal disciples.

Moses

. . .

Hillel and Shammai

Gamaliel	Johanan b. Zakki
Simeon b. Gamaliel	His disciples
Rabbi (Judah ha-Nasi)	(esp. Eliezer the Great
Gamaliel his son	and Joshua)

The double chain makes it appear that there was rivalry within the rabbinic movement between leaders who physically descended from Hillel and those who claimed better to reflect the teaching of both Hillel and Shammai. It is noteworthy, however, that the competitors all saw themselves as heirs of the pre-70 Pharisees.

The Mishnah offers an abundance of concrete detail about the substance of 'the tradition of the elders'. Some of the traditions may have originated as interpretation of biblical law, but some were independent of it. The authors of the Mishnah were fully aware of the distinction.

> [The rules about] release from vows hover in the air and have naught to support them; the rules about the Sabbath, Festal-offerings, and Sacrilege are as mountains hanging by a hair, for [teaching of] scripture [thereon] is scanty and the rules many; the [rules about] cases [concerning property] and the [Temple-]service, and the rules about what is clean and unclean and the forbidden degrees, they have that which supports them, and it is they that are the essentials of the Law. (*Hagigah* 1.8).

This list could have been extended on both ends. The rules about handwashing in the Mishnah are many, with no scriptural support. The agricultural laws have appreciable biblical support. And so forth.

Theologically, the most important question about traditions is their status. Scholars, following a phrase in late rabbinic literature, call the Pharisees' extra-biblical rules 'oral law'. They often write that the Pharisees claimed that their oral laws were of equal age and status with the written law: they were given to Moses on Mount Sinai. This is not what the Pharisees and early rabbis thought. Proving a negative is tedious, and so I shall only exemplify the point.[17] This is one of the rules that goes back to Moses:

> Nahum the Scrivener said: 'I have received a tradition from R. Measha, who received it from his father, who received it from the Pairs,[18] who received it from the Prophets as a *Halakah* given to Moses from Sinai that if a man sowed his field in two kinds of wheat and made them up into one threshing-floor, he grants one *Peah* [as charity]; but if two threshing-floors, he must grant two *Peahs*. (*Pe'ah* 2.6)

In the preface to this tradition, which concerns how many corners of the field to leave for gleaners, we learn that Rabban Gamaliel did not know it, that he had recourse to a rabbinical court to discover the answer, and that even then it was known by only one sage. This is a general characteristic of the rabbinic 'oral laws' that are attributed to Moses: only one rabbi knows each one, and often the academy continues to debate the issue after 'Moses' has been quoted.

A further example: some slightly conflicting views about tefillin and mezuzot are attributed to Moses in the Talmuds: according to *p. Megillah* 75c (4.9), the rule that tefillin had four corners and were black goes back to Moses; according to R. Isaac in *Menahot* 35a Moses decreed that their straps must be black. Others, however, argued that they could be green, black or white, and stories were told of rabbis who used blue or purple.[19] It is hard to read such rabbinic passages and conclude that well before these Rabbis, the Pharisees already believed that their own rules went back to Moses and had equal status with the written laws.

The Pharisaic/rabbinic traditions that are discussed as 'received traditions' or 'traditional halakhot' could be lost, or known only to a man in Babylonia, and in any case sometimes they were not considered authoritative. The few minor traditions or halakhot that are traced back to Moses serve to refute the idea that the Pharisees ascribed their major distinguishing practices to him. On the one hand, the rabbis carried on their debates about things that only later someone said had been handed down from Moses, thus showing that rules in this category were not generally taught and were not on a par with the law. On the other hand, rabbinic literature does not ascribe to Moses the major traditions that we know distinguished the Pharisees, such as ʿeruv (see below).

Another way of stating the matter is this: the theory of halakhot given to Moses is not put forward as 'legitimation' of the Pharisees' peculiar rules, as most scholars seem to think. Far from being the Pharisaic defence of their major non-biblical practices, attribution to Moses is rabbinic one-up-manship, a game played only among rabbis, not used by Pharisees against Sadducees. We might paraphrase rabbinic claims to Mosaic traditions thus: 'You spent all that time arguing about it. You could have asked me. I already knew the answer: it's as old as Moses.'

More seriously, however, the Pharisees did defend their major traditions by an appeal to *antiquity*. They were the 'traditions of the fathers'. This was important in a world in which novelty was scorned,[20] but it did not elevate the traditions to the status of Holy Scripture. On this point, the Pharisees were quite different from the Essenes. The latter had 'secrets' in the Law of Moses that had been revealed to the Zadokite priests, and they regarded transgression of these secret requirements as sin. There is no indication that the Pharisees thought this about their ancestral traditions. On the contrary, breaking a rule that had only 'scribal' or rabbinic authority was not considered a transgression.[21]

It is now time to look at some examples of the Pharisees' legal interpretation.

Work

1. *'Eruvin*. We saw above (p. 335) that the Pharisees invented a tradition that overcame one of the anti-social aspects of sabbath law. By constructing doorposts and lintels, they 'fused' several houses into one, so that dishes could be carried from one to the other. This is, I think, a major tradition. It is a relaxation of the law, and it distinguished Pharisees sharply from both Sadducees and Essenes, who were much stricter (*'Eruvin* 6.2; CD 11.7–9).

2. Work on festival days. During the festivals and the public fast (the Day of Atonement) there are six days that the Bible commands are to be treated like sabbaths, with one exception: it permits the work involved in the preparation of food that would be eaten that day (Lev. 23; Ex. 12.16).[22] The dual nature of the festival days made them the subject of numerous legal rulings. For example, it was debated whether or not one could move a ladder in order to bring down a dove from the dovecote when the menu called for fowl (*Betsah* 1.3). The work involved in carrying, slaughtering, plucking and cutting up the dove was accepted without comment as being obviously required, but moving the ladder was a contentious issue. It could have been done the day before. According to *T. Yom Tov* 1.8 the Houses agreed that the ladder could be moved to the dovecote, but disagreed over whether it could be returned to its original place. The question was, What work is strictly required for the day's food?

The debate on which there are more surviving Pharisaic opinions than on any other also concerns a festival day: whether or not one could lay one's hands on the head of a sacrificial animal on such a day (*Hagigah* 2.2–3; *Betsah* 2.4; important variants in *Betsah* 19a–b). This was an important issue. The festival days were semi-sabbaths, and observance of the sabbath is one of the Ten Commandments. The Bible also requires the worshipper to lay his hands on the head of his sacrificial victim (e.g. for the burnt offering, Lev. 1.14; for the shared sacrifice, Lev. 3.2, 8, 13).[23] The Pharisees classified laying hands on the animal's head as 'work', and so they needed to decide whether or not one commandment 'overrode' the other. If so, which? if not, how best to fulfil both laws? This was a live issue; the Essenes were of the view that festivals should never fall on the sabbath. Most Jews came to Jerusalem only occasionally, and most trips fell during one of the three pilgrimage festivals. Pilgrims who came to Jerusalem for one of the festivals naturally wanted to make one trip serve many purposes. Each family might wish to offer several sacrifices. They therefore needed to know whether or not they could offer one or more of their sacrifices on a festival day.

In the case of the Pharisees and sacrifices on festival days, the House of Shammai ruled that shared sacrifices could be brought, but without the laying on of hands, while burnt offerings could not be brought. The House of Hillel accepted both offerings and allowed hands to be laid on in both cases (*Hagigah* 2.3; *Betsah* 2.4).[24] These two sacrifices were singled out for discussion because on a festival day work is permitted if it supplies food for that day. Shared sacrifices provided food for the priest, the offerer and his or her family and friends. In most of the sub-categories of the shared sacrifice, however, the food was allowed to be eaten over a two-day period (Lev. 7.12–36). Private burnt offerings, on the other hand, were brought to atone for transgression (Lev. 1.4), and none of the animal served as food. This explains why the Shammaites permitted shared sacrifices but not burnt offerings.[25]

Neither of these topics regarding work on festival days (whether moving a ladder or laying hands on the head of a sacrifice) counts as *a* Pharisaic tradition, since late in the Pharisaic movement the Houses of Hillel and Shammai were still debating practice. These are legal discussions that might eventually have solidified and have become 'traditions of the elders'.

3. Penalties. There is no direct evidence about what Pharisees thought should be the penalty for intentional transgression of the sabbath. Inadvertent transgression is straightforward: it requires a sin offering (so Lev. 4.27–35; cf. *Shabbat* 7.1). In view of the Pharisees' leniency, what would be required for a transgression to be judged intentional and therefore to require the death sentence (Num. 15.32–6)? Probably deliberate transgression, carried out in full view of others, with the intention of defying God. The Mishnah implies that testimony in a capital case is excluded if the witnesses did not warn the transgressor in advance (*Sanhedrin* 5.1), and it defines unintentional transgressions in such a way that the *offender* would have to announce in advance that an action was a conscious transgression. A person might forget 'the principle of the Sabbath', or forget that a given activity was work, and owe only a sin offering (*Shabbat* 7.8). Possibly these views continue those of the Pharisees.

4. The sabbath year and the prosbul. The most famous and in some ways the most interesting Pharisaic tradition is the prosbul, which the Mishnah attributes to Hillel (*Shevi'it* 10.3). The prosbul facilitated lending and borrowing near the end of each seven year cycle. The Bible specifies that all loans are forgiven in the sabbatical (seventh) year (Deut. 15.2). The intention was to provide periodic relief to borrowers. The Deuteronomic legislators foresaw that, as the seventh year approached, lenders might become reluctant, and they urged people not to hold back their money because the seventh year was near (Deut. 15.9–11).[26] This admonition was not always sufficient, and lenders refused loans that could not be secured or collected. It is very probable that small farmers borrowed against the next season's crop, as they still do, and that loans were necessary. According to the early rabbinic

commentary on Deuteronomy, this was the formula that allowed loans to be collected in the seventh year.

> 'I declare unto you, So-and-so and So-and-so, judges in such-and-such place, that whatsoever debt is owed to me, I am to be free to collect it at any time I wish'; and the judges or the witnesses must sign below. (*Sifre Deut.* 113)[27]

The word 'prosbul' stands for the Greek phrase *pros boulē*, 'to the council' or 'before the council'. If the lender made a declaration before the city council, he could collect the loan even in the seventh year. Deut. 15.3 requires *individuals* to forgive debts in the seventh year, and this was evaded by having the individual lender declare to a public body that the debt would be collected. Apparently it was thought that this shifted the responsibility to a group, the council, which was not bound by the law, with the happy result that the necessary business of borrowing and lending could go on as usual.

The prosbul supports the view that the Pharisees were on the whole not among the aristocrats. It protects the lender, to be sure, but it is aimed at helping the small landowner or businessman. We do not know how many people accepted this legal device. It depends on the willingness of the council to participate in an avoidance of the written law, and also on the willingness of the debtor not to invoke the sabbath forgiveness of debts. That is, if it worked at all, the magistrates and lenders – possibly both aristocrats – had to accept it, and they had to trust the borrower also to accept it. This may have been an instance in which the Pharisees were able to affect public policy.

In discussing the topic, Neusner raised the question of whether or not people observed the sabbatical year. If they did not, the prosbul was not a legal device, but an academic exercise. Originally he reserved judgment: 'I know no evidence of what people actually did.'[28] More recently he has criticized Solomon Zeitlin's discussion of the prosbul, objecting that he '[took] for granted that the Sabbatical laws were everywhere enforced'.[29] There is in fact good evidence that Jews generally observed the sabbath day, as the earlier Neusner recognized: 'All Jews kept the Sabbath. It was part of the culture of their country'.[30] There is also good evidence that Jews in Palestine observed the sabbath year. We need only recall that John Hyrcanus, an adherent of the Sadducees, had once broken off a siege because of the arrival of the sabbatical year and that Julius Caesar exempted Jews in Palestine from taxes in the seventh year – thus he at least was persuaded that they kept it (above, pp. 161f.)

There is, finally, an interesting piece of archaeological evidence that bears on the prosbul. In a document found in the Judaean desert, dated the second year of Nero (13 Oct. 55–12 Oct. 56), a borrower promises to repay a loan, plus interest of one-fifth, 'even if it is a year of rest'.[31] This, of course, does not prove that it was Hillel who invented the prosbul, only that some decades after his death a similar legal device was in use. One of the difficulties in reading rabbinic literature is deciding when people did something because 'the rabbis had decreed it' and when common and widely accepted practices happen to be recorded in the Mishnah.

Tithes, purity and exclusivism

Many scholars have attributed to the Pharisees traditions that had the result of separating them from other Jews. The word 'Pharisee', in Hebrew *perûshîm*, is usually thought to be derived from *parash* in the meaning 'separate',[32] and it is thought that they physically separated themselves from others, constituting a sect. They did this, the proposal runs, by developing special rules for handling and eating food. Christian scholars have often cited these points to draw an extremely denigrating view of the Pharisees as self-righteous exclusivists, who avoided contact with non-Pharisees since it 'put at risk' their own purity and thus threatened their 'membership within the realm of the holy and the divine'.[33] Another scholar accused the Pharisees of practising apartheid and 'shun[ning] the non-Pharisee as unclean'.[34] The Pharisees' special knowledge, we are also told, caused them to despise the common people, since they held that 'it is forbidden to have mercy on one who has no knowledge'.[35] This last despite numerous rabbinic statements to the contrary.[36] How scholars who write such things can hold that it was the *Pharisees* who despised others and who were self-righteous is a mystery. The well known scholars whom I have just quoted inherited these misrepresentations from their predecessors, and they pass them on to junior scholars, who proceed to put them in their textbooks, where undergraduates read them as official 'knowledge'.[37]

We shall turn to some of the Pharisaic rules about food and purity in a moment. When we do so, we shall see that the proposal that the Pharisees formed a sect that had nothing to do with others, and that excluded ordinary people from the 'realm of the holy and the divine' is not correct. Here I wish to offer some general observations that count against the view of Jeremias, Black and others, a view that has recently been championed by Neusner.

It is not true that Pharisees would not come into contact with others. They took part in civic life and associated with other members of society. Paul, a Pharisee, persecuted the early Christians, and so must have come near them. He and (I suppose) other Pharisees travelled by land and sea, mixing with all and sundry. According to Matthew, Pharisees traversed sea and land in search of converts (Matt. 23.15). It is doubtful that this characterizes very many, but in any case they bought and sold, shopped in crowded markets, and walked along crowded streets. Pharisees are usually said to have sat on the Sanhedrin with non-Pharisees, and we know that Simeon b. Gamaliel co-operated with non-Pharisees during the revolt. Other Pharisees took active part in the war. And so on, as long as one wishes.

Not only did Pharisees not achieve apartheid, they seem not to have wished it: there is not a word about social isolation in any of the ancient literature. Josephus' silence on this point is especially striking. He liked recounting curious aspects of religious behaviour, and he wrote about the Essenes' food and purity laws, and their exclusivist separatism, at some length: they accepted neither clothing nor food from others (*War* 2.126), and they bathed after touching even a lower-ranking member of the order (2.150). Analogous practices on the part of the Pharisees would have deserved some comment from Josephus, but there is none. Similarly early Christians would have criticized their Pharisaic opponents for this kind of exclusivism, but Christian literature is as silent on such topics as is Josephus.[38] The Pharisees in the gospels bound around Galilee, mixing with others in synagogues, inviting Jesus to dine, inspecting his disciples' hands. There is no hint that they avoided contact with others. We can dismiss this kind of creative scholarship and its results.[39]

Tithes

One of the Pharisaic rules that is supposed to have cut them off from ordinary people is their strict view of tithing. They were less strict than the priestly aristocracy, which, as we saw above, expected farmers to separate fourteen tithes in each seven-year cycle, whereas the Pharisees required twelve. They did, however, think that these twelve should be set aside. Of the twelve, four were second tithe, eaten by the farmer and his family in Jerusalem, usually while enjoying a festival. Two were for charity. Six went to the priests and Levites: a tithe to the Levites, who in turn tithed to the priests. There were also minor gifts to the priests, first fruits, heave offering, and firstlings of animals.

Of all these contributions, the only one that the Pharisees suspected the common people of avoiding was first tithe – ten per cent of produce each year except the seventh. Even here, they suspected them of not contributing only the Levites' portion (nine-tenths of first tithe, nine one-hundredths of the crop). They thought that everybody could be trusted with regard to the other offerings, which went to the priesthood. They invented a legal category for food that they acquired from someone who may not have tithed it: *demai*-produce, 'produce that may or may not have been tithed'. Some

Pharisees thought that, when such produce came into their hands, they should tithe it, just to be on the safe side. They did *not*, however, regard even the intentional consumption of the Levites' share of first tithe as a capital offence (as they did in the case of first fruits and heave offering, *Bikkurim* 2.1). They would not themselves *intentionally* eat the Levites' share, but not even all Pharisees thought that they had to tithe *demai*-produce.

Although the existence of the category 'doubtful-if-tithed produce' shows that the Pharisees were enthusiastic about tithing, if necessary tithing what they bought as well as what they sold, they were not fanatical. The most substantial Pharisaic discussion in the Mishnah about tithing is this:

> *Demai*-produce may be given to the poor and to billeted troops to eat. Rabban Gamaliel used to give *demai*-produce to his labourers to eat. The School of Shammai say: Almoners should give what has been tithed to them that do not give tithe and what is untithed to them that do give tithe; thus all will eat of what is duly tithed. But the Sages say: Almoners may collect food and distribute it regardless [of the rules of *demai*-produce], and let him that is minded to tithe it [according to the rules of *demai*-produce] tithe it. (*Demai* 3.1)

This passage reveals what I regard as a characteristic Pharisaic trait: distinguishing between what is in the Bible and what not. The Bible does not say that people who buy food and doubt that it has been tithed must tithe it. The Bible commands *the farmer* to tithe or (if he consumes the tithe) to redeem it by paying its equivalent plus one-fifth to the temple (Lev. 27.30f.). To do more, to tithe food that one buys, is going beyond the law. Many Pharisees were here as elsewhere happy to go beyond it. But there were limits. The House of Shammai wanted charity organized so as to ensure that all food, whether bought or given away, was tithed. 'The Sages' (standing in for the Hillelites?) disagreed and left it to the individual. Further, Rabban Gamaliel II himself, son of the great Pharisee Simeon b. Gamaliel, gave doubtful-if-tithed food to his workmen. At most we may assume that many Pharisees made sure that food that they bought, ate and sold was tithed, if necessary tithing it again (possibly only partially, see below). They seem not to have patrolled the land, insisting that all food in the country be treated in the way they treated it. That is, they distinguished their own 'tradition' from the law.

The Hillelites' position in another passage also shows moderate enthusiasm: When one receives *demai*-produce, one should reserve and not eat *only* the 'heave offering of the tithe', that is, the priests' tenth of the Levites' tenth (*T. Ma'aser Sheni* 3.15). The buyer of the produce could eat the rest of first tithe – the Levites' 9/100ths, since only the priests' portion was holy.

These discussions reveal not only a good deal less fanaticism than most people attribute to the Pharisees, but also the degree to which they trusted the common people. There are no parallel categories for other holy food: food about which it was doubtful if second tithe, first fruits and heave offering had been deducted, or herds from which firstlings may not have been contributed.[40] Since heave offering, first fruits and firstlings were all, in the Pharisees' view, more sacred than the Levitical tithe, they would never have run the risk of eating them even accidentally.[41] The absence of these categories shows that they did not think that anyone would sell them food from which the other offerings had not been deducted. They worried only about the Levites' share of first tithe, and not all of them felt compelled to contribute that from food that they bought or acquired through trade.

These rules do not sound like the Pharisees of scholarly imagination: because of their tithing laws, they despised the common people, would not associate with them, considered them cut off from God's mercy, etc.

The existence of the category, *demai*-produce, does, of course, reveal scrupulousness and the intention to see that Levites as well as priests were supported. Tithes, in the post-70 rabbis' view, were still payable even after the temple was destroyed, and the desire to preserve the clergy accounts for the emphasis on tithing in rabbinic literature. This does not sound like the other Pharisees of scholarly imagination: people who opposed the priesthood and sacrifices, and who led the people away from them.

Purity: food

One very important aspect of Pharisaic legal discussions concerns holy food, and we may begin the discussion of purity with this sub-topic. Study of holy food also reveals what they thought about the purity of their own daily food. The Pharisees have often been defined as a group that ate their everyday food in purity, as if they were priests in the temple.

There are essentially five kinds of holy food: (1) what the priests ate inside the temple; (2) what the priests and their families ate outside the temple; (3) second tithe (eaten in Jerusalem by those who produced it); (4) the Passover meal; (5) the shared sacrifice. In practice, (3), (4) and (5) would have overlapped: people spent their second tithe money at the festivals. We saw above that, even before the Pharisees, and independently of them, people started handling the priests' food in purity (pp. 221f.). We find aspects of this practice in Isa. 66.20; Judith 11.13 (*c.* 150–125 BCE) and CD 11.18–20. Further, as we shall see, the Pharisees thought that many of the common

people kept certain impurities away from the priests' food. Here, then, the
Pharisees were neither innovators nor unique, but they shared in a broad
cultural development, within which they made special rules for themselves. I
shall mention only a few of the numerous passages on handling the priests'
food, and we shall also look at second tithe. These are the two sub-topics
where we see most clearly their view of themselves and of others. Were they a
separatist sect? Did they exclude ordinary people from the true commonwealth of Israel?

1. In discussing turning grapes into wine, the Houses of Hillel and
Shammai debated at what point the hands should be pure. The Shammaites
held that a man's hands must be pure when he put grapes into the wine vat,
while the Hillelites maintained that the grapes could be put in with impure
hands, but that heave offering of the wine must be separated with pure hands
(*Tohorot* 10.4).

2. The Houses also debated when the wine vat could be made impure,
whether after first tithe was removed, or only after second tithe had been
separated (*T. Terumot* 3.12).

3. May a woman during stage two of childbirth impurity touch 'Holy
Things' (eaten within the temple), eat second tithe (eaten by lay people in
purity), set apart dough offering or handle heave offering (eaten by priests'
families outside the temple) (*Niddah* 10.6f.)? The answer was 'yes', except for
'Holy Things'.

These are extremely interesting passages. The first reveals handwashing
as a purity practice, to which we shall return. All three show that the Pharisaic
Houses or Schools did not think that all food and wine should always be kept
pure. This is what scholars say that they thought, and Neusner has produced
an entire library making this claim.[42] But these passages, and many others,
show that they distinguished the handling of food before it was separated for
holy purposes (heave offering, first and second tithe) from the way it was
handled afterwards for their own consumption. The Houses debated only
what purity rule should apply at what point in the preparation of food while it
still contained the priests' portion. According to the first two passages, after
the offerings, including second tithe, came out, the grapes, the wine, and the
wine vat could all be impure, and the Pharisees would cheerfully drink the
wine.

The third passage cited above is especially interesting, since in this case
the Bible states that a woman in the second stage of childbirth impurity may
not touch 'any holy thing' (Lev. 12.4). For the Pharisees, the question was
which holy things this verse covered. The Mishnah takes the term to refer to
'Most Holy Things', eaten in the temple. For other holy food there was a
lower standard of purity.[43] Here they had a perfect chance to say that all their

food was holy and that no impure woman could touch it. They passed up the chance, and limited what she could not touch to only the most sacred food.

4. One passage shows that the Pharisees tried to keep corpse impurity away from the priests' food *from harvest on*. Corpse-impurity was especially important because it was the most virulent and anti-priestly impurity. This probably explains why the Pharisaic Houses began to keep this impurity away from food at the earliest possible point. In passage (1) above, the Houses debated whether their hands should be pure at the time when grapes were put into the press or only when the priests' share of the wine was separated. When it came to corpse-impurity, however, they agreed that they should harvest the grapes without infecting them, and they debated only how this could best be done. They posed this problem in a very interesting way: how shall we harvest grapes if the vine hangs over a grave area? Anyone walking into the graveyard would pick up corpse impurity and convey it to the grapes, which would be made into wine, some of which would reach the priests.

> How can they gather the grapes in a Grave-area? Men and vessels must be sprinkled the first and the second time; then they gather the grapes and take them out of the Grave-area; others receive the grapes from them and take them to the winepress. If these others touched the grape-gatherers they become unclean. So the School of Hillel. The School of Shammai say: They should hold the sickle with a wrapping of bast, or cut the grapes with a sharp flint, and let them fall into a large olive-basket and bring them to the winepress. (*Oholot* 18:1)

The solution of the House of Hillel to the problem of grapes in a graveyard is ingenious and shows a novelty of conception: the grape-gatherers and their baskets can be *inoculated* against corpse-impurity in advance. 'Sprinkled the first and the second time' refers to the rite for removing corpse-impurity, but here it is 'removed' beforehand. Then the grapes are pure, and so is the wine made from them, provided that the people who carry the grapes to the winepress do not touch the grape-gatherers. It must be doubted that farmers had immediate access to the special water used for corpse-impurity, and it is likely that the Hillelites had in mind sprinkling with ordinary water as a minor gesture.

The House of Shammai's proposal is only slightly less inventive: the gatherers should not touch the grapes themselves, but cut them and let them fall directly into the basket. Cutting should be done with flint (stone does not contract corpse-impurity), or with a sickle wrapped with bast. The bast (a fibrous material) probably was thought to serve as a 'vessel' around the sickle which prevented corpse-impurity from passing through the harvester to the sickle and then to the grapes. Those who followed the Shammaite's view were not protected against acquiring corpse-impurity themselves. It was not a problem if they had it; they just wanted to keep it away from the priests' wine.

5. Before leaving holy food, we should note that the Pharisaic Houses thought that the common people kept some forms of impurity away from it.[44] The common people were trusted to keep second tithe pure (*Tevel Yom* 4.5). If a priest or a member of his family left vessels in the care of an ordinary person, the vessels did not contract corpse-impurity, though they did contract a lesser impurity, *midras* impurity (*Tohorot* 8.2). (This is the secondary impurity acquired by touching a menstruant or a person with a discharge; it is defined more fully below).[45] The Houses also thought that the common people preserved the purity of wine and oil while they still contained the priests' portion.[46] This is not required by biblical law, and here we see the degree to which it had become commonly accepted that the priests' food should be handled in purity before it reached them – as well as, of course, the generally law-abiding character of the ordinary people, at least as judged by the Pharisees and rabbis.

Again we see that the Pharisees did not think that the common people were excluded from the sphere of the divine and sacred; they were just one step lower on the purity ladder than the Pharisees themselves, who were one step below priests outside the temple. This is what *Hagigah* 2.7, summarized below, explicitly says. Here I have not quoted this passage, or any other, as a single prooftext, but rather I have adduced much better evidence: in the earliest layer of rabbinic literature, the discussions of the priests' food, and the vessels in which it is stored, *presuppose* that Pharisees did not treat their own food as if it were holy, and also that the ordinary people kept the most obvious purity rules, including one that goes beyond the Bible.

The passages in nos. 1–4 refer to rules that the Pharisees imposed on themselves when handling the priests' food. Whether the priests worried about wine from grapes that had overhung a grave area we do not know. Very probably not: harvesting and handling the priests' food in purity are not biblical laws. The Pharisees' scrupulousness in this regard did not make them an isolated sect, since how they harvested and bottled did not affect dealings with other people. The priests and Levites collected the tithes, the Pharisees took their own first fruits to the temple; social relations with the populace in general were not an issue.

Their *attitude* towards others, however, is an issue for us. The only attitude towards the priests in the early layers of rabbinic literature is one of protection, support and respect. One cannot find passages that show that the Pharisees opposed the priests, thought that there were corrupt, and wanted to lead people away from worship in the temple. We find when discussing purity what we found when discussing tithes: complete support of the priesthood.

These signs of respect contrast greatly with the harsh criticisms of other pietists: the priests take menstrual blood into the temple (and the like).[47]

The attitude towards the ordinary people that is conveyed by such passages as *Tevel Yom* 4.5; *Tohorot* 8.2 (no. 5) is notably non-polemical and non-judgmental, and one of them explicitly contradicts the theory that Pharisees would not deal with ordinary people:

> Beforetime they used to say: They may exchange Second tithe [money in Jerusalem] for the produce of an *Am-haaretz*. Then they changed this and said: Also for money of his. (*Tevul Yom* 4.5)[48]

Biblical law requires that second-tithe produce be eaten in purity. The passage assumes that ordinary people (*ʿammê ha-ʾarets*) observe that law. They are not outcasts; one can buy holy food from them. *Tohorot* 8.2 does not criticize the ordinary people for allowing priests' vessels to acquire *midras* impurity. There is no campaign to go around the countryside trying to coerce non-Pharisees into keeping vessels free from all impurity. In this passage, as in many others, the Pharisees (in this particular case, possibly the early rabbis) simply want to know, to decide for themselves what assumptions they should make about vessels that had been in the possession of an ordinary person. If the ordinary person knew that the vessels belonged to a priest or a member of a priest's family, the Pharisees presumed them to be free of corpse impurity but not *midras* impurity; if the ordinary person thought that the vessels belonged to a layman, the presumption was that they had both corpse-impurity and *midras* impurity. A lot of the Pharisees' and early rabbis' discussions of impurity have to do with locating it, apparently for their own information, so that they will know what to presume if they have anything to do with the object in question.

6. There is, however, one purity law that affected commercial dealings with ordinary people.

> The School of Shammai say: A man may sell his olives only to an Associate. The School of Hillel say: Even to one that [only] pays Tithes. Yet the more scrupulous of the School of Hillel used to observe the words of the School of Shammai. (*Demai* 6.6; partial//*T. Maʿaserot* 3.13)

Olives and grapes (passage no. 1 above) required special consideration because they naturally become moist before they are ready to be pressed to produce oil and wine. Lev. 11.38 states that 'if water be put' on 'seed', the seed was susceptible to being made impure by the carcass of a dead 'swarming thing'. From this the Pharisees derived the following views: (1) 'seed' means 'any foodstuff'; (2) 'if water be put' means that a person must want liquid to be on the foodstuff; the rule applies to moisture that forms naturally, if the owner of the foodstuff wants it to be there; (3) moistened foodstuff is susceptible to lots of impurities, not just the impurity of a dead swarming thing.[49] Olives and grapes ooze, and since the owner desires them to do so, they are susceptible to impurity, and so they must be handled with care. Dry foodstuff, including foodstuff that becomes wet without the owner explicitly desiring it, is immune from impurity. These views are not explicitly stated, as I have just stated them, but are presupposed in hundreds and hundreds of rabbinic discussions. Once one knows the presuppositions, the discussions, otherwise opaque, become clear. These interpretations, then, are deep in rabbinic literature and they are assumed in the passages attributed to the Houses of Hillel and Shammai. Further, other people may have accepted the same views, or similar ones, as we saw in discussing the Essenes.[50] We can safely attribute to the Pharisees this understanding of food's susceptibility to impurity.

We do not know just what the ordinary people thought of all this. Obviously they did not entirely agree. My guess is that they did not accept the Pharisaic/pietist extension of 'if water be put' to include susceptibility to all impurities. They probably would have agreed that they should not moisten foodstuff themselves and then allow it to come into contact with dead mice. That is the sort of thing that Lev. 11 actually prohibits.

At any rate, we see why the Houses debated grapes when considering how to keep impurity away from the priests' food. Here they discuss selling olives: they do not want to sell olives to someone who may let them ooze, allow impurity to come into contact with them, and then press them to make oil. A Pharisee could buy dry food from even the least scrupulous person, as well as sell it to him.

It appears from this mishnah that the attempt to observe the purity laws of Lev. 11.32–8 imposed more restrictions on trade than did the rule about *demai*-produce. On the other hand, the sale of olives in bulk was probably not a very large part of a tradesman's business. A Pharisaic middleman, for example, could buy dry olives (not yet oozing), let them ripen, and then either crush them himself or sell them to someone whom he trusted to keep them covered. This, the most restrictive rule in the Pharisaic corpus, did not make the Pharisees an isolationist sect. We may recall that the Dead Sea group would not use oil at all, possibly for reasons of purity. Jews in general disliked foreign oil (p. 216). The Pharisees fall in between, more restrictive than Jews in general, less restrictive than the Dead Sea sect.

7. Finally, we note that Pharisees would not eat with ordinary people. According to *T. Shabbat* 1.15 the Houses of Hillel and Shammai debated whether or not a Pharisee who was impure because of genital discharge (spermatorrhoea) could eat with an ordinary person, an ʿam ha-ʾarets who had

the same impurity. The Hillelites permitted it and the Shammaites prohibited it. The debate, however, presupposes that when the Pharisee was pure, he would not dine with an ordinary person. If, when both the Pharisee and the ʿam ha-ʾarets were impure, the Houses debated whether they could eat together, we must assume that ordinarily they did not eat together. The objection from the Pharisaic viewpoint was probably that ordinary people had *midras* impurity. The Pharisees preferred to avoid this impurity when they could (see below).

I have dealt fairly extensively with food and purity because most scholars have defined the Pharisees as a lay group that ate ordinary food in purity, as if they were priests in the temple. I shall return to the question of defining them, and to the topic of living outside the temple as if one were in it. Was it, for example, their ideal? Whatever the answer to further questions, we have seen enough to be confident that they did not for one moment believe that their own food was kept as pure as the priests' *in* the temple, and not even as pure as the food eaten by priests and their families outside the temple (heave offering). With regard to olives, they exercised some caution. This is the principal purity law that affected their own food or that of other laity, except that they preferred not to dine with people who routinely had *midras* impurity.

Purity: handwashing

The only other purity practice that I wish to explain here is handwashing, which was adopted late in the Pharisaic movement for limited purposes. According to *Shabbat* 14b, 'Shammai and Hillel decreed uncleanness for the hands' in a particular context: handling heave offering (used by the rabbis as a generic term for holy food eaten by priests outside the temple and their families). We saw above that they disagreed about just when hands should be washed – whether before handling the moist grapes or only when separating the priests' portion of the wine – but they agreed that they should wash hands to keep impurity away from the priests' wine. The discussion in *Shabbat* 14b, unlike the Houses debate in *Tohorot* 10.4, is later reflection. Babylonian rabbis ask themselves why Hillel and Shammai decreed that hands could convey impurity, and their best answer is that it was to serve as an additional safeguard against contamination of heave offering (see the opening discussion in *Shabbat* 13b). We cannot improve on their research and knowledge of the tradition.

Handwashing could conceivably have come into Pharisaism earlier and from any one of several sources. Handwashing was already practised in the Diaspora (pp. 223f.). It could arise spontaneously because of the biblical use of 'clean hands' as a metaphor for innocence. In the song of David in II Sam.

22.21 'cleanness of my hands' is parallel to 'my righteousness', a parallel repeated in Ps. 18.20, 24. According to Ps. 24.4, one who goes to the temple should have 'clean hands and a pure heart'. Such passages as these could have led the Pharisees and other pietists to wash their hands frequently, especially before praying. It appears, however, that this was not their starting point, and that they did not wash their hands in connection with prayer,[51] but rather in connection with heave offering.

Apparently with this partial agreement between Hillel and Shammai as the beginning point, the later Houses of Hillel and Shammai applied handwashing to their own cups of wine on sabbaths and other holy days (*Berakhot* 8.2, 4; *T. Berakhot* 5.25–28).[52] There is no indication that they washed hands before other meals. Later rabbis debated whether or not hands should be washed before all meals (*T. Berakhot* 5.13, 27), on the whole regarding it as not compulsory. This weighs very heavily against the idea that before 70 all Pharisees had washed their hands before every meal.

It appears that the Pharisees also washed their hands after handling scripture (*Eduyot* 5.3; *Yadaim* 3.5). The reason is not clear; perhaps the scriptural books were *so* holy that they rendered hands impure by a kind of reverse logic. The rabbis of the Babylonian Talmud were puzzled by the rule, and one suggested that their predecessors had kept scrolls of the law near heave offering: both were holy, and so both required handwashing (*Shabbat* 14a).

Scholars treat handwashing as proof that the Pharisees wished to live 'like priests in the temple'. Handwashing, however, is not a priestly rule; it is not even biblical. Priests, before eating holy food, immersed. Further, the Pharisees did not wash their hands to protect their own food from impurity, but rather the priests' food, which shows perfectly clearly that they did not think of themselves as eating in priestly purity.

Did the Pharisees achieve priestly purity?

The Pharisees seem to have made minor gestures that partially imitated priestly purity: the avoidance of unnecessary corpse impurity and of *midras* impurity. The Bible orders priests to avoid corpse impurity completely, except when there is a death in the immediate family (Lev. 21.1–3). Pharisees did not observe this rule; on the contrary, rabbinic evidence is that joining a funeral cortège and mourning at the grave site were religious obligations that people fulfilled for non-family members (e.g. *Ketuvot* 17a; *Berakhot* 18a; so also Josephus, *Apion* 2.205). They tried, rather, to avoid accidental corpse-impurity, which could be incurred, for example, by leaning out of a window when a corpse was being carried down the street. This minor and partial avoidance could have several explanations, such as that they wanted to keep corpse impurity away from heave offering, some of which they might have in the house.[53] The introduction of corpse-impurity into a room required it to be purged by a priest over a seven-day period, and they may have been interested only in avoiding unnecessary domestic disruption. But their avoidance of accidental corpse-impurity might also be a minor gesture towards living a life of special sanctity.

Midras impurity is similar. This impurity is derived from contact with certain impure people. To take the most common case: a menstruant renders her bed and chair impure, and they in turn make anyone who touches them impure (Lev. 15.19–24). This derived impurity is not very severe: removing it requires immersion, washing the clothes, and waiting until sunset. Scholars, imagining that the Pharisees lived like priests, have thought that, to avoid this impurity, they expelled their wives from their houses when menstruating, and also after childbirth, the first stage of which is equivalent to menstruation. Nursing mothers, we are to imagine, lived either in sheds outside the main house or in separate encampments outside the city. Neusner made a slightly more reasonable proposal: menstruants and new mothers had separate sets of furniture. This furniture, of course, could not be touched by the Pharisee, since that is precisely what rendered him impure.[54]

While the woman was impure (these scholars further imagine), the male Pharisee, in addition to working in the field all day, had to grind grain, knead dough, bake bread, mend garments, and do all the other things that occupied women's lives.[55] When one adds this fantasy to the other fantasies about Pharisees – they ran the temple, served as scribes, taught in the schools and synagogues, manned judicial bodies, and functioned as legal experts, advising people on what to sacrifice when, what to do about a broken marriage agreement, how to sort out inheritances – and on and on – one will see that they were moderately busy. One must remember that they also had to study; otherwise they could not have done any of these things. Their early training would have been intense: mastery of agriculture or some other means of earning a livelihood, mastery of the law, and mastery of baking and weaving as well. Being a Pharisee's wife would have been a mixed blessing. She would get one week off every month from her regular chores, and further time off after childbirth, but the price of the leisure was that she was expelled from her house.

Besides the fact that this depiction of Pharisaic domestic life is fantastic, something else counts against it: rabbinic literature. It completely lacks the rules that living like priests would require: What *does* one do with a nursing mother in a house of four tiny rooms? Who carries the impure womans' special furniture? How does one manage to harvest and cook simultaneously?

Secondly, rabbinic literature is full of discussions of *midras* impurity, and the assumption is that one could acquire it at home. This proves that menstruants were not expelled from their houses. One Mishnaic passage discusses menstruation and the preparation of food, warning only against the menstruant's preparing food that requires purity – that is, not the family's ordinary food (*Niddah* 9.9).

The priests themselves could cope with handling and eating holy food in purity because they did not have to harvest it, press the olives, put the grapes into the vat, put oil and wine into vessels, grind grain into meal and flour, and so on. They had to be pure to eat holy food, but if the food was holy it had been given to them. Even so, priests did not always live in purity.[56] It would have been completely impossible for the Pharisees.

A passage referred to above, *Hagigah* 2.7, seems to me to describe real life precisely. An ordinary person's garments were more likely to have *midras* impurity than a Pharisee's, a Pharisee's more likely than a priest's when he was not in the temple, a priest's outside the temple more likely than a priest's inside the temple. Common people, one gathers from rabbinic discussions, did not worry about *midras* impurity, except when they entered the temple, and possibly then they did not worry about *midras* impurity on their clothes.[57] Pharisees tried to avoid it when they could, but they did not go to ridiculous lengths. Even the garments of priests outside the temple might have *midras* impurity. It is probable that priests and Pharisees alike immersed their clothes, bedding and chairs after the woman's menstrual period passed. Occasional immersion would also take care of other minor impurities.[58]

The evidence is that Pharisees aspired to a level of purity above the ordinary, but below that of priests and their families, and also well below that of the Qumran sect. One may say that they made minor gestures towards living like priests, but it is probably more accurate to say that purity was a common ideal, one held by many Jews and Gentiles alike, that the Pharisees shared the ideal, and that they pursued it more thoroughly than did most Jews.

Pharisaic associations?

Many scholars have thought that Pharisees formed '*closed communities*', called 'associations' (*ḥavûrôt*) and that they were themselves properly called 'associates' (*ḥaverîm*).[59] The terminology constitutes a difficult technical question that I have discussed several times and shall not discuss again.[60] With regard to the substantive issue, one can answer 'yes' or 'no', depending on *how* closed one imagines their communities to have been.

First, with regard to trade: they were cautious about selling olives (*Demai* 6.6), and apparently also about dealing in liquids, because of their interpretation of 'if water be put' (*Bekhorot* 30b; *T. Demai* 2.12). The existence of the category *demai*-produce shows that they did *not* buy produce only from other Pharisees, since otherwise they would not have needed to discuss what to do when they acquired produce that might not have been tithed. We may conclude that they exercised some care in trade, and that they preferred to trade only with people who kept these two parts of biblical law (moist foodstuff; tithing), but that sometimes they dealt with people who may not have tithed. I would call this not 'closed' but 'cautious' and 'partially restrictive'. Pharisees would deal in second tithe produce with the ordinary people, since they trusted them to keep the laws of second tithe (*Tevel Yom* 4.5).

With regard to eating, Pharisees did not, at least on average, eat with people below them on the purity scale. I think that Christian scholars make too much of this. They imagine that the Pharisaic meal was sacred and that exclusion from it was a kind of excommunication. 'Table-fellowship means fellowship before God'.[61] Apart from the fact that this may or may not be the case, depending on circumstances, it is incorrect to assume, as such statements do, that in the first century people thought that salvation depended on dining together: the Pharisees admitted only those with whom they ate into the people of God. The priests did not think that, in order for people to engage in 'fellowship before God', they, the priests, must eat with them. What the priests thought was that lay people who ate a shared sacrifice with other lay people partook of a sacred meal, one in which the priests and the altar participated, though in different physical locations. (The priests took their portion of the shared sacrifice home.) The ordinary people quite evidently thought the same thing, though with what level of sophistication we do not know.[62] The Pharisees doubtless agreed. No one thought that the *real* sacred moment came when the Pharisees sat down to eat, nor that the only way to experience 'fellowship with God' was to eat with Pharisees. The enormous devotion to the sanctity of the temple, which characterized all the major groups in Palestine, including the common people, shows that they thought that it was there, in the temple, that humans came closest to the divine. The Qumran sectarians found a substitute for worship in the temple, but even in Qumran it was not a meal that substituted for the temple, but prayers.[63]

In real life, most people do not eat with most other people. In communities today where the Methodists, for example, have church suppers, usually there are only Methodists there. At feasts and special occasions, one usually invites one's friends, associates, and other people of like mind. We may assume that when there was communal dining (for example, at Passover), the Pharisees ate only with their relatives and close friends. Some scholars think that the Pharisees routinely ate together.[64] The only evidence, however, is that those who happened to live in the same courtyard or alley ate together on the sabbath. A Sadducee might live in the alley, and he and his family would not eat with the Pharisees, since *the Pharisees* would be transgressing the sabbath law against carrying. They all still went to the same temple, and neither the Sadducees nor the Pharisees thought that, since they did not all eat the sabbath meal together, the members of the other party were excluded from Israel.

A lay Pharisee might have been delighted to be invited to dine with a non-Pharisaic priest, who would be at least as pure as the Pharisee. The Houses debated just who could share a firstling (*T. Bekhorot* 3.15; *Bekhorot* 5.2). If the priest decided that some Pharisees whom he liked were sufficiently pure, he could invite them, and they would presumably go.

On the sabbath, then, they would eat with nearby Pharisaic neighbours (nearby, because of the restrictions on carrying and their own rules of ʿeruvin); at festivals they, like everyone else, ate with relatives and friends. Non-Pharisees at a festival, dining on a shared sacrifice or the Passover lamb at their campsite, fresh from the temple, and having purified themselves for the occasion, did not feel excluded from the realm of the holy and divine because they were not eating at a Pharisee's campsite. They had their own sacred food, sanctified where it mattered.

This exhausts our knowledge of Pharisaic 'communities'; there were neighbourhood communities, based on the rules of ʿeruvin, and there were farmers and tradesmen with whom Pharisees could do business without worrying. There is no information about a Pharisaic 'quarter' of Jerusalem (contrast 'the gate of the Essenes'). Pharisees had neither secret enclaves, rites that set them off as the 'true Israel', nor special group worship (they said the Shemaʿ and prayed at home; they attended the common synagogue).

I wish to emphasize how different this is from the descriptions offered by two influential scholars, which are commonly accepted. What Jeremias and Neusner say about the Pharisees is true not of them, but of the Dead Sea sect. They describe the wrong group: the only true Israel, communal meals, meals eaten in purity, sacred food, closed societies, unwillingness to mingle with others because of fear of impurity, exclusion of everyone else from the realm of the sacred, hatred of other Jews, expulsion of people who transgress food and purity laws from the commonwealth of Israel.[65] These characteristics are found in the Dead Sea Scrolls and in Josephus' description of the Essenes. They are not found in any source that might conceivably come from or reflect the Pharisees. I hasten to add that Neusner recognized that there is no evidence for Pharisaic ritual meals, and he made rather a big point of it.[66] He also did not write that the Pharisees hated and despised other Jews. On these points, where he disagreed with Jeremias, he was completely right.

The Mishnah's presuppositions

Some of Neusner's most interesting work is his identification of the presuppositions of each Mishnaic tractate: what one must know in advance in order to comprehend the discussion. He has obscured his own contribution here, since he frequently denies that he finds any presuppositions, a denial that usually accompanies his attacks on other people who find them.[67] To conclude this brief treatment of Pharisaic traditions, however, we may resurrect some of the presuppositions that, according to his analysis, either lie at the earliest layer of the Mishnah, or are presupposed by it. It will be of interest to compare this list with his conclusion, that the Pharisees were a pure-food sect. Each of the following points is a 'tradition', a view that is not explicitly in the Bible but may be considered Pharisaic. Page numbers refer to Neusner's *Judaism: The Evidence of the Mishnah*, which is the summary of his 43 volumes, *History of the Mishnaic Law*.

1. The altar did not sanctify what was sacrificed on it by its own power, as if by magic. Rather, the worshipper should intend to make a proper sacrifice to God (p. 206).

2. The Bible requires both immersion and the setting of the sun for many impurities. The Mishnah presupposes a view that is not biblical: that the person who has immersed, but upon whom the sun has not yet set, 'is unclean in a diminished sense of uncleanness' (p. 213).

3. 'Long before the destruction of the temple' the group behind the Mishnah had worked out the sabbath law in much greater detail than is provided in the Bible (p. 89).

4. Rules for charity (leaving a 'forgotten sheaf' in the field) were developed before the Mishnah but after the completion of biblical law (p. 54). (Compare Deut. 24.19 and Mishnah *Pe'ah* 6.)

Following the analysis that leads to these results, Neusner concludes that 'if someone had set out to organize a "Mishnah" before 70, his single operative category would have been making meals' (p. 59). The conclusion simply does not tally with the evidence, none of which has to do with making meals, and we should accordingly change the definition of the Pharisees, the group most likely to have been behind the earliest stratum of the Mishnah. Pharisaic rules covered almost the entirety of the Bible and a good deal more.

The Pharisees were what they appear in Josephus to be: a group of mostly lay people who were concerned to study, interpret and apply the biblical law, and who did not fear to go beyond it. They conservatively called their innovations 'the traditions of the elders' (rather than the radical 'oral law' or 'new covenant'). Their close attention to law and tradition made them stand out, not because only they cared for the law, but because they were so exact and because they applied law and tradition to even more areas of life than did most Jews.

Precision, intention and closeness to God

Beginning with Josephus and the New Testament, we have offered numerous points that characterize the Pharisees. They can all be illustrated from the Mishnah, which, though written later, shows the influence of pre-70 Pharisaism. This does not mean that one can discover Pharisaic opinion on a given issue simply by turning to the Mishnah or other rabbinic literature. It does seem, however, that these works capture something of the flavour of pre-70 Pharisaism. Here I think above all of two main features of early rabbinic literature.

Josephus and the New Testament say that the Pharisees were 'precise' in their interpretation. We have seen above numerous examples, but I wish to emphasize one more aspect of precise interpretation, using rabbinic literature for illustrative purposes. One of the major aims of rabbinic legal exegesis was to define when a given law was fulfilled and when not. One example from thousands: According to Esther 9.26–8 'the Jews' took it upon themselves to observe the Feast of Purim each year in order to commemorate the victory over Haman that is the subject of the book. At some time or other it became traditional to read Esther, usually called simply 'the scroll', Megillah, once each year. Among some at least this came to be regarded as an obligation. People naturally needed to know when the obligation had been fulfilled: *precisely* what must be done to meet the requirement to read 'the scroll'? The Mishnaic rabbis undertook to answer the question, as this paragraph will show:

> If a man read [the Scroll] piecemeal or drowsily, he has fulfilled his obligation; if he was copying it, expounding it, or correcting a copy of it, and he directed his heart [to the reading of the Scroll], he has fulfilled his obligation; otherwise he has not fulfilled his obligation. (*Megillah* 2.2)

Whether this paragraph is Pharisaic or later I do not know. I propose, however, that this is the sort of discussion that ancient authors had in mind when they said that the Pharisees were 'strict' or 'precise' interpreters of the law, and that here we have something of the flavour of Pharisaism.

This kind of meticulous activity now strikes people in different ways, as it did also in the first century. Many see it in a negative light: it is casuistic, nitpicking and trivial. It was undertaken to limit one's response to God, allowing followers to feel self-righteous while in fact they followed such trivial pursuits instead of attending to weightier ones. Such charges were levelled at the Pharisees in the first century. Christian tradition represented Jesus as criticizing them for obeying insignificant rules and shirking 'the weightier matters of the law, justice and mercy and faith' (Matt. 23.23). According to Mark 7 Jesus accused the Pharisees of following 'the tradition of the elders' in order to avoid keeping the commandments of God (7.9). Throughout the early chapters of the synoptic gospels the Pharisees (and scribes) are depicted as harrassing Jesus over what we now regard as trivia, such as allowing his disciples to pluck grain on the sabbath (Mark 2.24). Another way of putting this sort of accusation was to say that the Pharisees observed only the externals of the law, such as washing cups, while being spiritually dead within; that is, they were hypocrites (Matt. 23.25).

I doubt that these particular passages are actually words of Jesus, but for the present point it does not matter. The accusations were made by someone. Were they true?

Let us first consider casuistry. A casuist is a person who studies and resolves moral problems in specific situations; by extension, in modern use the term 'casuist' often means that the person does this in an overly subtle way, so that finally the resolution is dishonest. To take an example: Lev. 19.18 says, 'love your neighbour as yourself'. A dishonest casuist might define 'neighbour' so as to exclude a given person and then proceed to do that person damage. The rabbis, and presumably the Pharisees, were certainly 'casuists' in a general sense: anyone is who tries to apply a law to a new situation. Portia, in *The Merchant of Venice*, is a good casuist; by applying the law 'a pound of flesh' literally, she evades it, and does so in a good cause.[68] Rabbinic literature is full of humane and generous casuistry. What if person A, in a fit of anger, vows to have no benefit from person B ('I don't *want* your money')? Let us imagine that B happens to find property that A had lost. Is A then bound not to accept it? No, ruled the rabbis; that is an exception to the rules about vows (*Nedarim* 4.2; see generally 4.1–8). What if a person swore an oath not to eat onions, since onions are bad for the heart? He can eat Cyprus onions, which are good for the heart, and according to some even all onions (*Nedarim* 9.8). Since vows and oaths are often rash, tractate *Nedarim* is full of casuistry that avoids unfortunate consequences, but this characterizes rabbinic exegesis as a whole. We should attribute the same sort of casuistry to the Pharisees; in fact, the prosbul, attributed to Hillel, is an example of benign casuistry.

We may take it as certain that most followers of Pharisaism were not conscious of basing their lives on hypocrisy: the pretence of serving God when in fact they were seeking only self-glorification (so the charge in Matt. 23.5–7). It is not credible that a major religious movement within Judaism was based on bad motives.

Religious polemic often assigns bad motives to the other side. It is a charge that is hard to disprove, and thus the enemies of a religious movement can hold it securely. To take a more recent example: Protestants have sometimes accused Roman Catholics of sinning with the intention of receiving formal absolution and then of repeating the transgression. It is true that in the Roman church there is a rite of absolution, and thus nothing is simpler than to impugn the motives of those who make use of it. Further, it may be supposed that there are and have been Roman Catholics who regard penance as only an external matter, one not requiring internal repentance. For true Roman Catholics, however, the relationship between the exterior rite and the interior attitude is seen quite differently: the rite gives the occasion for repentance and the resolution to mend one's ways.

Similarly with regard to the Pharisees: others could see their scrupulous definition and fulfilment of the laws as being merely external activity that masked inner hypocrisy and self-righteousness, but they did not themselves see it that way. They thought that God had given them his law and bestowed on them his grace, and that it was their obligation within the loving relationship with God to obey the law precisely.

How do we know that they saw it this way? Partly by common-sense inferences based on observation of other religious polemic and defences. There are, however, passages that show that Pharisees themselves (and their rabbinic successors) regarded love and devotion to God as standing at the centre of their attempt to obey the law in every detail. According to Josephus many people followed the Pharisees' rules of worship because they admired their high ideals, expressed 'both in their way of living and in their discourse' (*Antiq.* 18.15). Josephus saw them as being 'affectionate to each other', and he said that they cultivated 'harmonious relations with the community' – unlike the Sadducees (*War* 2.166). That is, the Pharisees paid attention to the part of the law that says to love God and the neighbour. These passages in Josephus do not precisely describe inner motive, but their general thrust is relevant. Josephus is claiming that the Pharisees were good and kind and that their devotion to God was admired. We should also recall the depth of that devotion, which we summarized above: the willingness to die rather than be false to what they believed.

Explicit statements about motive come in rabbinic literature. I know of no body of literature that so emphasizes the importance of right intention and pure motive, of acting in a spirit of love and humility. Thus Hillel, in a saying retained in Aramaic: 'A name made great is a name destroyed' (*Avot* 1.13). To Hillel is also attributed this statement: 'Be of the disciples of Aaron, loving peace and pursuing peace, loving mankind and bringing them nigh to the Law' (*Avot* 1.12). According to Hillel's predecessor Shemaiah, one should 'love labour and hate mastery' (*Avot* 1.10). The Pharisees did not regard themselves as observing the law for the sake of self-glorification.

The topic of motive, 'intention', is even more directly discussed by the post-70 rabbis, making use of the phrase 'directing the heart' (to God). The scholar who studies much is not superior to his fellow, the common person, provided that the latter 'directs the heart to Heaven' (*Berakhot* 17a). Similarly the size of an offering does not matter, and all are called 'an odour of sweet savour'. This is 'to teach that it is all one whether a man offers much or little, if only he directs his mind towards heaven' (*Menahot* 13.11). I do not know of any sayings of this sort that are attributed to pre-70 Pharisees, but rabbinic literature attributes relatively few sayings (as distinct from legal discussions) to pre-70 Pharisees. I propose, however, that here as elsewhere the rabbis were the spiritual heirs of the Pharisees.

We may conclude that the Pharisees did not see their meticulous definition and observance of the law as being hypocritical and that they were not consciously seeking self-glorification; they were motivated by true religious devotion and the desire to serve God.

The second aspect of rabbinic literature that I wish to emphasize as reflecting something of the flavour of Pharisaism is the feeling of closeness to God at which their rules of prayer and reflection on the scripture aimed. Some of these aspects of worship were probably followed by the Jewish populace generally, and it may be daily prayer life that Josephus had in mind when he wrote that the people in general followed the Pharisees in 'prayers and sacred rites of divine worship' (*Antiq.* 18.15). From the discussion of common piety, we may recall that the Shemaʿ (Deut. 6.4–9) was to be said twice each day, morning and evening. This is specified in the passage itself and taken for granted in the Mishnah; it was widely observed, and surely kept by all Pharisees. The passage urges Israel to love God and to recall his commandments in various ways, including posting mezuzot on the doorposts and wearing tefillin (above, pp. 195–7). The Pharisees actually did wear tefillin containing the commandments, as the criticism in Matt. 23.5 shows. There the complaint is that they were worn for show, but we may be sure that those who wore them did so in order to follow the scriptural injunction to be ever mindful of God's law. Josephus said that the motive for saying the

Shema', praying, and posting mezuzot and wearing tefillin was to thank God
and to demonstrate 'the loving care with which God surrounds' those who
worship him (*Antiq.* 4.212f.; quoted above, p. 276).

The prayers that accompanied the Shema' probably followed the main
themes of the Eighteen Benedictions. In discussing common piety I proposed
that some people besides Pharisees may have used the themes of these
prayers, but we may be more confident that the Pharisees did. The Mishnah
attributes to Rabban Gamaliel the statement that one should pray the
Eighteen Benedictions every day, while R. Joshua proposed only the
substance of them (*Berakhot* 4.3; both born before 70, flourished before 100).
These prayers focus on repentance, forgiveness, thanksgiving for the
election, and the hope of redemption. It is difficult to pray them every day and
not to be reminded of the basic theological themes of Judaism: love, mercy
and repentance. Further, they inculcate the feeling of the presence of God.
According to the later rabbis, study serves the same function: when one
studies the law it is as if one stood before God at Mount Sinai.[69]

Without being able to assign such sayings to pre-70 Pharisees, we may still
see that the daily life of prayer and study was a feature of Pharisaism, and then
it is not difficult to attribute to the Pharisees the religious motives that are
expressed by Josephus and the rabbis.

Influence

To conclude the discussion of the Pharisees, we shall return to the
question of the degree to which they controlled Palestinian society. We saw
above that, after the time of Salome Alexandra, they did not hold positions of
power; that Pharisaic influence over the populace was not so great that
significant numbers were always ready to take to the streets in order to
persuade the rulers to follow the Pharisees; that Herod, the Roman
administrators and the high priests in any case did not obey the crowd. We
have now to ask whether or not the Pharisees ruled *very* indirectly. People
agreed with them, and for this reason followed Pharisaic rules.[70]

In a recent book Martin Hengel notes Morton Smith's objection to the
theory of Pharisaic control. He does not discuss Smith's actual argument
(that Josephus' summaries about the Pharisees are not substantiated by
individual accounts), but he very helpfully singles out the page in Schürer
that persuades him that the Pharisees represented Palestinian Judaism and
that Josephus was right when he wrote that the Pharisees had 'determinative
influence'.[71] According to Schürer, the Pharisees were

the classical representatives of that trend which set the inner development of Israel in the post-exilic period generally. What applies to [Israelites] in general applies specifically to the Pharisaic party. This is the real nucleus of the people, which is distinct from the rest of the mass only by its greater strictness and consistency.[72]

This section of Schürer in general is one of the places in which Josephus' summaries of Pharisaic control are taken quite literally: whenever the Sadducees were in office, they had to follow the Pharisees, or else the people would have kicked them out. They even restrained Herod. I have shown above that this was not actually the case. But now we should consider the more general and subtle point, that the Pharisees were the true representatives of Israel, and that in this sense their views prevailed.

I think that this puts the matter the wrong way around. The general trend to which Schürer referred was certainly there: people were zealous to live according to God's law. The Pharisees shared in this trend. Their willingness and ability to step forward as leaders varied, and a distinct change can be discerned beginning with Herod's reign; the Pharisees never again had the public role that they had under Jannaeus and Salome Alexandra. On the topic of *public, religio-political* assertion of zeal, we can see that they *shared* it but that they were not the sole embodiments of it, nor were they the cause of the fact that other people held it. The Essenes did not submit bravely to torture, refusing to eat unlawful food, because of Pharisaic influence, nor was that what led the Sicarii to refuse to call Caesar 'master' even under 'every form of torture and laceration of body' (*War* 2.152f.; 7.418). Both Essenes and Sicarii were inspired in part by the hope of a better world (*War* 2.153; above, pp. 282f.), but that was a widely held hope, earlier than and much larger than the Pharisaic party.

The Pharisees shared a common spirit,[73] and like everyone else they had to decide when to risk their lives. There is *no* indication, after the time of Jannaeus, that the populace was guided in this by the Pharisees. In 66 CE, the leading Pharisees tried to *restrain* the populace; in other cases they were readier to die than were most. Some of them risked death over the eagle, some when they went along with Judas the Galilean, but in neither case did the crowd follow. The Pharisees neither created zeal for the law nor decided when other people would display it.

The best case for Pharisaic control, that they were representatives of the popular mood, and so maintained their place as the leaders of the nation, breaks down. When we look at the topics discussed in this chapter, we see even more clearly that the Pharisees did not control the people. It is striking that the same scholars say that the Pharisees *excluded* most Jews from 'true Israel' because the ordinary people would not follow them, and that they controlled the people, so that everyone did what they said, especially with regard to religious observances.[74] These statements are contradictory; besides, both are in error. The Pharisees' distinctive practices and beliefs did not cut them off from other people, nor lead them to the view that ordinary Jews were actually not members of the covenant. Yet they *did* have distinctive practices, which by definition were rejected by everyone else. In handling the priests' food they followed purity rules that others did not accept. They had distinctive views about moist olives and grapes, and they periodically immersed their garments. They seem to have had no popular following on these points, though the Qumran sectarians may have agreed. The immersing of garments, one of the Pharisees' most restrictive views, was probably inconvenient but nevertheless possible for people who used public pools. The ordinary people did not follow the views of the Pharisees because they did not think that it was necessary. They had their own views, probably what the priests taught, and they followed them.

The point of being a party is to have special rules. The Pharisees' special rules made them Pharisees; they did not, in their own opinion, make them the only true Jews, but they did make them different from most other Jews. Had other people adopted their distinctive practices, which they could have done without too much difficulty, they would have been Pharisees too. But other people did not adopt them. This is so clear that I cannot see why scholars insist that everyone did what the Pharisees thought they should do.

A large part of the view that the Pharisees both controlled and spoke for Jews in general is the unspoken assumption that it was the Pharisees who wanted to obey the law and that other people were motivated by them. I pointed out above that Martin Hengel assumes that the Theodotus inscription, which says that a family of priests built and maintained a synagogue in Jerusalem, is an indication of Pharisaic activity. The Pharisees were generally responsible for the development of synagogues in Palestine, and so he 'assume[s] that this foundation, too, had a Pharisaic background'. He further explains that 'the priestly nobility had no interest in creating competition for the temple'.[75] Yet the inscription says that the supporting family was priestly, and evidently it was rich. Priests as priests cared about the law. They did not have to be Pharisees to do so. They believed in it and they taught it. The assumption that the Pharisees were the only ones committed to the law, and that whenever anyone else showed commitment it was because of Pharisaic influence, pervades scholarly descriptions of second-temple Judaism, and consequently the Pharisees crop up everywhere. But if people will put that assumption aside and look again at the literature, they will see things in a truer light, and they will not be compelled to insert the Pharisees into every narrative. One of the main ambitions of this book is to encourage readers to see common Judaism and common Jews as devoted to the law. This is shown by all the evidence, including rabbinic literature.

Pharisees shared common Judaism, not only the general spirit of zeal for God and his law, but also obedience to the commandments in everyday life. They did not invent common Judaism, nor did other people share it because of the Pharisees' influence. On some points the Pharisees were distinctive. Here again they did not determine what Jews in general thought and did.

20

Other Pietists

Here I wish to take account of further literature from Palestine in the Roman period, literature that may be called generally 'pietist' but that cannot be definitely attributed to a known party. It was once the custom to attribute almost all Palestinian pietist literature to the Pharisees, on the grounds that belief in some form of afterlife is usually present. Now that we see more clearly that most Jews expected some form of 'renewed existence', and that the Sadducees stood alone or almost alone in denying it, we can be less certain of assigning literature to parties or sects.

Some literature that was produced before the Roman period, or even before the Hasmonean revolt, remained in use and seems to have exercised some influence. Two of the principal works in this category are *Jubilees* and *I Enoch* (or at least four of the five component parts that now constitute the latter). These works were read at Qumran, where fragments have been found, and they both have the calendar that the sectarians followed. They obviously had a wider readership, however, and have come down through channels apparently unconnected with the Essene movement.

For the present purpose, I wish to offer only a sample of literature that is pietist but not otherwise identifiable, and I have chosen two works that date from the early Roman period (63 BCE–66 CE): the *Psalms of Solomon* and the *Testament of Moses* (often called the *Assumption of Moses*).[1] These I take as representative of 'other pietists' in the chart on p. 28 above. I have used both works in two different sections of this book, ch. 14 ('Hopes for the Future') and ch. 10 (criticism of the priests). I shall here try to convey something of the flavour of the works as a whole, including their overall theological stance. The aim of the present section is to indicate the range of hope for the future and protest about the present that characterized much of Judaism in the Roman period.

The Psalms of Solomon[2]

These eighteen Psalms constitute a substantial body of literature from early in the Roman period. Some clearly reflect the conquest of Jerusalem by Pompey (63 BCE), and in one there is a reference to his death (48 BCE; *Ps. Sol.* 2.26f.). It is not possible to be certain that they were all written in these years, nor that they are all from one hand. The overall point of view, however, is consistent.

The *Psalms* speak for people who call themselves 'the pious' (2.36; 4.8; 14.3 and often) or 'the righteous' (e.g. 3.6).[3] They are not otherwise identified, and they reveal no distinctive characteristics of the known rigorous parties, the Pharisees and Essenes. There are, for example, no references to the tradition of the elders, nor any mention of Zadokite priests.

The pious authors recall that they (or their spiritual predecessors) had fled to the desert (17.16–17). This was true, of course, of some Essenes, but the desert was the traditional place of refuge, especially for pious groups. Most of the known instances are later than the *Psalms of Solomon*, but we must suppose that various people fled to the desert at various times, whether or not Josephus recounts the event.[4] Thus the reference to the wandering in the desert does not help fix the authorship of *Ps. Sol.* 17 precisely.

The Roman invasion seems to have been the occasion of the psalms, but the Romans do not bear the brunt of the psalmists' attack. Principal criticism is directed against the Jewish priesthood, and thus against the last of the Hasmonean priests (Hyrcanus II, Aristobulus II and Antigonus, Aristobulus' son) and the other priestly aristocrats of their day. The second psalm gives this context clearly. God did not restrain 'the sinner', who used battering rams on the walls. Foreigners even walked up to the altar. The cause of this was that 'the sons of Jerusalem' had defiled the 'holy things of the Lord' and had 'profaned the offerings to God with lawless deeds' (*Ps. Sol.* 2.1–3). 'The sinner' is Pompey, but the real culprits are 'the sons of Jerusalem', who defiled the sacrifices. In 17.6 the Hasmoneans are accused of setting up their own monarchy and laying 'waste the throne of David', even though God appointed David as king and promised the position to his descendants forever. It will be recalled that Eleazar the Pharisee had urged John Hyrcanus to give up the priesthood and remain as head of state (*Antiq.* 13.291). The pious of the *Psalms of Solomon* objected to the Hasmoneans on both grounds: they were corrupt priests and illegal kings.

In a way common to religious polemic, the opponents are also accused of sexual offences: the daughters of Jerusalem engaged in 'unnatural intercourse' (2.13). Sexual sin was mixed with other crimes, such as transgression of the purity rules of the pious and even outright theft (*Ps. Sol.* 8.9–13, more fully above, p. 185). God treated the Jewish sinners as they deserved. He turned away his face, did not pity them, and 'abandoned them into the hands of those who prevail' – the Romans (2.7–9), who were the instruments of God's wrath. The sinners received recompense for their deeds (2.16).

The pious themselves had suffered, but they were not destroyed. They did not despise 'the chastening of the Lord' (3.4), but rather were moved by it to repentance, and God responded with forgiveness. The righteous person, the author explains, makes atonement for sins of ignorance 'by fasting and affliction of his soul', and God counts the pious guiltless (3.8). This is the fullest expression of this point of their theology:

> He will purify a soul in sin when confession and acknowledgment is
>   made;
> For shame is upon us and upon our faces on account of all these
>   things.
> And to whom will he forgive sins, if it be not to those who have
>   sinned?
> Thou shalt bless the righteous and not call them to account for the
>   sins they have committed;
> And thy goodness is upon sinners when they repent. (9.6f.)

Further, God's judgment and mercy alike are eternal,

> And the inheritance of sinners is destruction and darkness,
>   And their iniquities shall pursue them to Sheol below:
> Their inheritance shall not be found by their children,
>   For sins shall devastate the houses of sinners;
> And sinners shall perish for ever on the day of the Lord's judgment,
>   When God visits the earth with his judgment.
> But those who fear the Lord shall find mercy on it,
>   And shall live by the compassion of their God;
>   But sinners shall perish eternally. (15.10–13)

Here as in the Dead Sea Scrolls we cannot determine precisely what kind of life after death the authors expected. Sinners will be pursued to Sheol (Hades) and eternally destroyed, while the righteous will live; more we do not know.

In the shorter term, the pious authors counted on God to stand by the covenant promises and preserve Israel – that is, Israel as represented not by the iniquitous Hasmoneans, but rather by the pious. The authors of the Psalms hoped for an earthly kingdom of freedom from foreign rule, for national sovereignty, and righteousness.

And no nation will prevail against us;
  For thou art our protector,
And we shall call upon thee, and thou wilt hear us;
  For thou wilt pity the race of Israel for ever . . . (7.6–8)

For thou didst choose the seed of Abraham above all the nations,
  And didst set thy name upon us, O Lord;
  And thou wilt never cast us off. (9.9)

The salvation of the Lord be upon Israel his servant for ever;
  And may sinners perish altogether at the presence of the Lord;
And may the holy ones of the Lord inherit the promises of the Lord.
    (12.6)

Most distinctively, however, Ps. 17 depicts the coming of a new Davidic king (17.21), who will 'destroy the lawless nations' (17.24), judge the tribes of Israel, distribute the land among them (17.26, 28), and even rule the Gentiles (17.30). The Gentiles will also 'come from the ends of the earth to see his glory', bringing with them the children of Israel 'who had fainted' (17.31). The son of David's victory, however, does not depend on military strength: 'he shall not put his trust in horse and rider and bow, . . . nor shall he concentrate his hopes on numbers for the day of battle' (17.33). The reason is that God himself is king. He will have mercy on the Gentiles who fear him (17.34). The son of David, ruling as God's viceroy, will be 'pure from sin' and will not weaken 'during his days' (17.36f.). This apparently means that he will be mortal.

We have in these psalms first-hand evidence that resistance to the Hasmoneans, a desire for purity and piety, and the hope for a sovereign state motivated many. 'Resistance', however, was moral and passive. The authors of the Psalms hoped for a divine miracle: God would call together the children of Israel from the four corners of the earth (11.2f.), apparently including all twelve tribes. The prediction that 'the tribes' would share the land (17.28) probably means that more than the two surviving tribes were in mind. The lost ten would also be found.

The Testament of Moses[5]

The *Testament of Moses*, like the *Psalms of Solomon*, speaks for an otherwise unidentifiable pietist or group of pietists. There are some dislocations in the text as it stands; it appears that an anti-Hasmonean document was revised after the death of Herod. The Hasmoneans are strongly criticized: kings who are called priests will 'be responsible for much ungodliness in the holy of holies' (6.1), but Herod is referred to in the next lines:

And an insolent king will succeed them, who will not be of priestly stock, an arrogant and a shameless man; and he will judge them as they deserve. And he will put their leaders to death with the sword, and bury them secretly so that no one should know where their bodies are. He will kill both old and young and spare no one. He will be the object of universal dread and detestation. And he will treat them ruthlessly . . . for thirty-four years . . . (6.2–5)

That is a perfect description of Herod and his systematic elimination of the Hasmoneans.

The author then states that Herod's children will rule for shorter periods than he (6.7). The next lines refer to Varus, the legate of Syria who put down the riots that erupted when Herod died (6.8). This fixes the date of the document as we have it. Herod was king from 40 to 4 BCE, thirty-six years (though his effective rule was three years less), but Antipas was Tetrarch from 4 BCE to 39 CE – forty-three years. The work was written before the length of Antipas' reign was known (it is called 'shorter' than Herod's), and the last clear reference is to Varus. Then we may date the version that survives to the period 4 BCE–30 CE.

The history of the period from the Hasmonean revolt to the death of Herod, though dismal from the author's point of view, was nevertheless planned by God.

He has foreseen what will happen to both them and us from the beginning of the creation of the earth to the end of the age; and nothing has been overlooked by him, not even the smallest detail, but he has foreseen everything and brought everything about. (12.4)

That God runs things was the natural assumption, and in this sense most Jews of the time believed in 'fate' (as Josephus called it). Whether the author of this passage would deny freedom of choice to individuals, however, is another question. We have seen that other Jews, such as the Pharisees and the Qumran sectarians, combined strong predestinarian statements with the assumption of individual choice and responsibility.

The author looked forward to the 'final consummation' (1.18). At the end a Levite, named Taxo, would arise and lead his sons to a cave, where they would die 'rather than transgress the commandments of the Lord of lords' (9.6). This resolve perfectly reflects an important part of the temper of the times. The curious chapter about Taxo may be from an earlier version, for we do not learn the result of his resolve to die rather than transgress. In ch. 10 the scene shifts: God himself will appear. He will punish the Gentiles, destroy their idols, and exalt Israel to be 'in heaven above the stars' (10.7–9). This does not mean that the world ends. From heaven the Israelites can look down and see their enemies (10.10).

The document reflects the hatred that some of the pious felt for the Hasmoneans and Herod. What is most striking is the other-worldly character of the redemption of Israel. There is no messiah, no king, no new temple, no regathered twelve tribes – unless they are all in heaven.

Conclusion

These two documents, like the Dead Sea Scrolls, give dramatic, first-hand views of several aspects of Jewish piety. They both embody the underlying common theology, covenantal nomism. God has chosen Israel and will redeem his nation by his own initiative. People should obey his law. He punishes sinners severely and chastises the righteous for their transgressions.

These documents show how passionately some Jews held these views: how fiercely they loved God; how much they hated subjection, both Jewish and Roman; how deeply they believed that the future was in God's hands and that finally all would come out as it should. These authors, like many, were outwardly pacifist: there is no call to arms. Even the battles of the Davidic king will be fought by God. We learn here what strong emotions could lurk in the hearts of the pious who were outwardly submissive. As we saw in ch. 4, there was a wide range of views about 'foreign policy' and the dominant military force, whether Hasmonean, Herodian or Roman. We cannot say how many Jews of our period looked at the world precisely as did the authors of these texts, but they represent more than just themselves. We can readily imagine that smouldering dislike could be fanned into flames and that those who were formerly passive could be roused to action. We may think of the followers of Judas the Galilean, the Pharisees as they waited and watched for their chance, and a whole multitude who finally launched the great revolt, having for years submitted to Rome. These documents reveal something of the temper of those who rose against Jannaeus, and they help explain why he so brutally repressed them. They also help explain Herod's fortresses and his secret police, and just what it was that the Romans faced as they sought to deal with their most difficult subjects. Rulers saw the potentially vicious, murderous side of many of the pietists, who, however, saw themselves as wanting only to fulfil God's will, and to be allowed to do as he wished.

Who Ran What?

It is usually difficult to know how things really get done and who actually decides; official titles can be misleading. In small towns nowadays, most people know who runs what, but as the scale gets larger uncertainty begins. In the 1940s and 1950s Harry Turner ran Grand Prairie, Texas. He was not always mayor, and he was probably not the largest landowner. But Harry Turner ran the town. What he wanted, happened; what he did not want, did not happen. Let us change the scale. Who runs the modern parliamentary democracies? The presidents, prime ministers, premiers and chancellors? Or backroom committees, steered by civil servants and swayed by lobbyists? Only insiders know who actually had the most influence in a given situation, and the public finds out decades later, when documents are opened to researchers. One cannot determine the power of the US President by reading the Constitution. In practice, the President runs as many things as he has time for, cares about, and can get away with. President after President has, in some extra-constitutional way or other, involved the nation in a series of conflicts, including the early years of World War II, when the US was officially neutral.[1] On the other hand, presidents are pragmatic; they cannot get too far ahead of public opinion.

Given enough documentation, historians can penetrate the fog. I do not think that it is completely impossible to find out who ran what in Jewish Palestine during the early Roman period, but we may be sure in advance that the answers will vary from time to time and issue to issue. How can we find out who decided what?

I wish first to look at two largely mythical sources of government, Pharisaic law and the Sanhedrin, before offering more constructive proposals.

The rabbis had laid it down

Most historians of Judaism, when they wish to state what people actually did in pre-70 Palestine, offer a rabbinic ruling: Jews did X or Y because the rabbis, Pharisees or 'sages' (a term that covers both) had 'laid it down' or 'decreed it'. I have argued extensively that the Pharisees governed neither directly nor indirectly. Since Jewish society has so long been described by quoting rabbinic passages, however, I wish to add a further demonstration of how erroneous the resulting descriptions often are, and also to comment further on the uses and abuses of rabbinic literature.

In ch. 19 we noted that many scholars are involved in a fundamental self-contradiction with regard to the binding force of rabbinic law. They maintain that the rabbis (or Pharisees or sages) governed every aspect of life, not only because they had a majority in the Sanhedrin, but also because they were so influential with the populace that public opinion forced non-Pharisees who held office to follow Pharisaic rules; yet the same scholars state that the rabbis looked down on the common people because they did *not* follow Pharisaic laws, especially those dealing with tithes and purity. This leads to an unrealistic view of life in Jewish Palestine, a view that becomes even more unrealistic when one examines the rules that such scholars say the people followed. We often read that the rabbis (or sages or Pharisees) *successfully* enforced unreasonable rules while failing to get the people to keep one of the major biblical commandments, the requirement to support the Levites. We shall first look at this self-contradiction and lack of realism.

Jeremias, for example, states that before the Day of Atonement the high priest had to spend several nights in 'his official room in the Temple on the south side of the priests' forecourt' because the Mishnah says so.[2] In the Sanhedrin the 'high priests with Sadducean sympathies had to accustom themselves to withholding their views in Council, and to carrying out the Temple rites according to Pharisaic traditions'.[3] There had to be three temple treasurers, since the Mishnah requires it.[4] Even Herod had to obey the Pharisees, since they had the support of the people (citing not the Mishnah, but rather Josephus on another point).[5] All rules were enforced by the Pharisees and cases were decided by judges who were Pharisees or who followed Pharisaic law.[6] *Yet*, on the other hand, the ordinary people 'did not observe the demands of religious laws as [the Pharisees] did';[7] specifically, they did not keep 'the rules laid down by Pharisaic scribes on tithes and purity'.[8] The Pharisees therefore did not consider the ordinary people to be part of the 'true Israel', and they despised them.[9]

I cite Jeremias on these points only because he is extreme on both sides: everybody obeyed the Pharisees all the time; they were so popular that even on official temple issues the high priest had to obey them; the ordinary people, however, did not obey the Pharisees on two quite large issues, and the Pharisees consequently regarded them as outside the covenant. These two contradictory positions can be readily illustrated from almost any secondary literature that deals with Jewish practice. I add an example just to illustrate the point. According to Schürer, both old and new, it is wrong to think that individual Pharisees, such as Hillel, governed Palestine, since the Sanhedrin did, as the Mishnah explicitly says (*Sanhedrin* 11.2); this, however, is a formal distinction, and the leading Pharisaic teachers were '*in fact* the deciding authorities'.[10] The Pharisaic 'ordinances' were 'legally binding'. Any halakhah that was decided by a 'majority of Torah scholars' 'would become binding'.[11] On the other hand, the ʿammê ha-ʾarets, ordinary people, were not expected to observe the law strictly, especially the parts that deal with 'Levitical purity and priestly dues'.[12] On whom, then, were the Pharisees' laws binding?

Scholars such as Schürer and Jeremias employed evidence in the following way: they began with a few second-century passages on the 'associates', which say that these people ate food in purity and tithed;[13] they equated the associates with pre-seventy Pharisees; they viewed the associates' tithing and purity rules as setting them off from the general populace; and so they proposed that these were the laws that the people disobeyed. Next, the prooftexts from Josephus came into play: everyone did what the Pharisees said. This then became a *legal* fact: rabbinic law governed the country. Pharisees passed legislation and enforced it (or they made other people pass it and enforce it).

In this long tradition of scholarship, at least on the Christian side, the two laws that the people would not obey, tithing and eating food in purity, are regarded as externalistic, ritualistic, snobbish, elitist, self-righteous rules. The Pharisees excluded those who would not keep such rules from Jewish religion and society.[14]

This view, which is standard in the handbooks (with some variations), offers a completely unrealistic picture. We saw above that it gives neither a credible view of the high priests, kings and other rulers (pp. 394–8), nor of the common people, who quite evidently did not think that they were outside the true Israel and that the only way in was to become Pharisees (p. 441). Now I wish to exemplify the erroneous *method* that is basic to this view of the government of first-century Palestine. After explaining that people had to obey the Pharisees' rules, scholars sometimes say what they were. The technique is to pull an opinion out of rabbinic literature and to say that it was a law, without paying any attention either to the nature of the literature or to social and economic reality. Many of these 'laws' would have been very detrimental to individuals and society as a whole (as I shall show immediately below), but nevertheless people had to obey them or suffer dire consequences. Joachim Jeremias here stands well above everyone else. He wrote

Jerusalem in the Time of Jesus, purporting to describe real life. I shall take a fairly typical example to illustrate the technique and its results.

In one section, Jeremias gives lists of 'despised trades'. People who engaged in numerous businesses and occupations were, he says, deprived of their rights by the 'ruling class', the Pharisees. (This has a theological point: the despised members of society were the very people whom Jesus admitted to the kingdom.[15] The more people excluded by the Pharisees, the better Jesus looks.) One of the despised trades was being a herdsman. (1) Those who herded 'small cattle' (sheep and goats) transgressed the rabbinic rule that allowed sheep and goats to be pastured only 'on the steppes' (Billerbeck's translation of 'deserts': *Bava Qamma* 7.7). This rule was not 'juristic': breeders of sheep and goats were social outcasts but retained legal rights.[16] (2) Herdsmen 'in the service of Jerusalemites' appear twice in Jeremias' lists of people who were despised, categories I and IV. Those in category I were looked down on, but people in category IV were in a worse situation. They were hated 'by the people; they were *de jure* and officially deprived of rights and ostracized . . . In other words [the herdsman] was deprived of civil and political rights to which every Israelite had claim.'[17] 'It was forbidden to buy wool, milk or kids from [herdsmen]'.[18]

Whereas in the case of breeders of small cattle Jeremias had a clear Mishnaic statement to cite (*Bava Qamma* 7.7, 'small cattle' cannot be raised in Israel, except in the deserts), his statements about herdsmen who were employed by Jerusalemites required more inventive use of sources. The two passages are *Sanhedrin* 25b[19] and *Ketuvot* 62b. The first of these is a gloss on Mishnah *Sanhedrin* 3.3 The passage in the Mishnah excludes usurers and others from being judges or witnesses. It contains three chronological layers: 'Beforetime', R. Simeon and R. Judah. 'Beforetime' may indicate a Pharisaic layer; R. Judah flourished *c.* 150 CE; R. Simeon comes in between. The gloss in *Sanhedrin* 25b, which the Talmud designates as 'Tannaitic' (before 220 CE), adds herdsmen and others to the list of people who could not perform certain legal functions. It implies that the fault of the herdsmen was that they pastured animals on other peoples' land. Jeremias regarded both *Sanhedrin* 3.3 and the Talmudic addition as 'Pharisaic', and he also thought that these passages constituted a *law* (unlike *Bava Qamma* 7.7). Thus far, however, we do not know that the herdsmen whom the Pharisees deprived of their rights were those who were employed by Jerusalemites. Jeremias found this point in *Ketuvot* 62b, which states that Akiba was once a shepherd in the employ of a Jerusalemite. There is no explanation of why these passages should be combined, nor of how they lead to Jeremias' conclusion, nor of why the combination constitutes a law.

I shall summarize Jeremias' errors: (1) He dipped into the Talmud (more precisely, the parts of it quoted by Billerbeck) and lifted two sentences about herdsmen (*Sanhedrin* 25b, *Ketuvot* 62b). He combined these two sentences and considered them Pharisaic with no explanation of why a story about a second-century rabbi defines a rule elsewhere in the Talmud, nor of why these two passages, once combined, should be considered Pharisaic. (2) He construed a rabbinic opinion (*Sanhedrin* 25b) as a *law*, even though Judah ha-Nasi did not put it in the Mishnah. (3) He supposed that the rabbis controlled the machinery of the state: they could actually deprive people of their ordinary rights. (4) He paid no attention to real life.

I have said enough about (3) in earlier chapters and shall here comment on the others. (1) With regard to lifting passages, combining them, and calling them Pharisaic: It is sometimes possible to infer backwards from the views of later rabbis to pre-70 Pharisaic opinions. To do this, however, one has to discover the underlying principles of the rabbinic view, especially what the Talmud presupposes, and consider the possibility of development. In the present case, one should first find the general rabbinic view, which is that herdsmen working for someone else were *not* suspected of pasturing their animals on other peoples' property. The Talmud applies to herdsmen 'the presumption . . . that a man will not commit a sin unless he stands to profit by it himself' (*Bava Metsi'a* 5b). This is a very reasonable presumption, and also a basic rule, one that should be taken into account when saying that sentences about herdsmen and other employees were Pharisaic laws.[20] If the Pharisees thought that it was *employees* who were dishonest, why did the rabbis believe this not to be the case? Were they ignorant of the Pharisees' views, or did they simply decide to hold the opposite opinion? Possibly there is an explanation. But it should be noted that *no* rabbi *or* Pharisee, to our knowledge, *ever* stated that herdsmen who worked for others were considered always to be dishonest. That is Jeremias' contribution, which is opposed to the general rabbinic view.

Jeremias' use of the Talmud is especially flawed, but even had he made better use of Talmudic passages on herdsmen, the method would still be faulty. The entire procedure rests on the assumption that 'the halakhah' of the rabbis was pre-existent. This is what accounts *in general* for the practice of reaching into rabbinic literature, pulling out sentences, and saying that these were the laws of pre-70 Palestine. The chronological divisions in *Sanhedrin* 3.3, concluding with R. Judah (*c.* 150), would have bothered none of the major scholars who have used rabbinic literature to describe Palestine in the late second-temple period, nor would it bother very many today. Schürer, to be sure, stated that the halakhah was open-ended and kept developing,[21] and in theory everyone knows that. Occasionally there is a slip, an explicit statement of the pre-existence of the rabbinic halakhah: 'in Josephus' day,

Mishnah and Talmud did not yet exist, but the oral material which went to make them up was already current'.[22] This opinion, though seldom so forthrightly expressed, has governed the work of generations of scholars. Thackeray, Rajak and other students of Josephus, both old and new, with only a few exceptions, explain agreements between his work and rabbinic literature as instances that show that he was dependent on rabbinic rules. The 'oral tradition' that made up the Babylonian Talmud was already known to and enforced by the omnipresent Pharisees of Josephus' time.[23] I have elsewhere explained the assumption that lay behind this view: Jewish material was all 'tradition', and no one ever forgot anything. Second- to sixth-century rabbis basically just passed on old material that the Pharisees had already created.[24] Accompanying this has been the view that it was the Pharisees who created all extra-biblical rules. Therefore *any* non-biblical rule in Josephus, Philo or elsewhere proves the spread of Pharisaism and the authority of the Pharisees. While most scholars today will grant, at least formally, that material should be dated, the view is still widespread that the world of the Mishnah, or of the Babylonian Talmud, is the real world of pre-70 Palestine, and that rabbinic passages reveal what people did.

(2) I shall comment more briefly on Jeremias' second major mistake, which is also common in the literature, that of taking a rabbinic opinion as a law. It is especially dubious to cite a gloss on the Mishnah as a Pharisaic law. Let us say that the gloss really is Tannaitic, that is, that it comes from the period between 70 and 220 CE. Either Judah ha-Nasi, the editor of the Mishnah, did not know it, or he decided that it was not worth including. In either case, one would have to conduct an argument to prove that once upon a time it had been a Pharisaic law.

There is also a more general point with regard to calling an opinion a law: once one starts quoting rabbinic statements as laws governing Palestine, one may draw absolutely *any* portrait of first-century Palestine that one wants. There are thousands and thousands of pages, filled with opinions. Jeremias' choice in this section of his book has the effect of making the rabbis look extremely mean and narrow. One could just as easily and more justifiably cite another set of views altogether.[25] I shall return to the general problem of construing rabbinic statements as laws (below, pp. 465–72).

(4) Perhaps the most important error is the fourth: leaving real life out of account. Jeremias' view of the role of sheep, goats and shepherds in pre-70 Palestine seems to have been this: the temple and the festivals, particularly Passover, required tens of thousands of sacrificial animals, especially sheep; sheep and goats also accounted for a high percentage of the gross national product (wool, hides, meat, butter and cheese); nevertheless, the pre-70 sages decided to outlaw them and banished them to the desert, which could

not possibly support enough to keep the temple going;[26] herdsmen faced the choice of *either* following their profession, supplying some of the essentials of life and worship, while being deprived of all rights, *or* of seeking other employment (perhaps cutting stones for the temple, which would soon go out of business for lack of sheep); decent people, who followed the Pharisees, did without wool, milk and cheese; yet these same people would not follow the Pharisees' purity and tithing laws, and so were excluded from the true Israel.

It would be much more reasonable to think that Palestine's graziers were respected, which is what Aristeas and Philo both imply.[27] Dishonest practices, whether stealing others' sheep or grazing one's own flock on someone else's land, would have been handled by different rulers in different ways; but there is no reason to think that owners of flocks or shepherds were deprived of their civil rights, much less that decent people were required to do without milk, cheese and wool.

Part of the problem of the academic field is simply a surfeit of bad judgment. Rabbinic literature *can* reveal social reality. The itemization of women's work in such passages as *Ketuvot* 5.5 (above, p. 122) very usefully reveals that many women ground grain at home. They did not do it because the rabbis required them to do it, but the rabbinic discussion reveals an assumption about society, and *social assumptions* are revealing. A rabbinic *legal assumption* might be similarly revealing. But this would require study that is divorced from the modern academic assumption that virtually any sentence in rabbinic literature reveals real life because the literature pre-existed and because the Pharisees could *require* people to do anything that they said, no matter how unreasonable – except, of course, to tithe and observe a few minor purity regulations. We should always bear in mind that rabbinic opinions were not necessarily Pharisaic laws; even if they were, they should be evaluated carefully before we pronounce on actual practice.

The scholar or reader who wishes to do real history must take into account all sorts of possibilities when he or she faces a rabbinic passage; the response, 'everybody did it because the rabbis laid it down', is seldom the correct one. To illustrate this point, I shall now discuss the range of things that a rabbinic debate might mean. For the sake of these illustrations, I shall largely ignore dates, and take passages from the entire Tannaitic period (ending *c.* 220 CE), because here I do not wish to establish Pharisaic law, nor to discover which rules in late literature were early, but rather to illustrate how many possibilities one must consider before saying that a rabbinic passage was a law that governed society, or even that it was meant to be such a law. I intentionally use several examples that we have met before, in order to reduce the amount of explanation. A few examples come from the work of Yigael Yadin. He shared the standard assumption, especially as articulated by Alon, that rabbinic law, even though appearing in late documents, was early and that it was 'in force' in pre-70 Palestine.[28] Yet on the other hand he dealt with real life. Consequently he was in a position to discuss the question of whether or not people followed rabbinic rules and recommendations.

I now itemize several of the possibilities that must be considered when analysing rabbinic legal discussions and trying to establish what people actually did.

1. A rabbinic decree might be no more than a simple description of common practice, which someone finally decided to write down. The 'tied deeds' of Babata, a former resident of Nabataea, correspond in general style to descriptions of such documents in the Mishnah and the Babylonian Talmud. It would be unreasonable to think that rabbinic law governed Nabataea, and Yadin (who discovered the documents) did not think that it did. He described the scribal technique as 'a very old and known practice of the ancient world'.[29] This system of safeguarding deeds from tampering was very widespread. It is not a case in which 'the rabbis laid it down, and so it was done'.

A second example: immediately above we noted *Ketuvot* 5.5, where the rabbis 'require' women to grind flour, bake and so on; society had not waited until the rabbis 'laid it down', but had already assigned women these tasks.

Dozens, hundreds of rabbinic 'regulations' fall into this category: common practice in the Near East, or sometimes in the former Hellenistic kingdoms, recorded by the rabbis. Yadin noted other cases.[30] He had the great advantage of knowing a lot about the Mediterranean and the Near East, and thus he could frequently distinguish common practice, coincidentally recorded by the rabbis, from rabbinic innovations. Surprisingly few historians of Judaism have made such distinctions, and most tend to treat correspondences as proving obedience to rabbinic law. Other scholars, however, have noted the point that I have just illustrated from Yadin's work. Martin Goodman, discussing the activities of Galilean rabbis in the second century, observed that agreement between rabbinic literature and other evidence, such as papyri, 'does not mean that rabbinic law-making was accepted, but rather that the rabbis codified the law *as it was actually practiced*'. 'What all the papyri show is that rabbinic law reflected actual law'; the actual law, in the cases of correspondence between papyri and rabbinic literature, preceded and was independent of rabbinic decisions. Goodman gives numerous examples.[31]

The importance of this category when considering 'who ran what' is very great. Simple correspondences between rabbinic rules and actual practice do not necessarily prove that people obeyed the rabbis, since in many cases the rabbis simply wrote down what people did. In these cases, rabbinic rules do correspond to real life, but other evidence shows that the rabbis' views were not unique; sometimes the other evidence may even establish that rabbinic rules followed a given practice rather than creating or controlling it.

2. A rabbinic halakhah might be a simple application of biblical law. Yadin noted that the cloth found in the Judaean caves did not combine diverse fabrics, such as wool and linen. 'Adherence to the *halakhoth* concerning [mixed fibres] among the Bar Kokhba insurgents . . . shows that all these rulings were truly kept by the *am-ha'ares*'.[32] This prohibition, however, is not a Pharisaic/rabbinic halakhah enforced on the common people, but rather biblical law (Lev. 19.19; Deut. 22.9–11). Yadin, of course, knew that, and he simply wrote a little carelessly. That the *'ammê ha-'arets* generally observed biblical law is evident in all the sources (though in very few scholarly works), and their observing one commandment that is twice repeated is not a surprise, much less a proof that they obeyed the halakhah of the sages.

There are, again, hundreds of such rules in rabbinic literature. The Pharisees and rabbis certainly would have liked to *enforce* biblical laws. In order to understand Pharisaism, however, we should remember that Pharisees tolerated disagreement. Apparently for exegetical reasons, they thought that Sadducean high priests were wrong when they put incense on the coals only after they entered the Holy of Holies. Nevertheless, the Pharisees continued to use the temple. Thus even discovering that a rule in rabbinic literature is biblical, or was thought to be biblical, does not quite tell us what people did. We can be sure, however, that the rabbis/Pharisees thought that people should obey the Bible, and they 'decreed' a lot of biblical rules.

3. Many Pharisaic/rabbinic laws were intended only for members of the party.[33] Of those that we discussed in the chapter on the Pharisees, three stand out: handwashing, *'eruvin*, and *demai*-produce. The Hillelites and Shammaites debated among themselves just when hands should be washed (for example, before or after mixing the cup of wine at the sabbath meal), but this is presented as an intra-party dispute. Eventually, the rabbis promoted handwashing, which is one of the two purity laws that survive to the present day. But the earliest layer of rabbinic literature shows no criticism of the ordinary people for not washing their hands. The handwashing passages in the Mishnah and Tosefta do not 'decree' that everyone must do it.

The case of *'eruvin* is even clearer. This is a substantial relaxation of the sabbath law, and it appears that some Sadducees tried to keep the Pharisees from resorting to it (*'Eruvin* 6.2), as well they might. There seems to have been no pressure from the Pharisees to make other people 'fuse' houses by building doorposts and lintels. *'Eruv* was a major Pharisaic tradition, and observing it marked one as a Pharisee; Pharisees did not require it of others before regarding them as law-abiding. The same is true of *demai*-produce. Some Pharisees tithed food that came into their possession if they doubted that it had been fully tithed. The law that the Pharisees wanted people to obey was the biblical law that ordains supporting the Levites (and, to a lesser extent, the priests) by tithing. Some Pharisees did more than the Bible requires, but there is no hint that they tried to get the populace to follow their rules for *demai*-produce.

4. Some rabbinic prohibitions prove that most people did something else. What was most often prohibited, one may usually assume, was widely practised. Yadin pointed out that the rabbis first prohibited the use of imitations of Tyrian purple and later ruled that garments containing that colour had to be bought from an expert. The cloth that he discovered in the 'Bar-Kokhba' cave used dye that imitated the colour.[34] He took this to show that not everyone obeyed the rabbinic halakhah. The rabbinic evidence, however, is much later than the cloth, and the rabbis may not have forbidden it at the time the cloth in the Judaean cave was made. Nevertheless, we may be confident that when they got around to it, the Babylonian rabbis railed against a common practice, while most people carried right on using an imitation based on indigo, much cheaper and easier to obtain than the shellfish that is used to make Tyrian purple.

Yadin's discovery of cloth provides another example. According to *Sifre Deut.*, 'A woman shall not wear white garments, and . . . a man shall not cover himself with coloured garments'. 'This *halakhah*', Yadin promptly points out, 'was possibly not strictly kept'.[35] His archaeological evidence shows that 'possibly' can be deleted, since men wore coloured garments (see above, p. 123 and n.17). In this case, later rabbis disagreed with the colour restrictions, probably bowing to actual practice.[36]

Once more, hundreds of rabbinic rules will fall into the category of practices routinely followed even though prohibited by rabbinic decree. It is so important an issue, however, that I shall cite a few more cases. One large sub-category consists of passages in which a rabbi acknowledges that people do not observe 'the halakhah'.

> R. Judah said, 'The halakhah is according to the words of the House of Shammai, but most people follow the opinion of the House of Hillel.' (*T. Terumot* 3.12)

> As the rite [of slaughtering the Passover lamb] was performed on a weekday so was it performed on a Sabbath, save that the priests swilled the Temple Court, which was not with the consent of the Sages. (*Pesahim* 5.8)

> After the *Omer* had been offered they used to go out and find the market of

Jerusalem full of meal and parched corn, though this was not with the consent of the Sages. (*Menahot* 10.5)

The men of Jericho used to reap [the crop before the *Omer*] with the consent of the Sages, but they stacked it against the consent of the Sages, and the Sages did not reprove them. (*Menahot* 10.8)

Several pages could be filled with such passages.

It is more difficult to be certain of general disobedience when the rabbis do not explicitly admit it, but I shall propose some instances. In an earlier chapter we noted that the Pharisees first forbade drawn water in immersion pools, but seemed willing to apply this only to their own pools, and that later the Shammaites decreed against other people's practice. The Shammaites' decree was aimed at the aristocratic priesthood. They ruled that the aristocrats' practice of having warm, clean water poured over them in a bathtub after they immersed made their heave offering unfit; that is, they could not eat it.[37] I venture the opinion that the aristocratic priests continued to bathe after immersing and also continued to eat heave offering.[38]

It is likely that the story of Creation and the chapter on the Chariot were expounded in ways of which the rabbis did not approve (*Hagigah* 2.1); that people carried on making vows that rabbis forbade and ignoring vows that they held binding (*Nedarim*); that the people of Jericho continued to pick up fallen fruit on the sabbath despite rabbinic rebuke (*Pesahim* 4.8); that some people continued saying a prayer for the sun after R. Judah forbade it (*T. Berakhot* 6[7].6).

In this category, however, most interest attaches to the question of official acts, especially temple practice. One of the most strongly held scholarly views is that Josephus told the truth, the whole truth and nothing but the truth when he wrote that the Sadducees, though they held positions of power, could never do what they wanted because of the Pharisees' hold on the populace, and that prayers and other acts of worship were performed according to Pharisaic rules (*Antiq.* 18.15, 17). I proposed in ch. 18 that this is not a correct description of practice in the second temple. Here I wish to observe that we have evidence before our eyes to show that these statements are exaggerated, to say the least. I shall list here four examples that we have already seen and add one more.

(*a*) Sadducean high priests did not follow the Pharisees with regard to the incense and the censer of coals (above).

(*b*) The priests swabbed the floor of the temple at times that were 'not with the consent of the sages' (above).

(*c*) The aristocrats did not accept the Pharisees' rules about immersion pools. While the aristocrats had private immersion pools, it was evidently publicly known that they did not follow Pharisaic rules, and thus were, according to the Pharisees, impure. They continued to serve in the temple (above).

(*d*) We may be sure that as late as 5 BCE the Pharisees did not, despite *Yoma* 1.4–7, control the movements of the high priest just before the Day of Atonement (p. 396).[39]

(*e*) In 62 CE the Sadducean high priest Ananus convened '*a* council (*synedrion*) of judges' (not '*the* judges of *the* Sanhedrin', which is the LCL's translation) and had James the brother of Jesus and probably others executed. Certain fair-minded, lenient citizens, those most precise about the laws, objected, but the execution took place. Many scholars, as I pointed out above, think that the objectors were Pharisees, and this seems to me likely. In any case, the protest was partially successful: Ananus was deposed (*Antiq.* 20.199–203). He was deposed, however, for transgressing the procurator's exclusive right to execute,[40] not for breaking Pharisaic rules about court procedure. The immediate point is that when there was no procurator in the country, a Sadducean high priest (which Ananus was) could do what he wished, despite the supposed fact that Sadducees always had to do what the Pharisees said. The rabbis 'laid it down' that sages should decide capital cases, that the condemned had to have been warned in advance of his deed by two witnesses, and so on (Mishnah *Sanhedrin*), but often in real life what they 'laid down' did not matter. Authority lay elsewhere.

5. We saw in ch. 1 that some rabbinic regulations apply to another time, apparently to an ideal age. I shall here quote the passage to which I referred:

> . . . they may not add to the [Holy] City or to the courts of the Temple save by the decision of a king, a prophet, Urim and Thummim and a Sanhedrin of one and seventy [judges] . . . (*Shevuʿot* 2.2)

No matter whether we date this passage 20 or 220 CE, the Urim and Thummim did not exist, and most likely the Pharisees or rabbis of the time thought that no adequately inspired prophet was available. Part of the rule, that is, is hypothetical or ideal. The rabbis liked to cover all contingencies, including ones that will not arise in this world. I think that many of the rules of Mishnah *Sanhedrin* are idealistic, and that the temple measurements in *Middot* are as well; in the latter case the idealism is based on Ezekiel. Different scholars will come to different opinions about different passages. We can argue our cases. Everyone will agree that this needs to be done when we read Josephus' summary of the law in *Antiq.* 4. Some of the time he is just passing on what is in the Greek translation of the Hebrew Scripture, sometimes he is idealizing. We have to examine cases. The point here is that rabbinic literature must be examined in the same way.

6. I would like here to give an instance of a Pharisaic decree that everyone followed. It is hard to be certain, since the precise chain of cause and effect can never be traced. But I offer, as a possible example, the prosbul. It is possible that Hillel was the first person to think of a way of overcoming an unfortunate side-effect of the biblical law on the sabbath year, and that thereafter it was widely adopted. It is also possible, however, that the legal device arose in some other way and was later attributed to Hillel. I should here emphasize that rabbinic literature shows no general drive to assign rules to the most famous sages. Very few are ascribed to Hillel. It sometimes happens, however, that a major decision is incorrectly attributed to a famous man. According to *T. Pisha* 4.12f., Hillel was the person who convinced the populace that Passover overrides the sabbath; when Passover falls on the sabbath, the Passover lamb should nevertheless be sacrificed, though sacrifice is work. This, however, had already been accepted. The *Covenant of Damascus* complains about it, and avoidance of an overlap was one of the main points of the dissident calendar that is known from *Jubilees* and *I Enoch*, which probably are earlier than the Hasmonean revolt. Attributions of famous rules to Hillel constitute a special case. We should not generally suspect rabbinic literature of this kind of pseudepigraphy. Nevertheless, since the prosbul was a famous law, and since Hillel was a special case, I hesitate to say definitely that he was the first to propose it. For the sake of our examples, however, I waive the point and use the prosbul as evidence for category 6: sometimes the populace followed Pharisaic innovations.

7. We now come to the most important point, one that will lead to consideration of the nature of rabbinic literature. The reader of rabbinic rules must bear in mind that it would have been extremely difficult to do 'what the sages decreed', since they disagreed among themselves. A very high percentage of the legal discussions in the earliest rabbinic literature lack a conclusion; the Houses of Hillel and Shammai state their views, and it appears that they agree to disagree. Are we to imagine the populace, desirous to do what the Pharisees said, one day obeying Shammai and the next day Hillel? We saw above disagreements about how much drawn water could be used in an immersion pool. In earlier chapters we have seen disagreements about sacrificing on festival days, an important issue. Perhaps most striking, the Shammaites and Hillelites disagreed on rules about vaginal bleeding and sexual intercourse. We recall that the *Covenant of Damascus*, the *Psalms of Solomon* and the Mishnah all accuse their enemies on this very ground. It turns out that the Shammaites and Hillelites could accuse one another, either of transgression or of requiring an incorrect sacrifice.[41]

A later rabbi who noted this and similar points commented on the significance of such disagreements:

yet the [men of] the House of Shammai did not refrain from marrying women from [the families of] the House of Hillel, nor the [men of] the House of Hillel from marrying women from [the families of] the House of Shammai. Despite all the disputes about what is clean and unclean wherein these declare clean what the others declare unclean, neither scrupled to use aught that pertained to the others in matters concerned with cleanness. (*Yevamot* 1.4)

The explanation of this is that the Pharisees, and later the rabbis, distinguished their own rules, about many of which they disagreed among themselves, from biblical law, and with only a few exceptions regarded biblical law, not their extra rules, as being generally binding.[42] A standard view in the Mishnah is that *there are no penalties for transgressing 'scribal' rules*. The principal passages are from the middle of the second century (e.g. *Parah* 11.4f.; *Tohorot* 4.7, 11), but it is very likely that the Pharisees had the same view. Their special rules made them Pharisees, not the only people who observed the law (see no. 3 above). That is why they could use the temple, administered by priests who immersed in the wrong sort of pool. They applied this same kind of thinking to their intra-party disputes. The Shammaites' rules made them Shammaites, not the only true Jews, nor even the only true Pharisees.

Once this simple fact is accepted, the *genre* of early rabbinic legal material becomes clear. It does not consist of set rules that governed society. It consists of debates. In the period of our study, a local Pharisee or group of Pharisees may have made a rule that people accepted. It is not inconceivable that a large landowner, who owned property in both Jewish Palestine and Syria, would have asked a nearby Pharisee what temple dues he owed.[43] We must remember, however, that there was a competing group of teachers, the priests, and on matters such as tithes and purity most people would have followed priestly law, though if a Pharisee offered a more lenient rule some farmers might have been willing to cite it in their favour. But if anybody could *enforce* tithes, it was the priests, and only they had any say over *general* rules of purification before worshipping in the temple. The Pharisees had views, lots and lots of views. As many views on some points as there were Pharisees. They could follow their own views on most issues, since few of their special topics applied to areas of life beyond individual control. Saying that people generally did what 'the sages had laid down' corresponds neither to the social realities of pre-70 Jewish Palestine nor to the nature of rabbinic literature.

To conclude: the Pharisees did not govern Jewish Palestine. They debated rules and they had opinions. Some Pharisee or Pharisees may have influenced the practice of one or many people on one or more points. The priests and Levites influenced far more, the Essenes fewer. In the end, ordinary practice was what ordinary priests and ordinary people agreed on, usually because it was in the Bible, sometimes because it had become traditional long ago, before the rise of the parties, and only occasionally because of the influence of one of the parties.

The Sanhedrin voted and thereby governed all Jews

The confidence of hundreds of scholars, of all persuasions, that in remote antiquity Jews instituted a representative parliament, and that this body endured through the Hasmonean revolt, Pompey's conquest, Herod's government, and Roman prefects, always operating on the basis of majority votes, is touching but not persuasive. Above I wrote that there are two ghosts in most accounts of Jewish Palestine, the omnipresent and omnipotent but seldom-mentioned Pharisees and the Sanhedrin.[44] We now come to the second ghost.

What follows is part of a study that I did in 1984 and the summers of 1985 and 1986. Some of this went into *Jesus and Judaism* (1985), but the main study has languished, waiting for the day that I can now say will never arrive. My study has been overtaken. Martin Goodman has published *The Ruling Class of Judaea* (1987), which covers some of the same ground and covers it much better (except, of course, for a few points!). James McLaren will soon publish his Oxford DPhil. thesis on Jewish participation in government in the Roman period.[45] It is much more thorough than my essay was. These three studies all have a connection with Oxford, but they are fundamentally independent, although by now we have all read one another's work. The consequence of this partial duplication of effort is that I do not need to cover the entire ground, and I shall give only a few samples of the evidence that has led McLaren, Goodman and me to very similar conclusions. These are taken, with fairly few changes (some suggested by Goodman and McLaren), from my original study.[46] I shall not compare our views, since this would lead to discussions that are not necessary for the present purpose. I shall mention only a few points where I disagree with Goodman.

First, a word about the two main terms. The Greek word *synedrion* passed into Hebrew as *sanhedrîn*, from which we derive the English word sanhedrin. A Greek *synedrion* is not necessarily a court, and is certainly not a legislative assembly; it is a gathering, either for consultation or trial, but the nature of the meeting can be determined only by context. The rabbis borrowed this Greek word, altering it to *sanhedrîn*, and used it in the Mishnah in discussing courts and trials. Hence 'the Sanhedrin' in modern European languages means 'the court described in the Mishnah or some other supreme court or council in first-century Jewish Palestine'.

The second principal Greek word, *boulē*, has a clearer meaning: it is a council, particularly of a *polis*, the Greek word for an independent city,[47] one that had its own constitution and institutions: always a *gymnasium* (an educational and athletic facility for boys and youths), usually a theatre and sometimes a hippodrome. The members of a *boulē* were elected by all eligible voters. The *boulē* of a *polis* was large: the early Athenian *boulē* had 400 members, later enlarged to 500. The Roman Senate (called in Greek the *boulē*) was, in the time of Julius Caesar, 900, but Augustus reduced it to 600. In Palestine, we know of one *boulē* of this size: the *boulē* of Tiberias had 600 members (*War* 2.641), which was not an uncommon number for city councils of the time. It appears from this that Antipas founded Tiberias as a *polis*.

It is confusing to use 'the Sanhedrin' every time the word *synedrion* appears in Greek or *sanhedrîn* appears in Hebrew. The following conventions will help us keep things straight:

synedrion	a common Greek noun referring to a meeting of some sort.
the Synedrion	the same word, when the noun is prefaced by the definite article, and when the assembly conducts a trial (as it does in the gospels, Acts and Josephus)
sanhedrin	a Hebrew word, borrowed from Greek, meaning a court or council.
the Sanhedrin	the Hebrew word used to refer to a special court, usually 'the Great Sanhedrin'. I shall write the term in this way when discussing scholarly views about a supreme Jewish court, as well as when referring to the court of the Mishnah.
Sanhedrin	the title of one of the tractates in the Mishnah.

In terms of size, the 'Great Sanhedrin' of the Mishnah had seventy-one members, and there are other references to Jewish judicial (not legislative) bodies of seventy members.[48] We also know that there was a *boulē* in Jerusalem: Josephus attributes three actions to the Jerusalem *boulē*, and he also refers to the death of the secretary of the *boulē* and the burning of its meeting room, the *bouleutērion*.[49] It is most unlikely that Jerusalem was a *polis*, since it lacked, among other things, a *gymnasium* and annual democratic elections to the *boulē*. Elections would have attracted attention in at least one of the sources, and in this case silence proves non-existence. Further, the role of the high priest would have been hard to fit into the constitution of a *polis*.[50] Thus we may assume that the Jerusalem *boulē* need not have had hundreds of members. It could have had seventy or so.

It is already clear, I think, that the topic is going to be complicated. What was the Jerusalem *boulē*, if not the council of a *polis*? Is the Jerusalem *boulē*, known from Josephus, the same as the Mishnah's Sanhedrin of seventy-one? Does either body correspond to the Synedrion mentioned in the gospels and Acts?

Then there is the question of composition. The Mishnah's court consists of sages or rabbis. It is possible for the high priest to judge or to be judged, but the Sanhedrin can do without him (*Sanhedrin* 2.1). The king, on the other hand, can neither judge nor be judged (2.2). In the Synedrion of the gospels and Acts, the high priest is in charge. In Josephus, as we shall see, the king or ethnarch is the convener. Can these differences be explained?

People who have tried to save all the evidence (Josephus, the gospels, Acts, and the Mishnah), and who have supposed that all sources give accurate descriptions of *something*, have devised two-sanhedrin and three-sanhedrin theories. For example: the one in the Mishnah is only for intra-Pharisaic issues; the one in the gospels and Acts decided 'governmental' matters.[51]

Most scholars have thought that the evidence can all be conflated into a one-sanhedrin theory.[52] Josephus' *boulē* is the Mishnah's Sanhedrin and also the New Testament's Synedrion. It consisted of seventy or seventy-one men, and it served as both a legislative assembly and a supreme court. Pharisees were admitted to it during the reign of Salome Alexandra.[53] Since it contained both Pharisees and Sadducees, it was a 'representative national body'.[54] From time to time the majority changed. After the reign of Salome Alexandra, the Pharisees were increasingly recognized as the only 'religious' authorities.[55] Some hold that by then the priests had lost all interest in the law.[56] Therefore when the issue was 'religious', a Pharisee presided (as in the Mishnah); when the issue was 'governmental' the high priest presided (as in the New Testament, where the court decides on the *religious* question of blasphemy!)[57] The Sanhedrin always existed, at least from about 135 BCE to 66 CE; its members were appointed for life; and they continued in office even when there was a change in the head of state.

The previous paragraph is a composite 'majority' opinion. Numerous scholars who support most of the above points doubt one or more, such as whether or not the members were appointed for life.[58] Some state that Herod smashed the power of the Sanhedrin, though later it was re-surrected.[59] Many doubt that the head of the Sanhedrin changed according to the subject matter.[60] One could go through the description clause by clause and list scholars who agree and disagree with some points, but who agree with the main conclusion: one supreme Jewish court, representing both parties, which decided issues by majority vote.

I shall not, however, lay out the arguments on each phrase of the above description, since I think that all these proposals are wrong: the theories of one, two, or three sanhedrins are in error. There was no body that combined judicial and legislative powers, there were no appointments for life, Palestinian Jews did not all line up behind one of the two parties (no one ever includes the Essenes), the two small parties did not seat representatives in a parliament, changes of government did not just shift the numerical balance of power in an otherwise unchanged body, and legislation was not passed by the majority vote of either one or more standing legislative and judicial bodies. This whole picture is a scholarly invention, put together partly from little hints in diverse sources scattered over a couple of centuries, but partly made from brand new cloth, woven from threads that were spun in the nineteenth century.[61]

There were, of course, both judicial and advisory bodies. (There were no legislative assemblies. This is not even in the Mishnah.) Every ruler had councillors and everyone believed that accused criminals should be formally tried according to some legal system. Towns and cities had magistrates and small councils. I cannot here attempt a new proposal about the names and numbers of all judicial and advisory councils in Palestine, but I shall mention two councils of whose existence I have no doubt. The early Hasmoneans had a *gerousia*, 'council of elders',[62] and in the period when Judaea was a Roman province Jerusalem had a *boulē*, a city council (though the city was not a *polis*, and the council was not a *boulē* in the Greek sense). Probably all governments in between had some sort of official body. In the Graeco-Roman world, every ruler had a council, or claimed to have one. Whether that official body ever did anything is another issue. What is more certain is that rulers could summon courts for a special purpose whenever they wished.

Before we can consider the partly formal but partly informal way in which things really worked, it will be necessary to show that there is not good evidence for the existence of 'the Sanhedrin', which most people think governed Palestine uninterruptedly for 200 years. I shall demonstrate the things it did not do that people attribute to it, and also show that judicial bodies were not parliamentary, based on party representation and majority votes.

1. The Sanhedrin's ghostly presence. Scholars often find the Sanhedrin where it is not mentioned. I shall give just two examples. According to Josephus, when Salome Alexandra came to the throne, she turned the government over to the Pharisees, who executed some of their enemies and forced others into exile. Salome finally compromised with the formerly 'eminent', including her more ambitious son, Aristobulus II, by letting them have fortified places outside Jerusalem, where the Pharisees could not get at

them (*War* 1.110–14; *Antiq.* 14.408–18.) The principal scholarly view is that at this time the Pharisees became a majority in the Sanhedrin.[63] A second view is that the Pharisees became a significant minority in the Sanhedrin.[64]

Our only source for this period, Josephus, says nothing at all about any legislative or judicial body. Scholars imagine one. The losers were not outvoted, they were executed and exiled from Jerusalem.

The second example is much more elaborate and shows the full exercise of scholarly ingenuity. In 37 BCE Herod, heavily supported by Roman troops, conquered Jerusalem. The city had held out for five months. When its defences were finally penetrated, the Romans, 'infuriated by the length of the siege', engaged in 'wholesale massacre', in which Herod's Jewish troops participated.

> Masses were butchered in the alleys, crowded together in the houses, and flying to the temple. No quarter was given to infancy, to age, or to helpless womanhood. Nay, though the king sent messengers . . ., entreating them to spare, none stayed his hand . .

Herod finally restored order and even stopped some of the pillaging earlier than was usual after a successful siege.[65] Then he went to work in earnest. He 'discriminated between the two classes of the city population, by the award of honours . . . [to] those who had espoused his cause, while he exterminated the partisans of Antigonus'. So Josephus, *War* 1.351–8.

In the *Antiquities*, Josephus continues and either supplements or revises the story. During the siege, Pollion the Pharisee and his disciple Samaias 'advised the citizens to admit' Herod, and after the conquest he rewarded them. One of these Pharisees had previously favoured executing Herod, in a story that I shall describe below, and had warned that if Herod's life were spared he would one day punish his judges. The narrative continues: After his conquest, and when he had got rid of the Roman troops, Herod collected all the money he could get his hands on in order to make gifts to Marc Antony and other Roman supporters. In this money-raising campaign, he killed 'forty-five of the leading men of Antigonus' party', and when the corpses were taken out of the city, he had them searched, in order to find wealth that their survivors might have tried to smuggle out (*Antiq.* 15.1–6).

We cannot tell whether the forty-five leading supporters of Antigonus were additional victims, after the preliminary slaughter – especially rich men, kept alive for a while to get their money, then finally killed – or whether Josephus exaggerated in the *War*: Herod slaughtered Antigonus' supporters (*War*), well, at least forty-five (*Antiquities*).

Some scholars, their minds fixed on the great permanent body of legislators, the Sanhedrin, find it in this story. The steps in their reconstruction are these: (1) Herod had been threatened by the Sanhedrin when Hyrcanus II was ethnarch (for the trial of Herod, see below). (2) When Antigonus conquered Jerusalem and became high priest and king (*Antiq.* 14.379), he could mutilate Hyrcanus, the high priest and ruler, but he could not touch Hyrcanus' Sanhedrin. These seventy or seventy-one members were secure for life, they could not be dismissed, and they became Antigonus' judicial and legislative assembly. (3) When Herod conquered Jerusalem, he inherited Antigonus' Sanhedrin – that is, Hyrcanus' Sanhedrin, that had once threatened him, Herod. Herod sent the high priest and king to be executed, but he could not dismiss the members of the Sanhedrin. Herod, however, took the bull by the horns and executed more-or-less two-thirds of them (forty-five). Since he could not govern without a seventy or seventy-one member Sanhedrin, and since government was by majority vote of this body, Herod, to get his legislation passed, had to create vacancies in the parliament/high court.[66]

So, when Herod took Jerusalem he did not slaughter a lot of his adversaries, he executed just forty-five of the members of the seventy-one member Sanhedrin. The Sanhedrin always ruled; the constitution could not be changed; the law ordaining the Sanhedrin was immutable; all Herod could do was pack the court with his own supporters. One assumes that this enduring representative assembly had already changed allegiance once, being first loyal to Hyrcanus and then to Antigonus. Herod must have thought that it would nevertheless hand him some uncomfortable parliamentary reverses. In any case, he inherited a pre-existing Sanhedrin, and he was the first person brave enough to create vacancies, though he dared create only enough to obtain a clear majority.

Several considerations count against this proposal. First, at this point in Josephus' entire history 'the Synedrion' has been mentioned only once, in the trial of Herod, where, further, it may be from an inferior source (as explained below). We would expect that such a powerful body, strong enough to last through two changes of government (Hyrcanus to Antigonus to Herod), would have done something previously, would have made an impact that deserved mention in Josephus. Secondly, the character of the rulers tells against the theory. Antigonus conquered Jerusalem, aided by Parthian arms, with appreciable loss of life, and he cut off Hyrcanus' ears. Why would he keep Hyrcanus' legislative/judicial body? And Herod: surely no one can believe that he kept even twenty-six members of a court that had once threatened him with death. Thirdly, any ruler would have wanted her or his own council. When Salome Alexandra came to power, she deposed Jannaeus' advisers and appointed her own. The theory that we are considering (like all theories that assume the permanence of 'the Sanhedrin', despite the accession of a new head of state) requires us to suppose that, between the reigns of Salome and her son (Hyrcanus II), membership in the council became a lifetime appointment.[67] Such a major revolution is unlikely, especially under Hyrcanus II or Aristobulus II, since each contested the other's claim to be high priest and king; neither was obedient to an independent governing body. It is much likelier that they appointed their own councils. Finally, to accept the theory means that we have to deny the story of the mass slaughter described in the *War* and imagine that judicial procedure reigned, except for the execution of the forty-five. It is more probable that Herod executed, among others, almost all the surviving members of Hyrcanus' Synedrion, which had threatened him (as is suggested by *Antiq.* 14.175), plus all the members of Antigonus' council, plus all his other principal supporters. Antigonus was responsible for Herod's brother's death and also had admitted the Parthians to Jerusalem. Herod would not have kept any of the supposed legislators who were implicated in these actions.

I do not doubt that Hyrcanus and Antigonus had councillors; what I doubt is the theory of an enduring body of legislators who could be removed only by death, and the hypothesis that Herod desperately needed a *majority* in some pre-existing council.

The theories of life-time membership, party representation, and legislation that depended on a majority vote, are simply imposed on the story. I should emphasize that these *are* scholarly inventions. No ancient source offers them anywhere. The Mishnah has votes, but not party representation and life-long membership. The theory of party representation depends primarily on Acts 23.6, which says that some of the members of the Synedrion that tried Paul were Pharisees and some Sadducees, possibly only a few of each.[68] It is first assumed that the entire assembly that tried Paul was composed of Pharisees and Sadducees, and then this supposed parliamentary system is retrojected to the time of the Hasmoneans and made into an immutable principle.

Here, then, we have another wraithlike appearance of the Sanhedrin. Finding it in the story of Herod's bloody conquest of Jerusalem is rather like reading the history of the French revolution and concluding that the peasants wanted to force Louis XVI to create new Dukedoms for enough of them so that they could form a majority in the (non-existent) Chambre des Seigneurs.

I desist. Instead of taking readers through every instance where scholars perceive this Sanhedrin of the mind, though the narrative excludes its existence, I shall mention the *only* two times that '*the* Synedrion' plays a role in Josephus.

2. What the Synedrion (or Sanhedrin) actually did.

(*a*) The trial of Herod. There are two accounts in Josephus:

(*i*) *War* 1.208–11: When Hyrcanus II was high priest and ethnarch, and Herod was in charge of Galilee, the latter caught and executed a brigand-chief and his followers. Hyrcanus' advisors ('malicious persons at court') urged him to act. Herod, they told him, had broken the national law by carrying out executions without warrant *from the head of state*.[69] Hyrcanus was persuaded and ordered Herod to appear to answer the charge. He came, with armed men. The legate of Syria prevented a disastrous encounter by instructing Hyrcanus to acquit Herod, which he did.

(*ii*) The Synedrion appears in the parallel (*Antiq.* 14.163–84). This time it is 'the leading Jews', or the 'first among the Jews' who urged Hyrcanus to try Herod. When they cited the law, instead of saying that Herod needed the authority of Hyrcanus (as in the *War*), they said that the law 'forbids us to slay a man, even an evildoer, unless he has first been condemned by the Synedrion to suffer this fate'. Hyrcanus then had Herod brought before the Synedrion. The Syrian legate, as in the first story, ordered Hyrcanus to release Herod. Despite this, Herod actually had to appear. In the hearing, Samaias warned that if Herod was released, as Hyrcanus wished, he would punish the members and Hyrcanus as well.[70] The consequence was that the Synedrion wished to execute Herod, but Hyrcanus postponed the trial to another day. He then advised Herod to withdraw, which he did. Subsequently, when Herod contemplated attacking Jerusalem to depose Hyrcanus, his father and brother urged him to remember that Hyrcanus had *acquitted* him (*Antiq.* 14.163–84).

This does not all run perfectly smoothly. The account in the *Antiquities* appears to combine two different versions. According to one, the Syrian legate ordered Hyrcanus to acquit Herod, and he did so (so also *War*). According to the other, Herod appeared before the Synedrion, which did not reach a decision the first day, and he escaped with Hyrcanus' sanction, but was formally neither condemned nor acquitted – though later in the *Antiquities* he is said to have been acquitted.

I do not think that we can know the full truth of this confusing event or series of events. I could well believe that the Synedrion trial is a fiction. The alternative account, which is in the *War*, and still easily visible in the *Antiquities* – that the legate ordered Hyrcanus to acquit Herod, and that he did so – is intrinsically more likely. On the other hand, the story of Samaias' bravery, and of Herod's hatred for the Synedrion, is not unreasonable. I favour the first but find the second credible.

What is clearer is the information about the Synedrion. We cannot derive from this section proof that the Synedrion was a standing body, of fixed number, with a known membership, though many read that theory into the evidence. But we do see one thing: when Josephus wrote the *Antiquities*, he thought that a court called in Greek the Synedrion, not just the head of state, *should* try capital cases. Further, if he had a source for the second version, that source thought the same thing.

(*b*) The second and only other use of 'the Synedrion' in Josephus is slightly less difficult. There are again two versions, this time of the trial of Hyrcanus. According to the first (*Antiq.* 15.161–73), after Herod became king, the time of his greatest insecurity was just after the battle of Actium, when Octavian's forces defeated those of Antony and Cleopatra. Herod, who had been championed by and had supported Antony, now as at other times went to elaborate lengths to protect himself from real and imaginary enemies, especially Hasmoneans. If he was afraid of what Octavian might do to him, however, he was not being paranoid, only realistic. Were the victorious Roman to decide to punish Antony's supporters, he could crush Herod with little exertion. Josephus tells us that Herod was apprehensive, and we may believe him.

As a practical man, Herod knew that, were Octavian to depose and either exile or execute him, Rome would then have to find another ruler of Judaea. Herod's best security was for there to be no good alternative to himself. He had already disposed of the most likely candidate, the handsome Hasmonean teenager, Aristobulus III. The only surviving Hasmonean male was Hyrcanus II, never strong, now aged, lacking one or both of his ears, but still a Hasmonean.[71] We know what happened next. The only question is, did Herod have Hyrcanus murdered, or did he arrange for a legal execution. Josephus replies, or rather his sources do, 'both'. According to one version Hyrcanus was made to realize his danger and wrote to a friendly Arab, asking for haven. The messenger gave the letter to Herod, who allowed the correspondence to go forward. He then intercepted the reply, which promised enough men to get Hyrcanus safely away; he showed the reply to the Synedrion; and then he had the former king executed (*Antiq.* 15.161–173).

That, Josephus illuminatingly remarks, is the version from Herod's own Memoirs. There was another version, according to which, at a banquet, Herod tricked Hyrcanus into saying that he had received four horses from the Arab king. Herod decided to consider this gift to be bribery and had Hyrcanus strangled (*Antiq.* 15.174–6).

Here our decision can be more certain: there was no trial before the Synedrion. We learn that at least one person thought that there should have been: Herod himself. His Memoirs, according to which he acted after presenting evidence to a court, are self-serving.

In neither of Josephus' two stories of the Synedrion does it do anything on its own. Taking the maximalist view of the evidence, the account of Herod's trial in the *Antiquities* and the account of Hyrcanus' execution in Herod's own

Memoirs, all the Synedrion did was consent to what the ruler decided. The Syrian legate told Hyrcanus to acquit Herod; Herod was not convicted, though the Synedrion contemplated it. Herod told the Synedrion that Hyrcanus was a traitor, and then he had Hyrcanus executed.

One would discover the same thing if one went through the stories of trials by the Synedrion in the gospels and Acts, taking the same maximalist view of the evidence: the high priest cried, 'Blasphemy! We need no further witnesses', and everybody went along (Mark 14.64). A Roman officer interrupted the trial of Paul, and so in that case there was no verdict (Acts 23.10). The only possible exception to the rule that the convener decided the outcome is Acts 5.27–40, where the reader may guess that the high priest wanted the apostles executed, and that he was thwarted by Gamaliel, who persuaded the Synedrion to flog them and release them. The text, however, does not state what outcome the high priest desired.

The conclusion is that the theory of party representation, of democratic voting, and of legislation for all Israel passed by the Sanhedrin – a permanent body of legislators and judges, deciding all capital cases and voting on correct observance of the law, even sending emissaries throughout the world to communicate decrees[72] – is completely without basis. The Synedrion was *or was supposed to be* convened for some capital cases (not all, as we shall see). Its decisions agreed with those of the man who summoned it. That exhausts the evidence of our narrative sources. They do not even mention legislation.

The Mishnah has *theories*, idealistic and unrealistic as they are, but still only theories about how cases were decided and sentences executed.[73] The Mishnah itself does not say that the issues with which it deals in its substantive tractates were settled by its theoretical Sanhedrin. Looking up *sanhedrîn* in the concordances to Tannaitic literature will be illuminating for those who wish to pursue the question. One may almost say that even in the Mishnah the Sanhedrin never tries a case.[74] 'The Sanhedrin voted and governed Israel' is even less likely than 'the sages laid it down'.

How things really happened

Case study is the only way to penetrate the fog that obscures who did what. That is true whether one studies modern or ancient societies. We do not have a Hasmonean, Herodian, or chief-priestly constitution, but if we had one, we still would not know who ran what when. I offered some case studies in *Jesus and Judaism*, Goodman has made use of case studies in his *Ruling Class*, and McLaren has written a thesis based entirely on case studies. I think that eventually we shall get the various issues sorted out:

issue*s*, because no one person, committee or assembly decided every case at any one time; and from time to time the rules changed.

I shall offer here, fairly briefly, a few of my favourite case studies as examples of how different sorts of things were done by different people at different times.

1. One of the meanings of *synedrion* is 'court', and there are several examples in Josephus in which a ruler assembled *a synedrion*, without the definite article. In these cases *synedrion* is used of an *ad hoc* court convened to reach a decision on a special case. Any ruler could convene such a *synedrion*, choosing its members as he wished (e.g. Augustus, according to *Antiq.* 17.301). Jewish leaders did the same. A few examples:

(*a*) Herod assembled a 'common' or 'joint *synedrion*' of *his own relatives and his provincial governors* to try two of his sons for treason (*War* 1.537). This course was recommended by Augustus. It gave a semblance of legality to the executions that followed. This case alone casts grave doubt on the theory that there was, or was even suposed to be, a single high court that conducted important trials. Augustus tried to maintain the forms of the Roman constitution, and it is most unlikely that, in such a delicate matter as the trial of two potential heirs to the throne in Judaea, he advised Herod to adopt a procedure that was irregular and against the Jewish 'constitution'. All we learn is that Augustus thought that there should be a trial: he did not want Herod to act entirely on his own. Herod empanelled a court that would return the decision that he thought was necessary.

(*b*) Similarly Herod convened a *synedrion* of his *friends and relatives* to consider the problem of his unnamed sister-in-law, Pheroras' wife. The *synedrion* did not do anything, since when Herod put to Pheroras a choice, between keeping his brother (Herod) or his wife, Pheroras chose his wife. That brave choice saved Pheroras' wife: Herod had no wish to execute his brother, and so he decided to execute no one. He then tried to make arrangements that would keep certain members of his family away from one another, so that they could not plot (*War* 1.571–3). That is, the *synedrion* made no decision, since Herod told it not to do so.

(*c*) In 64 or 65 Agrippa II assembled a *synedrion* to consider the issue of the Levites' robes. They had asked to be allowed to wear white, and this was permitted. Some were also granted the right to sing the Psalms by heart, not having to hold the heavy scrolls (*Antiq.* 20.216–18). Agrippa II was not king or ethnarch of Judaea. He held land in the north of Palestine, and he had the right to appoint the high priest. He had influence in Jerusalem, but no legal role in government. He could call a *synedrion* to consider a temple matter because he could appoint the high priest and he controlled the robe: that is, in temple matters he was supreme when and if he cared to exercise the right, though routinely the high priest ran things. At any rate, Agrippa II could not have been the regular head of the (supposed) one supreme Sanhedrin that always sat and judged cases in Jerusalem. He was, however, able to call a *synedrion* that could rule on quite important points governing the temple. It is possible that there was a special standing *synedrion* for temple matters, and that on this occasion Agrippa II took it over, but it is more likely that he chose who would attend. There was opposition to the outcome. Josephus, for one, bitterly resented the decision to let the Levites wear white, as if they were super-special priests. 'All this was contrary to the ancestral laws, and such transgression was bound to make us liable to punishment' (*Antiq.* 20.218). To get the right outcome, Agrippa had to choose the right *synedrion*.

(*d*) Just a few years earlier (62), the high priest Ananus had assembled 'a *synedrion* of judges', which sounds faintly like Herod's *synedrion* of his own provincial administrators, since most of the judges were probably priests and may have owed their position to the high priest. The *synedrion*, in any case, was rigged. As we saw above, it executed James the brother of Jesus, though many protested.

The conclusions about *a synedrion* (without the definite article) are the same as those about *the* Synedrion. A ruler convened a group for a special purpose, and it did what he wished.

2. There are instances in which rulers called a popular assembly. In Greek cities, the council (*boulē*) ordinarily ran things, but supreme power rested with the full assembly of citizens (*ekklēsia*). Goodman has quite correctly emphasized the importance of the assembly in Jewish history, as well as Greek, and has discussed its elimination during the period of direct Roman rule in Judaea.[75] I give examples to illustrate two ways in which a public assembly could function.

(*a*) Herod sometimes called assemblies, rather than a *synedrion* or court, when he wished to carry out executions. Josephus explains that he could bully the crowd into doing his will, since they feared that failure to oblige him would lead to a massacre. In one case he got the people themselves to bludgeon and stone the accused to death (*War* 1.550; cf. *Antiq.* 16.393).

(*b*) While Josephus may be partly right about Herod's motive in using public assemblies for executions, he was naive about the uses of power, and Herod was not. Herod could always have a rigged *synedrion* do what he wished, and scaring the crowd was not necessary if he simply wanted an execution. If an assembly of the populace condones an execution, it is *implicated*, and criticism of the ruler is very difficult. Having an assembly actually assist in an execution was an even more powerful tool.[76] Herod used an assembly for his most unpopular execution, that of the men who tore down the golden eagle (*War* 1.654f.; cf. *Antiq.* 17.160f.). Herod's own sons could be executed by a rigged *synedrion*, but not the esteemed teachers Judas and Matthias. They and their students were later publicly mourned, after Herod's death, and the people also complained to Archelaus; but while Herod lived, there was little the populace could say. An amphitheatre full of Jewish citizens had agreed. Herod probably doubted that he could persuade the assembly to carry out the executions, and so he contented himself with public agreement.

(*c*) Just before the revolt and during it, the Jewish leadership had recourse to public assemblies. The chief priests 'assembled the multitude in the temple' to urge them not to provoke the Romans (*War* 2.320). Agrippa II also convened an assembly to appeal for peace (2.346). After Cestius had withdrawn, and full revolt was inevitable, the people assembled in the temple to appoint the leaders and generals (2.562). Later, when the Zealots and Idumaeans challenged the previously elected leadership, Ananus and other leaders assembled the populace and denounced their internal foes (*War* 4.159). Calling an assembly did not guarantee the outcome. Despite the appeal of Agrippa II, the populace went to war. Despite the arguments of Ananus and his colleagues, the populace did not rise to their defence.

In all these cases, however, a full assembly functioned as 'the government'. Even when it was convened by officials, the assembly was the law. The persuasiveness of the appeal depended in part on circumstances. Herod argued with troops at his disposal and none that could be raised against him, and his arguments were felt to be very persuasive. Ananus argued against opponents who had more troops than he, and his eloquence could not save him. The whole populace would not put their lives on the line. Josephus claimed that 8,500 men died defending Ananus, but they faced Idumaean troops, and the temple guards were no match for a trained army.

3. We shall now consider briefly the *boulē* and the *koinon*. As we noted, Jerusalem had a council, called in Greek sources the *boulē*. It seems to have done very little, though it did carry out a few official acts in the events that led to the war. I shall describe these below. But there was, at least formally, a council.

After the revolt was underway, there are numerous references to the *koinon*. It is possible that this is simply another term for the *ekklēsia*, public assembly, though I incline to the view that it was an administrative council. I wish here neither to argue this nor insist upon it, but only to indicate the possibility. If it was a council, it was *koinon*, 'common', because it was more representative than the *boulē* had been. The Pharisee, Simon son of Gamaliel, was a member, and possibly John the Essene. I have said before, and shall demonstrate just below, that in the crisis the chief priests co-opted other leaders, including the leading Pharisees. All the leaders may have constituted the 'common council'. The principal references to the *koinon* are these: *Life* 65, 72, 190, 254, 341.

4. People who, because of birth, wealth, abilities, or position, were 'leaders' often acted on their own or collaboratively to get things done, with no reference to a formal body. This was usually the case in Judaea under direct Roman rule, since Roman rule was in fact indirect: most of the Romans were in Caesarea. They left the running of Jerusalem, and apparently also Judaea, to the only group they could identify as suitable: the native aristocracy. These people did not become officials; they had no titles (except the high priest); they were simply responsible to maintain order and see that tribute was paid.

The only way of explaining how the system worked is to give narrative accounts. One, the murder of a Galilean pilgrim in Samaria, I offered above (pp. 329f.); it would be helpful if the reader looked at it again. Here I shall repeat two pages from *Jesus and Judaism* (slightly expanded), in which I summarized Josephus' account of a crucial series of actions: the attempt of the aristocracy to mediate between the crowd and the last Roman procurator, Gessius Florus, in the year 66. This narrative includes the few references to action taken by the *boulē*.

Florus took seventeen talents from the temple treasury, possibly because of arrears in tribute, but possibly to cover extraordinary imperial expenses (*War* 2.293; for the tribute, see below).[77] This led some Jews to mock him, by taking up a collection for his benefit, and some shouted abuse at him (295). After using troops to cow the crowd (300), Florus called together the CHIEF PRIESTS, as well as the POWERFUL and the BEST KNOWN of the city. He demanded that they find those who were guilty (301f.). The leaders pointed out the impossibility of the task and urged Florus not to press the matter (302–304). He ordered the soldiers to sack the market. A massacre followed, during which Jews of even equestrian rank were scourged before Florus' tribunal and crucified (305–308). In the tumult of the next day, the POWERFUL, with the CHIEF PRIESTS, tried to prevail on the crowd not to provoke the procurator. To emphasize how desperate they were they rent their clothes, an act of mourning. 'The multitude promptly complied, alike out of respect for their petitioners, and in the hope that Florus would spare them further enormities' (316–317). Florus sent for the CHIEF PRIESTS and the BEST KNOWN MEN and told them that, to demonstrate their obedience, the people had to go along the road to meet arriving Roman troops (318). The CHIEF PRIESTS urged this action on 'the multitude' in the temple, with some success (320–5).[78] Unfortunately, when the crowd met the Romans, there were further outcries against Florus, which led to another massacre (326–9). Rebels seized the porticoes of the temple. Florus sent for the CHIEF PRIESTS and the BOULĒ, and 'told them that he intended to quit the city, but would leave them whatever garrison they desired. In reply, they undertook to maintain perfect order and to prevent any revolution, provided that he left them a single cohort' (331f.).

[It is noteworthy that, although the CHIEF PRIESTS and other leaders figured in the tumult as the intermediaries between the Romans and the Jerusalemites, the BOULĒ appears when Florus is about to do something official: leave a garrison in the control of the responsible Jewish body. Massacres, flogging and execution could take place without the involvement of the BOULĒ. But just before quitting the city, Florus summoned it.]

From the safety of Caesarea, Florus wrote to Cestius, the legate of Syria; and the MAGISTRATES[79] of Jerusalem also wrote, putting the blame on Florus (333). Cestius now took a direct hand. His emissaries met Agrippa II, who was just returning from Alexandria, at Jamnia. The Jewish leaders – the CHIEF PRIESTS, the POWERFUL and the BOULĒ – also went to Jamnia to seek Agrippa's help (333–37).

The story continues, and later we hear about the CHIEF PRIESTS and the BEST KNOWN MEN trying to persuade the (ordinary) priests who were in charge of the offerings not to stop the sacrifices for the Roman rulers (410). The priests were not persuaded, and the POWERFUL gathered with the CHIEF PRIESTS and the BEST KNOWN of the PHARISEES to consider the situation (411). In subsequent action the CHIEF PRIESTS continue to be mentioned as those who sought accommodation with Rome (422).

The impression is overwhelming that the CHIEF PRIESTS took the lead in mediating between the Romans and the populace: they were held responsible by the Romans, they asserted their authority and prestige in seeking accommodation, and they undertook to speak to the Romans on behalf of the nation. There was a BOULĒ (probably of seventy members), but it seems to have met formally only once during the events under Florus. When things reached a disastrous stage, and only then, did the priests assemble 'the BEST-KNOWN PHARISEES' to help consider the matter.

The BOULĒ then took one further step. The MAGISTRATES (or RULERS) and MEMBERS OF THE BOULĒ dispersed around Judaea to collect tribute (405).

The situation, of course, was extreme; but the account nevertheless shows who did what: the chief priests were active throughout; the formal *boulē* undertook a few duties. I think that it is impossible that Josephus made this up in order to impose a theory of government on the facts. The narrative is too long and too detailed. Given leisure to act, the *boulē* might have done more, though we know of no specific instances. There were other times of crisis, such as the clash between the Galileans and Samaritans, but in none of them does a council figure. During the period when Judaea was a Roman province, the main actors are *always* the chief priests, accompanied by 'the powerful'. Only in the last, fatal crisis does the *boulē* appear, and similarly only this one time did the chief priests feel compelled to call on the Pharisees for help.

This narrative is the most detailed we have, and it shows how things worked in an emergency: the *boulē* did very little. Men who may have held no formal positions tried to keep matters under control. We must always be open to the possibility that sometimes the *boulē* came to formal decisions and recommended them to the people and the procurator. Its absence from other narratives, however, makes this an extremely speculative possibility.

The story of the trial of Jesus shows the same system at work in different circumstances. This time, control of the crowd was not the issue, but only the control of a man who might excite the crowd, and the Roman prefect co-operated with the high priest. Nevertheless, the same governmental structure can be seen. The high priest ordered Jesus' arrest, he hastily convened a court, he interrogated the prisoner, he took the very extreme step of rending his garments while declaring Jesus guilty,[80] and he achieved the desired result (Mark 14.53–64; similarly Matthew and Luke). Scholars have laboured endlessly over the trial scene because it does not agree with Mishnah *Sanhedrin*. The gospel accounts do present problems, but disagreement with the Mishnah is not one of them.[81] For the present purpose it is not necessary to examine these stories critically. The system *as the gospels describe it* corresponds to the system that we see in Josephus. The trial of Jesus agrees very well with his stories of how things happened.[82]

Many of our best narratives describe events during the time of 'direct' Roman rule of Judaea, and they all agree: the high priest, with the support and assistance of the chief priests and some of the powerful lay people, handled local government. The system was informal, and the degree of consultation with others varied. There probably was an official council, but the high priest did not necessarily consult it as a body and in a formal way before taking action. For example, Ananus' *synedrion* of judges was probably not his council. That would be a strange phrase to use for the *boulē*.

Other rulers also ruled. According to the gospels, Antipas decided to execute John the Baptist without trial (Mark 6.17–29). Archelaus used his troops aainst the Jerusalem populace without a mandate from 'the Sanhedrin'.

There was, of course, an ideal of adequate deliberation before taking action and of trial by jury before execution. Each ruler had a council. We do not know, however, that even in theory the council served also as the court that tried major cases. As I indicated above, Herod's trial of two of his sons counts against the equation; in fact all the references in Josephus to *a* synedrion (in the sense of 'court') lead us to doubt that the idea of a supreme court was widely accepted. On the other hand, there are two references in Josephus to *the* Synedrion, and the authors of Matthew, Mark, Luke and Acts also refer to the Synedrion. The evidence does not permit a firm decision about the formal existence of a supreme court with a fixed and known membership. We can be certain, however, that, even if there was supposed to be such a court, rulers could nevertheless empanel a group of their supporters for a trial.

Prooftexts and reality

At conferences and in lectures, whenever I discuss with other scholars the role of the Pharisees and the chief priests, my interlocutor inevitably appeals to two statements by Josephus that we discussed in ch. 18. One says that 'all prayers and sacred rites . . . are performed' in accordance with the Pharisees' views (*Antiq.* 18.15), the other that the Sadducees submit to the Pharisees for fear of the masses (*Antiq.* 18.17).

When having to think on my feet, my first response is sometimes simply to quote the contrary prooftexts from the same author. In *Against Apion* Josephus attributes to Moses the creation of the world's best form of government, which the Greeks copied, but not entirely successfully, since their philosophy was addressed to the few rather than to the masses (*Apion* 2.168f.). Josephus had previously called this system of government an 'aristocratic oligarchy', 'rule by a few elite people' (*Antiq.* 11.111; cf. 4.223). In *Apion*, he coins a new Greek word for the government established by Moses, and observed by the Jews, except for a few regrettable periods when they had a king: 'theocracy', rule by God through his priests (2.165). The high priest, along with the other priests, had the responsibility not only to sacrifice, but also to 'safeguard the laws, adjudicate in cases of dispute, [and] punish those convicted of crime' (2.193–194). This is Josephus' fullest statement of the ideal form of government, the death of which he had so recently witnessed:

> Would you change the entire character of the constitution? Could there be a finer or more equitable polity than one which sets God at the head of the universe, which assigns the administration of its highest affairs to the whole body of priests, and entrusts to the supreme high-priest the direction of the other priests?

The men to whom God entrusted the ordering of divine worship as their first charge were those who were pre-eminently gifted with persuasive eloquence and discretion. But their responsibilities further embraced a strict superintendence of the Law and of the pursuits of everyday life; for the appointed duties of the priests included general supervision, the trial of cases of litigation, and the punishment of condemned persons.

Could there be a more saintly government than that? Could God be more worthily honoured than by such a scheme, under which religion is the end and aim of the training of the entire community, the priests are entrusted with the special charge of it, and the whole administration of the state resembles some sacred ceremony? (*Apion* 2.184–9)

When I quote this, or as much of it as I can remember, the reply is always that Josephus wrote in such terms just because he was a priest. I can then answer that he wrote that the Pharisees ran everything because he had become a Pharisee and a backer of the house of Gamaliel.

The Mishnah is the subject of slightly different exchanges. Someone will say to me that the Mishnah states that the Great Sanhedrin tried capital cases; therefore it did. My reply is that numerous rules in *Sanhedrin* did not govern real life, such as the rule that kings could not judge.

Some prooftexts are better than others. There is no doubt that Josephus' own preferred state was the 'theocracy' that he eulogizes in *Apion* 2.[83] Despite his undoubted bias, anyone who studies Jewish history will see that he did not entirely make it up. There is more to be said in favour of the 'theocracy' prooftexts than in favour of the 'Pharisaic thought-control' prooftexts.

The truth is, however, that we can and should get along without choosing always to believe one prooftext or other. We can, instead, notice when a summary passage happens to be right, without imposing summaries on every individual event. Scholarly love of consistency does a lot of damage to historical understanding. A theory derived from the Pharisaic-control prooftexts has been imposed on the major narrative sources by generations of scholars, beginning before the time of the original Schürer, just as has the theory of Sanhedrin-control. A few statements are abstracted, polished into a smooth system of legislative and judicial procedure, and then applied to concrete cases. I have attempted to show a few of the many things wrong with the theories of control by the Pharisees or the Sanhedrin.

We can study the narratives, and from them derive the *implied* and *presupposed* state of affairs. All that the gospels tell us about the trial of Jesus, for example, is that the high priest called together a group and interrogated him. The group agreed unanimously (so it appears) to recommend his execution to Pilate. Someone may have called this group 'the Sanhedrin', or simply 'a sanhedrin'. If the latter, it would quickly acquire the definite article:

it was *the* sanhedrin that met when Jesus was interrogated. According to our only source, the narrative of the gospels, none of the rules of Mishnah *Sanhedrin* applied. Why, then, do people who believe the narrative think that the Mishnaic tractate governed the country? Josephus offers an extremely large number of individual narratives, taken from different sources, and not one of them supports either the theory of Sanhedrin-control or Pharisaic-control. They can be analysed to discover what they do imply.

In the periods of direct Roman rule in Judaea, the chief priests, often joined by prominent laymen, were the leading actors. The priests, however, did not always run everything everywhere. Influence and control varied from time to time, from region to region, and from issue to issue. The government of Herod was quite different from the government of the prefects and procurators. The chief priests, unmentioned during Herod's time, rose to prominence after Archelaus was deposed. Judaea under procuratorial rule in the period 6–41 CE was unlike Galilee under Antipas in the same period. Priests probably preferred not even to enter Tiberias (though Josephus did, during the revolt). The only way to find out who ran what when is to study cases. One-line slogans – the Pharisees were the new ruling class[84] – are, by definition, wrong. This particular one turns out to be wrong in virtually all the cases that we can study. Pharisees are notably absent from the case studies, being either unmentioned or tangential. Nor can it be said that they *secretly* controlled all affairs and rites, as I demonstrated above.

Palestinian Judaism was a rich, diverse, multifaceted society, with a good deal of restless change. Birth and wealth counted, as they always have, but so did piety, learning and zeal. All of these qualities were useful in public life, and people who aspired to leadership demonstrated them in different degrees. There are no set rules about which of these qualities counted most strongly. Our narrative sources indicate that different individuals and groups had different degrees of influence at various times and on various issues. Who ran what? It varied.

22

Epilogue

A study of the history of Judaism, especially Palestinian Judaism, in the early Roman period raises the question of whether or not things might have turned out differently. It was probably unwise of the chief priests to consult others, such as the leading Pharisees, so seldom and, in the crisis with Florus, so late. As Goodman suggests, Rome may have been unwise to rely on the chief priests and the wealthy laity in the first place.[1] Perhaps greater use of the Pharisees and an effort to involve more members of the public would have prevented revolt.

The topic is entirely speculative, but speculation can help us see things in better perspective. 'What might have been', if considered in light of the basic realities of the eastern Mediterranean world, allows us to evaluate a little better what actually was. The first basic reality was that Rome was going to control Palestine. Secondly, it would do so, as far as possible, indirectly, by making use of Jewish allies and puppets. If there was a reliable and able client king, he would rule; if no one person was sufficiently able and trustworthy, there would be a division of the country among lesser men (ethnarchs and tetrarchs); if worse came to worst, Rome would send a governor, who would rule via a local group of responsible citizens. The third basic reality was that Jewish Palestine was on the whole more difficult to govern successfully than were most parts of the Roman Empire. Theologically, the doctrines of monotheism and the election made relations with pagan rulers potentially difficult. The conviction that God *cared* about *every* part of life meant that small disagreements could assume large proportions. I shall return to other special factors in Jewish Palestine just below.

Whatever system Rome employed would be subject to a basic reality of all human existence: some people are better than others, and weaknesses are not always evident in advance. The careers of Roman emperors, such as Gaius (Caligula) and Nero, both of whom seemed to promise great things, serve as examples that are near at hand. This means that *any* system might break down for human reasons.

All things considered, I think that there were bound to be uprisings, and I am not in the least surprised that one of these led to full revolt. On general grounds such as these, I think that we cannot say that the system of government that was devised for Judaea between 44 and 66 was more certainly doomed to failure than another system would have been. Perhaps a few more particular remarks about other possible mediators than the aristocratic priests will, however, be helpful.

The Romans were, of course, cautious about public assemblies, and the chief priests and other aristocrats would not have been allowed to assemble very many people very often.[2] Great crowds were allowed during the festivals, but Roman troops stood guard, being stationed even on the roofs of the porticoes. Despite quasi-democratic elements in Jewish history (the full assembly), there was no safe way in which Rome could have ruled Palestine through a broadly-based local government. Jewish crowds were always dangerous to public order, and this might have been true even of a *boulē* of 600, had Jerusalem been accorded the status of a *polis*. The history of the Pharisees does not give one confidence that they would have uniformly exerted themselves in favour of peace. They seem to have become more tolerant of others since the stormy days of Jannaeus and Salome Alexandra, and after the revolt failed they certainly adopted a 'catholic' policy. Further, it is not in the least impossible that, in his day, Simeon ben Gamaliel was the sagest man in Israel (I think of Josephus' extravagant praise). But we cannot know that as a group, and over a period of decades, they would have governed on Rome's behalf more wisely than did the chief priests.

Crucial to the question of what would have been the better course is an evaluation of the aristocratic priesthood. I disagree with Goodman about the popularity and influence of the aristocratic priests.[3] I think that few were despised, more were accepted as leaders. In the entire history of Israel, the longest period of tranquillity had been when the aristocratic priesthood governed Jerusalem, under the general overlordship of a remote empire (*c.* 520–175 BCE). I do not think that it was obviously wrong for Rome and the new aristocratic priests to try it again. It is true that the new aristocracy was partially discredited because high priests could be appointed and dismissed. Yet they retained a remarkable degree of influence.[4] In any case, no better *aristocracy* was available. By 6 CE it was no longer possible to re-establish the Zadokites, and Herod had eliminated the Hasmoneans. There is no doubt that Goodman is correct to stress the absence of a long-established, highly revered native aristocracy, but I think that the new aristocracy could have coped if the problems they faced had been less severe.

The real trouble was that the world had changed. The Roman empire impinged more strongly than had previous empires. Even though Palestine was not precisely 'occupied', there were troops in Caesarea and fortified areas in Jerusalem and elsewhere. The Roman empire seems to have imposed itself more on the populace than had the Persian empire and the Ptolemaic kingdom (though, of course, not more than Antiochus IV). More important, however, was the change in Jewish Palestine. In the Persian period, the Jewish state was a little theocracy, huddled in the Judaean hills around Jerusalem. Since then, Israel had grown, been powerful, seen its borders extended as far as David's. The Jewish religion had also been tampered with: something the Persians never did. People still remembered Antiochus IV Epiphanes. Gaius (Caligula) had recently tried to defile the temple in a way that recalled Antiochus' 'abmonination of desolation'. Then Nero came along. Who knew what would happen next? Tranquillity under native priests and a distant overlord was no longer possible. Too few people looked back to the Persian period as a model, too many back to the Hasmonean. Not that the Hasmoneans had been universally loved. On the contrary, some of them had fierce internal opposition. At the end of the Hasmonean period, the competition between Hyrcanus II and Aristobulus II had led to disenchantment on the part of some of the populace. Yet, Herod still feared that a member of the family might lead an uprising against him. Whether they were loved, feared or hated, the Hasmoneans had shown what was possible. Perhaps 'freedom' could be won again.

My guess is that what happened had to happen. The ambitions and hopes that had been roused by the Hasmoneans – roused among people who hated them as well as those who loved them – were powerful. The ideal of national sovereignty lived for 310 years, from 175 BCE to 135 CE. Until these hopes were completely crushed by the failure of the second major revolt, they posed a threat to the peace and stability of powerful neighbours. And the powerful neighbours could not leave the Jews alone, as the Persians had done.

The various actors in the period that we have surveyed are often the objects of moral censure. We shall understand them better if we view them sympathetically. I rather like the chief priests. I think that on the whole they tried hard and did better at staving off revolt and protecting the Jewish population from Roman troops than any other group could have done – except a succession of Herods. I even find things about Herod to like. He was no more ruthless than anyone else of his period who started as a minor governor and ended up as a king. Once in power, he raised Jewish Palestine to a new position in the world, he earned for Jews and Judaism the respect of Rome, he prevented uprisings and made the frontier safe, and so he kept Roman troops out of Palestine. He murdered the Hasmoneans, repressed the populace and executed anyone who crossed him. But there were no revolts, his magnificent building projects employed thousands of labourers, trade increased, and everything worked. Modern distaste for successful dictators, which I fully share, is based in part on an implied comparison with modern democracy. If one will study conquerors, kings and emperors of Herod's time, Herod will be seen in a better light.

I rather like the Pharisees. They loved detail and precision. They wanted to get everything just right. I like that. They loved God, they thought he had blessed them, and they thought that he *wanted* them to get everything just right. I do not doubt that some of them were priggish. This is a common fault of the pious, one that is amply displayed in modern criticism of the Pharisees. The Pharisees, we know, intended to be humble before God, and they thought that intention mattered more than outward show. Those are worthy ideals. The other pietists strike me as being less attractive than the Pharisees. The surviving literature depicts them as not having much of a programme for all Israel, and as being too ready to cultivate hatred of others: learn *our* secrets or God will destroy you. But probably they weren't all that bad, and we can give them credit for loving God and being honest.

Mostly, I like the ordinary people. They worked at their jobs, they believed the Bible, they carried out the small routines and celebrations of the religion: they prayed every day, thanked God for his blessings, and on the sabbath went to the synagogue, asked teachers questions, and listened respectfully. What could be better? Every now and again they took their hard-earned second tithe money to Jerusalem, devoutly performed their sacrifices, carried the meat out of the temple to share with their family and friends, bought some wine, and feasted the night away. Then it was back to the regular grind. This may not sound like much, but in their view they were living as God wished. The history of the time shows how firmly they believed in God, who gave them the law and promised them deliverance.

Notes

Part I: Context

1. Preview

1. On the date of the last battle of the first revolt against Rome, see *HJP* I, p. 512 n. 139.

2. See Josephus, *Life*. In this brief summary, I shall not cite individual paragraphs. Among the older literature on Josephus, I still find Bentwich's *Josephus* (1914) to be useful, despite the author's animosity towards his subject. More recently, and more sympathetically, see Rajak, *Josephus*, 1983.

3. Thucydides, *History of the Peloponnesian War* I.22.1: he 'adhered as closely as possible to the general sense of what was actually said', while composing the speech 'in the language in which . . . the several speakers would express . . . the sentiments most befitting the occasion'.

4. On using Josephus, see further Gibbs and Feldman, 'Josepus' Vocabulary for Slavery', *JQR* 4, 1986, 281–310. 'The highest degree of probability of Josephus' historical accuracy . . . occurs when Josephus and the Talmud (insofar as it transmits the oral tradition of Josephus' period and earlier times) agree, when Josephus and his Biblical sources agree, when Josephus and inscriptional evidence agree, when two or more separate works of Josephus agree, or when it has been possible to set aside any motivations that Josephus may have had . . .' (n. 4, pp. 283f.).

5. See Charlesworth, *OTP*, 2 vols; Sparks, *AOT*; the Apocryphal or Deutero-canonical works are also included in major English translations of the Bible. A very useful survey of some of the literature is provided by Nickelsburg, *Jewish Literature between the Bible and the Mishnah*.

6. Apocalypses usually contain 'eschatology' (ideas about the end), but it is incorrect to define apocalypses as simply eschatological. They reveal mysteries of numerous sorts. See, for example, Rowland, *The Open Heaven;* Hellholm (ed.), *Apocalypticism in the mediterranean World and the Near East*.

7. Rabbinic knowledge of esoteric subjects: *Hagigah* 2.1. Ezekiel's visionary chariot is mentioned in Ben Sira 49.8, not in Ezekiel. The term *merkavah* ('chariot') has been used to describe Ezekiel's vision of heavenly wheels (1.15–21) and later mystical speculations. Paul: expected the return of the Lord, I Thess. 4.16f.; visions, II Cor. 12.1; heard voices, II Cor. 12.8f.; made travel arrangements, II Cor. 12.14–18 and often; gave instructions about worship services, I Cor. 14.26–33. Note that three of these topics are all in the same chapter.

8. As Neusner has frequently proposed. See *JLJM*, ch. V, especially pp. 324–8.

9. I still do not know, after decades as a New Testament scholar, precisely what Paul meant when he said that women should cover their heads when praying or prophesying 'because of the angels' (I Cor. 11.10).

10. The term 'Pharisee' refers to a member of the Pharisaic party before the destruction of Jerusalem in 70 CE. 'Rabbis' were the post-70 scholars who inherited and developed Pharisaic traditions, finally creating 'rabbinic Judaism'. Some people, obviously, were both. Johanan b. Zakkai was a Pharisee who survived the war and became a leading Rabbi. The terminological distinction is early: in rabbinic literature Hillel, Shammai and other Pharisees are not given the honorific title 'rabbi'.

11. See more fully *JLJM*, pp. 166–73. A major point of academic dispute is the date of anonymous material (the s^etam). In *JLJM* I give several instances in which the s^etam is presupposed by Pharisaic debates, and thus may be regarded as early (pp. 185, 200, 210, 213, 218, 222, 224). A full study would reveal a great many more cases.

12. The presuppositions of post-70 discussions may imply a pre-70 Pharisaic view. See *JLJM*, pp. 250–2 for a list of presuppositions about purity, and the index to that work *s. v.* 'Presuppositions and consensus' for further discussion. For an example of my use of a fairly late rabbinic passage for illustrative purposes only, see below, p. 333 (on *Sanhedrin* 10.1).

13. See the provocative lecture by Wacholder, 'Messianism and Mishnah'. He gives numerous instances in which the Mishnah's rules, especially about the temple, 'refer primarily to a Halakhah of the First Temple which will be reinstituted in the Third Temple. These references to the Sanctuary do not necessarily embrace the Second Temple' (p. 24),

14. The Urim and Thummim in ancient times were on the high priest's ephod (an outer garment; see Added Note to ch. 6), or carried in his pocket. They were believed to disclose God's answers to direct questions (e.g. Num. 27.21). By the time of the Mishnah they had long since disappeared; see *Antiq.* 3.215–18; more fully below, p. 70.

15. For other scholars who hold the same view, see ch. 18 n. 45.

2. *The Issues that Generated Parties*

1. On the suitability of the term 'philosophy', see p. 50.

2. See, for example, Morton Smith, *Palestinian Parties and Politics*, pp. 101f.; 'The Dead Sea Sect in Relation to Ancient Judaism', *NTS* 7, 1961, pp. 347–60; Philip R. Davies, *The Damascus Covenant*, pp. 36–47.

3. There is some problem about what to call the area: many Jews use and have used 'the Land'; many Christians and others 'the Holy Land'. Some ancient authors spoke of 'Palestinian Syria'. 'Palestine' is the simplest and easiest compromise.

4. See *HJP*, pp. 135–63. For summaries, see Bruce, *Israel and the Nations*, pp. 128–42; Leaney, *The Jewish and Christian World 200 BC to AD 200*, pp. 83–8; Russell, *The Jews from Alexander to Herod*, p. 31–9.

5. See Kampen, *The Hasideans and the Origin of Pharisaism*.

6. On the Hellenistic cities, see *HJP* II, pp. 85–183.

7. Both purple and gold, however, were used in the vestments of the high priest. See the Added Note to ch. 6.

8. See e.g. Leaney, p. 91.

9. See the histories of the parties below, chs. 15, 16, 18.

10. See *HJP* III, pp. 145–7.

11. *HJP* III, pp. 145–7 and notes; Jeremias, *Jerusalem*, pp. 184–6 and notes.

12. See e.g. Le Moyne, *Les Sadducéens*, pp. 66f. and n. 1.

13. It is noted that this Onias had sided with the Ptolemies and thus had friends in Egypt (see e.g. Hoenig in *IDB, s.v.* Onias).

14. Full evidence in *HJP* III, pp. 145–7.

15. See the summaries by Busink, *Der Tempel von Jerusalem*, p. 816; Hengel, *Judaism and Hellenism* I, pp. 272–5, both of whom are inclined to favour the proposal.

16. Further passages in Vermes, *Perspectives*, p. 185; on messiahs, see also below, pp. 295–8.

17. *Jubilees* and parts of *I Enoch* are very close to the Dead Sea Sect in many respects. Especially important is the solar calendar of 364 days, which is common to *Jubilees*, *I Enoch* 72–82, and some of the Dead Sea Scrolls. It is possible that an early version of *Jubilees* and parts of *I Enoch* are pre-Hasmonean, and thus 'Essene' views may also be pre-Hasmonean. Some scholars have argued that parts of the *Covenant of Damascus* are also pre-Hasmonean. All these issues, however, are difficult and controverted. The position adopted here is that the Essene party as we know it originated in the early Hasmonean period, though it may have drawn on earlier sources. See further ch. 16 below.

18. Vermes, *The Dead Sea Scrolls in English*, 3rd ed., pp. 23–35; *Perspective*, pp. 137–62; Knibb, *The Qumran Community*, pp. 4–12.

19. On 'Sadducee', see Le Moyne, pp. 155–163.

20. Le Moyne, p. 67; Jeremias, *Jerusalem* pp. 192f. He was not, however, eminent, and this may count against the connection between the Zakokites and the Sadducees.

21. Neusner, *Rabbinic Traditions about the Pharisees* I, p. 64; III, p. 297.

22. The term 'scribe' has a range of overlapping meanings. See below, pp. 170f., 179–82.

23. There was possibly a legal/exegetical basis for this disagreement. Ex. 22.28 [Heb. v. 27] commands the people not to curse God or their ruler (the two words for 'curse' are different in Hebrew). Hyrcanus may have taken this to mean that the penalty for denigrating the ruler should be the same as for blaspheming God, while the Pharisees may have found some sort of distinction.

3. *Historical Outline of the Roman Period*

1. The discussion of this topic by Kasher (*Jews, Idumaeans, and Ancient Arabs*, pp. 126–30), like most others, supposes that the Mishnaic halakhah was the law of the land, and that the question of whether or not *people* doubted Herod's full Jewishness is to be decided by studying *rabbinic* law. See especially 127f., where Kasher decides that 'from a formal aspect there appears to have been no blemish on Herod's Jewishness'. It is better to accept Josephus' report that some people objected to Herod because he was only a 'half-Jew' (*Antiq.* 14.403).

2. I Kings 4.24 gives Solomon a very large domain, but this is exaggerated. Jannaeus' kingdom, and later Herod's, were, however, almost as big as the legendary kingdom of David and Solomon. One may compare Maps 104, 105, 213 and 220 in Aharoni and Avi-Yonah, *Bible Atlas*.

3. For variants on the story of mutilation, see Marcus' note to *Antiq.* 14.366. For biblical law on blemished priests, see Lev. 21.16–23.

4. *HJP* I, p. 286.

4. *The Context of Conflict*

1. See further ch. 14.

2. Neusner is inclined to doubt this. See *Messiah in Context*, pp. 5–16, and my attempt to analyse his various statements, *JLJM*, pp. 324–6.

Part II: Common Judaism

5. Common Judaism and the Temple

1. I am not competent to discuss the eastern Diaspora, but Mesopotamian Jews also shared in common Judaism. They paid the temple tax, and occasionally one learns that a priest or Pharisee moved from Mesopotamia to Palestine and could understand what was going on. Temple tax: *Antiq.* 18.312f.; priest from Babylon: *Antiq.* 15.22; the Pharisee Hillel: *Pesahim* 66a.

2. On communication between Palestine and the Diaspora, see e.g. II Macc. 1.10; Judith 11.14. This does not, however, mean that 'the Sanhedrin' in Jerusalem wrote the rules that Diaspora Jews followed. See *JLJM*, ch. IV; below, e.g. p. 223.

3. Smith, 'The Dead Sea Sect in Relation to Ancient Judaism', *NTS* 7, 1960–61, pp. 347–60, here p. 356. Cf. 'Palestinian Judaism in the First Century', pp. 73f. The term 'normative Judaism' in modern academic discussion stems from George Foot Moore, *Judaism*, who used the term to mean 'rabbinic', but he applied it to the chronological period *c.* 70–200 CE. See his comments in I, p. v and III, pp. v–vi; further my discussion *P&PJ*, p. 34 n. 11.

4. For the last two topics, see especially Burkert, pp. 75–84, 86f., 98, 110, 270. The principal book on Greek purification is René Ginouvès, *Balaneutikè. Recherches sur le bain dans l'antiquité grecque.* I have summarized a few points in *JLJM*, pp. 262f.

5. Most recently, see Beard and North, (eds), *Pagan Priests.* The diversity of Greek and Roman paganism makes it difficult to offer completely accurate generalizations that cover all priests, temples and cults. When one adds Egyptian religion and the Asian cults that penetrated the Roman empire, the difficulty is multiplied.

6. See e.g. Burkert, pp. 96f.

7. Lane Fox, *Alexander the Great*, pp. 112, 214, 231, 295.

8. Gordon, 'From Republic to Principate', *Pagan Priests*, p. 196f.

9. According to Pausanias, the worship of Artemis Laphria in Patrae included burning wild animals alive, but he said that this practice was unique (*Description of Greece* 7.18.8–13).

10. E.g. *War* 2.119; Philo, *Creation of the World* 128.

11. The topic of a 'canon' of Jewish Scripture is a complicated one, which I shall avoid. 'Inspired' is, I think, safe.

12. Marcel Simon, *Verus Israel*, ET p. 10 and n. 39; p. 31.

13. The author used a pseudonym, and thus he is properly called 'Pseudo-Aristeas', but for convenience I shall call him 'Aristeas'.

14. *HJP* II, pp. 272f.; III, pp. 54, 58, 122f.

15. A man who was a 'priest and teacher of wisdom' is mentioned in an inscription found at the synagogue in Sardis (fourth century CE). See Hanfmann, 'The Ninth Campaign at Sardis (1966)', *BASOR* 187, October 1967, p. 38.

16. Stephen's speech in Acts 7 is often taken to be critical of the temple, but the question is difficult: does it criticize the temple as such, or only some conceptions of it? See e.g. Craig Hill, *Hellenists and Hebrews: Reappraising Division within the Earliest Church*, Minneapolis 1991.

17. There are useful pictures and drawings of the temple complex in Kathleen and Leen Ritmeyer, 'Reconstructing Herod's Temple Mount in Jerusalem', *BAR* 15 (6, 1989), pp. 23–42.

18. Ben-Dov, *In the Shadow of the Temple*, p. 67.

19. See Wacholder, 'Hecataeus of Abdera', *Enc. Jud.* 8, cols. 236f.

20. Busink, *Der Temple von Jerusalem*, p. 832; similarly Aharoni and Avi-Yonah, *Bible Atlas*, rev. ed., map 204.

21. On 'Solomon's portico', see Busink, pp. 1198f.

22. Busink (p. 835) proposes that a porticoed outer court had first been built during the reign of Ptolemaios II Philadelphos in Egypt (285–245 BCE). The *stoa* reveals Hellenistic influence.

23. This verse does not show that 'the woman participated beside the man' in the ancient cult, as Busink thought (p. 1077).

24. Grafman, 'Herod's Foot and Robinson's Arch', *IEJ* 20, 1970, pp. 60–66. One assumes that, whatever unit of measurement was used, the builders employed obvious multiples of the unit: 1,000 feet rather than 1,001.25. On this assumption, Grafman's proposal makes sense of the temple walls. J. Maier has attemped to explain the history of the temple architecture on the assumption that builders used cubits of different lengths in different parts and at different times ('The Architectural History of the Temple').

25. Ben-Dov, *In the Shadow of the Temple*, p. 77. For the measurements, see Safrai, 'Temple', *Enc. Jud.* 15, col. 964.

26. Dalman, *Sacred Sites and Ways*, p. 286; cf. the plans in Scully, *The Earth, the Temple, and the Gods*, revised ed., figures 264, 265, 320.

27. Herod's was not quite 'the greatest temple of all times' or 'the largest site of its kind in the ancient world' (Ben-Dov, pp. 74, 77).

28. On the temple of Amun at Karnak, see Baines and Málek, *Atlas of Ancient Egypt*, pp. 90–2; W. Stevenson Smith, *The Art of Architecture of Ancient Egypt*, rev. W. K. Simpson, p. 366; Hobson, *Exploring the World of the Pharaohs*, pp. 136–8.

29. The largest Hindu temple complex, which is at Śrīraṅgam, is surrounded by a wall 2,475 feet × 2,880 – 755 metres × 878. The complex was built over a long period between the 13th and 18th centuries. See Basham, *The Wonder that was India*, pp. 201, 358.

30. For this calculation, see below. Josephus claimed that at points the workmen had to build up from a depth of 300 cubits, which would be about 150 metres (*War* 5.188). The context indicates that he may have had in mind the depth of the ravines. At no point is the temple platform supported by 150 metres of fill.

31. The obelisks of Rameses II are 25 metres high. Note also the size of the columns in the hypostyle hall in the temple of Amun (below). According to Busink, an unused stone at the temple of Baalbek is 21.72 metres × 4.3 × 5.3. For other massive stones, see Busink, pp. 1356f. Collectors of large stone lore will wish to know that the largest sarsen stones at Stonehenge are 6.6 metres high (*c.* 22 ft.) and weigh 45 tons.

32. Ben-Dov, p. 88.

33. See especially Busink, pp. 1532–8.

34. I can hardly hope to succeed if Vincent and Busink have failed. See Busink, pp. 1529–74; L. -H. Vincent, Le temple hérodien de'après la Mišnah', *RB* 61, 1954, pp. 5–35, 398–418. Vincent argues that *Middot* presents, on the basis of scriptural exegesis, 'an ideal sanctuary of the eschatological restoration' (p. 417).

35. Cf. Vincent, 'Le temple', p. 407: *Middot* eliminates non-liturgical aspects of the architecture, especially the elements that displayed 'the ostentatious wealth of the Idumaean monarch, [who was] too imbued with Hellenism . . .'. It is possible, however, that the Rabbis were not that conscious of Herod's temple, and were simply guided by Ezekiel, where it is difficult to find stoas (though the translators of the LXX tried: Ezek. 40.18; 42.3, 5).

36. I take this point from Bentwich, *Josephus*, pp. 121–3, who cites Schlatter, *Zur*

Topographie und Geschichte Palästinas, and Colonel Conder, *Tent Work in Palestine*, neither of which I have seen. The point, however, is readily confirmed. Josephus knew more about Herod's palace, Roman tactics and the Jews' defensive efforts when he wrote about Matsada, where he had not been, than he did about Jotapata, where he had fought. Bentwich regarded this as discrediting him: 'his very accuracy about some topographical details is suspicious'. I would urge that we can trust him as much on the temple as on Matsada, and for the very same reason: he had a good source. For a minor instance in which his source did not look quite carefully enough at the columns on Matsada, see below, n. 49 (2).

37. Thus in the later work, he says that the temple enclosure was four stades: one stade per side (*Antiq.* 15.340). This shows, I think, a reversion to the ideal theory of Ezekiel: the temple was square (Ezek. 42.16–20); so also *Middot* 2.1. Earlier, Josephus had known that Herod's temple enclosure was not square: *War* 6.311.

38. According to Lane Fox, Memnon, a Greek general who fought for the Persians against Alexander, was the 'deviser of the first field maps to be used in Greek warfare' (*Alexander the Great*, p. 118). My colleagues John Matthews and S. M. Barnish have kindly informed me that the question of Roman notebooks and files is a substantial one. My proposal requires only notebooks, not a filing system that would allow them to be retrieved decades later.

39. The Greek text has been often published. See e.g. Deissmann, *Light from the Ancient East*, p. 80. The translation is by Peretz Segal (see the next note). Cf. Josephus, *War* 5.193f.; 6.124–6.

40. Segal, 'The Penalty of the Warning Inscription from the Temple of Jerusalem', *IEJ* 39, 1989, pp. 79–84. 'Split his skull with clubs' is from *Sanhedrin* 9.6, which deals with a priest who served while impure.

41. According to *War* 5.200, there were porticoes around the inner wall, and possibly they provided an area where the women could stand and watch. On this part of the temple, see the next note.

42. The problems of reconstructing the Court of the Women are especially severe. The clear intent of *War* 5.198 is that this court was walled off (*diateteichismenou*). On the way in, men and women separated at the eastern gate. The men walked straight through to another gate and thus into the Court of the Israelites, while the women detoured to the south or north and entered one chamber or the other of the Court of the Women. Especially striking is Josephus' statement that the west end of the Women's Court had no gate (*War* 5.200). This means that it was not an open area between the two east-west gates (as Busink and everyone else have always assumed), but was enclosed, accessible only from the north and south. The men did not go through either chamber where the women were, but along a corridor that was in some sense 'walled', with the two chambers for women on either side. The walls along the corridor, of course, need not have been solid or higher than a person's head. According to *Antiq.* 15.418, men and women passed together through the eastern gate, but women had to stop before entering the Court of the Israelites. All of the reconstructions that I have seen accept *Antiq.* 15 and show the Court of the Women open also to men, not walled off. For the size and layout of the Court of the Women, most accept *Middot* 2.5. It seems to me likely, however, that *Antiq.* 15 is simplified and that *War* 5 is correct. Such details as that the Women's Court was 'walled off' and that it had no gate on its west side were probably not made up. Here Josephus describes the temple as he knew it.

43. Façade 100 cubits: *War* 5.207; 90 cubits: 5.209; interior 100: 5.221. On the difference of 10 cubits in height see Busink, pp. 1116f.

44. The relationship of the tapestry to the doors is very puzzling. If it actually hung *before* the doors (so *War* 5.212), they could not have been seen. Note also the description of 'hangings' on the doors in *Antiq.* 15.394. Busink proposed that, when Josephus wrote 'before the doors', he had mentally stepped through the doors and was standing in the first chamber (pp. 1117f.; cf. 1121). Though possible, this seems unlikely, and the problem of the tapestry remains.

45. *War* 5.200, on the inner porticoes and the treasury rooms, is especially difficult. See Busink's reconstructions, Abb. 242, p. 1064 and Abb. 24⁻, p. 1095, and his discussion, pp. 1097–1105.

46. On water for purification in the temple area, see Lev. 16.23f. Ben Sira 50.3 refers to a 'reservoir like the sea in circumference', but we do not know whether the water was used for washing away the blood or bathing or both. See further Mazar, *Mountain of the Lord*, pp. 128–30; below, pp. 117f.

47. On the inner rooms, see *Middot* 2.5; *Tamid* 1.1. On the council chamber, which is difficult to locate precisely, see *War* 5.144; 6.354.

48. Ben-Dov (pp. 124f.) states that 'the Greek term for a royal portico is a basilica and is derived from *basileus*, meaning king', and further that the 'royal portico' in Athens was called a basilica. In both cases the noun is *stoa*, modified by 'royal' (*Antiq.* 15.411, *basileia stoa*), as Ben-Dov also states on p. 125. The error is in supposing that 'basilica' is an alternative name. As Busink shows, a stoa is distinct from a basilica, and Herod built stoas (Busink, pp. 1219–30).

49. Busink, pp. 1187–1200. There are minor critical points. (1) Busink points out that the platform of the present Haram, built over the temple mount, declines by three metres from north to south (p. 1191). Presumably this was true in antiquity, in which case not all the columns along the east and west walls could have been the same height. (2) Josephus states that each column was cut from a single piece of marble. He gave a similar description of the columns in Herod's palace on Matsada, but modern excavations have shown this to be in error. There the columns were made of drums placed on top of one another and covered with stucco, so that they appeared to be monoliths (*War* 7.290; Yigael Yadin, *Masada* p. 46 and fig. p. 44; Busink, p. 1190). The historian could have made a similar mistake about the columns in the temple. Otherwise, he can be shown to be fairly accurate. Using ancient archaeological principles (Vitruvius), Busink calculated that the diameter of columns 11.5 metres high should have been 1.65 metres (p. 1193), though there might be some variation. (Josephus wrote 25 cubits, 12.5 metres, but one must allow for the capital, and not all the columns were the same height. Thus Busink used 11.5 metres.) Excavations have uncovered columns 1.5 metres in diameter (Ben-Dov, p. 92).

50. The description of the Royal Portico is taken from *Antiq.* 15.411–416. See Busink's detailed analysis, which justifies Josephus' description (pp. 1200–1230).

51. See n. 28.

52. This cannot be quite right, since 162 is not divisible by 4. For solutions to this puzzle, see Busink, pp. 1203–6.

53. The circumference of the columns was equal to the armspan of three men (immediately above). Busink (p. 1209) reckons a span of both arms at 1.85 metres × 3 = 5.55, which yields a diameter of 1.76 metres.

54. Josephus wrote that the columns were 27 feet high, but this is apparently an error for 27 cubits = 40.5 feet. Note that the columns of the other porticoes were 25 cubits high; those of the Royal Portico must have been higher. The overall height of the side aisles he put at 'over 50 feet'; that is, more than 15.5 metres (measurements in feet multiplied by .31, as suggested by Grafman). See on all this Busink, pp. 1212–14.

55. On the Royal Portico as a stoa, see Busink, pp. 1219–30.
56. I am indebted to Rabbi Solomon Bernards for the data from Temple Emanuel.
57. Ben-Dov, pp. 77, 92.
58. Ben-Dov, p. 92.
59. Ben-Dov, p. 103.
60. On Robinson's arch, see Mazar, *The Mountain of the Lord*, p. 132; Ben-Dov, pp. 121–33.
61. There were at least three 'palaces': Herod's, the Hasmoneans' and the high priests'. The quotation is from Pliny, *Natural History* 5.70, cited by Stern, *Greek and Latin Authors on Jews and Judaism* I, pp. 469, 471. I have changed 'famous' to 'illustrious' as the translation of *clarissima*.
62. The phenomenon ceased, according to Josephus, about 200 years before he wrote the *Antiquities*. This is approximately the time of Hyrcanus, about whom Josephus wrote, 'he was accounted by God worthy of three of the greatest privileges, the rule of the nation, the office of high-priest, and the gift of prophecy' (*Antiq.* 13.299; *War* 1.69). I am indebted to Rebecca Gray for this point.
63. It is not correct to say, as some do, that they governed only priests and the temple; below, pp. 217–22; *JLJM*, pp. 147f.

Added Note to Ch. 5: Gentiles, Purity and the Temple

1. On the Jewish impurities, see ch. 12 below.
2. *Niddah* 7.4; *T. Niddah* 6.15; *JLJM*, p. 156. The topic, whether or not blood found near a woman's bathhouse is impure, no matter what the answer of a given rabbi, reveals the assumption that Lev. 15 applies only to Jews.
3. This was the view of Adolf Büchler, 'The Levitical Impurity of Gentiles', *JQR* 17, 1927, pp. 1–81. It has been supported by numerous scholars, including Zeitlin and Hoenig; see Hoenig, 'Oil and Pagan Defilement', JQR 61, 1970, pp. 69f. and notes. On the other side, see Alon, 'The Levitical Uncleanness of Gentiles', *Jews, Judaism and the Classical world*, pp. 146–89; J. Baumgarten, 'The Essene Avoidance of Oil'. The question has been not 'did Jews behave towards Gentiles as if they were impure?' but 'when did the rabbis declare them to be impure?' Alon, however, while interested in the second question, also pointed out that most people did not observe the halakhah (as he took it to be) decreeing that Gentiles were impure.
On the 'eighteen decrees', see *Shabbat* 1.4; *Shabbat* 13b; *Zavim* 5.12. Some scholars interpret these as restrictive decrees, against association with Gentiles, hastily passed *c.* 65 CE. See e.g. Zeitlin, *The Rise and Fall of the Judaean State* II, pp. 358f.
4. J. Baumgarten cites this passage in his debate with Hoenig: *Studies in Qumran Law*, p. 97.
5. Cf. Ezek. 44.9.
6. On Herod and the Pharisees, see *Antiq.* 14.172 (conflict with Samaias, a Pharisee according to *Antiq.* 15.3); 17.41–6 (they were implicated in a plot against him).
7. See my fuller discussions, 'Jewish Association with Gentiles and Galatians 2:11–14'; *JLJM*, pp. 282f.
8. This is the likeliest construal of *War* 5.226.
9. Jews who had purified themselves in order to enter the temple probably tried to avoid touching anyone or anything that might be impure (cf. *Arist.* 106), but they could not be certain of avoiding all contact. My guess is that most people, even when about to enter the temple, did not worry too much about acquiring impurity by contact with Gentiles or with other Jews. (See the discussion of the ordinary people and *midras* impurity below,

pp. 229, 439f.) Official temple policy, however, was to reduce the chance that a worshipper would touch a menstruant. If the common opinion had been that Gentile impurity was highly contagious and prevented worship in the temple, one would have expected Gentiles to be prohibited from entering Jerusalem during festivals.

10. Mark 7.4; see further ch. 12.

6. *The Ordinary Priests and Levites*

1. When the Zealots overthrew the first leaders of the revolt, they also took over the appointment of the high priest. Lots were cast, and the choice fell on Phanni, who, though a priest, lived in a village and 'scarcely knew what the high priesthood meant' (*War* 4.155f.). The rabbis discussed this high priest; some proposed that he was brought in from cutting wood, some from cutting stone, and some from ploughing, the latter based on I Kings 19.19 (*T. Yom ha-Kippurim* 1.6). We cannot know what his actual circumstances were, but probably he was not a farmer. The best evidence that as a rule priests did not work the land is the lack of accusation that they did so.

2. Precisely when the 'theocracy' began is uncertain. Early in the Persian period, Zerubbabel, a descendant of David, was appointed governor (e.g. Zech. 3.8; 6.12). While there was a Davidic governor, of course, the high priest did not reign supreme. Further, Nehemiah was a strong but non-Davidic governor. When one adds to such points the fact that the dates of Zerubbabel, Nehemiah and Ezra (a Zadokite priest) are hard to sort out, one must hesitate before saying just when rule by the high priest, under a non-interfering Persian governor, began. To get a clearer picture of the problems, the reader may look up these proper names in the standard dictionaries and encyclopedias.

3. According to *T. Ta'aniyot* 2.2, there were between four and nine fathers' houses in each course, and there were diverse ways of dividing the week's work among them.

4. See the discussion of the daily sacrificial routine, p. 117 and n. 7.

5. Jeremias, *Jerusalem* p. 200. The further calculations on pp. 203f. are even more dubious. For example, he missed the change of shifts (discussed below).

6. 'He [Aristeas] intends the number 700 to represent the number of priests and Levites in the *weekly* course', Jeremias, p. 200. That is certainly not what Aristeas intended. He described how silent it was, even though 700 men were ministering (see below).

7. II Chron. 30.27 mentions prayer by the priests and Levites, but apparently not as a regular part of the temple service (though it may have been).

8. Translation by Andrews in Charles, *POT.* here as in other places in Shutt's translation of *Aristeas* in the *OTP*, there are remarkable mistranslations.

9. The passage in *Apion* refers to the sanctuary, but it may be that further guards at the inner wall turned back people who were carrying parcels. According to Mark 11.16, it was Jesus who forbade people to carry things *through* the temple. The author presumably had in mind some temple other than the one in Jerusalem, where the temple grounds could not have served as a shortcut between any two points. Carrying things into sacred precincts was commonly forbidden in the ancient world.

10. Eating in the temple: *Jubilees* 49.15–23 requires worshippers to eat the Passover lamb inside the temple area. This probably refers to the court in front of the temple, before it was enclosed with a wall and paved. Ezekiel imagined that in the future the outer court of the temple would have kitchens for cooking the people's sacrifices (46.21–4). J. Baumgarten (*Studies in Qumran Law*, pp. 65f.) proposes that 'the early halakhah' required all holy food to be eaten in the temple and that in a later period the priests allowed the Essenes to follow that practice, making available to them 'some isolated area' within

the temple complex so that they could participate in temple worship and eat the holy food in a holy place. I think that it is possible that, early in the second-temple period, when the population was quite small, the outer court, which was then not enclosed, was used for cooking the Passover lamb (the only holy food mentioned in *Jubilees* 49.15–23). I doubt, however, that *Jubilees* was 'the early halakhah'; it appears always to have been sectarian or semi-sectarian. Nevertheless, cooking in the outer court is possible for the early period. I do not regard this as a reasonable proposal for Herod's temple. It is most unlikely that lay people built fires and cooked meat inside the enclosed area during a festival, especially during Passover. The crowds were too great. Further, I think that the statements by Josephus and Philo to the effect that lay people did not eat and drink in the temple, that silence was maintained, and that it was not a place for making merry, refer to the entire temple complex. (Philo on the austerity of religion, *Spec. Laws* 1.74; p. 70 above.)

11. It is possible that the statement in the *Antiquities*, that some assassinations were carried out in the temple area, is a later exaggeration, which allows Josephus to make more forcefully one of his general points: that the temple had been profaned and needed to be purged with fire; in destroying it the Romans served as God's agents.

12. *Sheqalim* 5.1f.; *T. Sheqalim* 2.14; *T. Horayot* 2.10.

13. According to *Sheqalim* 5.2, there were always at least three treasurers, to guard against dishonesty. Josephus also speaks of 'treasurers' (of the temple) in *Antiq.* 15.408; 18.93. Other passages make it likely that there was one chief treasurer: *War* 6.390, discussed below; *Antiq.* 20.194, where the treasurer is named.

14. For the use of the Jerusalem temple for personal deposits, see II Macc. 3.6, 10f., 15, 22. We cannot know to what degree it served as a safe repository in untroubled times, but when war threatened the wealthy stripped their houses and deposited valuables in the temple (*War* 6.282).

15. According to *HJP* I, p. 269, 2,000 talents in gold. The official coinage for the temple tax and other cash taxes and fines was (according to the Mishnah, *Bekhorot* 8.7) the Tyrian shekel, which was silver. *Arist.* 40 depicts the pilgrims as bringing 100 talents in silver. On the other hand, Cicero (*Pro Flacco* 28.66–9) refers to the right of Diaspora Jews to send gold to the temple. (See below at n. 18.) One assumes, then, that the temple's income in coinage was mixed, some silver and some gold.

16. Smallwood, *The Jews under Roman Rule*, p. 197 n. 61.

17. Smallwood, p. 36, n. 50.

18. Cicero, *Pro Flacco* 28.66–9, cited in Stern, *Greek and Latin Authors* I, pp. 196–201.

19. Smallwood, p. 110; *Antiq.* 17.317–320.

20. A votive offering could be a monument, but it is doubtful that monuments were permitted in the Jerusalem temple.

21. If in *Antiq.* 3.228 one reads *de* as adversative (so Thackeray in the LCL), Josephus distinguishes thank offerings, which must be without blemish, from burnt offerings, which by implication might be blemished. In view of Lev. 22.18, however, this is probably a wrong construal of his meaning.

22. *Ta probata* in John 2.14f. is usually translated 'sheep'. The word can, however, also refer to goats. The only English term that includes both is 'flock'; thus the translation 'flock-animals'. (See e.g. Ex. 34.3, where the LXX translates the Hebrew *ts'on*, 'flock', as *ta probata*; elsewhere *probaton* translates *seh*, which can be either a lamb or a kid.) For a similar reason I translate *tous boas*, 'cattle', as 'herd-animals', since the cattle could be either cows or oxen.

23. Jeremias, *Jerusalem*, p. 49. The passage from Josephus is *Antiq.* 20.205, which

says that the former hgh priest Ananias was wealthy. How this supports the case that Annas pastured animals in the temple is not clear.

24. Edersheim, *The Life and Times of Jesus the Messiah* I, p. 370.

25. Abrahams, *Studies* I, p. 88.

26. Horsley, *Jesus and the Spiral of Violence*, p. 300.

27. Horsley, p. 281. Throughout this book, Horsley romanticizes the 'early' laws (apparently meaning Deuteronomy).

28. The question of the total expense of the national institution – sacrifices, tithes, first fruits and the like – will be taken up in ch. 9; as just indicated, personal immorality on the part of priests, especially aristocratic priests, will be discussed in chs 10 and 15.

29. Horsley thinks that the people on the whole did not support the temple system (*Spiral*, pp. 287, 299).

Added Note to Ch. 6: The Priestly Vestments

1. Shutt (in *OTP* II) mistranslates *byssos*, 'fine linen', as 'leather' and 'ankles' as 'loins', thus creating a new description of the priests' clothes: leather loincloths.

2. Subsequent notes will show that I think that the description by Haran ('Priestly Vestments', *Enc. Jud.* 13, cols. 1063–9) is not quite right, at least for the late second-temple period, and that the illustrations that he uses (from Moshe Levin's *Melekhet Hammishkan*, which I have not seen) contain errors.

3. LXX Ex. 36.34–6 is parallel to 39.27–9 in Hebrew and English.

4. Some of the turns of phrase can be paralleled in descriptions of priestly garments found in classical writers: e.g. *diazōma peri ta aidoia*, 'drawers around the private parts'; *pilos*, 'close-fitting cap made of felt'. Josephus may have had help in finding the precise descriptive phrases, but I doubt that they are purely literary artifice. More likely, parts of the apparel of the Jewish priests were like those of other priests.

5. In the *Enc. Jud.* (see n. 2), the sash is shown tied around the waist.

6. Cf. Yadin, *The Finds from the Bar-Kokhba Period in the Cave of Letters*, p. 209. Four fingers' breadth, on the ancient hand, was probably closer to 4 cm than to today's 6 or 7 cm (1½–2 inches rather than 2½–3). The *Enc. Jud.* depicts the sash as round, not flat, smaller than four fingers and also too small to be decorated with flowers.

7. The RSV and the NRSV translate *ma'aseh rôqem* in Ex. 28.39; 39.29 'embroidered with needlework'; the JB also uses 'embroider'. It is literally 'work of a variegator', and in BDB (*s. v. rqm*) it is clear that variegation was usually the task of a weaver, not an embroiderer. In any case Josephus describes the decoration as being the work of a weaver.

8. The curtain in front of the tabernacle was crimson (*Antiq.* 3.183), that in front of the sanctuary was scarlet (*War* 5.212f.). He did not intend to make a distinction, but rather used one word in one work, another in another. Similarly the priests' sash have crimson in *Antiq.* 3.154, while the high priest's sash has scarlet in *War* 5.232, though the sashes were the same (*Antiq.* 3.159). Cf. also *War* 6.390 with *Antiq.* 3.113, 124; *Antiq.* 4.80 with LXX Num. 19.6.

9. Yadin, *The Finds*, discussion pp. 182f.; the Appendix by Abrahams and Edelstein, p. 279; plates 58, 59. A colour photograph also appears in Yadin, *Bar Kokhba*, ET 1971, p. 83.

10. In an informative article Ziderman explains the process by which Tyrian purple was produced and also offers comments on the biblical colours ('Seashells and Ancient Purple Dyeing', *BA* 53, 1990, pp. 98–101). He proposes that they were blue-purple, red-purple and crimson (bluish red). Josephus' three terms in *Antiq.* 3.154 are *phoinix* (crimson),

porphura (Tyrian purple, a bluish purple) and *hyakinthos* (hyacinth blue). Thus it is possible that all three colours in the priests' sashes contained blue and that none was bright red. I am not sure, however, that the terms tell us precisely what the colours were. First- century Jews could make a wider range of reds than Ziderman takes into account, and it is possible that the reddish colour was brighter and less blue than crimson is. See Abrahams and Edelstein in Yadin, *The Finds*, pp. 278f.

11. Yadin, *The Finds*, chs 10 (on dyeing wool) and 12 (on linen fabric).

12. Yadin, *The Finds*, pp. 252, 254.

13. Yadin, *The Finds*, pp. 170, 204 and n. 1, 254, 262. The child's linen shirt had a band that was not decorated, which shows 'the distinct desire to avoid mixing of diverse kinds', while imitating the pattern (p. 257).

14. *JLJM*, p. 37.

15. Haran, col. 1068.

16.Ex. 28.4–39; 39.2–26; Ben Sira 45.7–12; *War* 5.231–7; *Antiq.* 3.159–78.

17. The *Enc. Jud.* depicts the ephod as a kind of skirt, open in the centre, but covering the buttocks, hips and thighs.

18. The word 'linen' does not occur, but *pilûsîn* is linen from Pelusium.

19. Haran, col. 1068.

7. Sacrifices

1. In his article on Sacrifice in the *Encyclopaedia Judaica*, Aaron Rothkoff correctly states that 'most of the discussion in the Mishnah and Talmud is post-Temple and is therefore largely academic'. But he regards *Tamid* and *Zevahim* 5 as giving good information about second temple practice (*Enc. Jud.* 14, col. 607). This distinction seems basically correct; see further nn. 6 and 16 below.

2. See also Josephus' description of a private burnt offering, *Antiq.* 3.225–7, quoted below. On whether all the parts were washed, or only the inwards and legs, see Thackeray's notes in the LCL.

3. See Jean-Louis Durand, 'Greek Animals: Toward a Topology of Edible Bodies', Detienne and Vernant (eds), *The Cuisine of Sacrifice among the Greeks*, pp. 87–118.

4. The word 'holocaust' is derived from the Greek *holokautōma* or *holokautōsis*, 'whole-burnt offering'.

5. The rabbinic view was that an ordinary Israelite, if pure, could slaughter any of the sacrificial animals (*Zevahim* 3.1). I offer a speculative explanation of Philo's view below, n. 14.

6. The Mishnah is of the view that laymen were required to enter the Court of the Priests in order to slaughter, wave (the breast of a shared offering) and lay hands on the head of the victim (*Kelim* 1.8). They laid on hands at the same spot they slaughtered (*Menahot* 9.8). According to one opinion in *Middot* 2.6, the Priests' Court stood 2 cubits (1.25 metres, 3 feet 9 inches) above the Israelites' Court (though there were other opinions). The Mishnaic rabbis also thought that the animals were slaughtered by being tied to one of twenty-four rings to the north of the altar (arranged either in four rows, one opinion, or six rows, another: *Middot* 3.5). These physical arrangements would require a lay person to enter the Priests' Court (by a staircase) in order to participate in slaughtering the sacrificial victim; thus the view that they did so, despite Num. 18.3, which forbade even Levites to come near the altar. In the actual temple, laymen could reach across the parapet, and the Priests' Court was not so much higher than the Israelites' Court that this would have been impossible.

7. The Septuagintal word for 'guilt offering' is *plemmeleia*, which Josephus uses in other contexts, but never to refer to a sacrifice.

8. In ch. 9 we shall see that the Mishnaic, and presumably Pharisaic interpretation of tithes was slightly less expensive than Josephus'. With regard to the added fifth, however, the Mishnah adds a penalty if the person who owes it attempts to reduce the amount by swearing falsely: *Bava Qamma* 9.7.

9. Mazar, *Mountain of the Lord*, p. 109.

10. Because of the wording of Lev. 5.6f., where 'guilt [offering]' appears, it might have been possible to construe the reduction from a quadruped to birds as applying also to guilt offerings. This is excluded, however, by Lev. 6.6 [Heb. 5.25]; Num. 5.8. The Mishnah (*Bava Qamma* 9.11), Philo and Josephus (in the passages cited in the text) agree that the guilt offering (or the 'sin offering' for an intentional transgression, as Josephus and Philo categorize it) had to be a ram.

11. It entered the manuscript tradition at *Antiq.* 3.219, where, however, 'relaxation' is to be preferred; a copyist knew the LXX.

12. Cf. the discussion of the priests' vestments in the Added Note to ch. 6.

13. According to the Pharisees and rabbis, a person who had immersed, but upon whom the sun had not yet set, was partially pure – not, however, pure enough to enter either the Women's Court or the Israelites' Court (*Kelim* 1.8). Thus even by rabbinic rules the couple would have to avoid sexual relations after sunset if they wanted to enter the temple the next day.

14. In the pagan world, money and position did not shield men from slaughtering animals with a knife: on the contrary, some priestly offices were a sign of worldly prestige and success, and people like Alexander the Great, Aristotle and Julius Caesar were expert and frequent sacrificers. (Alexander: above, p. 49; Aristotle: see Durand, 'Greek Animals', pp. 99f.). But a rich Diaspora Jew, like Philo, would have reason to slaughter only the annual Passover lamb. He might turn even that over to someone else, and he would do so if he feared that he could not do it well; animals were not supposed to suffer, but to die easily, from having the main arteries expertly slit. This may explain why Philo thought that the priests always cut the throat in Jerusalem; perhaps when he was a pilgrim a priest did it for him.

15. See Durand, 'Greek Animals', pp. 90–2.

16. I have at several points indicated my own and others' doubts that the Mishnaic rabbis offer accurate descriptions of the temple and its procedures. Partly they did not know. Partly, however, they did not intend to describe what actually happened. In the second and subsequent centuries they continued to discuss what *should* have been done. With regard to the daily burnt offering, however, we have no other source. Further, the main outline of *Tamid* must describe what happened, since it narrates things that had to be done (clean the altar, bring wood, etc.). One may doubt details of singing, praying, sounding trumpets, and some of the sequences; but, again, we know from other sources that the priests did offer blessings, that the Levites did sing, and so on. See also Rothkoff, n. 1 above.

17. According to *War* 6.299, priests entered 'the inner court of the temple by night, as their custom was in the discharge of their ministrations'. They could not have entered the temple complex at night, since the gates were kept closed. This passage supports the Mishnah's view that some slept over and started work in the interior just before sunrise. In *Apion* 2.105, however, Josephus states that priests entered 'in the morning, when the temple was opened . . ., and again at mid-day'. Possibly a shift entered in the morning and took over after the first sacrifice, while a new shift came on duty at mid-day, and completed the day's sacrifices; some of them slept over to prepare the altar before dawn.

18. The place of the scriptural passages and prayers mentioned in *Tamid* 5.1 is

uncertain. The Mishnah seems to put them at the time when the priests were in the Chamber of Hewn Stone, but the prayers are said to be 'with the people'. This part of the service was surely public, and I have repeated it at the end of the day.

19. A. Mazar, 'The Aqueducts of Jerusalem', *Jerusalem Revealed*, ed. Yadin, pp. 79–84. Joseph Patrich ('A Sadducean Halakha and the Jerusalem Aqueduct', *The Jerusalem Cathedra* 2 (ed. Levine), pp. 25–39) notes that the lower aqueduct passed through a grave area, which was permitted by the Sadducees and prohibited by the Pharisees (*Yadaim* 4.7). He finds it reasonable to think that Herod built it, but he also believes that the Pharisees dictated law to Herod. Thus he inclines to the view that it was built under John Hyrcanus I or Alexander Jannaeus. I think that the standard view, shared by Patrich, that a representative legislative body, the Sanhedrin, ruled Jewish Palestine, and that it was usually controlled by the Pharisees, is incorrect. The aqueduct, however, cannot be precisely dated: if it was not built in the heyday of the Hasmoneans, Herod would certainly have built it. Pilate also built an aqueduct, using some of the temple's money to do so (*War* 2.175–7).

8. *The Common People*

1. On the dominance of agriculture in Palestine, see Applebaum, 'Economic Life in Palestine', *CRINT* 1.2, pp. 631f.

2. For the theory that there were few sheep and goats in Palestine, because of rabbinic decree, see n. 33. For evidence to the contrary, in addition to the statements by Aristeas, Philo and Josephus, note also the requirements of the temple. There is a good discussion of the point by Applebaum, 'Economic Life', p. 655.

3. Pliny, *Natural History* 12.54 § 111–123. For balsam as the source of the famous balm, see John Bostock and H. T. Riley, *The Natural History of Pliny* III, London, 1885, p. 147. For problems with Pliny's discussion, see ibid., p. 149 n. 76; R. K. Harrison, 'Balm', *IDB* 1, p. 344. On Jericho as crown land, see below, p. 164.

4. According to G. A. Smith, tourists and pilgrims from Muslim countries have generally been favourably impressed by Judaea, while Europeans have not. See Smith, *Jerusalem* I, p. 297. He pointed out that Judaea never supported large timber trees; the soil was used for olives, grapes and figs (pp. 298–305).

5. There is a clear account, with excellent maps and illustrations, in Connolly, *Greece and Rome at War*, Appendix 2; on circumvallation, see pp. 292–4; on Jerusalem, see pp. 298–300.

6. Broshi, 'The Diet of Palestine in the Roman Period – Introductory Notes', *The Israel Museum Journal* 5, 1986, pp. 41–56, here p. 44.

7. Yadin, *The Finds from the Bar-Kokhba Period*, p. 169.

8. The Appendix on textiles by David H. Abrahams and Sidney M. Edelstein in Yadin's *Finds*, p. 279.

9. Yadin, *Finds*, p. 178.

10. For expertise in tailoring, see Yadin, *Finds*, p. 211 (though housewives could have been expert tailors); note also the weavers' 'signatures', p. 225 and plate 69.

11. Yadin, *Finds*, p. 170.

12. Yadin, *Finds*, pp. 207–9.

13. Yadin, *Finds*, p. 205.

14. Referring to classical Greece, Mary Houston wrote that 'on elderly men and on ceremonial occasions the tunic fell to the feet, but for younger men and manual workers it reached only to mid thigh' (*Ancient Greek, Roman and Byzantine Costume and Decoration*, p. 47). Apparently women's tunics fell to the feet (see the illustrations, pp. 32–6).

15. At each corner: see Yadin, *Finds*, p. 238.

16. For men's and women's mantles, Yadin, *Finds*, pp. 227–9. His generalization about colours seems a bit too broad; some of the women's mantles were quite light; see nos. 43, 46, 47 on table 17, p. 226.

17. Yadin, *Finds*, table 17, p. 226.

18. Egypt: M. C. C. Edgar, *Graeco-Egyptian Coffins, Masks and Portraits*, 1905. See Plate VII no. 33126 (1st century CE); Plate XXI nos. 33154 (3rd century CE) and 33155 (125–150 CE); Plate XXIX no. 33209 (1st or 2nd century); Plate XLV no. 33272 (sometime between 200 BCE and 200 CE!). I take the dates from Edgar's introduction, pp. vii-x, xvii. The art that adorned the synagogue at Dura-Europos, which had been recently completed when the city was destroyed in 256 CE, has been often published. See, for example, E. R. Goodenough, *Jewish Symbols in the Greco-Roman Period*, vols 9–11. On the date of the synagogue, see most conveniently Hopkins, *The Discovery of Dura-Europos*, pp. 140–77.

19. Notched bands have been found at Muraba'at, Dura-Europos, and Palmyra (Yadin, *Finds*, pp. 221–3); gammas have been found at Dura-Europos, Palmyra and Karanis in Egypt (p. 223). Notched bands disappear in the fourth century CE (p. 230).

20. Yadin points to five illustrations from Graeco-Egyptian coffins that have the same decoration that he discovered in the Judaean wilderness (listed above, n.18). On two of these the name survives: Sambathion and Herakleon. He argues somewhat indirectly that these are Jewish names. On p. 231 he indicates that he thinks that Christian artists who drew notched bands and gammas used 'older, illustrated, Jewish sources', which indicates that he understood these designs, at least at some period, to have been characteristically Jewish. The two names, however, leave the question open. Tcherikover (whom Yadin cites, *Finds*, p. 229 nn. 55, 56) stated that Sambathion was derived from 'sabbath', but that it came to be used by non-Jewish Egyptians who kept the sabbath. Herakleon is pagan (derived from Herakles), but came to be used by Jews as well. See Tcherikover and Fuks, *Corpus Papyrorum Judaicarum* I, pp. 29, 94–6.

21. Carcopino, *Daily Life in Ancient Rome*, pp. 176–80.

22. Ibid., p. 180.

23. Any picture book of the Graeco-Roman world will illustrate these remarks. There is a compact collection of hairstyles in Cynthia Thompson, 'Hairstyles, Head-coverings, and St Paul. Portraits from Roman Corinth', *BA* 51, June 1988, pp. 99–115. See also the artists' renditions of New Testament characters, based on surviving depictions of Jews and other first-century residents of the Near East, in Sanders and Woodrow, *People from the Bible*, pp. 117–74.

24. On the source of Josephus' geographical knowledge, see pp. 59f. above. The circumference of a city is not the sort of thing that one knows just because one lives there: he relied on expert information.

25. On 24 October 1988, the number of people outside the Lithuanian Cathedral was put at 20,000 by the *Independent* and 5,000 by the *International Herald Tribune*. Larger variations can also be found, especially when hostile groups estimate crowds (e.g. both the police and leaders of demonstrations).

26. Avi-Yonah in *CRINT* I.1, pp. 108–110. Avi-Yonah's calculations are based on accepting Josephus' account of how many troops he raised to fight the Romans (60,000) and on assuming that these men constituted 8% of the whole population; this yields a Jewish population of 750,000 in Galilee. One must suspect Josephus of exaggerating the size of his force, and we may also suppose that more than 8% of the population was considered fit to fight; it was a national emergency.

27. Jeremias (*Jerusalem*, p. 205) proposed 500,000 to 600,000 Jews in Palestine in the first century. Magen Broshi puts the total population of the country (Jews and Gentiles) at 1,000,000 at its peak (*c.* 600 CE). Two methods (study of the size of inhabited areas and estimate of wheat production) lead to the same result. See 'The Population of Western Palestine in the Roman-Byzantine Period', *BASOR* 236, 1979, pp. 1–10; 'Estimating the Population of Ancient Jerusalem', *BAR* 4, 1978, pp. 10–15.

28. Josephus wrote that at Passover the greatest number of sacrifices was offered, which need not require the largest number of pilgrims, but the general context seems to indicate that more people attended Passover than any other festival.

29. Mohamed Amin, *Pilgrimage to Mecca*, p. 21.

30. Amin, *Pilgrimage to Mecca*, p. 18.

31. The fact that there were more Muslims in the early twentieth century than Jews in the first century is not, I think, a significant factor; proximity and ease and safety of travel are more important.

32. The Theodotus inscription will be discussed below, pp. 176f.

33. There is a very helpful survey of foodstuff by Broshi, 'Diet of Palestine'. I have just a few reservations about it: (1) He includes eggs but otherwise leaves fowl out of account. For fowl as a festival but non-sacrificial meal, see the debate between the Hillelites and Shammaites in *Betsah* 1.3; cf. also the debate on fowl and cheese served together (*Hullin* 8.1). (2) In discussing sheep and goats, he gives too much weight to the rabbinic decree prohibiting raising 'small cattle' (*Bava Qamma* 7.7, Broshi, p. 48). The same decree prohibits raising fowls in Jerusalem. The temple, however, consumed tens of thousands of lambs each year and many more doves and pigeons. Here as elsewhere, rabbinic theory did not govern life, especially before 70. (See Applebaum, 'Economic Life in Palestine', *CRINT* 1.2., p. 655). (3) Broshi does not take account of the importance of shared sacrifices in providing occasional red meat for the laity.

34. According to Ex. 12.2, Passover falls in the first month of the year. By the first century, however, the common reckoning was that the Jewish year began in the autumn and that Passover fell in the seventh month. Philo noted the problem and explained that 'this month [of Passover] comes seventh . . . as judged by the cycle of the sun, but in importance it is first, and therefore is described as first in the sacred books' (*Spec. Laws* 2.151). In fact, different biblical authors had different views about whether the year began in the spring or autumn. See Lev. 23.5, 23 (first month in spring, seventh in autumn); Ex. 23.16; 34.22 (first month in autumn). Philo's discussion indicates that in his day the second view (first month in autumn) had prevailed. Josephus conflates the biblical evidence in another way, and his view may reflect the official views of the temple priesthood: Nisan (in the spring) begins the year for festivals and 'for everything relating to divine worship', while 'for selling and buying and other ordinary affairs' 'the ancient order' – that the year began in the autumn – was maintained (*Antiq.* 1.81). Many modern scholars think that this is correct, and that the older system was that the year began in the autumn. The present Jewish calendar begins in the autumn.

35. For exceptions, see below, under the Essenes.

36. We noted above that the early Biblical name for the month of Passover was 'spring', Aviv. In exile in Babylonia, the Jews picked up the name Nisan from the Babylonian Nissanu, the first month of the year. For Nisan as the *first* month, see Esth. 3.7; I Esdras 5.6; *Antiq.* 3.248; 11.109; cf. n. 34 above. For use of the name Nisan, see also Neh. 2.1; Add. Esth. 1.1; *Antiq.* 1.81; 2.311; 3.201. See Wiesenberg, 'Nisan', *Enc. Jud.* 12, cols. 1175f.

37. See, for example, Ernst Kutsch, 'Passover. Critical View', *Enc. Jud.* 13, cols. 169–72.

38. Ex. 12.5: a *seh* from the sheep or goats. The Hebrew *seh* and the Greek *probaton*, which often translates it, can be either a lamb or a kid; similarly *tso'n* in 12.21. According to Deut. 16.2, however, the animal could be either from the flock or herd; that is, it could be a lamb, a kid or a bullock. These traditions are apparently conflated in II Chron. 35.7, according to which king Josiah contributed as Passover offerings 30,000 lambs and kids and 3,000 bullocks. For the most part people offered lambs, which were more plentiful and thus cheaper. (There were more lambs than kids, because sheep have more uses than goats.)

39. *Antiq.* 2.317. Thackeray thought that 2.317 (eight days) contradicts 3.248f. (seven days), but in the first passage Josephus does not distinguish Passover from Unleavened Bread. See also *Antiq.* 9.271: 'When the festival of Unleavened Bread came round, they sacrificed the *Phaska*, as it is called, and offered the other sacrifices for seven days': the Passover lamb one day, other sacrifices seven days, all called 'Unleavened Bread'. In *War* 5.100 he even calls the 14th of Xanthicus (=Nisan) 'the day of unleavened bread'. In other passages, however, Passover is the dominant term and includes Unleavened Bread (e.g. *Antiq.* 17.213). Note *Antiq.* 18.29: 'When the Festival of Unleavened Bread, which we call Passover, was going on . . .'. I am grateful to Fabian Udoh for clarifying Josephus' usage.

40. This construes *kekatharmenon* as middle rather than passive. Philo probably does not have in mind the priestly sprinkling that removed corpse impurity: see the next note.

41. *JLJM*, pp. 263–70. See especially, *Spec. Laws* 1.261; 3.205f.

42. *Spec. Laws* 2.145; so also *Moses* 2.224.

43. Alan Mendelson, *Philo's Jewish Identity*, p. 64. Similarly Goodenough, *By Light, Light*, pp. 261f. ('as far as we know'). Heinemann stated that Philo's meaning, 'that for the Passover sacrifice the laity take over *all* the functions of the priests', 'is doubtless false'. Philo (according to Heinemann) simply followed Ex. 12.24, which says that the Passover rite described there (no priests, no temple) is 'perpetual'. Philo took this to mean that it continued to be performed as it had been the first time, without priests (*Philons griechische und jüdische Bildung*, pp. 33f.). Heinemann does not explain how Philo could hold such a false view while knowing that actual practice was different.

44. *JLJM*, pp. 263–70. On Philo's view of the mixture of ashes and water, see immediately below and further p. 252.

45. Juster (*Les Juifs dans l'empire romain* I, p. 357 n. 1) thought that some Jews ate the Passover lamb in the Diaspora during the days of the temple, the same view as taken here, but his evidence is not completely convincing. He cited parallels to *Betsah* 23a, which do not quite say that someone sacrificed the Passover lamb outside of Jerusalem, and *Antiq.* 2.312f., where Josephus wrote that 'we keep this sacrifice in the same customary manner' as in the Exodus story. This probably takes Josephus' phrase *kata to ethos houtōs thuomen* too literally. There has been academic discussion of an analogous legal problem, whether or not some Jews continued to sacrifice after the destruction of the temple. See, for example, Alexander Guttmann, 'The End of the Jewish Sacrificial Cult', *HUCA* 38, 1967, pp. 137–48. He argues that the community sacrifices ceased entirely but that some people continued private sacrifices. For a negative opinion on both possibilities, see *HJP* 1, pp. 522f.

46. Elsewhere Josephus wrote that Passover began on the fourteenth of Xanthicus (*Antiq.* 2.311; 3.248), which simply equates Xanthicus with Nisan.

47. We shall see in ch. 9 that the new barley was offered during Unleavened Bread; thus the new grain at Weeks was probably wheat.

48. 'Young males from the herd' (Num. 29.13) may be either oxen or bulls.

49. Rabbinic literature contains references to an occasion when an ordinary priest, not a high priest, was pelted with citrons, because he did not carry out a rite correctly. (The rite is somewhat obscure, but it usually goes under the name of the 'water libation'.) The Mishnah (*Sukkah* 4.9; *Yoma* 2.5) clearly indicates that the priest in question was an ordinary priest, but he is not otherwise identified. According to the Tosefta, he was a Boethusian (*T. Sukkah* 3.16), according to the Babylonian Talmud he was a Sadducee (*Sukkah* 48b near end). That is, in the later rabbinic sources there was an attempt to make the priest an aristocratic priest. Scholars generally conflate all these passages, though they drop the point that the priest who performed the water libation was an ordinary priest. Actually, we are told, he was the Saducean high priest Jannaeus, and the reason the people, led by the Pharisees, attacked him was that he broke one of their more minor rules. This is true even of Le Moyne, though he carefully laid out the evidence (*Les Sadducéens*, pp. 283–9) and was aware of the chronological sequence: Josephus, Mishnah, Tosefta, Babylonian Talmud. I do not doubt that the rabbis who discussed pelting with citrons remembered, more-or-less accurately, the occasion when the crowd attacked Jannaeus. That does not mean, however, that we can derive independent information about the attack on Jannaeus from the Babylonian Talmud (*c.* sixth century), where it departs from its sources (the Mishnah and Tosefta) and conclude that an event just prior to a serious civil war had as its basis a detail about pouring water. Rabbinic literature tries to reduce history to a question of legal detail. Josephus' story, by contrast, indicates that the people were seriously opposed to Jannaeus; they not only pelted him, they questioned his ancestry. Very serious bloodshed was to follow.

50. For the range of dates, see Booths in the chart above, p. 132; on which month is first and which seventh, see n. 34 above.

51. Some voluntary fasts involved only abstention from food, but 'affliction' implies more than this; see *JLJM*, pp. 81–3.

52. On the changes of clothing, a complicated topic, see the Added Note on Priestly Vestments, pp. 100–102.

53. Rhoads, *Israel in Revolution*, p. 33.

9. *Tithes and Taxes*

1. *JLJM*, pp. 44f. and notes.

2. See the summary in Danby, *The Mishnah*, p. 66 n. 9; 73 n. 6.

3. These two passages say that the consequence of the thefts was that some of the ordinary priests starved. Puzzling over this, I previously suggested that possibly the priests interpreted the biblical passages that forbid them to have 'any portion' as meaning that they could eat *only* sacrifices, tithes and other holy food (*JLJM*, pp. 24–6). Hyam Maccoby has persuaded me that this was not the reason for their starving, since there was good precedent for eating forbidden food to avoid starvation (I Sam. 21.1–6). He proposes instead that the priests in Josephus' stories were simply destitute; they had no money and were forced to rely entirely on the temple dues. The stories are still puzzling, since (as I observed before) one would expect that the populace would have given more food to keep priests from starving.

4. So Ex. 13.13; 34.20. This is accepted as standard in Mishnah *Bekhorot*. Num. 18.15f., however, specifies a redemption price of five shekels. Josephus (*Antiq.* 4.71) states the rules of 1½ shekels for impure animals and 5 shekels for a son. Philo also does not distinguish the ass from other impure animals (*Spec. Laws* 1.135).

5. This was the understanding in the Greek-speaking world: LXX Num. 18.15; Philo, *Spec. Laws* 1.135, specifying 'horses, asses and camels'.

6. The conclusion is assumed in *Bekhorot* 1, but the reasoning is not given. The exegetical argument appears in *Sifre Num.* 118: 'I might have thought that one redeems the rest of the impure beasts . . ., but Scripture teaches, "redeem an ass with a lamb" (Ex. 13.13).' It seems to me intrinsically likely that in this case exegesis led to the rabbinic halakhah.

7. Thackeray, following the French translator Weill, proposes that Josephus derived the technique that he describes from the tradition found in *Menahot* 6.4 (LCL, note to *Antiq.* 3.251). *Menahot*, however, deals not with the first measure or sheaf of grain, but rather with meal offerings that accompany or substitute for an animal sacrifice. For the present topic, grain or dough at Passover, see *Hallah* 1.1f.

8. See Yadin, *Temple Scroll* I, pp. 102f.

9. So also Maccoby, *Early Rabbinic Writings*, pp. 68f.

10. Some scholars find a reference to heave offering in the repetition of *aparchē*, 'first fruits', in *Spec. Laws* 1.132–4, 141. See *JLJM*, p. 292 and notes.

11. On the terminology and related problems, see *JLJM*, pp. 289–94 and p. 365 n. 19.

12. Note their exegetical difficulty in *Terumot* 3.7.

13. *JLJM*, p. 291.

14. A drachma was approximately equivalent to a denarius, and a denarius serves as a daily wage in Matt. 20.2. For a drachma a day, see also Tobit 5.14. The sporadic evidence indicates that there was a range of wages, but one drachma or denarius is as good a figure as any. See the evidence assembled by Daniel Sperber, 'Costs of Living in Roman Palestine', *JESHO* 8, 1965, pp. 248–71.

15. On the identification of this sum as the temple tax, see *JLJM*, p. 293.

16. *JLJM*, pp. 49–51; 297–9. William Horbury ('The Temple tax', *Jesus and the Politics of his Day*, pp. 265–86) argues that the temple tax was such a late innovation that it was still being disputed in Jesus' day, and that Jesus allied himself with its critics, such as the Qumran community. This is an interesting argument, though I think that it is incorrect. The evidence cited in the text indicates that Jews virtually without exception paid the temple tax. I offer a few quick points about Horbury's argument: (1) The temple tax was based on a conflation of Neh. 10.32 [Heb. 10.33], which requires an annual tax of one-third shekel, and the half-shekel tax required at a time of census by Ex. 30.11–16. This is pretty solid biblical support. Biblical passages on such topics were routinely conflated, and I do not see how the first-century reader could have regarded this tax as ill supported by the Bible. (2) Horbury is incorrect in saying that the tax is not referred to in *Aristeas*; see the previous note. (3) Horbury proposes that only Pharisees supported the temple tax, but Josephus, Philo and Vespasian all assumed that every adult male Jew in the world paid it. (4) A different interpretation at Qumran does not add up to much: the Qumran community differed from the mass of the populace on almost every point touching the temple and the priesthood. (5) If it is true that the priests thought that they should be exempt from the temple tax, as it probably is, this does not mean that there was resistance to the tax in other quarters. The priests were a special case.

Horbury's argument has been used for a different purpose by Horsley, who proposes that Jesus thought that any and all taxation 'in the name of God was illegitimate' (Horsley, *Spiral of Violence*, pp. 281f.). He cites Horbury among others as agreeing ('so also', n. 53 on p. 346). But Horbury wrote nothing of the sort, nor did the others whom Horsley cites. Horsley further proposes that the view that all the Jewish taxes were illegitimate was a common and popular view in first-century Jewish Palestine (pp. 281–3), which requires drastic treatment of the evidence.

17. Applebaum, 'Economic Life in Palestine', *CRINT* I.2, pp. 661f.

18. Applebaum, p. 665, referring to Herod's will (*Antiq.* 17.317–24), which actually indicates that his annual income as over 960 talents.

19. Richard Horsley, *Jesus and the Spiral of Violence*, p. 237. Further page numbers are given in the text.

20. Horsley and Hanson, *Bandits, Prophets and Messiahs*, pp. 60f.

21. I shall not discuss loans, mortgages, interest and foreclosure, except to say that we have very little direct evidence about interest and foreclosure, and that the indirect evidence is difficult to interpret. I believe that it is premature to offer such generalizations.

22. Compare Horsley, *Spiral*, p. 288, 'all the various tithes'.

23. Borg, *New Vision*, pp. 84f.

24. Grant, *Economic Background*, n. 3 to p. 90, on p. 91. The statement that the Jews should pay Hyrcanus and his sons a tithe was simply Caesar's confirmation that the high priest could continue to collect the tithe; the context is assurance that Hyrcanus' previous rights will be respected.

25. Cf. Horsley, *Bandits*, pp. 56f.: in 6 CE the chief priests 'no longer needed to maintain military forces and a complete political administration of an independent state' out of the tithes.

26. Applebaum, 'Economic Life', p. 661.

27. Grant, p. 89.

28. The discussion by Stern ('The Province of Judaea', *CRINT* I.1, p. 334f.) assumes that Rome imposed these special requirements (the *angaria*) throughout the period. He does not refer to Caesar's remission of them, and the evidence that he cites is not convincing. For example, the setting of Matt. 5.41 was not Roman Judaea; if Jesus said it, the setting was Antipas' Galilee.

29. Rostovtzeff, *The Social and Economic History of the Roman Empire*, 1926, pp. 461f.; 2nd ed., I, pp. 514f. It is unfortunate that Grant's study was published the same year as Rostovtzeff's great work. I am sure that Grant would have read it, and this would have prevented some of the errors of subsequent New Testament scholars.

30. Pilate's aqueduct: *War* 2.175–7; Florus' confiscation: *War* 2.293f. The commentators note that, according to 2.403, Judaea was behind in its payment of tribute, and Florus may only have been making good the deficit.

31. Applebaum, pp. 661f.

32. E.g. Stern, 'Province of Judaea', p. 332; *HJP* I, p. 372.

33. Cf. Stern, 'Province of Judaea', pp. 330f.

34. Horsley, *Spiral*, p. 281. He seems to be thinking here of the difference in tithing laws between Deuteronomy on the one hand and Leviticus, Numbers and Nehemiah on the other.

35. Horsley goes much further than this. Once upon a time, ancestral land had supported all the descendants of a family (*Spiral*, p. 232). This would mean that no family ever produced more than one heir.

36. Applebaum, p. 678.

37. *HJP* I, pp. 298–300, 302.

38. Applebaum, 'Economic Life', pp. 665, 667–9. On Caesarea, see *Antiq.* 15.331–41.

39. Applebaum, pp. 666f.

40. Applebaum, p. 666.

41. Applebaum, p. 637.

42. Applebaum, p. 691. His reference to Stern, 'Province of Judaea', pp. 366–72, is not to the point.

43. So, for example, Horsley and Hanson, *Bandits*, pp. 48–87.

44. *War* 1.311–13, pp. 37f. above.

45. See pp. 6f and, more fully, pp. 385, 409 below.

46. *JSJ*, p. 240.

47. Above, pp. 35f., 40.

48. *War* 2.232–44, discussed more fully in ch. 15.

49. 'Province of Judaea', p. 331.

50. *HJP* I, p. 402.

51. Caesar gave Hyrcanus Joppa, a valuable and largely non-Jewish port city, allowed him to tax the residents, and charged him tribute (*Antiq.* 14.205f.). Such arrangements with regard to crown lands presumably existed between the emperor and later Jewish rulers.

52. Stern, 'Province of Judaea', p. 332. I must confess that I am dubious about the produce tax in *Antiq.* 14.203, which is missing from the Latin. The wording is extremely puzzling, both in grammar and content. *kai hina* does not follow grammatically. It is most strange that 'they', the Jews, should be required to hand over produce 'in the second year at Sidon', since this seems to be a direct tax on the farmers, not mediated through Hyrcanus. Ordinarily, as we noted, Rome required the local ruler to pay tribute (p. 162 above). Here Caesar requires the Jews to pay Rome (i.e., the troops in Syria) directly.

53. See n. 14.

54. *HJP* I, p. 373.

55. See Stern, 'Province of Judaea', p. 332.

10. *The Priests and Levites Outside the Temple*

1. Jeremias, *Jerusalem*, p. 194 n. 146; Freyne, *Galilee from Alexander the Great to Hadrian*, p. 165.

2. Miller shows the evidence to be indecisive: *Studies in the History and Traditions of Sepphoris*.

3. Vermes, *Perspectives*, p. 185.

4. See Rebecca Gray, *Prophetic Figures in Late Second Temple Jewish Palestine: The Evidence from Jospehus*, Oxford 1992.

5. *HJP* II, p. 324 ('already complete'); *JPJC* II.1, p. 313 ('fully completed').

6. *Jerusalem*, pp. 234. He believed that the scribes were named in rabbinic literature, and so he could count them; see below.

7. Jeremias, p. 236. The words omitted in this quotation are citations from Billerbeck.

8. Rabbinic legal material routinely puts 'scribal' rulings below those of the Bible. Transgression of a scribal prohibition brings no penalty (in the rabbis' view) and does not require atonement. For example, people who are impure according to the 'words of torah' are guilty if they enter the temple, while those who are impure according to the 'words of the scribes' are not (*Parah* 11.4f.). See *JLJM*, ch. II.

9. Jeremias, p. 237.

10. Jeremias, p. 254.

11. I write 'generally' because there has to be a point at which one stops looking up passages, none of which says what is claimed.

12. Jeremias, pp. 233–5.

13. Jeremias, pp. 254f.

14. Jeremias, pp. 379f.

15. Maccoby, *Revolution in Judaea*, p. 61.

16. Maccoby, pp. 61f.

17. Rajak, *Josephus*, p. 29.
18. Below, pp. 462f.
19. Rajak, *Josephus*, p. 19.
20. Deissmann, *Light from the Ancient East*, pp. 439–41.
21. Hengel, *Between Jesus and Paul*, pp. 16–18.
22. See *HJP* II, pp. 322–36, on the work of 'Torah scholars', called first 'scribes' then 'Rabbis'; these Torah scholars are named, using rabbinic literature (pp. 356–80). In the original ET of Schürer (*JPJC* II.1), the relevant pages are 313–28 ('scribism') and 351–79 (the names of the 'scribes'). I have not tried to discover who invented the curious practice of writing down rabbis' names and then saying that we know who 'the scribes' were.
23. Pages 52f. above.
24. See the stories in Josephus about Essene and unclassified teachers who were probably Pharisees: *War* 1.78–80; 1.648–50; *Antiq.* 13.311–13.
25. The statement that, whoever held a position, he had to follow Pharisaic views, raises a different issue, discussed in ch. 18. Here the subject is who held the offices.
26. See more fully chs 15, 21.
27. Rajak, p. 30: Josephus' early education was 'broadly Pharisaic'.
28. See ch. 6 n. 1 above, on the high priest appointed by the Zealots.
29. Yadin, *Bar-Kokhba*, ch. 16.
30. Yadin, *Bar-Kokhba*, pp. 229f. For the history of this scribal practice, see Naphtali Lewis, *The Documents from the Bar Kokhba Period*, pp. 6–11.
31. Yadin, *Bar-Kokhba*, p. 236.
32. It is possible that Ben Sira was a priest: Stern, 'Aspects of Jewish Society: the Priesthood and other Classes', *CRINT* I.2, pp. 590f.
33. *HJP* II, pp. 322–5. Ben Sira is depicted as standing near the beginning of the transfer of power to the laity.
34. Jeremias, *Proclamation*, p. 145.
35. Avigad, *Jerusalem*, pp. 130f.
36. Bamberger, 'Money-Changer', *IDB* III, pp. 435f., here p. 435.
37. Maccoby, *Revolution in Judaea*, p. 56.
38. Rajak, *Josephus*, p. 22.
39. This accusation does not appear in all manuscripts. See Charles' translation in *POT* p. 313, note to 14.6.
40. Nickelsburg (*Faith and Piety*, p. 68) dates them to 'the Hellenistic period'.
41. Josephus wrote that Alexander and his concubines were feasting 'in a conspicuous place'. That it was a balcony is my own contribution to the story.
42. See *JLJM*, pp. 209–13.
43. I leave aside here examples of marriages between closely related Herodians, all of which fell (barely) within the letter of the biblical law. The Herodians were not priests, but it is possible that some priestly families intermarried in the same way.
44. See *JSJ*, pp. 66f. and notes. I erred in writing that Mark 11.17 is the only reference in the New Testament that accuses the priests themselves of dishonesty. Even it does not accuse them of being directly dishonest (though indirect dishonesty is implied).
45. This is based on taking the phrase 'seekers of smooth things' to refer to the Pharisees.
46. Gray, 'The Psalms of Solomon', *POT*, p. 628.
47. On Josephus' view of government and priests, see below, pp. 488f. and n. 83.
48. The passage is quoted above, p. 92.

49. Lane Fox, *Alexander the Great*, pp. 249, 454.

50. See ch. 13 n. 28.

11. *Observing the Law of God I*

1. See Gordon, 'From Republic to Principate: priesthood, religion and ideology', *Pagan Priests*, ed. Beard and North, p. 193.

2. Smith, 'The Dead Sea Sect'.

3. E.g. *T. Yom ha-Kippurim* 4[5].5; Mekilta *Bahodesh* 7 (Lauterbach, vol. II, pp. 249–51). See *P&PJ* pp. 157–60; 179.

4. The division of five commandments governing behaviour towards God and five governing behaviour towards other humans is, of course, schematic. Philo proceeded to put honour of father and mother (the fifth commandment) on the borderline, since it includes honour of God the Father (*Heir* 171). He and others also knew that the sabbath commandment (no. four) benefits people, animals and the land.

5. 'Piety' is *eusebeia*; 'holiness' *hosiotēs*; 'love of humanity' *philanthrōpia*; 'justice' *dikaiosynē*.

6. The rabbis interpreted the 'stranger' of Lev. 19.34 ('love the stranger as yourself') to mean 'proselyte', which is the commonest meaning of *ger* in rabbinic Hebrew. See *Sifra Qedoshim* pereq 8. (There are various attitudes towards Gentiles in rabbinic literature, on the whole rather favourable, except in the periods shortly after the two revolts. See *P&PJ*, pp. 206–12.) Further, the LXX translates *ger* as 'proselyte' in Lev. 19.34. The use of the term *philanthrōpia* in the Greek-writing authors, however, reveals that many Jews derived the commandment to love all humans – not just Jews and proselytes – from the Bible.

7. For similar passages in Josephus, using alternative terms to represent the two tables, see *Antiq.* 7.356, 374, 384; 8.280, 300, 394; 9.236. I am indebted to Rebecca Gray for these passages.

8. Both Philo and Josephus give longer virtue lists. Our present concern is only with the division between duty to God and duty to other humans. While *eusebeia* and *dikaiosynē* are the most frequent two terms in this context, there are others, some of which appear in the passages just cited. *Hosiotēs* ('holiness') often accompanies *eusebeia* and sometimes replaces it. *Theosebeia*, 'fear of God' is a third possibility. *Philanthrōpia* similarly accompanies or replaces *dikaiosynē*. 'Self-control' (*egkrateia*) is frequent in Philo; in one instance it is paired with *eusebeia* (*Spec. Laws* 1.193) and in one with *theosebeia* (*Moses* 1.303). There is an interesting three-fold categorization in *Spec. Laws* 4.97: self-restraint, love of other humans, piety towards God. In view of Philo's strong attack on passion and desire (e.g. *Spec. Laws* 4.79–99), it is surprising that he does not give the three-fold formula more often; for him, virtue began with self-control. This view, which could be called either 'Stoic' or 'Platonic', is seen also in *Arist.* 277f. (people lack self-control, yearn for pleasure, and therefore fall into injustice; a person who has self-control will treat others with justice). Aristobulus also summarized the law with the three-fold formula *eusebeia*, *dikaiosynē* and *egkrateia* (Aristobulus Fragment 4 (13.12.8); *OTP* II, p. 841, where 13.13 is a typographical error). The relative frequency of the two-fold formula, with one term indicating behaviour towards other humans and the other behaviour towards God, shows how firmly fixed the division of the law into two tables was.

9. This was pointed out many years ago by Lake, *Beginnings* V, p. 207, but not often heeded.

10. See e.g. Simon, *Verus Israel*, pp. 163–6.

11. E.g. Rhoads, *Israel in Revolution*, p. 34.

12. *JLJM*, pp. 71f. and notes.

13. *JLJM*, pp. 72–7.

14. A few people doubt that synagogues existed in Palestine before 70. I pointed out some of the errors in these arguments in *JLJM*, nn. 28 and 29, pp. 341–3. Below we shall see the positive evidence that shows that synagogues were common.

15. For a longer list of names of the buildings that we usually call synagogues, see Levine, 'The Second Temple Synagogue: the Formative Years', *The Synagogue in Late Antiquity*, ed. Levine, p. 13.

16. Page 50 above.

17. Ma'oz, 'The Synagogue of Gamla and the Typology of Second-Temple Synagogues', *Ancient Synagogues Revealed*, ed. Levine, pp. 35–41, quotations from p. 41. The estimates of seating capacity, however, are mine, not Ma'oz's.

18. Ma'oz, p. 40; cf. G. Foerster, 'The Synagogues at Masada and Herodium', pp. 24–9 in the same volume.

19. On Howard Kee's recent attempt to re-date the Theodotus inscription and to raise doubts about the existence of first-century synagogues in Palestine ('The Transformation of the Synagogue after 70 CE', *NTS* 36, 1990, pp. 1–24), see *JLJM*, nn. 28 and 29, pp. 341–3.

20. Hanfmann, 'The Ninth Campaign at Sardis (1966)', *BASOR* 187, October 1967, p. 38.

21. See Fiensy, *Prayers Alleged to Be Jewish*. He proposes a date between 150 and 300 CE (pp. 220–28).

22. Quoted from Heinemann, *Prayer in the Talmud*, pp. 26–9. A genizah is a storeroom in which were put texts which were no longer usable but which contained the name of God and therefore could not be destroyed. The Cairo Genizah, found in the nineteenth century, contained about a quarter of a million documents.

23. Vermes here translates *tsidqôt* 'righteousness', but 'mercy' is more likely; see the next note.

24. Vermes translates 'by the righteousness of God' (*bᵉtsidqat'el*). *Tsedaqah* in this hymn is parallel with *ḥasidim*, 'mercy', and is best translated in the same way. The lines quoted are 1QS 10.11f., 16; 11.2f., 11f. See Vermes, *DSSE*, 3rd ed., pp. 76–80.

25. 1QH 7.26–31; ET *DSSE³*, p. 186.

26. *Apion* 2.196f. (quoted below, p. 277), the Eighteen Benedictions, and many of the individual prayers scattered throughout the literature.

27. *DJD* VII, pp. 105–136. The text was edited by Maurice Baillet and published in 1982. It was not, however, a complete surprise that there were fixed prayers at Qumran. See Talmon, 'The Emergence of institutionalized Prayer in Israel in the Light of the Qumrân Literature'.

28. Since communal prayer is not biblical, and since private prayer was well established, the origin of praying together in a congregation requires explanation. See, for example, Talmon, 'The Emergence of institutionalized Prayer'. In a private communication, Rabbi Solomon Bernards has suggested that the origin of communal prayer is the priestly prayer in the temple referred to in *Tamid* 5.1. This was imitated by lay Israelites, who (according to rabbinic sources) divided themselves into twenty-four courses, represented by delegates who either went to Jerusalem with the priestly course or who stayed at home and prayed together at the times fixed by the temple. (On the courses of laymen, the *'anshê ma'amad*, see Moore, *Judaism* II, pp. 12f.) The large and unanswered question is whether priestly prayers in the temple preceded the practice of praying in 'houses of prayer', which probably began in the Diaspora, not Palestine. Only if the dates could be settled – which seems impossible – could we begin to establish the lines of influence.

29. Levine, 'The Second Temple Synagogue', p. 22.

30. Levine (ibid., pp. 15–23) thinks that prayer was part of services in Diaspora synagogues but not in Jerusalem synagogues. He leaves open the question of synagogal prayer in the rest of Palestine.

31. *Life* 294f.; above, p. 199.

32. Whittaker, *Jews and Christians: Graeco-Roman Views*, pp. 63–73.

33. On festival days, semi-sabbaths, see *JLJM*, pp, 9–13.

34. This raises the question of Gentile 'God-fearers' and what parts of the Jewish law, if any, they accepted. Were some sympathetic but completely non-observant? Did some accept the sabbath but not monotheism? These difficult questions lie outside the scope of our study, though we shall see below the theology that could make room for 'righteous Gentiles'. On God-fearers, see A. T. Kraabel, 'Synagoga Caeca', *'To See Ourselves as Others See Us'*, ed. Neusner and Frerichs, pp. 219–46; J. Reynolds and R. Tannenbaum, *Jews and Godfearers at Aphrodisias*, esp. p. 88. There is a very helpful exchange of views in the *Biblical Archaeology Review*, including a bibliography: Robert S. MacLennan and A. Thomas Kraabel, 'The God-Fearers – a Literary and Theological Invention', *BAR* 12 (5, 1986), pp. 46–57; Louis Feldman, 'The Omni-Presence of the God-Fearers', *BAR* 12 (5, 1986), pp. 58–69. Feldman hopes soon to complete a major study, which is much needed.

35. Simon, *Verus Israel*, p. 325; cf. p. 375.

36. On conscription, see further *Antiq.* 14.228, 232, 237.

37. Unfortunately it is not possible to be sure whether this means the right to send money to Jerusalem or the right to contribute money for local observance of the festivals. 'Make offerings for their sacrifices' (14.227) might conceivably mean either. I am inclined to think that these passages refer to permission to remit the temple tax to Jerusalem, a right that was highly prized. Philo attributes it to Augustus (*Embassy* 156f.; 291; 311–16). It had, however, been exercised earlier (*Arist.* 34, 40 and 42). See *JLJM*, pp. 293f.

38. Cited by Marcus in a note to *Antiq.* 14.215 (LCL).

12. *Observing the Law of God II*

1. See Stern, *Greek and Latin Authors on Jews and Judaism* I, pp. 2–4 (Herodotus). For later passages, see 'circumcision' in the index (vol. III).

2. Outsiders: Stern, vol. I, pp. 325 (Horace), 436 (Persius), 441 (Petronius' *Satyricon*) and elsewhere. Insiders: see immediately below.

3. *HJP* I, pp. 537–40; III, p. 123. It appears that Hadrian forbade circumcision prior to the second revolt, and that the ban was one of its causes.

4. Mendelson, *Philo's Jewish Identity*, p.57.

5. Philo, *Migration* 89–93. What is uncertain is whether the allegorizers had actually abandoned circumcision (and sabbath and festivals), or whether Philo feared that their theorizing tended in this direction: 'It is true that receiving circumcision does indeed portray the excision of pleasure and all passions . . .: but let us not on this account repeal the law laid down for circumcising' (92).

6. See Whittaker, *Jews and Christians: Graeco-Roman Views*, pp. 73–80.

7. See Stern, *Greek and Latin Authors* II, p. 665. The saying, like many witticisms, cannot be regarded as belonging beyond question to its supposed author. Macrobius lived in the fifth century CE, and the setting that he gave for Augustus' saying is not correct: he stated that when Herod had the babes of Bethlehem slaughtered (Matt. 2.16), one of his own sons was among them. Conceivably, of course, Augustus really did make the statement about Herod's execution of his own sons, but Macrobius did not know the

actual context. Macrobius wrote in Latin, but the saying is cleverer in Greek: it would have been a play on *huios*, 'son' and *hus*, 'pig'. This favours a Greek origin and indicates that Macrobius inherited the saying.

8. Seneca, *Moral Letters* 108.98.22; Whittaker, p. 76.

9. Many scholars take this passage to refer to the right to send tithes to Jerusalem. Diaspora Jews, however, did not send a tithe of their produce to Jerusalem, and the passage is best understood as dealing with the Jews' own food supply in Miletus. See *JLJM*, pp. 296f.

10. See more fully *JLJM*, 277–82.

11. For making sure that the animal does not choke when its throat is slit, see *Hullin* 1.2. In *JLJM*, pp. 278f. and n. 24 (p. 363), I proposed that this worry lay behind the prohibition of meat that was 'strangled' (see Acts 15.20, 29; 21.25; cf. *Jos. and Asen.* 8.5; 21.14). I noted that the Greeks accused the Scythians of strangling animals with a noose, but I thought it unlikely that this was in mind in Acts 15.20. I overlooked, however, *Spec. Laws* 4.122, where Philo castigates 'some of the type of Sardanapalus', who 'prepare meat unfit for the altar by strangling and throttling the animals, and entomb in the carcase the blood which is the essence of the soul and should be allowed to run freely away'. In view of this, we must think that strangling animals with a noose, or garroting them, was practised outside of Scythia, and consequently that Acts 15.20 may refer to it.

12. Diaspora Jews seem not to have worried about Gentiles *handling* their meat, oil and wine. Note that in Sardis the council ordered the pagan market manager to supply the Jews with suitable food. Either the Jews did not think that Gentiles were impure, or they regarded Gentile impurity as non-contagious. Cf. the Added Note to ch. 5 above. Hoenig has correctly argued that the problem with Gentile oil was its association with pagan gods, not its susceptibility to impurity ('Oil and Pagan Defilement', *JQR* 61, 1970–71, pp. 63–75, esp. 65–9). Goodman attributes the refusal to use Gentile oil to 'a pervasive religious instinct' 'to avoid gentile foodstuffs of various common kinds', an instinct that 'was all the more powerful for its lack of rationale' ('Kosher Olive Oil in Antiquity', *A Tribute to Geza Vermes*, pp. 227–45, quotation from 240. J. Baumgarten, however, argues that the problem with oil was the special susceptibility of liquids to impurity: *Studies in Qumran Law*, pp. 88–97. I think that Baumgarten may be right in his main argument, which concerns the Essenes. This does not, however, prove that there was a single halakhah on oil and impurity that was accepted by Jews all over the world.

13. For a range of reluctance about Gentile food, see Dan. 1.8–16; Tob. 1.10f.; Judith 10.5; 12.2, 9f., 19; 13.8; Add. Esther 14.17: III Macc. 3.4–7; *Jos. and Asen.* 7.1; 8.5; 18.5; 20.8; *Life* 14.

14. On the general issue of Jewish association with Gentiles, see my essay 'Jewish Association with Gentiles and Galatians 2:11–14'.

15. We recall that Josephus thought that a sin (or purification) offering should be a lamb *and* a female kid (*Antiq.* 3.231), which is more expensive than the Bible requires (above, p. 108). Thus the offering of two animals in the present case was not excessively expensive in his own view. The requirement of sacrifices in the case of failure to remove corpse impurity, however, is an expensive addition to biblical law.

16. There are further carcass rules; see *JLJM*, pp. 140, 142 and the lists on pp. 137–9, 147f., 151.

17. Hyam Maccoby has persuaded me that I misinterpreted the 'swarming things' of Lev. 11 when I proposed that flying insects as well as earth-bound swarming things created the impurities listed in Lev. 11.32–38 (*JLJM*, pp. 32f.; 165f.; 199–205; 246f.). It is a question of whether or not to distinguish the impurity of *sherets ha-ʿoph* (Lev. 11.20)

from that of *sherets ha-sherets 'al-ha-'arets* (11.29). I erred in not distinguishing them. This means that dead insects did not render vessels, moist food and liquid impure; that was the effect only of dead weasels, rodents and the like.

18. On improper mixtures as impure, see Douglas, *Purity and Danger*, ch. 3: what is whole is pure; the purity laws exclude what is anomalous or ambiguous. This interpretation explains leprosy, and the exclusion of shellfish from the diet, but not very many of the purity laws.

19. The Pharisees or early rabbis debated just which foods a woman with stage one of childbirth impurity could touch (*Niddah* 10.6f.).

20. On trusting the common people, see *JLJM*, pp. 238f.; Maccoby, *Early Rabbinic Writings*, p. 96.

21. Mazar, *Mountain of the Lord*, p. 146.

22. See the Theodotus inscription, above, p. 176.

23. Some of the passages in Philo are cited immediately below; see further *JLJM*, pp. 263–71.

24. The clearest presentation is in Philippe Bruneau, *Recherches sur les cultes de Délos à l'époque hellenistique et à l'époque impériale*, 1970, pp. 480–93, esp. pp. 481f., 490f; plates B, C, G, H; cf. Bruneau, '"Les Israélites de Délos" et la juiverie déliens', *Bulletin de Correspondence Hellénique* 106, 1982, pp. 465–504; see pp. 491–5 and the illustrations on pp. 500f. The original excavator, A. Plassart, pointed out that the pool cannot have been a cistern, since the walls were not plastered (though miqva'ot in Palestine did have plastered walls): Plassart, 'Fouilles de Délos', *BCH* 40, 1916, pp. 145–256, citation from 240. The pool consists of a natural fault in the rock, fed by an underground source of water, into which a shaft was sunk. There are no steps, but Bruneau points out that a wooden ladder could have given access to the pool. There was a similar pool, but with steps of porous stone, in a private house that seems to have belonged to a Jew (Bruneau, *Recherches*, p. 491 n. 2; Lysimachus is mentioned in an inscription found in the house and also in one found in the synagogue). These are the only two 'cisterns' in Delos where it was possible to go down into the water. Bruneau thought that a possible objection to his theory was that there was no way of draining the used water (*Recherches*, p. 491); but Palestinian miqva'ot cannot be drained. As far as I know, no student of Palestinian miqva'ot has examined the pools in Delos. Bruneau's arguments, made prior to the explosion of knowledge about Palestinian immersion pools, seem persuasive. They at least merit further investigation.

With regard to the identification of the building as a synagogue, I find Plassart and Bruneau completely convincing. Plassart's identification was accepted by Goodenough, *Jewish Symbols* 2, pp. 71–5.

25. E. L. Sukenik, *Ancient Synagogues in Palestine and Greece*. See further *JLJM*, p. 360 n. 8 (ch. IV.B).

26. For more details and references to secondary literature, see *JLJM*, pp. 214–27 and notes.

27. On the history of the identification of stepped pools as miqva'ot, see *JLJM*, pp. 215f. and notes.

28. The existence of public immersion pools indicates that many people did not observe rules of garment-purity. Several impurities render the clothes impure. How can one walk to a public pool in impure clothes, immerse, and not touch one's impure clothes again? On the Pharisees' view that the garments of ordinary people were impure, see *Hagigah* 2.7 and other passages below, p. 440.

29. The miqveh + 'otsar pool in Jericho is in the Hasmonean palace, and it pre-

sumably comes from a time when the Pharisees had influence at court. On Jericho, see *JLJM*, p. 218 and nn. 28, 43 and 48 (pp. 355f.).

30. This is a controversial topic. See *JLJM*, pp. 220–7.

31. Cf. *Berakhot* 1.1, where the rabbis refer to the time when the priests enter their houses (not the temple; Danby's interpretation is incorrect) to eat heave offering. The discussion concerns the time for saying the evening Shema‘, and this statement assumes that priests entered their houses to eat at about sunset. The Pharisees considered that a person who bathed but upon whom the sun had not yet set was half pure. Pharisaic priests may have been able to eat before sunset. Maccoby (*Early Rabbinic Writings*, p. 98) thinks that priests immersed in the morning but waited until evening to eat. A quick dip in the miqveh just before sunset is much more likely. Then they would not have to worry about what they touched during the day.

32. Above, n. 28; below, p. 440f.

33. Neusner, *Reading and Believing*, p. 54.

34. See *Demai* 6.6 (protection of moist olives before they are pressed for oil); *Hagigah* 2.7 (*midras* impurity); *Hagigah* 3.4f. (wine, oil and heave offering); *Tevul Yom* 4.5 (second tithe). Of these, *Hagigah* 3.4f. is anonymous and may not be Pharisaic, but the others probably are.

35. *JLJM*, ch. IV.B.

36. See Stern, *Greek and Latin Authors* I, p. 446; II, pp. 433–5.

37. See the introduction to ch. 11 above.

38. For example, Jeremias, *Jesus' Promise to the Nations*, pp. 40f., 61f.; Sanders, *P&PJ*, pp. 206–12.

39. On the interpretation of Ex. 22.28 [Heb. 27], see below, p. 242. Our evidence for Palestine is mostly indirect. Pagans and Jews lived together in Caesarea, for example, and the Jews seem not to have attacked the pagan temples.

40. Not all Jews had this ideal: Qumran was an exception.

41. Cecil Roth, 'England', *Enc. Jud.* 6, cols. 747–58, here 756.

42. Rhoads, *Israel in Revolution*, p. 33.

43. Stern, *Greek and Latin Authors* II, p. 159; similarly Julian the Apostate (fourth century; Stern, II, pp. 551f.).

44. The quotations from Book 37 are by Whittaker, *Jews and Christians*, pp. 55, 69; that from Book 66 is by Cary in the LCL. For full texts and translations, see Stern, *Greek and Latin Authors*, pp. 349–51, 371–5.

13. *Common Theology*

1. See *Antiq.* 4.207; *Apion* 2.237; *Spec. Laws* 1.53; *Moses* 2.205.

2. On Hasmonean designs, see Meshorer, *Ancient Jewish Coinage* I, pp. 60–8; on Herod's coins, which pose several difficulties, see vol. II, pp. 18–30.

3. Meshorer, vol. II, pp. 44–6.

4. Meshorer, vol. II, pp. 51–64.

5. Meshorer, vol. II, pp. 35–41.

6. Meshorer, vol. II, pp. 5–9. Meshorer proposes that Herod and his successors actually minted the 'Tyrian' silver coins from 19 BCE to CE66 (pp. 6f.).

7. I and others have occasionally supposed that the coinage required by the temple did not have a 'graven image', and here I wish to rectify the error. For the mistake, see *J&J*, p. 64; note also Hamburger's hesitation in *IDB*, *s.v.* money, pp. 428f.

8. Meshorer, vol. II, p. 8.

9. So Meshorer, vol. II, p. 8.

10. *Encylopedia of Archaeological Excavations in the Holy Land* II, p. 606.

11. Dothan, 'The Synagogue at Hammath-Tiberias', *Ancient Synagogues Revealed*, ed. Levine, pp. 63–9; *Encyclopedia of Archaeological Excavations*, pp. 1178–84. Unfortunately, neither publication shows Helios and the Zodiac clearly. The floor is difficult to photograph, as I can attest. The clearest depiction that I have seen is in Dennis Groh, 'Jews and Christians in Late Roman Palestine. Towards a New Chronology', *BA* 51, June 1988, p. 80–96, here pp. 88f.

12. Translation by M. Smith, 'Helios in Palestine', *Eretz-Israel. Archaeological, Historical and Geographical Studies* 16, H. M. Orlinsky Volume, 1982, pp. 199–214.

13. Smith, 'Helios', pp. 200–2.

14. Cited by Smith, 'Helios', p. 210.

15. Goodenough, *Jewish Symbols in the Greco-Roman Period*, 13 vols. See, for example, his discussion of 'The Lingua Franca of Symbolism', vol. 4, pp. 37f.

16. On Paul as a source for knowledge of pre-70 Jewish theology, see George Carras, *Paul, Josephus and Judaism: The Shared Judaism of Paul and Josephus*, unpubl. Oxford D. Phil. thesis, 1989.

17. For other instances of cosmic symbolism as interpreted by Philo and Josephus, see Thackeray's note to *War* 5.218.

18. On providence in Philo, see Mendelson, *Philo's Jewish Identity*, pp. 46–8.

19. 'Dualism' is an adequate title, even when people believed in a lot of evil beings, since there were still basically only two sides: God versus the forces of evil.

20. See Shaul Shaked, 'Iranian influence on Judaism: first century B.C.E. to second century C.E.' *Cambridge History of Judaism* I, pp. 308–25.

21. I have discussed the interplay of dualism and monotheism more fully in SIN/SINNERS (NT), *Anchor Bible Dictionary*, forthcoming.

22. Rajak, *Josephus*, p. 99.

23. See *P&PJ*, pp. 257–70.

24. See, for example, *P&PJ*, pp. 261, 264f., 268.

25. Similarly Philo, *Quest. Ex.* 1.2.

26. See 'Intention' and Repentance' in the subject index to *P&PJ*.

27. Above, pp. 111f.

28. According to Philo, Augustus Caesar had ordered that burnt offerings be sacrificed each day, at his own expense, 'as a tribute to the most high God' (*Embassy* 157; cf. 232, 317). It is possible that these sacrifices are not the same as those offered by the Jews, and at their expense, on behalf of Rome (*Apion* 2.77; cf. *War* 2.197, 409). Some scholars, however, equate them, proposing that Josephus correctly said that the Jews paid for the offerings and that Philo was in error (e.g. Rajak, *Josephus*, p. 118 n. 34).

29. Above, pp. 193f.

30. On loving both the neighbour and the stranger, see above, pp. 193f., on *koinōnia* (fellowship with other Jews) and *philanthrōpia* (love of all humans). On their combination in epigrammatic epitomes, see *JLJM*, pp. 70, 90.

31. See Sanders, *Paul: Past Master*, pp. 86–91.

32. Heinemann, *Prayer in the Talmud*, p. 30.

33. Heinemann, pp. 31–5.

34. Heinemann, pp. 32f.

35. Fergus Millar, noting 'Palestinian Judaism' in the title of *P&PJ*, criticizes me for not 'giving a central (or indeed any) place to the communal worship and sacrifice at the Temple', which means that I left out the corporate aspects of 'Palestinian Judaism' and made it a purely personal religion ('Reflections on the Trial of Jesus', pp. 379f.). It would

have been better had he noted the book's subject matter (pp. 16f.: how the religion was conceived by its adherents to function; not what they did on a day-to-day basis, but how they *understood* 'getting in and staying in'). The phrase 'or indeed any' leaves out of account the several discussions of sacrifice – part of what Jews thought they should do to 'stay in': pp. 80, 162–8 (how the rabbis understood sacrifice), 299 (sacrifice in the *Covenant of Damascus*, 302–4 (substitutions for sacrifice at Qumran), 338–41 (Ben Sira on sacrifice), 379f. (*Jubilees*), 398 (the absence of sacrifice from the *Psalms of Solomon*). With regard to my elimination of the corporate aspect of religion: I wrote that 'the corporate conception was maintained'. There are 'statements to the effect that an individual's sin brings punishment on all Israel'. 'The pattern of religion which we have been discussing demonstrates how individual and collective religion were combined. We note that the individual's place in God's plan was accomplished by his being a member of the group. Thus we find virtually no individual quest for salvation in Rabbinic literature. The question is whether or not one is an Israelite in good standing' (p. 237). Similarly pp. 367; 547.

36. Joseph Fitzmyer criticizes me for thinking that rabbinic literature is 'representative of the "Palestinian Judaism" with which Paul would have been in contact' (in J. Reumann, *Righteousness in the New Testament*, p. 217). What I wrote was that I was searching for what was common in a four hundred year span of Palestinian Judaism (e.g. pp. 422f.), that rabbinic literature of the Tannaitic period was the latest body of literature in the comparison, and that I took most of it to date from the period 135–200 (pp. 24, 60f.). I did not propose that rabbinic literature *represents* Palestinian Judaism, but only that it is one of several sources (e.g. *P&PJ*, pp. 18, 24f.; the book contains more than one chapter). Nor did I say anything about the kind of Judaism that Paul was in *contact* with. The comparison was a comparison, not a study of the sources of Paul's thought (*P&PJ*, pp. 10f., 19 and often).

37. Presupposition is proved when a point that is not stated informs a given discussion: see, for example, the discussion of means of atonement (pp. 416f.). For other examples in this book, see pp. 198, 434, 493f. One must study material in order to know when the lack of an explicit statement proves dissent, when it proves acceptance, and when it proves neither. See e.g. *JLJM*, pp. 179f., 322–4.

38. As most scholars realize, the covenant idea was central to all forms of Judaism. Thus Geza Vermes observed that 'the key to any understanding of Judaism must be the notion of the covenant' (*Perspectives*, pp. 163–164), and Alan Segal describes 'covenant' as 'the root metaphor underlying Hebrew society' (*Rebecca's Children*, p. 4).

39. See more fully my essay 'Jewish Association with Gentiles'.

40. We have seen several times that one may also doubt that Jews considered Gentiles impure; or, if they did think so, that they regarded the impurity as contagious.

41. Josephus' version of the purpose of circumcision (Gen. 17) was 'that [Abraham's] posterity should be kept from mixing with others' (*Antiq.* 1.192). 'Mixing' probably refers to intermarriage. This is probable partly becaue of the part of the body that is circumcised, but partly because of Josephus' other references to marriage and sexual intercourse.

42. For instances of Christian reluctance or refusal to associate with pagans, to intermarry, or to participate in civic activities (because of idolatry), see Peter Brown, *The Body and Society*, pp. 191, 285f., 342, 358.

43. On this section of Romans as relying on standard Diaspora Jewish homiletical material, see my *Paul, the Law and the Jewish People*, pp. 123–35.

44. Moore, *Judaism* I, p. 279; II, pp. 385f.; III, p. 205 (correcting a mistranslation); *P&PJ*, pp. 206–12.

45. Ch. 12, n. 11.

46. Understanding the various views of Greeks and Romans about what sexual practices were in accord with 'nature' lies beyond the scope of this book. See Dover, *Greek Homosexuality*; Richlin, *The Garden of Priapus*.

47. Compare the discussion of God-fearers, ch. 11 n. 34.

48. See e.g. Whittaker, pp. 90f.

49. In this section, as in some others, I for the most part avoid citing material that I used in *P&PJ*, where copious references will be found.

50. For further passages, see Nickelsburg, *Jewish Literature between the Bible and the Mishnah*, the index under 'Prayer'; *P&PJ*, the index under 'Repentance'.

51. For rabbinic passages on suffering as atoning, see *P&PJ*, pp. 168–72; on worrying if one does not suffer in this world, *Sifre Deut.* 32; *Mekilta Bahodesh* 10 (Lauterbach vol. II, pp. 280–2).

52. *Ps. Sol.* 8.25f.; 10.1; and often; 1QS 8.3f.; Wisd. Sol. 12.2, 20–2; for rabbinic passages, see the previous note.

53. See *J&J*, p. 412 n. 31, on Barrett, 'The Background of Mark 10:45', *New Testament Essays*, ed. Higgins, pp. 1–18.

54. On reward and punishment in the world to come, see *P&PJ*, pp. 125–8.

55. See *P&PJ*, pp. 92–7; note 'indicative and imperative', p. 27. I also argued extensively that grace was perceived to be prior to the law (e.g. pp. 85–7, 176–9, 291–8, 419–23, 543, 548f.).

56. Most Christian scholars, I am happy to report, have agreed with my argument, but some have objected. A few objections have been fuelled by anger that I dare call a non-Christian religion a religion of grace, and some insist that, despite all the evidence, Judaism really was a legalistic religion of merit that opposed grace. I think that in some cases, however, readers have been misled by the terms I used.

57. Daube, 'Standing in for Jack Coons', *Rechtshistoriches Journal* 7, pp. 179–90, quotation from 180.

58. *P&PJ*, p. 99.

59. *P&PJ*, p. 86.

14. *Hopes for the Future*

1. Horsley and Hanson note that 'a few distinguished American scholars' have pointed out that Sicarii were not Zealots, that the Zealots were not a party that continued from 6 to 74 CE (but rather originated in the winter of 67–68 CE), and that many of the characteristics attributed to the supposed Zealot party were common (*Bandits, Prophets, and Messiahs*, xi–xxviii, quotation from xiii). The scholars who made these observations are Foakes Jackson and Lake, *The Beginnings of Christianity* I, pp. 421–5; Zeitlin, 'Zealots and Sicarii', *JBL* 81, 1962, pp. 395–8; Morton Smith, 'Zealots and Sicarii: Their Origins and Relations', *HTR* 64, 1971, pp. 1–19. Kirsopp Lake and F. J. Foakes Jackson were British.

2. Rhoads, *Israel in Revolution*, pp. 47–59. He terminates the period of quiesence at 44 CE because then Judas' sons appear. Since Josephus still does not mention the 'sect', 'no more can be inferred from the narrative than that it was probably one of the more important groups of brigands and *sicarii* active in the period' (p. 59). This infers too much. There is no evidence for 'sect' apart from Josephus' calling Judas' movement a 'philosophy'.

3. Goodman adduces evidence that the philosophy did not lead to total anarchy, though he regards that as its 'logical conclusion' (*Ruling Class*, pp. 93f.).

4. See Goodman, *Ruling Class*, pp. 186–92.

5. The *War Rule* is discussed more fully below, pp. 296f.

6. On providence, see above, pp. 249–51.

7. 'The race endowed with vision' 'is called Israel' (*Unchangeableness of God* 144). This rests on a supposed etymology: Israel = *'ish ra'ah 'el*. See Wolfson, *Philo* II, pp. 51, 84. On the ambiguity in Philo between a mystical goal, which was universalistic and individualistic, and the standard covenantal conception of common Judaism, see Sanders, 'The Covenant as a Soteriological Category', pp. 25–39.

8. On the importance of Palestine, see W. D. Davies, *The Gospel and the Land*.

9. E.g. Simon, *Verus Israel*, p. 8; cf. p. 328.

10. E.g. Beasley-Murray, *Jesus and the Kingdom of God*, pp. 52–62. Much of the evidence that he cites is general, lacking the word 'messiah' and not mentioning David.

11. The *Covenant of Damascus* mentions one messiah from Aaron and Israel combined (e.g. 14.19; 20.1). I do not know whether this shows a different view among ancient Essenes, or reveals that a later copyist could not make sense of two messiahs. Two messiahs, one of Judah and one of Levi, also appear in the *Testaments of the Twelve Patriarchs*, e.g. *T. Sim.* 7.2. The descendant of Levi is given a possibly eschatological role in *T. Reub.* 6.10–12, and a certainly eschatological role in *T. Levi* 18. The problem with using messianic references in these *Testaments* is that they have been heavily revised by Christian scribes. The passages that emphasize Levi are, by definition, less likely to be Christian than those that emphasize the messiah from Judah (Jesus was given a Davidic ancestry, stemming from Judah).

12. 4Q174 1.11–13; *DSSE³*, p. 294.

13. 4Q174 1.11–13; *DSSE³*, p. 294.

14. 4QPBless; *DSSE³*, p. 260.

15. 1QSb 3.22–4.28 (the Zadokite priests), column 5 (the Prince of the Congregation (*DSSE³*, pp. 236f.). This is a different work from the one cited in the previous note.

16. Special encouragement from the 'priest destined for the appointed time of vengeance', 1QM 15.6 (apparently different from the head priest, 15.4); later the head priest comes forward, 1QM 16.11; for Michael, see 17.6–8; angels, 1.10; 12.4f. It is sometimes hard to tell when God is striking blows and when strengthening the hands of his elect. Thus in 1QM 11.8f. God fells 'the troops of Belial' 'by the hand of the poor ones that are to be redeemed', but the swords that strike are not the swords of men (11.11f.). This may be metaphorical, but in other passages it seems that the sectarians hoped for very concrete help from both the angels and God. See 1QM 18.1–3, 10–13; cf. 11.8–12, 17; 13.12–16; 14.16.

17. It is hard to explain the importance of Jesus' Davidic descent in the New Testament. When it was thought that all Jews longed for a messiah descended from David, the only problem was why Jesus was thought to be *messiah*. A Davidic messiah should be a military figure, and so it was not clear how early Christians reconciled this expectation with their view of Jesus, who was not a warrior. Now that we know that hope for a son of David was not universal among Jews, the question is all the more difficult. Why emphasize 'son of David' at all?

18. See the classic study by Erwin Rohde, *Psyche: The Cult of Souls and Belief in Immortality among the Greeks*. Numerous of Rohde's views have, of course, been challenged or even refuted. Nevertheless, the book reveals a range of opinions and also the diversity of terms and formulations.

19. See Boyce, 'Persian religion in the Achemenid age' and Shaked, 'Iranian influence on Judaism', *Cambridge History of Judaism* I, pp. 301, 323.

20. See also *Heir* 69–73; 111; 264f.; *Spec. Laws* 3.1–6. The degree to which the mind could escape the body that entrapped it, while the body yet lived, is a difficult topic in Philo, and fortunately one that we do not need to explore.

21. See, for example, Sandmel, *Philo of Alexandria*, p. 117.

22. See Rohde, *Psyche*, ch. 2.

23. Rohde attributes the view to the Orphics (pp. 342f., 346f.), Pythagoras (p. 375), Pindar (pp. 415f.), Plato (p. 467), and the Thracians (pp. 263f.).

24. 1QS 2.5–8; *DSSE³*, p. 63. Several passages about destruction are listed in *P&PJ*, p. 272.

25. They are conveniently collected in *OTP* I. Besides the apocalypses, some of the testaments also have heavenly tours (e.g. *Testament of Abraham*).

26. E.g. *Megillah* 4.10; *Hagigah* 2.1 (discouraging discussion of the heavenly chariot). See above, pp. 7f.; below, p. 372.

Part III: Groups and Parties

15. *Aristocrats and Sadducees*

1. *Antiq.* 13.293–8. It is reasonable to think that intra-Jewish struggles during the Hasmonean period were also conflicts of the two main parties. See pp. 28f., 381f., 390f.

2. See ch. 21 below.

3. On the Hasmonean coins the title is 'great priest', *kôhen gadôl* or *ha-kôhen ha-gadôl*; see e.g. Meshorer, *Coinage* I, p. 84. Similarly in Ben Sira 50.1 the adjective is *gadôl* in Hebrew, *megas* in Greek. This all agrees with the Hebrew and Greek of Lev. 21.10. In the *War Scroll*, however, the term is 'head priest', *kôhen ha-r'ôsh* (1QM 15.4). Other Greek sources use *arch-*, discussed below.

4. Meshorer, *Coinage* I, gives examples from the coins of four Hasmoneans. See e.g. p. 123 (Jannaeus), 134 (Aristobulus II), 136 (Hyrcanus II), 155 (Antigonus).

5. Meshorer I, pp. 47f. and notes.

6. See ch. 3. n. 3.

7. For a list of who appointed which Jewish high priest, see *HJP* II, pp. 229–32 (with references); Bruce, *Israel and the Nations*, pp. 234f.

8. I am grateful to Martin Goodman for advice on this paragraph.

9. On 'self-government', see ch. 21 below.

10. This high priest is called 'Annas' in the New Testament (e.g. Luke 3.2; John 18.3), but 'Ananus' by Josephus. Since one of his sons was named Ananus (Josephus: Ananus son of Ananus), I have decided to use the New Testament version of the father's name.

11. Goodman (*Ruling Class*, p. 138 n. 2) points out that the text reads as translated here, rather than 'between the high priests, on the one hand, and the priests and the leaders of the populace . . . on the other' (so Feldman in the LCL). Feldman seems to follow the Epitome, which is cited in the notes (E).

12. See Goodman, *Ruling Class*, pp. 140–7.

13. E.g. Rajak, *Josephus*, p. 22.

14. In *Antiq.* 20.6, Josephus specifies the full-length tunic 'and the sacred garb' (*stolē*), the latter term perhaps referring to the ephod and crown (Added Note to ch. 6). Mostly, however, he uses only the general word *stolē*, evidently as a collective noun, as also in *Antiq.* 3.158, 180. Thus, in English, 'vestments'.

15. Goodman, *Ruling Class*, p. 40.

16. See n. 3 above. 1QM 2.1 refers to 'the head priests' or 'chiefs of the priests' (*r'oshî ha-kôhanîm*).

17. Jeremias (*Jerusalem*, pp. 177f.) proposed that in Hebrew the chief priests were called 'sons of the high priests'. He cites 1QM 2.1 as if it supports this theory, but it points

the other way. The only distinction is between the singular and the plural.

18. That there were a few such families is indicated by Josephus in *War* 4.148; analysis of the high priests' names and descent leads to the conclusion that four families supplied most of the high priests, though the families of a few cannot be identified. See *HJP* II, p. 234; Jeremias, *Jerusalem*, p. 194.

19. Jeremias, *Jerusalem*, p. 179.

20. See *HJP* II, pp. 232–5, which gives both Schürer's original view and an assessment of Jeremias' criticism; see further Goodman, *Ruling Class*, p. 120. One may note that Jeremias' rabbinic passages are irrelevant.

21. Some details are different in *Antiq.* 20.118–36.

22. I shall summarize this section, highlighting the participants, in ch. 21; cf. *J&J*, pp. 314f.

23. For this sequence, see *War* 2.428, 556; 4.159, 327, 335f., 358; 5.420, 424, 439, 527–33; 6.113–15.

24. Above, pp. 160, 185.

25. Above, pp. 85–9, 185f.

26. For the discussion that follows, see *JLJM*, pp. 97–108, where there are further examples.

27. Daube, 'Example and Precept: From Sirach to R. Ishmael', pp. 16–20, here p. 18.

28. In this passage, the law is the Pentateuch; the line is missing in some manuscripts.

29. See Herr, 'Oral Law', *Enc. Jud.* 12, 1439–42.

30. *JLJM*, ch. II.

31. On intercalation, see above, pp. 131f.

32. *Yoma* 19b and parallels; see below, pp. 396f.

33. See Lauterbach, *Rabbinic Essays*, pp. 51f.

34. See Safrai, 'Oral Tora', *The Literature of the Sages* (CRINT II.3.1), p. 41.

35. Above, pp. 182f.

36. This depends on the possibility that 4QMMT, a document detailing legal arguments between Qumran and the Jerusalem authorities, may actually have been sent to a high priest. See *JLJM*, p. 37 & n. 12 (336). For a preview of the letter, see Schiffman, 'The New Halakhic Letter (4QMMT) and the Origins of the Dead Sea Sect', *BA* 53, 1990, pp. 64–73.

37. Horsley, *Spiral of Violence*, p. 249.

38. Rajak, *Josephus*, p. 22.

39. Goodman, *Ruling Class*, pp. 199–206.

40. Rajak, *Josephus*, pp. 153f.

16. *The Essenes and the Dead Sea Sect I*

1. Geza Vermes, *The Dead Sea Scrolls. Qumran in Perspective* (cited as *Perspective*); *The Dead Sea Scrolls in English*, 3rd ed. (cited as *DSSE³*); Michael A. Knibb, *The Qumran Community* (cited as *Community*); Philip Davies, *Behind the Essenes*.

2. See P. Davies, *The Damascus Covenant*, p. 19.

3. E.g. Knibb, *Community*, p. 10. This assumes that Josephus was wrong when he said that there was no high priest. If Josephus was entirely dependent on I Maccabees, his statement was only an inference from the silence of his source.

4. See, for example, several articles by Murphy-O'Connor (cited and discussed in the following books); P. Davies, *The Damascus Covenant*, 1982; *Behind the Essenes*, 1987; Callaway, *The History of the Qumran Community*, 1988.

5. On 11QT, see n. 24 below.

6. In the graves near the Qumran settlement, which have not been fully excavated, bones of a few women and children were found. Vermes (*Perspective*, pp. 97, 108) suggested that the entire Essene party may have met at Qumran annually, and that over the years a few children and women died while they were there. On the basis of present knowledge, I regard this as the best explanation. There is, however, another possibility. In an early article, Morton Smith thought that it was possible that around the main Qumran settlement there were 'pious hangers-on', possibly including women who 'ministered to the needs of the members' ('Dead Sea Sect', p. 347). The *Temple Scroll*, we shall see below, assumes that no women will reside in the new Jerusalem, but it does not command resident males to be celibate. Wives could reside outside the walls, and couples could occasionally have intercourse in the wives' camp, though the couple would then be impure and neither could enter the city for three days. Women could enter Jerusalem whenever they were pure. It is possible that some such rule was applied at Qumran, though only further finds of the remains of women and children would make this probable.

7. See Beall, *Josephus' description of the Essenes illustrated by the Dead Sea Scrolls*, and the important review by P. Davies, *JTS* 41, 1990, pp. 164–9.

8. There are a lot of cautions in scholarly literature about avoiding the premature identification of the community known from the Scrolls with the Essenes of Philo and Josephus (e.g. Talmon, *The World of Qumran*, pp. 20f.). In my discussion of the Dead Sea sect in *P&PJ* I observed this caution, and I did not use Philo or Josephus at all. I took them to be external witnesses to the same movement, whose information was often in error. I now think that their descriptions are better than that. I continue to define the Essenes by the scrolls, but Josephus' summary offers great organizational advantages for the purpose of this book, and I shall make considerable use of it. For combining Josephus and the Scrolls, see also Beall, *Josephus' description of the Essenes illustrated by the Dead Sea Scrolls*.

9. The handwriting of existing manuscripts does not determine the date of original composition. Some of the Scrolls, or earlier versions of them, could be pre-Roman.

10. The original excavators proposed 150–200, and this is widely accepted (e.g. Vermes, *Perspective*, p. 88). More recent studies suggest as many as 300–400 (for bibliography: Schiffman, *Sectarian Law*, p. 209 n. 104). I have no opinion of my own.

11. The LCL has 'occupy no one city, but settle in large numbers in every town'. The word 'town', however, is missing; Josephus wrote 'no one city, but settle . . . in each'; that is, in each city. The word 'city', of course, may be used loosely.

12. On the 'gate of the Essenes', see *War* 5.145 and especially Yadin's discussion, *Temple Scroll* I, pp. 301–4. NB: two of Yadin's books are titled *The Temple Scroll*, a short description published in 1985 and a 3 volume edition published in 1983 (ET; the Hebrew ed. was published in 1977). References to the 3 volume work are distinguished only by the use of a volume number (*Temple Scroll* I). Where possible, I refer to the short single volume, which is more readily accessible. See n. 24 for an example in which both works are cited.

13. For the sexual practices of the Essenes, see above, p. 344; below p. 353; n. 17 below; ch. 17, p. 368.

14. I take the view that 1QS 8.20–9.2 deals with a select group within the sect, the 'men of perfect holiness', who are judged more strictly than other members. See *P&PJ*, pp. 284f.

15. For details and complications in these penal codes, see Schiffman, *Sectarian Law*, pp. 73–88.

16. For prostration in the temple, see e.g. *Antiq.* 9.269; Ben Sira 50.17. On the difficult passage CD 11.21f., see Rabin's note and Schiffman, 'The Dead Sea Scrolls and the Early History of Jewish Liturgy', *The Synagogue in Late Antiquity*, ed. Levine, pp. 7–31, here p. 25.

17. I do not think that this is adequately explained by saying that the enlarged temple of 11QT would cover most of the city, and that therefore CD's legislation assumes that anyone in Jerusalem would actually be in the (true) temple area (so P. Davies, 'The Temple Scroll and the Damascus Document', p. 208, appealing to J. Maier, 'The Architectural History of the Temple in Jerusalem in the Light of the Temple Scroll', both in *Temple Scroll Studies*). The outside wall of the temple of 11QT was to be 1604 cubits on each side, in round numbers about 800 metres (Yadin, *Temple Scroll*, p. 253; similarly Maier, pp. 24f.). That would cover a lot of the city, but by no means all. Maier seems not to have included the very large northern suburb, but even without it 11QT's temple would not by any means cover the whole city. In any case, this suggestion does not explain the rule in 11QT that, when things were built and organized correctly, semen impurity would require laymen to withdraw from the *city* – not just from the temple precincts (p. 368 below). It seems that Jerusalem as a city was to be pure. Note also the requirements that other cities be almost as pure (ibid.).

18. E.g. Vermes, *Perspective*, pp. 95f., 182; Knibb, *Community*, pp. 111, 121f.

19. *Perspectives*, p.182; cf. Knibb, *Community*, p. 116.

20. So Schiffman, *Sectarian Law*, p. 191: 'exclusion from the pure food of the community meant that offenders were unable to eat everyday meals with their fellows at the same table'.

21. 'And' is visible after 'bread' in 1QSa 2.19. See *DJD* I, plate 24.

22. *Sectarian Law*, pp. 191f.

23. *Sectarian Law*, p. 192.

24. See Yadin, *Temple Scroll*, pp. 91f.; *Temple Scroll* I, pp. 108–11. If one accepts that 11QT (the *Temple Scroll*) is sectarian in the narrow sense, rather than simply a scroll in the sect's library, the interpretation of 1QS 6.4f. as referring to first fruits is certain. It is possible that different parts of 11QT were written at different times or by different people, and this leads some to say that it is not sectarian in the strict sense. I am most impressed, however, with its unity and the close relations to other Scrolls. In these chapters, I use 11QT for festivals and purity at Qumran, and on these topics it fits in very well indeed. It seems to me much more dubious to continue to cite, as many do, CD as governing Qumran. Two issues, marriage and sacrifice, make that impossible. The marriages of 11QT, on the other hand, lie in the future. On 11QT, besides Yadin's magnificent publications, see *Temple Scroll Studies*, ed. George J. Brooke, 1989. H. Stegemann in particular queries Yadin's view ('The Literary Composition of the Temple Scroll and its Status at Qumran', pp. 123–48). Barbara Thiering ('The Date of Composition of the Temple Scroll', pp. 99–120) has a succinct list of the connections between it and other scrolls from Qumran (pp. 101f.).

25. Schiffman, *Sectarian Law*, p. 192; p. 203 n. 12. Licht, *The Rule Scroll*, p. 140.

26. *Re'shît leḥem*, 'first fruits of bread', is not a biblical term, but the sectarians did use *leḥem* in discussing first fruits: 11QT 18.14. See Yadin, *Temple Scroll* II, p. 79; I, p. 105.

27. See Yadin, *Temple Scroll*, pp. 89–96; *Temple Scroll* I, pp. 99–122. For subsequent debate, see Marvin A. Sweeney, 'Sefirah at Qumran: Aspects of the Counting Formulas for the First-Fruits Festivals in the Temple Scroll', *BASOR* 251, 1983, pp. 61–6.

28. *Temple Scroll*, p. 93.

29. On oil, see above, p. 216. The view that liquid rendered things susceptible to impurity is discussed in ch. 19.

30. *Temple Scroll*, p. 95.

31. J. Baumgarten, 'The Essene Avoidance of Oil and the Laws of Purity', *Studies in Qumran Law*, pp. 88–97. Baumgarten's restoration of CD 12.15–17 is convincing.

32. Above, p. 228.

33. Below, pp. 439f. and n. 58.

34. See Yadin, *Temple Scroll*, pp. 170–7.

35. See further, p. 368 below.

36. *Apolouesthai* is 'bathe', not 'wash', and therefore means 'immerse'. On the distinction of terms, see *JLJM*, p. 267.

37. See 4Q512, fragment 11, *DSSE³*, p. 238, where 'seven days' may refer to removal of corpse impurity.

38. Yadin offers a superbly clear description of the calendar in *Temple Scroll*, pp. 84–90.

39. Talmon, *The World of Qumran*, p. 149.

40. For the argument that the temple and sacrificial rules are not merely theoretical, see Davies, 'The Ideology of the Temple in the Damascus Document', *JJS* 33, 1982, pp. 287–301.

41. Yadin, *Temple Scroll*, pp. 87f.

42. Note also CD 16.2–4, which refers to 'the Book of the Divisions of Times into their Jubilees and Weeks', the document that we now call *Jubilees*. The precise meaning of the sentence is somewhat obscure. It appears that CD regards *Jubilees* as giving the correct divisions of time, but does not require that festivals be held according to its calendar.

43. Davies, 'Ideology of the Temple', p. 290. Cf. J. Baumgarten, *Studies*, p. 71.

44. Cf. Smith, 'The Dead Sea Sect'.

45. So e.g. Knibb, *Community*, p. 96. 'Guardian' is *mᵉbaqqer*; 'Master' or 'wise leader' is *maskkil*. CD 13.6f. counts in favour of equating the two titles: 'the Guardian . . . instructs' is in Hebrew *hammᵉbaqqer . . . yaskkil*.

17. *The Essenes and the Dead Sea Sect II*

1. Vermes, *Perspectives*, pp. 101f.

2. On purity laws in the *Temple Rule*, see Yadin, *Temple Scroll* I, pp. 277–307; *Temple Scroll*, pp. 170–91.

3. *P&PJ*, p. 294 and n. 156.

4. *DSSE³*, pp. 290–2, 262f.

5. There is a list of names of angels in 1QM 9.15f., and Michael plays a major role in the war. For Raphael, see Tob. 3.17.

6. In his very good discussion of angels in the Scrolls, Ringgren opens by accepting this view, correctly saying that it is 'well known' (*The Faith of Qumran*, p. 81).

7. It is an error to think that 'transcendent' means 'inaccessible'. This is an old debate. See my previous review of this as an issue in the study of rabbinic literature (*P&PJ*, pp. 212–33).

8. Above, pp. 249f.

9. Carol Newsom, *Songs of the Sabbath Sacrifice*; *DSSE³*, pp. 221–30.

10. 4Q400, *DSSE³*, p. 222.

11. 4Q405 20 ii 21f., *DSSE³*, p. 228.

12. Ch. 1 n. 7 above.

13. Stoic philosophers knew that there was a problem about holding fate and freewill together (see e.g. Max Pohlenz, *Die Stoa* I. p. 101). Josephus knew about the Stoics and their view of fate, but he and most other Jews did not grapple with the philosophical problems that the doctrine raised.

14. *P&PJ*, pp. 266f.

15. *P&PJ*, pp. 287–98.

16. *P&PJ*, pp. 157–82.

17. On votive offerings, *anathēmata*, see *JLJM*, p. 294 and n. 34.

18. Joseph Baumgarten, thinking (as do many scholars) that CD governed Qumran, has made two attempts to find a time when it did so, and thus when all the Essenes sacrificed. In the course of these studies he correctly disposed of the idea that the Essenes had their own altar at Qumran or elsewhere, and he also made interesting observations on the reading of *Antiq.* 18.19. Once one grants, however, that the marrying and sacrificing Essenes of CD were not the same people as the Qumran sectarians, the problems vanish. See Baumgarten, 'Sacrifice and Worship among the Jewish Sectarians of the Dead Sea (Qumran) Scrolls', originally publ. 1953; 'The Essenes and the Temple – A Reappraisal', both in *Studies in Qumran Law*, 1977.

19. 1QS 5.7–11; CD 15.5–16.6 (pp. 361f. above).

20. E.g. *Temple Scroll*, p. 89.

21. Schiffman (*Sectarian Law*, pp. 16f.) has a different view. He seems to overlook 'return to the Law of Moses' and the 'secrets' that were revealed to the Zadokite priests.

18. The Pharisees I

1. 'Seekers of smooth things' are in Hebrew *dôrshê ha-halaqôt*, apparently a pun for 'seekers of correct behaviour', *dôrshê ha-halakhôt*. The latter phrase is a good description of the Pharisees, and the Qumran sectarians, by changing two letters, accused them of being too lenient in their practice of the law.

2. Lohse, *The New Testament Environment*, p. 75. Among recent literature, see also Horsley, *Spiral of Violence*, p. 69: Salome Alexandra 'brought the Pharisees into participation and perhaps into dominance in her government'; they shared (with the eminent?) 'a certain degree of political power'.

3. Ch. 3 n. 3.

4. The singular 'Pharisee' points towards a leader, but there is no indication of who he was.

5. The section *Antiq.* 17.41–5 is difficult to unravel. I take 17.41f. to be a 'flashback' to the loyalty oath of *Antiq.* 15.370, and 17.43f. to explain the role of the Pharisees in Pheroras' wife's plot. I am indebted to Rebecca Gray for this interpretation of the passage.

6. Ch. 19 n. 16.

7. I have changed the tense of the verbs.

8. I here take *koinon* to mean 'common council', rather than 'public assembly', as some understand it. We shall return to the question in ch. 21. Joseph son of Gorion is called Gorion son of Joseph in *War* 4.159.

9. In his very interesting and useful analysis of Josephus' passages on the Pharisees, Steve Mason makes one suggestion that is especially unfortunate: that in *Life* 12, usually translated 'I began to govern my life by the rules of the Pharisees', Josephus meant that, being desirous of entering upon a career in public life, he followed the Pharisees, since that was necessary for a public career in the mid-50s (Mason, *Flavius Josephus on the Pharisees*, pp. 347–56). This is based on the common assumption that the Pharisees ran everything. Becoming a Pharisee in order to seek public office, however, would have made Josephus unique. Only in 66 did Ananus, a Sadducee, and the other chief priests consult the Pharisees, as our nos. 6 and 7 show. Only one Pharisee, Simon b. Gamaliel, seems to have achieved public prominence in this period. Ananus, it must be remembered, was not only the leading figure during the early days of the revolt, but also Josephus' hero, and Josephus seems to have been a follower of Ananus in the mid-60s (e.g. *War* 4.158–60, 318–25). During this part of Josephus' account, he refers several times to Pharisees and several times to chief priests, but he draws no connection between them except the

common desire to calm the populace (before the revolt was fully underway) and to fend off the Zealots (when they attacked the revolutionary government). The other chief priests who played a leading role, then, were not Pharisees. Josephus' qualifications for public life were that he was an aristocratic priest and that he knew the law (e.g. *Life* 29; 189–98). The last passage shows that during the revolt Pharisees were active, and thus Josephus' allegiance did him no damage. In the mid-50s, however, public roles were not conditional on following the Pharisees.

10. Neusner, *From Politics to Piety*, ch. 3; the quotation is from p. 66. The chapter has been often reprinted under slightly different titles.

11. We saw above (pp. 323, 327.) that the high priest and the chief priests as a group played virtually no role in Josephus' two accounts of Herod. The chief priests are not mentioned at all in *War* 1.354–2.13 or *Antiq.* 14.482–17.192, the sections that deal with Herod. One learns only that the high priest was appointed or deposed (*Antiq.* 15.22; 17.164–165), and one reads the story of the high priest's vestments (e.g. *Antiq.* 15.403, 408), but that is all. Cf. Rhoads (*Israel in Revolution*, p. 39) on the non-appearance of the Sadducees.

12. See e.g. Safrai, 'Oral Tora', CRINT II.3.1, pp. 35–42.

13. According to Josephus, Hyrcanus I did not take the title 'king' (e.g. *War* 1.70). I do not cite this point as proving that *Antiq.* 13.288 does not refer to Hyrcanus I, since Josephus and other ancient authors sometimes used titles loosely.

14. See, for example, Stern, 'Nicholas of Damascus', *Enc. Jud.* 12, col. 1140f.; cf. Schwartz, 'Josephus and Nicolaus on the Pharisees', *JSJ* 14, 1983, pp. 157–71.

15. See above, p. 346. The explanation of why Herod excused them is not certain. For this suggestion, see A. I. Baumgarten, '*Korban* and the Pharisaic *Paradosis*', p. 9; *JLJM*, p. 53.

16. Jannaeus' execution of the 800: *War* 1.97; the Pharisees retaliate against the eminent, who are defended by Aristobulus II: *War* 1.114; *Antiq.* 13.410f.; Aristobulus seizes throne: *War* 1.121f.; Antipater and sons (Herod and Phasael) support Hyrcanus II: *War* 1.124–6, 199–207; Antigonus and Parthians responsible for Phasael's death: *War* 1.254–60, 271f.; Herod besieges Antigonus in Jerusalem: 1.342–53.

17. See the full analysis by James McLaren, *Power and Politics in Palestine*.

18. See *HJP* I, p. 296, for this summary statement.

19. *HJP* I, p. 296, citing *Antiq.* 15.176.

20. *HJP* II, p. 402, citing *Antiq.* 17.41.

21. Jeremias, *Jerusalem*, pp. 262f.

22. Mason (*Flavius Josephus on the Pharisees*, pp. 45–8 and throughout) proposes that, if Josephus used sources, he completely rewrote them, and thus the statements about the Pharisees in *Antiq.* 13.288, 298 reflect his own view (though Mason also sometimes appeals to the theory of imperfect redaction of sources, e.g. pp. 219, 228f.). He further argues that in their literary context these passages show disapproval of the Pharisees: 'their participation in power was a disaster and sealed the doom of the Hasmonean house' (p. 250). This is an important argument, which is partially persuasive. It reveals, however, Nicolaus' view, not Josephus'. Nicolaus was probably responsible for all the references to the Pharisees in the Hasmonean and Herodian periods; that is why they are internally consistent. I shall make three points with regard to Mason's treatment of the summaries about the Pharisees and Josephus' view of the party. (1) Mason does not note the number of times that Josephus deletes the Pharisees from stories of rebellion, thus protecting their reputation (further below, pp. 410f.). It is necessary to take this into account when considering Josephus' own assessment, which was more favourable than that of Nicolaus.

(2) Mason focuses on the question of whether or not a reference to the Pharisees shows them in a favourable or unfavourable light, not on the problem of the conflict between summaries that say that the Pharisees were all-powerful and individual narratives that show that they were not. My argument is based primarily on this point: there was no time at which these summaries (at least as they are usually understood) were true, except the period of Salome Alexandra's reign. In what socio-political context can we situate them? The best is that of Herod, when the Pharisees proved to be a nuisance, when their period as chief trouble-makers was still fresh in peoples' memories, and when Nicolaus of Damascus wrote his history. In this setting, they do not prove that the Pharisees determined all policies, but that they had enough support to annoy Herod. (3) In his discussion of *Antiq.* 13.288–98, Mason seriously misconstrues §288. He takes it to say that the Pharisees *initially* opposed Hyrcanus, and then he finds it to be in conflict with what follows (pp. 216–18). It is in fact an opening summary that gives the *conclusion*: the Pharisees became hostile towards Hyrcanus *and his sons*. This cannot be their initial attitude, but rather it is the consequence of a series of events during Hyrcanus' reign and thereafter. One anecdote then follows, which partially explains how the Pharisees came to oppose Hyrcanus. The conclusion of 13.296 repeats the point of 13.288: enmity arose between Hyrcanus and the people because of his conflict with the Pharisees. Mason's mis-reading allows him to propose that 13.288, which is unfavourable towards the Pharisees, is Josephus' own view, which stands in contradiction to the rest of the passage. Once we see how 13.288 relates to the subsequent paragraphs, we also see that it does not stand apart as Josephus' hostile editorial statement that does not fit the narrative. With regard to attitude, it agrees with the rest of the passage: hostility developed between Hyrcanus and the Pharisees, and the Pharisees were in general trouble-makers.

23. *Antiq.* 15.268–79.

24. Schalit (*König Herodes*, pp. 463f., 471) derives the attitude of the 'extreme' Pharisees from the *Psalms of Solomon*: the son of David would put an end to Herod's reign.

25. Acts 7.58–60; 12.2; *Antiq.* 20.200.

26. Conflict with the Pharisees: Mark 2.1–3.6; crowds: Mark 1.37; 2.2; 3.7 and often. I have discussed the conflict passages in *JLJM*, ch. 1.

27. *Antiq.* 18.36–8, 109–119, 245–521; *Life* 65.

28. Executions and massacres: nos. 3 and 4 above; people who complained to Archelaus (pp. 402f. below); Theudas and his followers; the Egyptian's followers (both above, p. 39.); some of the people on both sides of the fighting between Galileans and Samaritans (pp. 329f.); some of the protesters against Florus (below, pp. 485f.); Jesus, Stephen, and the two Jameses – among others. Herod had secret police, and he forbade most meetings and assemblies. He consequently did not have to resort to the use of troops very often, but he did employ exemplary executions. He also sometimes staged show-trials, in which a large crowd approved executions, or even carried them out. See below, pp. 483f.

29. See e.g. Rhoads, *Israel in Revolution*, pp. 51f.

30. Rajak, *Josephus*, p. 31. On 'the sages laid it down', see pp. 458–72.

31. As is often the case, there is probably *something* behind *part* of this discussion in the Mishnah. It is possible that after Herod's time the high priest actually did stay awake all night, since *c.* 5 BCE a nocturnal emission disqualified the high priest from sacrificing on the Day of Atonement (*Antiq.* 17.165f.). I doubt that many high priests chose Pharisees to keep them awake. This story simultaneously proves that, despite Herod's alleged submission to the Pharisees, they did not in fact control his high priests on the day before the Day of Atonement.

32. The debate is discussed above, p. 335.

33. Cf. *Sifra Ahare Mot* pereq 3.11; *Yoma* 53a.

34. Neusner, *Rabbinic Traditions about the Pharisees before 70*, III, pp. 296f., 307; *JLJM*, pp. 12, 244f. For a rare instance in which the Houses of Hillel and Shammai debate what the priests should do, see *Sheqalim* 8.6, (discussed *JLJM*, p. 193, where 8.5 is a typographical error). Neusner also observed that stories and traditions about the temple are more frequent in passages attributed to Pharisees before Hillel than in the more abundant House of Hillel/House of Shammai materials (ibid., I, p. 64; III, p. 307). The evidence is so slight, however, that it is difficult to draw hard conclusions from it. Further, much of the early material consists of stories rather than rules.

35. Neusner, *Rabbinic Traditions* III, pp. 289f.

36. *Apion* 2.108; *Antiq.* 17.42.

37. Mason, 'Priesthood in Josephus and the "Pharisaic Revolution"', *JBL* 107, 1988, pp. 657–61.

38. Above, pp. 345f., 516 n.24.

39. *JLJM*, ch. IV.

40. Above, pp. 223f.

41. Alexander Guttmann, *Ancient Synagogues*, pp. 3f.

42. Hyam Maccoby, *Revolution in Judaea*, p. 164–7. Maccoby's view of what the crowd wanted when Jesus was before Pilate is complex, and it lies beyond the present topic.

43. Maccoby, *Revolution in Judaea*, pp.26 (the Hasidim were later called Pharisees), 98 (Jesus was a Pharisee), 59–64 (Pharisees led Israel), pp. 203–6 (Jesus' teaching on love etc. was Pharisaic), pp. 56f. (second-century rabbis were Pharisees).

44. I give several examples in *JEJ*, pp. 200–202, 274–81.

45. Morton Smith, 'Palestinian Judaism in the First Century', repr. in H. A. Fischel, (ed.), *Essays in Greco-Roman and Related Talmudic Literature*, pp. 183–97, esp. 190–7; Jacob Neusner, 'Josephus' Pharisees: A Complete Repertoire', *Formative Judaism* 3rd Series, pp. 61f. (at least some earlier printings of the article did not specify the indebtedness to Smith); Shaye J. D. Cohen, *Josephus in Galilee and Rome*; Sanders, *JEJ*, pp. 309–17; Goodman, *Ruling Class*. That Pharisees did not control Galilee is clearly implied in Goodman's earlier work, *State and Society in Roman Galilee*, esp. pp. 78, 93.

46. See above, pp. 172f., 182, 191f., 363f.

47. Louis Ginzberg, *On Jewish Law and Lore*, 1962; Louis Finkelstein, *The Pharisees*, 3rd. ed., 1962.

48. Neusner, *Judaism: The Evidence of the Mishnah*, pp. 166, 235.

49. On tithes, see above pp. 149f.; for first fruits and firstlings, see pp. 151f.

50. Goodman (*Ruling Class*, p. 154) points out that this was a symbolic action that had no practical effect, since lenders had copies. The leaders of the revolt, who managed the crowds fairly well, were also aristocrats.

51. I Macc. 2.38; *War* 1.311–13.

52. The identification was headline news in Israel, and orthodox Rabbis came to Matsada to verify that the pools met the Talmudic specifications (Yadin, *Masada*, pp. 164–7).

53. Several parts of these sections in the *Antiquities* show mastery of rhetoric and thus point to Nicolaus as the author: e.g. *Antiq.* 13.411–15.

54. Possibly they were effectively in control before Hyrcanus I and during the reign of Hyrcanus II.

19. *The Pharisees II*

1. *JLJM*, p. 133 and notes.

2. We can learn a lot about Judaism from Paul, and I cited him fairly frequently on some topics of common Jewish theology. For example, he believed in one God, and he also thought that there were demons and other spiritual powers. This was not specifically Pharisaic, but was common to a lot of Jews.

3. Discussed more fully in *JLJM*, pp. 166–73.

4. E.g. *Judaism: the Evidence of the Mishnah*, p. 86.

5. See *JLJM*, ch. III.

6. A few of the presuppositions of the earliest material, as established by Neusner, are listed below, pp. 443f. See also my effort to list presuppositions in one area of law, purity: *JLJM*, pp. 250–52.

7. Josephus' favourable bias was not so great as to prevent him from quoting negative summaries about the Pharisees from a source; above, p. 392.

8. Above, pp. 249–51, 299–302.

9. *P&PJ*, p. 68, citing principally J. N. Epstein.

10. *P&PJ*, pp. 84–107.

11. *Mekhilta Bahodesh* 7, ed. Lauterbach, vol. II, p. 249.

12. Pages 249–51.

13. Martin Goodman has pointed out to me that 'strict concerning the laws', while it could mean 'strict with regard to observance of the Jewish law', might also mean strict with regard to the Roman regulations, which reserved the death sentence for the Roman procurator. Cf. strict with regard to piety, said of anyone, whether Gentile or Jewish (*Apion* 2.144); 'strict superintendence of the law', said with regard to the priests (*Apion* 2.187); 'strictly . . . to observe their laws', said of the Spartans (*Apion* 2.227). I still incline to the majority view, that those who protested the action of Ananus were the Pharisees, but certainty is not possible.

14. I am indebted to Peretz Segal for this point; cf. ch. 5 n. 40 above.

15. Mark 14.63f.; *Antiq.* 20.200f.

16. On the use of the word 'strict' or 'precise' with regard to the Pharisees, see A. I. Baumgarten, 'The Name of the Pharisees', *JBL* 102, 1983, pp. 411–428. Baumgarten proposes that the name 'Pharisees' may derive not from the meaning 'separate', which is one possible meaning of *prsh*, but rather from another possible meaning, 'specify': *parôshîm*, 'specifiers', rather than *pᵉrûshîm*, 'separatists'.

17. See *JLJM*, ch. II, where I agree with and extend Neusner's proposal in *Torah: From Scroll to Symbol*.

18. The Pharisees who are listed in sets of two in *Avot* 1.4–12.

19. See e.g. *Shabbat* 108a; 79b/*Menahot* 32a.

20. See A. I. Baumgarten, 'The Pharisaic *Paradosis*', *HTR* 80, 1987, pp. 63–77.

21. These paragraphs on 'oral law' are adapted from *JLJM*, pp. 122–4, where there are full references to halakhot from Moses, 'received traditions' and the like.

22. Two of the festival days fall in Passover (Ex. 12.16; Lev. 23.7f.), one during Weeks (Lev. 23.21) and two during booths (Lev. 23.35f.). (The sixth 'festival day', in this case better called a 'fast day', is the Day of Atonement: Lev. 23.28–32).

23. On the question of women and the laying on of hands, see above, pp. 109f.

24. According to *T. Hagigah* 2.10, the Shammaites laid hands on the head of a shared sacrifice on the day before the festival day.

25. Adapted from *JLJM*, pp. 9–11.

26. Neusner, *Politics to Piety*, p. 15.

27. The wording of *Sifre Deut.* is to be preferred to that of *Shevi'it* 10.4, since the former more adequately accounts for the title. The translation is that of Hammer. For

further discussions of the prosbul, see *T. Shevi'it* 8.3–11.

28. 'The Matter of Hillel', quoted here from *Judaism in the Beginning of Christianity*, p. 67, but written much earlier.

29. Neusner, *Reading and Believing*, pp. 57f.

30. *Rabbinic Traditions* III, pp. 288f.

31. *DJD* II, 1961, pp. 100–104, no. 18.

32. For an alternative, see n. 16 above.

33. Jeremias, *Proclamation*, pp. 118f., quoting and agreeing with O. Betz, *What do we Know About Jesus?*, p. 74.

34. Black, 'Pharisees', *IDB* 3, p. 776b.

35. Jeremias, *Proclamation*, p. 118.

36. For example: The scholar who studies much is not superior to his fellow, the common person, provided that the latter 'directs the heart to Heaven' (*Berakhot* 17a). See further *P&PJ*, pp. 96, 149, 152–7.

37. E.g. Johnson, *The Writings of the New Testament*, p. 52: the Pharisees thought that the ordinary folk were 'not fully part of the people' of Israel. This was the result of their purity and tithing laws (pp. 46, 54).

38. Although not a criticism of Pharisees, Acts 10.28 states that Jews would not come near Gentiles. See my discussion in 'Association with Gentiles', n. 11.

39. I am sure that it is true that Pharisees would not *eat* with people whom they regarded as heinous sinners. On the significance of eating, see below, pp. 441f. The present point is that in order to criticize Jesus and his disciples, they travelled from Jerusalem to Galilee, probably passing through Samaria, and went up to Jesus and his companions and inspected their hands (Mark 7.1f., 5). I do not suppose that this happened just as Mark presents it; I simply note that, in one of the passages that people say proves that Pharisees practised apartheid, they are actually depicted as coming into contact with quite a lot of impure people and places.

40. See Maccoby, *Early Rabbinic Writings*, pp. 68f.; *JLJM*, p. 304.

41. On the degrees of sanctity of holy food, see *JLJM*, p. 303.

42. *JLJM*, pp. 152–84.

43. The Bible uses both 'Most Holy Things', eaten by the priests in the temple (Lev. 6.16f.; Num. 18.9), and also 'Holy Things', referring to any of the gifts and offerings that the priests ate, whether in the temple or at home with their families (Lev. 22.1–16). The rabbis sometimes distinguished the 'Most Holy Things' (things eaten in the temple, plus the whole-burnt offering) from the 'Minor Holy Things' (eaten by priests and families outside the temple, or by lay people, after having been brought to the temple: peace offerings, Passover lamb, etc.): see *Zevahim* 5.4–8; 10.6 (5.5 lists Most Holy Things, though the term is lacking). They did not, however, always distinguish holy food by these terms. In *Niddah* 10.6f. 'Holy Things' refers to 'Most Holy', and the 'Minor Holy Things' are listed rather than designated by this term.

44. Maccoby, *Early Rabbinic Writings*, pp. 71, 96.

45. See p. 439.

46. *Hagigah* 3.4; see further *Demai* 1.3, and on this point *JLJM*, p. 238; 304 and n. 62.

47. Above, pp. 182–7.

48. On 'Beforetime' passages, see *JLJM*, p. 238 and n. 3 (p. 358).

49. This is a correction of my explanation in *JLJM*; see ch. 12 n. 17.

50. Above, pp. 357f.

51. See Alon, 'The Bounds of the Laws of Levitical Cleanness', p. 201. Alon notes that washing of hands for prayer is 'taught in the Talmud only by Amoraim' (that is, after

220 c.e.). He argues that 'the halakah' is early, citing Diaspora evidence. It is better to note that Diaspora and Pharisaic practices were different.

52. On these difficult passages, see *JLJM*, pp. 203f., 229, drawing on Alon's explanation.

53. For passages and various possible reasons for the Pharisees' concern, see *JLJM*, pp. 184–8.

54. For these proposals of domestic apartheid, see *JLJM*, pp. 155–62 (pre-Neusner); 174–6 (Neusner).

55. According to Neusner, 'the ritual uncleanness that prevents sexual relations also makes a woman unclean for the preparation of food': *Rabbinic Traditions* III, p. 295.

56. Maccoby, *Early Rabbinic Writings*, p. 98.

57. Above, p. 225 and n. 28.

58. In *Betsah* 2.2 the Houses of Hillel and Shammai debate when vessels and people must be immersed to be ready for the sabbath. They agree that vesels must be immersed the previous day; but they disagree about when people should immerse, the Shammaites arguing for the previous day, the Hillelites permitting immersion on the sabbath day itself. This indicates that Pharisees did not immerse every day. On the 'morning bathers', who were not Pharisees, see *JLJM*, p. 231 and n. 74 (p. 357), referring to Alon.

59. Jeremias *Jerusalem*, pp. 246–52, his emphasis.

60. *P&PJ*, pp. 61f., 152–7; *J&J*, pp. 186–8; *JLJM*, p. 250.

61. Jeremias, *Proclamation*, p. 115.

62. On the difficult question of how people thought about participating in the altar, see above, pp. 255f.

63. Schiffman correctly argues that the supposed meal in 1QS 6.4f. was not 'sacral': *Sectarian Law*, pp. 191–210. On prayer as substituting for sacrifice, see p. 376. above.

64. Alan Segal, *Rebecca's Children*, p. 125; cf. 52, 58, 117.

65. Jeremias, *Jerusalem*, pp. 246–67. He found close parallels between the Pharisees and CD and 1QS (pp. 259f.), all in error with regard to the Pharisees. See also Neusner, *Rabbinic Traditions* III, pp. 286–300, comparing the Pharisees with the Dead Sea sect and the early Christians. This is the section of Neusner's work where he says that laws have to do with eating ordinary food in priestly purity, when in fact they deal with other topics (*JLJM*, ch. III).

66. Neusner, *Rabbinic Traditions* III, p. 297.

67. *JLJM*, pp. 319; 334 n. 11.

68. Daube, 'Standing in for Jack Coons', pp. 187f.

69. *P&PJ*, pp. 221f., drawing on Urbach.

70. This is where we left the topic above, p. 407.

71. Hengel, *The Pre-Christian Paul*, n. 226 on pp. 131f. 'Determinative influence' is Hengel's summary of the passages in Josephus that we quoted above, pp. 389f.

72. Quoted from the *The Pre-Christian Paul*, ET by John Bowden, pp. 131f. The quotation is from E. Schürer, *Geschichte des jüdischen Volkes im Zeitalter Jesu Christi* II, p. 456. Hengel also refers to *HJP* II, p. 402.

73. See pp. 407–9. on the partial overlap of Pharisaic ideology with that of the Sicarii, especially on facing death and hoping for a better future.

74. See further pp. 459f. below.

75. Hengel, *The Pre-Christian Paul*, p. 57.

20. *Other Pietists*

1. It is likely that most of *T. Moses* was written during the Hasmonean period rather than the Roman, but since ch. 6 clearly refers to Herod and shows that the work was updated in the Roman period, I shall include it. On the date, see Priest in *OTP* I, pp. 920f. and the references to Licht and Nickelsburg (p. 926). For the clearest brief account of whether what we have is the *Assumption* or *Testament of Moses*, see Sparks, *AOT*, pp. 601f.

2. The translation quoted is that of S. P. Brock in Sparks, *AOT*; the translation by R. B. Wright in *OTP* II is sometimes cited.

3. In Brock's translation 'the holy ones', in Wright's 'the devout'.

4. See, for example *War* 1.311–13.

5. Quotations are from Sweet's revision of Charles' translation in Sparks, *AOT*.

21. *Who Ran What?*

1. See Bailey and Ryan, *Hitler vs. Roosevelt*; Wormuth and Firmage, *To Chain the Dog of War*.

2. *Jerusalem*, p. 153f.

3. *Jerusalem*, p. 159. Jeremias gives a whole list of rites that the priests had to do in accordance with Pharisaic wishes on p. 264, citing rabbinic evidence from the third to the sixth century.

4. *Jerusalem*, p. 166.

5. *Jerusalem*, p. 263.

6. E.g. *Jerusalem*, p. 237.

7. *Jerusalem*, p. 259.

8. *Jerusalem*, p. 266.

9. *Jerusalem*, pp. 259, 266f. On despising and hating, see Jeremias, *Proclamation*, p. 118.

10. *HJP* II, p. 332; *JPJC*, II.1, p. 322.

11. *HJP* II, pp. 341f.; *JPJC* II.1, pp. 333f.

12. *HJP* II, p. 398; *JPJC* II.2, p. 22.

13. The two main passages are *Demai* 2.2f.; *T. Demai* 2.2. The Mishnaic passages on the 'associates' are quoted in *HJP* II, pp. 386f., and they are basic to the definition of the Pharisees that follows; for some reason the Tosefta passages are not quoted. These passages are central to Jeremias' discussion of the supposedly closed Pharisaic communities (*Jerusalem*, p. 259).

14. E.g. Jeremias, *Proclamation*, p. 118; *Jerusalem*, pp. 246, 259, 266 ('as the true Israel [the Pharisees] drew a hard line between themselves and the masses . . .').

15. *Jerusalem*, p. 312.

16. *Jerusalem*, pp. 307f. On Billerbeck's translation of 'deserts' (*midbarôt*) as 'steppes', see n. 26. Jeremias' discussion in this section is very confusing. Breeders of small cattle are in list 1a on p. 307. On the next page he states that lists 1a–c are not 'juristic', and then adds that people pursuing the trades in 1b–c were not necessarily social outcasts. I think that the result is that breeders of small cattle were social outcasts.

17. Jeremias, *Jerusalem*, pp. 311f., referring to category IV on p. 304.

18. *Jerusalem*, p. 305.

19. In *Jerusalem*, p. 311 n. 44, Jeremias gives the passage as *Sanhedrin* 24b; the passage is correctly cited on p. 305 n. 14. The incorrect citation, 24b, probably depends on Billerbeck, *Kommentar* III, p. 599; the text and correct citation appear several times in Billerbeck, e.g. vol. I, p. 498.

20. Although Billerbeck gave the passages on herdsmen from *Sanhedrin* several times, he did not cite *Bava Metsi'a* 5b.

21. *HJP* II, p. 342; *JPJC* II.1, p. 334.

22. Rajak, *Josephus*, p. 28.

23. Rajak, p. 33; see her n. 63 for some of the history of scholarship.

24. *JLJM*, pp. 243f.

25. Jeremias was handicapped because he was dependent on the selection of Talmudic passages provided by Billerbeck. Some of his misrepresentation of general rabbinic opinion is actually to be laid at Billerbeck's door.

26. After 70 there might have been reason to try to reduce the number of sheep and goats, which are in some ways detrimental to basic agriculture. While the temple stood, the area around Jerusalem would have produced a lot of wool and dairy products, probably too great a quantity for local consumption. Thus there might have been circumstances after 70 that made reducing the grazing area of flocks advantageous. I do not know anyone other than Jeremias who has taken *Bava Qamma* 7.7 as a law that governed pre-70 Palestine. Everyone else has perceived that this would be a problem while the temple stood. Applebaum, for example, understood the passage to apply 'in the main to conditions after 70' ('Economic Life', p. 670). Billerbeck (*Kommentar* I, p. 493) may have been slightly troubled by the lack of realism that he attributed to the Pharisees; this may explain why he wrote 'steppes' (prairies) where the text has 'deserts'. Quite a few sheep could be pastured on steppes.

27. Above, pp. 119f.

28. For example, *Temple Scroll* I, p. 307.

29. Yadin, *Bar-Kokhba*, pp. 229f.; see above, p. 179.

30. For a similar case, the re-use of scroll-wrappers for burial shrouds, see *Finds*, p. 244.

31. Goodman, *State and Society*, pp. 159–63 and notes.

32. Yadin, *Finds*, p. 170.

33. Neusner correctly pointed out that the Pharisaic rules were mostly in-house regulations, though he erred in thinking that they governed principally the Pharisees' own food (*JLJM*, ch. III).

34. Yadin, *Finds*, p. 185; above, pp. 122f.

35. *Finds*, p. 229.

36. *Finds*, p. 229 n. 51.

37. Page 227 above.

38. *JLJM*, pp. 224–6.

39. That he did so is cited as a fact by Jeremias (n. 2 above) and Rajak (*Josephus*, p. 30), because 'it is laid down'.

40. Who had the right to execute is a contentious point of long standing, but I think that it should not be. Roman historians whom I have consulted think that Sherwin-White (*Roman Society and Roman Law in the New Testament*) was correct in arguing that in equestrian provinces (like Judaea), only the prefect or procurator had the power of life and death. The argument is supported by *War* 2.117. A speech that Josephus attributes to Titus supplies interesting evidence. Trying to persuade the defenders of Jerusalem to surrender, he asked, 'And did we not permit you to put to death any who passed [the balustrade in the temple], even if he were a Roman?' (*War* 6.126). The precise wording seems to imply that permission to execute anyone who trespassed the barrier was a special benefit, though the weight falls on the clause 'even a Roman'. Execution by mob violence, of course, was another matter (as in Acts 7.57f.). If no harm (i.e. disruption) came of it, it

might be overlooked.

41. *JLJM*, pp. 209–13.

42. My most extensive argument in favour of this point is *JLJM*, ch. II. See also pp. 213f. for a possible instance in which the Pharisees regarded one of their rules as binding.

43. See *JLJM*, pp. 209–303.

44. Page 388.

45. McLaren, *Power and Politics in Palestine*.

46. Some of the comments by Goodman and McLaren influenced which parts I left out, as well as helping me clarify the points I left in. I am grateful to them both.

47. 'Independent', from the time of Philip of Macedonia on, could mean at best 'semi-autonomous'. Alexander and his successors kept up the tradition of founding 'independent' cities, but in the Hellenistic kingdoms and the Roman empire city rights were limited.

48. Two passages in Josephus point to the number seventy. (1) When Josephus took command of Galilee he 'selected . . . seventy persons of mature years and the greatest discretion and appointed them magistrates (*archontoi*) of the whole of Galilee', and also seven individuals in each city to deal with petty cases, referring important matters and capital cases to himself and the seventy (*War* 2.570f.). We do not hear of the seventy in Galilee actually doing anything. They are mentioned again only when Josephus took them hostage (*Life* 79). This shows that they were respected and eminent; all the decisions seem to have been taken by Josephus himself, or by one of the other leaders of revolution. (2) When the Zealots were in charge in Jerusalem, they wished to eliminate Zacharias, 'one of the most eminent of the citizens'. They ordered seventy of the 'leading citizens' to compose a court, and they accused Zacharias of treason. He defended himself and, so doing, braced the seventy to share his fate. They acquitted him. The Zealots killed him and threw his body into the ravine. They did not kill the seventy, but rather drove them from the temple, 'sparing their lives for the sole reason that they might disperse through the city and proclaim to all the servitude to which they were reduced' (*War* 4.334–44).

It may be assumed that Josephus modelled his organization on another, and that the Zealots were mocking regular courts. This points to the use of a seventy man court to hear important cases, and seven local magistrates in each town or village. The numbers seventy and seven, of course, are important symbolic numbers, which makes them especially suitable for courts and delegations. Thus, for example, Batanaea sent seventy spokesmen to Agrippa II (*War* 2.482) and Ecabatana sent seventy delegates to Varus (*Life* 56–58).

The Mishnah's number, seventy-one, is an interesting bit of exegesis: seventy elders of Israel (Num. 11.16), plus Moses. My guess is that the standard exegesis fixed on seventy, and that the Mishnah is simply being a bit cleverer.

49. The secretary: *War* 5.532; the council chamber: *War* 6.354; cf. 5.144. The *boulē* itself is discussed below.

50. Tcherikover, 'Was Jerusalem a "Polis"?', *IEJ* 14, 1964, pp. 61–78; Safrai, 'Jewish Self-Government', pp. 389f.

51. The most convenient and clearest presentation of the two-sanhedrin theory is Ellis Rivkin's in *What Crucified Jesus?*

52. The account of the Sanhedrin in *HJP* II, pp. 199–226 is a penetrating analysis of the various theories and a judicious statement of the majority view, one that lacks some of the weakest points that I here include in 'the majority opinion'. See nn. 58, 60.

53. *HJP* I, p. 230; II, p. 210; Jeremias, *Jerusalem*, pp. 223, 262.

54. Alon, *The Jews in their Land* I, p. 44.

55. Safrai, 'Jewish Self-Government', p. 384.

56. Rajak, *Josephus*, p. 19.

57. Cf. Falk, *Introduction to Jewish Law* I, pp. 55f.; Safrai, 'Jewish Self-Government', pp. 388f.

58. *HJP* II, p. 211: 'the members were not changed yearly and elected by the people, as in the case of the democratic councils of the Greek cities, but held office for a longer period, perhaps for life'.

59. E.g. Alon, *The Jews in their Land* I, p. 44. Falk, who defines 'the Sanhedrin' in traditional rabbinic terms, recognizes that rulers may not have consulted it (*Jewish Law* I, p. 56).

60. *HJP* II, pp. 215–17.

61. Goodman's doubts are more-or-less equally thoroughgoing (*Ruling Class*, pp. 113–16).

62. Possibly the *gerousia* was called *hever* in Hebrew: see Meshorer, *Coinage* I, pp. 47f. and notes; above, p. 319.

63. Safrai, 'Jewish Self-Government', p. 384; Russell, *The Jews from Alexander to Herod*, p. 74.

64. Lohse, *The New Testament Environment*, p. 75.

65. On the Roman view of the need for mass slaughter after a siege, followed by regulated pillaging, see Connolly, *Greece and Rome at War*, p. 295.

66. A. Momigliano, 'Herod of Judaea', *CAH* 10, 1936, pp. 316–39, here p. 322. I am here filling in the steps that would be necessary to support his conclusions.

67. I am indebted to James McLaren for this point.

68. According to Acts 23.7, there was an upheaval (*stasis*) of the Pharisees and Sadducees, with the result that 'the assembly' (*plēthos*) was divided. This falls short of saying that the assembly consisted only of Pharisees and Sadducees; rather, their disagreement divided the assembly.

69. Josephus at this point calls Hyrcanus 'king', though Pompey had demoted him to 'ethnarch'. Josephus' titles are not always precise. He (and other Greek-writing authors) sometimes called the Roman emperor 'king'; our term, 'emperor', is itself not correct. I shall leave such niceties aside.

70. According to *Antiq.* 15.4 Pollion made this warning. There are variant readings in the manuscripts; Josephus may have forgotten which Pharisee it was.

71. On the mutilation, see ch. 3 n. 3.

72. 'In consequence of its importance, the Sanhedrin had links with the entire world of Jewry, and joined every little village in Judaea administratively with Jerusalem', Jeremias, *Jerusalem*, p. 74.

73. For one example, see above, p. 420.

74. The rabbis thought that there had been a 'chamber of hewn stone' from which halakhic rulings sometimes emanated (e.g. *Pe'ah* 2.6; there are only a few more passages). They also held that there were three *bet dins*, courts, that handed down rulings (*Sanhedrin* 11.2). If one accepts all such statements and then combines them as referring to 'the Sanhedrin', one will be able to find a *few* rulings by 'the Sanhedrin', which, however, is not called that. Very few scholars, whether Christian or Jewish, have been fundamentalistic enough to make all these equations and combinations. If one does not make them, 'the Sanhedrin' decided no cases. If one makes them, the *bet din* = the court that met in the chamber of hewn stone = the Sanhedrin decided a few cases.

75. *Ruling Class*, p. 110. On popular assemblies see also Falk, *Jewish Law* I, pp. 50f.

76. Cf. Lane Fox's comments on Alexander's use of stoning, *Alexander the Great*, p. 284.

77. On the usual 'right' of an empire to levy charges over and above tribute, see above, pp. 161f.

78. At this point Goodman underestimates the effectiveness of the chief priests: 'the pleas of the Jewish leaders to the rioters proved useless. Florus could not rely on them to keep order and decided not to try' (*Ruling Class*, p. 153). If events had stopped where this note is placed, the chief priests would have been effective.

79. *Hoi archontes* can be either 'magistrates' or, more generally, 'officials', 'administrators', or 'rulers'. For present purposes, I assume them to be 'magistrates', without trying to decide just what relation, if any, they bore to 'judges' (*kritoi*).

80. Lev. 21.10 forbids the high priest to rend his clothes. In the story of the crisis with Florus, Josephus states that the chief priests rent their clothes trying to persuade the crowd, but he does not explicitly say that the high priest did so: *War* 2.316, 322. In *War* 2.237 (the Galilean – Samaritan clash) the 'magistrates' wore sackcloth and put ashes on their heads. Public acts of mourning by high-ranking men seem to have been an effective device for swaying a court or a crowd.

81. There is a large body of literature on the synoptic accounts of the trial of Jesus. The version in John is substantially different.

82. This point is made very forcefully by Rivkin, *What Crucified Jesus?*

83. See his historical descriptions in *Antiq.* 4.186, 214–24, 304; 11.111; 12.138–42; 13.166. Kings should be ruled by priests and the council; it was the Hasmoneans who, by becoming kings, ruined it (14.41).

84. Jeremias, *Jerusalem*, p. 267.

22. Epilogue

1. *Ruling Class*, esp. pp. 34–50.
2. Goodman, *Ruling Class*, p. 110.
3. *Ruling Class*, esp. pp. 111, 124; see ch. 21 n. 78 above.
4. Above, pp. 329f., 339, 485–7 and n. 78.

Bibliography*

1 Editions and Translations Cited or Quoted

Apocrypha and Pseudepigrapha

The Apocryphal Old Testament, ed. H. F. D. Sparks, Oxford 1984. (Cited as *AOT*.)

The Apocrypha and Pseudepigrapha of the Old Testament in English, vol. II *Pseudepigrapha*, ed. R. H. Charles, Oxford 1913; repr. 1963. (Cited as *POT*.)

The Old Testament Pseudepigrapha, vol. I *Apocalyptic Literature and Testaments*; vol. II *Expansions of the 'Old Testament'*, etc., ed. James H. Charlesworth, New York 1983, 1985. (Cited as *OTP* I & II.)

The Dead Sea Scrolls

The Dead Sea Scrolls in English, tr. Geza Vermes, 3rd, revised and augmented ed., Harmondsworth 1987. (Cited as *DSSE³*.)

Discoveries in the Judaean Desert II: Les grottes de Murabbaʿât, ed. P. Benoit, J. T. Milik and R. de Vaux, Oxford 1961. (Cited as DJD II.)

Discoveries in the Judaean Desert VII: Qumrân Grotte 4, vol. III, ed. Maurice Baillet, Oxford 1982. (Cited as DJD VII.)

The Scroll of the War of the Sons of Light against the Sons of Darkness, ed. Yigael Yadin, ET Oxford 1962.

Songs of the Sabbath Sacrifice: A Critical Edition, ed. and tr. Carol Newsom, Atlanta 1985.

The Temple Scroll, ed. Yigael Yadin, 3 vols + supplementary plates, English ed., Jerusalem 1983.

The Zadokite Documents, ed. and tr. Chaim Rabin, 2nd ed., Oxford 1958. (This text is now more commonly called *The Covenant of Damascus* or *The Damascus Rule*; cited as CD.)

Rabbinic Literature

The Babylonian Talmud, Soncino ed., general ed. I. Epstein, 35 vols, London 1935–52, repr. in 18 vols, London 1961.

The Mekilta, ed. and tr. Jacob Z. Lauterbach, 3 vols, Philadelphia 1933–1935.

The Mishnah, tr. Herbert Danby, Oxford 1933.

Sifra d'Be Rab. Hu' Sefer Torat Kohanim, Jerusalem 1959.

Sifre. A Tannaitic Commentary on the Book of Deuteronomy, ET Reuven Hammer, New Haven and London 1986.

The Tosefta, tr. Jacob Neusner and others, 6 vols, New York 1977–1986.

*For fuller bibliographies of reference works and texts, see *P&PJ*; *JLJM*.

Other Jewish Literature and Texts
Corpus Papyrorum Judaicarum, 3 vols, ed. Victor A. Tcherikover and Alexander Fuks, Cambridge MA and Jerusalem 1957, 1960 and 1964.
The Documents from the Bar Kokhba Period in the Cave of Letters, ed. Naphtali Lewis, Yigael Yadin and Jonas C. Greenfield, Jerusalem 1989.
Josephus, *Works*, ed. and tr. H. St J. Thackeray (vols 1–5), Ralph Marcus (vols 5–8) and Louis Feldman (vols 9–10), LCL, London and Cambridge MA 1926–1965.
Philo, *Works*, ed. and tr. F. H. Colson (vols 1–10) and G. H. Whitaker (vols 1–5), LCL, London and Cambridge MA 1929–1943.

Other Ancient Literature
Bibliographical details are not given for the works available in the Loeb Classical Library, unless another edition is cited.
Dio Cassius, *Roman History*: LCL.
Greek and Latin Authors on Jews and Judaism, ed. Menahem Stern, 3 vols, 1974–1984.
Herodotus, *History*: LCL.
Pausanius, *Description of Greece*: LCL.
Philostratus, *The Life of Apollonius of Tyana*: LCL.
Pliny, *Natural History*, ed. John Bostock and H. T. Riley, 6 vols, London 1855–1857; also LCL.
Seneca, *Moral Letters*: LCL.
Suetonius, *Lives of the Caesars*: LCL.
Tacitus, *Annals* and *Histories*: LCL.
Thucydides, *History of the Peloponnesian War*: LCL.

2 Reference Works Cited or Quoted

Atlas of Ancient Egypt, ed. John Baines and Jaromír Málek, New York 1980.
The Cambridge History of Judaism, ed. W. D. Davies and Louis Finkelstein, vol. I: *Introduction; the Persian Period*, Cambridge 1984; vol. II: *The Hellenistic Age*, Cambridge 1989.
Encyclopedia of Archaeological Excavations in the Holy Land, ed. Michael Avi-Yonah, 4 vols, Jerusalem and Oxford 1975–1978.
Encyclopaedia Judaica, 16 vols, ed. in chief Cecil Roth, corrected ed., Jerusalem n.d.; vol. 17, Supplement, 1982.
Hebrew and English Lexicon of the Old Testament, ed. Francis Brown, S. R. Driver and C. A. Briggs, Oxford 1907, rvsd. 1953.
The Interpreter's Dictionary of the Bible, 4 vols, gen. ed. G. A. Buttrick, Nashville 1962; Supplementary Volume, gen. ed. Keith Crim, 1976.
The MacMillan Bible Atlas, ed. Yohanan Aharoni and Michael Avi-Yonah, rev. ed., New York 1977.

3 General

Abrahams, I., *Studies in Pharisaism and the Gospel*, First and Second Series, Cambridge 1917, 1924 (repr. New York 1967).

Alon, Gedalyahu, 'The Bounds of the Laws of Levitical Cleanness', *Jews, Judaism and the Classical World*, ET Jerusalem 1977, pp. 190–234.

Alon, Gedalyahu, *The Jews in their Land in the Talmudic Age (70–640 C.E.)*, 2 vols, ET Jerusalem 1980, 1984.

Alon, Gedalyahu, 'The Levitical Uncleanness of Gentiles', *Jews, Judaism and the Classical World*, pp. 146–89.

Amin, Mohamed, *Pilgrimage to Mecca*, London 1978.

Applebaum, S., 'Economic Life in Palestine', *The Jewish People in the First Century*, ed. Safrai and Stern (CRINT 1.2), pp. 631–700.

Applebaum, S., 'The Social and Economic Status of the Jews in the Diaspora', *The Jewish People in the First Century*, ed. Safrai and Stern (CRINT 1.2), pp. 701–27.

Avigad, Nahman, *Discovering Jerusalem*, New York 1983.

Bailey, Thomas A. and Paul B. Ryan, *Hitler vs. Roosevelt: The Undeclared Naval War*, New York 1979.

Bamberger, B. J., 'Money-Changer', *IDB* III, pp. 435f.

Barrett, C. K., 'The Background of Mark 10:45', *New Testament Essays: Studies in the Memory of Thomas Walter Manson*, ed. A. J. B. Higgins, Manchester 1959, pp. 1–18.

Bashem, Arthur L., *The Wonder that was India*, London 1967.

Baumgarten, A. I., '*Korban* and the Pharisaic *Paradosis*', *Ancient Studies in Memory of Elias Bickerman. The Journal of Ancient Near Eastern Society* 16–17, 1984–1985, pp. 5–17.

Baumgarten, A. I., 'The Name of the Pharisees', *JBL* 102, 1983, pp. 411–28.

Baumgarten, A. I., 'The Pharisaic *Paradosis*', *HTR* 80, 1987, pp. 63–77.

Baumgarten, J. M., *Studies in Qumran Law*, Leiden 1977.

Beall, Todd S., *Josephus' description of the Essenes illustrated by the Dead Sea Scrolls*, Cambridge 1988.

Beard, Mary and John North, eds, *Pagan Priests: Religion and Power in the Ancient World*, London 1990.

Beasley-Murray, G. R., *Jesus and the Kingdom of God*, Grand Rapids 1986.

Ben-Dov, Meir, *In the Shadow of the Temple*, ET New York 1985.

Bentwich, Norman DeMattos, *Josephus*, Philadelphia 1914.

Betz, O., *What do we Know About Jesus?*, ET London 1968.

Black, Matthew, 'Pharisees', *IDB* III, pp. 774–81.

Borg, Marcus J., *Jesus, a New Vision: Spirit, Culture, and the Life of Discipleship*, New York 1984.

Boyce, Mary, 'Persian religion in the Achemenid age', *CHJ* I, pp. 279–307.

Brooke, George J., ed., *Temple Scroll Studies*, Sheffield 1989.

Broshi, Magen, 'Estimating the Population of Ancient Jerusalem', *BAR* 4/2, 1978, pp. 10–15.

Broshi, Magen, 'The Diet of Palestine in the Roman Period – Introductory Notes', *The Israel Museum Journal* 5, 1986, pp. 41–56.

Broshi, Magen, 'The Population of Western Palestine in the Roman-Byzantine Period', *BASOR* 236, 1979, pp. 1–10.

Brown, Peter, *The Body and Society. Men, Women, and Sexual Renunciation in Early Christianity*, New York 1988.

Bruce, F. F., *Israel and the Nations from the Exodus to the Fall of the Second Temple*, Exeter 1973.

Bruneau, Phillippe, '"Les Israélites de Délos" et la juiverie déliens', *BCH* 106, 1982, pp. 465–504.

Bruneau, Phillipe, *Recherches sur les cultes de Délos à l'époque Hellenistique et à l'époque impériale*, Paris 1970.

Brunt, P. A., *Roman Imperial Themes*, Oxford 1990.

Büchler, Adolf, 'The Levitical Impurity of Gentiles', *JQR* 17, 1926–27, pp. 1–81.

Burkert, Walter, *Greek Religion*, ET Oxford 1985.

Busink, Th. A., *Der Tempel von Jerusalem*, 2 vols, Leiden 1970, 1980.

Callaway, Philip R., *The History of the Qumran Community*, Sheffield 1988.

Carcopino, Jérôme, *Daily Life in Ancient Rome*, ET New Haven 1940.

Carras, George, *Paul, Josephus and Judaism: The Shared Judaism of Paul and Josephus*, unpubl. Oxford D. Phil. thesis, 1989.

Cohen, Shaye J. D., *Josephus in Galilee and Rome*, Leiden 1979.

Conder, Claude Reignier, *Tent Work in Palestine*, London 1878.

Connolly, Peter, *Greece and Rome at War*, London 1981.

Dalman, Gustaf, *Sacred Sites and Ways*, ET New York 1935.

Daube, David, 'Example and Precept: From Sirach to R. Ishmael', *Tradition and Interpretation in the New Testament*. Essays in Honor of E. Earle Ellis, ed. Gerald F. Hawthorn with Otto Betz, Grand Rapids and Tübingen 1987, pp. 16–20.

Daube, David, 'Standing in for Jack Coons', *Rechtshistorisches Journal* 7, pp. 1979–90.

Davies, Philip R., *Behind the Essenes: History and Ideology in the Dead Sea Scrolls*, Atlanta 1987.

Davies, Philip R., Review of *Josephus' Description of the Essenes* by Todd Beall, *JTS* 41, 1990, pp. 164–9.

Davies, Philip R., *The Damascus Covenant*, Sheffield 1982.

Davies, Philip R., 'The Ideology of the Temple in the Damascus Document', *JJS* 33, 1982, pp. 287–301.

Davies, Philip R., 'The Temple Scroll and the Damascus Document', *Temple Scroll Studies*, ed. Brooke, pp. 201–10.

Davies, Philip R. and Richard T. White, eds, *A Tribute to Geza Vermes: Essays on Jewish and Christian Literature and History*, Sheffield 1990.

Davies, W. D., *The Gospel and the Land*, Berkeley 1974.

Deissmann, Adolf, *Light from the Ancient East*, ET London 1910, repr. 1965.

Detienne, Marcel and Jean-Paul Vernant, eds, *The Cuisine of Sacrifice Among the Greeks*, ET Chicago 1989.

Dothan, M., 'The Synagogue at Hammath-Tiberias', *Ancient Synagogues Revealed*, ed. Levine, pp. 63–9.

Dothan, M., 'Tiberias, Hammath', *Encyclopedia of Archaeological Excavations*, pp. 1178–84.

Douglas, Mary, *Purity and Danger. An Analysis of the Concepts of Pollution and Taboo*, London 1966, repr. 1984.

Dover, Kenneth J., *Greek Homosexuality*, London 1978.

Durand, Jean-Louis, 'Greek Animals: Toward a Topology of Edible Bodies', *The Cuisine of Sacrifice*, ed. Detienne and Vernant, pp. 87–118.

Edersheim, Alfred, *The Life and Times of Jesus the Messiah*, 2 vols, Grand Rapids 1936.

Edgar, M. C. C., *Graeco-Egyptian Coffins, Masks and Portraits*, Catalogue Général des antiquités Egyptiennes du musée du Caire, Cairo 1905.

Falk, Ze'ev W., *Introduction to Jewish Law of the Second Commonwealth*, 2 vols, Leiden 1972, 1978.

Feldman, Louis, 'The Omni-Presence of the God-Fearers', *BAR* 12, 1986, pp. 58–69.

Fiensy, David A., *Prayers Alleged to be Jewish*, Chico CA 1985.

Finkelstein, Louis, *The Pharisees. The Sociological Background of their Faith*, 2 vols, 3rd ed. with suppl., Philadelphia 1962.

Fitzmyer, Joseph A., see Reumann, John.

Foakes Jackson, Frederick J. and Kirsopp Lake eds, *The Beginnings of Christianity*, 5 vols, London 1920–33.

Foerster, G., 'The Synagogues at Masada and Herodium',*Ancient Synagogues Revealed*, ed. Levine, pp. 24–9.

Fortna, Robert and Beverly Gaventa, eds, *The Conversation Continues: Studies in Paul and John in Honor of J. Louis Martyn*, Nashville 1990.

Freyne, Sean, *Galilee from Alexander the Great to Hadrian, 323 B.C.E. to 135 C.E.: A Study of Second Temple Judaism*, Wilmington 1980.

Gibbs, John G. and Louis H. Feldman, 'Josephus' Vocabulary for Slavery', *JQR* 4, 1986, pp. 281–310.

Ginouvès, René, *Balaneutikè. Recherches sur le bain dans l'antiquité grecque*, Bibliothèque des Ecoles Françaises d'Athènes et de Rome 200, Paris, 1962.

Ginzberg, Louis, *On Jewish Law and Lore*, Cleveland 1962.

Goodenough, Erwin R., *By Light, Light: The Mystic Gospel of Hellenistic Judaism*, London 1935.

Goodenough, Erwin R., *Jewish Symbols in the Greco-Roman Period*, 13 vols, New York 1953–68.

Goodman, Martin, 'Kosher Olive Oil in Antiquity',*A Tribute to Geza Vermes*, ed. Davies and White, pp. 227–45.

Goodman, Martin, *State and Society in Roman Galilee, A.D. 132–212*, Totowa NJ 1983.

Goodman, Martin, *The Ruling Class of Judaea: The Origins of the Jewish Revolt Against Rome, A.D. 66–70*, Cambridge and New York 1987.

Gordon, Richard, 'From Republic to Principate: priesthood, religion and idealogy', *Pagan Priests*, ed. Beard and North, pp. 177–98.

Grafman, R., 'Herod's Foot and Robinson's Arch', *IEJ* 20, 1970, pp. 60–66.

Grant, Frederick C., *The Economic Background of the Gospels*, London 1926.

Gray, Rebecca, *Prophetic Figures in Late Second Temple Jewish Palestine: The Evidence from Josephus*, Oxford 1992.

Groh, Dennis, 'Jews and Christians in Late Roman Palestine: Towards a New Chronology', *BA* 51, 1988, pp. 80–96.

Guttmann, Alexander,*Ancient Synagogues: The State of Research*, Atlanta 1981.

Guttmann, Alexander, 'The End of the Jewish Sacrificial Cult', *HUCA* 38, 1967, pp. 137–48.

Hanfmann, George M. A., 'The Ninth Campaign at Sardis', *BASOR* 187, 1967, pp. 9–62.

Haran, Menahem, 'Priestly Vestments', *Enc. Jud.* 13, cols 1063–9.

Harrison, R. K., 'Balm', *IDB* I, p. 344.

Heinemann, Isaak, *Philons griechische und jüdische Bildung*, Hildesheim 1962 (= Breslau 1929, 1930, 1932).

Heinemann, Joseph, *Prayer in the Talmud: Forms and Patterns*, ET Berlin and New York 1977.

Hellholm, David, ed.,*Apocalypticism in the Mediterranean World and the Near East*, Tübingen 1983.

Hengel, Martin, *Between Jesus and Paul: Studies in the Earliest History of Christianity*, ET London 1983.

Hengel, Martin, *Judaism and Hellenism: Studies in their Encounter in Palestine during the Early Hellenistic Period*, 2 vols, ET London 1974.

Hengel, Martin, in collaboration with Roland Deines, *The Pre-Christian Paul*, ET London 1991.

Herr, Moshe David, 'Oral Law', *Enc. Jud.* 12, cols 1439–42.

Hill, Craig, *Hellenists and Hebrews: Reappraising Division within the Earliest Church*, Minneapolis 1991.

Hobson, Christine, *Exploring the World of the Pharaohs*, London 1987.

Hoenig, Sidney B., 'Oil and Pagan Defilement', *JQR* 61, 1970, pp. 63–75.

Hoenig, Sidney B., 'Onias', *IDB* III, pp. 603f.

Hopkins, Clark, *The Discovery of Dura-Europos*, New Haven 1979.

Horbury, William, 'The Temple tax', *Jesus and the Politics of his Day*, ed. Ernst Bammel and C. F. D. Moule, Cambridge 1984, pp. 265–86.

Horsley, Richard, *Jesus and the Spiral of Violence: Popular Jewish Resistance in Roman Palestine*, San Francisco 1987.

Horsley, Richard and John S. Hanson, *Bandits, Prophets, and Messiahs: Popular Movements at the Time of Jesus*, Minneapolis 1985.

Houston, Mary, *Ancient Greek, Roman and Byzantine Costume and Decoration*, London 1931.

Jeremias, J., *Jerusalem in the Time of Jesus*, ET London and Philadelphia 1969.

Jeremias, J., *Jesus' Promise to the Nations*, ET London and Nashville 1958.

Jeremias, J., *The Proclamation of Jesus*, ET London 1971.

Johnson, Luke Timothy, *The Writings of the New Testament: An Interpretation*, Philadelphia 1986.

Juster, Jean, *Les Juifs dan l'empire romain. Leur condition juridique, économique et sociale*, 2 vols, Paris 1914.

Kampen, John, *The Hasideans and the Origins of the Pharisees: A Study in I and II Maccabees*, Atlanta 1988.

Kasher, Aryeh, *Jews, Idumaeans, and Ancient Arabs*, Tübingen 1988.

Kee, Howard, 'The Transformation of the Synagogue after 70 CE: Its Import for Early Christianity', NTS 36, 1990, pp. 1–24.

Knibb, Michael A., *The Qumran Community*, Cambridge 1987.

Kraabel, A. T., 'Synagoga Caeca', *To See Ourselves as Others See Us*, ed. Jacob Neusner and Ernest Frerichs, Chico, CA 1985, pp. 219–46.

Kutsch, Ernst, 'Passover. Critical View', *Enc. Jud.* 13, cols 169–172.

Lane Fox, Robin, *Alexander the Great*, London 1975.

Lauterbach, Jacob Z., *Rabbinic Essays*, Cincinnati 1951.

Le Moyne, Jean, *Les Sadducéens*, Paris 1972.

Leaney, Alfred Robert Clare, *The Jewish and Christian World 200 BC to AD 200*, Cambridge 1984.

Levine, Lee I., ed., *Ancient Synagogues Revealed*, Jerusalem 1981.

Levine, Lee I., ed., *The Jerusalem Cathedra: Studies in the History, Archaeology, Geography and Ethnography of the Land of Israel* II, Jerusalem and Detroit 1982.

Levine, Lee I., 'The Second Temple Synagogue: the Formative Years', *The Synagogue in Late Antiquity*, ed. Levine, pp. 7–31.

Levine, Lee I., ed., *The Synagogue in Late Antiquity*, Philadelphia, ASOR 1987.

Licht, Jacob, *The Rule Scroll. A Scroll from the Wilderness of Judaea: 1QS, 1QSa, 1QSb*, Jerusalem 1965 (Hebrew).

Lohse, Eduard, *The New Testament Environment*, ET Nashville 1976.

Maccoby, Hyam, *Early Rabbinic Writings*, Cambridge 1988.

Maccoby, Hyam, *Revolution in Judaea*, 2nd ed., New York 1980.

MacLennan, Robert S. and A. Thomas Kraabel, 'The God-Fearers – a Literary and Theological Invention', *BAR* 12, 1986, pp. 46–57.

McLaren, James, *Power and Politics in Palestine: The Jews and the Governing of their Land. 100 BC–AD 70*, Sheffield 1991.

Maier, Johann, 'The Architectural History of the Temple in Jerusalem in the Light of the Temple Scroll', *Temple Scroll Studies*, ed. Brooke, pp. 23–62.

Maʿoz, Z., 'The Synagogue of Gamla and the Typology of Second-Temple Synagogues', *Ancient Synagogues Revealed*, ed. Levine, pp. 35–41.

Mason, Steve N., 'Priesthood in Josephus and the "Pharisaic Revolution"', *JBL* 107, 1988, pp. 657–61.

Mason, Steve N., *Flavius Josephus on the Pharisees. A Composition-Critical Study*, Leiden 1991.

Mazar, A., 'The Aqueducts of Jerusalem', *Jerusalem Revealed*, ed. Yadin, pp. 79–84.

Mazar, Benjamin, *The Mountain of the Lord*, Garden City NY 1975.

Mendelson, Alan, *Philo's Jewish Identity*, Atlanta 1988.

Meshorer, Yaʿakov, *Ancient Jewish Coinage*, 2 vols, Dix Hills NY 1982.

Millar, Fergus, 'Reflections on the Trial of Jesus', *A Tribute to Geza Vermes*, ed. Davies and White, pp. 355–81.

Miller, Stuart S., *Studies in the History and Traditions of Sepphoris*, Leiden 1984.

Momigliano, A., 'Herod of Judaea', *Cambridge Ancient History* 10, Cambridge 1936, pp. 316–39.

Moore, George Foot, *Judaism in the First Centuries of the Christian Era*, 3 vols, Cambridge MA 1927–1930.

Neusner, Jacob, *From Politics to Piety: The Emergence of Pharisaic Judaism*, Englewood Cliffs NJ 1973.

Neusner, Jacob, 'Josephus' Pharisees: A Complete Repertoire', *Formative Judaism* 3rd Series, Chico, CA. 1983, pp. 61–82.

Neusner, Jacob, *Judaism in the beginning of Christianity*, Philadelphia 1984.

Neusner, Jacob, *Judaism: The Evidence of the Mishnah*, Chicago 1981.

Neusner, Jacob, *Messiah in Context: Israel's History and Destiny in Formative Judaism*, Philadelphia 1984.

Neusner, Jacob, *The Rabbinic Traditions about the Pharisees before 70*, 3 vols, Leiden 1971.

Neusner, Jacob, *Reading and Believing: Ancient Judaism and Contemporary Gullibility*, Atlanta 1986.

Neusner, Jacob, *Torah: From Scroll to Symbol in Formative Judaism*, Philadelphia 1985.

Nickelsburg, George W. E., *Faith and Piety in Early Judaism: Texts and Documents*, Philadelphia 1983.

Nickelsburg, George W. E., *Jewish Literature between the Bible and the Mishnah*, Philadelphia 1981.

Patrich, Joseph, 'A Sadducean Halakha and the Jerusalem Aqueduct', *The Jerusalem Cathedra* 2, ed. Levine, pp. 25–39.

Plassart, André, 'Fouilles de Délos, *BCH* 40, 1916, pp. 145–256.

Rajak, Tessa, *Josephus: The historian and his Society*, London 1983.

Reumann, John, with Joseph A. Fitzmyer and Jerome D. Quinn, *"Righteousness" in the New Testament: "Justification" in the United States Lutheran-Roman Catholic Dialogue*, Philadelphia 1982.

Reynolds, J. and R. Tannenbaum, *Jews and Godfearers at Aphrodisias*, Cambridge Philological Society Supplementary Volume 12, Cambridge 1987.

Rhoads, David M., *Israel in Revolution, 6–74 C.E.: A Political History Based on the Writings of Josephus*, Philadelphia 1976.

Richlin, Amy, *The Garden of Priapus*, New Haven 1983.

Ringgren, Helmer, *The Faith of Qumran: Theology of the Dead Sea Scrolls*, ET Philadelphia 1963.

Ritmeyer, Kathleen and Leen Ritmeyer, 'Reconstructing Herod's Temple Mount in Jerusalem', *BAR* 15/6, 1989, pp. 23–42.

Rivkin, Ellis, *What Crucified Jesus?*, Nashville 1984 and London 1986.

Rohde, Erwin, *Psyche: The Cult of Souls and Belief in Immortality among the Greeks*, ET London 1925.

Rostovtzeff, M., *The Social and Economic History of the Roman Empire*, Oxford, 1926; 2nd ed., 2 vols, Oxford 1957, corrected repr. 1971.

Roth, Cecil, 'England', *Enc. Jud.* 6, cols 747–72.

Rothkoff, Aaron, 'Sacrifice', *Enc. Jud.* 14, cols 599–615.

Rowland, Christopher, *The Open Heaven. The Study of Apocalyptic in Judaism and Early Christianity*, London and New York 1982.

Russell, D. S., *The Jews from Alexander to Herod*, London 1967.

Safrai, Shmuel, 'Jewish Self-Government', *The Jewish People in the First Century* (CRINT I.1), ed. Safrai and Stern, pp. 377–419.

Safrai, Shmuel, 'Oral Tora', *The Literature of the Sages* (CRINT II.3.1), ed. Safrai, Assen and Philadelphia 1987, pp. 35–119.

Safrai, Shmuel and Michael Avi-Yonah, 'Temple, Second: Structure', *Enc. Jud.* 15, cols 960–69.

Safrai, Shmuel and M. Stern, eds, *The Jewish People in the First Century*, 2 vols (CRINT I.1,2), Assen and Philadephia 1974, 1976.

Sanders, E. P., 'The Covenant as a Soteriological Category and the Nature of Salvation in Palestinian and Hellenistic Judaism', *Jews, Greeks and Christians: Religious Cultures in Late Antiquity. Essays in Honor of William David Davies*, ed. Robert Hamerton-Kelly and Robin Scroggs, Leiden 1976, pp. 11–44.

Sanders, E. P., *Jesus and Judaism*, London and Philadelphia 1985.

Sanders, E. P., 'Jewish Association with Gentiles and Galatians 2:11–14', *The Conversation Continues*, ed. Fortna and Gaventa, pp. 170–88.

Sanders, E. P., *Jewish Law from Jesus to the Mishnah: Five Studies*, London and Philadelphia, 1990.

Sanders, E. P., *Paul and Palestinian Judaism*, London and Philadelphia 1977.

Sanders, E. P., *Paul: Past Master*, Oxford 1991.

Sanders, E. P., SIN/SINNERS (NT), *Anchor Bible Dictionary*, forthcoming.

Sanders, E. P., and Martin Woodrow, *People from the Bible*, London 1987.

Sandmel, Samuel, *Philo of Alexandria*, New York 1979.

Schalit, Abraham, *König Herodes: Der Mann und sein Werk*, Berlin 1969.

Schiffman, Lawrence H., 'The Dead Sea Scrolls and the Early History of Jewish Liturgy', *The Synagogue in Late Antiquity*, ed. Levine, pp. 33–48.

Schiffman, Lawrence H., 'The New Halakhic Letter (4QMMT) and the Origins of the Dead Sea Sect', *BA* 53, 1990, pp. 64–73.

Schiffman, Lawrence H., *Sectarian Law in the Dead Sea Scrolls: Courts, testimony and the penal code*, Chico CA 1983.

Schürer, Emil, *Geschichte des jüdischen Volkes im Zeitalter Jesu Christi*, 2nd ed., 1886–1890; 3rd and 4th eds, 1901–1909.

Schürer, Emil, *The Jewish People in the Time of Jesus Christ*, 6 vols, ET of the 2nd German ed., Edinburgh, 1885–1891. (Cited as *JPJC*.)

Schürer, Emil, *The History of the Jewish People in the Age of Jesus Christ (175 B.C.–A.D. 135)*, rev. and ed. by Geza Vermes, Fergus Millar and others, 3 vols in 4 parts, Edinburgh 1973–1987. (Cited as *HJP*.)

Schwartz, Daniel R., 'Josephus and Nicolaus on the Pharisees', *JSJ* 14, 1983, pp. 157–71.

Scully, Vincent, *The Earth, the Temple, and the Gods: Greek Sacred Architecture*, rev. ed. New Haven 1979.

Segal, Alan F., *Rebecca's Children: Judaism and Christianity in the Roman World*, Cambridge, MA 1986.

Segal, Peretz, 'The Penalty of the Warning Inscription from the Temple of Jerusalem', *IEJ* 39, 1989, pp. 79–84.

Shaked, Shaul, 'Iranian influence on Judaism: First century B.C.E. to second century C.E.', *CHJ* I, pp. 308–25.

Sherwin-White, Adrian, *Roman Society and Roman Law in the New Testament*, Oxford 1963.

Simon, Marcel, *Verus Israel*, ET New York 1986.

Smallwood, Mary, *The Jews under Roman Rule from Pompey to Diocletian. A Study in Political Relations*, Leiden 1976; repr. 1981.

Smith, George Adam, *Jerusalem: The Topography, Economics and History from the Earliest Times to A.D. 70*, 2 vols, London 1907–8.

Smith, Morton, 'Helios in Palestine', *Eretz-Israel. Archaeological, Historical and Geographical Studies* 16, H.M. Orlinsky Volume, 1982, pp. 199–214.

Smith, Morton, 'Palestinian Judaism in the First Century', repr. in *Essays in Greco-Roman and Related Talmudic Literature*, ed. H. A. Fischel, New York 1977, pp. 183–97.

Smith, Morton, 'The Dead Sea Sect in Relation to Ancient Judaism', *NTS* 7, 1960–61, pp. 347–60.

Smith, Morton, *Palestinian Parties and Politics that Shaped the Old Testament*, New York and London 1971.

Smith, Morton, 'Zealots and Sicarii: Their Origins and Relations', *HTR* 64, 1971, pp. 1–19.

Smith, W. Stevenson, *The Art and Architecture of Ancient Egypt*, rev. by W. K. Simpson, London 1981.

Sperber, Daniel, 'Costs of Living in Roman Palestine', *JESHO* 8, 1965, pp. 248–71.

Stegeman, H., 'The Literary Composition of the Temple Scroll and its Status at Qumran', in *Temple Scroll Studies*, ed. Brooke, pp. 123–48.

Stern, Menahem, 'Aspects of Jewish Society: The Priesthood and other Classes', *The Jewish People in the First Century*, ed. Safrai and Stern (CRINT I.2), pp. 561–630.

Stern, Menahem, 'Nicholas of Damascus', *Enc. Jud.* 12, cols 1140f.

Stern, Menahem, 'The Province of Judaea', *The Jewish People in the First Century*, ed. Safrai and Stern (CRINT I.1), pp. 308–76.

Sukenik, E. L., *Ancient Synagogues in Palestine and Greece*, London 1934.

Sweeney, Marvin A., 'Sefirah at Qumran: Aspects of the Counting Formulas for the First-Fruits in the Temple Scroll', *BASOR* 251, 1983, pp. 61–6.

Talmon, Shemaryahu, 'The Emergence of Institutionalized Prayer in Israel in the Light of the Qumran Literature', *Qumran. Sa piété, sa théologie et son milieu*, ed. M. Delcor, Paris and Leuven 1978, pp. 265–84.

Talmon, Shemaryahu, *The World of Qumran from Within*, Jerusalem 1989.

Tcherikover, Victor A., 'Was Jerusalem a "Polis"?', *IEJ* 14, 1964, pp. 61–78.

Thiering, Barbara, 'The Date of Composition of the Temple Scroll', *Temple Scroll Studies*, ed. Brooke, pp. 99–120.

Thompson, Cynthia, 'Hairstyles, Head-coverings, and St. Paul. Portraits from Roman Corinth', *BA* 51, June 1988, pp. 99–115.

Vermes, Geza, *The Dead Sea Scrolls: Qumran in Perspective*, London 1977.

Vincent, L. H., 'Le temple herodien d'après la Misnah', *RB* 61, 1954, pp. 5–35, 398–418.

Wacholder, Ben Zion, 'Hecataeus of Abdera', *Enc. Jud.* 8, cols 236f.

Wacholder, Ben Zion, 'Messianism and Mishnah: Time and Place in the Early Halakhah', The Louis Caplan Lecture on Jewish Law, Hebrew Union College Press 1979.

Whittaker, Molly, *Jews and Christians: Graeco-Roman Views*, Cambridge 1984.

Wiesenberg, E. J., 'Nisan', *Enc. Jud.* 12, cols 175f.

Wolfson, Harry A., *Philo: Foundations of Religious Philosophy in Judaism, Christianity and Islam*, 2 vols, Cambridge MA 1947.

Wormuth, Francis D. and Edwin B. Firmage, *To Chain the Dog of War. The War Power of Congress in History and Law*, 2nd ed., Urbana 1989.

Yadin, Yigael, *Bar-Kokhba: The Rediscovery of the Legendary Hero of the Second Jewish Revolt Against Rome*, New York 1971.

Yadin, Yigael, ed., *Jerusalem Revealed: Archaeology in the Holy City, 1968–1974*, Jerusalem 1975.

Yadin, Yigael, *Masada: Herod's Fortress and the Zealot's Last Stand*, New York 1966.

Yadin, Yigael, *The Finds from the Bar-Kokhba Period in the Cave of Letters*, Jerusalem 1963.

Yadin, Yigael, *The Temple Scroll*, London 1985.

Zeitlin, Solomon, *The Rise and Fall of the Judaean State*, 3 vols, Philadelphia 1962–1978.

Zeitlin, Solomon, 'Zealots and Sicarii', *JBL* 81, 1962, pp. 395–8.

4 Comments on Histories of Judaism

The history of Judaism in the period 175 BCE–135 CE is that of Emil Schürer, as revised by Geza Vermes, Fergus Millar and others (*The History of the Jewish People in the Age of Jesus Christ*, cited as *HJP*). There are numerous short accounts, all largely dependent on Schürer. I find the following three most useful:

F. F. Bruce, *Israel and the Nations from the Exodus to the Fall of the Second Temple*, Exeter 1969; often reprinted.

This is a very good historical survey of the period 1300 BCE–70 CE in Palestine. It includes unusually comprehensive tables of dates and names.

A. R. C. Leaney, *The Jewish and Christian World 200 BC to AD 200*. (Cambridge Commentaries on Writings of the Jewish and Christian World 200 BC to AD 200), Cambridge 1984.

Part I gives a historical sketch of the Jewish Diaspora and of Italy, Syria, Judaea and Egypt. Greece is omitted since Jews did not settle there. Part II treats aspects of Jewish and Christian literature and religion. The appendices contain lists of names, dates and literature, as well as two genealogical tables.

D. S. Russell, *The Jews from Alexander to Herod*, Oxford 1967; often reprinted.

Part I sketches the history of Palestine from Alexander the Great to the death of Herod. Part II treats a few main points of Jewish religion, with an emphasis on speculative theology. Part III describes some of the Palestinian Jewish literature. It treats apocalyptic and wisdom literature in greater detail than do most other short introductions. There are chronological tables and two genealogies.

There is not much to choose between these works with regard to the history of Palestine in the Hasmonean and Roman periods, except that Russell stops with the death of Herod. Individual advantages: *Bruce* covers the history of Israel during the biblical period; *Leaney* treats the Diaspora and the histories of neighbouring countries; *Russell* discusses some of the Jewish literature in greater detail than do the others.

Index of Names

Index of Passages

BIBLE

HEBREW BIBLE / JEWISH SCRIPTURE

NEW TESTAMENT

JOSEPHUS

RABINNIC LITERATURE

MISHNAH

BABYLONIAN TALMUD

PALESTINIAN TALMUD

DEAD SEA SCROLLS

PHILO

APOCRYPHA AND PSEUDEPIGRAPHA

OTHER ANCIENT LITERATURE

Index of Subjects

Adultery, charged against priests, 183
Advice, legal, 180, 181
'Affliction', on Day of Atonement, 141; and atonement, 454
Afterlife, belief in, 42f., 284, 298–303, 333, 369f., 416, 421, 452, 454; *see also* Heaven, World to come
Akribeia and cognates, *see* Experts, Strict
'Ammê ha-'arets, see People, ordinary
Allegorizers, 213f., 519 n.5
Angel of Light, Angel of Darkness, 373
Angels, depictions of, 242f.; Iranian influence on conception of, 249, 371; role of, in eschatological war, 296f., 526 n.16; in Dead Sea Scrolls, 370–72
Animals, in Jewish law, 194, 248
Antiquity, Pharisees' appeal to, 424
Apocalypses, apocalypticism, 7–10, 302f.
Aqueducts, in Jerusalem, 118, 508 n.19
Archaeology, of Qumran, 345
Aristocracy, as constituting the Jewish ruling class, 187, 383, 389, 485–90; *see also* Priests, high; Priests, chief; Leading citizens; Theocracy
Aristocrats, 280; ch. 15; whether they mistreated the ordinary people, 331f.; activities and behaviour at the time of the revolt, 328f., 330, 338f.; responsibility to keep Roman troops and Jewish crowds apart, 330, 331, 337f., 339; less ruthless than Herod, 336; moral criticisms of, 336 (cf. 182–9); moral evaluation of, 337–40; did not disappear after 70, 339; could appeal to masses, 406; *see also* Aristocracy, Leading citizens; Priests, chief; Priests, high; Wealth
Art, *see* Decoration
Assarius, 154
Assembly, public, 212, 492; *see also* Sabbath, Synagogue; as governing body, 483f.
Associates, Associations, Pharisaic, 440–42,

461; *see also* Exclusivism
Astrology, 244
Atheism, unusual in ancient world, 20, 144f., 236f.; charge against Socrates, 51; conceivable charge against God-fearers, 270; *see also* Belief in God
Atonement, 192f., 252f., 415–17, 454; *see also* Day of Atonement
Autocracies, 395, 403
'Autonomy', *see* 'Freedom' and Theocracy
Avowal, The (in Deut. 26), 138, 139, 153, 154, 157, 251f.

Balance of payments, 163f.
Balsam, 120
Bandits, in Josephus, *see* 'Brigands'
Banquets, and shared sacrifices, 110f., 114
Barley, 152f.
Bath tubs, 224; bathing quarters, 225
Bathing, as purification, 71, 72, 73, 76, 358–60; *see also* Miqva'ot; Purification
'Beforetime', in Mishnah, 461
Behaviour, correct, *see* Orthopraxy
Belief in God, in ancient world, 236f. (*see also* Atheism); in Judaism, entails obedience, 195, 229, 236f.
'Best known', The, *see* Leading citizens
Bible, *see* Scripture, Jewish
Birds, as sacrificial victims, 68, 88–90, 91, 110, 185
Blasphemy, 194
Blemishes, on sacrificial animals, 86, on people, 359
Blood, significance of, 115; disposal of, in the temple, 117f.; consumption of, 193, 194; atones (in Judaism and Christianity), 252; *see also* Sacrifice
Body-soul dualism, 298f.
Booths, Feast of, 127, 139–41; and first fruits, 153; *see also* Uprisings

Dead Sea Sect, 14; chs 16, 17; *see also* Dead
Sea Scrolls; Essenes; Qumran
Death, as atoning, 417
Decoration, of temple, 242f., 244; of Antipas'
palace, 243
Decrees, supposedly emanating from
Sanhedrin, 481
Deeds (legal documents), 465
Defecation, 359f.
Deities, pagan, *see* Demons, Idolatry
Demai-produce (produce that may or may not
have been tithed), 429–31, 441, 466f.
Demons, 247; and Iranian influence, 249
Deuteronomy, rules about taxes in, 163
Deliverance, history of and hope for, 135,
138; *see also* Redemption
Democracy, at Qumran, 365f.; modern, 458;
see also Parliament
Desert, traditional place of refuge, 453; as a
place of pastureage, 461–4, 539 n.16
Devotion to God, in Pharisaism, 417, 421
Diaspora Judaism, included within common
Judaism, 47f., 144f., 236–8, 298, 498 n.1
(eastern Diaspora); solidarity with
Palestinian Jews, 47, 256f., 265; role of
priests in, 52f., 177, 201; and temple tax,
47, 52, 163f., 237, 256f., 265; esteem for
temple, 52–4, 256f., 265; pilgrimage, 47,
127, 128, 130, 256f.; Passover sacrifices in
the Diaspora, 133f.; extent of the income
from, 163f.; views on 'justice and piety',
193f.; religious observance: 197, 201f.,
236f., 351 (prayer), 197f., 202, 236f. (study
of scripture), 198, 199f., 201, 202, 207,
208 (attendance at synagogues), 202, 207
(religious meals?), 209f., 237 (sabbath),
215–17 (food), 218, 223f., 237 (purity),
224, 237, 437 (handwashing); special legal
rights granted to, 211f.; and Gentiles,
233f., 265f., 267–70; were not concerned
about Gentiles handling their food, 520
n.12; and Pharisees, 399; and Sanhedrin,
173; Paul as an example of a Diaspora
Pharisee, 413; *see also* the passage index to
Philo, Paul's letters, and other Greek-
language Jewish literature
Diet, 129 and n.33 (510)
Dikaiosynē, see Justice
'Directing the heart', 447
Discharge (an impurity), 89, 184, 219, 436f.;
cf. Menstruation
Disputes, legal, among parties or groups of
Jews, 183–5
Diversity, *see* Unity and diversity

Documents, legal, need of professional pre-
paration, 179f., 181
Doorways, *see* Mezuzot
Doves, dove-sellers, *see* Birds
Dreams, 172
Drink, The, in Dead Sea Scrolls, 354
Dualism, 249f.; *see also* Body, Demons,
Monotheism
Dyeing, 122f. and notes

Eagle over the gate of the temple, 38, 242,
280, 284, 322, 384, 402f., 483f.
Economic development, under Herod, 164f.
Education, of priests and laypeople, 171f.,
178f., 182, 187, 191f., 363f., 404
Eighteen Benedictions, 142f., 197, 203–5;
260–62, 448
Ekklēsia, see Assembly . . . as governing body
Elders, 171, 177; *see also* Council of elders,
Leading citizens
Election, of Israel, 213, 241, 261, 262–7, 276,
415f., 419, 448, 457; of Essenes, 374
Elections, 174f.
'Eminent', The, 325, 382, 391; *see also* Lead-
ing citizens
Employment and unemployment, 85
Enemies, treatment of, 194, 233–5
Engineering, theoretical, 191
Epitomes of law, *see* Law, summaries of
'Eruv, 'Eruvin (changing the sabbath
limits), 335, 425, 442, 466f.
Eschatology, and apocalypses, 495 n.6;
Jewish, *see* ch. 14, Essenes, Future,
Jerusalem, Land, Rabbis, Visions
Essenism, Essenes, sources, 529 n.8; chs 16
and 17; general characteristics, 13f.; origin
of, 24f.; and temple, 53, 352, 362f.; dress
of, 96–8; as teachers, 177; as religious
polemicists, 186; and sun worship, 245f.,
351; view of fate, 251; views on afterlife,
299–302; ch. 15; history and development
of, 341–49; evidence for, 342–5; and
marriage, 344, 529 n.6; literary references
to, 345–9; absent from Josephus' history
for several decades, 346; participation in
revolt, 346f.; pacifism, 347; numbers of,
347; where resident, 347; sexual rules of,
347, 352; occupations of, 347; charity,
poverty and property, 348; rules of admission and membership, 349–51; oaths, 349,
351; monastic rules, 350; punishments for
misdeeds, 350, 353f., 367; worship, 351;
prayers, 196f., 206f., 351, 376f.; exclusivism, 352–63, 442; food and purity,

Righteousness, hope for, 289–98; *see also* Justice

Riots, *see* Uprisings

Ritual, in Judaism and other ancient religions, *see* Religion; 'ritual' as a division of the Jewish law, 194, 259

Roman administrators, 280, 323, 346, 394, 404, 483, 485–7, 490; *see also* Government; Priests, high; Judaea

Roman Catholicism, 446

Roman taxes, 161–64, 514f. nn.28, 29, 51, 52, 166, 168, 280f.

Roman troops, at temple, 138 (Passover); billeting of, 161; need to keep apart from Jewish mob, 331, 337; and pillage, 476, 542 n.65

Rome, and Hasmoneans, 21; and Palestine, chs 3, 22; Jewish sacrifices on behalf of, 189, 255f., 523 n.28; religion in, 190; compared to Persians and Ptolemies, 493

Rome, Romans, in *Psalms of Solomon*, 453

'Rulers', *see* Leading citizens, Magistrates

Sabbath, 194; general observance of, 237 (*see also* Observance); assembly and study on, 197–9, 207f., 201, 211, 236; prohibition of fighting on, 26, 203, 209, 210, 211; carrying burdens on, 208; buying and selling on, 208; penalties for transgression of, 208; generally observed, 209, 211, 236f., 427; empire-wide right to assemble on, 209f., 212; pagan views of, 209f.; special rules of the Pharisees regarding, 210; sexual intercourse on, 211; and the theology of creation, 248; and sacrifice, 335, 362; among Essenes, 367, among Pharisees, 425–8, 443; *see also* Scripture, Study, Synagogues, Worship

Sabbatical year, 147f., 161, 162, 168, 209, 426–8; generally observed, 427

Sacrifice, sacrifices, in ancient religion, 49f.; in Jerusalem, 79–81; supply of animals for, 85–90; categories and technique, ch. 7; Jewish sacrifice compared to Greek, 105, cf. 107; and thanksgiving, 106, 111f.; as placating God, 106; as honouring God, 106; as a common religious activity, 114–116; theology of, 251–7; among Essenes, 376f.; in Pharisaism, 416; defilement of, 453; *see also* Community sacrifices, Individual sacrifices, Burnt offerings, Guilt offerings, Shared sacrifices, Sin offerings, Thank offerings, Festivals, Slaughter

Sadduceanism, Sadducees, general characteristics, 13f.; origin of, 25f.; scribes, 174; and fate, 251; hopes for future, 280, 287; views on afterlife, 299–301; ch. 15; religious principles, 332–6; harshness of, 332f., 419f; views on resurrection, 332f.; views on 'tradition', 333–6; on sabbath, 335; on incense on the Day of Atonement, 335, 396f., 466; 'book of decrees', 335; conflict/disagreement with Pharisees, 380, 393, 396, 449, 466, 527 n.1; membership in supposed Sanhedrin, 474f., 478

Sages, wise men, 173, 176f.; required money and leisure, 181f.; used as synonymous with Pharisees and Rabbis, 459

Samaritans, involved in civil unrest, 165; clash with Galileans, 329f.

Sanhedrin, 173, 382, 394, 420, 469, 472–81; the things the Sanhedrin did not do, 475–8; Sanhedrin and Herod, 477f.; theory of membership for life, 474, 477f.; narratives in which (i.e. the Synedrion) actually does something, 479–81; most views of it without basis in narrative sources, 481, 489f.; in theory should have been convened for trials, 481; limited role even in Mishnah, 481; *see also* Council, Government, Parliament, *Synedria*, Synedrion, Trials

Sanhedrin (Mishnaic tractate), 420, 469, 473, 487, 489f.

Scape-goat, 142

Scholars, modern, misattribute common Jewish views to Pharisees alone, 195; Christian, use Pharisees as a foil, 400

Schools (educational institutions), 176; supposedly run by Pharisees, 388; *see also* Synagogues (sometimes called 'schools')

Scribal rules, no punishment for transgression of, 424, 471, 515 n.8

Scribes, 170–77; sacred (priestly) scribes, 172; lay and priestly scribes, 172–7; types and divisions of, 179–82; numbers of, 180f.; among the Essenes, 347; *see also* Sages, Teachers

Scripture, Jewish, role of in common Judaism, 47f.; in the temple service, 80, 117; at festivals, 133, 137f., 140, 142f.; weekly study of, 197f., 207f., 236; at Qumran, 363f.; touching, and handwashing, 438

Second tithe, 113, 148–50, 157, 166f., 431, 432, 435, 441

Secrecy, among Essenes, 361, 424